ScottForesman
LITERATURE
AND INTEGRATED STUDIES

Middle School: Grade Six

Middle School: Grade Seven

Middle School: Grade Eight

Forms of Literature

World Literature

American Literature

English Literature

The cover features a detail of Grace Carpenter Hudson's
Ka-tat (1922), a painting of a Pomo Indian boy which appears
in full on this page. Born and raised among the Pomo, a
Native American people that lived in the coastal valleys of
northern California, Hudson devoted her career to capturing
their culture. *Grace Hudson Museum, Ukiah, California*

ScottForesman
LITERATURE
AND INTEGRATED STUDIES

Grade Six

Senior Consultants

Alan C. Purves
State University of New York at Albany

Carol Booth Olson
University of California, Irvine

Carlos E. Cortés
University of California, Riverside (Emeritus)

Judith A. Brough
Gettysburg College, Gettysburg

Edward N. Brazee
University of Maine

ScottForesman

Editorial Offices: Glenview, Illinois
Regional Offices: San Jose, California • Tucker, Georgia • Glenview,
Illinois • Oakland, New Jersey • Dallas, Texas

ACKNOWLEDGMENTS

Texts

xxiv "Zlateh the Goat" from *Zlateh the Goat and Other Stories* by Isaac Bashevis Singer. Text Copyright © 1966 by Isaac Bashevis Singer. Reprinted by permission of HarperCollins Publishers. **6** Reprinted by permission of Norma Fox Mazer 1995. From *Short Takes: A Short Story Collection for Young Readers*, originally published by William Morrow. Copyright © 1986 by Norma Fox Mazer. All rights reserved. **14** "Thinking" by Lorna Dee Cervantes edited by Sylvia Cavazos Pena is reprinted with permission from the publisher of *Kikiriki: Stories and Poems in English and Spanish for Children* (Houston: Arte Publico Press-University of Houston, 1981). **19** "Whatif" from *A Light in the Attic* by Shel Silverstein. Copyright © 1981 by Evil Eye Music, Inc. Reprinted by permission of HarperCollins Publishers. **20** "Life Doesn't Frighten Me" from *And Still I Rise* by Maya Angelou. Copyright © 1978 by Maya Angelou. Reprinted by permission of Random House, Inc. **23** "The Six Rows of Pompons" from *Yokohama, California* by Toshio Mori. Reprinted by permission of The Caxton Printers, Ltd. **31** "Stolen Day" by Sherwood Anderson, *This Week Magazine*, 1941. Copyright © 1941 by United Newspaper Magazine Corp. Renewed 1968 by Eleanor Copenhaver Anderson. Reprinted by permission of Harold Ober Associates Incorporated. **38** "September 10, 1990 to September 14, 1990" from *The Diary of Latoya Hunter* by Latoya Hunter. Copyright © 1992 by Latoya Hunter. Reprinted by permission of Crown Publishers, Inc. **44** Adapted from "Should I Be Worried?" *Current Health® 1*, Volume 17, No. 4, December 1993. Reprinted by permission from Weekly Reader Corporation. Copyright © 1993 by Weekly Reader Corporation. All rights reserved. **50** "Emily" from *When Learning Is Tough: Kids Talk About Their Learning Disabilities* text copyright © 1994 by Cynthia Roby. Photographs copyright © 1994 by Elena Dorfman. Published with permission of Albert Whitman & Company. All rights reserved. **52** "Arithmetic" from *The Complete Poems of Carl Sandburg*, copyright © 1950 by Carl Sandburg and renewed 1978 by Margaret Sandburg, Helga Sandburg Crile, Janet Sandburg, reprinted by permission of Harcourt Brace & Company. **56** "The Circuit" by Francisco Jimenez, *The Arizona Quarterly*, Autumn 1973. Reprinted by permission of the author. **62** "Campesinos/Fieldworkers" (Spanish/English) from *Voices From the Fields* by S. Beth Atkin. Text and Photographs Copyright © 1993 by S. Beth Atkin. By permission of Little, Brown and Company. **67** "The Dandelion Garden" by Budge Wilson. Reprinted by permission of Philomel Books and the author from *The Dandelion Garden and Other Stories,* copyright © 1995 by Budge Wilson. **78** "Change" from *River Winding* by Charlotte Zolotow. Copyright © 1970 by Charlotte Zolotow. Reprinted by permission of Scott Treimel New York on behalf of the author. **79** "Dust of Snow" by Robert Frost, from *The Poetry of Robert Frost* edited by Edward Connery Lathem. Copyright 1951 by Robert Frost. Copyright © 1923, 1969 by Henry Holt and Co., Inc. Reprinted by permission of Henry Holt and Co., Inc. **82** From *The Ancestor Tree* by T. Obinkaram Echewa. Copyright © 1994 by T. Obinkaram Echewa. Used by permission of Lodestar Books, an affiliate of Dutton Children's Books, a division of Penguin USA Inc. **92** From *How It Feels When Parents Divorce* by Jill Krementz. Copyright © 1984 by Jill Krementz. Reprinted by permission of Alfred A. Knopf Inc. **112** "Raymond's Run" from *Gorilla, My Love* by Toni Cade Bambara. Copyright © 1971 by Toni Cade Bambara. Reprinted by permission of Random House, Inc. **124** "In the Beginning Was The" from *Sprints & Distances* by Lillian Morrison. Copyright © 1965, renewed 1993 by Lillian Morrison. Used by permission of Marian Reiner for the author. **125** "To James" by Frank Horne from *Haverstraw*, London, 1963. Reprinted by permission of Paul Breman, Ltd. **126** "The Sprinters" from *Sprints & Distances* by Lillian Morrison. Copyright © 1965, renewed 1993 by Lillian Morrison. Reprinted by permission of Marian Reiner for the author.

continued on page 670

ISBN: 0-673-29451-X

Copyright © 1997
Scott, Foresman and Company, Glenview, Illinois
All Rights Reserved. Printed in the United States of America.

http://www.sf.aw.com

3 4 5 6 7 8 9 10 DR 03 02 01 00 99 98 97

iv

ScottForesman
LITERATURE
AND INTEGRATED STUDIES

Grade Six

Senior Consultants

Alan C. Purves
State University of New York at Albany

Carol Booth Olson
University of California, Irvine

Carlos E. Cortés
University of California, Riverside (Emeritus)

Judith A. Brough
Gettysburg College, Gettysburg

Edward N. Brazee
University of Maine

ScottForesman

Editorial Offices: Glenview, Illinois
Regional Offices: San Jose, California • Tucker, Georgia • Glenview,
Illinois • Oakland, New Jersey • Dallas, Texas

Visit ScottForesman's Home Page at http://www.scottforesman.com

ACKNOWLEDGMENTS

Texts

xxiv "Zlateh the Goat" from *Zlateh the Goat and Other Stories* by Isaac Bashevis Singer. Text Copyright © 1966 by Isaac Bashevis Singer. Reprinted by permission of HarperCollins Publishers. **6** Reprinted by permission of Norma Fox Mazer 1995. From *Short Takes: A Short Story Collection for Young Readers,* originally published by William Morrow. Copyright © 1986 by Norma Fox Mazer. All rights reserved. **14** "Thinking" by Lorna Dee Cervantes edited by Sylvia Cavazos Pena is reprinted with permission from the publisher of *Kikiriki: Stories and Poems in English and Spanish for Children* (Houston: Arte Publico Press-University of Houston, 1981). **19** "Whatif" from *A Light in the Attic* by Shel Silverstein. Copyright © 1981 by Evil Eye Music, Inc. Reprinted by permission of HarperCollins Publishers. **20** "Life Doesn't Frighten Me" from *And Still I Rise* by Maya Angelou. Copyright © 1978 by Maya Angelou. Reprinted by permission of Random House, Inc. **23** "The Six Rows of Pompons" from *Yokohama, California* by Toshio Mori. Reprinted by permission of The Caxton Printers, Ltd. **31** "Stolen Day" by Sherwood Anderson, *This Week Magazine,* 1941. Copyright © 1941 by United Newspaper Magazine Corp. Renewed 1968 by Eleanor Copenhaver Anderson. Reprinted by permission of Harold Ober Associates Incorporated. **38** "September 10, 1990 to September 14, 1990" from *The Diary of Latoya Hunter* by Latoya Hunter. Copyright © 1992 by Latoya Hunter. Reprinted by permission of Crown Publishers, Inc. **44** Adapted from "Should I Be Worried?" *Current Health® 1,* Volume 17, No. 4, December 1993. Reprinted by permission from Weekly Reader Corporation. Copyright © 1993 by Weekly Reader Corporation. All rights reserved. **50** "Emily" from *When Learning Is Tough: Kids Talk About Their Learning Disabilities* text copyright © 1994 by Cynthia Roby. Photographs copyright © 1994 by Elena Dorfman. Published with permission of Albert Whitman & Company. All rights reserved. **52** "Arithmetic" from *The Complete Poems of Carl Sandburg,* copyright © 1950 by Carl Sandburg and renewed 1978 by Margaret Sandburg, Helga Sandburg Crile, Janet Sandburg, reprinted by permission of Harcourt Brace & Company. **56** "The Circuit" by Francisco Jimenez, *The Arizona Quarterly,* Autumn 1973. Reprinted by permission of the author. **62** "Campesinos/Fieldworkers" (Spanish/English) from *Voices From the Fields* by S. Beth Atkin. Text and Photographs Copyright © 1993 by S. Beth Atkin. By permission of Little, Brown and Company. **67** "The Dandelion Garden" by Budge Wilson. Reprinted by permission of Philomel Books and the author from *The Dandelion Garden and Other Stories,* copyright © 1995 by Budge Wilson. **78** "Change" from *River Winding* by Charlotte Zolotow. Copyright © 1970 by Charlotte Zolotow. Reprinted by permission of Scott Treimel New York on behalf of the author. **79** "Dust of Snow" by Robert Frost, from *The Poetry of Robert Frost* edited by Edward Connery Lathem. Copyright 1951 by Robert Frost. Copyright © 1923, 1969 by Henry Holt and Co., Inc. Reprinted by permission of Henry Holt and Co., Inc. **82** From *The Ancestor Tree* by T. Obinkaram Echewa. Copyright © 1994 by T. Obinkaram Echewa. Used by permission of Lodestar Books, an affiliate of Dutton Children's Books, a division of Penguin USA Inc. **92** From *How It Feels When Parents Divorce* by Jill Krementz. Copyright © 1984 by Jill Krementz. Reprinted by permission of Alfred A. Knopf Inc. **112** "Raymond's Run" from *Gorilla, My Love* by Toni Cade Bambara. Copyright © 1971 by Toni Cade Bambara. Reprinted by permission of Random House, Inc. **124** "In the Beginning Was The" from *Sprints & Distances* by Lillian Morrison. Copyright © 1965, renewed 1993 by Lillian Morrison. Used by permission of Marian Reiner for the author. **125** "To James" by Frank Horne from *Haverstraw,* London, 1963. Reprinted by permission of Paul Breman, Ltd. **126** "The Sprinters" from *Sprints & Distances* by Lillian Morrison. Copyright © 1965, renewed 1993 by Lillian Morrison. Reprinted by permission of Marian Reiner for the author.

continued on page 670

ISBN: 0-673-29451-X

Copyright © 1997
Scott, Foresman and Company, Glenview, Illinois
All Rights Reserved. Printed in the United States of America.

http://www.sf.aw.com

3 4 5 6 7 8 9 10 DR 03 02 01 00 99 98 97

Senior Consultants

Alan C. Purves

Professor of Education and Humanities, State University of New York at Albany; Director of the Center for Writing and Literacy. Dr. Purves developed the concept and philosophy of the literature lessons for the series, consulted with editors, reviewed tables of contents and lesson manuscript, wrote the Assessment Handbooks, and oversaw the development and writing of the series testing strand.

Carol Booth Olson

Director, California Writing Project, Department of Education, University of California, Irvine. Dr. Olson conceptualized and developed the integrated writing strand of the program, consulted with editors, led a team of teachers in creating literature-based Writing Workshops, and reviewed final manuscript.

Carlos E. Cortés

Professor Emeritus, History, University of California, Riverside. Dr. Cortés designed and developed the multiculturalism strand embedded in each unit of the series and consulted with grade-level editors to implement the concepts.

Judith A. Brough

Chair, Department of Education; Professor of Education; Supervisor of Student Teachers; Gettysburg College, Gettysburg.

Edward N. Brazee

Associate Professor of Education, University of Maine. Founder and Director, Middle Level Education Institute; Founder and Executive Director, Maine Association for Middle Level Education.

Drs. Brough and Brazee advised on middle school philosophy, the needs of the middle school student, and requirements of the middle school curriculum. In addition they reviewed selections, tables of contents, and lessons and developed prototypes and outlines for all middle school unit projects.

Series Consultants

Visual and Media Literacy/Speaking and Listening/Critical Thinking

Harold M. Foster. Professor of English Education and Secondary Education, The University of Akron, Akron.

Dr. Foster developed and wrote the Beyond Print features for all levels of the series.

ESL and LEP Strategies

James Cummins. Professor, Modern Language Centre and Curriculum Department, Ontario Institute for Studies in Education, Toronto.

Lily Wong Fillmore. Professor, Graduate School of Education, University of California at Berkeley.

Drs. Cummins and Fillmore advised on the needs of ESL and LEP students, helped develop the Building English Proficiency model for the program, and reviewed strategies and manuscript.

Life Skills/Personal Development

David J. DePalma. Partner, Life Skills Consultants; developmental psychologist.

Charlotte Wright DePalma. Partner, Life Skills Consultants; former high school and university teacher.

Andrea Donnellan White. Partner, Life Skills Consultants; former elementary teacher.

W. Brent White. Partner, Life Skills Consultants; former middle school teacher.

The Whites and DePalmas conceptualized the Life Skills sequence for the program and wrote pupil book activities as well as the Life Skills book for each middle school grade.

Reviewers and Contributors

Pupil Edition/Teacher Edition

Valerie Aksoy, El Dorado Intermediate School, Concord, California **Sylvia Alchediak,** Burney Simmons Elementary School, Plant City, Florida **Doris Ash,** Dolan Middle School, Stamford, Connecticut **Camille Barnett,** Pioneer Middle School, Cooper City, Florida **Beverly Bradley,** W. Mack Lyon Middle School, Overton, Nevada **Candice Bush,** O'Callaghan Middle School, Las Vegas, Nevada **Colleen Fleming,** Charles Shaw Middle School, Gorham, Maine **Philip Freemer,** Hall High School, West Hartford, Connecticut **Ellen Golden,** Hammocks Middle School, Miami, Florida **Anita Hartgraves,** Martin Middle School, Corpus Christi, Texas **Lea Heyer,** Burney Simmons Elementary School, Plant City, Florida **Linda Holland,** Medinah Middle School, Roselle, Illinois **Mary Howard,** Valley Center Middle School, Valley Center, California **Kathy Jesson,** Hammocks Middle School, Miami, Florida **Christina Kenny,** Hill Middle School, Long Beach, California **Kathy Knowles,** Alamo Junior High School, Midland, Texas **J. Chris Leonard,** Southridge Middle School, Fontana, California **Sandra Litogot,** O.E. Dunckel Middle School, Farmington Hills, Michigan **Sue Mack,** Gregory

CONTENTS

UNIT 1

CHANGE

PART ONE: GROWING PAINS

PART TWO: MAKING ADJUSTMENTS

UNIT 3

RELATIONSHIPS

THEME OVERVIEW   **216**

PART ONE: KEEPING TRADITIONS

PART TWO: WHAT REALLY MATTERS

Literature

Exploring the Theme through Folklore

Integrated Studies

UNIT 4

$\mathcal{E}$NVIRONMENT

THEME OVERVIEW   **338**

PART ONE: APPRECIATING YOUR WORLD

Part Two: Protecting Your World

Literature

Integrated Studies

$\mathcal{J}$USTICE

THEME OVERVIEW 429

PART ONE: FACING PREJUDICE

PART TWO: WHAT'S FAIR, WHAT'S NOT

Literature

Exploring the Theme through Folklore

Integrated Studies

UNIT 6

CONFLICT AND RESOLUTION

PART ONE: FACING THE PROBLEM HEAD-ON

PART TWO: FINDING SOLUTIONS

Literature

Exploring the Theme through Folklore

Integrated Studies

Glossaries, Handbooks, and Indexes

Genre Overview

Short Stories

Nonfiction

Poetry

FEATURE OVERVIEW

Interdisciplinary Studies

Reading Mini-Lesson

Writing Mini-Lessons

Language Mini-Lessons

Writing Workshops

Indicates workshops found in the Unit Resource Books—Teacher's Resource File

Beyond Print

Model for Active Reading

Good readers tend to read actively. They jump right in, getting involved, picturing the action, and reacting to the characters or ideas. They question, evaluate, predict, and in other ways think about the story or article they are reading. These three sixth-grade students shared their thoughts as they read "Zlateh the Goat." You might not have the same questions or ideas that they did about this story. However, their ways of responding will give you ideas for how you can get actively engaged as you read literature.

ANDREW PANAHON I like to read science fiction which is my favorite. I play the violin, and I like playing chess.

COURTNEY UNDERWOOD I'm eleven years old and an avid reader. I like mysteries, because I like the suspense. I also like to play volleyball.

EMMANUEL RAGUAY I play on a
baseball team. I'm really into sports. I also
like reading, especially mysteries.

Six Reading Strategies

Following are some of the techniques that
good readers use, often without being aware
of them.

Question Ask questions that come to mind
as you read.

Example: Why did Aaron have to take the
goat to market?

Predict Use what has happened so far. Make
reasonable guesses about what might
happen next.

Example: I wonder what will happen to Aaron
when the weather changes?

Clarify Clear up confusion and answer
questions.

Example: Aaron could survive because he
had snow to eat and milk to drink.

Summarize Review what has happened so far.

Example: Well, Aaron thinks he's saved when
he finds the hay, but I wonder how long they
can last.

Evaluate Use your common sense and
evidence in the selection to arrive at sound
opinions and valid conclusions.

Example: I think Aaron was still a good son
even though he had to disobey his parents.

Connect Compare the text with something in
your own experience, with another text, or
with ideas within the text.

Example: If I were Aaron, I would have tried to
go back home when the weather started to
change.

ZLATEH THE GOAT

▲ Do you think this goat painted by Marc Chagall could help you survive a snowstorm?

ISAAC BASHEVIS SINGER

At Hanukkah time the road from the village to the town is usually covered with snow, but this year the winter had been a mild one. Hanukkah had almost come, yet little snow had fallen. The sun shone most of the time. The peasants complained that because of the dry weather there would be a poor harvest of winter grain. New grass sprouted, and the peasants sent their cattle out to pasture.

For Reuven the furrier it was a bad year, and after long hesitation he decided to sell Zlateh the goat. She was old and gave little milk. Feivel the town butcher had offered eight gulden for her.

ANDREW I remember that Hanukkah is a holiday for Jewish people. (connect)

ANDREW I bet something is going to happen to the goat. (predict)

EMMANUEL What does the goat's name mean? (question)

Such a sum would buy Hanukkah candles, potatoes and oil for pancakes, gifts for the children, and other holiday necessaries for the house. Reuven told his oldest boy Aaron to take the goat to town.

Aaron understood what taking the goat to Feivel meant, but had to obey his father. Leah, his mother, wiped the tears from her eyes when she heard the news. Aaron's younger sisters, Anna and Miriam, cried loudly. Aaron put on his quilted jacket and a cap with earmuffs, bound a rope around Zlateh's neck, and took along two slices of bread with cheese to eat on the road. Aaron was supposed to deliver the goat by evening, spend the night at the butcher's, and return the next day with the money.

While the family said goodbye to the goat, and Aaron placed the rope around her neck, Zlateh stood as patiently and good-naturedly as ever. She licked Reuven's hand. She shook her small white beard. Zlateh trusted human beings. She knew that they always fed her and never did her any harm.

When Aaron brought her out on the road to town, she seemed somewhat astonished. She'd never been led in that direction before. She looked back at him questioningly, as if to say, "Where are you taking me?" But after a while she seemed to come to the conclusion that a goat shouldn't ask questions. Still, the road was different. They passed new fields, pastures, and huts with thatched roofs. Here and there a dog barked and came running after them, but Aaron chased it away with his stick.

The sun was shining when Aaron left the village. Suddenly the weather changed. A large black cloud with a bluish center appeared in the east and spread itself rapidly over the sky. A cold wind blew in with it. The crows flew low, croaking. At first it looked as if it would rain, but instead it began to hail as in summer. It was early in the day, but it became dark as dusk. After a while the hail turned to snow.

In his twelve years Aaron had seen all kinds of weather, but he had never experienced a snow like this one. It was so dense it shut out the light of the day. In a short time their path was completely covered. The wind became as cold as ice. The road to town was narrow and winding. Aaron no longer knew where he was. He could not see through the snow. The cold soon penetrated his quilted jacket.

At first Zlateh didn't seem to mind the change in weather. She, too, was twelve years old and knew what winter meant. But when her legs sank deeper and deeper into the snow, she began to turn her head and look at Aaron in wonderment. Her mild eyes seemed to ask, "Why are we out in such a storm?" Aaron hoped that a peasant would come along with his cart, but no one passed by.

The snow grew thicker, falling to the ground in large, whirling flakes. Beneath it Aaron's boots touched the softness of a plowed

COURTNEY Why did Aaron have to go to town and not the father? (question)

EMMANUEL It seemed like an easy task just to take the goat and get some food. (evaluate)

field. He realized that he was no longer on the road. He had gone astray. He could no longer figure out which was east or west, which way was the village, the town. The wind whistled, howled, whirled the snow about in eddies. It looked as if white imps were playing tag on the fields. A white dust rose above the ground. Zlateh stopped. She could walk no longer. Stubbornly she anchored her cleft hooves in the earth and bleated as if pleading to be taken home. Icicles hung from her white beard, and her horns were glazed with frost.

Aaron did not want to admit the danger, but he knew just the same that if they did not find shelter they would freeze to death. This was no ordinary storm. It was a mighty blizzard. The snow had reached his knees. His hands were numb, and he could no longer feel his toes. He choked when he breathed. His nose felt like wood, and he rubbed it with snow. Zlateh's bleating began to sound like crying. Those humans in whom she had so much confidence had dragged her into a trap. Aaron began to pray to God for himself and for the innocent animal.

Suddenly he made out the shape of a hill. He wondered what it could be. Who had piled snow into such a huge heap? He moved toward it, dragging Zlateh after him. When he came near it, he realized that it was a large haystack which the snow had blanketed.

Aaron realized immediately that they were saved. With great effort he dug his way through the snow. He was a village boy and knew what to do. When he reached the hay, he hollowed out a nest for himself and the goat. No matter how cold it may be outside, in the hay it is always warm. And hay was food for Zlateh. The moment she smelled it she became contented and began to eat. Outside, the snow continued to fall. It quickly covered the passageway Aaron had dug. But a boy and an animal need to breathe, and there was hardly any air in their hideout. Aaron bored a kind of window through the hay and snow and carefully kept the passage clear.

Zlateh, having eaten her fill, sat down on her hind legs and seemed to have regained her confidence in man. Aaron ate his two slices of bread and cheese, but after the difficult journey he was still hungry. He looked at Zlateh and noticed her udders were full. He lay down next to her, placing himself so that when he milked her he could squirt the milk into his mouth. It was rich and sweet. Zlateh was not accustomed to being milked that way, but she did not resist. On the contrary, she seemed eager to reward Aaron for bringing her to a shelter whose very walls, floor, and ceiling were made of food.

Through the window Aaron could catch a glimpse of the chaos outside. The wind carried before it whole drifts of snow. It was completely dark, and he did not know whether night had already come or whether it was the darkness of the storm. Thank God that in the

COURTNEY I began questioning how they would survive. (question)

EMMANUEL It seemed as if Aaron and the goat might die with all the chaos going on around them. (predict)

hay it was not cold. The dried hay, grass, and field flowers exuded the warmth of the summer sun. Zlateh ate frequently; she nibbled from above, below, from the left and right. Her body gave forth an animal warmth, and Aaron cuddled up to her. He had always loved Zlateh, but now she was like a sister. He was alone, cut off from his family, and wanted to talk. He began to talk to Zlateh. "Zlateh, what do you think about what has happened to us?" he asked.

"Maaaa," Zlateh answered.

"If we hadn't found this stack of hay, we would both be frozen stiff by now," Aaron said.

"Maaaa," was the goat's reply.

"If the snow keeps on falling like this, we may have to stay here for days," Aaron explained.

"Maaaa," Zlateh bleated.

"What does 'maaaa' mean?" Aaron asked. "You'd better speak up clearly."

"Maaaa, maaaa," Zlateh tried.

"Well, let it be 'maaaa' then," Aaron said patiently. "You can't speak, but I know you understand. I need you and you need me. Isn't that right?"

"Maaaa."

Aaron became sleepy. He made a pillow out of some hay, leaned his head on it, and dozed off. Zlateh, too, fell asleep.

When Aaron opened his eyes, he didn't know whether it was morning or night. The snow had blocked up his window. He tried to clear it, but when he had bored through to the length of his arm, he still hadn't reached the outside. Luckily he had his stick with him and was able to break through to open air. It was still dark outside. The snow continued to fall and the wind wailed, first with one voice and then with many. Sometimes it had the sound of devilish laughter. Zlateh, too, awoke, and when Aaron greeted her, she answered, "Maaaa." Yes, Zlateh's language consisted of only one word, but it meant many things. Now she was saying, "We must accept all that God gives us—heat, cold, hunger, satisfaction, light, and darkness."

Aaron had awakened hungry. He had eaten up his food, but Zlateh had plenty of milk.

For three days Aaron and Zlateh stayed in the haystack. Aaron had always loved Zlateh, but in these days he loved her more and more. She fed him with her milk and helped him keep warm. She comforted him with her patience. He told her many stories, and she always cocked her ears and listened. When he patted her, she licked his hand and his face. Then she said, "Maaaa," and he knew it meant, I love you, too.

The snow fell for three days, though after the first day it was not as thick and the wind quieted down. Sometimes Aaron felt that

COURTNEY I don't know what "maaaa" means. Does Aaron understand Zlateh? (question)

ANDREW Since Aaron left home, he has had to find a safe place to stay during the snowstorm and food for Zlateh and for himself. (summarize)

there could never have been a summer, that the snow had always fallen, ever since he could remember. He, Aaron, never had a father or mother or sisters. He was a snow child, born of the snow, and so was Zlateh. It was so quiet in the hay that his ears rang in the stillness. Aaron and Zlateh slept all night and a good part of the day. As for Aaron's dreams, they were all about warm weather. He dreamed of green fields, trees covered with blossoms, clear brooks, and singing birds. By the third night the snow had stopped, but Aaron did not dare to find his way home in the darkness. The sky became clear and the moon shone, casting silvery nets on the snow. Aaron dug his way out and looked at the world. It was all white, quiet, dreaming dreams of heavenly splendor. The stars were large and close. The moon swam in the sky as in a sea.

On the morning of the fourth day Aaron heard the ringing of sleigh bells. The haystack was not far from the road. The peasant who drove the sleigh pointed out the way to him—not to the town and Feivel the butcher, but home to the village. Aaron had decided in the haystack that he would never part with Zlateh.

Aaron's family and their neighbors had searched for the boy and the goat but had found no trace of them during the storm. They feared they were lost. Aaron's mother and sisters cried for him; his father remained silent and gloomy. Suddenly one of the neighbors came running to their house with the news that Aaron and Zlateh were coming up the road.

There was great joy in the family. Aaron told them how he had found the stack of hay and how Zlateh had fed him with her milk. Aaron's sisters kissed and hugged Zlateh and gave her a special treat of chopped carrots and potato peels, which Zlateh gobbled up hungrily.

Nobody ever again thought of selling Zlateh, and now that the cold weather had finally set in, the villagers needed the services of Reuven the furrier once more. When Hanukkah came, Aaron's mother was able to fry pancakes every evening, and Zlateh got her portion, too. Even though Zlateh had her own pen, she often came to the kitchen, knocking on the door with her horns to indicate that she was ready to visit, and she was always admitted. In the evening Aaron, Miriam, and Anna played dreidel. Zlateh sat near the stove watching the children and the flickering of the Hanukkah candles.

Once in a while Aaron would ask her, "Zlateh, do you remember the three days we spent together?"

And Zlateh would scratch her neck with a horn, shake her white bearded head, and come out with the single sound which expressed all her thoughts, and all her love.

COURTNEY I was surprised when they were found so soon. (summarize)

ANDREW If Zlateh had been saved right away, the story would have been boring! (evaluate)

COURTNEY I liked the story because it had a happy ending. (evaluate)

ANDREW It was a pretty good story because it reminded me of *Jack and the Beanstalk.* (evaluate/connect)

Discussion After Reading

Once they've finished a selection, active readers reflect and respond in a variety of ways.

How would you grade Aaron on the following character traits on a scale of 1 to 5, with 1 being good?

Responsible; Obedient; Problem solver

ANDREW I would give him a 1 for being responsible because I think he made the right decisions. I would give him a 2 for being obedient. He never went to town with the goat. As a problem solver, I would give him a really high grade if 1 wasn't the highest. He knew what to do when he found the haystack.

COURTNEY I would definitely give him a 1 for being responsible. For obedience, maybe a 2 1/2. As a problem solver, I would give him much higher than a 1.

EMMANUEL I would give him a 1 for responsibility. I would give him about a 3 for obedience. He really didn't take the goat to town. I would have done the same thing. I would give him a 1 for problem solving.

Which character in the story does the author develop best—Aaron or Zlateh? Explain.

ANDREW I think the author developed Aaron best. All the goat said was "Maaa."

EMMANUEL I agree that the goat didn't have much to say.

COURTNEY Aaron was developed best because of all the actions he took.

Zlateh produced food, but she was also a pet. Would you have sold a beloved pet to buy other things that you and your family might need more? Why?

COURTNEY I would have sold the goat to a neighbor so that I could have easy access to it. Pets are pets and they can always get another home, but people can't.

EMMANUEL If both my parents had jobs and I thought we could get by, I wouldn't sell the pet.

ANDREW I would have sold the goat because the family needed more stuff.

Zlateh the Goat **xxix**

Change

Growing Pains

Making Adjustments

Talking About
CHANGE

Change involves physical and mental growth, and it affects everyone. We will all need to make adjustments as long as we live. Often we want to keep things the way they are, only to find that some change has made life better.

Change is also a theme in many works of literature. Notice how the quotations from selections you will read reflect the same ideas as the comments from young people across the United States.

The thought of having to move to Fresno and knowing what was in store for me there brought tears to my eyes.

from "The Circuit" by Francisco Jiménez, page 57

The garden was no longer in full bloom, and there is nothing sadder than a withered flower.

from "The Dandelion Garden" by Budge Wilson, page 70

The dreaded Freshman Day is drawing near.

from "My First Day in Junior High" by Latoya Hunter, page 39

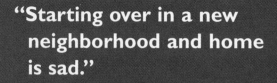

"Starting over in a new
neighborhood and home
is sad."

Tran – Madison, WI

"Why can't things that are
beautiful stay the same?"

Jennifer – Spokane, WA

"How can we deal with
change and make the
best of it?"

Jordan – Little Rock, AR

Part One

Growing Pains

No one ever said growing up was easy. In fact, people once thought it was normal for children and teenagers to feel physical discomfort as their arms and legs grew. *Growing pains*, they called it. Today, we use the expression to mean the sometimes difficult, sometimes funny, experiences that are a natural part of growing up. In the selections that follow, you will meet other young people struggling toward adulthood. You may find you have a lot in common.

Multicultural Focus **Change** naturally occurs as you grow older. This sometimes leads to tension, misunderstanding, fear, and even conflict. As you read, notice how the characters deal with such changes.

Before Reading

Tuesday of the Other June

by Norma Fox Mazer

Norma Fox Mazer
born 1931

Among other jobs, Norma Fox Mazer worked as a radio-station secretary and a cashier before deciding to devote herself to writing. Since 1971, she has written more than twenty novels and collections of short stories about the challenges of growing up. Describing her own growth as a person and a writer, she says, "That girl who was, as I remember her, insecure, unsure, dreaming, yearning, longing, that girl who was hard on herself, who was cowardly and brave, who was confused and determined—that girl who was me—still exists. I call on her when I write. I am the me of today—the person who has become a woman, a mother, a writer. Yet I am the me of all those other days as well."

Building Background

What's in a Name? In "Tuesday of the Other June" names are very important. Think about your own name. Why were you given it? What does it say about you? Do you like it, or do you wish you could change it? How do you feel when you meet someone who has the same name?

Getting into the Story

Writer's Notebook One of the characters in "Tuesday of the Other June" is a bully. In your notebook, write about a bully you have known. Tell who the person was and why you consider him or her a bully. Use a made-up name if you wish. Describe an incident in which the bully bothered you or someone you cared about.

Reading Tip

Predicting Sometimes, you can easily predict what a story will be about; other times, predicting is a bit trickier. It makes sense to begin the prediction process with the title of the story. When you see the title "Tuesday of the Other June," what is the first thing that comes to your mind? Now consider what else *June* might refer to, and how that might change the meaning of the title.

Below are some words and phrases that appear in the story. Use them to make up a story that could be titled "Tuesday of the Other June." After you have read the selection, compare your story with Norma Fox Mazer's.

pool	punch	growl	Awfulday
moving	hateful	no more	Fish Eyes

Tuesday of the Other JUNE

Norma Fox Mazer

"Be good, be good, be good, be good, my Junie," my mother sang as she combed my hair; a song, a story, a croon, a plea. "It's just you and me, two women alone in the world, June darling of my heart, we have enough troubles getting by, we surely don't need a single one more, so you keep your sweet self out of fighting and all that bad stuff. People can be little-hearted, but turn the other cheek, smile at the world, and the world'll surely smile back."

We stood in front of the mirror as she combed my hair, combed and brushed and smoothed. Her head came just above mine; she said when I grew another inch she'd stand on a stool to brush my hair. "I'm not giving up this pleasure!" And she laughed her long honey laugh.

▲ Andrew Wyeth is best known for his realistic, almost photographic-like paintings, like *Siri* done in 1970. As you read the story, does this painting reinforce how you visualize June?

My mother was April, my grandmother had been May, I was June. "And someday," said my mother, "you'll have a daughter of your own. What will you name her?"

"January!" I'd yell when I was little. "February! No, November!" My mother laughed her honey laugh. She had little emerald eyes that warmed me like the sun.

Every day when I went to school, she went to work. "Sometimes I stop what I'm doing," she said, "lay down my tools, and stop everything, because all I can think about is you. Wondering what you're doing and if you need me. Now, Junie, if anyone ever bothers you—"

"—I walk away, run away, come on home as fast as my feet will take me," I recited.

"Yes. You come to me. You just bring me your trouble, because I'm here on this earth to love you and take care of you."

I was safe with her. Still, sometimes I woke up at night and heard footsteps slowly creeping up the stairs. It wasn't my mother, she was asleep in the bed across the room, so it was robbers, thieves, and murderers, creeping slowly . . . slowly . . . slowly toward my bed.

I stuffed my hand into my mouth. If I screamed and woke her, she'd be tired at work tomorrow. The robbers and thieves filled the warm darkness and slipped across the floor more quietly than cats. Rigid under the covers, I stared at the shifting dark and bit my knuckles and never knew when I fell asleep again.

In the morning we sang in the kitchen. "Bill Grogan's GOAT! Was feelin' FINE! Ate three red shirts, right off the LINE!" I made sandwiches for our lunches, she made pancakes for breakfast, but all she ate was one pancake and a cup of coffee. "Gotta fly, can't be late."

I wanted to be rich and take care of her. She worked too hard, her pretty hair had gray in it that she joked about. "Someday," I said,

"I'll buy you a real house and you'll never work in a pot factory again."

"Such delicious plans," she said. She checked the windows to see if they were locked. "Do you have your key?"

I lifted it from the chain around my neck.

"And you'll come right home from school and—"

"—I won't light fires or let strangers into the house and I won't tell anyone on the phone that I'm here alone," I finished for her.

"I know, I'm just your old worrywart[1] mother." She kissed me twice, once on each cheek. "But you are my June, my only June, the only June."

She was wrong, there was another June. I met her when we stood next to each other at the edge of the pool the first day of swimming class in the Community Center.

"What's your name?" She had a deep growly voice.

"June. What's yours?"

She stared at me. "June."

"We have the same name."

"No we don't. June is *my* name, and I don't give you permission to use it. Your name is Fish Eyes." She pinched[2] me hard. "Got it, Fish Eyes?"

The next Tuesday, the Other June again stood next to me at the edge of the pool. "What's your name?"

"June."

"Wrong. Your—name—is—Fish—Eyes."

"June."

"Fish Eyes, you are really stupid." She shoved me into the pool.

The swimming teacher looked up, frowning, from her chart. "No one in the water yet."

Later, in the locker room, I dressed quickly and wrapped my wet suit in the towel. The Other June pulled on her jeans. "You guys see

---

1. **worrywart** (wėr′ē wôrt′), *n.* person who worries too much.
2. **pinch** (pinch), *v.* squeeze with thumb and forefinger.

that bathing suit Fish Eyes was wearing? Her mother found it in a trash can."

"She did not!"

The Other June grabbed my fingers and twisted. "Where'd she find your bathing suit?"

"She bought it, let me go."

"Poor little stupid Fish Eyes is crying. Oh, boo hoo hoo, poor little Fish Eyes."

After that, everyone called me Fish Eyes. And every Tuesday, wherever I was, there was

. . . she stepped on my feet, **pinched** my arms, . . . and knotted my braids together.

also the Other June—at the edge of the pool, in the pool, in the locker room. In the water, she swam alongside me, blowing and huffing, knocking into me. In the locker room, she stepped on my feet, pinched my arms, hid my blouse, and knotted my braids together. She had large square teeth, she was shorter than I was, but heavier, with bigger bones and square hands. If I met her outside on the street, carrying her bathing suit and towel, she'd walk toward me, smiling a square, friendly smile. "Oh well, if it isn't Fish Eyes." Then she'd punch me, *blam!* her whole solid weight hitting me.

I didn't know what to do about her. She was training me like a dog. After a few weeks of this, she only had to look at me, only had to growl, "I'm going to get you, Fish Eyes," for my heart to slink[3] like a whipped dog down into my stomach. My arms were covered with bruises. When my mother noticed, I made up a story about tripping on the sidewalk.

My weeks were no longer Tuesday, Wednesday, Thursday, and so on. Tuesday was Awfulday. Wednesday was Badday. (The Tuesday bad feelings were still there.) Thursday was Betterday and Friday was Safeday. Saturday was Goodday, but Sunday was Toosoonday, and Monday—Monday was nothing but the day before Awfulday.

I tried to slow down time. Especially on the weekends, I stayed close by my mother, doing everything with her, shopping, cooking, cleaning, going to the laundromat. "Aw, sweetie, go play with your friends."

"No, I'd rather be with you." I wouldn't look at the clock or listen to the radio (they were always telling you the date and the time). I did special magic things to keep the day from going away, rapping my knuckles six times on the bathroom door six times a day and never, ever touching the chipped place on my bureau[4]. But always I woke up to the day before Tuesday, and always, no matter how many times I circled the worn spot in the living-room rug or counted twenty-five cracks in the ceiling, Monday disappeared and once again it was Tuesday.

The Other June got bored with calling me Fish Eyes. Buffalo Brain came next, but as soon as everyone knew that, she renamed me Turkey Nose.

Now at night it wasn't robbers creeping up the stairs, but the Other June, coming to torment[5] me. When I finally fell asleep, I dreamed of kicking her, punching, biting, pinching. In the morning I remembered my dreams and felt brave and strong. And then I remembered all the things my mother had taught me and told me.

Be good, be good, be good, it's just us two women alone in the world . . . Oh, but if it weren't, if my father wasn't long gone, if we'd had someone else to fall back on, if my mother's mother

---

3. **slink** (slingk), *v.* move in a sneaking, guilty manner.
4. **bureau** (byur′ ō), *n.* chest of drawers for clothes.
5. torment (tôr ment′), *v.* worry or annoy very much.

and daddy weren't dead all these years, if my father's daddy wanted to know us instead of being glad to forget us—oh, then I would have punched the Other June with a frisky heart, I would have grabbed her arm at poolside and bitten her like the dog she had made of me.

One night, when my mother came home from work, she said, "Junie, listen to this. We're moving!"

Alaska, I thought. Florida. Arizona. Someplace far away and wonderful, someplace without the Other June.

"Wait till you hear this deal. We are going to be caretakers, troubleshooters[6] for an eight-family apartment building. Fifty-six Blue Hill Street. Not janitors, we don't do any of the heavy work. April and June, Troubleshooters, Incorporated. If a tenant has a complaint or a problem, she comes to us and we either take care of it or call the janitor for service. And for that little bit of work, we get to live rent free!" She swept me around in a dance. "Okay? You like it? I do!"

So. Not anywhere else, really. All the same, maybe too far to go to swimming class? "Can we move right away? Today?"

"Gimme a break, sweetie. We've got to pack, do a thousand things. I've got to line up someone with a truck to help us. Six weeks, Saturday the fifteenth." She circled it on the calendar. It was the Saturday after the last day of swimming class.

Soon, we had boxes lying everywhere, filled with clothes and towels and glasses wrapped in newspaper. Bit by bit, we cleared the rooms, leaving only what we needed right now. The dining-room table staggered on a bunched-up rug, our bureaus inched toward the front door like patient cows. On the calendar in the kitchen, my mother marked off the days until we moved, but the only days I thought about were Tuesdays—Awfuldays. Nothing else was real except the too fast passing of time, moving toward each Tuesday . . . away from Tuesday . . . toward Tuesday . . . .

And it seemed to me that this would go on forever, that Tuesdays would come forever and I would be forever trapped by the side of the pool, the Other June whispering *Buffalo Brain Fish Eyes Turkey Nose* into my ear, while she ground her elbow into my side and smiled her square smile at the swimming teacher.

And then it ended. It was the last day of swimming class. The last Tuesday. We had all passed our tests and, as if in celebration, the Other June only pinched me twice. "And now," our swimming teacher said, "all of you are ready for the Advanced Class, which starts in just one month. I have a sign-up slip here. Please put your name down before you leave." Everyone but me crowded around. I went to

. . . I would be forever **trapped** by the side of the pool . . .

the locker room and pulled on my clothes as fast as possible. The Other June burst through the door just as I was leaving. "Good-bye," I yelled, "good riddance to bad trash!" Before she could pinch me again, I ran past her and then ran all the way home, singing, "Good-bye . . . good-bye . . . good-bye, good riddance[7] to bad trash!"

Later, my mother carefully untied the blue ribbon around my swimming class diploma. "Look at this! Well, isn't this wonderful! You are on your way, you might turn into an Olympic swimmer, you never know what life will bring."

"I don't want to take more lessons."

---

6. **troubleshooter** (trub′ əl shü′tər), *n.* person who discovers and eliminates causes of trouble.

7. **good riddance**, exclamation expressing relief that something or somebody has been removed.

How might you have handled the Other June at the pool?

"Oh, sweetie, it's great to be a good swimmer." But then, looking into my face, she said, "No, no, no, don't worry, you don't have to."

The next morning, I woke up hungry for the first time in weeks. No more swimming class. No more Baddays and Awfuldays. No more Tuesdays of the Other June. In the kitchen, I made hot cocoa to go with my mother's corn muffins. "It's Wednesday, Mom," I said, stirring the cocoa. "My favorite day."

"Since when?"

"Since this morning." I turned on the radio so I could hear the announcer tell the time, the temperature, and the day.

Thursday for breakfast I made cinnamon toast, Friday my mother made pancakes, and on Saturday, before we moved, we ate the last slices of bread and cleaned out the peanut-butter jar.

"Some breakfast," Tilly said. "Hello, you must be June." She shook my hand. She was a friend of my mother's from work, she wore big hoop earrings, sandals, and a skirt as dazzling as a rainbow. She came in a truck with John to help us move our things.

John shouted cheerfully at me, "So you're moving." An enormous man with a face covered with little brown bumps. Was he afraid his voice wouldn't travel the distance from his mouth to my ear? "You looking at my moles?"[8] he shouted, and he heaved our big green-flowered chair down the stairs. "Don't worry, they don't bite. Ha, ha, ha!" Behind him came my mother and Tilly balancing a bureau between them, and behind them I carried a lamp and the round, flowered Mexican tray that was my mother's favorite. She had found it at a garage sale and said it was as close to foreign travel as we would ever get.

The night before, we had loaded our car, stuffing in bags and boxes until there was barely room for the two of us. But it was only when we were in the car, when we drove past Abdo's Grocery, where they always gave us credit, when I turned for a last look at our street—it was only then that I understood we were truly going to live somewhere else, in another apartment, in another place mysteriously called Blue Hill Street.

Tilly's truck followed our car.

"Oh, I'm so excited," my mother said. She laughed. "You'd think we were going across the country."

Our old car wheezed up a long steep hill. Blue Hill Street. I looked from one side to the other, trying to see everything.

My mother drove over the crest of the hill. "And now—ta da!—our new home."

"Which house? Which one?" I looked out the window and what I saw was the Other June. She was sprawled on the stoop of a pink house, lounging back on her elbows, legs outspread, her jaws working on a wad of gum. I slid down into the seat, but it was too late. I was sure she had seen me.

My mother turned into a driveway next to a big white building with a tiny porch. She leaned on the steering wheel. "See that window there, that's our living-room window . . . and that one over there, that's your bedroom. . . ."

We went into the house, down a dim cool hall. In our new apartment, the wooden floors clicked under our shoes, and my mother showed me everything. Her voice echoed in the empty rooms. I followed her around in a daze. Had I imagined seeing the Other June? Maybe I'd seen another girl who looked like her. A double. That could happen.

"Ho yo, where do you want this chair?" John appeared in the doorway. We brought in boxes and bags and beds and stopped only to eat pizza and drink orange juice from the carton.

"June's so quiet, do you think she'll adjust[9] all right?" I heard Tilly say to my mother.

"Oh, definitely. She'll make a wonderful adjustment. She's just getting used to things."

But I thought that if the Other June lived on the same street as I did, I would never get used to things.

That night I slept in my own bed, with my own pillow and blanket, but with floors that creaked in strange voices and walls with cracks I didn't recognize. I didn't feel either happy or unhappy. It was as if I were waiting for something.

Monday, when the principal of Blue Hill Street School left me in Mr. Morrisey's classroom, I knew what I'd been waiting for. In that room full of strange kids, there was one person I knew. She smiled her square smile, raised her hand, and said, "She can sit next to me, Mr. Morrisey."

"Very nice of you, June M. Okay, June T, take your seat. I'll try not to get you two Junes mixed up."

I sat down next to her. She pinched my arm. "Good riddance to bad trash," she mocked.[10]

I was back in the Tuesday swimming class only now it was worse, because everyday

---

8. **mole** (mōl), *n.* a spot on the skin, usually black or brown.

9. **adjust** (ə just′), *v.* accommodate oneself; get used to something.

10. **mock** (mok), *v.* make fun of by copying or imitating.

would be Awfulday. The pinching had already started. Soon, I knew, on the playground and in the halls, kids would pass me, grinning. "Hiya, Fish Eyes."

The Other June followed me around during recess that day, droning[11] in my ear, "You are my slave, you must do everything I say, I am your master, say it, say, 'Yes, master, you are my master.'"

I pressed my lips together, clapped my hands over my ears, but without hope. Wasn't it only a matter of time before I said the hateful words?

"How was school?" my mother said that night.

"Okay."

She put a pile of towels in a bureau drawer. "Try not to be sad about missing your old friends, sweetie, there'll be new ones."

The next morning, the Other June was waiting for me when I left the house. "Did your mother get you that blouse in the garbage dump?" She butted me, shoving me against a tree. "Don't you speak anymore, Fish Eyes?" Grabbing my chin in her hands, she pried open my mouth. "Oh, ha, ha, I thought you lost your tongue."

We went on to school. I sank down into my seat, my head on my arms. "June T, are you all right?" Mr. Morrisey asked. I nodded. My head was almost too heavy to lift.

The Other June went to the pencil sharpener. Round and round she whirled the handle. Walking back, looking at me, she held the three sharp pencils like three little knives.

Someone knocked on the door. Mr. Morrisey went out into the hall. Paper planes burst into the air, flying from desk to desk. Someone turned on a transistor radio.[12] And the Other June, coming closer, smiled and licked her lips like a cat sleepily preparing to gulp down a mouse.

I remembered my dream of kicking her, punching, biting her like a dog.

Then my mother spoke quickly in my ear:

Turn the other cheek, my Junie, smile at the world and the world'll surely smile back.

But I had turned the other cheek and it was slapped. I had smiled and the world hadn't smiled back. I couldn't run home as fast as my feet would take me, I had to stay in school—and in school there was the Other June. Every morning, there would be the Other June, and every afternoon, and every day, all day, there would be the Other June.

She frisked down the aisle, stabbing the pencils in the air toward me. A boy stood up on his desk and bowed. "My fans," he said, "I greet you." My arm twitched and throbbed, as if the Other June's pencils had already poked through the skin. She came closer, smiling her Tuesday smile.

"No," I whispered, *"no."* The word took wings and flew me to my feet, in front of the Other June. *"Noooooo."* It flew out of my mouth into her surprised face.

The boy on the desk turned toward us. "You said something, my devoted fans?"

"No," I said to the Other June. "Oh, no! No. No. No. No more." I pushed away the hand that held the pencils.

The Other June's eyes opened, popped wide like the eyes of somebody in a cartoon. It made me laugh. The boy on the desk laughed, and then the other kids were laughing too.

"No," I said again, because it felt so good to say it. "No, no, no, no." I leaned toward the Other June, put my finger against her chest. Her cheeks turned red, she squawked something—it sounded like "Eeeraaghyou!"—and she stepped back. She stepped away from me.

The door banged, the airplanes disap-

---

11. **drone** (drōn), *v.* talk or say in a monotonous voice.
12. **transistor radio**, a usually small, battery-operated radio equipped with electronic devices called transistors.

peared, and Mr. Morrisey walked to his desk. "Okay. Okay. Let's get back to work. Kevin Clark, how about it?" Kevin jumped off the desk and Mr. Morrisey picked up a piece of chalk. "All right, class—" He stopped and looked at me and the Other June. "You two Junes, what's going on there?"

I tried it again. My finger against her chest. Then the words. "No—more." And she stepped back another step. I sat down at my desk.

"June M," Mr. Morrisey said.

She turned around, staring at him with that big-eyed cartoon look. After a moment she sat down at her desk with a loud slapping sound.

Even Mr. Morrisey laughed.

And sitting at my desk, twirling my braids, I knew this was the last Tuesday of the Other June.

Another Voice

Thinking

Lorna Dee Cervantes

I think I grew up last year.
Or maybe today
is just a phase,
like Autumn's bright red foliage
5 just before Winter's death.
Sometimes I think that maybe
life
is nothing but
one big phase
10 waiting for the next,
and death
is what you have
when you run out of phases.
I think that maybe
15 I did grow up . . .
some.

After Reading

Making Connections

1. List three words that describe your thoughts as you finished the story.

2. How did the story compare to your prediction?

3. Suppose the Other June had a different name—Jessica, for example. Do you think she would have been less cruel to June? Why or why not?

4. 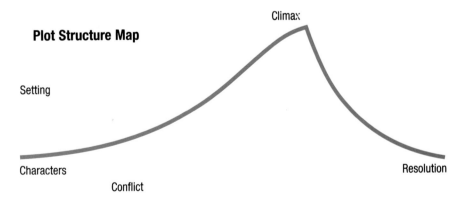 What **changes** in June's life influence the way she responds to the Other June?

5. Do you think the story would have been different if the author had made any of the main characters male? Why?

6. Suppose you asked the author what the "message" of the story is. What do you think she would say?

7. In small groups, discuss the best ways to deal with a bully. Report your conclusions to the class.

Literary Focus: Plot

The **plot** of a story is made up of the events that the author uses to present and then resolve a conflict. Often, a story's plot has a structure like that in the diagram. First, the author establishes the setting or place, characters, and conflict to be resolved. As the story goes on, events build to the climax, or turning point.

Copy the diagram on a sheet of paper. Look back at the story, and record the characters and the conflict in the appropriate places in the diagram. Summarize the climax.

Plot Structure Map

Climax

Setting

Characters

Conflict

Resolution

Vocabulary Study

On your paper, write the word from the list that best completes the meaning of the sentence.

adjust
troubleshooter
torment
drone
mock

1. Even in June's sleep, the Other June's voice would _____ in her ear.

2. When a tenant in June and April's building had a leaky faucet, he called the _____ for help.

3. "I wonder if a person can _____ to being treated so hatefully," June said.

4. June wished she could _____ the Other June by punching and biting her.

5. Worst of all, the Other June would _____ June by repeating everything she would say.

Expressing Your Ideas

Writing Choices

A Word from the Other June You are June M, the Other June. Write a **diary entry** for the day June T stood up to you in school. What happened, from your point of view? How do you feel about it?

Goodday, Badday June renamed the days of the week based on her dread of seeing the Other June. Invent new names for the seven days of the week based on your own feelings about each day. Write **dictionary entries** for the new names. You may want look at real dictionary entries first.

After "The End" Books and televisions stories often have epilogues explaining what happens to the characters. How do you think each June has grown from her experience? Write an **epilogue** for this story.

Other Options

"What If" Skit The story could have ended differently than it did. June might have knuckled under as before, or the Other June might have refused to back down. With a small group, imagine a new ending. Prepare and perform a **skit** in which you act it out. Afterwards, poll your classmates. Do they like your imagined ending more or less than the actual ending?

A June Melody Hollywood is making a movie of "Tuesday of the Other June." You have been asked to put together the musical score. Choose three scenes from the story. Then select **music** to accompany each scene. The music should fit the action and mood of the scenes. Play recordings of the music for the class and explain the thinking behind your choices.

Writing Mini-Lesson

Setting Up Your Working Portfolio

What Is a Working Portfolio? A working portfolio is a collection of the writing you've done throughout the school year. Think of your working portfolio as a road map. It can show you and others where you've been and where you're heading as a writer. Later in the year, you'll create a presentation portfolio to display your best writing.

What to Keep in Your Working Portfolio

- Working drafts of your writing including lists, charts, other planning pieces, and first drafts

- Final drafts of your writing, including pieces that have been revised and edited as a record of your completed work

- Other completed assignments that are not pieces of writing, such as videotapes or audiotapes

- Self-evaluations in which you examine ways you've improved and ways you can still improve as a writer

- Reflections in which you consider how the writing you've done has helped you grow as a student and as a person

How to Get Started

Start by setting some writing goals. Find out from your teacher what the course goals are for the first grading period. Then, get together with a group of students and discuss how you plan to meet those goals. Where do you think you need to work the hardest? Write a statement of goals to post at the front of your portfolio.

Then decide what to use for your working portfolio. You might try a three-ring binder, an expandable folder, or a report folder. You, your group, or your teacher might have other ideas.

Finally, create a cover for your portfolio. You could draw it, use a photograph, or make a collage. In planning your cover illustration, think about how to show who you are as a person and as a writer.

Before Reading

Whatif by Shel Silverstein
Life Doesn't Frighten Me by Maya Angelou

Shel Silverstein
born 1932

"I never planned to write or draw for kids," says Shel Silverstein. That may be why his work appeals to readers of all ages. In his poems and stories, Silverstein combines humor with insight into young people's concerns.

Maya Angelou
born 1928

Although she has succeeded in a variety of fields—from acting to teaching—Angelou is best known for her books, plays, and poems. "You may encounter many defeats, but you must not be defeated. I believe all things are possible . . ."

Building Background

Invented Words *Whatif* is an example of an invented, or made-up, word. Authors often use such words to make a point, especially in humorous writing. Have you read any poems or stories with made-up words? Do you have any made-up words of your own?

Getting into the Poems

Writer's Notebook Both poems list some doubts and fears that a young person might feel. In your notebook, make a chart with these headings:

Fears Then	Fears Now	Fears in the Future
darkness		

In the first column, list some fears you remember experiencing as a six-year-old. In the second column, list some fears you experience now. In the third column, list some fears you think you might experience five years from now. As you read, note whether any of the fears in the poems are ones you have had.

Reading Tip

Oral Reading Reading a poem aloud can add to your enjoyment as well as your understanding of it. Speak in a natural voice, and move ahead steadily until you come to punctuation. Then pause, stop, or do whatever else is appropriate for that type of punctuation. Most of all, enjoy yourself!

Whatif

Shel Silverstein

Last night, while I lay thinking here,
Some Whatifs crawled inside my ear
And pranced and partied all night long
And sang their same old Whatif song:
5 Whatif I'm dumb in school?
Whatif they've closed the swimming pool?
Whatif I get beat up?
Whatif there's poison in my cup?
Whatif I start to cry?
10 Whatif I get sick and die?
Whatif I flunk that test?
Whatif green hair grows on my chest?
Whatif nobody likes me?
Whatif a bolt of lightning strikes me?
15 Whatif I don't grow taller?
Whatif my head starts getting smaller?
Whatif the fish won't bite?
Whatif the wind tears up my kite?
Whatif they start a war?
20 Whatif my parents get divorced?
Whatif the bus is late?
Whatif my teeth don't grow in straight?
Whatif I tear my pants?
Whatif I never learn to dance?
25 Everything seems swell, and then
The nighttime Whatifs strike again!

Life Doesn't Frighten Me

Maya Angelou

Shadows on the wall
Noises down the hall
Life doesn't frighten me at all
Bad dogs barking loud
5 Big ghosts in a cloud
Life doesn't frighten me at all.

Mean old Mother Goose[1]
Lions on the loose
They don't frighten me at all
10 Dragons breathing flame
On my counterpane[2]
That doesn't frighten me at all,

I go boo
Make them shoo[3]
15 I make fun
Way they run
I won't cry
So they fly
I just smile
20 They go wild
Life doesn't frighten me at all.

Tough guys in a fight
All alone at night
Life doesn't frighten me at all.
25 Panthers in the park
Strangers in the dark
No, they don't frighten me at all.

That new classroom where
Boys all pull my hair
30 (Kissy little girls
With their hair in curls)
They don't frighten me at all.

Like the poem, the boy in *Freedom* by Charles White (1966-67) appears to be thinking that "life doesn't frighten me." What changes do you think he's experienced to come to this conclusion?

Don't show me frogs and snakes
And listen for my scream,
35 If I'm afraid at all
It's only in my dreams.

I've got a magic charm
That I keep up my sleeve,
I can walk the ocean floor
40 And never have to breathe.

Life doesn't frighten me at all
Not at all
Not at all.
Life doesn't frighten me at all.

---

1. **Mother Goose**, a character associated with many old nursery rhymes and fairy tales.
2. **counterpane** (koun′tər pān), *n.* an outer covering for a bed; bedspread.
3. **shoo** (shü), *v.* scare or drive away by calling "Shoo!"

After Reading

Making Connections

1. Which fears in each poem are similar to fears that you have had?

2. The speaker in "Whatif" is afraid of many things, while the speaker in "Life Doesn't Frighten Me" claims to be totally unafraid. Do you suppose the speaker in the second poem really feels that way? Explain.

3. Both poems list a variety of fears. List the fears in each poem under the categories below. Then compare your answers with those of your classmates.

realistic   ⟵   ⟶   important

4. Look back at the chart you made in your Writer's Notebook. Do you see **changes** in the kinds of fears you have? If so, why?

5. Can you make a connection between your fears and the fears of the characters in "Tuesday of the Other June"?

Literary Focus: Rhyme

Many poems have **rhyme**, in which words—usually at the ends of lines—have the same last sounds. Poets use rhyme to create various effects, including humorous ones. Rhyme also adds to the enjoyment of reading a poem aloud.

Patterns of rhyme can vary greatly. "Whatif" and "Life Doesn't Frighten Me" have two very different patterns. Look at the poems. Which poem has the simpler pattern? How does each pattern affect the mood, or feeling, of the poem?

Expressing Your Ideas ———

What If It Rhymes? With a partner, write a **poem** about fears that uses the same rhyme pattern as "Whatif" or as "Life Doesn't Frighten Me."

Face to Face The boy pictured on page 20 is thinking of how he can conquer a great fear. What is his fear and what **changes** will he experience to overcome it? Write a **speech** from his point of view.

Poetry Corner Ask permission to read the poems to a class of first graders. Remember to use the reading tip on page 18.

Before Reading

The Six Rows of Pompons

by Toshio Mori

Toshio Mori
1910–1980

With tenderness and sympathy, Toshio Mori wrote about the lives of Japanese Americans in northern California. Born in Oakland, young Mori worked ten to twelve hours each day in his family's nursery and then forced himself to write for four hours more. He once described the life this way: "Since I had to get up at dawn every morning to prepare flowers for the market, I slept only a few hours. During the day, I thought about characters and themes for stories. I used to work so hard I thought I would fall by the wayside. . . . It was six years and many rejection slips later when my first story was finally accepted for publication."

Building Background

Immigration "The Six Rows of Pompons" is about a Japanese American family living near Oakland, California, before World War II (1939-1945). Seeking jobs, many people from Japan came to the United States in the late 1800s. Most of these immigrants settled in California.

Getting into the Story

Discussion This story describes how older family members deal with a high-spirited seven-year-old. In a small group, share your recent baby-sitting or other experiences with young children.

Reading Tip

Making Inferences Although "The Six Rows of Pompons" is written in the first person, you are never really given any specific information about who the narrator is. You can make inferences about or figure out who the narrator is from clues the author gives you. As you read the story, look for clues. Write them down. When you have finished reading, use the clues to piece together a mental picture of the narrator.

San Francisco–Oakland Area

San Francisco–Oakland Bay Bridge

Oakland

San Francisco

San Francisco Bay

PACIFIC OCEAN

miles
0   5
kilometers
0   8

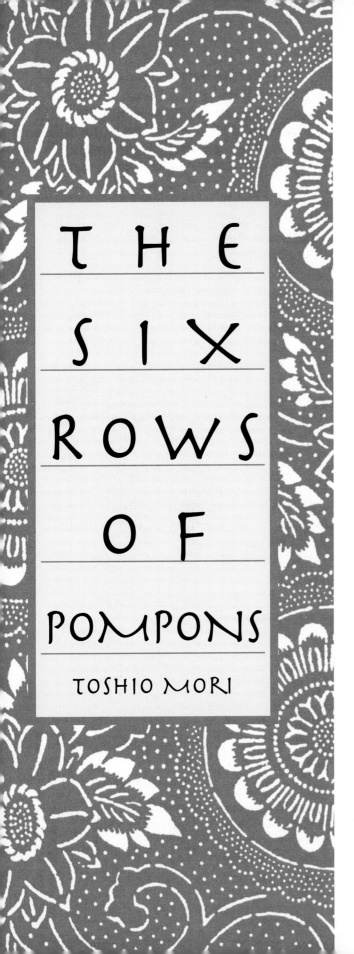

THE SIX ROWS OF POMPONS

TOSHIO MORI

When little Nephew Tatsuo[1] came to live with us he liked to do everything the adults were doing on the nursery,[2] and although his little mind did not know it, everything he did was the opposite of adult conduct, unknowingly destructive and disturbing. So Uncle Hiroshi[3] after witnessing several weeks of rampage[4] said, "This has got to stop, this sawing the side of a barn and nailing the doors to see if it would open. But we must not whip him. We must not crush his curiosity by any means."

And when Nephew Tatsuo, who was seven and in high second grade, got used to the place and began coming out into the fields and pestering us with difficult questions as "What are the plants here for? What is water? What are the bugs made for? What are the birds and why do the birds sing?" and so on, I said to Uncle Hiroshi, "We must do something about this. We cannot answer questions all the time and we cannot be correct all the time and so we will do harm. But something must be done about this beyond a doubt."

"Let us take him in our hands," Uncle Hiroshi said.

So Uncle Hiroshi took little Nephew Tatsuo aside, and brought him out in the fields and showed him the many rows of pompons growing. "Do you know what these are?" Uncle Hiroshi said. "These things here?"

---

1. **Tatsuo** (tät sü′ō).
2. **nursery** (nėr′sər ē), *n.* place where plants are raised for transplanting or sale.
3. **Hiroshi** (hə rō′shē).
4. rampage (ram′pāj), *n.* fit of rushing wildly about; spell of violent behavior.

"Yes. Very valuable," Nephew Tatsuo said. "Plants."

"Do you know when these plants grow up and flower, we eat?" Uncle Hiroshi said.

Nephew Tatsuo nodded. "Yes," he said, "I knew that."

"All right. Uncle Hiroshi will give you six rows of pompons," Uncle Hiroshi said. "You own these six rows. You take care of them. Make them grow and flower like your uncles'."

"Gee!" Nephew Tatsuo said.

"Do you want to do it?" Uncle Hiroshi said.

"Sure!" he said.

"Then jump right in and start working," Uncle Hiroshi said. "But first, let me tell you something. You cannot quit once you start. You must not let it die, you must make it grow and flower like your uncles'."

"All right," little Nephew Tatsuo said, "I will."

"Every day you must tend[5] to your plants. Even after the school opens, rain or shine," Uncle Hiroshi said.

"All right," Nephew Tatsuo said. "You'll see!"

So the old folks once more began to work peacefully, undisturbed, and Nephew Tatsuo began to work on his plot. However, every now and then Nephew Tatsuo would run to Uncle Hiroshi with much excitement.

"Uncle Hiroshi, come!" he said. "There's bugs on my plants! Big bugs, green bugs with black dots and some brown bugs. What shall I do?"

"They're bad bugs," Uncle Hiroshi said. "Spray them."

"I have no spray," Nephew Tatsuo said excitedly.

"All right. I will spray them for you today," Uncle Hiroshi said. "Tomorrow I will get you a small hand spray. Then you must spray your own plants."

Several tall grasses shot above the pompons and Uncle Hiroshi noticed this. Also, he saw the beds beginning to fill with young weeds.

"Those grasses attract the bugs," he said. "Take them away. Keep the place clean."

It took Nephew Tatsuo days to pick the weeds out of the six beds. And since the weeds were not picked cleanly, several weeks later it looked as if it was not touched at all. Uncle Hiroshi came around sometimes to feel the moisture in the soil. "Tatsuo," he said, "your plants need water. Give it plenty, it is summer. Soon it will be too late."

Nephew Tatsuo began watering his plants with the three-quarter hose.[6]

"Don't hold the hose long in one place and short in another," Uncle Hiroshi said. "Keep it even and wash the leaves often."

In October Uncle Hiroshi's plants stood tall and straight and the buds began to appear. Nephew Tatsuo kept at it through summer and autumn, although at times he looked wearied and indifferent.[7] And each time Nephew Tatsuo's enthusiasm lagged Uncle Hiroshi took him over to the six rows of pompons and appeared greatly surprised.

"Gosh," he said, "your plants are coming up! It is growing rapidly; pretty soon the flowers will come."

"Do you think so?" Nephew Tatsuo said.

PREDICT: How do you think the six rows of pompons will turn out?

"Sure, can't you see it coming?" Uncle Hiroshi said. "You will have lots of flowers. When you have enough to make a bunch I will sell it for you at the flower market."

"Really?" Nephew Tatsuo said. "In the flower market?"

Uncle Hiroshi laughed. "Sure," he said.

---

5. **tend** (tend), *v.* take care of; look after; attend to.
6. **three-quarter hose**, hose that is three-fourths of an inch in diameter.
7. **indifferent** (in dif′ər ənt), *adj.* not caring one way or the other; having or showing no interest.

Tatsuo is enthusiastic at first about his garden. Explain how you would feel about tending flowers like the ones in the photograph.

"That's where the plant business goes on, isn't it?"

One day Nephew Tatsuo wanted an awful lot to have us play catch with him with a tennis ball. It was at the time when the nursery was the busiest and even Sundays were all work.

"Nephew Tatsuo, don't you realize we are all men with responsibilities?" Uncle Hiroshi said. "Uncle Hiroshi has lots of work to do today. Now is the busiest time. You also have lots of work to do in your beds. And this should be your busiest time. Do you know whether your pompons are dry or wet?"

"No, Uncle Hiroshi," he said. "I don't quite remember."

"Then attend to it. Attend to it," Uncle Hiroshi said.

Nephew Tatsuo ran to the six rows of pompons to see if it was dry or wet. He came running back. "Uncle Hiroshi, it is still wet," he said.

"All right," Uncle Hiroshi said, "but did you see those holes in the ground with the piled-up mounds of earth?"

"Yes. They're gopher holes," Nephew Tatsuo said.

"Right," Uncle Hiroshi said. "Did you catch the gopher?"

"No," said Nephew Tatsuo.

"Then attend to it, attend to it right away," Uncle Hiroshi said.

One day in late October Uncle Hiroshi's pompons began to bloom. He began to cut and bunch and take them early in the morning to the flower market in Oakland. And by this time Nephew Tatsuo was anxious to see his pompons bloom. He was anxious to see how it feels to cut the flowers of his plants. And by this time Nephew Tatsuo's six beds of pompons looked like a patch of tall weeds left uncut through the summer. Very few pompon buds stood out above the tangle.

Few plants survived out of the six rows. In some parts of the beds where the pompons had plenty of water and freedom, the stems grew strong and tall and the buds were big and round. Then there were parts where the plants looked shriveled[8] and the leaves were wilted and brown. The majority of the plants were dead before the cool weather arrived. Some died by dryness, some by gophers or moles, and some were dwarfed by the great big grasses which covered the pompons altogether.

When Uncle Hiroshi's pompons began to flower everywhere the older folks became worried.

"We must do something with Tatsuo's six beds. It is worthless and his bugs are coming over to our beds," Tatsuo's father said. "Let's cut it down and burn them today."

"No," said Uncle Hiroshi. "That will be a very bad thing to do. It will kill Nephew Tatsuo. Let the plants stay."

So the six beds of Nephew Tatsuo remained intact, the grasses, the gophers, the bugs, the buds and the plants and all. Soon after, buds began to flower and Nephew Tatsuo began to run around calling Uncle Hiroshi. He said the flowers are coming. Big ones, good ones. He wanted to know when can he cut them.

"Today," Uncle Hiroshi said. "Cut it today and I will sell it for you at the market tomorrow."

Next day at the flower market Uncle Hiroshi sold the bunch of Nephew Tatsuo's pompons for twenty-five cents. When he came home Nephew Tatsuo ran to the car.

"Did you sell it, Uncle Hiroshi?" Nephew Tatsuo said.

"Sure. Why would it not sell?" Uncle

---

8. **shriveled** (shriv′əld), *adj.* dried up; withered.

Hiroshi said. "They are healthy, carefully cultured[9] pompons."

Nephew Tatsuo ran around excitedly. First, he went to his father. "Papa!" he said, "someone bought my pompons!" Then he ran over to my side and said, "The bunch was sold! Uncle Hiroshi sold my pompons!"

At noontime, after the lunch was over, Uncle Hiroshi handed over the quarter to Nephew Tatsuo.

"What shall I do with this money?" asked Nephew Tatsuo, addressing all of us, with shining eyes.

"Put it in your toy bank," said Tatsuo's father.

"No," said Uncle Hiroshi. "Let him do what he wants. Let him spend and have a taste of his money."

"Do you want to spend your quarter, Nephew Tatsuo?" I said.

"Yes," he said.

"Then do anything you wish with it," Uncle Hiroshi said. "Buy anything you want. Go and have a good time. It is your money."

On the following Sunday we did not see Nephew Tatsuo all day. When he came back late in the afternoon Uncle Hiroshi said, "Nephew Tatsuo, what did you do today?"

"I went to a show, then I bought an ice cream cone and then on my way home I watched the baseball game at the school, and then I bought a popcorn from the candy man. I have five cents left," Nephew Tatsuo said.

"Good," Uncle Hiroshi said. "That shows a good spirit."

Uncle Hiroshi, Tatsuo's father, and I sat in the shade. It was still hot in the late afternoon that day. We sat and watched Nephew Tatsuo riding around and around the yard on his red tricycle, making a furious dust.

"Next year he will forget what he is doing this year and will become a wild animal and go on a rampage again," the father of Tatsuo said.

"Next year is not yet here," said Uncle Hiroshi.

"Do you think he will be interested to raise pompons again?" the father said.

EVALUATE: Why does everyone think Tatsuo will not change?

"He enjoys praise," replied Uncle Hiroshi, "and he takes pride in good work well done. We will see."

"He is beyond a doubt the worst gardener in the country," I said. "Probably he is the worst in the world."

"Probably," said Uncle Hiroshi.

"Tomorrow he will forget how he enjoyed spending his year's income," the father of Tatsuo said.

"Let him forget," Uncle Hiroshi said. "One year is nothing. We will keep this six rows of pompon business up till he comes to his senses.[10]

We sat that night the whole family of us, Uncle Hiroshi, Nephew Tatsuo's father, I, Nephew Tatsuo, and the rest, at the table and ate, and talked about the year and the prospect of the flower business, about Uncle Hiroshi's pompon crop, and about Nephew Tatsuo's work and, also, his unfinished work in this world.

---

9. **cultured** (kul′chərd), *adj.* helped to grow by labor and care; cultivated.
10. sense (sens′), *n.* normal, sound condition of mind.

After Reading

Making Connections

1. Who do you think really has growing pains in this story—Nephew Tatsuo or the adults? Explain.

2. How would you rate Uncle Hiroshi's method of child raising? Explain.

3. What do you think is meant by the phrase "his unfinished work in this world" in the last sentence of the story?

4. Nephew Tatsuo and Uncle Hiroshi are the only fully developed **characters** in the story. Why do you suppose the author tells us so little about the narrator and other members of the family?

5. How do you think the author's experiences as a child might have influenced the **plot** of this story?

6. Imagine your next encounter with a young child you know. Will you behave differently as a result of reading this story? Why or why not?

Literary Focus: Characterization

Like most authors, the author of "The Six Rows of Pompons" does not directly tell you what the characters are like. Instead, he reveals the **characterization** by providing clues you can use to draw conclusions and to compare one character with another. For example, you can compare Tatsuo's father and Uncle Hiroshi.

Look back to the story to find the two situations described in the chart below. Copy the chart. Then complete it with your own ideas.

Situation	How Tatsuo's Father Reacts	How Uncle Hiroshi Reacts	My Conclusion About the Two Men
Bugs from Tatsuo's rows spreads to other beds	He suggests cutting down and burning		
Tatsuo spends the money from sale of his flowers			

Vocabulary Study

The sentences below come from a story that Uncle Hiroshi might have written for Nephew Tatsuo. For each underlined word or phrase, choose the word from the list that has the same meaning and write it on your paper.

rampage
tend
indifferent
shriveled
senses

1. Once there was an <u>uncaring</u> gardener.
2. He would rather ride his tricycle than <u>care for</u> his plants.
3. Without water, the <u>withered</u> plants drooped in the hot sun.
4. When the young gardener saw the condition of his plants, he began a <u>violent fit</u>, with much shouting, running back and forth, and chasing the animals from the plants.
5. After a while, the boy came to his <u>right mind</u> and settled down to care for his plants.

Expressing Your Ideas ——————

Writing Choices

Ways of Growing Write a brief **essay** that describes how this story fits into the theme "Growing Pains." Consider who and what grows, how they grow, and the difficulties they encounter.

In Praise of Hiroshi You are Tatsuo, many years later. Uncle Hiroshi has died, and you will deliver a **eulogy**, or speech of praise, at his funeral. Write the eulogy. Be sure to note how Hiroshi helped you become who you are today.

Step by Step Write a list of **directions** for growing the pompons. Use the story as well as other sources for information.

Other Options

Flower Power What do you think happened at the flower market when Uncle Hiroshi took Tatsuo's pompons there? With a partner, prepare a **skit** in which one of you plays Uncle Hiroshi and the other plays the person to whom he wants to sell the pompons. Perform your skit for the class.

Fill in the Blanks In the last paragraph of the story, the narrator refers to "the whole family of us, Uncle Hiroshi, Nephew Tatsuo's father, I, Nephew Tatsuo, and the rest." Use these and other hints—and your imagination—to create Uncle Hiroshi's **family tree.** Include a small portrait of each person, his or her name, and his or her relationship to the other family members.

Growth Spurt Make a **drawing** of the six rows of pompons as they looked when Tatsuo wasn't really paying much attention to them. Then draw the six rows of pompons as they looked when he was tending them.

Before Reading

Stolen Day

by Sherwood Anderson

Sherwood Anderson
1876–1941

Sherwood Anderson concentrated on portraying believable characters in real-life situations. For inspiration, Anderson drew on the people and incidents of his own Ohio boyhood. He referred to the main characters in his fiction as "split-off sections" of himself. In *A Story Teller's Story*, one of his three autobiographies, he described the experience of writing fiction this way: "Sometimes I had been seated writing all night at my desk and could not have told whether I had been there two hours or ten. Then the morning light streamed in at my window and my hands trembled so that I could no longer hold the pen. What a sweet clean feeling."

Building Background

In Sickness and in Health If you're like most people, you sometimes imagine you're sick when, in fact, you're perfectly healthy. For example, you may hear about some rare disease with a peculiar set of symptoms. Before long, you feel sure you're experiencing those exact symptoms! People who frequently feel this way, and whose lives are seriously affected by their feelings, are said to suffer from *hypochondria*. Hypochondriacs are not pretenders or fakes; they truly believe they are ill.

Getting into the Story

Writer's Notebook In the story, the narrator "steals" a school day for himself. Have you ever stolen time for yourself? That is, have you avoided or put off doing something you were supposed to do in favor of something you wanted to do? Write about it in your notebook.

Reading Tip

Keeping Track of Sequence "Stolen Day" is written as if the narrator were thinking aloud. At various points in the story, his thoughts skip from the present to the past to the future and back again. To keep track of sequence in the story, make a chart of past, present, and future events. When you read a passage in which the sequence is a bit confusing, go back and carefully reread the passage. Jot down the events described in the passage under the appropriate headings in your chart. See the example below.

Past Events	Present Events	Future Events
Drowned child found by narrator's mother	Narrator considers going fishing	Narrator might drown; mother will feel bad

SHERWOOD ANDERSON

It must be that all children are actors. The whole thing started with a boy on our street named Walter, who had inflammatory rheumatism.[1] That's what they called it. He didn't have to go to school.

Still he could walk about. He could go fishing in the creek or the waterworks[2] pond. There was a place up at the pond where in the spring the water came tumbling over the dam and formed a deep pool. It was a good place. Sometimes you could get some big ones there.

I went down that way on my way to school one spring morning. It was out of my way but I wanted to see if Walter was there.

He was, inflammatory rheumatism and all. There he was, sitting with a fish pole in his hand. He had been able to walk down there all right.

It was then that my own legs began to hurt. My back too. I went on to school but, at the recess time, I began to cry. I did it when the teacher, Sarah Suggett, had come out into the schoolhouse yard.

She came right over to me.

"I ache all over," I said. I did, too.

I kept on crying and it worked all right.

"You'd better go on home," she said.

So I went. I limped painfully away. I kept on limping until I got out of the schoolhouse street.

Then I felt better. I still had inflammatory rheumatism pretty bad but I could get along better.

I must have done some thinking on the way home.

"I'd better not say I have inflammatory rheumatism," I decided. "Maybe if you've got that you swell[3] up."

---

1. **inflammatory rheumatism** (in flam′ə tôr′ē rū′mə tiz′əm), a disease of the joints usually marked by heat, redness, swelling, and pain.
2. **waterworks** (wô′tər wėrks′), *n.* system of pipes, reservoirs, pumps, and so on for supplying a city or town with water.
3. swell (swel), *v.* become larger or thicker.

How does this fishing scene painted by Adam Emory Albright in 1906 add to the mood of the story?

I thought I'd better go around to where Walter was and ask him about that, so I did—but he wasn't there.

"They must not be biting today," I thought.

I had a feeling that, if I said I had inflammatory rheumatism, Mother or my brothers and my sister Stella might laugh. They did laugh at me pretty often and I didn't like it at all.

"Just the same," I said to myself, "I have got it." I began to hurt and ache again.

I went home and sat on the front steps of our house. I sat there a long time. There wasn't anyone at home but Mother and the two little ones. Ray would have been four or five then and Earl might have been three.

It was Earl who saw me there. I had got tired sitting and was lying on the porch. Earl was always a quiet, solemn little fellow.

He must have said something to Mother for presently she came.

"What's the matter with you? Why aren't you in school?" she asked.

I came pretty near telling her right out that I had inflammatory rheumatism but I thought I'd better not. Mother and Father had been speaking of Walter's case at the table just the day before. "It affects the heart," Father had said. That frightened me when I thought of it. "I might die," I thought. "I might just suddenly die right here; my heart might stop beating."

On the day before I had been running a race with my brother Irve. We were up at the fairgrounds after school and there was a half-mile track.

"I'll bet you can't run a half mile," he said. "I bet you I could beat you running clear around the track."

And so we did it and I beat him, but afterward my heart did seem to beat pretty hard. I remembered that lying there on the porch. "It's a wonder, with my inflammatory rheumatism and all, I didn't just drop down dead," I thought. The thought frightened me a lot. I ached worse than ever.

"I ache, Ma," I said. "I just ache."

She made me go in the house and upstairs and get into bed.

It wasn't so good. It was spring. I was up there for perhaps an hour, maybe two, and then I felt better.

I got up and went downstairs. "I feel better, Ma," I said.

Mother said she was glad. She was pretty busy that day and hadn't paid much attention to me. She had made me get into bed upstairs and then hadn't even come up to see how I was.

I didn't think much of that when I was up there but when I got downstairs where she was, and when, after I had said I felt better and she only said she was glad and went right on with her work, I began to ache again.

I thought, "I'll bet I die of it. I bet I do."

I went out to the front porch and sat down. I was pretty sore at Mother.

"If she really knew the truth, that I have inflammatory rheumatism and I may just drop down dead any time, I'll bet she wouldn't care about that either," I thought.

I was getting more and more angry the more thinking I did.

"I know what I'm going to do," I thought; "I'm going to go fishing."

I thought that, feeling the way I did, I might be sitting on the high bank just above the deep pool where the water went over

the dam, and suddenly my heart would stop beating.

And then, of course, I'd pitch[4] forward, over the bank into the pool and, if I wasn't dead when I hit the water, I'd drown sure.

They would all come home to supper and they'd miss me.

"But where is he?"

Then Mother would remember that I'd come home from school aching.

She'd go upstairs and I wouldn't be there. One day during the year before, there was a child got drowned in a spring. It was one of the Wyatt children.

Right down at the end of the street there was a spring under a birch tree and there had been a barrel sunk in the ground.

Everyone had always been saying the spring ought to be kept covered, but it wasn't.

So the Wyatt child went down there, played around alone, and fell in and got drowned.

Mother was the one who had found the drowned child. She had gone to get a pail of water and there the child was, drowned and dead.

This had been in the evening when we were all at home, and Mother had come running up the street with the dead, dripping child in her arms. She was making for[5] the Wyatt house as hard as she could run, and she was pale.

She had a terrible look on her face, I remembered then.

"So," I thought, "they'll miss me and there'll be a search made. Very likely there'll be someone who has seen me sitting by the pond fishing, and there'll be a big alarm and

---

4. **pitch** (pich), *v.* fall or plunge forward.
5. **making for**, going toward.

Stolen Day   **33**

all the town will turn out and they'll drag[6] the pond."

I was having a grand time, having died. Maybe, after they found me and had got me out of the deep pool, Mother would grab me up in her arms and run home with me as she had run with the Wyatt child.

I got up from the porch and went around the house. I got my fishing pole and lit out for[7] the pool below the dam. Mother was busy—she always was—and didn't see me go. When I got there I thought I'd better not sit too near the edge of the high bank.

By this time I didn't ache hardly at all, but I thought:

"With inflammatory rheumatism you can't tell," I thought.

"It probably comes and goes," I thought.

"Walter has it and he goes fishing," I thought.

I had got my line into the pool and suddenly I got a bite. It was a regular whopper: I knew that. I'd never had a bite like that.

I knew what it was. It was one of Mr. Fenn's big carp.[8]

Mr. Fenn was a man who had a big pond of his own. He sold ice in the summer and the pond was to make the ice. He had bought some big carp and put them into his pond and then, earlier in the spring when there was a freshet,[9] his dam had gone out.[10]

So the carp had got into our creek and one or two big ones had been caught—but none of them by a boy like me.

The carp was pulling and I was pulling and I was afraid he'd break my line, so I just tumbled down the high bank, holding onto the line and got right into the pool. We had it out, there in the pool. We struggled. We wrestled. Then I got a hand under his gills and got him out.

He was a big one all right. He was nearly half as big as I was myself. I had him on the bank and I kept one hand under his gills and I ran.

I never ran so hard in my life. He was slippery, and now and then he wriggled out of my arms; once I stumbled and fell on him, but I got him home.

So there it was. I was a big hero that day. Mother got a washtub and filled it with water. She put the fish in it and all the neighbors came to look. I got into dry clothes and went down to supper—and then I made a break that spoiled my day.

There we were, all of us, at the table, and suddenly Father asked what had been the matter with me at school. He had met the teacher, Sarah Suggett, on the street and she had told him how I had become ill.

"What was the matter with you?" Father asked, and before I thought what I was saying I let it out.

"I had the inflammatory rheumatism," I said—and a shout went up. It made me sick to hear them, the way they all laughed.

It brought back all the aching pain again, and like a fool I began to cry.

"Well, I *have* got it—I *have*, I *have*," I cried, and I got up from the table and ran upstairs.

I stayed there until Mother came up. I knew it would be a long time before I heard the last of the inflammatory rheumatism. I was sick all right, but the aching I now had wasn't in my legs or in my back.

---

6. **drag** (drag), *v.* search, as by pulling a net or hook through water.
7. **lit out for,** went quickly toward.
8. **carp** (kärp), *n.* bony freshwater fish that lives in ponds and slow streams.
9. **freshet** (fresh′it), *n.* flood caused by heavy rains.
10. **gone out,** washed away.

After Reading

Making Connections

1. Copy the diagram below in your Writer's Notebook. Mark the scale to show how much you could or could not identify with the **narrator** of the story. Then tell why you feel as you do.

Could identify with him									Could not identify with him
1	**2**	**3**	**4**	**5**	**6**	**7**	**8**	**9**	**10**

2. Do you think the **narrator** truly believed he had inflammatory rheumatism? Explain.

3. The narrator seems to want attention, especially from his mother. What would you suggest he do to get more attention?

4. Some parts of the story, like the following, read as though they were never edited: "I went down that way on my way to school one spring morning." Why do you think the author used this **style?**

5. Did the **sequence,** which skips around around from event to event, make the story more interesting? Explain.

6. If you could steal a day for yourself, what would you do?

Literary Focus: Characterization

In "The Six Rows of Pompons" you learned how the author revealed characterization by contrasting two characters. Authors have several methods for revealing characterization. An author may describe a character's actions, "quote" the character's words or thoughts, or tell how others react to the character.

Copy the web below. On the lines, write three traits you feel that the narrator of "Stolen Day" has. For each trait, write an example from the story that revealed the trait to you.

Narrator of "Stolen Day"

Vocabulary Study

The narrator wondered if inflammatory rheumatism made a person swell up, and he imagined how it would be if his heart stopped and he pitched into the pool. What other words come to mind when you think of **swell** and **pitch**? On a sheet of paper, write five related words for *swell* and *pitch*.

Expressing Your Ideas

Writing Choices

A Likely Story Imagine you are the narrator. Write a **letter** to your teacher in which you explain why you decided to miss school and apologize for your absence.

A Different Angle Imagine you are your parents. Would you have been sympathetic to the narrator? Would you have wanted to punish the narrator? In a **diary entry**, write down what actions you will take toward the narrator.

Thoughts into Words Write a first-person **narrative** of a time when you put off doing something in favor of an activity you wanted to do, such as the one shown in the picture. As the author did in "Stolen Day," write as if you were thinking aloud, even if it means skipping back and forth from present to past to future.

Other Options

Carp Cartoon Prepare a **comic strip** about the narrator's experience catching and bringing home the big carp. No speech is necessary, but you may want to include a few "sound effects."

Later That Evening The last paragraph of the story indicates that the narrator's mother went up to his room sometime after supper. With a partner, create and present the **dialogue** that might have occurred between mother and son.

A Change of Scenery Imagine that you have stolen a day. What would the setting be if you were the character? Draw a **mural** for your story.

Before Reading

My First Year in Junior High

by Latoya Hunter

Latoya Hunter
born 1977–

"The world is waiting for Latoya!" That comment, written on her sixth-grade report card, launched Latoya Hunter into the world of publishing. The comment was quoted in a newspaper article about Latoya's school. A book editor read the article and contacted Latoya. Would she like to keep a diary during her first year in junior high, and get paid for it? Latoya's diary was published in 1992.

Building Background

Kinds of Schools In the United States, some students attend junior high schools. These schools usually have seventh and eighth grades and sometimes ninth grade. Other students attend middle schools which have sixth, seventh, and eighth grades. Other students go to elementary schools that have grades Kindergarten through eighth grades. What grades make up your school? Do you like the present arrangement, or do you think a different organization would be better? Explain.

Getting into the Selection

Discussion In a small group, share your experiences with new situations, such as entering a new school, moving to a new neighborhood, or trying a new activity. How did you feel beforehand? Who or what helped you get through it? How did you feel when the newness wore off? As you read the selection, compare your feelings with Latoya's.

Reading Tip

Diary Entries Reading someone else's diary entries may be a new experience. To get the most out of your reading, keep these things in mind:

- Many diary keepers write once a day every day. Others write only when they have time or something special to say.

- Diary writers usually feel free to reveal their most private thoughts and opinions, even if those opinions are negative.

- Diary entries often contain references that are clear to the writer but confusing to the reader. In Latoya's diary, JH, J.H.S., and J.H.S. 80 refer to the junior high school she attends. Public schools in New York City, where Latoya lived, are numbered.

- Many diary writers think of their diaries as people who can listen, understand, and give comfort. Thus, diary entries often resemble letters to a close friend.

My First Year in Junior High

Latoya Hunter

September 10, 1990

Dear Diary,

It is hard to believe that this is the day I have anticipated and looked forward to for such a long time. The sun still rose in the East and set again in the West, the crisis in Iraq is still going strong and Oprah Winfrey still preached at 4:00 about other people's business. This may sound funny but somewhere in the back of my mind I thought the world would stop for my first day of JH. The day proved me wrong and I've grown to realize that nothing will be quite as I dreamed them up.

My teachers are one of my biggest disappointments. In this crazy dream world of mine my teachers were cool and calm and bright and welcoming. They were really just normal people making their livings. Ms. Johnson is the science teacher. She is Australian-Chinese. I have never met a teacher who gave so many rules. Her rules for the year took up at least 3 pages of my notebook. All my other teachers are just average. They aren't, or don't seem to be nothing above or under that. Maybe during the year they'll prove to be above, or hopefully not under. My other courses are math, English, French, social studies, and Home and Careers. There are none I'm really excited about.

Diary, there isn't much of a welcoming committee at this school. However, there's a day 8th & 9th graders set out to show freshmen how they feel about us. They call it Freshman Day. It may sound sweet but it's not at all. What they set out to do is terrorize us. They really seem to want to hurt us. It's a tradition I guess. I hope with God's help that I'll be able to make it through without any broken bones.

Well, today I think I could say J.H.S. is almost like an earthly version of hell.

September 11, 1990

Dear Diary,

I never thought I'd get desperate enough to say this but I envy you. You don't have to live in this troubled world; all you do is hear about it. You don't have to go to J.H. and watch the clock, praying for dismissal time to come. You also don't have to go through a situation like sitting in a cafeteria watching others laughing and talking and you don't know anyone. To sit there and eat the food that is just terrible because there's nothing else to do.

You don't do any of those things. All you do is listen to pathetic twelve-year-olds like me tell you about it.

I guess you can tell how my day went. Diary, what am I going to do? My best friend left to go to another school. I wish she could be with me. We had so much fun together. She moved right before summer started. She doesn't live anywhere close so it would be much easier if she stayed at the school closest to her. That's the only part of it that's easy. The hardest part is not being together.

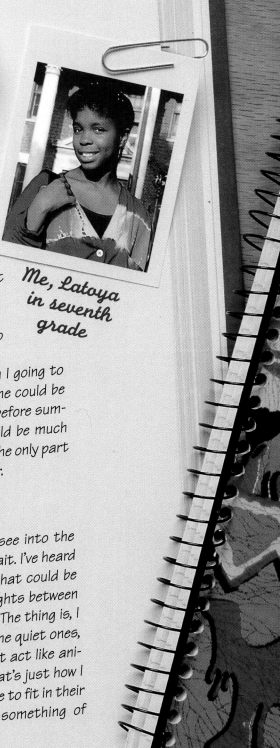

Me, Latoya in seventh grade

September 12, 1990

Dear Diary,

The dreaded Freshman Day is drawing near. I can see into the deranged minds of the 8th & 9th graders. They can't wait. I've heard rumors that they attack kids in the hall. I wonder if that could be true. Are they that cruel? I feel there will be a lot of fights between freshmen and seniors, I hope I won't be in any of them. The thing is, I know the kind of people they'll be aiming for. They are the quiet ones, the ones who aren't into the crowd, the kids who don't act like animals on the street. That's the kind of person I am. That's just how I am and how I'll leave J.H.S. 80. I'm not about to change to fit in their dead-in-an-alley-headed crowd. I intend to make something of myself. Life is too precious to waste.

September 13, 1990

Dear Diary,

Is it strange for someone to want to get sick so they can't leave their house for a day? Well, I do and you know why—it's Freshman's Day eve and tis not the season to be jolly. The older kids are really trying to make us believe like we're trespassing on their property. Well, it isn't theirs alone.

If there is a special diary way of praying, pray I'll come home in one piece. I'll write to you tomorrow. If I survive.

September 14, 1990

Dear Diary,

I can't believe I'm here writing to you with no scratches or bruises. I actually made it! Something must have snapped in the minds of the older kids. Maybe they remembered when they were freshmen themselves because there were only a few fights today. I witnessed one of them with a geeky looking boy who really fought back, badly as he did. They didn't really bother girls. I think that was decent of them. I'm really relieved as you may guess.

In the morning, Mr. Gluck, the principal announced that if anyone even thought of touching us it would mean suspension. Maybe that was why this Freshman Day was so much calmer. Whatever reason why, I appreciate it.

Well Diary, what I assume was the worst week of J.H. is over. I hope things will get better next week. It has to. It can't get any worse . . . or can it?

After Reading

Making Connections

1. Predict Latoya's attitude about junior high at the end of the school year, and explain your prediction.

2. Latoya had a publishing contract that called for her to produce a diary. Even without the contract, do you think she would have kept a diary? Explain.

3. ☺ Have you had school experiences similar to Latoya's? Explain how you reacted to these **changes** in your life.

Literary Focus: Point of View

The term **point of view** refers to an author's choice of a speaker to tell what is happening in a story. Most stories are written either in the first person, in which a character tells a story, or in the third person, in which story events are told by an outside observer. Of course, diary entries like Latoya's are always written in the first person, and they reflect the writer's own perspective on events.

Reread Latoya's first diary entry. Now consider Latoya's first day from a different point of view. Imagine yourself as Ms. Johnson, the science teacher. Write your answers to these questions.

- Why did you give three pages of rules to your classes?

- What were your first impressions of your students in general? Of Latoya Hunter in particular?

Expressing Your Ideas

Help! You are an advice columnist for a teen magazine. You receive a letter from a student who is nervous about the first day of junior high. Write a **letter of advice** to that student explaining how he or she can be prepared for the new school year.

Your Turn A publisher asks you to keep a diary. Of course you realize that someday the whole world will read it. With that in mind, write **diary entries** for the next seven days. Then read them to the class.

Latoya's Room Imagine what Latoya's room at home might look like. Draw or paint a **picture** of it.

Life Is Precious What does Latoya's statement that "Life is too precious to waste" mean to you? Use pictures and objects to make a **collage** that shows your appreciation of life.

Growing Pains

Stepping Up

Rites of Passage

Anthropology Connection
Most peoples around the world celebrate rites of passage. Many different ceremonies honor young people as they step up from childhood to adulthood and begin a new stage of life.

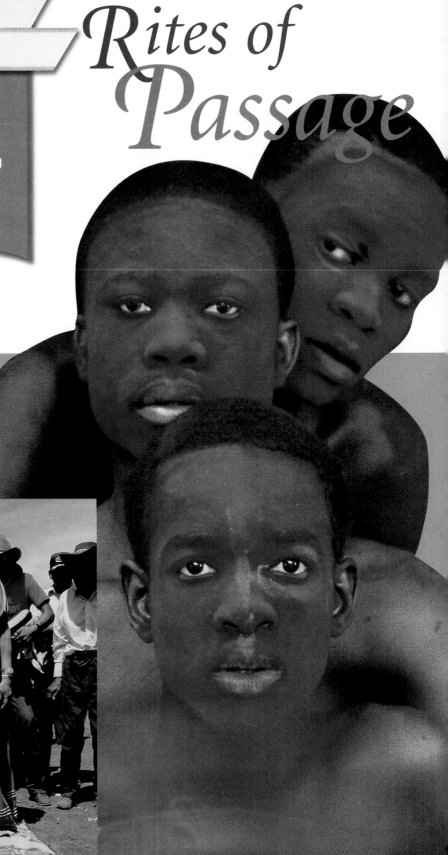

In a coming of age ceremony, Kota boys, who live in the Congo, paint their faces blue. The color blue symbolizes the death of childhood. The boys are reminded that before they become adults, the child in each of them must die. ➤

A young Apache girl comes of age. ▼

◄ **A Mexican American girl celebrates quinceañera, her fifteenth birthday, with a beautiful gown and lavish party.**

⋀ **In India, boys take part in a Hindu *sannyas* ceremony. The ten- to twelve-year-old boys become students of a swami, a Hindu spiritual leader. They leave their homes to live with the master, who teaches practical skills as well as the sacred literature. In return, the boys do menial tasks for the master.**

Growing up happens slowly. Every day you grow. Some days you hardly notice a change, and other days you seem to be a whole new person.

All over the world people observe rites of passage. In a very public way, these ceremonies celebrate growth and change—physical or spiritual. Birthdays, graduations, and weddings honor passage into a new stage of life. Christian confirmation and Jewish bar mitzvah celebrate reaching spiritual maturity.

Although rites of passage take many forms, they all have something in common. They say good-by to the old and welcome the new. The ceremonies help people to accept their new place and new responsibilities in society.

Responding

1. What do all the young people in these pictures have in common?

2. Describe some of the rites of passage that your family celebrates.

Should I Be Worried?

Wednesday was the big math test. Teresa was worried. She had knots in her stomach and couldn't even concentrate enough to study.

When you worry, it doesn't feel good. You can't stop thinking about what's bothering you. You may have stomachaches. You can't seem to concentrate on anything else and, like Teresa, the worrying just makes things worse.

Big Worries,
Little Worries

Worries come in different sizes. Some are little: you worry that the store may be sold out of the record you want. Like Teresa's math test, some are medium-size: you might not have enough money saved up to buy the presents you want. Finally, there are big ones—you worry that your dad may lose his job, that the kids in the new school that you are going to won't like you, that your sick dog may die soon. The bigger the worry, the more it seems to take over how you feel.

Not only do worries come in different sizes, they also come in different types. Most worries are based on real problems. Teresa worries about the math test if she hasn't done her homework; you worry about Christmas money if Christmas is two weeks away and you only have $2.33. Once you solve the problem, the worrying goes away.

The other kinds of worries are the ones that usually aren't based on real problems. You worry that your dog is going to die even though he's young and healthy, you worry that your hair is too short even though other people have told you how cute it is. You may have one particular worry that pops up every now and then, often out of nowhere. These worries usually come up when you are feeling down or tired or sad or upset about something else, or when you just don't feel good about yourself. When your mood improves or your self-confidence comes back, the worry usually goes away.

A lot of times it helps just to figure out what kind of worry it is. If it's a worry that comes up now and then and seems to reflect your mood, look for ways to feel better. Do something you like, spend some fun time with your family, get some rest. If it's based on a real problem, figure out what you can do to solve it.

Worrywarts:
Put Your Worry to Work!

Solving the problem isn't always easy. Here are some ideas:

Come up with a plan.
If you are worried about going to a new school, figure out a way to check it out ahead of time. Maybe you can meet some of the kids who will be in your class.

Get help.
If Teresa isn't sure about some of the math, she can call a friend who can explain it to her. If you are not even sure how to begin to tackle a problem, ask a parent or teacher for ideas.

Don't wait until the last minute.
A lot of problems can be prevented by not putting things off. If Teresa starts studying as soon as she knows about the test, she won't panic the night before.

Worries sure don't do you any good. They don't go away by themselves, but you can learn to shake them. The most important thing is to do *something*. If you think you worry too much, try these ideas:

Realize that you can only control you.
Some people worry about other people's problems or about what everyone thinks about them. Even though you can help others, you can't fix their problems for them. Even though you want others to like you, you can't make everybody happy. Do what's important for you.

Allow yourself to make mistakes.
Some people worry if they don't always get A's, run the fastest mile, or get the biggest part in the school play. Pushing yourself too hard can keep you worrying all the time. Give yourself permission to not always have to be the star.

Reduce your stress.
Exercise, take a break, have some fun. Worries get bigger as your stress goes up.

Talk to someone.
Talking to someone else helps to keep things from getting bottled up inside you. Try talking to a parent, a friend, a teacher, or your guidance counselor.

Responding

1. What can you do to tame your worries?

2. Write down something that worries you right now. What three things might you do to get rid of that worry?

Safety Connection

A driver's license! Is there any better proof that a teen has finally changed from a child to an adult? The chart below tells you when you will be able to get a driver's license in your state.

When Can I DRIVE?

State	Age Requirement for Regular License
Alabama	16
Alaska	18
Arizona	16
Arkansas	18
California	21
Colorado	16
Connecticut	18
Delaware	18
District of Columbia	18
Florida	16
Georgia	18
Hawaii	17
Idaho	18
Illinois	18
Indiana	18
Iowa	16
Kansas	18
Kentucky	16
Louisiana	17
Maine	18
Maryland	17
Massachusetts	18
Michigan	18
Minnesota	15
Mississippi	

State	Age Requirement for Regular License
Missouri	16
Montana	18
Nebraska	16
Nevada	18
New Hampshire	18
New Jersey	17
New Mexico	16
New York	17
North Carolina	18
North Dakota	16
Ohio	18
Oklahoma	16
Oregon	16
Pennsylvania	16
Rhode Island	16
South Carolina	16
South Dakota	16
Tennessee	16
Texas	16
Utah	16
Vermont	18
Virginia	18
Washington	18
West Virginia	18
Wisconsin	18
Wyoming	18

Source: AAA, 1994 and The MacMillan Almanac for Kids

Responding

1. How old do you have to be to get a driver's license in your state?

2. Find out the earliest age you can receive a restricted license in your state.

*In many states, drivers' licenses are available at ages younger than those shown, for people who have completed driver's education or who qualify because of other circumstances.

Reading Mini-Lesson

Recognizing Topics, Main Ideas, and Supporting Details

To get the point of an article, think about the relative importance of the ideas in it. You can use the title and headings as clues. For example, look at "Should I Be Worried?" Notice that the title and two headings in dark type all include a form of the word worry. The **topic** of the article—what it is about—is "worry." The topic of an article can usually be stated in a word or two.

Next, ask yourself about the **main idea** of the article. The main idea is the author's message about the topic. Sometimes a main idea is stated by the author, but often you must put the message into your own words. Which of the following sentences do you think best describes the main idea of the entire article?

1. Worries come in different sizes.

2. People can work to overcome all kinds of worries.

3. People should worry about all their worries.

Not only does the article have a main idea, but the parts of it and the paragraphs also have main ideas. **Details** are small pieces of information that tell about and support the main idea.

An outline of the information under the heading "Big Worries, Little Worries" might look like this:

(topic)	**KINDS**
(main idea)	**Worries come in different sizes and types.**
(details)	small, medium, or big
(details)	realistic or unrealistic

Activity Options

1. You can also use an outline to show the main ideas and supporting details for the information under the second heading in "Should I Be Worried?"

2. Find another short article in a newspaper or magazine and show the topic, main ideas, and details of the article by making an outline.

Part Two

Making Adjustments

If your clothes don't fit you, you might adjust a button. But have you ever adjusted your life? In the selections that follow, characters have to make changes in their lives. Some face situations that they can't avoid. Others decide on their own to make changes that cause improvement.

Multicultural Focus **Interactions** often involve contact between people of different backgrounds. Some people may treat others as inferior or as outsiders. How do the characters develop ways of dealing with these situations?

Emily

by Cynthia Roby

Cynthia Roby
born 1946
Imagine this. You are a parent, and your child is struggling in school. How can you help your child cope with a learning disability? Journalist Cynthia Roby had one answer: write a book. She dedicated her book to her son Nick "whose resilience and positive spirit in the face of his learning problems inspired this project." *When Learning Is Tough* is a collection of eight portraits of young people with learning disabilities. Emily Keegin, the subject of "Emily," was in sixth grade when she was interviewed by Roby. By writing this book, Roby helps people realize that learning disabilities are a challenge for many students—a challenge each person faces in his or her own unique way.

Building Background

Different Strokes for Different Folks Everyone has a special way of learning. Some people learn best by reading. Others pick up information more quickly when they hear it. Others do their most effective learning by studying pictures, maps, and illustrations. Still others need to use the information in a practical, hands-on way to really understand it. These are just a few of the many different learning styles people use to succeed in school and at their jobs.

Some people have difficulties learning specific types of things. Such difficulties are called **learning disabilities.** For example, people with **dyslexia** often confuse letters and numbers and read letters and words out of order. They can use different learning styles to help them overcome their learning disabilities.

Getting into the Selection

Writer's Notebook Make a space in your notebook for boasting. What kinds of things are you really good at? How do these natural abilities help you in school, in sports, and with making and keeping friends? Now, look at the flip side. What kinds of things give you trouble? How do your weaknesses make some subjects or situations difficult?

Reading Tip

Taking Notes Taking notes can be an important way to help you get more out of your reading especially if you have trouble reading. It can be as simple as jotting down your thoughts, impressions, and reactions as you read. Or you can take notes on a particular topic.

Keep your notebook at your side as you read "Emily," and take notes on the selection. You might want to focus your note-taking on one of the following topics: Emily's learning disability and learning styles, her strengths and weaknesses, how Emily expresses herself, or what you can learn from Emily.

EMILY

CYNTHIA ROBY

I guess you could say that my personality[1] is smack dab in the middle of my two parents'. My mother, who is an artist and designs greeting cards, is very overprotective. My father, who is a lawyer, is more carefree. They don't care that I have learning disabilities; they totally understand. Both of my parents have, maybe not learning disabilities, but different ways of learning. And they are not wonderful spellers. My whole family is that way.

I have two sisters. My older sister isn't home much now. My younger sister can be fun to be with. Other times I want to kill her. For fun I like to hang out with my friends downtown and look in stores but never buy anything.

Music really gets my spirits up. I play the trumpet. It's actually kind of hard to play, but it is easier for me because I have musical experience from playing the piano. I also love art. If I were painting a tree I might put some pink and purple in it, or some blue, just to make it more interesting. I've written tons of stories this year, and I love poetry. But it has been hard for me because I can't spell as well as the other kids.

When I first started school, I thought I must just be dumb. Why shouldn't I be learning this stuff? Sometimes I would even spell the word *in* wrong. I would spell it *en.* I thought, "I am so stupid!" For hours sometimes I would cry in my room. People would say, "You are not stupid. You're wonderful." and I'd say, "Yeah, right!" Now I know my learning problems don't have anything to do with my basic intelligence.[2]

---

1. **personality** (pėr′sə nal′ə tē), *n.* the individual quality that makes one person act differently from another person.
2. **intelligence** (in tel′ə jəns), *n.* ability to learn and know; quickness of understanding.

▲ Emily playing a trumpet.

When I was younger, I started falling further and further behind. In the fourth grade, when I started going to a tutor,[3] I didn't tell any of my friends. Some kids whispered, "She's going to a tutor," and then it seemed like everyone found out and said to me, "Oh, gosh. Is she nice?" and stuff. I didn't really care what the other kids thought because I knew that was what I needed. After a time some other kids started going, too. The tutor was great and really helped me.

My biggest dread was that I was going to have to stay back and repeat a grade. I thought that would be really awful. Kids I knew who had stayed back lost all their friends and had to make new friends. Everyone thought they were stupid. Fortunately,[4] I didn't have to stay back after all.

I've had a lot of testing and have found out that if I hear something I do a lot better than if I just see it. If you say six plus six equals twelve, or whatever, I keep saying it to myself and hearing it, and then I start remembering it. I learn from my ear, from hearing. Sometimes I make up rhymes to help me remember things like multiplication tables.

I usually know what's going on in school but sometimes I don't get concepts.[5] I would like to tell my teachers, "Teach more by talking to me than by giving me lots of pieces of paper and telling me to read them and to know things by tomorrow."

When I do my homework, I try to be really organized and work at my desk, but I usually end up propped against my bed. When I study for exams, I go over old tests. History comes naturally. In math, I just have to go over and over the problems until I know them.

After I finish school, the learning disabilities won't be as much a part of my life. Computers will help me with any written work. They already have spell checkers, and by then we will probably be able to talk to a computer and it will type.

Reading
by Emily Keegin

When I read I feel the words
Wash around my head
Like music of a butterfly
A flower starting to grow
5 I read of adventure
Mysteries too
Sports and poems
So can you
I go to my room
10 sit upon my bed
and feel the
music wash around
my head.

I can't wait until I am about twenty-six or thirty, especially if I am doing something like art or if I am some kind of superstar. I'm in plays at school, and I love acting. If I am an actress, the learning difficulties won't matter as much because I could listen to the script and then repeat it.

I have lots of ideas about what I want to be when I grow up. I will be slightly tall, like my Dad. I would like to be some kind of wonderful star. An actress, an artist, or a writer. I love history, so I might be an historian. I'd love to be some kind of sports person or maybe just do sports as a hobby. I love putting things together so I might be a model maker, doing something like models of houses. I'd like to be a designer. Interior designing is my favorite. I've decorated two doll houses. It's hard to decide right now. I've gone through so many ideas.

---

3. **tutor** (tü′tər), *n.* a private teacher.
4. **fortunately** (fôr′chə nit lē), *adv.* luckily.
5. **concept** (kon′sept), *n.* big idea or general notion.

Painted in 1928 by Charles Demuth, *I Saw the Figure 5 in Gold* is his impression of the No. 5 engine roaring through a lamplit street of a dark and rainy city. How do the floating numbers in the painting set the mood for the poem?

Arithmetic

Carl Sandburg

Arithmetic is where numbers fly like pigeons in and out
    of your head.
Arithmetic tells you how many you lose or win if you
    know how many you had before you lost or won.
5 Arithmetic is seven eleven all good children go to heaven
    —or five six bundle of sticks.
Arithmetic is numbers you squeeze from your head to
    your hand to your pencil to your paper till you get
    the answer.
10 Arithmetic is where the answer is right and everything is
    nice and you can look out of the window and see
    the blue sky—or the answer is wrong and you
    have to start all over and try again and see how
    it comes out this time.
15 If you take a number and double it and double it again
    and then double it a few more times, the number
    gets bigger and bigger and goes higher and higher
    and only arithmetic can tell you what the number
    is when you decide to quit doubling.
20 Arithmetic is where you have to multiply—and you
    carry the multiplication table in your head and
    hope you won't lose it.
If you have two animal crackers, one good and one bad,
    and you eat one and a striped zebra with streaks
25   all over him eats the other, how many animal
    crackers will you have if somebody offers you five
    six seven and you say No no no and you say Nay
    nay nay and you say Nix nix nix?
If you ask your mother for one fried egg for breakfast
30   and she gives you two fried eggs and you eat both
    of them, who is better in arithmetic, you or your
    mother?

After Reading

Making Connections

1. Imagine Emily was a new student at your school. Would you try to get to know her? Why or why not?

2. From reading "Emily," what did you find out about learning disabilities that you didn't know before?

3. Pick three words to describe Emily's attitude toward her learning problems. If you had similar difficulties, do you think you would have the same attitude she has? Explain.

4. Do you think Emily will be successful as an adult? Explain.

5. ☝ **Interactions** involve contact between people of different backgrounds. How did Emily's attitude help to change how her classmates perceived people with learning disabilities?

6. If you have a learning disability, did reading "Emily" change the way you think about or cope with it? Explain. If you don't have a learning disability, did reading the selection inspire you to think differently about or change the way that you respond to people with learning disabilities? Explain.

Literary Focus: Diction

Read a paragraph or two of "Emily" out loud. Can you "hear" Emily talking? The author used Emily's own words to give you a feeling of what Emily is like as a person. **Diction** involves choosing words to clearly express ideas and feelings. Reread "Emily," paying special attention to the way words and expressions are used. Find three or more examples in which you think Emily expressed herself very well. For each example, tell why you think her choice of words was so effective. Find three or more examples in which you think Emily could have improved her diction. Rewrite each example in a way that you feel makes it more effective.

Vocabulary Study

concept
fortunately
intelligence
personality
tutor

Below are learning tips Emily might have written. Write the word from the list that best completes each one.

Learning Tip 1 Your personal learning is probably related to your ___. Do you like to study alone, or do you prefer to be with others?

Learning Tip 2 Even if you have learning disabilities, don't worry about your ___. Many people who have learning disabilities are actually smarter than people who don't have them.

Learning Tip 3 If you have difficulty learning a ____ by reading, ask questions and try talking about the idea with your teacher.

Learning Tip 4 If you are having trouble with a particular subject in school, you might work with a ___ who can give you extra help. It's best to go to someone who isn't just good in the given subject but also has training with different learning styles.

Learning Tip 5 You are not alone with your learning disability. ____ , most states have organizations that can help you. To find out which ones are active in your state, contact the Clearinghouse on Disability Information, 330 C Street SW, Room 3132, Washington, D.C., 20202-2524.

Expressing Your Ideas

Writing Choices

Learning Your Own Way Make a **chart** of study tips Emily uses when she works at different subjects. Use the notes you took. In a separate column, write down the study tips you use for each subject listed. Compare your tips with Emily's. **Interaction** with your classmates can also help you discover other study tips. Try any new study tips you think will work well for you.

A Poet Who Doesn't Know It Write a **poem** about something you are good at or something that causes you difficulty.

Other Options

For All Learners Research different learning styles that people have. Then, design a **display** that demonstrates different ways people might learn.

Tough for You Too Pick an experience in which you had trouble with something and found a way to overcome it. Discuss this experience with one or more friends. Talk about what adjustments you made. Then make a **tape** about your experience and what you learned from it. Pay attention to effective diction.

Before Reading

The Circuit

by Francisco Jiménez

Francisco Jiménez
born 1943

The 1958 crop-picking season was over and fifteen-year-old Francisco Jiménez was attending Santa María High School in California. Police officers came to one of his classes to arrest him. His family had come to the United States without proper papers and they all were sent back to Mexico.

Within two months, they got permanent-resident visas and returned to California. Francisco graduated from high school in 1961 and went on to college. He is now a professor of literature and writes both in Spanish and in English. His works are autobiographical, painting a bittersweet picture of life as a migrant worker.

Building Background

Moving Around In the United States, many fruit and vegetable crops are harvested by hand. Farmers often hire **migrant workers** to pick the crops.

Migrant workers travel across the country going from one seasonal job to the next. Whole families often spend at least half the year picking fruit or harvesting vegetables.

Getting into the Story

Discussion Have you ever had to move someplace else? How did it feel? If you haven't moved yourself, talk with a friend or family member who has. Ask that person to share his or her feelings.

Reading Tip

Using Graphic Aids A family of migrant workers is the subject of the story "The Circuit." What do you already know about harvesting crops and about migrant workers? What would you like to find out about these topics? A graphic aid, the K-W-L chart, can be an excellent learning tool.

Before you read "The Circuit," make your own K-W-L chart in your notebook. Fill in the first two columns with what you know and what you want to know about migrant workers. Look for answers to your questions as you read. After you read, complete the last column of your chart.

What I **Know** K	What I **Want** to Know W	What I **Learned** L
Migrant workers pick crops.	What kind of homes do migrant workers live in?	

◄ *On the Arrowback* was painted by Ken Danby in 1975. Predict what this boy's mood might have to do with the story.

THE CIRCUIT

FRANCISCO JIMÉNEZ

It was that time of year again. Ito, the strawberry sharecropper,[1] did not smile. It was natural. The peak of the strawberry season was over and the last few days the workers, most of them *braceros*,[2] were not picking as many boxes as they had during the months of June and July.

As the last days of August disappeared, so did the number of *braceros*. Sunday, only one—the best picker—came to work. I liked him. Sometimes we talked during our half-hour lunch break. That is how I found out he was from Jalisco,[3] the same state in Mexico my family was from. That Sunday was the last time I saw him.

When the sun had tired and sunk behind the mountains, Ito signaled us that it was time to go home. "*Ya esora,*"[4] he yelled in his broken Spanish. Those were the words I waited for twelve hours a day, everyday, seven days a week, week after week. And the thought of not hearing them again saddened me.

As we drove home Papa did not say a word. With both hands on the wheel, he stared at the dirt road. My older brother, Roberto, was also silent. He leaned his head back and closed his eyes. Once in a while he cleared from his throat the dust that blew in from outside.

Yes, it was that time of year. When I opened the front door to the shack, I stopped. Everything we owned was neatly packed in cardboard boxes. Suddenly I felt even more the weight of hours, days, weeks, and months of work. I sat down on a box. The thought of having to move to Fresno[5] and knowing what was in store for me there brought tears to my eyes.

That night I could not sleep. I lay in bed thinking about how much I hated this move.

A little before five o'clock in the morning, Papa woke everyone up. A few minutes later, the yelling and screaming of my little brothers and sisters, for whom the move was a great adventure, broke the silence of dawn. Shortly, the barking of the dogs accompanied them.

While we packed the breakfast dishes,

---

1. **sharecropper** (sher′krop/ər), *n.* person who farms land for the owner in return for part of the crops.
2. *braceros* (brä sä′rōs), Mexican migrant farm workers.
3. **Jalisco** (hä lēs′kō), a state in west-central Mexico.
4. *Ya esora* (yä es ō′rä), Spanish for "It's time."
5. **Fresno** (frez′nō), city in central California.

Papa went outside to start the "Carcanchita."[6] That was the name Papa gave his old '38 black Plymouth. He bought it in a used-car lot in Santa Rosa[7] in the winter of 1949. Papa was very proud of his car. *"Mi Carcanchita,"* my little jalopy, he called it. He had a right to be proud of it. He spent a lot of time looking at other cars before buying this one. When he finally chose the "Carcanchita," he checked it thoroughly before driving it out of the car lot. He examined every inch of the car. He listened to the motor, tilting his head from side to side like a parrot, trying to detect any noises that spelled car trouble. After being satisfied with the looks and sounds of the car, Papa then insisted on knowing who the original owner was. He never did find out from the car salesman. But he bought the car anyway. Papa figured the original owner must have been an important man because behind the rear seat of the car he found a blue necktie.

"We have work! Mr. Sullivan said WE CAN STAY there the whole season . . ."

Papa parked the car out in front and left the motor running. *"Listo"* [8] (ready), he yelled. Without saying a word, Roberto and I began to carry the boxes out to the car. Roberto carried the two big boxes and I carried the two smaller ones. Papa then threw the mattress on top of the car roof and tied it with ropes to the front and rear bumpers.

Everything was packed except Mama's pot. It was an old large galvanized pot she had picked up at an army surplus store in Santa Maria[9] the year I was born. The pot was full of dents and nicks, and the more dents and nicks it had, the more Mama liked it. *"Mi olla"* [10] (my pot), she used to say proudly.

I held the front door open as Mama carefully carried out her pot by both handles, making sure not to spill the cooked beans.

When she got to the car, Papa reached out to help her with it. Roberto opened the rear car door and Papa gently placed it on the floor behind the front seat. All of us then climbed in. Papa sighed, wiped the sweat off his forehead with his sleeve, and said wearily: *"Es todo"* [11] (that's it).

As we drove away, I felt a lump in my throat. I turned around and looked at our little shack for the last time.

At sunset we drove into a labor camp near Fresno. Since Papa did not speak English, Mama asked the camp foreman if he needed any more workers. "We don't need no more," said the foreman, scratching his head. "Check with Sullivan down the road. Can't miss him. He lives in a big white house with a fence around it."

When we got there, Mama walked up to the house. She went through a white gate, past a row of rose bushes, up the stairs to the front door. She rang the doorbell. The porch light went on and a tall husky man came out. They exchanged a few words. After the man went in, Mama clasped her hands and hurried back to the car. "We have work! Mr. Sullivan said we can stay there the whole season," she said gasping and pointing to an old garage near the stables.

The garage was worn out by the years. It had no windows. The walls, eaten by termites, strained to support the roof full of holes. The loose dirt floor, populated by earthworms, looked like a gray road map.

That night, by the light of a kerosene

---

6. **Carcanchita** (kär kän chē′tä), an affectionate term for the car.
7. **Santa Rosa**, California city north of San Francisco; fruit shipping center for the Sonoma Valley.
8. *Listo* (lēs′tō).
9. **Santa Maria**, city in Santa Barbara County, California.
10. *Mi olla* (mē ō′yä).
11. *Es todo* (es tō′dō).

lamp, we unpacked and cleaned our new home. Roberto swept away the loose dirt, leaving the hard ground. Papa plugged the holes in the walls with old newspapers and tin can tops. Mama fed my little brothers and sisters. Papa and Roberto then brought in the mattress and placed it on the far corner of the garage. "Mama, you and the little ones sleep on the mattress. Roberto, Panchito, and I will sleep outside under the trees," Papa said.

Early next morning Mr. Sullivan showed us where his crop was, and after breakfast, Papa, Roberto, and I headed for the vineyard to pick.

Around nine o'clock the temperature had risen to almost one hundred degrees. I was completely soaked in sweat and my mouth felt as if I had been chewing on a handkerchief. I walked over to the end of the row, picked up the jug of water we had brought, and began drinking. "Don't drink too much; you'll get sick," Roberto shouted. No sooner had he said that than I felt sick to my stomach. I dropped to my knees and let the jug roll off my hands. I remained motionless with my eyes glued on the hot sandy ground. All I could hear was the drone of insects. Slowly I began to recover. I poured water over my face and neck and watched the black mud run down my arms and hit the ground.

I still felt a little dizzy when we took a break to eat lunch. It was past two o'clock and we sat underneath a large walnut tree that was on the side of the road. While we ate, Papa jotted down the number of boxes we had picked. Roberto drew designs on the ground with a stick. Suddenly I noticed Papa's face turn pale as he looked down the road. "Here comes the school bus," he whispered loudly in alarm. Instinctively, Roberto and I ran and hid in the vineyards. We did not want to get in trouble for not going to school. The yellow bus stopped in front of Mr. Sullivan's house. Two neatly dressed boys about my age got off. They carried books under their arms. After they crossed the street, the bus drove away. Roberto and I came out from hiding and joined Papa. *"Tienen que tener cuidado"*[12] (you have to be careful), he warned us.

After lunch we went back to work. The sun kept beating down. The buzzing insects, the wet sweat, and the hot dry dust made the afternoon seem to last forever. Finally the mountains around the valley reached out and swallowed the sun. Within an hour it was too dark to continue picking. The vines blanketed the grapes, making it difficult to see the bunches. *"Vámonos,"*[13] said Papa, signaling to us that it was time to quit work. Papa then took out a pencil and began to figure out how much we had earned our first day. He wrote down numbers, crossed some out, wrote down some more. *"Quince"*[14] (fifteen dollars), he murmured.[15]

When we arrived home, we took a cold shower underneath a waterhose. We then sat down to eat dinner around some wooden crates that served as a table. Mama had cooked a special meal for us. We had rice and tortillas with *carne con chile,*[16] my favorite dish.

The next morning I could hardly move. My body ached all over. I felt little control over my arms and legs. This feeling went on every morning for days until my muscles finally got used to the work.

It was Monday, the first week of November. The grape season was over and I could now go to school. I woke up early that morning and lay in bed, looking at the stars and savoring[17] the thought of not going to work and of starting sixth grade for the first time that year.

---

12. *Tienen que tener cuidado* (tyen′ en kā te ner′ kwē ꞔHä′ ꞔHō).
13. *Vámonos* (vä′mō nōs), Spanish for Let's go.
14. *Quince* (kēn′sā).
15. murmur (mėr′mər), v. say in a soft, low, indistinct voice.
16. *carne con chile* (kär′nā kōn chē′lā), Spanish for "meat with chile."
17. savor (sā′vər), v. enjoy very much.

Since I could not sleep, I decided to get up and join Papa and Roberto at breakfast. I sat at the table across from Roberto, but I kept my head down. I did not want to look up and face him. I knew he was sad. He was not going to school today. He was not going tomorrow, or next week, or next month. He would not go until the cotton season was over, and that was sometime in February. I rubbed my hands together and watched the dry, acid-stained skin fall to the floor in little rolls.

When Papa and Roberto left for work, I felt relief.[18] I walked to the top of a small grade next to the shack and watched the "Carcanchita" disappear in the distance in a cloud of dust.

Two hours later, around eight o'clock, I stood by the side of the road waiting for school bus number twenty. When it arrived I climbed in. No one noticed me. Everyone was busy either talking or yelling. I sat in an empty seat in the back.

I was startled. I HAD NOT HEARD ENGLISH for months. I looked at the lady who waited for an answer.

When the bus stopped in front of the school, I felt very nervous. I looked out the bus window and saw boys and girls carrying books under their arms. I felt empty. I put my hands in my pants pockets and walked to the principal's office. When I entered I heard a woman's voice say: "May I help you?" I was startled.[19] I had not heard English for months. I looked at the lady who waited for an answer. My first instinct was to answer her in Spanish, but I held back. Finally, after struggling for English words I managed to tell her that I wanted to enroll in the sixth grade. After answering many questions, I was led to the classroom.

Mr. Lema, the sixth-grade teacher, greeted me and assigned me a desk. He then introduced me to the class. I was so nervous and scared at that moment when everyone's eyes were on me that I wished I were with Papa and Roberto picking cotton. After taking roll, Mr. Lema gave the class the assignment for the first hour. "The first thing we have to do this morning is finish reading the story we began yesterday," he said enthusiastically. He walked up to me, handed me an English book, and asked me to read. "We are on page 125," he said politely. When I heard this, I felt my blood rush to my head; I felt dizzy. "Would you like to read?" he asked hesitantly.[20] I opened the book to page 125. My mouth was dry. My eyes began to water. I could not begin. "You can read later," Mr. Lema said understandingly.

For the rest of the reading period I kept getting angrier and angrier with myself. I should have read, I thought to myself.

During recess I went into the restroom and opened my English book to page 125. I began to read in a low voice, pretending I was in class. There were many words I did not know. I closed the book and headed back to the classroom.

Mr. Lema was sitting at his desk correcting papers. When I entered he looked up at me and smiled. I felt better. I walked up to him and asked if he could help me with the new words. "Gladly," he said.

The rest of the month I spent my lunch

---

18. **relief** (ri lēf′), *n.* the lessening of or freeing from a burden.
19. **startled** (stär′tld), *adj.* surprised.
20. **hesitantly** (hez′ə tənt′lē), *adv.* undecidedly or with uncertainty.

hours working on English with Mr. Lema, my best friend at school.

One Friday during lunch hour Mr. Lema asked me to take a walk with him to the music room. "Do you like music?" he asked me as we entered the building.

"Yes, I like Mexican *corridos*,"[21] I answered. He then picked up a trumpet, blew on it and handed it to me. The sound gave me goose bumps. I knew that sound. I had heard it in many Mexican *corridos*. "How would you like to learn how to play it?" he asked. He must have read my face because before I could answer, he added: "I'll teach you how to play it during our lunch hours."

That day I could hardly wait to get home to tell Papa and Mama the great news. As I got off the bus, my little brothers and sisters ran up to meet me. They were yelling and screaming. I thought they were happy to see me, but when I opened the door to our shack, I saw that everything we owned was neatly packed in cardboard boxes.

---

21. ***corridos*** (kō rē′THōs), Mexican folk ballads, usually telling of a hero's adventures.

Campesinos

Leobardo V. Cortéz

Temprano,
cuando sale el sol,
bultos se mueven por los campos como
relojes en cada amanecer
5 hasta que la luna sale.

Sus manos de bronce
saludan
como
rifles en una guerra.

10 Luchando
para sobrevivir
un nuevo mañana
para nuestros hijos. . . .

Los chalecos blancos
15 de nuestra inocencia
pureza
y riqueza. . . .

Ven niño, deja tu vida sobre la tierra.
Yo soy
20 el esclavo de mis hijos.

Yo soy
también su dueño.
¡Sí!

Yo soy
25 el campesino
en los campos. . . .

Fieldworkers

Leobardo V. Cortéz

Early,
when the sun comes out,
lumps move throughout the fields like
clockwork every sunrise,
5 until the moon comes.

Their bronze hands
wave
like
rifles in a war.

10 Fighting
for survival
a new tomorrow
for our children. . . .

The white vests
15 our innocence
purity
and wealth. . . .

Come child, leave your life upon the
    land.
I am
20 the slave of my children.

I am
their owner as well.
Yes!

I am
25 the campesino
in the fields. . . .

In *Campesino,* painted by Daniel DeSiga in 1976, the endless field symbolizes the farm laborer's work which comes to an end only with the harvest.

After Reading

Making Connections

1. If you had been in the same situation as the narrator, would you have shared with your family your feelings about leaving your new school?

2. Reread the author biography on page 59. How do you think Jiménez's experiences affected the story?

3. Why do you think the author didn't explain why the family had to pack up and leave at the end of the story?

4. The ending of the story is similar to the beginning. How does this relate to the story's **title?**

5. Complete your K-W-L chart and make **generalizations** about migrant workers' experiences. Include any ideas you get from reading the poem on page 62.

6. **Interactions** involve contact between people of different backgrounds. Based on what you have read about migrant workers, how would you act toward students who you know will only be in your class a short time?

7. If you had a choice, would you rather work most of the year or go to school? Why?

Literary Focus: Personification

The river murmured a gentle welcome to my hot, tired feet.

Writers of poetry and fiction sometimes give human traits to animals or objects. This type of literary device is known as **personification.** The sentence above is an example. In this sentence, the writer compares a river to a person uttering a soft greeting.

Francisco Jiménez uses personification several times in "The Circuit." Look through the story to find examples of personification. Copy them in your notebook.

Below is a story from the point of view of another young migrant worker. Select the word from the list that best completes each incomplete sentence. Write your answers on a sheet of paper.

murmur
relief
hesitantly
savor
startle

Not expecting good news, my father __(1)__ walks up to the back door of the big, white house. When he returns, he looks very tired and discouraged. He shakes his head and said, "No work here."

"Let's go down the road," I __(2)__ softly. We climb into our car, which rattles and shakes as we bump along. We pull up next to a barn. A thin stooped man appears suddenly. The man smiles with __(3)__ and says, "I hope I didn't __(4)__ you. I have been worried about getting my artichoke crop harvested and extra hands would be welcome." Then, he suggests we consider staying through February. My dad can help pick the cotton. "Hurray! We may get to stay here awhile," I say wanting to __(5)__ the idea.

Expressing Your Ideas

Writing Choices

Help Wanted Write an **advertisement** for a farmer who needs migrant workers to pick his or her crop. List the hours the workers will work. Tell the wages, either per hour or per box or bag of fruit picked. Describe living arrangements that will be made for workers and their families. Include any benefits of the job. Post your advertisement on the class bulletin board.

Struggles, Strikes, and Songs Do research on migrant farm workers in the United States and how they have tried to improve working conditions for themselves and their families. Look for information on César Chávez, Dolores Huerta, and the United Farm Workers. Try to find newspaper or magazine articles on current issues involving migrant workers. Write a **report** based on your research. Include a time line, pictures, and other visual aids to make your report interesting.

Other Options

Mapping the Circuit Study a detailed road map of California while you reread "The Circuit." Try to trace the route the narrator's family followed from job to job. Scan the footnotes for more information. Work with your classmates to make your own **map** of the circuit.

New Kid on the Block Think of a time when you entered a new class or school. Lead a **discussion** about how you and your classmates have felt. Think of advice you might give other new students that would improve **interactions** between you and new students.

Before Reading

The Dandelion Garden

by Budge Wilson

Budge Wilson
born 1927

Like the young boy in "The Dandelion Garden," author Budge Wilson is a very creative, hard-working person. She started her career as an artist and only later became a writer. Once she started writing, the motivation to keep writing came from within. According to Wilson, "Writing centers me and makes me peaceful. If I haven't written anything for a while, I start to feel like a jigsaw puzzle before it has been made up."

Wilson was born in Nova Scotia and has lived there for most of her life. Many of her stories are set in that province of Canada.

Building Background

Friend or Foe If you just examined a single dandelion, you might consider it one of the world's loveliest flowers. The bloom is as bright as the sun. The leaves are delicious in salads, and the seeds are tiny parachutes that are fun to blow off the stem. The dandelion flourishes throughout most of North America.

However, the dandelion has a horrible reputation as a weed. It can take over any garden or lawn, because its wide-based, flat leaves shade out grass and other small plants and its thick, strong taproot takes up water from deep in the soil. Dandelions can bloom from the earliest days of spring well into the late fall.

Getting into the Story

Writer's Notebook Have you ever worked hard on something and been very proud of your work only to show it to a friend or relative and be disappointed in the reaction you got? Describe your experience in your notebook. How did you feel while you were working on your project? How did you feel after the other person's disappointing reaction? Were you motivated to work on a similar project again? Or did the lack of response or negative response from someone else discourage you? As you read, compare your experiences to those of the main character, Hamlet.

Reading Tip

Figuring Out Unfamiliar Words from Context "The Dandelion Garden" has many words that will be probably be unfamiliar to you. Don't let the unfamiliar terms discourage you. Use context clues to help you figure the meanings of new words. For example, the first sentence of the story describes two people of *humble means*. This phrase may be unfamiliar to you, but the next sentence gives a clue as to its meaning. "Although low in funds, the father was . . . " You can infer from the second sentence that *humble means* refers to being low in funds, or having little money.

The Dandelion Garden

Budge Wilson

*I*n a land not far away and not so long ago, a son was born to two people of humble means. Although low in funds, the father was high in pretensions, and named his son Hamlet.[1] "For," he explained, "this is no ordinary boy. He is our firstborn, and I intend that he shall be profound and inscrutable and undeniably great."

Hamlet displayed a notable lack of profundity during the first five years of his life. He did all the usual things. This pleased his father, who, like all parents, regarded usual things as unusual when performed by his own child. He developed remarkable and miraculous skills: he learned how to unbutton his shoes, to go to the bathroom, to throw a ball, to catch beetles, and to color between the lines. "Clearly," said the father, as he watched this singular development from nothing to something, "this is no ordinary child."

Then, in the spring of one memorable year, Hamlet had his fifth birthday. On the day after his birthday, when he was just five years and twenty-four hours old, he took a spade into the garden, with the intention of increasing his collection of beetles. Upon entering the garden, however, he stopped short, with one of his legs suspended two inches from

---

1. **Hamlet** (ham′lit), a difficult to understand character in a play of that name by William Shakespeare.

Dandelion

This painting is an example of illuminated text. When books were hand lettered, artists often decorated letters to help break up the monotony of endless rows of words.

the ground. He dropped his spade, as the delight of his discovery drained the strength from his arms. He sat down so that he might survey[2] the miracle at closer range. The lawn was a lawn no longer. It was a sea of sunshine, and the flowers that made up the infinity of yellowness were everywhere. When he recovered from the initial shock, Hamlet snatched one of the flowers from its stem and rushed into the house.

"What is it?" he demanded of his mother, thrusting the flower before her eyes.

"A dandelion, of course," said his mother, looking at the flower with distaste.

He hardly dared ask the next question. At last he summoned the courage. "Is it strong?" he asked nervously. "Will it grow easily?"

His mother searched about in her mind for an adjective capable of describing the gargantuan[3] strength of dandelions. Finally she resorted to the force of simplicity and gave her answer. *"Very,"* she replied.

The boy's relief was enormous. For a moment it was enough to know that the flowers would endure and come again. But soon the desire to possess the object of his love overcame him. "Could I," he faltered. "May I . . . *take* some?"

"Please, do," said his mother with feeling, and disappeared upstairs to make the beds.

Beetles were forgotten. So also were balls, swings, crayons, and Sunday-school picnics. He applied himself with concentration and devotion and toil and delicacy[4] to the planting of a dandelion garden. He chose a spot at the back of the yard behind the hedge, where

2. **survey** (sər vā′), *v.* look over; examine.
3. **gargantuan** (gär gan′chü ən), *adj.* huge.
4. **delicacy** (del′ə kə sē), *n.* fineness of feeling for small differences; precision.

he might work unnoticed and undisturbed. "I'm making a surprise, I'm making a surprise," he chanted over and over to himself, as he thrust his spade into the earth; then he made up a little tune to go with the words. He dug up the plants one by one from the lawn, removing each one with such care that not a leaf was harmed. This took a long time. Next he made a soft roomy hole, deposited the plant, sprinkled it with fertilizer, and watered it carefully, generously, and accurately. Then he patted it lovingly into the ground. By the end of two weeks, he had forty-two plants in his garden. He was satisfied. The display was adequate in numbers and very splendid in effect. It was five o'clock, and he was tired.

He chose his mother first. He chose her because he loved her, and also because there was no one else around at the time. He dashed, he tore, he flew into the kitchen, and, pulling at his mother's apron, gasped, "Come! Come! Come quickly to the garden and see my surprise!"

Hamlet's mother paused for a moment in the middle of her preparations for the evening meal. She looked at him and failed to notice the visionary glitter in his eyes. "Your face," she said, "is dirty. Go wash and tidy yourself before going any further."

Washed and combed, he returned, still aglow. "Come with me," he begged. "Come. Please. To the garden."

"Not now," she said, puncturing the balloon of his delight. "I have no time. I must peel the potatoes, heat the water, scrape the carrots, pour the milk, set the table, whip the cream, cook the meat, sweep the floor, and change my clothes before dinner. Tomorrow I will come. Not now. I have no time."

Hamlet shivered. But he answered, because he had no choice, "Yes, Mother, we will go tomorrow."

The next day, the dandelions were wilted and bent. Even dandelions will not last indefinitely, and their season was past. "Next year," said the boy, "is forever. But I will wait and build another garden in another spring, and this time I will take my father to see it. He will come."

The year passed, another spring arrived, and Hamlet was six. At the first appearance of the dandelions, he started to work with great haste. This time he planted his garden with even more care, arranging the flowers in special groups, curves, and circles. It took him two weeks to complete it, and when it was done he stood back and surveyed it with joy and with pride.

He had learned something the previous year. He washed his hands and face carefully, and waited for the right moment to approach his father. When his father seemed comfortably occupied in doing nothing at all, Hamlet walked quickly up to him.

EVALUATE: Why do you think Hamlet felt he needed to hurry as he approached his father?

"Father," he began. "Father, please come with me. I have a surprise to show you—a fine thing I have made all by myself. It has taken me two weeks to finish it." He pulled at his father's arm.

"Fine, my son," said his father, already guessing at the nature of the surprise. It would be a tree house, a handmade steam engine, or a car fashioned from orange crates. Truly, Hamlet was a remarkably creative child. He followed his son into the backyard.

Hamlet was overwhelmed by his father's willingness to come. He could bear the suspense no longer. "Father," he cried, "my surprise is a dandelion garden!"

His father stopped walking. "A garden?" he thought, with deep dismay. "My son, my firstborn—a wimp!" He turned to his son in anger, and then checked himself. "This is a problem of great delicacy," he argued to himself. "As a wise father, I will handle it with control and with calm." Thus he congratulated himself.

"Let us have a little talk, first," said his father, placing a hand upon Hamlet's shoulder. Despite the warmth of the afternoon, Hamlet could feel a chilly wind on the back of his neck. "All right, Father," he replied, his eyes fastened upon the hedge.

"Boys," said the father, "are different from girls. They like climbing trees and building boats and throwing balls and playing marbles and going fishing and making forts and having snowball fights. Boys are not interested in flowers. Sometimes men plant gardens, but this is in order to improve the value of their property. Your mother is calling us in to dinner." Then his father, in a generous welling-up of understanding and wisdom, once more placed his hand upon Hamlet's shoulder. "I'm sure," he concluded, "that we understand one another."

EVALUATE: Why do you think the father stereotypes what boys and girls can do? Do you think he is fair to his son? Explain.

That evening Hamlet looked lovingly at his garden. He already possessed it, but now the desire to share it with someone else was a flood straining to be loosed. Tomorrow he would find that person.

But the next day was the fifteenth day, and it was too late. The garden was no longer in full bloom, and there is nothing sadder than a withered flower. "Next year," sighed Hamlet, "is forever and ever, but I will make another garden and show it to a gardener. A gardener is a lover of flowers and will understand."

The leaves fell and the snow passed, and it was spring again. In greatest secrecy, Hamlet planted his garden, more intricate[5] and magnificent than ever before. On the fourteenth day, he gazed upon the blooms and knew that this was more beautiful than the other gardens. The dandelions were tall and strong; their blooms were like the rays of the sun; the design of their arrangement was marvelous to see. He went forth in search of a gardener.

"Gardener," he said when he finally found one, "I have made a garden. Will you come to see it?"

"Good," exclaimed the gardener. "I would like very much to see your garden. No doubt the flowers are very beautiful. I trust that you have eliminated all the weeds."

"What is a weed?" asked Hamlet.

"A weed," said the gardener, "is a very terrible thing, and the worst kind of weed is a dandelion. It tries hard to grow in every flower garden. It even invades the lawns. Everyone knows that each blade of grass must be rescued from the ravages[6] of a dandelion. I have in my pocket a very effective weed-killer. Since you are interested in gardens, you may have this bottle. Sprinkle a little on every dandelion tonight, and by morning each one will be twisted and wilted and completely dead. Now—take me to see your garden."

The gardener looked around in surprise. The boy was gone. He shrugged his shoulders and returned to his job of grafting[7] two rare rosebushes.

It was six o'clock now, and too late for Hamlet to find someone else before the dawning of the fifteenth day. He spent the evening watering his garden. He wore a heavy sweater, because he felt very cold.

And so it came to pass that each year

---

5. **intricate** (in′trə kit),   *adj.* complex.
6. **ravage** (rav′ij),   *n.* destruction or great damage.
7. **grafting** (graf′ting), *n.* the practice of putting a shoot from one plant into a slit in the other, so that it will grow there permanently.

▲ *Dandelion Seed Heads and the Moon* was painted by Charles Burchfield. Do you think
this artist agrees with Hamlet about the beauty of dandelions?

The Dandelion Garden 71

Hamlet spent two weeks making a dandelion garden. Every year it was finer than it had been the year before. On the fourteenth day he always looked for one person with whom he could share it.

One year he asked a schoolteacher to come and admire his blooms. "How long has it taken you to tend this garden?" she asked.

"Two weeks," he replied.

"And how much time have you spent on arithmetic and spelling and history and geography and grammar?" she inquired.

"Not much time at all," he answered. "But a dandelion is a wonderful thing. You can lick the end of it and make the stem curl into a hundred different curves and wiggles."

"That," she said, "is of no educational value, and is therefore of no significance."

He spoke one spring to a businessman of great wealth and prominence. "This is an idle way to spend your time, my boy," said the man. "You must apply yourself to life in a practical way, collecting enough knowledge and skill to make yourself wealthy and important."

"But," argued Hamlet, "a dandelion is a very useful thing. When it has gone to seed you can blow the seeds away and find out what time it is."

"Ah," sighed the man, "but you may blow the wrong number of times, and therefore be confused as to the correct time. To a man of business, the correct time is of prime importance. The reason you give for valuing a dandelion is of no significance at all."

A clergyman admonished him for spending his time in a useless way, asking if he had done any good works or said any prayers during the two-week interval. Hamlet could recall neither good works nor prayers. However, he replied, "Dandelions can be used for good purposes. You can poke holes in their stems, put other dandelions in the holes, weave them together, and make a flower chain. This can be presented as a gift to one's grandmother, to place about her neck."

"This is a very frivolous[8] purpose," replied the clergyman, "and cannot be regarded as of any significance."

Finally he found an artist. "Surely," he felt, "she will come to see my garden and will marvel at its great beauty."

"Most flowers are lovely," she told him, "but if there is any flower that can be regarded as commonplace, it is the dandelion. Why do you not plant roses?"

"But the dandelion is the first flower of the year," he replied, "and it is also of a perfect and symmetrical form."

"It matters not at all if a flower arrives in May or December," she argued, "and besides, a dandelion is too perfect. Were I to paint a field of dandelions, I could put dabs of yellow paint at random throughout the grass on my picture, and everyone would say, 'Yes, those are dandelions.' But were I to paint a rose, I would have to paint each petal with infinite care."

Hamlet did not bother to reply. Her arguments, he felt, were of no significance at all. Besides, he was tired. He was tired of arguing, tired of searching, tired of planting. He was, in fact, tired of being young. He was eleven years old that spring.

PREDICT: Do you think Hamlet will plant his garden again next spring? Why or why not?

The next year an old man came wandering through the land. No one knew where he came from or where he was going, but he seemed to be looking for someone. Finally he reached the town in which Hamlet lived. It was the fifteenth day of the garden, and

---

8. frivolous (friv′ə ləs), *adj.* silly; lacking in seriousness.

Hamlet was sitting by the hedge, building a steam engine out of soup cans.

"I have been looking for you," said the man. "I am a dandelion grower. I am a hundred and ninety-nine years old and I have spent my life in the cultivation[9] and care of dandelions. I have twenty-two acres of land on which are planted eighty-eight million dandelions. Every year I go on a long journey, searching for one other person with whom I can share my flowers. You are the person."

With listless eyes, Hamlet looked up at the man. "It is too late," he replied. "I used to be a grower of dandelions myself, but now I am a builder of steam engines. I am twelve years old, and I now know that the cultivation of dandelions is an unmanly pursuit. Dandelions are useless, time-consuming, frivolous, and much too common. Besides, they are weeds. Last night, I, too, returned from my search for a person with whom to share my garden. Finding myself unsuccessful for the eighth time, I came back home and in great wrath stamped upon my flowers until they were all dead. I am twelve years old now, and very wise, and a maker of steam engines." The boy looked at him with such fierce determination that the old man knew it was useless to argue. He turned away from Hamlet and wept.

So Hamlet grew up to be a very efficient and successful engineer. By developing a habit of averting[10] his eyes when in the presence of dandelions, he became moderately content; indeed, in the course of time, he grew to be quite fond of engines and machines and bridges and dams. His father, of course, was both relieved and delighted by this turn of events. Nobody knows what became of the old man. There were not even any rumors, because no one was very interested. However, you may have noticed that dandelions are, if anything, on the increase. This fact may be of some significance.

On the other hand, it may mean nothing at all.

---

9. **cultivation** (kul′tə vā′shən), *n.* preparing land and growing plants.
10. **avert** (ə vėrt′), *v.* turn aside.

After Reading

Making Connections

1. Each person Hamlet shared his garden with had a different opinion of its value. What is your opinion of the garden?

2. What do you admire the most about Hamlet? the least about Hamlet?

3. ✋ **Interactions** involve contact between people of different backgrounds. What differences does the author show between the world of children and the world of adults?

4. Why do you think the author loaded her sentences with words that are close in meaning, as in the following example?

   Next he made a roomy hole, deposited the plant . . . and watered it *carefully*, *generously*, and *accurately*.

5. If you read "The Six Rows of Pompons," how would you compare the way Tatsuo took care of his garden to the way Hamlet took care of his?

6. What do you think is the **theme** or message of this story?

7. Hamlet made an adjustment in the story. How does his adjustment compare with adjustments you've made as you've grown up?

Literary Focus: Metaphor

A **metaphor** is a comparison between two unlike things without using any words of comparison. Writers use metaphors to help readers see things in a new way. Study the following example. Then find other metaphors in "The Dandelion Garden," and list them in a chart like the one below.

Sentence with Metaphor	Comparison Made	Effect of the Metaphor
"Not now," she said, puncturing the balloon of his delight.	Hamlet's feelings to a balloon	Boy's sense of accomplishment is deflated.

Vocabulary Study

On a sheet of paper, write the letter of the word or phrase that is most nearly the same in meaning as the capitalized word.

**avert
cultivation
delicacy
frivolous
survey**

1. SURVEY: **a.** draw   **c.** sway
             b. examine   **d.** call

2. CULTIVATION: **a.** caring for   **c.** harvesting of
                 b. fencing in   **d.** depositing of

3. AVERT: **a.** say   **c.** turn away
             b. hold   **d.** delay

4. DELICACY: **a.** strength   **c.** clumsiness
              b. precision   **d.** decency

5. FRIVOLOUS: **a.** not serious   **c.** not normal
               b. not pleasant **d.** not common

Expressing Your Ideas

Writing Choices

I Owe It All to . . . Write a **speech** about someone's positive or negative reaction to something you have done. In the speech, tell how that person's reaction motivated you to continue or quit. Review your Writer's Notebook for ideas.

What Would You Say? Imagine that seven-year-old Hamlet has chosen to show you this dandelion garden. Write a **dialogue** in which you give him your response.

Other Options

Flower or Weed? In a **debate** with other class members, take a stand on the issue of whether the dandelion should be considered a flower or a weed. Refer to your teacher or to a panel of your classmates to decide the winner of the debate.

3-D Garden With clay, fabric, yarn, or other materials, create a **collage** of how you think Hamlet's garden looked. Glue materials to a cardboard backing or ask your art teacher for other suggestions.

Language Mini-Lesson

Identifying Common Misspellings

Including all the Letters Say the word *restaurant.* Like many people, you might have said *restrant.* However, this pronunciation leaves out a lot of the word. If you don't hear all the letters when you say a word, you might leave letters out when you write the word. In this way knowing how to pronounce a word can help you spell it.

Spelling Strategy Sometimes exaggerating the pronunciation of troublesome letters will help you remember them when you write the word. For example, say the *h* in *vehicle* whenever you write it. With a word like *conductor,* remember the *o* by pronouncing the last syllable like *or* when you're writing.

Activity Options

1. Letters are missing in each word below. Work with a partner to supply the missing letters and spell each word correctly.

   - probly
   - asprin
   - avrage
   - twelth
   - seprate
   - cabnet

2. Using the list of words from the first activity, work with a partner to make up pronunciation strategies that will help you spell each word correctly in your writing. Share your strategies with the rest of the class.

3. Look back over the writing you've done for your classes so far this year. Identify words you've misspelled because you didn't hear all the letters. Make up a secret pronunciation for each word and keep the list in your portfolio. Add to the list throughout the year and make up secret pronunciations for each new word.

Before Reading

Change by Charlotte Zolotow
Dust of Snow by Robert Frost

Charlotte Zolotow
born 1915

In her fifty-year-long career as a writer and editor of children's books, there is hardly a subject Charlotte Zolotow hasn't explored. Her portrayal of simple feelings helps us keep in touch with the child-poet alive in each of us.

Robert Frost
1875–1963
Pulitzer-prize-winning poet, Robert Frost took as much pride in his farm as in his writing. Daily rambles across the fields and through the woods were the inspiration for many of his most well-known poems.

Building Background

Seasons Come and Go In many parts of the United States, seasonal changes occur four times a year. Winter is the cold season, when few plants grow and snow may blanket the ground. Spring is the season when trees sprout leaves, plants pop out of the ground, and many young birds and animals are born. During the summer, the warmth brings living things into full bloom. The cool temperatures of autumn cause plants to die or become dormant. In some parts of America, there are two seasons: a wet season, when rains fall and plants grow rapidly, and a dry season, when plant growth may slow down. Seasonal changes are commonly used to create mood or to emphasize a theme in literature.

Getting into the Poems

Discussion Wherever you live, changes occur each and every year. What kinds of changes do you see around you? How do these changes affect you, your feelings, your moods, and what you like to do? Talk about these changes in the world around you with your classmates. Then, think about how you yourself have changed over the years. Talk about these inner changes or write about them in your notebook.

Reading Tip

Identifying Point of View Although poems don't always have characters, every poem is told from a point of view. The first-person point of view uses the pronoun *I*. The second-person point of view is signaled by the use of *you*. The third-person point of view uses *he*, *she*, *it*, and *they*. Most poems are written from the first-person point of view. Identify the point of view of each poem as you read it. Make a sketch or write a description of what you think the speaker in each poem is like.

Change

Charlotte Zolotow

The summer
still hangs
heavy and sweet
with sunlight
5 as it did last year.

The autumn
still comes
showering gold and crimson
as it did last year.

10 The winter
still stings
clean and cold and white
as it did last year.

The spring
15 still comes
like a whisper in the dark night.

It is only I
who have changed.

March Thaw painted by John Carlson in 1936 portrays an everyday scene between seasons. What words and phrases in the poems could you use to describe the picture?

Dust of Snow

Robert Frost

The way a crow
Shook down on me
The dust of snow
From a hemlock tree[1]
5 Has given my heart
A change of mood
And saved some part
Of a day I had rued.[2]

---

1. **hemlock tree**, an evergreen tree related to the
pine, with flat needles and small cones.
2. **rue** (rü), *v.* be sorry for; regret.

After Reading

Making Connections

1. Which of these poems better describes something you have felt? Explain your answer.

2. Of all the characters you have read about in this book, which do you think would be most likely to write a poem like "Change"? like "Dust of Snow"? Explain.

3. How does each poet use a season or seasons to express a **mood?**

4. Why do you think the author of "Change" made the last stanza different from the other four stanzas?

5. Do you think change is good or bad? What in either or both of these poems supports your point of view?

Literary Focus: Mood

The poems "Change" and "Dust of Snow" have different **moods**—that is, each expresses a different feeling or creates a different atmosphere. "Change" has a thoughtful mood. The speaker in the poem is thinking about personal changes. "Dust of Snow" has a more joyful mood. Tell how each poet used images that appeal to the senses of sight, smell, sound, taste, and touch to create mood.

Expressing Your Ideas

Writing Choices

Some Like It Hot Write a **poem** with the first-person point of view to describe your favorite season. Use words that will appeal to your senses of sight, smell, sound, taste, and touch.

Rain Drops Keep Falling on My Head Even when the weather does not change a lot from season to season, for example, summer to autumn—certain events mark the arrival of a season. Make a **list** of your associations of your favorite season.

Other Options

To Everything, There Is a Season Find three pieces of **music** about seasons to share with the class. You can play the music or bring in tapes or other recordings, if you wish. Talk about the music with your class. Compare the moods and the messages of the various pieces.

Weather or Not First choose a season. Then draw or paint a **picture** that would describe the weather and activities of that season.

Before Reading

The Ancestor Tree

by T. Obinkaram Echewa

T. Obinkaram Echewa

"Everyone, in time, becomes an ancestor, even thieves and murderers." This statement by a character in a novel that Echewa wrote became the inspiration for "The Ancestor Tree." Echewa, a Nigerian native, calls the story an original contemporary folk tale because it builds on existing traditional African stories to make them relevant to young people of this generation.

Echewa moved to the United States when he was twenty-one years old. He currently teaches English at West Chester University in Pennsylvania.

Building Background

Nigerian Village The **setting,** or place, of "The Ancestor Tree" is the imaginary African village of Amapu. In an actual Nigerian village, most of the people are farmers. The town has a central square, where the local government—a village council—meets. The village council is traditionally made up of all the older men in the village.

Getting into the Story

Writer's Notebook Think about an older person of whom you are fond, perhaps a relative or a neighbor. Use your notebook to write about special things that you have learned from this person.

Reading Tip

Names The names in the story are in Igbo, a language spoken by the Ibo people of Nigeria. The chart lists some of the names, their pronunciations, and their meanings. As you read, take notes on whether the characters' names give any clues about them.

Igbo Names in "The Ancestor Tree"			
Name	**Pronunciation**	**Male or Female**	**Meaning**
Adanma	ä′dän mä′	Female	daughter of beauty
Aham-Efula	ä′häm ef ü′lä	Male	may my name not be lost
Amadi	ä mä′dē	Male or Female	in honor of the sun god
Nna-nna	ən ä′ ən ä′	Male	father of the father
Okoro	ōkôr′ō	Male	glad to have a son
Ozurumba	ō′zù rùm′bä	Male	international
Ugochi	ugō′chē	Female	most precious gift of God

The Ancestor TREE

T. Obinkaram Echewa

Nna-nna was the oldest man in the village of Amapu.[1] He was so old that no one knew how old he really was or remembered a time when he was young. He was old, yes, but full of life. Often sick, yes, and sometimes unable to walk because of his painful joints, but always full of jokes and laughter. Often tired, yes, but never too tired to tell a story. And when he had a story to tell, the children stood in a group in front of him, joking and laughing.

His full nickname was Nna-nna Anya M'ele,[2] which meant Grandfather the Onlooker,[3] a funny nickname since he was blind.

"Who is blind?" Nna-nna would ask, pretending to be angry. "All I do now is *see*. I see, whether my eyes are open or closed, whether it is night or day, whether I have a lamp or not!"

It was true! Nna-nna could "see" quite well. He did not use a cane to get around, and yet he rarely stumbled. When the children came to visit him in the shed in front of the house where he spent his days, he usually greeted them by name before they even said a word. If the children had an argument while they were playing and came running to Nna-nna to settle it, he had no difficulty deciding who had started the trouble, who had first called the other person a bad name, or who had struck the first blow.

Ask or tell Nna-nna anything, his eyes would stretch or crinkle and his tongue would waggle back and forth across his lips. And then he would give a clever answer. Sometimes, the children, especially Adindu,[4] Aham-Efula, and

---

1. **Amapu** (ä mä′ pü).
2. **Nna-nna Anya M'ele** (ən ä′ ən ä′ än′yä mel′ē).
3. onlooker (ôn′lừk′ər), *n.* person who watches without taking part; spectator.
4. **Adindu** (ä din′ dü).

Ugochi, tried to sneak up on Nna-nna, but none of them could fool him.

Every morning, even before the sun came up, Nna-nna was already sitting in his shed, scrubbing his teeth with a chewing stick, spitting into the dust, and swatting flies with his towel. The children ran up to the shed to say "good morning" to him as soon as they emerged[5] from their houses. Adindu was usually the first one up, followed by Ugochi, Aham-Efula, and the others.

"Nna-nna, good morning!" Adindu would say.

"Nna-nna, *ifutala ulo!*"[6] Ugochi would say.

"Nnn-nna, *ibola chi!*"[7] Aham-Efula would call out.

One by one, the children would kneel down in front of Nna-nna and open their hands in the shape of a bowl to receive his blessing.

"May you live a long life," Nna-nna would say, blowing into Adindu's hands.

"Ugochi, may your bowl overflow with blessings all day long! Aham-Efula, may Luck smile on you all day today."

"Thank you," each child would say in turn. "The same to you, Nna-nna."

A short time later, one of the children would say, "Nna-nna, tell us a story! Tell us how we used to act when we were little babies!"

"Let me see," Nna-nna would say, and then he would begin calling the children's names one by one.

"Adindu, on the day you were born, you were so eager to come into the world that your mother nearly had you at the farm."

The children would burst out laughing, even though they had heard all this before. "What about me? What about me?" they would all say at the same time.

"Ugochi, you have always been a troublemaker. Even while you were in your mother's womb, you used to kick so much it looked like there was a war going on in there. Everyone thought your mother was carrying twins and that two of you were fighting.

"Aham-Efula, everyone knows of your loud voice! When you were born, all of the villagers heard your first cry—it was so loud!"

"Nna-nna, what about me?" the other children would shout excitedly.

"Nna-nna, how did I crawl when I was a baby?"

"Nna-nna, what was the first word I ever said?"

"Nna-nna, was I bald or did I have a lot of hair when I was born?"

Nna-nna would answer all the children's questions one by one by one.

At night, when it was time to go to bed, the children would beg Nna-nna for another story. "Just one more!" they would say as their mothers came to drag them away.

"All right, just one more," Nna-nna would agree. But as soon as he finished that story, another child would say, "Just one more, Nna-nna."

"No more, no more," Nna-nna would finally reply, laughing. "It will soon be morning, and you can all come back then."

For Adindu, Ezinna, Chidinma, Aham-Efula, Okoro, Ugochi, Adanma, Amadi, Okezia, and all the other children in the village, Nna-nna was like the sky—always there. He was there early in the morning when they woke up, during the middle of the day while they were playing, and late at night when they got ready to go to bed. It seemed that he would always be there.

Then, one day, Nna-nna became very sick. He no longer came out to the shed to sit beside his log fire, but instead lay grunting and groaning inside his house. Adults began telling the children to stay away from his door

---

5. **emerge** (i mėrj′), *v.* come out.

6. **ifutala ulo** (ē′ fü tä′lä ü′lō).

7. **ibola chi** (ē bō′lä chē′).

▲ During a trip to Africa, William Vincent painted *Zanzibar, Tanzania*. How does this setting compare to the one you visualized when you began reading the story?

and not to bother him with their noise and anxious questions. From the secret whispers of the adults, the children began to suspect that Nna-nna was about to die.

On a day when no adults were around, the children, led by Adindu, went inside Nna-nna's house.

"Ah," Nna-nna said, as soon as he "saw" the children. He turned on his cot and began to call their names one by one. "I am very glad you have all come to visit me," he said.

"We are sorry that you are sick," Adindu said on behalf of the other children. "Is there anything we can do for you?"

"No, thank you, Adindu," Nna-nna replied, trying to shake his head. "My time has finally come, and I am going to die. But that is not why I am sad."

Several of the children began to cry.

"Why are you sad?" Adindu asked.

"Mmmmh," Nna-nna grunted. "You are children. I do not think you would understand."

"Tell us about it, Nna-nna," Adindu said, trying not to cry. "Tell us about it. We will understand!"

Nna-nna bit down on his lip as he said, "I am afraid that after I am dead no one will remember me."

"No! No! Never! No!" the children said

together. "We will always remember you. We will never, never, never forget you! We will always remember the stories you told us. Your songs and your jokes. All the games and riddles."

"Is that so?" Nna-nna asked. His voice had the hint of a laugh in it, and his eyes were crinkled, the way they always were when he was about to tell a joke.

"Yes! Yes! Yes!" the children replied.

"In that case, then," Nna-nna said, trying to laugh, "each of you must tell me a story, a joke, or a riddle—your favorite—by which you will remember me after I am dead. Adindu," Nna-nna said, "why don't you take the first turn?"

There was one condition for planting an Ancestor Tree: The person who died had to have living children.

After Adindu had told his story, the other children took turns telling jokes, stories, and riddles. When they were finished, Nna-nna said, "Thank you very much, children. Thank you. As long as you remember and repeat all those stories, jokes, and riddles, I guess I will never be forgotten."

But then after a while, Nna-nna's face became sad again. The children noticed tear drops at the corners of his eyes.

"Nna-nna, why are you still crying?" Adindu asked, wiping the tears from his own eyes.

"The reason I am sad is that after I die my Navel Tree will be cut down from the Forest of the Living, and no Ancestor Tree will be planted for me in the Forest of the Ancestors!"

"O-o-oh," the children gasped. All of them knew about the old custom of planting Navel Trees and Ancestor Trees. Their village had two sacred forests, the Forest of the Living and the Forest of the Ancestors. Whenever a child was born in the village, a piece of that child's navel cord[8] was planted together with

a young tree in the Forest of the Living. And whenever anyone from the village died, that person's Navel Tree was cut down; and a new tree, called an Ancestor Tree, was planted for the person in the Forest of the Ancestors. However, there was one condition[9] for planting an Ancestor Tree: The person who died had to have living children.

Nna-nna had no living children.

"Do not cry, Nna-nna," Adindu said. "I am sure there is something we can do."

"There is nothing you can do," Nna-nna replied. "Custom is custom. I cannot say that it should be changed because of me."

"We will always remember you, Nna-nna, no matter what," Adindu said.

"Yes," Ugochi agreed. "We will never, never forget you!"

Aham–Efula spoke next. He said, "If the adults do not plant an Ancestor Tree for you, we will sneak into the Forest of the Ancestors and plant one. By the time anyone finds out, your tree will already be there!"

"Yes," Adindu agreed. "All of us will sneak into the forest together, and we will not be afraid. And if we cannot plant an Ancestor Tree for you right away, we will plant one for you when we grow up."

"I appreciate your kind thoughts, children," Nna-nna said. "I may not have a tree in the Forest of the Ancestors, but I am glad to

---

8. **navel cord**, cordlike structure that connects the navel of an embryo or fetus with the placenta of the mother. It carries nourishment to the fetus and carries away waste.
9. condition (kən dish′ən), *n.* thing on which something else depends.

know that I will be alive in your memories. All of you together will be my Ancestor Tree."

About a week later, Nna-nna died. That same night, his old Navel Tree was cut down.

For days afterward, all the children in the village were sad. When they woke up in the morning, Nna-nna was no longer in the shed waiting to say "good morning" to each of them and blow a blessing into their hands. At night, when they finished their moonlight games and were about to go bed, Nna-nna was no longer there to tell them "just one more story," or to call out funny good-nights to them as their mothers dragged them to bed.

Every day, the children gathered in Nna-nna's shed to talk about him and tell his stories and riddles to one another. Sometimes, they held contests to see who remembered more of Nna-nna's jokes. At other times, they took turns pretending to be Nna-nna, saying and doing the things he used to say and do.

Inside their homes, when they were with their fathers and mothers or uncles and aunts, the children kept asking, "How come Nna-nna can't have a tree in the Forest of the Ancestors?"

"It is an ancient custom," Adindu's father said when Adindu asked him.

"How come there is such a custom?" Adindu asked.

"That's just the way things are. Custom is custom is custom," Adindu's father replied.

"How do customs begin?" Adindu persisted.[10]

"I do not know. Most customs are so old they started even before I was born."

"Do customs ever change?" Adindu asked.

"Enough questions!" Adindu's father replied angrily. "Go and find something to do."

One day, while the adults were holding a Village Council meeting nearby and the children were playing in Nna-nna's shed, Ugochi said, "Nna-nna has been dead now for many weeks, and still no Ancestor Tree has been planted for him."

"That is true," Aham-Efula said, "But what can we do? We are only children."

"But we promised Nna-nna that we would do something," Ugochi reminded everyone.

"That is true," Adindu said, holding his head in his hands and thinking deeply.

"But what can we do?" Aham-Efula asked again.

"Let us be bold," Adindu said suddenly, his eyes burning with determination. "The adults are having their meeting. Why don't we go over there now and ask them to plant an Ancestor Tree for Nna-nna?"

"No-oh," many of the children said, shrinking back in fear. "Children are not allowed at the adults' meeting."

"I know," Adindu said, "but are we going to break our promise to Nna-nna?" When Adindu asked this question, many of the children became silent and sad. After a while, they agreed to go with Adindu and began walking slowly toward the Village Council.

"What is the matter?" asked Ozurumba, the oldest man at the Council. "Why are you children walking around with such sad faces? We realize that your friend, Nna-nna, died recently, but everyone dies sooner or later, and Nna-nna lived a very long life."

Adindu raised his hand, and Ozurumba nodded to him to speak. "We are sad," Adindu said, "not only because of Nna-nna's death but because no Ancestor Tree has been planted for him in the Forest of the Ancestors."

"That is true," Ozurumba said. "We cannot plant an Ancestor Tree for Nna-nna because he is not an ancestor. He has no living children."

"But all the children want Nna-nna to be

---

10. **persist** (pər sist′), v. continue stubbornly, firmly, or without letting up.

our ancestor," Adindu said. "All of us feel like his children and grandchildren."

"Is that so?" Ozurumba asked, his eyes widening with surprise.

"Yes," Adindu replied.

Usually, adults teach and children learn, but in this case, we have the opposite.

"I see," Ozurumba said. He and the other adults in the Council were surprised by the children's boldness and, for a long time, continued to shake their heads in disbelief. After talking for a while among themselves, they told the children to come back in a week to hear the decision of the Council.

The children were very excited as they walked away.

A week later, the children returned.

"*Ezi, amuru!*"[11] Ozurumba said, as the children held their breaths in anticipation.[12] "Teach and learn. Usually, adults teach and children learn, but in this case, we have the opposite. Children are teaching and adults are learning. You children have taught us that customs have a beginning, customs can change, and sometimes, customs come to an end. We have decided to end one custom and begin another. We will plant a tree for Nna-nna in the Forest of the Ancestors. It is true that he has no living children, but it is also obvious that he has left something of himself in all of you, which, after all, is what it means to be an ancestor."

Ozurumba continued: "We have also decided that, from this day onward, we will change the way we select which ancestors to honor. Beginning today, only people who have lived honorable lives, people whose spirits are noble, will have trees planted for them in the Forest of the Ancestors. *Ezi, amuru* indeed!"

The children were very happy. They jumped up and down, hugged one another, and exchanged pumping handshakes. But above all, they were proud of what they had accomplished. Nna-nna would not be forgotten.

---

11. *Ezi, amuru!* (ez′e ä mur′ü).

12. anticipation (an tis′ə pā′shən), *n.* expectation or a looking forward to something.

After Reading

Making Connections

1. Who do you think made the biggest adjustments in the story— Nna-nna, the children, or the Village Council? Explain your answer.

2. Look back at the chart of names. Why was the meaning of Nna-Nna's name important to the story?

3. Customs are really unwritten rules. What are some customs you follow in your home or your school?

4. 👣 In the village, the elders were respected and children really didn't have a say in village matters. How did the children improve **interactions** between themselves and the village council?

5. Some people think African villages like the one in the story show how well democracy can work on a local level. Do you think democracy works as well in your town, city, or region? Explain.

Literary Focus: Folk Tales

The author of "The Ancestor Tree" calls this story a "contemporary folk tale." To understand what he means, you first need to know the definition of a **folk tale.** It is a traditional story that has been told for centuries before it is written down. Traditional folk tales have simple **plots,** lively action, and **characters** without a lot of depth. The **themes** of folk tales often revolve around needs people have.

   As a contemporary folk tale, "The Ancestor Tree" has not been passed down for many generations. How well does this story fit the folk-tale mold? Reread "The Ancestor Tree" and mark rating scales like the ones below that you have drawn in your notebook.

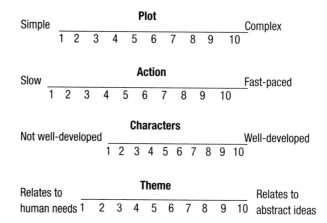

Plot
Simple _____ Complex
1 2 3 4 5 6 7 8 9 10

Action
Slow _____ Fast-paced
1 2 3 4 5 6 7 8 9 10

Characters
Not well-developed _____ Well-developed
1 2 3 4 5 6 7 8 9 10

Theme
Relates to _____ Relates to
human needs 1 2 3 4 5 6 7 8 9 10 abstract ideas

Vocabulary Study

For each underlined word or phrase, choose the vocabulary word that is closest in meaning. Write your answers on a sheet of paper.

anticipation
condition
emerge
onlooker
persist

1. Adindu, you were always a good bargainer. If anyone asked you for a favor, you always listed one thing you needed before agreeing to do the favor.

2. Looking forward to things is your best friend, Ezinna. Someday, you will learn to enjoy the moment without planning for it.

3. You are rarely ever just a spectator, Aham-Efula. You will always be involved in making decisions.

4. Before you were born, Okoro, your mother was worried that you would come out feet first. You were born with your arms extended above your head, which is why you are such a good swimmer.

5. Ugochi, whether you are awake or asleep, you continue in being active. Your family tells me that you keep them awake nights.

Expressing Your Ideas

Writing Choices

On the Beat in Africa Pretend you are a reporter in Amapu. Write a **newspaper article** about how the children of the village were able to change an ancient custom. Remember to answer the questions, "Who, how, when, where, and why."

Let's Work Together With a small group, think of a custom in your school or community that you would like to see changed. Then, draft a **petition** describing the custom, explaining what you don't like about it and how you think the custom should be changed. Then ask fellow classmates or others in your community to support you by signing it.

Other Options

Here Lies Nna-nna Design a **memorial plaque** for Nna-nna. On the plaque, include both a picture and a saying that you think Nna-nna would want to be remembered by. Try to make your saying humorous and sincere, as Nna-nna's sayings were.

Would You Like to Hear a Story? "The Ancestor Tree" is perfect for storytelling. Read through the story several times, looking for ways to use different voices and mannerisms, ways to use simple props, and ways to involve the audience in the story. Finally, do a **storytelling performance** in front of a group of friends, your family, or your class.

Making Adjustments

Stressed Out

Health Connection

Growing up means change. Change brings stress. Everyone experiences stressful situations, and everyone makes adjustments differently. Try to discover the stress busters that work best for you.

Stressful Situations

The Coddington Life Events Scale for Adolescence (abridged)

Events	Weight*
Death of a parent	108
Death of a brother or sister	88
Divorce of your parents	70
Marital separation of your parents	62
Death of a grandparent	52
Hospitalization of a parent	52
Remarriage of a parent to a step-parent	51
Birth of a brother or sister	50
Loss of a job by a parent	46
Major increase in parents' income	41
Major decrease in parents' income	43
Start of a new problem between your parents	41
End of a problem between your parents	30
Being told you are very attractive by a friend	26
Going on the first date of your life	42
Finding a new dating partner	34
Breaking up with a boy/girl friend	39
Being told to break up with a boy/girl friend	35
Start of a new problem between you and your parents	43

Events	Weight
End of a problem between you and your parents	35
Beginning the first year of high school	19
Moving to a new school district	41
Failing a grade in school	47
Suspension from school	34
Graduating from high school	33
Being accepted at the college of your choice	39
Recognition for excelling in a sport or other activity	24
Getting your first driver's license	32
Being responsible for an automobile accident	36
Appearance in a juvenile court	31
Failing to achieve something you really wanted	32
Getting a summer job	35
Getting your first permanent job	40
Deciding to leave home	41
Being hospitalized for illness or injury	50
Death of a close friend	63

Source: Coddington, 1983

This boy is concentrating on his math test. You read about Emily's and Panchito's challenges in school. You too might feel the pressure in some classes.

Weight–the numbers in this column are units that show how stressful each event can be.

Even though parent-child disagreements are normal and expected, they can be a strain on any teen. Trying to understand your parents' point of view, even if you don't agree with it, often helps ease the stress.

The death of a loved one is the most stressful event a young person might have to endure. Support from friends and family members is especially important at this time.

Moving to a new home means starting over in school, finding new friends, and trying to fit into an unfamiliar neighborhood. Courage and determination can turn this stressful situation into an adventure.

Surviving the Stress of Parents' Divorce:
Tito, age 11

Jill Krementz

It seems like my parents were always fighting. The biggest fight happened one night when we were at a friend's house. Mommy was inside the house crying, and Daddy was out on the sidewalk yelling and telling my mother to come down, and my little sister, Melinda, and I were outside with a friend of my father's. We were both crying because we were so frightened. Then Daddy tried to break the door down, so Mommy came downstairs. And then the police cars came and Daddy begged Mommy to stay quiet and not say anything and to give him another chance, but she was so unhappy that she got into one of the cars. But just before she got into the car she came over to where we were standing, Melinda and I, and took us. That's when my father grabbed my arm and tried to take me back. He didn't want Mommy to leave and figured that if he could keep me, she'd have to stay, too. But the policeman took me and put me into the car on Mommy's lap. After Daddy realized that we weren't going to get out of the car,

© Jill Krementz

he went away, and after a little while Mommy and Melinda and I got out of the police car and went to a cousin's house. I was only four but I remember everything.

We stayed with our cousin for about two months, and during this time I saw my father whenever he visited us at my grandmother's house. Mommy didn't want to cut us off entirely from him because she worried that we might resent her if she did that. I was always happy to see him, but sometimes it made me feel sad, too, because I would look forward to our visits so much and then when we were together it could never be as perfect as I was hoping it would be. He was still so angry at Mommy's leaving him that it was hard for him to feel anything else for anybody.

He kept trying to talk her into coming back, and I really wanted them to get back together—I would beg her to try again because Daddy kept promising that he would change. But she didn't believe him, and this got me angry at her and made *her* look bad in my eyes. It's so weird because I realize now that it was my father who was causing most of the problems, but back then, as soon as he was away from us and there wasn't any fighting, I would get mad at my Mom for not letting him back. Now that I'm older I know that if she had let him come home we would have been right back where we were before, with all the fighting and violence. I guess I just missed him so much that I wanted him home. I kept begging Mommy, "Give him one more chance, and if he doesn't change, you can divorce him." But Mommy wouldn't change her mind and after a while we moved in with her mother. When I was six my parents finally got a divorce, and right after it was final my Dad moved to Puerto Rico. Since then I've hardly seen him at all. He's remarried now and has two children.

About the time of the divorce I started to get into fights with other kids, and my mother got worried. She thought I must be feeling very angry and having a hard time expressing my feelings, so she took me to a therapist. His name was Dr. Gray and I saw him once a week after school. We got really close and he'd talk to me about my problems with my Dad. This went on for about two years, and during that time he helped me realize that the divorce was better for me in the long run because our home was more relaxed and there wasn't so much tension in the air.

The other thing that happened around this time was that my mother found out about an organization called Big Brothers, where I could have another male figure in my life—someone besides Dr. Gray. The way it works is that you go there and talk to a social worker, who matches you up with someone they think you'll be able to talk to and get along with. They paired me off with a guy named Pat Kelly, and we've been getting together every weekend for a couple of years. It's been great for me because my Mom tends to be too over-protective of me—she feels she has to be two parents—and I need a chance to get out on my own. Pat and I do a lot of things like play baseball or video games and eat hot dogs. But the best thing we do is talk—like when I do something good in school I can tell him, and if I feel sad I can talk about that, too. His parents got

> In a way I wish there hadn't been so many changes in one year, but I do feel happier than I've ever felt before.

divorced when he was twelve, and so we have a lot of the same feelings. Mostly, we talk about things that guys like to talk about—things like sports and girlfriends and personal stuff that I need advice on. It makes me feel that I don't have to depend upon my mother a hundred percent of the time, and, best of all, that I don't have to feel so lonesome for my Dad. I still miss him, but at least there's someone who's like a father in my life, some-one I can see and be with on a regular basis. Once in a while I think I'd like to move to Puerto Rico and live with my Daddy.

Even though Mommy got remarried last year, which means I have a new stepfather, I still feel closer to Pat in a lot of ways because we've had more time together and because I've never had to share him with my Mom. This past year has been very complicated but mostly very good. I'm getting to know my stepfather better every day, and I have a new house, new friends, a new school, and, as of two months ago, a brand-new baby brother. In a way I wish there hadn't been so many changes in one year, but I do feel happier than I've ever felt before. I feel especially lucky to have Pat in my life. He's like my best friend—someone who's always there for me—and I don't have to share him with anybody. Sometimes I look at my little brother and I think that one day he'll be my age and I can be a big brother to him. But I hope that he won't have to experience all the pain and loneliness I went through when my parents got a divorce.

How Can You Deal with Stress?

Can you imagine a life without any stress at all? This is unrealistic since some stress is a natural part of daily life. Sometimes you might be able to avoid stressful situations. However, you must face and deal with many of them. The more stress that a person has to deal with, the greater the chance it might eventually affect the person's health. Learning how to deal with stress effectively is an important step to maintaining good health.

The National Mental Health Association suggests the following ways to deal with the anxieties and tensions of everyday life.

Talk It Out

Sharing your problems and feelings with a family member or someone else you trust and respect can help relieve emotional stress. Sometimes another person can help you see a new side to your problem that you have not yet considered. Perhaps, too, another person can help you find a new solution.

Sometimes stress can become too much for one person to handle alone. Even family and friends might not be able to provide relief for a heavy burden of emotional stress. If this happens, a guidance counselor or psychologist can provide assistance. Seeking skilled help is not an admission of defeat. Rather, it indicates that a person is wise enough to know when to get help.

Get Away for a While

Sometimes when things are going wrong, it helps to get away from the situation for a short while. If you can forget about your problem by getting involved with a hobby, game, book, or movie, you can return to the problem later when you feel refreshed.

Work Off Your Anger

If you are angry or upset with someone, take time to cool off before you both discuss the problem. Find something else to do with your pent-up energy. Try exercise. Walking, bicycling, or any other active exercise will help relieve symptoms of tension. Your mind and body will feel more relaxed. Then you can deal with the situation in a more calm and sensible way.

FoxTrot   by Bill Amend

Give in Now and Then

Quarreling can be a source of stress and a waste of energy. Although you need to stand up for what you think is right, remember that no one is right all the time. Instead of arguing, try to see the other person's point of view. If you yield occasionally, you might find that others will too.

Do Something for Others

Instead of worrying about your own problems, take time to help someone else. Not only will this give you a chance to get away from your own stress, but it will give you a feeling of accomplishment as well.

Take One Task at a Time

At times you might think you have so many responsibilities that you can not possibly handle them all. This overwhelmed feeling might cause you to panic. A logical approach to this problem can help you overcome your stress. Determine which tasks are most urgent and difficult. Take care of these first. When you complete the more difficult tasks, you will see that the remaining ones are much simpler in comparison. These too can then be tackled one at a time.

Avoid the "Superperson Self-Image"

Sometimes, you can feel unnecessary stress because you expect too much of yourself. No one can be perfect in everything. Try not to be too hard on yourself if you cannot achieve every goal you set. Rather, set realistic goals for yourself and do the best you can to accomplish them.

Go Easy with Criticism

Just as you should not expect perfection of yourself, try not to expect perfection of others. If you always expect perfection, you might feel upset or angry if others do not meet your expectations. Remember that each person has his or her own good points, values, and shortcomings. Each person has a right to develop as an individual just as you do.

Give the Other Person a Break

When people are experiencing tension, they often feel hurried and under pressure for time. Life becomes one big race in which all the participants are trying to "get there first." When this happens, someone is bound to get hurt in the competition—physically or emotionally.

Competition in appropriate situations can be a great source of challenge and fun. However, when competition becomes a part of every aspect of your life, stress can result. Learn to give others a break sometimes. Cooperate rather than compete.

Make Yourself Available

Sometimes you might feel worried or anxious because you think that you are being left out or rejected. In reality, others might be eager for you to make the first move. Instead of waiting to be asked, make yourself available.

Balance Work and Recreation

Be sure to include time in your life for having fun. All work and no play can lead to a very stressful life. Develop a hobby—one that gives you pleasure and helps you forget for a time the daily tasks you must do. Getting involved in active games and sports will help put some fun in your life.

Responding

1. Look at the Coddington Life Events Scale of stressful situations on page 88. Which of these have you dealt with in the past year?

2. What helped Tito cope with the loss of his father when his parents divorced? Think about what helped you get through your last stressful experience.

3. Write down three stressful situations in your life right now. Under each one, make a list of ways you might cope with the problem. Use the list above for ideas.

Reading Mini-Lesson

Understanding Sequence

When you read a story or watch a movie or television show, it is important to understand the order or sequence of events taking place. Since no writer or film maker tells you *everything* in order, you have to be prepared to skip from one event to another. Words like *then*, *after*, and *just before* are time markers. They help you follow the sequence of events, even when they aren't told in the exact order in which they happened.

You also need to see the connection between main events and the smaller ones that make them up. For example, think of a week in school as a story. Each school day is a main event in your story. Class periods are small events in each day. If someone asked you what happened last week, you might say, "I had a huge test in Math on Wednesday. *After that*, the week was easy. *Before the test*, however, all I did was worry and study."

You can think of a story as a sequence of related events that show one main action. A story's action is made up of several main events, usually told in the order in which they take place. Look at "Surviving the Stress of Parents' Divorce." The main action of the article is, "Tito makes adjustments to his parents' divorce." Each paragraph tells you one main event in Tito's story, and that main event is made up of many smaller events.

Activity Options

Main Event	Tito remembers parents' biggest fight
Smaller event	Mommy inside friend's house, Daddy outside yelling
Smaller event	Police come

1. To determine the sequence of main events for Tito's story, you can make a main event story map. Read each paragraph and summarize the main event in a few words. You will have six main events in your list. Then make a list of the smaller events under each main event. A start for the first paragraph is in the chart at the left.

2. If you were taking pictures to go along with Tito's story, how could you best show the change from early to late in the story? Draw two sketches of the pictures you would take and explain what part of the story each belongs with.

3. Work with a friend and list 20 words or groups of words that serve as time markers in Tito's story.

Writing Workshop

Exploring Changing Attitudes

Assignment You've read about characters who learn to make adjustments in their attitudes and ways of life. Now become one of these characters and explore the adjustment you made.

WRITER'S BLUEPRINT

Product   A series of three journal entries

Purpose   To describe, from a character's point of view, experiences that lead to an adjustment in attitude or way of living

Audience   The character you chose

Specs   To write successful journal entries, you should:

❑ Choose a character from a selection who makes a successful adjustment in attitude or way of life. Write as if you are that character using the first person ("I") point of view.

❑ Begin by writing a journal entry that reflects the character before he or she made any adjustment in attitude or way of living.

❑ Continue with a second journal entry that reveals changes in attitude or way of life and explores what brought about these changes.

❑ Conclude with a third journal entry in which the character reflects on these changes and what he or she might have learned from the experience.

❑ In each journal entry, show the character or the changes through the character's reflections on daily events rather than simply telling what happens.

❑ Follow the rules for correct grammar, usage, spelling, and mechanics. Watch for agreement between pronouns and antecedents.

The instructions that follow will help you write a successful series of journal entries.

1 PREWRITING

Analyze the literature to become familiar with the kinds of adjustments that characters in the selections had to make. What situation confronted the character? What had to be done about it? What did the character learn?

OR . . .
If you've already selected the character for whom you wish to write journal entries, move on to the **open mind** step.

Character	Situation	Adjustment	Lesson Learned
Emily	Has learning disabilities	Works with a tutor to acquire different learning styles	To compensate for her disability in order to achieve a career

Choose a character whose identity you'd like to assume. Refer to the chart you just created and select the character with whom you most identify or whom you find most interesting. Remember, from this point on, you are the character.

Create three open mind diagrams to show what you, as the character, think and feel before, during, and after the experience. Draw images and symbols that represent your thoughts about what you had to do to make the adjustment and what you learned from the experience. Beneath each diagram, write a statement that describes your state of mind at each stage of the adjustment.

Share your open mind diagrams with a partner. Discuss the symbols you included and ideas about how you felt about the situation and the adjustment you had to make. Read your statements and elaborate if necessary.

Plan your journal entries using your chart, diagrams, and other notes to arrange the events in order for your entries. To help you plan, draw a time line and place the events on it.

Choose a key event from the beginning of the time line, one from the middle, and one from the end. Then, complete a writing plan like the one below. Remember, you're writing as your character, so write in the first-person using "I" and "me" throughout.

Beginning: Journal Entry 1
Date
- What is happening at the beginning of the selection?
- Present attitude/way of life

- Feelings
- Details from the story so that the reader will experience what the character did

Middle: Journal Entry 2
Date
- How is the situation changing?
- How is attitude/way of life changing?
- Feelings
- Details from the story

End: Journal Entry 3
Date
- What my character learned or how the character's attitude or way of life changed
- Feelings
- Details from the story

  DRAFTING

Before you write, review your notes, plans, and graphics from the Prewriting stage. Look at the Writer's Blueprint again. To make your writing lively and interesting, don't just tell your reader what happened. Show it, too. For tips on how to do this, look ahead to the Revising Strategy on Showing, not Telling on page 100.

COMPUTER TIP
When writing a piece such as a journal entry, use the formatting functions of your software, such as margin changes or changes in spacing, to make your piece look more like a real entry.

Here are some ideas for getting started on your draft:

- Start each entry with a vivid detail about the day, such as what the weather was like or what you ate for lunch.

- Launch right into a description of the problem, including details about the setting and other people involved.

- Write a statement about how you are feeling today.

REVISING

Ask your partner for comments on your draft before you revise it.

✔ Do I write the way my character would?

✔ Do I show the changes in my character's attitude?

✔ Do I show that the character reflects on the lesson he or she learns?

✔ Do I show rather than tell my character's thoughts and feelings?

Revising Strategy

Showing, not Telling

To make your writing more interesting and entertaining, try to show your readers what is happening rather than telling them. To show rather than tell, use concrete details that show what you're trying to communictate.

Telling: We had a spelling bee today and I was really nervous.

Showing: We had a spelling bee today. My hands were dripping with sweat while I waited to take my turn. When Mrs. Timmer asked me to spell *designer,* my voice wavered and quaked with every letter.

In the Literary Source, Francisco Jiménez uses concrete details to show the condition of the garage. Notice how the writer of the journal entry below shows different reactions from the children.

STUDENT MODEL

I would tell stories over and over. When I told a funny story, children would burst out laughing even though they had heard all this before. When I said it was time to go to sleep, the children would scream and yell. "Tell just one more story!" they wailed. I would tell a final story and then watch as the children's mothers dragged them away.

4 EDITING

Ask a partner to review your revised draft before you edit. When you edit, pay special attention to agreement between pronouns and their antecedents.

Editing Strategy

Pronoun/Antecedent Agreement

Pronouns agree in number and gender with their antecedents. Remember, the antecedent of a pronoun is the noun it refers to. In the sentence *Jack took the book with him, him* is the pronoun and *Jack* is the antecedent.

When a pronoun and its antecedent are close together, as in the example above, correct agreement isn't a problem. Sometimes words or phrases that come between the pronoun and antecedent can cause confusion. Look at the example in which the plural pronoun *they* mistakenly refers to the singular noun *person*.

If a **person** wants to spell better, **they** should try putting the spelling list on tape.

To be sure your pronouns and their antecedents agree, try this:

- First, find the antecedent of the confusing pronoun.

- If the antecedent is singular, make sure the pronoun is singular.

- If the antecedent is plural, make sure the pronoun is plural.

Notice how the writer of the journal entry below fixed an agreement problem between a pronoun and its antecedent.

> This idea came up many times, but it just didn't happen. "If they
> notice the tree, they will cut (them) *it* down," Andeau told the kids.

FOR REFERENCE . . .
More rules for pronoun and antecedent agreement are listed in the Language and Grammar Handbook.

STUDENT MODEL

5 PRESENTING

Here are two ideas for presenting your journal entries.

- Have a read-around with a group. After each person reads his or her journal entries aloud, discuss the adjustments that the character made and describe times that you may have experienced similar adjustments.

- Gather all the entries in the class that were done for one particular character. Put the entries for each character in one folder entitled "My Journal." Leave the journals in a central place for sharing.

6 LOOKING BACK

Self-evaluate. What grade would you give your paper? Look back at the Writer's Blueprint and evaluate yourself on each point, from 6 (superior) down to 1 (weak).

Reflect. Think about what you learned from writing your journal entries as you write answers to these questions.

✔ How has your attitude toward the character you became changed since you began this assignment?

✔ What adjustments do you expect to face in the near future?

For Your Working Portfolio: Add your journal entries and your reflection responses to your working portfolio.

Beyond Print

An Oral History

You have many interesting true stories to tell. You could tell stories about school, home, friends, and trips. You could also tell stories about happy, sad, and scary times.

When you are much older, the stories you have today will be more interesting because children will want to know what it was like back in the nineties. Older people that you know have fascinating stories about their lives. A person over seventy-five lived during serious world events like World War II, the Great Depression, and the assasination of President John F. Kennedy. Also older people spent part of their lives without television, fast food, computers, and rock music.

Conducting an Interview

Do you know a person who is over seventy-five years of age? Ask if you can interview him or her. Prepare some questions ahead of time. Here are a few suggestions.

- Did you suffer during the Great Depression?
- How did you get information about local and world events?
- How did the World War II change your life?
- What do you remember about the John F. Kennedy assassination?
- Do you remember sixth grade? What was school like?
- What kinds things did you do for fun?
- What did you like best about growing up?
- What did you like the least?

Listening Hints

- Listen carefully to each answer.
- Take notes.
- After each answer, summarize what was said.

Activity Options

1. Select four or five of the most interesting questions and answers from your interview. Share them with your classmates.

2. Use the answers from your interview to write an oral history. Remeber that the oral history should read as though the person you interviewed was actually telling a story. Combine your work with that of your classmates to make a class book of oral histories to be displayed and read by family, visitors, and other students in your school.

Projects for Collaborative Study

Theme Connection

Growing Pains No doubt you are bombarded daily with suggestions and advice on how to grow healthy and strong. What are the things that you feel you need to do? What are the things that you don't think you really need to do?

■ Have a class discussion about the types of habits one should follow to grow up healthy, including types of foods one should eat and types of activities one should participate in.

■ As a group, prepare an ideal daily plan for a healthy adolescent. Include healthy menus for three meals. Include activities before and after school that contribute to keeping healthy. Try to follow the plan for one day and compare what you did with your classmates.

Literature Connection

Characterization In this unit, the ways the authors develop the characters are really important to how the stories move along. In "The Six Rows of Pompons," for example, we find out about the main character by the ways other characters respond to him. In "Tuesday of the Other June," we learn about June mainly through her own words. Choose two or three selections in the unit, and in a small group, discuss how each character was developed.

■ Work in a small group to extend one of the selections in the unit using the method of characterization you like best. Together, write your story, dramatize it, or tell it aloud to the class.

Life Skills Connection

Changing Your View of the Seasons Change can be predictable or unpredictable. A change in the seasons is predictable. Each new season brings changes in weather, hours of sunlight, and the range of activities available for you to pursue.

Which season is your favorite, and what do you like about it? Which season is your least favorite, and what about it don't you like?

■ As a class, form a human graph according to people's preferences for their favorite season. Then, form a human graph that illustrates people's preferences for their least favorite season.

■ As a class, discuss what reasons people used to make their selection. Afterwards, identify a way to make your least favorite season more enjoyable for you.

Multicultural Connection

Personal Growth Change occurs in you and in your life because of your **interactions** with others. Every year new students join your class. With a group of your classmates, prepare a handbook of things you can do to welcome a new classmate.

■ Include activities or other things that will make the new student comfortable and respected.

■ Include activities that provide opportunities for the new student to share his or her past experiences with the class.

Read More About Change

A Wrinkle in Time (1962) by Madeleine L'Engle. In this science-fiction classic, a brother and sister face tremendous odds to rescue their father from another planet.

Going Home (1986) by Nicholasa Mohr. Felita spends a summer in Puerto Rico, where she must learn to blend the traditions of New York City with the traditions of Puerto Rico.

More Good Books

Bridge to Terabithia (1977) by Katherine Paterson. Jess has to work through his grief when he tragically loses a new-found friend.

The Summer of the Swans (1970) by Betsy Byars. When Sara's brother disappears, she must depend on the one person she doesn't like.

The Mouse Rap (1990) by Walter Dean Myers. Mouse and his friends engage in a mock bank robbery that actually uncovers $50,000 stolen during a real robbery in Harlem in the 1930s.

A Friend Like That (1988) by Alfred Slote. Robbie has to contend with losing a person he likes and being around someone he hates.

The Squeaky Wheel (1990) by Robert K. Smith. Mark has to adjust to his parents' divorce and face a bully every day at school.

Challenges

The Race Is On!

Incredible Journeys

Talking About
CHALLENGES

Munich Olympic Games, by Jacob Lawrence, 1971.

We will face many kinds of challenges in our lives. Some challenges will involve races against time and other people. Other challenges are actually dangerous travels across time and space. And some challenges are only journeys within the mind. Each challenge that we meet successfully increases our ability to face new challenges.

On these two pages, sixth-graders talk about challenges in their lives. Below their comments are passages from the stories in this unit.

" **Consider what will happen if you fail to meet the challenge.**

Peter–Skokie, IL

Walt lay in the snow, thinking rapidly. He was only a boy, but in the face of the threatened injustice to old lame Loren Hall he felt that he must do something.

from "The King of Mazy May"
by Jack London, page 132

"How can we encourage other people to challenge themselves?"

Brigitte—Redondo Beach, CA

If you have a chance to do something good, be sure to do it. Happiness will come back to you.

from The Ch'i-lin Purse" by Linda Fang, page 199

"When the challenge is too great, sometimes people give up."

Andrew—Valentine, NE

. . . This is a dead end. We can't find jobs. We don't have any more money. Nothing. We're going to have to jump into the river.

from "Amitabh" by Janet Bode, pages 187–188

"How do people react to challenges?"

Alma—Silver City, NM

Now some people like to act like things come easy to them, won't let on that they practice. Not me.

from "Raymond's Run" by Toni Cade Bambara, page 113

Part One

The Race Is On!

Is it any wonder that we call ourselves the human race? We race against time, against other people, against ourselves. We race for pride, for glory, for freedom, for love. Sometimes, we ask ourselves, "Is winning what it's all about, or is there something that's more important?" The following selections all center on people—and animals—who race to meet a challenge, overcome an obstacle, or reach a goal. You'll find out who wins, of course. But you may discover that the suspense is more thrilling than the outcome!

Multicultural Connection Because of their **individuality** people may face challenges of many types. Sometimes those challenges involve group pressures and responsibilities. In these selections, how do the individuals meet such group challenges successfully?

Before Reading

Raymond's Run

by Toni Cade Bambara

Toni Cade Bambara
1939-1995

Toni Cade Bambara grew up in various neighborhoods in New York City, including Harlem, and in Jersey City, New Jersey. She has become known not only as a writer, but also as a professor and as an activist who is especially concerned with issues affecting African American women. "I can't remember a time when I was not writing," Bambara says. "I can't really say I have a motive for writing now. I'm compelled. I don't think I could stop if I wanted to."

Building Background

On Broadway "Raymond's Run" takes place in Harlem, a section of New York City. Harlem was originally a Dutch settlement. It grew from an area of farms to a residential district. Today, it is one of the world's largest urban African American communities. Many famous writers, artists, actors, and musicians have worked in Harlem. As you read "Raymond's Run," look for clues about the place or **setting**. Notice the role the setting plays in the story.

Getting into the Story

Discussion The narrator of "Raymond's Run" has a special talent. Talk about something you do especially well. It may be playing soccer, singing, solving math problems, or cooking. Do you have a natural talent for it, or do you have to work hard at it?

Reading Tip

Narrator's "Voice" The narrator of "Raymond's Run" has a distinctive "voice"—a way of expressing herself that is personal and unique. She "speaks" like most of us do when we're among friends. She uses slang. She also invents humorous words and phrases. The chart gives the meanings of some words and phrases the narrator uses. Are any familiar to you?

Words and Phrases in Story	Meanings
play the dozens	trade insults for fun
in my face	annoying me; arguing with me
high-prance	raise the knees in an exaggerated way while walking
one of those Dodge City scenes	face-to-face meeting like one between a sheriff and a gang of outlaws in a town of the Old West
feature	tolerate; put up with
signify	gain the advantage over someone with an insult

Raymond's RUN

Toni Cade Bambara

I don't have much work to do around the house like some girls. My mother does that. And I don't have to earn my pocket money by hustling; George runs errands for the big boys and sells Christmas cards. And anything else that's got to get done, my father does. All I have to do in life is mind my brother Raymond, which is enough.

Sometimes I slip and say my little brother Raymond. But as any fool can see he's much bigger and he's older too. But a lot of people call him my little brother 'cause he needs looking after 'cause he's not quite right. And a lot of smart mouths got lots to say about that too, especially when George was minding him. But now, if anybody has anything to say to Raymond, anything to say about his big head, they have to come by me. And I don't play the dozens or believe in standing around with somebody in my face doing a lot of talking. I much rather just knock you down and take my chances, even if I am a little girl with skinny arms and a squeaky voice, which is how I got the name Squeaky. And if things get too rough, I run. And as anybody can tell you, I'm the fastest thing on two feet.

There is no track meet that I don't win the first place medal. I used to win the twenty-yard dash when I was a little kid in kindergarten. Nowadays, it's the fifty-yard dash. And tomorrow I'm subject to run the quarter-meter relay all by myself and come in first, second, and third. The big kids call me Mercury[1] 'cause I'm the swiftest thing in the neighborhood. Everybody knows that—except two people who know better, my father and me. He can beat me to Amsterdam Avenue with me having a two fire-hydrant head start and him running with his hands in his pockets and whistling. But that's private information. 'Cause can you imagine some thirty-five-year-old man stuffing himself into PAL shorts to race little kids? So as far as everyone's concerned, I'm the fastest and that goes for Gretchen too, who has put out the tale that she is going to win the first-place medal this year. Ridiculous. In the second place, she's got short legs. In the third place, she's got freckles. In the first place, no one can beat me and that's all there is to it.

I'm standing on the corner admiring the weather and about to take a stroll down Broadway so I can practice my breathing exercises, and I've got Raymond walking on the inside close to the buildings, 'cause he's subject to fits of fantasy and starts thinking he's a circus performer and that the curb is a tightrope strung high in the air. And sometimes after a rain he likes to step down off his tightrope right into the gutter and slosh around, getting his shoes and cuffs wet. Then I get hit when I get home. Or sometimes if you don't watch him, he'll dash across traffic to the island in the middle of Broadway and give the pigeons a fit. Then I have to go behind him apologizing to all the old people

sitting around trying to get some sun and getting all upset with the pigeons fluttering around them, scattering their newspapers and upsetting the waxpaper lunches in their laps. So I keep Raymond on the inside of me, and he plays like he's driving a stage coach, which is O.K. by me so long as he doesn't run me over or interrupt my breathing exercises, which I have to do on account of I'm serious about my running, and I don't care who knows it.

SUMMARIZE: What is Squeaky's attitude toward Raymond?

Now some people like to act like things come easy to them, won't let on that they practice. Not me. I'll high-prance down 34th Street like a rodeo pony to keep my knees strong even if it does get my mother uptight so that she walks ahead like she's not with me, don't know me, is all by herself on a shopping trip, and I am somebody else's crazy child. Now you take Cynthia Procter for instance. She's just the opposite. If there's a test tomorrow, she'll say something like, "Oh, I guess I'll play handball this afternoon and watch television tonight," just to let you know she ain't thinking about the test. Or like last week when she won the spelling bee for the millionth time: "A good thing you got *receive*, Squeaky, 'cause I would have got it wrong. I completely forgot about the spelling bee." And she'll clutch the lace on her blouse like it was a narrow escape. Oh, brother. But of course when I pass her house on my early morning trots around the block, she is practicing the scales[2] on the piano over and over and over and over. Then in music class she

---

1. **Mercury**, in Roman myths, messenger of the gods, known for his speed of travel.
2. **scales** (skālz), *n.* series of tones arranged according to rising or falling pitch.

always lets herself get bumped around so she falls accidentally on purpose onto the piano stool and is so surprised to find herself sitting there that she decides just for fun to try out the ole keys. And what do you know— Chopin's waltzes[3] just spring out of her fingertips and she's the most surprised thing in

I'm ready to fight, . . .I much prefer to just knock you down. . .

the world. A regular prodigy.[4] I could kill people like that. I stay up all night studying the words for the spelling bee. And you can see me any time of day practicing running. I never walk if I can trot, and shame on Raymond if he can't keep up. But of course he does, 'cause if he hangs back someone's liable to walk up to him and get smart, or take his allowance from him, or ask him where he got that great big pumpkin head. People are so stupid sometimes.

So I'm strolling down Broadway breathing out and breathing in on counts of seven, which is my lucky number, and here comes Gretchen and her sidekicks:[5] Mary Louise, who used to be a friend of mine when she first moved to Harlem from Baltimore and got beat up by everybody till I took up for her on account of her mother and my mother used to sing in the same choir when they were young girls, but people ain't grateful, so now she hangs out with the new girl Gretchen and talks about me like a dog; and Rosie, who is as fat as I am skinny and has a big mouth where Raymond is concerned and is too stupid to know that there is not a big deal of difference between herself and Raymond and that she can't afford to throw stones. So they are steady coming up Broadway and I see right away that it's going to be one of those Dodge City scenes 'cause the street ain't that big and they're close to the buildings just as we are. First I think I'll step into the candy store and look over the new comics and let them pass. But that's chicken and I've got a reputation[6] to consider. So then I think I'll just walk straight on through them or even over them if necessary.

But as they get to me, they slow down. I'm ready to fight, 'cause like I said I don't feature a whole lot of chit-chat, I much prefer to just knock you down right from the jump and save everybody a lotta precious time.

"You signing up for the May Day races?" smiles Mary Louise, only it's not a smile at all. A dumb question like that doesn't deserve an answer. Besides, there's just me and Gretchen standing there really, so no use wasting my breath talking to shadows.

"I don't think you're going to win this time," says Rosie, trying to signify with her hands on her hips all salty, completely forgetting that I have whupped her behind many times for less salt than that.

EVALUATE: Is Squeaky as sure of herself as she seems to be?

"I always win 'cause I'm the best," I say straight at Gretchen, who is, as far as I'm concerned, the only one talking in this ventriloquist-dummy routine. Gretchen smiles, but it's not a smile, and I'm thinking that girls never really smile at each other because they

---

3. **Chopin's waltzes**, pieces of piano music for the waltz (a smooth, even, gliding dance) written by Frédéric Chopin, a Polish composer of the early 1800s.
4. **prodigy** (prod′ə jē), *n.* person with amazing brilliance or talent, especially a remarkably talented child.
5. **sidekick** (sīd′kik′), *n.* partner or close friend.
6. **reputation** (rep′yə tā′shən), *n.* what people think and say the character of a person is.

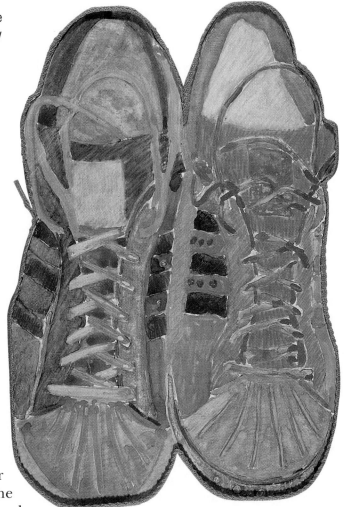

Shoe Series 2 painted by Marilee Whitehouse Holm. Are these the kind of running shoes you visualized Squeaky wearing? ➤

don't know how and don't want to know how and there's probably no one to teach us how, 'cause grown-up girls don't know either. Then they all look at Raymond, who has just brought his mule team to a standstill. And they're about to see what trouble they can get into through him.

"What grade you in now, Raymond?"

"You got anything to say to my brother, you say it to me, Mary Louise Williams of Raggedy Town, Baltimore."

"What are you, his mother?" sasses Rosie.

"That's right, Fatso. And the next word out of anybody and I'll be *their* mother too." So they just stand there and Gretchen shifts from one leg to the other and so do they. Then Gretchen puts her hands on her hips and is about to say something with her freckle-face self but doesn't. Then she walks around me, looking me up and down, but keeps walking up Broadway, and her sidekicks follow her. So me and Raymond smile at each other and he says, "Giddyap" to his team and I continue with my breathing exercises, strolling down Broadway toward the ice man of 145th with not a care in the world 'cause I am Miss Quicksilver[7] herself.

I take my time getting to the park on May Day because the track meet is the last thing on the program. The biggest thing on the program is the May Pole dancing, which I can do without, thank you, even if my mother thinks it's a shame I don't take part and act like a girl for a change. You'd think my mother'd be grateful not to have to make me a white organdy dress with a big satin sash and buy me new white baby-doll shoes that can't be taken out of the box till the big day. You'd think she'd be glad her daughter ain't out there prancing around a May Pole getting the new clothes all dirty and sweaty and trying to act like a fairy or a flower or whatever you're supposed to be when you should be trying to be yourself, whatever that is, which is, as far as I am concerned, a poor black girl who really can't afford to buy shoes and a new dress you only wear once a lifetime 'cause it won't fit next year.

I was once a strawberry in a Hansel and

---

7. **Quicksilver**, another name for the element mercury, named for Mercury in Roman myths.

Gretel pageant when I was in nursery school and didn't have no better sense than to dance on tiptoe with my arms in a circle over my head doing umbrella steps and being a perfect fool just so my mother and father could

I am not a strawberry. I do not dance on my toes.

come dressed up and clap. You'd think they'd know better than to encourage that kind of nonsense. I am not a strawberry. I do not dance on my toes. I run. That is what I am all about. So I always come late to the May Day program, just in time to get my number pinned on and lie in the grass till they announce the fifty-yard dash.

I put Raymond in the little swings, which is a tight squeeze this year and will be impossible next year. Then I look around for Mr. Pearson, who pins the numbers on. I'm really looking for Gretchen if you want to know the truth, but she's not around. The park is jam-packed. Parents in hats and corsages and breast-pocket handkerchiefs peeking up. Kids in white dresses and light-blue suits. The parkees unfolding chairs and chasing the rowdy kids from Lenox as if they had no right to be there. The big guys with their caps on backwards, leaning against the fence swirling the basketballs on the tips of their fingers, waiting for all these crazy people to clear out the park so they can play. Most of the kids in my class are carrying bass drums and glockenspiels and flutes. You'd think they'd put in a few bongos or something for real like that.

Then here comes Mr. Pearson with his clipboard and his cards and pencils and whistles and safety pins and fifty million other things he's always dropping all over the place with his clumsy self. He sticks out in the crowd because he's on stilts. We used to call him Jack and the Beanstalk to get him mad. But I'm the only one that can outrun him and get away, and I'm too grown for that silliness now.

"Well, Squeaky," he says, checking my name off the list and handing me number seven and two pins. And I'm thinking he's got no right to call me Squeaky, if I can't call him Beanstalk.

"Hazel Elizabeth Deborah Parker," I correct him and tell him to write it down on his board.

"Well, Hazel Elizabeth Deborah Parker, going to give someone else a break this year?" I squint at him real hard to see if he is seriously thinking I should lose the race on purpose just to give someone else a break. "Only six girls running this time," he continues, shaking his head sadly like it's my fault all of New York didn't turn out in sneakers. "That new girl should give you a run for your money." He looks around the park for Gretchen like a periscope in a submarine movie. "Wouldn't it be a nice gesture if you were . . . to ahhh . . ."

EVALUATE: Is Mr. Pearson serious, or is he joking?

I give him such a look he couldn't finish putting that idea into words. Grown-ups got a lot of nerve sometimes. I pin number seven to myself and stomp away, I'm so burnt. And I go straight for the track and stretch out on the grass while the band winds up with "Oh, the Monkey Wrapped His Tail around the Flag Pole," which my teacher calls by some other name. The man on the loudspeaker is calling everyone over to the track and I'm on my back looking at the sky, trying to pretend I'm in the country, but I can't, because even

▲ *Runners II* was painted by Diana Ong. Do you feel this painting adds to the suspense of the upcoming race between Sqeaky and Gretchen?

grass in the city feels hard as sidewalk, and there's just no pretending you are anywhere but in a "concrete jungle"[8] as my grandfather says.

The twenty-yard dash takes all of two minutes 'cause most of the little kids don't know no better than to run off the track or run the wrong way or run smack into the fence and fall down and cry. One little kid, though, has got the good sense to run straight for the white ribbon up ahead so he wins. Then the second-graders line up for the thirty-yard dash and I don't even bother to turn my head to watch 'cause Raphael Perez always wins. He

wins before he even begins by psyching[9] the runners, telling them they're going to trip on their shoelaces and fall on their faces or lose their shorts or something, which he doesn't really have to do since he is very fast, almost as fast as I am. After that is the forty-yard dash, which I used to run when I was in first grade. Raymond is hollering from the swings 'cause he knows I'm about to do my thing 'cause the

---

8. **concrete jungle**, term for a city, emphasizing the idea that survival is difficult.
9. **psych** (sīk), *v.* deliberately confuse or upset someone.

man on the loudspeaker has just announced the fifty-yard dash, although he might just as well be giving a recipe for angel food cake 'cause you can hardly make out what he's saying for the static.[10] I get up and slip off my sweat pants and then I see Gretchen standing

. . .the pistol shot explodes in my blood and I am off and weightless again, . . .

at the starting line, kicking her legs out like a pro. Then as I get into place I see that ole Raymond is on line on the other side of the fence, bending down with his fingers on the ground just like he knew what he was doing. I was going to yell at him but then I didn't. It burns up your energy to holler.

PREDICT: Who will win the race?

Every time, just before I take off in a race, I always feel like I'm in a dream, the kind of dream you have when you're sick with fever and feel all hot and weightless. I dream I'm flying over a sandy beach in the early morning sun, kissing the leaves of the trees as I fly by. And there's always the smell of apples, just like in the country when I was little and used to think I was a choo-choo train, running through the fields of corn and chugging up the hill to the orchard. And all the time I'm dreaming this, I get lighter and lighter until I'm flying over the beach again, getting blown through the sky like a feather that weighs nothing at all. But once I spread my fingers in the dirt and crouch over the Get on Your Mark, the dream goes and I am solid again and am telling myself, Squeaky, you must win, you must win, you are the fastest thing in the world, you can even beat your father up

Amsterdam if you really try. And then I feel my weight coming back just behind my knees then down to my feet then into the earth and the pistol shot explodes in my blood and I am off and weightless again, flying past the other runners, my arms pumping up and down and the whole world is quiet except for the crunch as I zoom over the gravel in the track. I glance to my left and there is no one. To the right, a blurred Gretchen, who's got her chin jutting out as if it would win the race all by itself. And on the other side of the fence is Raymond with his arms down to his side and the palms tucked up behind him, running in his very own style, and it's the first time I ever saw that and I almost stop to watch my brother Raymond on his first run. But the white ribbon is bouncing toward me and I tear past it, racing into the distance till my feet with a mind of their own start digging up footfuls of dirt and brake me short. Then all the kids standing on the side pile on me, banging me on the back and slapping my head with their May Day programs, for I have won again and everybody on 151st Street can walk tall for another year.

"In first place . . ." the man on the loudspeaker is clear as a bell now. But then he pauses and the loudspeaker starts to whine. Then static. And I lean down to catch my breath and here comes Gretchen walking back, for she's overshot the finish line, too, huffing and puffing with her hands on her hips taking it slow, breathing in steady time like a real pro, and I sort of like her a little for the first time. "In first place . . ." and then three or four voices get all mixed up on the loudspeaker and I dig my sneaker into the

---

10. **static** (stat'ik), *n.* noise or other interference with reception on radio or television or in a public address system.

grass and stare at Gretchen, who's staring back, we both wondering just who did win. I can hear old Beanstalk arguing with the man on the loudspeaker and then a few others running their mouths about what the stop-watches say. Then I hear Raymond yanking at the fence to call me and I wave to shush him, but he keeps rattling the fence like a gorilla in a cage like in them gorilla movies, but then like a dancer or something he starts climbing up nice and easy but very fast. And it occurs to me, watching how smoothly he climbs hand over hand and remembering how he looked running with his arms down to his side and with the wind pulling his mouth back and his teeth showing and all, it occurred to me that Raymond would make a very fine runner. Doesn't he always keep up with me on my trots? And he surely knows how to breathe in counts of seven 'cause he's always doing it at the dinner table, which drives my brother George up the wall. And I'm smiling to beat the band 'cause if I've lost this race, or if me and Gretchen tied, or even if I've won, I can always retire as a runner and begin a whole new career as a coach with Raymond as my champion. After all, with a little more study I can beat Cynthia and her phony self at the spelling bee. And if I bugged my mother, I could get piano lessons and become a star. And I have a big rep[11] as the baddest thing around. And I've got a roomful of ribbons and medals and awards. But what has Raymond got to call his own?

So I stand there with my new plans, laughing out loud by this time as Raymond jumps down from the fence and runs over with his teeth showing and his arms down to the side, which no one before him has quite mastered as a running style. And by the time he comes over I'm jumping up and down so glad to see him—my brother Raymond, a great runner in the family tradition. But of course everyone thinks I'm jumping up and down because the men on the loudspeaker have finally gotten themselves together and compared notes and are announcing, "In first place—Miss Hazel Elizabeth Deborah Parker." (Dig that.) "In second place—Miss Gretchen P. Lewis." And I look over at Gretchen, wondering what the *P* stands for. And I smile. 'Cause she's good, no doubt about it. Maybe she'd like to help me coach Raymond; she obviously is serious about running, as any fool can see. And she nods to congratulate me and then she smiles. And I smile. We stand there with this big smile of respect between us. It's about as real a smile as girls can do for each other, considering we don't practice real smiling every day, you know, 'cause maybe we too busy being flowers or fairies or strawberries instead of something honest and worthy of respect . . . you know . . . like being people.

---

11. **rep** (rep), *n.* reputation.

After Reading

Making Connections

1. What scene from the story sticks in your mind the most? Why?

2. Suppose Gretchen had won the race. How do you think Squeaky would have felt? Why?

3. What changes do you think will occur in the relationship between Squeaky and Raymond after the race?

4. What role does the urban **setting** play in the story?

5. How do you think the author's own experiences might have influenced some of the words and phrases Squeaky uses?

6. Do you think the author's choice of **title** for the story is a good one? Why or why not?

7. 🐾 Squeaky finds traditional female activities ridiculous, and she thinks most girls behave in phony ways. How do you think her **individuality** affects her relationship with Gretchen?

8. Do you agree with the thought, "It doesn't matter whether you win or lose, but how you play the game"? Would Squeaky agree with you? Why or why not?

Literary Focus: Imagery

We say an author uses **imagery** when he or she writes words that help us experience the way things look, sound, smell, taste, or feel. Imagery can make characters and settings seem comfortably real and familiar, or strangely and delightfully new.

"Raymond's Run" contains many examples of powerful imagery, especially in the description of the race. Look back at the story and find at least six examples. For each example, consider which of your senses—sight, hearing, smell, taste, or touch—is most important for experiencing what the author describes. Use a chart like the one below to record your ideas.

Example of Imagery	Most Important Sense
even grass in the city feels hard as sidewalk	touch
arms pumping up and down	sight

Vocabulary Study

Write the word from the list that best completes the meaning of each sentence.

prodigy
scales
sidekick
reputation
static

1. Cynthia doubted that Squeaky had the patience to sit and practice _____ on the piano each day.

2. When Squeaky won the twenty-yard dash in kindergarten, her parents knew they had a _____ for a daughter.

3. Squeaky thought her _____ as a great runner would be ruined if she lost the May Day race this year.

4. Mr. Pearson kept tapping the microphone, but the _____ made it hard for the audience to hear him.

5. Gretchen hoped that Squeaky would be her _____ from now on.

Expressing Your Ideas

Writing Choices

Raymond's Next Run Write an **epilogue** or conclusion to the story, from Squeaky's point of view. Describe Raymond's training for, and participation in, the Fourth of July races.

Practice Makes Perfect Write **slogans** for Squeaky and the other characters. A slogan is a word or phrase used by a person or group to express its purpose or goal. One example is "Be prepared."

Express Yourself Colorful expressions show your own **individuality**. Create a dictionary of expressions that you and your classmates use.

Other Options

Raymond Speaks Up In the story, Raymond does not speak. Give a short **speech** in which you present Raymond's point of view about what it is like to have Squeaky as a sister.

Special Olympics With a small group, find out about the Special Olympics: what they are, how they got started, how often they are held, who participates, and so on. Present your findings in a **bulletin board display** that includes illustrations that you find or create.

The Race Is On Make a poster to advertise the track meet.

Writing mini-Lesson

Using Tone in Writing

Recognizing Tone Tone in writing has much the same purpose as the tone of voice we use when we speak: it helps readers get a sense of a writer's attitude toward his or her subject. Tone can be humorous, sad, terrifying, or dull. One way writers express tone is through their choice of words. Compare the tone in these two sentences about the same situation:

- The couple enjoyed a romantic stroll home bathed in the warm glow of the moonlight.

- Two people nervously hurried home trying to avoid the eerie glow of the moonlight.

What is the tone of each sentence? How are the tones different? What words or phrases change the tone?

Writing Strategy To express tone in your own writing, you must first determine how you feel about your subject and what you'd like to communicate to readers. For example, do you like your topic? Is it boring? exciting? frightening? Once you know the feelings you'd like to convey, choose words or phrases that capture these feelings.

Activity Options

1. What scene do you see outside your classroom door or window? Work with a partner to write two descriptions of the scene using different tones—one silly and one serious. Share your scenes with the class.

2. Think about a movie you have seen recently, either in a theater or on television. What was the movie's tone and how was it conveyed? How did the movie's tone affect your reaction to it? Have a class discussion about tone in movies and make a chart listing the movies, their tones, and ways that tone was conveyed.

3. With a partner, make a list of words and phrases that convey a particular tone. Then, exchange lists with another pair of partners and write a description or scene that reflects the same tone as the new list.

Before Reading

In The Beginning Was The by Lillian Morrison

To James by Frank Horne

The Sprinters by Lillian Morrison

Lillian Morrison
born 1917

Many of Lillian Morrison's poems celebrate the effort and beauty of athletics. She once wrote this about the connections between sports and poetry: "Each is a form of play; each is a form of ritual. . . . They go together naturally wherever there is zest for life."

Frank Horne
1899–1974

Frank Horne was a track star in college. As a teacher, he also coached the school track team. By the time "To James" was published in 1929, he had developed an illness that would hinder his ability to use his legs for the rest of his life.

Building Background

Running Two of the poems you are about to read—"To James" and "The Sprinters"—focus on track events, which take place on outdoor or indoor courses. Track events include short races, or sprints, and distance races. Sprinters run at top speed, while distance racers vary their speed in order to last the entire race. In recent years, both sprinters and distance racers have done what was once thought impossible. Improved tracks and training methods have contributed to this progress.

Getting into the Poems

Writer's Log Many people—from children to adults—get pleasure out of running, even if they don't race or play a sport like football. Why does running appeal to them? Copy the web below in your notebook, and complete it with as many ideas as you can. Draw on your own and others' experiences.

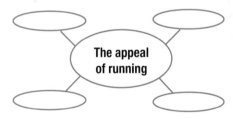

The appeal of running

Reading Tip

Free Verse It's likely that many of the poems you've read follow fixed, regular patterns of rhyme (in which certain words have the same ending sounds) and rhythm (in which stressed and unstressed sounds occur in a certain pattern). Be prepared for something different in the three poems that follow. Each poem is an example of free verse: poetry that breaks free from regular rhyme and rhythm patterns. To appreciate the special way that each poem is structured, listen to yourself as you read. If necessary, read each poem several times until it sounds "right" to you.

In The Beginning Was The

Lillian Morrison

In the beginning was the

Kickoff.
The ball flew
looping down true
5   into the end zone
where it was snagged,[1]
neatly hugged
by a swivel-hipped back
who ran up the field
10 and was smeared.[2]

The game has begun.
The game has been won.
The game goes on.
Long live the game.
15 Gather and lock
tackle[3] and block
move, move,
around the arena
and always the beautiful
20 trajectories.[4]

▲ *Ohio State University Stadium* was painted by William Hawkins in 1984.

---

1. **snag** (snag), *v.* catch or obtain by quick action.
2. **smear** (smir), *v.* overwhelm; defeat (in this case, bring to the ground by other players).
3. **tackle** (tak′əl), *v.* seize and stop, or throw to the ground. In football, players try to tackle the opposing player who has the ball.
4. **trajectory** (tra jek′tər ē), *n.* curved path of a projectile, such as a football that has been thrown or kicked into the air.

To James

Frank Horne

Do you remember
how you won
that last race . . . ?
how you flung your body
5 at the start . . .
how your spikes
ripped the cinders
in the stretch . . .
how you catapulted[1]
10 through the tape[2] . . .
do you remember . . . ?
Don't you think
I lurched with you
out of those starting holes . . . ?
15 Don't you think
my sinews[3] tightened
at those first
few strides . . .
and when you flew into the stretch
20 was not all my thrill
of a thousand races
in your blood . . . ?
At your final drive
through the finish line
25 did not my shout
tell of the
triumphant ecstacy
of victory . . . ?
Live

30 as I have taught you
to run, Boy—
it's a short dash.
Dig your starting holes
deep and firm
35 lurch out of them
into the straightaway
with all the power
that is in you
look straight ahead
40 to the finish line
think only of the goal
run straight
run high
run hard
45 save nothing
and finish
with an ecstatic burst
that carries you
hurtling
50 through the tape
to victory . . .

---

1. **catapult** (kat′ə pult), *v.* shoot forward or up suddenly; spring.
2. **tape** (tāp), *n.* string or strip of cloth stretched across a race track at the finish line.
3. **sinew** (sin′yü), *n.* tendon.

The Sprinters

Lillian Morrison

The gun explodes them.
Pummeling,[1] pistoning they fly
In time's face.
A go at the limit,
5 A terrible try
To smash the ticking glass,
Outpace the beat
That runs, that streaks away
Tireless, and faster than they.

10 Beside ourselves
(It is for us they run!)
We shout and pound the stands
For one to win,
Loving him, whose hard
15 Grace-driven stride
Most mocks the clock
And almost breaks the bands[2]
Which lock us in.

---

1. **pummel** (pum′əl), v. hit; strike; beat.
2. **band** (band), n. real or imaginary thing that
   binds or limits people.

▲ *Munich Olympic Games* was painted by Jacob Lawrence in 1971.
How does the style of this painting of runners compare to the
style of the painting shown on page 117?

After Reading

Making Connections

1. Which is more important: winning or participating? Why?

2. Do you think the **free-verse** style of the poems works well, or would you prefer that the poems were more regular in rhyme and rhythm? Explain.

3. Both "The Sprinters" and "To James" compare life to a competition. If you were going to describe your life, what sport would you compare it to?

Literary Focus: Imagery

In all three poems, the poets use imagery to create the setting, establish the mood, and dramatize the action.

Imagine that you attended the race or game in one of the poems. Write what you would say to a friend who did not attend. Use your own imagery. Appeal to your friend's senses of sight, hearing, taste, touch, and smell.

pummel
snag
smear
catapult
tackle

Vocabulary Study

Each word in the list is a verb that can be used to talk about sports or other activities. Use each word in a sentence.

Expressing Your Ideas

You Be the Poet Think about how your **individuality** will help you achieve a goal. Write a **poem** in free verse that describes how you hope to achieve that goal.

And Now, the Sports Report Attend a sporting event in your community. Write a **newspaper article** about the event that makes your readers feel as if they were there.

Preserve a Poem With a partner, make a **tape recording** of one of the poems. One of you should read the poem aloud while the other creates sound effects. Play your recording for the class.

Poetry in Motion Create a **dance** interpretation of one of the poems. Choose recorded music to accompany your dance. Then perform your dance for the class.

Before Reading

The King of Mazy May

by Jack London

Jack London
1876–1916

Like so many others, Jack London left his home in California to try to strike it rich in the Klondike gold rush. He failed to find gold in Canada, but his experiences—and those of other prospectors and trappers he met—gave him the ideas for many of the exciting stories he wrote about "the frozen north." London said this about his writing: "Naturally, my reading early bred in me a desire to write, but my manner of life prevented me attempting it. I have no literary help or advice of any kind—just been sort of hammering around in the dark till I knocked holes through here and there and caught glimpses of daylight."

Building Background

The Klondike "Gold!" That cry went up in the Klondike region of northwestern Canada in 1896. As fast as they could, prospectors claimed pieces of land by driving sticks called stakes into the ground. Once a claim was staked, a prospector had to travel to a town to have the claim legally recorded. Often, while the prospector was away, claim-jumpers seized the land.

Getting into the Story

Writer's Notebook "The King of Mazy May" is an adventure story. In your notebook, copy the word web shown below. Write five words that come to your mind when you think of adventure. Compare your web with those of your classmates.

Reading Tip

Context Clues "The King of Mazy May" contains many words that may be unfamiliar to you. Although some words are defined on the page, you will need to figure out the meanings of other words as you read. When you come to a word you aren't sure of, try to use the overall meaning of the sentence to guess at the meaning of the difficult word. Reread the sentence, replacing the difficult word with your guess. If it makes sense, you're on the right track.

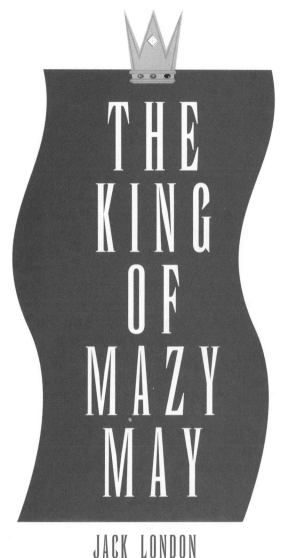

THE KING OF MAZY MAY

JACK LONDON

Walt Masters is not a very large boy, but there is manliness in his make-up, and he himself, although he does not know a great deal that most boys know, knows much that other boys do not know. He has never seen a train of cars nor an elevator in his life, and for that matter he has never once looked upon a cornfield, a plow, a cow, or even a chicken. He has never had a pair of shoes on his feet, nor gone to a picnic or a party, nor talked to a girl. But he has seen the sun at midnight, watched the ice jams on one of the mightiest of rivers, and played beneath the northern lights,[1] the one white child in thousands of square miles of frozen wilderness.

Walt has walked all the fourteen years of his life in suntanned, moose-hide moccasins, and he can go to the Indian camps and "talk big" with the men, and trade calico and beads with them for their precious furs. He can make bread without baking powder, yeast, or hops, shoot a moose at three hundred yards, and drive the wild wolf dogs fifty miles a day on the packed trail.

Last of all, he has a good heart, and is not afraid of the darkness and loneliness, of man or beast or thing. His father is a good man, strong and brave, and Walt is growing up like him.

Walt was born a thousand miles or so down the Yukon, in a trading post below the Ramparts. After his mother died, his father and he came on up the river, step by step, from camp to camp, till now they are settled down on the Mazy May Creek in the Klondike

---

1. **northern lights**, streamers or bands of light appearing in the northern sky at night; also called aurora borealis.

country. Last year they and several others had spent much toil and time on the Mazy May, and endured great hardships; the creek, in turn, was just beginning to show up its richness and to reward them for their heavy labor. But with the news of their discoveries, strange men began to come and go through the short days and long nights, and many unjust things they did to the men who had worked so long upon the creek.

Si Hartman had gone away on a moose hunt, to return and find new stakes driven and his claim jumped. George Lukens and his brother had lost their claims in a like manner, having delayed too long on the way to Dawson to record them. In short, it was the old story, and quite a number of the earnest, industrious[2] prospectors had suffered similar losses.

But Walt Masters's father had recorded his claim at the start, so Walt had nothing to fear now that his father had gone on a short trip up the White River prospecting for quartz. Walt was well able to stay by himself in the cabin, cook his three meals a day, and look after things. Not only did he look after his father's claim, but he had agreed to keep an eye on the adjoining one of Loren Hall, who had started for Dawson to record it.

Loren Hall was an old man, and he had no dogs, so he had to travel very slowly. After he had been gone some time, word came up the river that he had broken through the ice at Rosebud Creek and frozen his feet so badly that he would not be able to travel for a couple of weeks. Then Walt Masters received the news that old Loren was nearly all right again, and about to move on afoot for Dawson as fast as a weakened man could.

Walt was worried, however; the claim was liable[3] to be jumped at any moment because of this delay, and a fresh stampede had started in on the Mazy May. He did not like the looks of the newcomers, and one day, when five of them came by with crack[4] dog teams and the lightest of camping outfits, he could see that they were prepared to make speed, and resolved to keep an eye on them. So he locked up the cabin and followed them, being at the same time careful to remain hidden.

He had not watched them long before he was sure that they were professional stampeders, bent on jumping all the claims in sight. Walt crept along the snow at the rim of the creek and saw them change many stakes, destroy old ones, and set up new ones.

In the afternoon, with Walt always trailing on their heels, they came back down the creek, unharnessed their dogs, and went into camp within two claims of his cabin. When he saw them make preparations to cook, he hurried home to get something to eat himself, and then hurried back. He crept so close that he could hear them talking quite plainly, and by pushing the underbrush aside he could catch occasional glimpses of them. They had finished eating and were smoking round the fire.

"The creek is all right, boys," a large, black-bearded man, evidently[5] the leader, said, "and I think the best thing we can do is to pull out tonight. The dogs can follow the trail; besides, it's going to be moonlight. What say you?"

"But it's going to be beastly cold," objected one of the party. "It's forty below zero now."

"An' sure, can't ye keep warm by jumpin' off the sleds an' runnin' after the dogs?" cried an Irishman. "An' who wouldn't? The creek's as rich as a United States mint! Faith, it's an ilegant chanst to be gettin' a run fer yer money! An' if ye don't run, it's mebbe you'll not get the money at all, at all."

"That's it," said the leader. "If we can get to Dawson and record, we're rich men; and

---

2. **industrious** (in dus′trē əs), *adj.* working hard and steadily; diligent.
3. **liable** (lī′ə bəl), *adj.* likely; unpleasantly likely.
4. **crack** (krak), *adj.* excellent; first-rate.
5. **evidently** (ev′ə dənt lē), *adv.* plainly; clearly.

▲ *The Home Guard* was painted by Sydney Laurence in 1917. What words and phrases in the story could you use to describe this picture?

there's no telling who's been sneaking along in our tracks, watching us, and perhaps now off to give the alarm. The thing for us to do is to rest the dogs a bit, and then hit the trail as hard as we can. What do you say?"

Evidently the men had agreed with their leader, for Walt Masters could hear nothing but the rattle of the tin dishes which were being washed. Peering out cautiously, he could see the leader studying a piece of paper. Walt knew what it was at a glance—a list of all the unrecorded claims on Mazy May. Any man could get these lists by applying to the gold commissioner[6] at Dawson.

"Thirty-two," the leader said, lifting his face to the men. "Thirty-two isn't recorded, and this is thirty-three. Come on; let's take a look at it. I saw somebody had been working on it when we came up this morning."

Three of the men went with him, leaving one to remain in camp. Walt crept carefully after them till they came to Loren Hall's shaft. One of the men went down and built a fire on the bottom to thaw out the frozen gravel, while the others built another fire on the dump and melted water in a couple of gold pans. This they poured into a piece of canvas stretched between two logs, used by Loren Hall in which to wash his gold.

_____

6. **commissioner** (kə mish′ə nər), *n.* official in charge of some department of a government.

The King of Mazy May **131**

In a short time a couple of buckets of dirt were sent up by the man in the shaft, and Walt could see the others grouped anxiously about their leader as he proceeded to wash it. When this was finished, they stared at the broad streak of black sand and yellow gold grains on the bottom of the pan, and one of them called excitedly for the man who had remained in camp to come. Loren Hall had struck it rich and his claim was not yet recorded. It was plain that they were going to jump it.

Walt lay in the snow, thinking rapidly. He was only a boy, but in the face of the threatened injustice[7] to old lame Loren Hall he felt that he must do something. He waited and watched, with his mind made up, till he saw the men begin to square up new stakes. Then he crawled away till out of hearing, and broke into a run for the camp of the stampeders. Walt's father had taken their own dogs with him prospecting, and the boy knew how impossible it was for him to undertake the seventy miles to Dawson without the aid of dogs.

Gaining the camp, he picked out, with an experienced eye, the easiest running sled and started to harness up the stampeders' dogs. There were three teams of six each, and from these he chose ten of the best. Realizing how necessary it was to have a good head dog, he strove to discover a leader amongst them; but he had little time in which to do it, for he could hear the voices of the returning men. By the time the team was in shape and everything ready, the claim-jumpers came into sight in an open place not more than a hundred yards from the trail, which ran down the bed of the creek. They cried out to Walt, but instead of giving heed to them he grabbed up one of their fur sleeping robes, which lay loosely in the snow, and leaped upon the sled.

"Mush! Hi! Mush on!" he cried to the animals, snapping the keen-lashed whip among them.

The dogs sprang against the yoke straps, and the sled jerked under way so suddenly as to almost throw him off. Then it curved into the creek, poising[8] perilously[9] on one runner. He was almost breathless with suspense, when it finally righted with a bound and sprang ahead again. The creek bank was high and he could not see the men, although he could hear their cries and knew they were running to cut him off. He did not dare to think what would happen if they caught him; he just clung to the sled, his heart beating wildly, and watched the snow rim of the bank above him.

Suddenly, over this snow rim came the flying body of the Irishman, who had leaped straight for the sled in a desperate attempt to capture it; but he was an instant too late. Striking on the very rear of it, he was thrown from his feet, backward, into the snow. Yet, with the quickness of a cat, he had clutched the end of the sled with one hand, turned over, and was dragging behind on his breast, swearing at the boy and threatening all kinds of terrible things if he did not stop the dogs; but Walt cracked him sharply across the knuckles with the butt of the dog whip till he let go.

It was eight miles from Walt's claim to the Yukon—eight very crooked miles, for the creek wound back and forth like a snake, "tying knots in itself," as George Lukens said. And because it was so crooked the dogs could not get up their best speed, while the sled ground heavily on its side against the curves, now to the right, now to the left.

Travelers who had come up and down the Mazy May on foot, with packs on their backs, had declined to go round all the bends, and instead had made shortcuts across the narrow necks of creek bottom. Two of his pursuers had gone back to harness the remaining dogs,

---

7. injustice (in jus′ tis), n. lack of fairness or rightness; being unjust.
8. poise (poiz), v. balance.
9. perilously (per′ə ləs lē), adv. dangerously.

but the others took advantage of these shortcuts, running on foot, and before he knew it they had almost overtaken him.

"Halt!" they cried after him. "Stop, or we'll shoot!"

But Walt only yelled the harder at the dogs, and dashed round the bend with a couple of revolver bullets singing after him. At the next bend they had drawn up closer still, and the bullets struck uncomfortably near him; but at this point the Mazy May straightened out and ran for half a mile as the crow flies. Here the dogs stretched out in their long wolf swing, and the stampeders, quickly winded, slowed down and waited for their own sled to come up.

Looking over his shoulder, Walt reasoned that they had not given up the chase for good, and that they would soon be after him again. So he wrapped the fur robe about him to shut out the stinging air, and lay flat on the empty sled, encouraging the dogs, as he well knew how.

At last, twisting abruptly between two river islands, he came upon the mighty Yukon sweeping grandly to the north. He could not see from bank to bank, and in the quick-falling twilight it loomed a great white sea of frozen stillness. There was not a sound, save the breathing of the dogs, and the churn of the steel-shod sled.

No snow had fallen for several weeks, and the traffic had packed the main river trail till it was hard and glassy as glare ice. Over this the sled flew along, and the dogs kept the trail fairly well, although Walt quickly discovered that he had made a mistake in choosing the leader. As they were driven in single file, without reins, he had to guide them by his voice, and it was evident the head dog had never learned the meaning of "gee" and "haw."[10] He hugged the inside of the curves too closely,

"Halt!" they cried after him. "Stop, or we'll shoot!"

often forcing his comrades behind him into the soft snow, while several times he thus capsized[11] the sled.

There was no wind, but the speed at which he traveled created a bitter blast, and with the thermometer down to forty below, this bit through fur and flesh to the very bones. Aware that if he remained constantly upon the sled he would freeze to death, and knowing the practice of Arctic travelers, Walt shortened up one of the lashing thongs, and whenever he felt chilled, seized hold of it, jumped off, and ran behind till warmth was restored. Then he would climb on and rest till the process had to be repeated.

Looking back he could see the sled of his pursuers, drawn by eight dogs, rising and falling over the ice hummocks like a boat in a seaway. The Irishman and the black-bearded leader were with it, taking turns in running and riding.

Night fell, and in the blackness of the first hour or so Walt toiled desperately with his dogs. On account of the poor lead dog, they were continually floundering[12] off the beaten track into the soft snow, and the sled was as often riding on its side or top as it was in the proper way. This work and strain tried his strength sorely. Had he not been in such haste he could have avoided much of it, but he feared the stampeders would creep up in the darkness and overtake him. However, he could hear them yelling to their dogs, and knew from the sounds they were coming up very slowly.

When the moon rose he was off Sixty Mile,

10. **gee . . . haw**, commands given to sled dogs to turn right (gee) or left (haw).
11. capsize (kap sīz′), v. overturn.
12. flounder (floun′dər), v. struggle awkwardly without making much progress.

dog, and he knew he could easily run away from them if he could only change the bad leader for the good one. But this was impossible, for a moment's delay, at the speed they were running, would bring the men behind upon him.

When he was off the mouth of Rosebud Creek, just as he was topping a rise, the report[13] of a gun and the ping of a bullet on the ice beside him told him that they were this time shooting at him with a rifle. And from then on, as he cleared the summit[14] of each ice jam, he stretched flat on the leaping sled till the rifle shot from the rear warned him that he was safe till the next ice jam was reached.

Now it is very hard to lie on a moving sled, jumping and plunging and yawing like a boat before the wind, and to shoot through the deceiving moonlight at an object four hundred yards away on another moving sled performing equally wild antics. So it is not to be wondered at that the black-bearded leader did not hit him.

After several hours of this, during which, perhaps, a score of bullets had struck about him, their ammunition began to give out and their fire slackened.[15] They took greater care,

▲ *Trapper and Dog Team* was painted by Frank Schoonover in 1937. Do you think this boy could outwit the claim-jumpers?

and Dawson was only fifty miles away. He was almost exhausted, and breathed a sigh of relief as he climbed on the sled again. Looking back, he saw his enemies had crawled up within four hundred yards. At this space they remained, a black speck of motion on the white river breast. Strive as they would, they could not shorten this distance, and strive as he would, he could not increase it.

Walt had now discovered the proper lead

13. **report** (ri pôrt), *n.* sound of a shot or an explosion.
14. **summit** (sum′it), *n.* highest point; top.
15. **slacken** (slak′ən), *v.* become less active, vigorous, or brisk; become slower.

and shot at him at the most favorable opportunities. He was also leaving them behind, the distance slowly increasing to six hundred yards.

Lifting clear on a crest of a great jam off Indian River, Walt Masters met with his first accident. A bullet sang past his ears, and struck the bad lead dog.

The poor brute plunged in a heap, with the rest of the team on top of him.

Like a flash Walt was by the leader. Cutting the traces with his hunting knife, he dragged the dying animal to one side and straightened out the team.

He glanced back. The other sled was coming up like an express train. With half the dogs still over their traces, he cried "Mush on!" and leaped upon the sled just as the pursuers dashed abreast of him.

The Irishman was preparing to spring for him—they were so sure they had him that they did not shoot—when Walt turned fiercely upon them with his whip.

He struck at their faces, and men must save their faces with their hands. So there was no shooting just then. Before they could recover from the hot rain of blows, Walt reached out from his sled, catching their wheel dog by the forelegs in midspring, and

The ping of a bullet on the ice beside him told him that they were this time shooting at him with a rifle.

throwing him heavily. This snarled the team, capsizing the sled and tangling his enemies up beautifully.

Away Walt flew, the runners of his sled fairly screaming as they bounded over the frozen surface. And what had seemed an accident proved to be a blessing in disguise. The proper lead dog was now to the fore, and he stretched low and whined with joy as he jerked his comrades along.

By the time he reached Ainslie's Creek, seventeen miles from Dawson, Walt had left his pursuers, a tiny speck, far behind. At Monte Cristo Island he could no longer see them. And at Swede Creek, just as daylight was silvering the pines, he ran plump into the camp of old Loren Hall.

Almost as quick as it takes to tell it, Loren had his sleeping furs rolled up, and had joined Walt on the sled. They permitted the dogs to travel more slowly, as there was no sign of the chase in the rear, and just as they pulled up at the gold commissioner's office in Dawson, Walt, who had kept his eyes open to the last, fell asleep.

And because of what Walt Masters did on this night, the men of the Yukon have become proud of him, and speak of him now as the King of Mazy May.

After Reading

Making Connections

1. Below is a Survival Report Card. Copy the card on your paper. Then grade Walt in each category. Explain each grade.

Character Trait	Grade
Courage	
Skill	
Determination	
Common Sense	

2. 🐾 Because of his **individuality**, Walt felt obligated to prevent the stampeders from jumping Loren Hall's claim. If you were in Walt's place, what do you think you would have done? Explain.

3. After the long, exciting chase, the author wraps up the story quickly and neatly. Why do you suppose he does that?

4. "The King of Mazy May" is a violent story. Some people think such stories, TV shows, and movies encourage people to be violent. Do you agree? Why or why not?

Literary Focus: Setting

Setting is the time and place in which the events of a story occur. A setting may be described in detail or only suggested. It may be important or unimportant to the events of the story.

With a partner, reread "The King of Mazy May" and write down everything the author tells you about the setting. Discuss the following questions:

- What does the author say about where the story occurs? What doesn't he say about it?

- What image of the place does the author give you?

- What does the author say about when the story occurs?

- Why do you suppose the author gives so much more information about place than about time?

- How important is the specific setting? That is, could the events of the story occur anywhere and anytime? Why or why not?

Vocabulary Study

The paragraphs below are from a news account of a recent dog-sled race. Use context clues to decide which word from the list best completes each unfinished sentence. Write the word.

liable
evidently
injustice
poising
perilously
capsize
flounder
summit
slacken
industrious

The U.S. dog-sled team came __(1)__ close to serious injury or death in yesterday's race. The team was leading and had just passed over the __(2)__ of a hill when a moose appeared on trail below.

Jane Snow, driver of the team, later reported, "From the way he stared at us, the moose __(3)__ was as surprised as we were. But I knew we had more to fear because a moose is __(4)__ to kick or charge when startled. I brought the dogs to such a sudden stop that I thought the sled would __(5)__ , tossing me off. The dogs left the trail and began to __(6)__ through the deep snow toward the woods.

"I faced the moose alone, __(7)__ on one foot because my other ankle was painfully twisted. I was angry that this silly moose would make us lose, when we've been so __(8)__ about training every day. Without thinking, I started shouting about the __(9)__ that the moose was doing to us. He began to charge, but almost immediately, he began to __(10)__ his pace, and then he stopped.

"It was as if he understood what I was saying! He turned and disappeared. I called to the dogs, and soon we were on our way. We finished in third place, but I'm just glad we survived."

Expressing Your Ideas

Writing Choices

Now Showing Write an **advertisement** for the movie about "The King of Mazy May." Use words from the web you made on page 128 to emphasize that the story is an exciting adventure.

Weather Report Details in "The King of Mazy May" help you experience the cold of the Klondike. Write a detailed **description** of the most extreme weather condition you've experienced, such as a violent storm, intense cold or heat, or flooding.

Other Options

Gold Fever Work in a small group to research gold rushes in North America in the 1800s. Create a **museum exhibit** that answers questions like these: Where did the prospectors come from? What tools and methods did they use? How long did they stay? How many struck it rich?

Mush, You Huskies! Find out about the famous Iditarod dog-sled race, and make an **oral report** to the class about it. Include visual materials, such as a map of the route or drawings of the types of dogs that participate.

Before Reading

The Pacing White Mustang

by Jean Craighead George

Jean Craighead George
born 1919

As children, Jean Craighead George and her twin brothers spent their summers swimming, fishing, and playing softball on farmland owned by their family. Imaginative adventurers, the twins dominated those summers. "With two such brothers," George once said, "a younger sister *had* to be a writer to find her niche [place] and survive." As a writer, George has combined her loves of nature and literature to create many books of fiction and nonfiction for young people. George enjoys doing firsthand research, whether it means tramping through a dense rain forest or observing the 150-plus pets her family has had over the years.

Building Background

Mustang Heritage When Christopher Columbus made his second voyage to the Americas in 1493, his passengers included horses. In the 1500s, Hernán Cortés and other Spanish explorers began arriving on the North American mainland, and they too brought horses. Native Americans soon realized how useful horses could be for transportation, hunting, and war.

Today, about twenty thousand descendants of the early Spanish horses roam freely in the western United States. We call these horses mustangs. Hunting mustangs is now illegal, but it still occurs.

Getting into the Selection

Discussion "The Pacing White Mustang" describes a horse who could run incredibly fast. In a small group, talk about some of the advantages of speed, for both animals and humans. What disadvantages can you think of? As you discuss, fill in a chart like the one below.

	Advantages of Speed	**Disadvantages of Speed**
For Animals	escaping from danger	
For Humans		

Reading Tip

Nonfiction Fiction and nonfiction have some things in common. Either may include descriptions of scenes, people, animals, or objects. Either may tell the story of an event. But fiction deals with imaginary people and events, while nonfiction deals with real people, real events, and the real world. As you read "The Pacing White Mustang," look for clues that tell you it is nonfiction.

The Pacing White Mustang

Fastest Horse in the West

JEAN CRAIGHEAD GEORGE

In the days when there were still buffalos, Native Americans, and U.S. Cavalry on the Great Plains, the Pacing White Mustang lived in wild splendor somewhere "out west." He sped like a tornado across the prairie and commanded his herd like a general. Stories were written about his strength and beauty, and prizes were offered for his capture. But no one could rope him.

His speed was legendary. He moved his front and back legs simultaneously, first on one side and then on the other, in a dynamic gait called "pacing." Other horses alternately put forward the front right with back left legs, then the front left with the back right. The pacer fairly flew.

He was as wild as the cornflower and as beautiful as snow on the mountains. The Osage Indians said he was a ghost. Cowboys said he was a mirage.

But he was out there and he was real. Washington Irving removed all doubt. In 1832 he sighted the magnificent white stallion while on a tour of the prairies with the Commissioner of Indian Affairs. A few years later an army general and one of his captains were awakened by a night battle between wild horses and wolves. At daylight they rode out to catch the horses for the army.

About a mile downstream they came upon the howling wolves and a herd of about 150 horses. Rising above them all, flailing[1] his feet

---

1. **flail** (flāl), *v.* beat; thrash.

Does this painting of *The Wild Horses of Nevada* by Maynard Dixon remind you of the author's description of the mustang? ➤

as he commanded, was the Pacing White Mustang. He had formed the mares in a circle facing inward so they could kick the enemy with their hoofs. Protected inside the circle were the foals[2] and yearlings.[3] What was most extraordinary was that the white mustang ruled the other stallions.[4] At his command they charged the wolves who were attacking the herd.

Upon scenting the men, the wolves ran off, and the men went after the horses. The Pacing White Mustang instantly signaled his stallions. They turned, pawed the ground in front of the mares and neighed. The mares opened their circle. The colts and yearlings ran out and the stallions led them off. The mares followed the colts.

The white stallion brought up the rear and took on the men. He would let a rider come to within twenty yards of him, then pull swiftly away, fall back, and let another horseman approach. In this manner he held off the horse raiders until his herd was out of sight. Then he vanished. Even the disappointed general had to admit that he and all the others who had tried, but had failed, to capture the white stallion had been outsoldiered by the Pacing White Mustang.

---

2. **foal** (fōl), *n.* horse less than one year old.
3. **yearling** (yir′ling), *n.* one-year-old horse.
4. **stallion** (stal′yən), *n.* adult male horse.

After Reading

Making Connections

1. Was speed or intelligence more important in the way that the white mustang "outsoldiered" the soldiers? Explain your thinking.

2. Suppose you had not known ahead of time that the selection was **nonfiction**. What clues would have helped you figure it out?

3. How do you think the author's feelings about animals influenced her attitude toward "The Pacing White Mustang"? Explain.

4. What challenges do today's wild animals face? Explain.

Literary Focus: Simile

To create a "picture," authors often point out ways in which two very different things are actually alike. When such a comparison includes the word *like* or *as*, it's called a **simile**. *Life is like a roaring sea* is one example of a simile.

Find as many similes in the selection as you can. Record them in a chart like the one below. For each simile, write a replacement that could be used to make the same comparison.

Author's Simile	My Idea for a Simile
He sped like a tornado.	He sped like a locomotive.

Expressing Your Ideas

Animal Comparisons Choose a real team or product with an animal name, or make one up. Write an **advertisement** for the team's next event or for the product. Tell why the team or product is a good one, based on the characteristics it shares with the animal.

Extraordinary Horses With a group of classmates, research some famous horses in history and legend, such as Marengo (French emperor Napoleon's white stallion) and Pegasus (the flying horse in Greek myths). Present brief **oral reports** on the various horses.

Poster Art Create a **poster** comparing a bicycle or skates to a mustang.

Before Reading

The Quest for the Golden Apples

retold by Josephine Preston

Background

All About Myths "The Quest for the Golden Apples" retells a myth of ancient Greece. Myths are old stories, often involving supernatural beings. Many myths explain something about nature.

   The gods and goddesses of Greek myths possessed extraordinary powers. Yet, they had human personality traits and emotions. In fact, Greek myths tell stories of gods and goddesses helping humans or interacting with them in other ways. When the Romans conquered Greece, they adopted many Greek gods and goddesses. The Roman goddess Venus, for example, was based on the Greek goddess Aphrodite. "The Quest for the Golden Apples" includes both Greek and Roman names.

Getting into the Story

Writer's Notebook Have you or someone you know or have heard about ever taken on an apparently impossible challenge? In your notebook, write about this experience. What was the challenge? What was the result? How do you think those involved felt?

Reading Tip

Visualizing A myth like "The Quest for the Golden Apples" may seem unrelated to your everyday life. After all, long-ago, faraway settings and characters with extraordinary powers are quite removed from your own experiences. You'll enjoy the story more if you try to visualize the setting and characters. Combine the clues the author gives with your imagination to form mental pictures. Make a chart the like the one below, and fill it in as you read.

Character	The Clues the Author Gives	What I Visualize
Atalanta		
Venus		
Hippomenes		

THE QUEST FOR THE GOLDEN APPLES

Josephine Preston

A talanta, a great huntress, was resolved to live unwed after learning that her father abandoned her because she had not been born a boy. And at last she devised a plan to be rid of all her suitors. She was known far and wide as the swiftest runner of her time; and so she said that she would only marry that man who could outstrip[1] her in a foot race, but that all who dared to try and failed must be put to death.

This threat did not dishearten all of the suitors, however, and to her grief, for she was not cruel, they held her to her promise. On a certain day the few bold men who were to try their fortune made ready, and chose young Hippomenes as judge. He sat watching them before the word was given, and sadly wondered that any brave man should risk his life merely to win a bride. But when Atalanta stood ready for the contest, he was amazed by her beauty. She looked like Hebe, goddess of young health, who is a glad serving-maiden to the gods when they sit at feast.

The signal was given, and, as she and the suitors darted away, flight made her more enchanting than ever. Just as a wind brings sparkles to the water and laughter to the trees, haste fanned[2] her loveliness to a glow.

Alas for the suitors! She ran as if Hermes had lent her his winged sandals. The young men, skilled as they were, grew heavy with

---

1. outstrip, (out strip′) v. go faster than; leave behind in a race.
2. fan (fan), v. stir up; arouse.

weariness and despair. For all their efforts, they seemed to lag like ships in a calm, while Atalanta flew before them in some favoring breeze—and reached the goal!

To the sorrow of all onlookers, the suitors were led away; but the judge himself, Hippomenes, rose and begged leave to try his fortune. As Atalanta listened, and looked at him, her heart was filled with pity, and she would willingly have let him win the race to save him from defeat and death; for he was comely and younger than the others. But her friends urged her to rest and make ready, and she consented, with an unwilling heart.

Meanwhile Hippomenes prayed within himself to Venus: "Goddess of Love, give ear, and send me good speed. Let me be swift to win as I have been swift to love her."

Now Venus, who was not far off—for she had already moved the heart of Hippomenes to love—came to his side invisibly, slipped into his hand three wondrous golden apples, and whispered a word of counsel[3] in his ear.

The signal was given; youth and maiden started over the course. They went so like the wind that they left not a footprint. The people cheered on Hippomenes, eager that such valor should win. But the course was long, and soon fatigue seemed to clutch at his throat, the light

THE PEOPLE CHEERED ON HIPPOMENES, EAGER THAT SUCH VALOR SHOULD WIN

shook before his eyes, and, even as he pressed on, the maiden passed him by.

At that instant Hippomenes tossed ahead one of the golden apples. The rolling bright thing caught Atalanta's eye, and full of wonder she stooped to pick it up. Hippomenes ran on. As he heard the flutter of her tunic close behind him, he flung aside another golden apple, and another moment was lost to the girl. Who could pass by such a marvel?[4] The goal was near and Hippomenes was ahead, but once again Atalanta caught up with him, and they sped side by side like two dragonflies. For an instant his heart failed him; then, with a last prayer to Venus, he flung down the last apple. The maiden glanced at it, wavered, and would have left it where it had fallen, had not Venus turned her head for a second and given her a sudden wish to possess it. Against her will she turned to pick up the golden apple, and Hippomenes touched the goal.

So he won that perilous[5] maiden; and as for Atalanta, she was glad to marry such a valorous man. By this time she understood so well what it was like to be pursued that she had lost a little of her pleasure in hunting.

---

3. **counsel** (koun′səl), *n.* advice.
4. **marvel** (mär′vəl), *n.* something wonderful; astonishing thing.
5. **perilous** (per′ə ləs), *n.* dangerous.

After Reading

Making Connections

1. Knowing the penalty for losing, would you have accepted the challenge and raced Atalanta? Explain.

2. 🐾 Atalanta didn't show **individuality** when others pressured her to race. What would you have done in her place?

3. Many cultures, especially cultures of the past, have valued sons above daughters. Do you think this fair? Explain.

Literary Focus: Plot

The **plot** of a story consists of the events that the author uses to present and then resolve a problem. In a carefully constructed plot, the events are arranged so that each event follows from the one before it. The pattern of events leads to the **climax,** or turning point, of the story. The problem is solved in the **conclusion.**

A chart like the one below can help you understand plot. Copy the chart. Look back at the story, and fill in the information. Be sure to list the main events in order. Also be sure that what you write under *Solution* relates to what you write under *Problem*.

Title:

Setting:

Characters:

Problem:

Events

Solution:

Vocabulary Study

The first word in each of the following pairs comes from the story. Decide if the pairs of words are synonyms, words that have similar meanings, or antonyms, words that have opposite meanings. On a sheet of paper, write *S* for Synonyms or *A* for Antonyms.

counsel
fan
marvel
outstrip
perilous

1. perilous – safe
2. counsel – advice
3. outstrip – pass
4. marvel – wonder
5. fan – weaken

Expressing Your Ideas

Writing Choices

Another Possibility The story could have developed differently. Someone might have won the race before Hippomenes got his chance. Atalanta could have changed the rules of the race or Venus's magic might not have worked. Imagine one of these possibilities, or another one that occurs to you. Write a new **plot outline** for the story, and share it with your classmates.

Right or Wrong Imagine that this story took place today. Write a **newspaper article** about the race and the scandal that is involved with the discovery of Hippomenes cheating by throwing apples all over the course.

Other Options

Run for Your Wife You have been hired to create an eye-catching **poster** to advertise the race to potential husbands. Make the poster. Be sure to include a headline.

And They're Off Imagine you are a sportscaster. Do a live, play-by-play **broadcast** of the race between Atalanta and Hippomenes. Spice up your broadcast with observations about the setting of the race and the contestants.

Act It Out With a partner or small group, prepare and perform a short **play** based on one of the scenes in the story. If you like, wear costumes and have appropriate background music playing as you perform.

The Race Is On!

Going for It!

Mathematics Connection
Everyone faces life challenges, both large and small. Some shy away from those challenges. Others race to meet them head-on. Those are the champions.

The Olympics

After Edwin Moses won the title for the 400-meter hurdles at the Montreal Olympics in 1976, he seemed unstoppable. Moses claimed 105 victories in his sport in the next seven years.

Sites of Olympic Games

Summer		Winter	
1896	Athens, Greece	1924	Chamonix, France
1900	Paris, France	1928	St. Moritz, Switzerland
1904	St. Louis, U.S.	1932	Lake Placid, NY, U.S.
1908	London, England	1936	Garmisch-Partenkirchen, Germany
1912	Stockholm, Sweden		
1920	Antwerp, Belgium	1948	St. Moritz, Switzerland
1924	Paris, France	1952	Oslo, Norway
1928	Amsterdam, Netherlands	1956	Cortina d'Ampezzo, Italy
1932	Los Angeles, U.S.	1960	Squaw Valley, CA, U.S.
1936	Berlin, Germany	1964	Innsbruck, Austria
1948	London, England	1968	Grenoble, France
1952	Helsinki, Finland	1972	Sapporo, Japan
1956	Melbourne, Australia	1976	Innsbruck, Austria
1960	Rome, Italy	1980	Lake Placid, NY, U.S.
1964	Tokyo, Japan	1984	Sarajevo, Yugoslavia
1968	Mexico City, Mexico	1988	Calgary, Alberta, Canada
1972	Munich, W. Germany		
1976	Montreal, Canada	1992	Albertville, France
1980	Moscow, USSR	1994	Lillehammer, Norway
1984	Los Angeles, U.S.		
1988	Seoul, S. Korea		
1992	Barcelona, Spain		

Source: The World Almanac and Book of Facts 1994

The settings for modern Olympics are very different from this ancient arena in Olympia, Greece. However, the challenges of competition remain the same.

She was a three-time medal winner in the 1988 Olympics. Seventeen-year-old Janet Evans didn't flinch in the face of her challenge. She beat older and more experienced swimmers.

Canadian David Steen reached new heights when he broke an Olympic record in the pole vault at the 1988 Games in Calgary, Alberta, Canada.

MEN'S POLE VAULT

Year	Height
1988	19 ft. 9.25 in.
1980	18 ft. 11.5 in.
1972	18 ft. .5 in.
1964	16 ft. 8.75 in.
1956	14 ft. 11.5 in.
1948	14 ft. 1.25 in.
1920	13 ft. 5 in.
1908	12 ft. 2 in.
1904	11 ft. 5.75 in.
1896	10 ft. 10 in.

Source: The World Almanac and Book of Facts 1994

WOMEN'S LONG JUMP

1952 20 ft. 5.7

1956 20 ft. 9.75 in.

1960 20 ft. 10.75 in.

1968 22 ft. 4.25 in.

1980 23 ft. 2 in.

1988 24 ft. 3.5 in.

Source: The World Almanac and Book of Facts 1994

Considered by many to be one of the world's best athletes, Jackie Joyner-Kersee is a winner. Shown here in the long jump, she challenges herself not only to win the Olympic gold, but to beat her own personal best.

A professional basketball player, Larry Bird was not afraid to accept the challenge of Olympic competition in the 1992 Barcelona Games.

Meeting the challenge of short track speed skating requires strength, strategy, and concentration as well as speed.

In the 1932 Olympics, Babe Didrickson was the only woman on the U.S. track team. Her 143 ft. 4 in. javelin throw set a new world record.

Slalom skier Alberto Tomba became the first Olympian skier to successfully defend his championship.

Responding

1. Compare the pole vault chart to the long jump chart. In which sport did the record vault or jump increase by the greatest percentage from the first to the last year listed?

2. What is the difference between the 1988 women's long jump record and the winning jump in 1956?

History Connection

From the beginning, the race was on for Wilma Rudolph. She learned that to be the best she had to keep challenging herself. Wilma decided to go for it, and she got it — the Olympic Gold. She kept challenging herself until her death in 1994.

Racing for the Gold

by Wilma Rudolph

That taste of winning I had gotten the year before never left me. I was more serious about track now, thinking deep down inside that maybe I had a future in the sport if I tried hard enough. So I thought nothing of cutting classes and going out to run. But one day I got a call to report to the principal's office. I went in, and he said, "Wilma, all of us here know just how important running track is to you. We all know it, and we are all hoping that you become a big success at it. But you can't keep cutting classes and going out to run." I was, well, mortified; the principal had found me out. He finally said that if I continued cutting classes, he would have to tell my father, and I knew what that meant. So I stopped. Even so, I was the first girl out there at practice and the last one to leave, I loved it so. We had some playday-type meets early that season, and I kept on winning all the races I was in. I felt unbeatable.

Then came the big meet at Tuskegee, Alabama. It was the big meet of the year. Girls from all over the South were invited down there to run, and the competition was the best for high school kids. It was a whole weekend type of thing, and they had dances and other things planned for the kids when they weren't out running. Coach Gray was going to

drive us all down there to Tuskegee Institute, where the meet was held, and I remember we brought our very best dresses. We all piled into his car until there wasn't an inch of empty space in that car. Mrs. Allison, my old teacher, came with us; she was going to chaperon us at the big dance after the meet.

All the way down to Alabama, we talked and laughed and had a good time, and Coach Gray would tell us how tough the competition was going to be, especially the girls from Atlanta, Georgia, because they had a lot of black schools down there, and they had these track programs that ran the whole year because of the warm weather. When we got there, all of us were overwhelmed, because that was the first college campus any of us ever saw. We stayed in this big dorm, and I remember just before the first competition, I started getting this nervous feeling that would stay with me for the rest of my running career. Every time before a race, I would get it, this horrible feeling in the pit of my stomach, a combination of nerves and not eating.

When we got to the track, these girls from Georgia really looked like runners, but I paid them no mind because, well, I was a little cocky. I did think I could wipe them out because, after all, I had won every single race I had ever been in up to that point. So what happens? I got wiped out. It was the absolute

worst experience of my life. I did not win a single race I ran in, nor did I qualify for anything. I was totally crushed. The girls from Georgia won everything. It was the first time I had ever tasted defeat in track, and it left me a total wreck. I was so despondent that I refused to go to any of the activities that were planned, including the big dance. I can't remember ever being so totally crushed by anything.

On the ride back, I sat in the car and didn't say a word to anybody, I just thought to myself about how much work was ahead of me and how I would like nothing better in the whole world than to come back to Tuskegee the next year and win everything. When I got home, my father knew immediately what had happened, and he didn't say anything. Every time I used to come home after a meet, I would rush into the house all excited and bubble over with, "I won. . . I won." This time I didn't say a word. I just walked in quietly, nodded to my father who was sitting there, and went into my room and unpacked.

After so many easy victories, using natural ability alone, I got a false sense of being unbeatable. But losing to those girls from Georgia, who knew every trick in the book, that was sobering. It brought me back down to earth, and it made me realize that I couldn't do it on natural ability alone, that there was more to track than just running fast. I also realized it was going to test me as a person—could I come back and win again after being so totally crushed by defeat?

When I went back to school, I knew I couldn't continue to cut classes to practice or else I'd be in big trouble. So I would fake sickness, tell the teacher that I didn't feel well and could I please go home? They would let me go, and then I would go over to the track and run. When that stopped working, when they realized that I looked

pretty good for being sick all the time, I simply asked them point-blank, "Look, could I cut this class today and go out and run?" Believe it or not, a lot of teachers said, "Okay, Wilma, go, but don't tell anybody."

I ran and ran and ran every day, and I acquired this sense of determination, this sense of spirit that I would never, never give up, no matter what else happened. That day at Tuskegee had a tremendous effect on me inside. That's all I ever thought about. Some days I just wanted to go out and die. I just moped around and felt sorry for myself. Other days I'd go out to the track with fire in my eyes, and imagine myself back at Tuskegee, beating them all. Losing as badly as I did had an impact on my personality. Winning all the time in track had given me confidence; I felt like a winner. But I didn't feel like a winner any more after Tuskegee. My confidence was shattered and I was thinking the only way I could put it all together was to get back the next year and wipe them all out.

But looking back on it all, I realized somewhere along the line that to think that way wasn't necessarily right, that it was kind of extreme. I learned a very big lesson for the rest of my life as well. The lesson was, winning is great, sure, but if you are really going to do something in life, the secret is learning how to lose. Nobody goes undefeated all the time. If you can pick up after a crushing defeat, and go on to win again, you are going to be a champion someday. But if losing destroys you, it's all over. You'll never be able to put it all back together again.

Responding
Think about the challenges you are facing right now. What might you do to deal with those situations? Think about the people you have just met in your reading. Perhaps you can use some of their ideas.

153

Reading Mini-Lesson

Using Comparison and Contrast

Comparing and **contrasting** are important skills. Before buying a compact-disc player, you would probably look at several different ones before you make a decision. First, you would compare them and discover how they are alike. Then, you would contrast them and discover how they are different. A difference might be the most important factor in deciding which one you will buy.

Comparing and contrasting skills are also helpful when reading. By seeing similarities and differences, you can better understand what you are reading and relate new information to what you already know.

"Racing for the Gold" on page 152 contrasts Wilma Rudolph as a winner with Wilma as a loser. Wilma sums up what she learned in one sentence: ". . . winning is great, sure, but if you are really going to do something in life, the secret is learning how to lose."

One way to recognize and understand similarities and differences in a selection is to use a compare-contrast frame like the one at the left.

Compare-Contrast Frame

Central Issue:
1. Record the central issue of the selection.

(+)

2. List the positive features associated with the central issue.

(−)

3. List the negative features associated with the central issue.

Conclusion
4. Record your conclusion.

Activity Options

1. Copy the chart at the left. Follow the steps to help you understand how Wilma's defeats at the meet in Alabama affected her. In the conclusion box, tell which results you think were more important, the positive or the negative.

2. Make a chart listing the differences and similarities between Wilma the Winner (before the big meet at Tuskegee) and Wilma the Loser (after Tuskegee). Include these features: her attitude before a race, the emotional effect on her after a race, the way she greeted her father after returning home, and the image she had of herself as a runner.

3. Have you ever thought you were the best at something, only to find out in a larger competition that others were better? Compare your experience with Wilma's by writing two summaries. For Wilma's story and for yours, include these ideas in the summary: the sport or activity, early successes, the tougher competition, and the lesson learned from losing.

Part Two

Incredible Journeys

If you could travel anywhere in the world—or in the universe for that matter—where would you go? To a sparkling city of the future, with moving sidewalks and flying cars? To a serene, blue-green lake, where rare and colorful birds serenade you from the trees?

Whether you ever get to take your dream vacation or not, you will go on many journeys throughout your life.

The selections that follow also describe journeys—both real and imaginary. Grab your bags and enjoy the tour!

 Multicultural Connection **Communication** often involves learning to see things differently as you overcome barriers to understanding. As you read, notice how the characters are helped along their journeys by better understanding themselves and others.

The Wish

by Roald Dahl

Roald Dahl
1916–1990

Roald Dahl turned down his mother's offer to attend college with this reply: "No thank you. I want to go to work for a company that will send me to faraway places like Africa or China." At age 16, he got his wish and went off to Tanzania (then Tanganyika) to work for an oil company. At the outbreak of World War II, Dahl joined Britain's Royal Air Force as a fighter pilot. His writing career began when he took notes for an interview about his own experience shooting down enemy planes. The interviewer sent Dahl's notes to the *Saturday Evening Post*. About this experience, Dahl wrote, "becoming a writer was pure fluke. Without being asked to, I doubt if I'd ever have thought of it."

Building Background

Magic Carpets Notice the colors, patterns, and details on the tapestry rug in the picture on page 158. Tapestry rugs, like this one, are often highly valued works of art. Museums put them on display. Art collectors pay thousands of dollars for them. Families pass these treasured rugs from generation to generation. With their dazzling colors and vibrant designs, tapestry rugs aren't just crusty, old pieces of carpet. They fuel the imagination, and show up as features of fanciful and exotic tales. Stare at the rug in the picture and let your mind wander as you follow the swirls of shapes, colors, and forms.

Getting into the Story

Writer's Notebook People have many customs and superstitions about wishes. A wish on a falling star is sure to come true. Your birthday wish won't come true if you talk between blowing out the candles and taking your first bite of cake. Do you have your own customs or superstitions about wishes? What are they? Did someone tell you these customs or superstitions or did you make them up? How do you feel if you do something that goes against your own superstitions? Explore these questions in your notebook.

Reading Tip

Visualizing The rug is a key element in "The Wish," and to fully appreciate the story it is helpful to visualize, or create a mental picture of the tapestry. Study the picture on page 158 to learn about the general design of most tapestry rugs. As you read the story, look for details about the design, color, and size of the rug and try to picture the rug as you put these details together. You may even want to make a sketch of the rug or jot down information about the rug in your notebook.

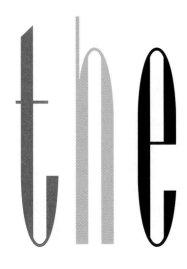

Roald Dahl

Under the palm of one hand the child became aware of the scab of an old cut on his kneecap. He bent forward to examine it closely. A scab was always a fascinating thing; it presented a special challenge he was never able to resist.[1]

Yes, he thought, I will pick it off, even if it isn't ready, even if the middle of it sticks, even if it hurts like anything.

With a fingernail he began to explore cautiously around the edges of the scab. He got the nail underneath it, and when he raised it, but ever so slightly, it suddenly came off; the whole hard brown scab came off beautifully, leaving an interesting little circle of smooth red skin.

Nice. Very nice indeed. He rubbed the circle and it didn't hurt. He picked up the scab, put it on his thigh and flipped it with a finger so that it flew away and landed on the edge of the carpet, the enormous red and black and yellow carpet that stretched the whole length of the hall from the stairs on which he sat to the front door in the distance. A tremendous carpet. Bigger than the tennis lawn. Much bigger than that. He regarded it gravely, settling his eyes upon it with mild pleasure. He had never really noticed it before, but now, all of a sudden, the colors seemed to brighten mysteriously and spring out at him in a most dazzling way.

You see, he told himself, I know how it is. The red parts of the carpet are red-hot lumps of coal. What I must do is this: I must walk all the way along it to the front door without touching them. If I touch the red, I will be burnt. As a matter of fact, I will be burnt up completely. And the black parts of the carpet . . . yes, the black parts are snakes, poisonous snakes, adders

---

1. **resist** (ri zist′), *v.* keep from doing or stop oneself from doing.

Designers of rugs **communicate** different ideas through their patterns. What do you

mostly, and cobras, thick like tree trunks round the middle, and if I touch one of *them*, I'll be bitten and I'll die before tea time.[2] And if I get across safely, without being burnt and without being bitten, I will be given a puppy for my birthday tomorrow.

He got to his feet and climbed higher up the stairs to obtain a better view of this vast tapestry of color and death. Was it possible? Was there enough yellow? Yellow was the only color he was allowed to walk on. Could it be done? This was not a journey to be undertaken lightly; the risks were too great for that. The child's face—a fringe[3] of white-gold hair, two large blue eyes, a small pointed chin—peered down anxiously over the banisters. The yellow was a bit thin in places and there were one or two widish gaps, but it did seem to go all the way along to the other end. For someone who had only yesterday triumphantly[4] traveled the whole length of the brick path from the stables to the summer house without touching the cracks, this carpet thing should not be too difficult. Except for the snakes. The mere thought of snakes sent a fine electricity of fear running like pins down the backs of his legs and under the soles of his feet.

He came slowly down the stairs and advanced to the edge of the carpet. He extended one small sandaled foot and placed it cautiously upon a patch of yellow. Then he brought the other foot up, and there was just enough room for him to stand with the two feet together. There! He had started! His bright oval face was curiously intent, a shade whiter perhaps than before, and he was holding his arms out sideways to assist his balance. He took another step, lifting his foot high over a patch of black, aiming carefully with his toe for a narrow channel of yellow on the other side. When he had completed the second step, he paused to rest, standing very stiff

and still. The narrow channel[5] of yellow ran forward unbroken for at least five yards and he advanced gingerly[6] along it, bit by bit, as though walking a tightrope. Where it finally curled off sideways, he had to take another long stride, this time over a vicious-looking mixture of black and red. Halfway across he began to wobble. He waved his arms around wildly, windmill fashion, to keep his balance, and he got across safely and rested again on the other side. He was quite breathless now, and so tense he stood high on his toes all the time, arms out sideways, fists clenched. He was on a big safe island of yellow. There was lots of room on it, he couldn't possibly fall off, and he stood there resting, hesitating, waiting, wishing he could stay forever on this big safe yellow island. But the fear of not getting the puppy compelled[7] him to go on.

> He got to his feet and climbed higher up the stairs to obtain a better view of this vast tapestry of color and death.

Step by step, he edged further ahead, and between each one he paused to decide exactly where next he should put his foot. Once, he had a choice of ways, either to left or right, and he chose the left because although it seemed the more difficult, there was not so much black in that direction. The black was what made him nervous. He glanced quickly over his shoulder to see how far he had come. Nearly halfway. There could be no turning

---

2. **tea time**, in England, the time in the late afternoon or early evening during which a light meal is served.
3. fringe (frinj), *n.* an edging of hanging threads or cords.
4. triumphantly (trī um′fənt lē), *adv.* successfully.
5. channel (chan′l), *n.* usually the bed of a stream, river, etc., but in this case a narrow strip of color in the rug.
6. gingerly (jin′jər lē), *adv.* with extreme care or caution.
7. compel (kəm pel′) *v.* drive or urge with force.

back now. He was in the middle and he couldn't turn back and he couldn't jump off sideways either because it was too far, and when he looked at all the red and all the black that lay ahead of him, he felt that old sudden sickening surge[8] of panic in his chest—like last Easter time, that afternoon when he got lost all alone in the darkest part of Piper's Wood.

Another snake slid up noiselessly beside the first, raised its head, two heads now, two pairs of eyes staring at the foot . . .

He took another step, placing his foot carefully upon the only little piece of yellow within reach, and this time the point of the foot came within a centimeter of some black. It wasn't touching the black, he could see it wasn't touching, he could see the small line of yellow separating the toe of his sandal from the black; but the snake stirred as though sensing the nearness, and raised his head and gazed at the foot with bright beady eyes, watching to see if it was going to touch.

"I'm not touching you! You mustn't bite me! You know I'm not touching you."

Another snake slid up noiselessly beside the first, raised its head, two heads now, two pairs of eyes staring at the foot, gazing at a little naked place just below the sandal strap where the skin showed through. The child went high up on his toes and stayed there, frozen stiff with terror. It was minutes before he dared to move again.

The next step would have to be a really long one. There was this deep curling river of black that ran clear across the width of the carpet, and he was forced by his position to cross it at its widest part. He thought first of trying to jump it, but decided he couldn't be sure of landing accurately[9] on the narrow band of yellow on the other side. He took a deep breath, lifted one foot, and inch by inch he pushed it out in front of him, far far out, then down and down until at last the tip of his sandal was across and resting safely on the edge of the yellow. He leaned forward, transferring his weight to this front foot. Then he tried to bring the back foot up as well. He strained and pulled and jerked his body, but the legs were too wide apart and he couldn't make it. He tried to get back again. He couldn't do that either. He was doing the splits and he was properly stuck. He glanced down and saw this deep curling river of black underneath him. Parts of it were stirring now, and uncoiling and sliding and beginning to shine with a dreadful oily glister. He wobbled, waved his arms frantically[10] to keep his balance, but that seemed to make it worse. He was starting to go over. He was going over to the right, quite slowly he was going over, then faster and faster, and at the last moment, instinctively[11] he put out a hand to break the fall and the next thing he saw was this bare hand of his going right into the middle of a great glistening mass of black and he gave one piercing cry of terror as it touched.

Outside in the sunshine, far away behind the house, the mother was looking for her son.

---

8. **surge** (sėrj), *n.* a swelling wave or something like such a wave.
9. **accurately** (ak′yər it lē), *adv.* without errors or mistakes.
10. **frantically** (fran′tik lē), *adv.* with wild fear.
11. **instinctively** (in stingk′tiv lē), *adv.* following a natural tendency.

Halfway Down

A. A. Milne

Halfway down the stairs
Is a stair
Where I sit.
There isn't any
5 Other stair
Quite like
It.
I'm not at the bottom,
I'm not at the top;
10 So this is the stair
Where
I always
Stop.

Halfway up the stairs
15 Isn't up,
And it isn't down.
It isn't in the nursery,
It isn't in the town.
And all sorts of funny thoughts
20 Run round my head:
"It isn't really
Anywhere!
It's somewhere else
Instead!

After Reading

Making Connections

amused   sad   anxious   bored   surprised

1. Pick a word from the list above or choose another word that best describes your reaction to the ending of this story. What caused you to respond this way?

2. Who are the other members in this child's family? Explain why you imagine the family this way.

3. Do you think the **main character** is a happy person? Why or why not?

4. What do you learn about the boy's **character** from the way he amuses himself?

5. The author contrasts the child in the darkness of the indoors with the mother in the light of the outside. How does this add to the mood and message of the story?

6. Have you ever invented games so that you wouldn't be bored? Explain.

Literary Focus: Point of View

The **point of view** of a story is the perspective from which the author tells the story. The easiest way to identify the point of view of a story is to identify its narrator and notice what pronouns the narrator uses. The pronouns in the chart below show the different points of view and the types of writing in which they are often found.

Pronouns	Point of View	Type of Writing
I, we	First-person	Diaries, letters, some fiction
You	Second-person	How-to books, rarely in fiction
He, she, it, they	Third-person	Newspapers, most fiction

   Although the author of "The Wish" generally uses the third-person point of view in this story, he occasionally changes to first-person. Make a list of places where the author uses the first-person point of view. What generalization can you make about these times? Why do you think the author chose to write the story combining both third-person and first-person points of view?

Vocabulary Study

Below is a letter a girl might have written to describe her previous day's adventure crossing the bricks between the stables and the barn. On a sheet of paper write the word from the list that completes each sentence.

accurately
channel
compel
frantically
fringe
gingerly
instinctively
resist
surge
triumphantly

Dear George,

Yesterday, something happened to __(1)__ me to undertake an incredible journey. The path between the stables and the barn turned into a seething __(2)__ of rushing water. I couldn't __(3)__ the challenge of crossing it. Scattered bricks were my only stepping stones. As I crossed, I felt the __(4)__ of powerful waves crashing over the bricks. I had to jump from brick to brick landing __(5)__ in the middle of each one. I knew __(6)__ that hungry sharks swam just below the surface of the water. And in the __(7)__ of grass that borders the path were huge, snapping clams that could swallow me whole! I had to step on tiptoe __(8)__ over the tall grasses between the bricks, as these were waving corals with poison tips. I almost didn't make it. I waved my arms __(9)__ after I almost lost my balance. But, in the end, I __(10)__ made my way across the deadly water and lived to tell the tale!

Sincerely yours,

Heather

Expressing Your Ideas

Writing Choices

Snake Jumping Suppose the boy in "The Wish" wants to leave directions for his cousin, who is sleeping upstairs, on how to cross the rug safely. Using the story as your source, write a numbered set of detailed **instructions** for how to get across the rug stepping only on the yellow parts. You may want to include a sketch with the directions.

A Day to Remember or Forget Do you have a birthday wish? What would have to happen for your birthday wish to come true? Write a **story** about it. Use the notes from your notebook.

Other Options

Rug of Terror The rug in the story seemed to come alive for the boy. Make a **painting** of the rug as it appears in the boy's imagination as he makes his way across it.

In the Mime's Eye Mimes exaggerate everyday actions to express the feelings behind the actions. Work with a group to present a **pantomime** of "The Wish." One person can outline the events in the presentation; one person can direct the presentation; and one person can be the mime. Work together to create and practice the presentation. Then perform it for the class.

Language Mini-Lesson

Punctuating for Clarity

Using Commas The use of punctuation marks, especially commas, helps to clarify information for readers. Compare these sentences with and without commas by reading them aloud. Which are easier to understand? Why?

For Reference

For more information about using commas, see the Language and Grammar Handbook.

WITHOUT COMMAS
Inside the air was cool.
Jack's chili has tomatoes onions mushrooms and peppers.
If you get an A I'll treat you to ice cream.

WITH COMMAS
Inside, the air was cool.
Jack's chili has tomatoes, onions, mushrooms, and peppers.
If you get an A, I'll treat you to ice cream.

Writing Strategy How do you know when you need a comma to clarify your writing? One way is to listen for a natural break when you read your sentences to yourself. When you read the sentence *Yesterday I returned home,* you should hear a brief pause after *Yesterday.* That's where a comma should go. When using this strategy make sure you read *naturally,* or you might hear breaks where there aren't any.

Activity Options

1. On separate slips of paper, write ten sentences that need commas to make them clear. Put commas in half of them, and leave commas out of the rest. Combine your slips of paper with those of some other students and then take turns choosing sentences and reading them aloud.

2. Look through the selections you've read to find passages where commas clarify meaning. Share your favorite example with the class.

3. Write a paragraph explaining how to make your favorite sandwich. Exchange it with a partner and then check your partner's paragraph for places where commas are needed.

Before Reading

Lob's Girl

by Joan Aiken

Joan Aiken
born 1924

Do you like neat, predictable stories where all questions raised are answered in the end? If you do, you might find British writer Joan Aiken challenges your taste. For her, "a sense of mystery and things left unexplained—references that are not followed up on, incidents and behavior that have to be puzzled over," are all important elements of a good story. Known for her unusual and fantastic tales, Aiken has written short stories and novels for children for more than forty years. Her father, Conrad Aiken, was a well-known American poet who moved his family to England before the birth of Joan, his third child.

Building Background

Resort Town The story "Lob's Girl" is set in the English county of Cornwall. Cornwall's coast has magnificent cliffs that tower above the sea. Small, scenic fishing villages are nestled in Cornwall's sheltered bays. Cornwall has a relatively warm climate compared with other parts of England. Palm trees even grow in the region! Because of the dramatic scenery, the beautiful beaches, and the warm climate, Cornwall has many resort towns along the coast.

Getting into the Story

Discussion One of the main characters in the story is a pet. Many people have pets with whom they have strong bonds. Have you ever had a pet that you felt strongly about? If not, what kind of animal would you most like for a pet?

Reading Tip

British English If you have ever talked to anyone from England, or watched a British actor or actress, you probably realize that people from England pronounce words differently and, they also use expressions different from those we commonly use in the United States. The characters in "Lob's Girl" use many British expressions and phrases, which may be unfamiliar to you. As you read, make a chart like the one below to write British terms or expressions you notice. Try to figure out what these words or phrases mean in context. Look for footnotes that give further explanations of the words or expressions. How would Americans say the same thing?

Term	How Used	Meaning in Context	Definition/How We Say It
much	they were *much* mistaken	very	*quite* mistaken, *sorely* mistaken, *very* mistaken

LOB'S Girl

Joan Aiken

Some people choose their dogs, and some dogs choose their people. The Pengelly family had no say in the choosing of Lob; he came to them in the second way, and very decisively.

It began on the beach, the summer when Sandy was five, Don, her older brother, twelve, and the twins were three. Sandy was really Alexandra, because her grandmother had a beautiful picture of a queen in a diamond tiara and high collar of pearls. It hung by Granny Pearce's kitchen sink and was as familiar as the doormat. When Sandy was born, everyone agreed that she was the living spit[1] of the picture, and so she was called Alexandra and Sandy for short.

On this summer day she was lying peacefully reading a comic and not keeping an eye on the twins, who didn't need it because they were occupied in seeing which of them could wrap the most seaweed around the other one's legs. Father—Bert Pengelly—and Don were up on the Hard[2] painting the bottom boards of the boat in which Father went fishing for pilchards.[3] And Mother—Jean Pengelly—was getting ahead with making the Christmas puddings[4] because she never felt easy in her mind if they weren't made and safely put away by the end of August. As usual, each member of the family was happily getting on with his or her own affairs. Little did they guess how soon this state

1. **living spit**, expression that means "looks just like"; a more common American expression is *spitting image*.
2. **the Hard**, a British term meaning "boat launch."
3. **pilchard** (pil′chərd), *n.* any of various small ocean-dwelling fishes.
4. **Christmas pudding**, a Christmas pudding is like a fruit cake.

A *Cornish Estuary* was painted by Alexander Forbes. How does this village compare to the one described on page 168?

of things would be changed by the large new member who was going to erupt into their midst.

Sandy rolled onto her back to make sure that the twins were not climbing on slippery rocks or getting cut off by the tide.[5] At the same moment a large body struck her forcibly in the midriff and she was covered by flying sand. Instinctively she shut her eyes and felt the sand being wiped off her face by something that seemed like a warm, rough, damp flannel. She opened her eyes and looked. It was a tongue. Its owner was a large and bouncy young Alsatian, or German shepherd, with topaz eyes, black-tipped prick ears, a thick, soft coat, and a bushy black-tipped tail.

"*Lob!*" shouted a man farther up the beach. "Lob, come here!"

But Lob, as if trying to atone[6] for the surprise he had given her, went on licking the sand off Sandy's face, wagging his tail so hard while he kept on knocking up more clouds of sand. His owner, a gray-haired man with a limp, walked over as quickly as he could and seized him by the collar.

"I hope he didn't give you a fright?" the man said to Sandy. "He meant it in play—he's only young."

---

5. **cut off by the tide**, put in a dangerous place because the water in the ocean is increasing in depth.
6. **atone** (ə tōn′),*v.* make up for an unkind act or a mistake.

Lob's Girl   **167**

"Oh, no, I think he's *beautiful,*" said Sandy truly. She picked up a bit of driftwood and threw it. Lob, whisking easily out of his master's grip, was after it like a sand-colored bullet. He came back with the stick, beaming, and gave it to Sandy. At the same time he gave himself, though no one else was aware of this at the time. But with Sandy, too, it was love at first sight, and when, after a lot more sticking-throwing, she and the twins joined Father and Don to go home for tea, they cast many a backward glance at Lob being led firmly away by his master.

"I wish we could play with him every day," Tess sighed.

"Why can't we?" said Tim.

Sandy explained. "Because Mr. Dodsworth, who owns him, is from Liverpool, and he is only staying at the Fisherman's Arms till Saturday."

"Is Liverpool a long way off?"

"Right at the other end of England from Cornwall, I'm afraid."

It was a Cornish fishing village where the Pengelly family lived, with rocks and cliffs and a strip of beach and a little round harbor, and palm trees growing in the gardens of the little whitewashed stone houses. The village was approached by a narrow, steep, twisting hill-road, and guarded by a notice that said LOW GEAR FOR 1 1/2 MILES, DANGEROUS TO CYCLISTS.

The Pengelly children went home to scones[7] with Cornish cream and jam, thinking they had seen the last of Lob. But they were much mistaken. The whole family was playing cards by the fire in the front room after supper when there was a loud thump and a crash of china in the kitchen.

Lob stood on his hind legs and plastered Sandy's face with licks.

"My Christmas puddings!" exclaimed Jean, and ran out.

"Did you put TNT[8] in them, then?" her husband said.

But it was Lob, who, finding the front door shut, had gone around to the back and bounced in through the open kitchen window, where the puddings were cooling on the sill. Luckily only the smallest was knocked down and broken.

Lob stood on his hind legs and plastered Sandy's face with licks. Then he did the same for the twins, who shrieked with joy.

"Where does this friend of yours come from?" inquired Mr. Pengelly.

"He's staying at the Fisherman's Arms—I mean his owner is."

"Then he must go back there. Find a bit of string, Sandy, to tie to his collar."

"I wonder how he found his way here," Mrs. Pengelly said, when the reluctant[9] Lob had been led whining away and Sandy had explained about their afternoon's game on the beach. "Fisherman's Arms is right round[10] the other side of the harbor."

Lob's owner scolded him and thanked Mr. Pengelly for bringing him back. Jean Pengelly warned the children that they had better not encourage Lob anymore if they met him on the beach, or it would only lead to more trouble. So they dutifully took no notice of him the next day until he spoiled their good resolutions[11] by dashing up to them with joyful

---

7. **scone** (skōn), *n.* small, rich, biscuitlike pastry.
8. **TNT**, *n.* abbreviation for trinitrotoluene, an explosive.
9. **reluctant** (ri luk′tənt), *adj.* unwilling.
10. **right round**, British expression meaning *clear around* or *all the way around.*
11. **resolution** (rez′ə lü′shən), *n.* vow or thing firmly decided upon.

barks, wagging his tail so hard that he winded[12] Tess and knocked Tim's legs from under him.

They had a happy day, playing on the sand.

The next day was Saturday. Sandy had found out that Mr. Dodsworth was to catch the half-past-nine train. She went out secretly, down to the station, nodded to Mr. Hoskins, the stationmaster, who wouldn't dream of charging any local[13] for a platform ticket, and climbed up on the footbridge that led over the tracks. She didn't want to be seen, but she did want to see. She saw Mr. Dodsworth get on the train, accompanied by an unhappy-looking Lob with drooping ears and tail. Then she saw the train slide away out of sight around the next headland, with a melancholy wail that sounded like Lob's last good-bye.

Sandy wished she hadn't had the idea of coming to the station. She walked home miserably, with her shoulders hunched and her hands in her pockets. For the rest of the day she was so cross and unlike herself that Tess and Tim were quite surprised, and her mother gave her a dose of senna.

A week passed. Then, one evening, Mrs. Pengelly and the younger children were in the front room playing snakes and ladders.[14] Mr. Pengelly and Don had gone fishing on the evening tide. If your father is a fisherman, he will never be home at the same time from one week to the next.

Suddenly, history repeating itself, there was a crash from the kitchen. Jean Pengelly leaped up, crying, "My blackberry jelly!" She and the children had spent the morning picking and the afternoon boiling fruit.

But Sandy was ahead of her mother. With flushed cheeks and eyes like stars she had darted into the kitchen, where she and Lob were hugging one another in a frenzy of joy. About a yard of his tongue was out, and he

was licking every part of her that he could reach.

"Good heavens!" exclaimed Jean. "How in the world did *he* get here?"

"He must have walked," said Sandy. "Look at his feet."

They were worn, dusty, and tarry. One had a cut on the pad.

"They ought to be bathed," said Jean Pengelly. "Sandy, run a bowl of warm water while I get the disinfectant."

"What'll we do about him, Mother?" said Sandy anxiously.

Mrs. Pengelly looked at her daughter's pleading eyes and sighed.

"He must go back to his owner, of course," she said, making her voice firm. "Your dad can get the address from the Fisherman's tomorrow, and phone him or send a telegram. In the meantime he'd better have a long drink and a good meal."

Lob was very grateful for the drink and the meal, and made no objection to having his feet washed. Then he flopped down on the hearthrug and slept in front of the fire they had lit because it was a cold, wet evening, with his head on Sandy's feet. He was a very tired dog. He had walked all the way from Liverpool to Cornwall, which is more than four hundred miles.

The next day Mr. Pengelly phoned Lob's owner, and the following morning Mr. Dodsworth arrived off the night train, decidedly put out,[15] to take his pet home. That parting was worse than the first. Lob whined, Don walked out of the house, the twins burst out crying, and Sandy crept up to her bedroom afterward and lay with her face pressed

---

12. **wind**, *v.* cause to be out of breath.
13. **local**, *n.* an informal term meaning a person from a particular, given locality.
14. **snakes and ladders**, a popular children's board game.
15. **put out**, inconvenienced or bothered.

into the quilt, feeling as if she were bruised all over.

Jean Pengelly took them all into Plymouth to see the circus the next day and the twins cheered up a little, but even the hour's ride in the train each way and the Liberty horses and performing seals could not cure Sandy's sore heart.

She need not have bothered, though. In ten days' time Lob was back—limping this time, with a torn ear and a patch missing out of his furry coat, as if he had met and tangled with an enemy or two in the course of his four-hundred-mile walk.

Bert Pengelly rang up Liverpool again. Mr. Dodsworth, when he answered, sounded weary. He said, "That dog has already cost me two days that I can't spare away from my work—plus endless time in police stations and drafting newspaper advertisements. I'm too old for these ups and downs. I think we'd better face the fact, Mr. Pengelly, that it's your family he wants to stay with—that is, if you want to have him."

Bert Pengelly gulped. He was not a rich man; and Lob was a pedigreed[16] dog. He said cautiously, "How much would you be asking for him?"

"Good heavens, man, I'm not suggesting I'd *sell* him to you. You must have him as a gift. Think of the train fares I'll be saving. You'll be doing me a good turn."

"Is he a big eater?" Bert asked doubtfully.

By this time the children, breathless in the background listening to one side of this conversation, had realized what was in the wind and were dancing up and down with their hands clasped beseechingly.[17]

"Oh, not for his size," Lob's owner assured Bert. "Two or three pounds of meat a day and some vegetables and gravy and biscuits—he does very well on that."

Alexandra's father looked over the telephone at his daughter's swimming eyes and

trembling lips. He reached a decision. "Well, then, Mr. Dodsworth," he said briskly, "we'll accept your offer and thank you very much. The children will be overjoyed and you can be sure Lob has come to a good home. They'll look after him and see he gets enough exercise. But I can tell you," he ended firmly, "if he wants to settle in with us, he'll have to learn to eat a lot of fish."

So that was how Lob came to live with the Pengelly family. Everybody loved him and he loved them all. But there was never any question who came first with him. He was Sandy's dog. He slept by her bed and followed her everywhere he was allowed.

Nine years went by, and each summer Mr. Dodsworth came back to stay at the Fisherman's Arms and call on his erstwhile dog. Lob always met him with recognition and dignified pleasure, accompanied him for a walk or two—but showed no signs of wishing to return to Liverpool. His place, he intimated,[18] was definitely with the Pengellys.

In the course of nine years Lob changed less than Sandy. As she went into her teens he became a little slower, a little stiffer, there was a touch of gray on his nose, but he was still a handsome dog. He and Sandy still loved one another devotedly.

One evening in October all the summer visitors had left, and the little fishing town looked empty and secretive. It was a wet, windy dusk. When the children came home from school—even the twins were at high school[19] now, and Don was a full-fledged fisherman—Jean Pengelly said, "Sandy, your Aunt

---

16. **pedigreed** (ped′ə grēd′), *adj.* said of a purebreed animal whose ancestry is known and recorded.

17. **beseechingly** (bi sēch′ ing lē), *adv.* in a begging or imploring manner.

18. **intimate** (in′tə māt), *v.* hint or suggest indirectly.

19. **high school**, a school in England that starts in what would be sixth grade or seventh grade in the United States.

Would this German shepherd, painted by Barbara Banthien, have the same effect on you as Lob had on Sandy?

Aunt Rebecca says she's lonesome because Uncle Will Hoskins has gone out trawling,[20] and she wants one of you to go and spend the evening with her. You go, dear; you can take your homework with you."

Sandy looked far from enthusiastic.

"Can I take Lob with me?"

"You know Aunt Becky doesn't really like dogs—Oh, very well." Mrs. Pengelly sighed. "I suppose she'll have to put up with him as well as you."

Reluctantly Sandy tidied herself, took her schoolbag, put on the damp raincoat she had just taken off, fastened Lob's lead to his collar, and set off to walk through the dusk to Aunt Becky's cottage, which was five minutes' climb up the steep hill.

The wind was howling through the shrouds[21] of boats drawn up on the Hard.

"Put some cheerful music on, do," said Jean Pengelly to the nearest twin. "Anything to drown that wretched sound while I make your dad's supper." So Don, who had just come in, put on some rock music, loud. Which was why the Pengellys did not hear the

---

20. **trawl** (trôl), *v.* fish using a special kind of net that is dragged along the bottom of the sea.
21. **shroud** (shroud), *n.* rope that stretches from the mast to the sides of the boat to support the mast.

truck hurtle[22] down the hill and crash against the post office wall a few minutes later.

Dr. Travers was driving through Cornwall with his wife, taking a late holiday before patients began coming down with winter colds and flu. He saw the sign that said STEEP HILL. LOW GEAR FOR 1 1/2 MILES. Dutifully he changed into second gear.

"We must be nearly there," said his wife, looking out of her window. "I noticed a sign on the coast road that said the Fisherman's Arms was two miles. What a narrow, dangerous hill! But the cottages are very pretty—Oh, Frank, stop, *stop!* There's a child, I'm sure it's a child—by the wall over there!"

Dr. Travers jammed on his brakes and brought the car to a stop. A little stream ran down by the road in a shallow stone culvert, and half in the water lay something that looked, in the dusk, like a pile of clothes—or was it the body of a child? Mrs. Travers was out of the car in a flash, but her husband was quicker.

"Don't touch her, Emily!" he said sharply. "She's been hit. Can't be more than a few minutes. Remember that truck that overtook us half a mile back, speeding like the devil? Here, quick, go into that cottage and phone for an ambulance. The girl's in a bad way. I'll stay here and do what I can to stop the bleeding. Don't waste a minute."

Doctors are expert at stopping dangerous bleeding, for they know the right places to press. This Dr. Travers was able to do, but he didn't dare do more; the girl was lying in a queerly crumpled heap, and he guessed she had a number of bones broken and that it would be highly dangerous to move her. He watched her with great concentration, won-

Its attendants lifted the child onto the stretcher...

dering where the truck had got to and what other damage it had done.

Mrs. Travers was very quick. She had seen plenty of accident cases and knew the importance of speed. The first cottage she tried had a phone; in four minutes she was back, and in six an ambulance was wailing down the hill.

Its attendants lifted the child onto the stretcher as carefully as if she were made of fine thistledown. The ambulance sped off to Plymouth—for the local cottage hospital did not take serious accident cases—and Dr. Travers went down to the police station to report what he had done.

He found that the police already knew about the speeding truck—which had suffered from loss of brakes and ended up with its radiator halfway through the post-office wall. The driver was concussed and shocked, but the police thought he was the only person injured—until Dr. Travers told his tale.

At half-past nine that night Aunt Rebecca Hoskins was sitting by her fire thinking aggrieved thoughts about the inconsiderateness of nieces who were asked to supper and never turned up, when she was startled by a neighbor, who burst in, exclaiming, "Have you heard about Sandy Pengelly, then, Mrs. Hoskins? Terrible thing, poor little soul, and they don't know if she's likely to live. Police have got the truck driver that hit her—ah, it didn't ought to be allowed, speeding through the place like that at umpty[23] miles an hour, they ought to jail him for life—not that that'd be any comfort to poor Bert and Jean."

---

22. **hurtle** (hėr′tl), *v.* drive or rush violently.
23. **umpty** (ump′tē), *adj.* an informal expression meaning "many."

Horrified, Aunt Rebecca put on a coat and went down to her brother's house. She found the family with white shocked faces; Bert and Jean were about to drive off to the hospital where Sandy had been taken, and the twins were crying bitterly. Lob was nowhere to be seen. But Aunt Rebecca was not interested in dogs; she did not inquire about him.

"Thank the lord you've come, Beck," said her brother. "Will you stay the night with Don and the twins? Don's out looking for Lob and heaven knows when we'll be back; we may get a bed with Jean's mother in Plymouth."

"Oh, if only I'd never invited the poor child," wailed Mrs. Hoskins. But Bert and Jean hardly heard her.

That night seemed to last forever. The twins cried themselves to sleep. Don came home very late and grim-faced. Bert and Jean sat in a waiting room of the Western Counties Hospital, but Sandy was unconscious, they were told, and she remained so. All that could be done for her was done. She was given transfusions to replace all the blood she had lost. The broken bones were set and put in slings and cradles.

"Is she a healthy girl? Has she a good constitution?"[24] the emergency doctor asked.

"Aye, doctor, she is that," Bert said hoarsely. The lump in Jean's throat prevented her from answering; she merely nodded.

"Then she ought to have a chance. But I won't conceal from you that her condition is very serious, unless she shows signs of coming out from this coma."[25]

But as hour succeeded hour, Sandy showed no signs of recovering consciousness. Her parents sat in the waiting room with haggard faces; sometimes one of them would go to telephone the family at home, or to try to get a little sleep at the home of Granny Pearce, not far away.

At noon next day Dr. and Mrs. Travers went to the Pengelly cottage to inquire how Sandy was doing, but the report was gloomy:

"Still in a very serious condition." The twins were miserably unhappy. They forgot that they had sometimes called their elder sister bossy and only remembered how often she had shared her pocket money with them, how she read to them and took them for picnics and helped with their homework. Now there was no Sandy, no Mother and Dad, Don went around with a gray, shuttered face, and worse still, there was no Lob.

The Western Counties Hospital is a large one, with dozens of different departments and five or six connected buildings, each with three or four entrances. By that afternoon it became noticeable that a dog seemed to have taken up position outside the hospital, with the fixed intention of getting in. Patiently he would try first one entrance and then another, all the way around, and then begin again. Sometimes he would get a little way inside, following a visitor, but animals were, of course, forbidden, and he was always kindly but firmly turned out again. Sometimes the guard at the main entrance gave him a pat or offered him a bit of sandwich—he looked so wet and beseeching and desperate. But he never ate the sandwich. No one seemed to own him or to know where he came from; Plymouth is a large city and he might have belonged to anybody.

At tea time Granny Pearce came through the pouring rain to bring a flask of hot tea with brandy in it to her daughter and son-in-law. Just as she reached the main entrance the guard was gently but forcibly shoving out a large, agitated,[26] soaking-wet Alsatian dog.

"No, old fellow, you can *not* come in. Hospitals are for people, not for dogs."

---

24. **good constitution**, strong nature or physical makeup.
25. **coma** (kō/mə), *n.* prolonged period of unconsciousness often caused by a serious injury.
26. **agitated** (aj/ə tā/ tid), *adj.* excited or disturbed.

Lob's Girl   **173**

▲ *Spring Afternoon* was painted by Allan R. Banks in 1984. Do you think Lob could have become as attached to this girl as he was to Sandy? Why?

"Why, bless me," exclaimed old Mrs. Pearce. "That's Lob! Here, Lob, Lobby boy!"

Lob ran to her, whining. Mrs. Pearce walked up to the desk.

"I'm sorry, madam, you can't bring that dog in here," the guard said.

Mrs. Pearce was a very determined old lady. She looked the porter in the eye.

"Now, see here, young man. That dog has walked twenty miles from St. Killan to get to my granddaughter. Heaven knows how he knew she was here, but it's plain he knows. And he ought be have his rights! He ought to get to see her! Do you know," she went on, bristling, "that dog has walked the length of England—twice—to be with that girl? And you think you can keep him out with your fiddling[27] rules and regulations?"

"I'll have to ask the medical officer," the guard said weakly.

"You do that, young man." Granny Pearce sat down in a determined manner, shutting her umbrella, and Lob sat patiently dripping at her feet. Every now and then he shook his head, as if to dislodge something heavy that was tied around his neck.

Presently a tired, thin, intelligent-looking man in a white coat came downstairs, with an impressive,[28] silver-haired man in a dark suit, and there was a low-voiced discussion. Granny Pearce eyed them, biding her time.

"Frankly . . . not much to lose," said the older man. The man in the white coat approached Granny Pearce.

"It's strictly against every rule, but as it's such a serious case we are making an exception," he said to her quietly. "But only *outside* her bedroom door—and only for a moment or two."

Without a word, Granny Pearce rose and stumped upstairs. Lob followed close to her skirts, as if he knew his hope lay with her.

They waited in the green-floored corridor outside Sandy's room. The door was half shut. Bert and Jean were inside. Everything was terribly quiet. A nurse came out. The white-coated man asked her something and she

---

27. **fiddling** (fid′ling), *adj.* useless or silly.
28. impressive (im pres′iv), *adj.* having a strong effect on the mind or feelings of others.

shook her head. She had left the door ajar and through it could now be seen a high, narrow bed with a lot of gadgets around it. Sandy lay there, very flat under the covers, very still. Her head was turned away. All Lob's attention was riveted on the bed. He strained toward it, but Granny Pearce clasped his collar firmly.

"I've done a lot for you, my boy, now you behave yourself," she whispered grimly. Lob let out a faint whine, anxious and pleading.

At the sound of that whine Sandy stirred just a little. She sighed and moved her head the least fraction. Lob whined again. And then Sandy turned her head right over. Her eyes opened, looking at the door.

"Lob?" she murmured—no more than a breath of sound. "Lobby, boy?"

The doctor by Granny Pearce drew a quick, sharp breath. Sandy moved her left arm—the one that was not broken—from below the covers and let her hand dangle down, feeling, as she always did in the mornings, for Lob's furry head. The doctor nodded slowly.

"All right," he whispered. "Let him go to the bedside. But keep a hold of him."

Granny Pearce and Lob moved to the bedside. Now she could see Bert and Jean, white-faced and shocked, on the far side of the bed. But she didn't look at them. She looked at the smile on her granddaughter's face as the groping fingers found Lob's wet ears and gently pulled them. "Good boy," whispered Sandy, and fell asleep again.

Granny Pearce led Lob out into the passage again. There she let go of him and he ran off swiftly down the stairs. She would have followed him, but Bert and Jean had come out into the passage, and she spoke to Bert fiercely.

"*I* don't know why you were so foolish as not to bring the dog before! Leaving him to find the way here himself—"

"But, Mother!" said Jean Pengelly. "That can't have been Lob. What a chance to take! Suppose Sandy hadn't—" She stopped, with her handkerchief pressed to her mouth.

"Not Lob? I've known that dog nine years! I suppose I ought to know my own granddaughter's dog?"

"Listen, Mother," said Bert. "Lob was killed by the same truck that hit Sandy. Don found him—when he went to look for Sandy's schoolbag. He was—he was dead. Ribs all smashed. No question of that. Don told me on the phone—he and Will Hoskins rowed a half mile out to sea and sank the dog with a lump of concrete tied to his collar. Poor old boy. Still—he was getting on. Couldn't have lasted forever."

"*Sank him at sea?* Then what—?"

Slowly old Mrs. Pearce, and then the other two, turned to look at the trail of dripping-wet footprints that led down the hospital stairs.

In the Pengellys' garden they have a stone, under the palm tree. It says: "Lob. Sandy's dog. Buried at sea."

After Reading

Making Connections

1. What surprised you most about the conclusion of the story?

2. What conclusions did you come to about the presence of the dog at the hospital?

3. What clues did the author give as to how the **plot** would develop in the story?

4. What role did the **setting** play in the story?

5. 🐾 Refer to your chart of British expressions. **Communication** often breaks down barriers. In what respects did the author's use of British words and phrases help you understand some aspects of British culture?

6. Based on what happened in this story, do you think people's pets should be allowed to visit hospital patients? Explain.

Literary Focus: Mood

The **mood** of a story is its atmosphere, or feeling. In "Lob's Girl," the author creates one type of mood in the first part of the story and a quite different mood in the second part. Find the place in the story where you think the mood changes.

One way that the author of "Lob's Girl" created two different moods is through her choices of words. Copy each word or phrase in the list below and decide whether it helps create the mood of the first part or the second part of the story. If necessary, look up unfamiliar words in a dictionary. After you have finished classifying the words, use them to help you come up with a few additional adjectives to describe the mood in each part.

aggrieved	dangerous hill	devotedly
wet, windy dusk	joyful barks	happily
beaming	empty	playing cards by the fire
overjoyed	forbidden	lonesome
bounced in	grimly	serious
circus	grateful	beach
coma	shuttered face	dancing up and down

Vocabulary Study

Imagine Lob could tell the story from his point of view. Below are some details he might include. On a sheet of paper write the word from the list that completes each sentence.

coma
impressive
pedigreed
reluctant
resolution

1. My name is Lob. I am a ____ German shepherd dog.

2. My first owner never wanted to play with me. So, I made a ____ that I would find a new owner.

3. I was ____ to hurt my owner's feelings.

4. However, when I met Sandy, she was really ____ !

5. We had wonderful times together. Then one day a truck ran over us. Sandy lay in a ____ . Before I died, I promised Sandy that I would visit her. And I did.

Expressing Your Ideas _____

Writing Choices

Dog: Lost and Found Imagine you are Mr. Dodsworth. Write an **advertisement** you might place after Lob ran away, describing him and explaining how to contact you if the dog were found.

Had a Dog, His Name Was Lob With a group, work together to compose a **song** about Sandy and Lob. In your song, tell how Sandy and Lob met and how Lob came to be Sandy's dog. Invent other adventures for the two, if you wish. End the song by describing the accident and what happened at the hospital. You can make up your own tune or use the tune of a familiar folk song or popular song.

Lob's Girl: The Sequel What do you think happened to Sandy? Write a continuation of the **story** that incorporates your ideas of what happened to Sandy and to her family.

Other Options

Lob's Eye View of England Take Lob's point of view and draw a **map** of his different journeys mentioned in "Lob's Girl." Indicate where various events mentioned in the story occurred. Also, imagine some of the adventures Lob might have had while traveling across the country and indicate where these imagined events occurred. Make your map accurate in terms of city location and scale; also include a scale of miles on your map. You can use the map on page 165 for reference.

Pets Make the Paper Collect newspaper and magazine stories about pets and their owners. After you have collected a number of stories, work together with a small group to make a **scrapbook** of pet stories. If you have a pet, you may want to include a story about you and your pet. Illustrate your scrapbook with drawings, photographs, and quotes.

Before Reading

The Walrus and the Carpenter by Lewis Carroll
What We Said Sitting Making Fantasies by James Berry

Lewis Carroll
1832–1898

Lewis Carroll's most famous story, *Alice's Adventures in Wonderland,* was published in 1865. The poem "The Walrus and the Carpenter" appears in the book *Through the Looking Glass.*

James Berry
born 1925

Born in Jamaica, James Berry came to England when he was in his early twenties. This move made him realize, "No one has reported our stories, or the way we saw things. It's the function of writers and poets to bring in the left-out side of the human family."

Building Background

Fantasies A fantasy can be a daydream, and it often includes the fulfillment of a wish that may never come true. Fantasy can be a dream that you have at night, in which all kinds of supernatural or otherwise impossible things happen.

Literature, too, can be fantasy. For instance, both "The Walrus and the Carpenter" and "What We Said Sitting Making Fantasies" include unreal objects or impossible events.

Getting into the Poems

Writer's Notebook In your notebook, write about some of your own fantasies. Are they daydreams or the dreams you have when you sleep? Which kind of fantasy do you find most fun or enjoyable? From which type of fantasy do you learn the most about yourself?

Reading Tip

Recognizing Different Types of Poetry Three types of poetry are epic, narrative, and lyric. The chart below defines these types. As you read, look for details that will help you classify the poems on the following pages as epic, narrative, or lyric.

Epic Poem	Narrative Poem	Lyric Poem
long poem that centers on a hero; often describes events of historic or mythic nature	poem with a plot that focuses on action and and has well-developed characters	poem that focuses on emotions or subjects of a personal nature

The Walrus and the Carpenter

LEWIS CARROLL

The sun was shining on the sea,
  Shining with all his might:
He did his very best to make
  The billows[1] smooth and bright—
5 And this was odd, because it was
  The middle of the night.

The moon was shining sulkily,
  Because she thought the sun
Had got no business to be there
10 After the day was done—
"It's very rude of him," she said,
  "To come and spoil the fun!"

The sea was wet as wet could be,
  The sands were dry as dry.
15 You could not see a cloud, because
  No cloud was in the sky:
No birds were flying overhead—
  There were no birds to fly.

The Walrus and the Carpenter
20 Were walking close at hand;
They wept like anything to see
  Such quantities of sand:
"If this were only cleared away,"
  They said, "it would be grand!"

25 "If seven maids with seven mops
  Swept it for half a year,
Do you suppose," the Walrus said,
  "That they could get it clear?"
"I doubt it," said the Carpenter,
30 And shed a bitter tear.

"Oysters, come and walk with us!"
  The Walrus did beseech.
"A pleasant walk, a pleasant talk,
  Along the briny[2] beach;
35 We cannot do with more than four,
  To give a hand to each."

---

1. **billow**, *n.* great, swelling wave.
2. **briny** (brī′nē), *adj.* very salty.

The eldest Oyster looked at him,
But never a word he said:
The eldest Oyster winked his eye,
40 And shook his heavy head—
Meaning to say he did not choose
To leave the oyster-bed.[3]

But four young Oysters hurried up,
All eager for the treat:
45 Their coats were brushed, their faces
washed,
Their shoes were clean and neat—
And this was odd, because, you know,
They hadn't any feet.

Four other Oysters followed them,
50 And yet another four;
And thick and fast they came at last,
And more, and more, and more—
All hopping through the frothy waves,
And scrambling[4] to the shore.

55 The Walrus and the Carpenter
Walked on a mile or so,
And then they rested on a rock
Conveniently low:
And all the little Oysters stood
60 And waited in a row.

"The time has come," the Walrus said,
"To talk of many things;
Of shoes—and ships—and sealing wax[5]—
Of cabbages—and kings—
65 And why the sea is boiling hot—
And whether pigs have wings."

"But wait a bit," the Oysters cried,
"Before we have our chat;
For some of us are out of breath,
70 And all of us are fat!"
"No hurry!" said the Carpenter.
They thanked him much for that.

"A loaf of bread," the Walrus said,
"Is what we chiefly need:
75 Pepper and vinegar besides
Are very good indeed—

Now if you're ready, Oysters dear,
We can begin to feed."
"But not on us!" the Oysters cried,
80 Turning a little blue.[6]
"After such kindness, that would be
A dismal[7] thing to do!"
"The night is fine," the Walrus said,
"Do you admire the view?

3. **oyster-bed**, *n.* a place such as a rock where many oysters attach themselves to live.
4. scramble (skram′bəl), *v.* climb or walk quickly over rough ground.
5. **sealing wax**, *n.* a wax that is melted for use as a seal on letters, packages, etc.
6. **turning a little blue**, a pun on *blue* meaning "sad" or—when referring to seafood—"spoiled."
7. dismal (diz′məl), *adj.* miserable.

◄ Drawing of Walrus and Carpenter from *Alice Adventures in Wonderland* by Sir John Tenniel

85 "It was so kind of you to come!
    And you are very nice!"
The Carpenter said nothing but
    "Cut us another slice:
I wish you were not quite so deaf—
90   I've had to ask you twice!"

"It seems a shame," the Walrus said,
    "To play them such a trick,
After we've brought them out so far,
    And made them trot so quick!"
95 The Carpenter said nothing but
    "The butter's spread too thick!"

"I weep for you," the Walrus said:
    "I deeply sympathize."[8]
With sobs and tears he sorted out
100   Those of the largest size,
Holding his pocket-handkerchief
    Before his streaming eyes.

"O Oysters," said the Carpenter,
    "You've had a pleasant run!
105 Shall we be trotting home again?"
    But answer came there none—
And this was scarcely odd, because
    They'd eaten every one.

8. **sympathize** (sim′pə thīz), *v.* feel someone else's sorrow or unhappiness.

The Walrus and the Carpenter   **181**

What We Said Sitting Making Fantasies

James Berry

1

I want a talking dog wearing a cap
who can put on gloves
and go to my mum when I'm playing
and she wants a job done.

2

5 I'd like a great satellite-looking dish[1]
in my garden, drawing together all
        sounds
of birds' voices, cats' mewing and
        fighting
crickets' chirping, dogs' barking and
        fighting
frogs' croaking, guineapigs' squeaking
10 bicycle-bells ringing, babies' crying
trains' passing, firecrackers' bursts and
        bangs
into one loud orchestral work
playing once every hour day and night
a new composition[2] every time
15 so an audience overbrims[3] my garden.

3

At last I have my anger breathalyser[4]
that shows them all—
parents, teachers, friends—
the fires they start
20 when they make me cross.
I just whip out
my Angerlyser.[5]
Offender[6] watches me blow
hard into it

25 and sees it swell
its fierce balloon of green
then black then red
and sees it drop and burst
into a flame, three colours
30 of horned heads and teeth
flaring, jumping, hissing
popping, spluttering—
all round the culprit's feet.
And I just walk away.

4

35 I'd like a white bull with one horn only
and it's black, and one eyepatch that's
        black,
and one stripe of red like a bright sash
all around his throat, side and back.
And my bull windowshops from shop to
        shop
40 on High Street on his own. And when
my bull moves, his whole red sash flashes
buttons of white lights

---

1. **satellite-looking dish**, a large, dish-shaped antenna.
2. **composition** (kom/pə zish/ən), *n.* a piece of music, such as a symphony.
3. **overbrim**, *v.* flow over the brim, overflow.
4. **breathalyser** (breth/l īz/ər), *n.* a trademarked device used to measure the amount of alcohol in someone's breath; the American spelling is *breathalyzer*.
5. **Angerlyser** (ang/gər līz/ər), *n.* a made-up word based on the word breathalyser; a device that measures anger when a person breathes into it.
6. **offender** (ə fen/dər), *n.* person who does wrong or offends in some way.

Childhood's Garden was painted by Charles Burchfield in 1917. Imagine taking a journey to this garden. What would you discover?

advertising my mum's curtain and
    wallpaper
shop, saying, PICTURES NOT
    CURTAINS. PETALS
45 NOT PAPER. FLORAL HOUSE FOR
    FASHION.

5
My first solo trial flight, you see.
I'm in my flying craft I made myself,
strapped in my seat. Gyrocompass,[7] like
every clockface instrument,
50 every switch, button and lever, is handy.
In constructing my craft I considered
all problems that affect flying stability.
I considered the aircraft's 'angles of
    attack.'
I considered its 'lift-drag ratio.'
55 I considered its 'total reaction.'
Yet when I operate the craft to go
forward, it zooms upward, climbing.
I operate it to descend, it levels
itself, it shoots away forward.
60 I operate it to climb, my craft spins
round and round and dives
to a perfect touchdown
and settles itself, purring like a cat.
I press a button, I'm unstrapped.
65 I press a button, I'm flicked up
and out, ejected on to my feet, in front
of the Queen, with her dogs in her
    garden.
'Hello,' she says. 'You must be Robin
    Flyer!'
'Yes, mam,' I say. She walks forward.
70 'Last week, your great-granma was a
    hundred.'
'Yes, mam. Your telegram came. We
    celebrated.'

'In her letter of thanks, your gran said
not to be surprised if you dropped
in. And here you are! Well—
75 stay for tea. Won't you? All
my grandchildren are coming.'
Naturally, I stay for tea, with dogs
and everybody there in the garden.

6
I'd like to have a purple pigeon
80 who flies up to heaven
and comes back rose-red
flying with trails of pale rainbow ribbons
straight through my window
into my bedroom.

7
85 I have a three-legged donkey.
I have my three-legged donkey just to
    see
how he dips his head when he walks
and quickens it up when he gallops.

8
I'd like to see cats with stubby wings
90 who just before their wings get raised
for a leap on to a bird, they set off
the loudest high pitched siren sound
from the cat's mouth. O, it's a scream
something earsplitting terrible.
95 Often you see cats losing distance
flying in desperation behind birds
and their on-and-on wailing
scream goes on, cracking up the air.

---

7. **Gyrocompass** (jī′rō kum/pəs), compass that helps
steady a ship or an airplane.

After Reading

Making Connections

1. Which of the characters in "The Walrus and the Carpenter" would you choose to be? What traits do you find most attractive?

2. What hints does the author give in "The Walrus and the Carpenter" that the poem is not to be taken seriously?

3. Why do you think the author didn't use rhyme in "What We Said Sitting Making Fantasies"?

4. Look at the chart in the Reading Tip on page 178. How would you classify each poem? Explain.

5. Discuss the similarities and differences between your own fantasies and the ones in the second poem. Use your notes from your notebook.

Vocabulary Study

Use the words from the list to complete the poem.

composition
dismal
offender
scramble
sympathize

The oysters had to (1) ,
   And run with all their might.
They couldn't believe they'd come so far
   For such a (2) plight.
"O Carpenter, please, (3) ,
   We can't survive out here!
The sea lions and the octopi
   Will eat us up, we fear."
After reading this sad (4) ,
   Which (5) was to blame?
The Walrus who thought up the plot
   Or the Carpenter with no shame?

Expressing Your Ideas

Kidnappers at Large Write a "Wanted" **poster** to hang in the local post office to alert other oysters about the Walrus and the Carpenter.

Off-the-Wall Scenes With a group, create a **mural** that portrays scenes from one of the poems.

Before Reading

Amitabh

by Janet Bode

Janet Bode
born 1943

Listening to people telling their own stories is a main interest of freelance writer Janet Bode. She has put together several oral histories. These are written versions of taped interviews in which people share important experiences in their lives. The one in which Amitabh's account first appears is called *New Kids on the Block: Oral Histories of Immigrant Teens*. Bode also writes articles for magazines. She lives in New York City.

Building Background

India Until he was ten years old, a boy named Amitabh (amə′tab) lived with his family in the Indian city of Bhaunagar (bun a gär) in the state of Gujarat (guj′a rat′) in western India. Bhaunagar is a modern seaport, with a population of about 350,000 people, as well as highways, factories, and many different types of businesses.

Getting into the Selection

Writer's Notebook Immigrants are people who leave one country, usually their homeland, and go to live in another country. The United States is considered a land of immigrants, because so many Americans or their ancestors came here from other lands. Do you know anyone who has recently immigrated to the United States? Have you yourself ever moved or changed schools? In your notebook, write about your experiences or the experiences of people you know.

Reading Tip

Comparison and Contrast Amitabh describes many similarities and differences between India and the United States. When he discusses similarities, he is making comparisons; when he describes differences, he is making contrasts. Make a Comparison/Contrast chart like the one below. As you read, fill in your chart with details that Amitabh mentions as he discusses his move and his adjustments to life in the United States.

Similarities Between India and the United States	Differences Between India and the United States
electricity, running water, traffic jams	kinds of food

Amitabh

JANET BODE

India is a sprawling nation, a peninsula with the Arabian Sea to the west, the Indian Ocean to the south, and the Bay of Bengal to the east. Its other borders touch six separate countries: Pakistan, China, Nepal, Bhutan, Burma, and Bangladesh. Archaeologists have found evidence of civilization[1] dating back at least 4,500 years. India today reflects its past: the Dravidians, its earliest known inhabitants; the Sanskrit-speaking tribes; the Moguls; and the British, from whom it gained independence in 1947. This densely populated land is the birthplace of the Buddhist and Hindu religions and the home of many others—Muslim, Christian, Sikh, and Jains. Five years ago, when Amitabh was ten, he and his parents and two brothers moved here from Bhaunagar. Now his American dream is a career in the Air Force in aviation electronics. One day after his ROTC[2] class, we met in his high school library. He recalled his first months after arriving in the Washington, D.C., suburbs.[3]

It is really bad for us in the beginning. We were five in a two-room apartment. Every day my parents would get up and go out to look for jobs. They knew they had to start all the way at the bottom, that people here didn't count any experience from India. But my father had been a biologist. My mother was a chemistry professor at a university. In India they were both making good money.

Now, though, they would come home every evening and they wouldn't have found anything. They would be very, very sad. They didn't know the bus systems or the subway systems here. They'd get lost. They'd get to some place and it would be too late. The job would be gone. They'd go to another place and the answer would be, no. One day, my parents said, "This is a dead end. We can't find jobs. We don't have any more money. Nothing. We're

---

1. **civilization** (siv′ə lə zā′shən), *n.* advanced stage in the development of a society.
2. **ROTC (or R.O.T.C.),** an abbreviation standing for "Reserve Officers' Training Corps; a program for students who plan to be officers in the U.S. Army.
3. **suburb** (sub′ėrb′), *n.* smaller town or village just outside or near a city.

Amitabh **187**

going to have to jump into the river." I wanted to think that they were not being serious, but I still would feel so sad for them and so sad for us.

I couldn't always understand why we had come here. Why would they leave the country where they had been born, where their children had been born? Bhaunagar was a modernized city on the northwest side of India. It had a lot of factories, apartment houses, and private homes. Our home was three stories high and we lived together with my uncle, my aunt, and my grandparents. My grandparents had another house in a small city called Mehsana. Every summer and during other vacations, we'd go there.

The weather was very warm. In the winters it would get cool enough to wear sweaters, but that was it. No snow. It also used to rain quite a bit. There was a dry and a rainy season, with monsoons[4] that occurred every year at a certain time. We had a good life there.

I know that people think that in India everybody is poor, that everything is backward. It's not that backward, and it's probably improved since I've been here. We had electricity and running water and traffic jams. I went to a good school. They taught the same subjects as over here, like art, general science, and math, and also some of the different languages of India. I think there are fifteen or sixteen languages. At home we spoke Gujarati,[5] and I learned how to speak Hindi, too.

I was happy. I knew the way things were done in India. I knew we were Hindu. In that religion we had many, many gods, some that I didn't even know. We had a lot of religious festivals. We used to go to temple. We could go any time we wanted. We believed in "karma"; how we acted in past lives decides who we will be born in future lives.[6] My family god was a god named Siva. It was a good god. He had many arms. He was very powerful and had snakes around him.

I knew the food. I loved cooked okra, the vegetable, and pouri, the bread. I had a favorite kind of curry.[7] I knew my future. I knew that when I got married, I would bring my wife to live with my parents. The bride's family would provide a dowry, money and silverware and things like that.

My parents said, though, that we would move to America because us kids would have more opportunities[8] for the future. This was a long time planning. I don't even remember the first time they told me. At first it went so slow. I did not know anything about America. Once, a friend of mine who was Christian took me to this place to get American hot dogs. At that time I had no idea what they were. I took a bite and I spit it out. It tasted disgusting!

But then sometimes I would get interested in coming here. I heard there were big buildings and fast cars. My older brother told me, "Over there in the United States you never see the sun. It's always snowing. When the sun does shine, it's a holiday." I thought like WOW! About a month before we left, my parents said, "We're moving to America." That's how they told me. And I said, "Yes." I told my friends in school and they said, "Yeah, sure, sure." I said, "Really. Watch."

We took a train from our home in Bhaunagar to Bombay, a city, my father said, about the size of New York. Then we flew from Bombay to the country of Kuwait and then on

---

4. **monsoon** (mon sün′), *n.* seasonal wind of the Indian Ocean and southern Asia.
5. **Gujarati** (gù̇j′ə rä′tē) and Hindi (hin′dē), two of India's sixteen official languages.
6. **karma . . . future lives,** Hindus believe in reincarnation—in the rebirth of the soul after death.
7. **curry** (kėr′ē), *n.* a peppery sauce popular in India and other parts of Asia.
8. opportunity (op′ər tü′nə tē), *n.* chance for advancing in life.

to London, England. I'd never been on an airplane before, so I didn't know what to expect.

Just before we were supposed to land in London, the whole plane started shaking all over. People who were standing up fell. Tea was spilling all over the place. I was crying. My mother was telling us, "Pray. Pray." Luckily, everything became all right. There had been an air cap. It's some technical word, I don't know what it means. We landed and then flew to Kennedy Airport in New York City and then National Airport in Washington, D.C.

After the first few months my parents found jobs, but the work was very tough on them. My father worked as a messenger, more a job for a boy than a man. He delivered letters and carried packages all over the city. Again, he would get lost the way he had when he was looking for work. He lasted about three or four months doing that until he found another job, and another job. All small jobs. Then he met an Indian man who owned a laboratory[9] who hired him. Now he's sort of back in the area of biology, where he used to work.

My mother started working at a store. She had to fold clothes, mostly. Then she got a better job watching patients at a senior citizens' home. Eventually, she became the dietitian[10] there. And now it's okay for me, too. Kids don't look at me strangely the way they did in

---

9. **laboratory** (lab′rə tôr′ē), *n.* place where scientific work is done or where drugs, medicines, or other chemicals are manufactured
10. **dietitian** (dī′ə tish′ən), *n.* person trained to plan meals that have the right amounts of the different nutrients.

▲ How does this street in India compare to a busy street where you live?

Amitabh **189**

the beginning. I had my first hamburger and said, "Forget it!" I threw it out. Eventually, though, I got used to it. Now I eat anything. I eat hot dogs, hamburgers, chicken, and french fries. I love pizza. In India I remember that once we had a fair and they had pizza, a small triangle, for eight rupees, about twenty-five cents. "It was better than the hot dog," I thought then.

Now we live in the suburbs in a big house with four bedrooms. I have my own bedroom with military posters all over the place. My middle brother and I have a computer. We have more than six hundred games for it. He wants to work in computers. My older brother is in college, the University of Maryland. He wants to be a surgeon.

I'm in the tenth grade. ROTC is my favorite class. I'm planning to go into the military right after I finish high school. It should help me out a lot because ROTC trains us for the military. Since when I was in India, my ambition was to make the military a career. I remember every time my father would take us to a shop, I'd want to buy military-colored clothes. Just yesterday I was looking at some photographs taken at my aunt and uncle's wedding in India. There I was, just a kid, in a military uniform. I don't know why I'm into it so much.

My parents don't mind, since I like it. I considered the Air Force Academy, but I talked to a recruiter who said I had to have at least a ninety average to make it. My average is seventy-five to eighty. What I have to do, though, right after school is out for the summer, is see how to be a citizen.[11] If I join the Air Force without being a U.S. citizen, I'm offered jobs, but not as many as if I am a citizen. The job I want, aviation electronics,[12] requires citizenship.

My father wants to become a citizen, too. My mother wants to stay Indian. Still, we are all changing. When we lived in Bhaunagar, my mother wore a sari.[13] She used to put a bindi, that little dot, on her forehead. Now only when we go to some festival, like every August 15 is Indian Independence Day and there's a big parade, then she will wear her sari and have a bindi. Mostly, she wears pants and a blouse.

They keep up on the news, what's happening in India. Back when the prime minister, that's like the president, Indira Gandhi, was murdered by her Sikh bodyguards, we were all shocked. There were phone calls going around in the whole Indian community here. That was something that we never imagined would happen. I guess for us it was the same as when someone tried to kill President Reagan. Except with Mrs. Gandhi, they succeeded.

I'm more Americanized than my parents. I still speak Gujarati at home, but now there's English mixed in a lot. I'm trying to get out of my accent as much as possible. And now I have what I guess you could call an American mouth: I have braces. I'd never seen braces in India. I hate wearing them!!! Just like American kids.

---

11. **citizen** (sit′ə zən), *n.* a person who is or becomes a member of a nation.
12. **aviation electronics**, branch of study that relates to the invention, development, and repair of television, radio, radar, and computer equipment for aircraft.
13. **sari** (sär′ē), *n.* the outer garment of Hindu women that consists of a long piece of cotton or silk worn wound around the body with one end thrown over the head or shoulder.

After Reading

Making Connections

1. What impressed you the most about Amitabh's story of his move and his adjustment to life in the United States?

2. What are some **comparisons** and **contrasts** Amitabh makes between life in India and life in the United States? Use the notes from your chart.

3. 👁 Amitabh feels that Americans have stereotypes about India and tells us how they are wrong. How did his **communication** of these ideas help you to see things differently?

4. Do you think it is fair that many immigrants with college educations or professional experience have to start at the bottom when they move to the United States?

5. Amitabh describes his "American dream" of having a career in the military. Think about your own American dream. What will you have to do to fulfill it?

6. What adjustments did you or someone you know have to make because of a change, such as moving or going to a new school? Use your notes from your notebook.

Literary Focus: Oral Histories

As you read this selection, did you feel as if you were actually listening to Amitabh talking? If so, you shouldn't be surprised. "Amitabh" is an **oral history**, a written version of a taped interview Amitabh had with author Janet Bode in which he recalls his own experiences. "Amitabh" shares certain characteristics with other oral histories:

- It is written from a first-person point of view.
- It includes informal language.
- It sometimes skips from one subject to another or from past to present to future, just as a person talking might.

Find examples of each of these characteristics of writing in "Amitabh" and record them in a chart like the one below.

First-Person Point of View	Informal Language	Skipping Around
It is really bad for us . . .	Forget it!	

Vocabulary Study

citizen
civilization
laboratory
opportunity
suburb

Read the imaginary diary entries that Amitabh might have written. Fill in the word from the list that best completes each entry.

October 10 Sometimes I wonder why my parents moved from India. They say that we will have an __(1)__ for more careers here in the United States.

October 13 Today I am very happy. My father found a job in a __(2)__. He gets to use his knowledge of biology in his work. I gave my report on India today. Many kids in the class were surprised to learn how advanced early Indian __(3)__ was. I told them that there is evidence that India developed the world's first flush toilets. Everyone was impressed.

October 20 I took the bus to downtown Washington. Then I rode it back to the __(4)__ where I live.

October 30 At the library, I found a book telling all the things you need to know to become a __(5)__ of the United States. I'm going to read the whole thing.

Expressing Your Ideas

Writing Choices

What Happened to You? Imagine you are author Janet Bode. Write a set of **interview questions** for Amitabh to find out about his experience as an immigrant to the United States. Include additional questions you have for Amitabh based on what he said in the selection.

Writing Back Home Imagine that you are visiting India. Write a **letter** to a friend back home. Tell your friend about your experiences. Tell about stereotypes people have about the United States and how you tried to change these stereotypes through **communication.** Tell about misconceptions you had about India and how things were different than you thought they would be.

Other Options

Tell Your Own Story With a partner, take turns doing **oral histories** with each other. Prepare a set of interview questions. These questions should be open-ended and help the person tell about significant memories or events in his or her life. Show your partner your questions so that he or she can think about what to say. If possible, get a tape recorder with a microphone.

Passage from India Make a **map** showing the route Amitabh's family took when they moved from India to the United States. Find the distance between each of their stops and write these distances in on your map. Compute the total distance from Bhaunagar to Washington, D.C.

The Ch'i-lin Purse

by Linda Fang

Linda Fang
born 1944

The book in which "The Ch'i-lin Purse" first appeared is a collection of ancient Chinese folk tales. It is Linda Fang's first book. To find the stories for this collection, Fang and her father spent many hours pouring over original Chinese writings. Fang's keen interest in folk tales is hardly surprising. She is a storyteller of national fame who has performed all over the country. Linda Fang lives in Washington, D.C.

Building Background

Chinese Words "The Ch'i-lin Purse" is set in ancient China. If the Chinese terms and phrases in the the story are unfamiliar to you, don't be put off. First of all, the author always provides the meaning of the Chinese terms and phrases. Second, most Chinese words are short, only one syllable long. So they are fairly easy to pronounce. Most begin with a consonant and end with a vowel.

Getting into the Story

Writer's Notebook "The Ch'i-lin Purse" has two characters who are described as "spoiled." What does this term mean to you? Do you know anyone or have you ever met anyone who seemed spoiled? How did they act or what did they do that made you think of them as spoiled? Do you think spoiled children always turn into unpleasant adults? Write your answers in your notebook.

Reading Tip

Sequence of Events The story "The Ch'i-lin Purse" has a fairly complex sequence of events, or series of actions that occur in a set order. A chart like the one below, can help you keep track of and review the story's sequence of events. Copy the chart. As you read, record each event. Each time you record an event in your chart, predict what might happen next. Check your predictions when you record the next event. After you finish reading the story, look over your chart and make sure you have recorded all the key events.

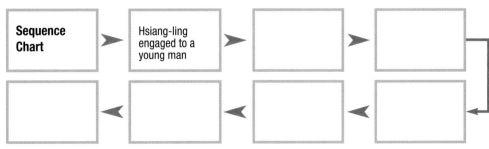

Sequence Chart → Hsiang-ling engaged to a young man → ☐ → ☐

☐ ← ☐ ← ☐ ← ☐

The Ch'i-lin Purse

Linda Fang

An embroidered silk pouch made in the late 19th or early 20th century.

It is said that many years ago in China, in a small town called Teng-chou,[1] there lived a wealthy widow, Mrs. Hsüeh. She had only one daughter, Hsüeh Hsiang-ling.[2] Hsiang-ling was beautiful and intelligent, and her mother loved her dearly. But since everything Hsiang-ling wanted was given to her, she became rather spoiled.

When Hsiang-ling was sixteen years old, her mother decided that it was time for her to marry. Through a matchmaker, Hsiang-ling was engaged to a young man from a wealthy family in a neighboring town.

Mrs. Hsüeh wanted to prepare a dowry[3] for Hsiang-ling that no girl in town could match. But Hsiang-ling was hard to please. Almost everything her mother bought for her was returned or exchanged at least two or three times.

When the dowry was finally complete, Mrs. Hsüeh decided to add one more item to it. It was the Ch'i-lin Purse, a red satin bag embroidered on both

---

1. **Teng-chou** (dung′ jou′).
2. **Hsüeh Hsiang-ling** (kew kyong ling), note that the family name comes first in Chinese.
3. **dowry** (dou′rē), *n.* money or property that women in some cultures bring to their husbands when they get married.

sides with a *ch'i-lin*,[4] a legendary animal from ancient times. The *ch'i-lin* had scales all over its body and a single horn on its head. In the old Chinese tradition, the *ch'i-lin* is the symbol of a promising male offspring.[5] Mrs. Hsüeh wanted to give Hsiang-ling the purse because she hoped that her daughter would give birth to a talented son.

When the purse Mrs. Hsüeh had ordered was ready, a family servant brought it home. But Hsiang-ling was not satisfied at all. "I don't like the pattern, take it back!" she said.

The servant returned to the store and ordered another. But when it was brought home, Hsiang-ling merely glanced at it and said, "The colors of the *ch'i-lin* are too dark, take it back!"

The servant went to place another order, but the new purse still did not please her. This time the servant broke down in tears.

"I won't go back again, young mistress. The people in the store laugh at me. They say I am hard to please. This is not true. You are the one who is hard to please. If you don't want this purse, I am going to leave you and work for someone else."

Although Hsiang-ling was spoiled, she was not a mean-spirited person. She somehow began to feel sorry for the old man, who had been with her family for more than forty years. So she looked at the purse and said, "All right, I will have this one. You may go and pay for it." The servant went back to the store, paid for the purse, and gave it to Mrs. Hsüeh.

EVALUATE: What does this incident show you about Hsiang-ling's personality?

Hsiang-ling's wedding fell on the eighteenth day of the sixth month according to the lunar calendar.[6] It was the day Hsiang-ling had longed for since her engagement. She was very excited and yet a bit sad, because she

▲ Do you think this Chinese bride is as spoiled as Hsiang-ling? Why?

knew she was leaving her mother and the home she had lived in for sixteen years.

Hsiang-ling wore a red silk dress and a red silk veil over her head. As she sat in her *hua-chiao*,[7] a sedan chair draped with red satin, and waited to be carried to her new home, her mother came to present her with the Ch'i-lin Purse.

4. *ch'i-lin* (chee leen).
5. offspring (ôf′spring′), *n.* the young of a person, animal, or plant.
6. lunar calendar, the Chinese lunar calendar is divided into 12 months of 29 or 30 days each; the new moon marks the beginning of the month. The new year is celebrated at the first new moon after the beginning of winter (between January 21 and February 19). This means that Hsiang-ling's wedding occurred sometime in July by the Western calendar.
7. *hua chiao* (kwa jyow), *n.* a canopied sedan chair with curtains, in which the bride is carried during an old-fashioned Chinese wedding.

"My dear child," she said as she lifted up the satin curtain in front, "this is your *ta-hsi-jih-tzu*,[8] your big, happy day. I am delighted to see you get married even though I will miss you terribly. Here is the Ch'i-lin Purse. I have put some wonderful things in it. But don't open it now. Wait until you are in your new home, and you will feel that I am with you."

Hsiang-ling was hardly listening. She was thinking about the wedding and wondering about her husband-to-be, whom she had never met. She took the purse and laid it on her lap. A few minutes later, four footmen came. Picking up the *hua-chiao*, they placed it on their shoulders, and the wedding procession began.

As the procession reached the road, it started to rain. Soon it was pouring so heavily that the footmen could not see well enough to continue. The wedding procession[9] came to a halt, and the *hua-chiao* was carried into a pavilion[10] that stood alongside the road.

There was another *hua-chiao* in the pavilion. It was shabby, with holes in the drapes. Hsiang-ling could hear a girl sobbing inside. This annoyed her, because she believed that a person crying on her wedding day could bring bad luck. So she told her maid to go and find out what was wrong.

"The bride is very sad," the maid said when she returned. "She is poor and has nothing to take to her new home."

PREDICT: What do you think Hsiang-ling will do?

Hsiang-ling couldn't help feeling sorry for the girl. Then her eyes fell on the Ch'i-lin Purse in her lap. She realized that she was lucky to have so many things, while this girl had nothing. Since she wasn't carrying any money with her, she handed the Ch'i-lin Purse to her maid. "Give this to the girl, but don't mention my name."

So the maid went over and gave the purse to the other bride. The girl stopped crying at once. Hsiang-ling had given away her mother's wedding gift without ever finding out what was inside.

A few minutes later, the rain stopped, the footmen picked up Hsiang-ling's *hua-chiao*, and the procession continued on its way. In an hour, Hsiang-ling arrived at her new home. She was happily married that evening, and to her delight she found her husband to be a wonderful and handsome young man. In a year's time, when she became the mother of a little boy, she felt she was the happiest woman in the world.

But six years later, there came a terrible flood. Hsiang-ling and her family lost their home and everything they owned. When they were fleeing their town, Hsiang-ling became separated from her husband and young son in the crowds of other townspeople. After

8. *ta-hsi-jih-tzu* (dä′ shē′ chē ′ jē′).
9. procession (prə sesh′ən), *n.* a group of persons moving along in a formal, orderly way.
10. pavilion (pə vil′yən), *n.* a building, for shelter, usually somewhat open.

A Paper shadow puppets in a wedding procession, carrying the bride in the traditional sedan.

searching for them in vain, Hsiang-ling followed a group of people to another town called Lai-chou.[11] She had given up hope that she would ever see her husband and child again.

As Hsiang-ling sat, exhausted and alone, at the side of the road leading to Lai-chou, a woman came up to her and said, "You must be hungry. Don't you know that a *li*[12] down the road there is a food-distribution shack? Yüan-wai Lu has opened it to help the flood victims. Talk to his butler. I am sure you can get something to eat there."

Hsiang-ling thanked the woman, followed her directions, and found the place. A long line of people with bowls in their hands were waiting to get a ration[13] of porridge. Hsiang-ling had never done such a thing in her life. As she stood in line holding a bowl and waiting her turn, she felt distraught[14] enough to cry, but she forced herself to hold back the tears.

Finally, when it was her turn, Yüan-wai Lu's butler scooped the last portion of porridge into her bowl and said to the rest of the people in line, "Sorry, no more porridge left. Come back early tomorrow."

The person behind Hsiang-ling began to sob. Hsiang-ling turned around and saw a woman who reminded her of her mother, except that she was much older. Without a word, she emptied her porridge into the woman's bowl and walked away.

The butler was surprised at what Hsiang-ling had done. Just as she had made her way back to the road, he caught up with her and said, "Young lady, I don't understand. Why did you give away your porridge—are you not hungry?"

---

11. **Lia-chou** (lē′ä′ jou′)
12. *li*, a traditional Chinese measure of distance equivalent to about 550 yards or almost one-third of a mile.
13. ration (rash′ən), *n.* a fixed allowance of food.
14. distraught (dis trôt), *adj.* very upset.

"I am hungry," said Hsiang-ling, "but I am young and I can stand hunger a bit longer."

"You are very unselfish," said the man. "I would like to help you. My master, Yüan-wai Lu, is looking for someone to take care of his little boy. If you are interested, I would be happy to recommend you."

Hsiang-ling gratefully accepted his offer and was brought to the house where Yüan-wai Lu and his wife lived.

Yüan-wai Lu, a man in his early thirties, was impressed with Hsiang-ling's graceful bearing, and he agreed to hire her. "My wife's health is very delicate and she seldom leaves her room. Your job is to take care of our son. You may play with him anywhere in the garden, but there is one place you must never go. That is the Pearl Hall, the house that stands by itself on the east side of the garden. It is a sacred[15] place, and if you ever go in there, you will be dismissed immediately."

CONNECT: If you were Hsiang-ling, would you want to go into the Pearl Hall? Why or why not?

So Hsiang-ling began her life as a governess. The little boy in her care was very spoiled. Whenever he wanted anything, he wanted it right away, and if he didn't get it, he would cry and cry until he got it. Hsiang-ling was saddened by his behavior; it reminded her of how spoiled she had been as a child.

One day, Hsiang-ling and the little boy were in the garden. Suddenly, the ball they were playing with disappeared through the window of the Pearl Hall. The boy began to wail. "I want my ball, I want my ball! Go and get my ball!"

"Young Master, I cannot go into the Pearl Hall," said Hsiang-Ling. "Your father doesn't allow it. I will be dismissed if I do."

But the little boy only cried louder, and finally Hsiang-ling decided that she had no choice. She walked over to the east side of the garden and looked around. No one was in sight. She quickly walked up the steps that led to the Pearl Hall and again made sure that no one was watching. Then she opened the door and stepped in.

She found herself standing in front of an altar, where two candles and some incense sticks were burning. But in the place where people usually put the wooden name-tablets of their ancestors was the Ch'i-lin Purse! Instantly she recalled the events of her wedding day and how happy she had been. She thought of her wonderful husband and her own son and how much she missed them. She had had everything then, and now she had nothing! Hsiang-ling burst into tears.

Suddenly, she felt a hand on her shoulder. When she turned around she found herself face-to-face with Mrs. Lu, her mistress, and a young maid.

"What are you doing here?" Mrs. Lu asked angrily.

"Young Master told me to come here and pick up his ball," Hsiang-ling replied.

"Then why were you weeping at the altar?"

"Because I saw the purse that once belonged to me."

Mrs. Lu looked startled. "Where are you from?" she asked, as she took the purse from the altar and sat down on a chair that leaned against a long table. There was a tremble in her voice.

"I am from Teng-chou."

"Bring her a stool," said Mrs. Lu, motioning to her maid. Not wanting to wait on another servant, the maid grudgingly[16] brought a stool and put it to Mrs. Lu's right. "You may sit down," said Mrs. Lu. Somewhat

---

15. **sacred** (sāk′rid), *adj.* holy.
16. **grudgingly** (gruj′ing lē), *adv.* unwillingly.

"You may sit down," said Mrs. Lu. Somewhat confused, Hsiang-ling sat down.

PREDICT: What do you think will happen to Hsiang-ling now?

"What was your maiden name?"[17]

"Hsüeh Hsiang-ling."

"When were you married?"

"On the eighteenth day of the sixth moon, six years ago."

"Bring her a chair and put it to my left," Mrs. Lu ordered her maid. Hsiang-ling was told to move to the chair. She was surprised to see herself treated as a guest of honor.

"Tell me how you lost the purse," said Mrs. Lu.

"It was a gift from my mother. My wedding procession was stopped on the road because of a storm, and my *hua-chiao* was carried into a pavilion. There was another *hua-chiao* in it, and the bride was crying."

"Move her chair to the middle and move mine to the right side," ordered Mrs. Lu. The chairs were switched, and once again Hsiang-ling was told to sit down. She was astonished[18] to find herself sitting in the middle seat—the place of the highest honor.

"Please continue," said Mrs. Lu.

"I gave the bride my purse. I never saw it again, and I have no idea how it got here."

Mrs. Lu dropped to her knees in front of Hsiang-ling and cried, "You are my benefactor! All these years I have been praying here for your well-being. When I got to my new home, I opened the purse and found it full of valuables, including this." She opened the purse and took out a piece of jade.[19] "My husband and I were able to pawn[20] it for a large amount of money. Using the money, we started a business and have now become very wealthy. So I reclaimed the jade and have kept it in the purse since. We also built the Pearl Hall to house the purse and to honor you.

"I knew that you lived in the Teng-chou area, so when I heard about the flood I prayed day and night in that direction, begging Buddha[21] to protect you from harm. I was hoping that one day I would find you and show you my gratitude.[22] And here you are, taking care of my son! I know what we must do. We shall divide our property and give you half of it. That will make us all very happy."

Hsiang-ling was speechless as Mrs. Lu placed the purse in her hands. That same day, Yüan-wai Lu sent out servants in all directions to look for Hsiang-ling's husband and son. Soon they were found, in a village not far from Teng-chou.

A great friendship developed between the two families. Later, whenever Hsiang-ling told people the story about her purse, she would always end the tale by saying, "If you have a chance to do something good, be sure to do it. Happiness will come back to you."

---

17. **maiden name,** the family name a woman has before she gets married.
18. astonish (ə ston′ish), *v.* greatly surprise or amaze.
19. jade (jād), *n.* precious stone that is highly valued in China.
20. pawn (pôn), *v.* leave an object with another person as security that borrowed money will be repaid.
21. **Buddha** (bü′də), *n.* religious teacher of northern India and founder of Buddhism.
22. gratitude (grat′ə tüd), *n.* thankfulness.

After Reading

Making Connections

1. This story has many different twists and turns. Which turns of **plot** surprised you the most?

2. Do you agree with Hsiang-ling that "If you have a chance to do something good, be sure to do it. Happiness will come back to you"? Why or why not?

3. Do you think the Lu child will act spoiled when he grows up? Why or why not?

4. Do you learn more about the **characters** from their words and actions or from the author's description of them? Explain.

5. Do you think this story would have ended the same way if it had been set in modern America? Explain.

6. Fate—a power that controls events—plays a large role in "The Ch'i-lin Purse." What role, if any, do you think fate plays in your life?

7. Based on this story and what you yourself have learned about life, would you do something good just so that in return something good would happen to you? Explain why or why not.

Literary Focus: Folk Tales

If you lived in China you might hear this story rather than read it in a book. It is a **folk tale**—one that has been told, with slight variations, for many centuries. Folk tales tend to have the following elements:

- Characters: simple rather than complex; some characters may have little personality and only serve to move events along.

- Plot: fast-moving and lively with one event quickly following another; the story generally ends quickly or immediately after a dramatic climax.

- Point of View: Usually is told from the third-person point of view.

- Theme: Often comments on human nature or human needs.

Reread "The Ch'i-lin Purse," and evaluate ways in which the story has the elements of a folk tale. For each of the elements above, give examples from the story.

Vocabulary Study

The following are sayings you might find in Chinese fortune cookies. Complete each saying with the word from the list that best fits with the meaning of the saying. Write the words on a sheet of paper.

astonished
distraught
gratitude
grudgingly
offspring
pavilion
pawn
procession
ration
sacred

1. Give willingly of your time, money, and love and you will be blessed with many ____.

2. May your funeral march follow your wedding ____ only after many years.

3. When the rains come, you need a sturdy ____ to keep dry.

4. If you work hard, you will have an extra ____ of food.

5. If you give ____, then you will receive in the same mean spirit.

6. If you have a bad day, don't be ____. A better day will soon follow.

7. If you break a ____ promise, you will regret it.

8. Don't be ____ at the generosity your own unselfish actions inspire.

9. Don't ____ all your valuables without keeping something.

10. Generosity to others brings their ____.

Expressing Your Ideas

Writing Choices

Don't Forget to Say . . . Imagine you are Mrs. Lu. Write a **thank-you note** to Hsiang-ling for the purse. Use details from the story to tell about your plans, your hopes, and your gratitude.

Wisdom of the Ages The last two sentences of "The Ch'i-lin Purse" are a proverb—a wise saying often about human actions or human nature. Make up another **proverb** that would apply to this story. Read and discuss your proverbs with your classmates and decide whether you think they apply to real life.

Happy New Moon Research a lunar calendar and write an **explanation** of what it is.

Other Options

Do Your Part With a group, select a scene from the story and perform it as a **skit.** Pick out the characters and decide who will play each part. Work out what each character will say and do. If possible, assemble costumes and make scenery for your skit. Perform your skit for the class. If different groups choose different scenes, perform them in sequence to make the play.

Thank You Very Much Explore the ways that people in different cultures show gratitude. Make a **chart** of the information you find.

Incredible Journeys

Links to China's Past

History Connection

Journeys can take many forms. You can travel cross-country by train, car, plane, or even camel. Or, you can journey in your mind from reality to the world of fantasy. Whatever your journey, make it a challenge, an adventure.

The Silk Road

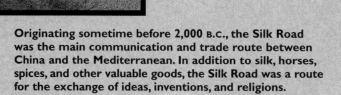

Originating sometime before 2,000 B.C., the Silk Road was the main communication and trade route between China and the Mediterranean. In addition to silk, horses, spices, and other valuable goods, the Silk Road was a route for the exchange of ideas, inventions, and religions.

Traders traveled through Xinjiang (shin′ jē läng) Province in western China. These desert lands, which were often bordered by high mountains, made travel challenging. Few caravans completed the entire journey.

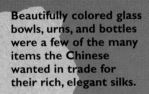

Beautifully colored glass bowls, urns, and bottles were a few of the many items the Chinese wanted in trade for their rich, elegant silks.

A merchant sells her wares in Rajasthan, India. The eggplant, onions, and ginger shown here are all native to Asia. Many foods came to the western world as a result of trade on the 5,000-mile Silk Road.

Camels adapt easily to a dry climate. They are strong and can survive longer than other pack animals without water. For this reason, they were used in trading caravans to carry goods and supplies.

Jade is a deeply colored stone used for centuries by the Chinese for carvings and jewelry. The sacred green and white jade was transported to the West from China by way of the Silk Road.

Opened in 2,000 B.C. or earlier, the Silk Road was a main avenue of communication between the East and the West for more than 4,000 years. This figurine from the Tang Dynasty, the 8th century A.D., is the type of artifact that might have been traded on the Silk Road.

Responding

1. Study the map and pictures. What problems do you think traders might have faced in their travels?

2. Those who braved the dangers of travel on the Silk Road were true pioneers. Are there any places left where one can be a pioneer today?

Art Connection

Learning something new can be a journey for the mind. Let your imagination travel the Silk Road as you practice writing Chinese numbers.

How to Write Chinese Numbers

In most parts of East Asia (China, Japan, and Korea), calligraphy has always been considered an art. A person who does calligraphy well is highly respected. Calligraphy is a lot like painting. However, the strokes must be done in a strong manner. There can be no retouching. To become a good calligrapher takes years of study and practice.

The traditional tools of the calligrapher are a brush, inkstick, and inkstone. To make the ink, a small amount of the inkstick is rubbed on the stone with water. Nowadays, however, the ink comes ready-ground. Instead of the traditional wolf-hair brushes, soft, felt-tipped brushmarkers can be used.

Chinese characters represent pictures and ideas. They are made up of strokes that are written in a particular order. The general rule is to make the strokes of a character from left to right and from top to bottom. When a horizontal stroke and another stroke cross, the horizontal one usually comes first.

Traditional Chinese writing in books and scrolls was written in columns from top to bottom and across the page from right to left. But in China today, the practice is to write horizontally across the page from left to right in the same manner as Westerners.

Chinese numbers are the easiest characters to write. On a sheet of paper, use an ordinary pen or a flexible felt tip pen. Follow the direction of the arrows in making the strokes. Practice the strokes, position, and size for each number.

The number 11 is written like this.

十一

Write these numbers.

12   13

14   15

16   17

18   19

Responding

1. Practice writing Chinese numbers until you feel comfortable with your results.

2. With your classmates, make a bulletin board display of Chinese characters.

Reading Mini-Lesson

Taking Notes and Outlining

Taking notes on what you read involves thinking. It is pointless to copy everything you read into your notebook. Decide what is most important to remember and how to organize your notes.

To take notes, you might make an outline of the most important ideas to help you remember and organize the information. The form of your outline will depend on your reading purpose, the kind of selection, and the future use of your notes. For example, if you were reading an editorial in a newspaper, you might organize your notes by outlining opinions and reasons. If you were reading a recipe in a cookbook, you might outline the ingredients and the steps to follow.

A good way to determine what is important is to reread the material. Below is an example of how you could begin to outline the article "How to Write Chinese Numbers," on page 202.

How to Write Chinese Numbers

A. Background of Calligraphy
B. Tools of the Calligrapher
C. Chinese Writing
D. Procedures for Writing Chinese Numbers

Activity Options

1. Complete the outline above. Copy the topics (with spaces between them) on your own paper. Fill in some details below each subtopic.

2. The heads below are often found in teaching materials that show you how to do something. In your science book or technology book, find a set of directions and outline the information under these headings:

   Background   Materials   Procedures

3. The picture essay "The Silk Road" on page 205 is meant to tell you *about* something. Make an outline of the information. Use the headings *Who, What, When, Where, Why,* and *How* to organize your outline.

Writing Workshop

A Poetic Journey

Assignment You've read about some journeys, real and imaginary, simple and complicated. Draw upon your imagination or experience and write a poem about a journey of your own.

WRITER'S BLUEPRINT

Product	A descriptive poem
Purpose	To describe a journey—real or imaginary—during which you face some kind of obstacle
Audience	Classmates, friends, family
Specs	A successful poem should include:

❑ An explanation of your journey: Where are you going? How will you get there? What lies at the end of your journey?

❑ A description of the obstacles you face and how you deal with them

❑ Your feelings at different parts of your journey

❑ Details that help the reader see, hear, taste, smell, and feel what you do

❑ Adjectives and adverbs that enhance your descriptions

The instructions that follow are designed to help you develop a successful poem.

STEP 1 PREWRITING

Reread the poems in this part. Be alert to language and form. How do the poems sound? What do they look like?

Brainstorm journeys you've made. In the poem "Halfway Down," Christopher Robin makes a journey down the stairs. Think of journeys you've made, real or imaginary, simple or complicated. Make a web of those journeys to record important details such as destination, obstacles along the way, and how you felt along the journey. Then choose a journey you'd like to write a poem about.

List sensory details about your journey that will enable your readers to experience what you did. Organize your descriptive words and phrases in a chart like the one below. At this point, you might want to look ahead to the Revising Strategy about imagery on page 210 to help you with your descriptions.

OR . . .
You may already have selected a journey that you wish to write a poem about. If you have, move ahead to the List sensory details step.

Journey	I See	I Hear	I Smell	I Taste	I Feel
a walk through my neighborhood	tall trees, leaves on the ground, cars, planes, people	planes, cars, dogs barking, people yelling	dead leaves, car exhaust	car exhaust	the ground, rough cement of the porch

Try a quickwrite. Spend a few minutes jotting down phrases and images you'd like to include in your poem. Remember, the lines in your poem do not have to rhyme. And a line in a poem does not have to be a complete sentence. In fact, maybe your entire poem is just one sentence that describes what happened along your journey.

OR . . .
Instead of listing details, you might want to make a map of your journey. Draw pictures of the events on your map and add words and phrases to describe what you hear, see, taste, feel, and smell along the journey.

STEP  DRAFTING

If you have trouble getting started, you might want to use the following poetry frame. Use your completed frame as an outline for your poem.

I travel on a *(type of vehicle–real or imaginary)* . . .
Through *(describe what you see)* . . .
It takes me away from *(that which you are escaping)* . . .
I journey to *(your destination)* . . .
Seeking *(what you hope to find)* . . .
I am *(your emotions)* . . .
I smell *(sensory details)* . . .
I see *(sensory details)* . . .
I feel *(sensory details)* . . .
Here, I am able to *(tell what's different about this new place)* . . .

3 REVISING

Ask your partner for comments on your draft before you revise. Ask your partner to highlight vivid details. Then concentrate on those lines that contain no highlighting.

✔ Do I include my feelings about my journey?

✔ Do I include my obstacles and how I deal with them?

✔ Do I create images that appeal to the senses?

Revising Strategy

Imagery

LITERARY SOURCE
"Parts of it were stirring now, and uncoiling and sliding and beginning to shine with a dreadful oily glister."
from "The Wish" by Roald Dahl

Imagery is the use of language that appeals to the senses. *The freezing wind stirred the snow into a whirling fan of ice* is more likely to make a reader feel the cold than the statement *The wind blew the snow around.* Look at how Roald Dahl describes a patch of carpet in the Literary Source. When you revise, try to include words that help the reader see, hear, smell, taste, or touch what you are describing.

Try revising these descriptions using imagery.

- The road was long.

- She carried her full suitcase to the car.

Notice how the writer of the passage below revised language to include more descriptive phrases.

STUDENT MODEL

Dogs bark wildly and

cars zoom past.

Leaves crunch under my feet.

trucks wail Fire ~~sirens~~ and a small silence,

then the action goes on.

roar Planes ~~fly~~ above and voices yell to be heard.

4 EDITING

Ask a partner to review your revised draft before you edit. When you edit, watch for errors in grammar, usage, spelling, and mechanics. If you're using adjectives or adverbs in your poem, make sure you've used the correct forms.

Editing Strategy

FOR REFERENCE . . .
More rules for comparative forms of adjectives and adverbs are listed in the Language and Grammar Handbook.

Forms of Adjectives and Adverbs

When writing descriptions in poetry, you'll probably use many adjectives and adverbs. Most adjectives and adverbs have three different forms—positive, comparative, and superlative—depending on how they're being used. The positive form describes one thing, the comparative compares two things, and the superlative compares three or more. Notice that endings or words can be added to change the forms and that spelling changes can occur.

	Positive	Comparative	Superlative
Adjectives	Weary Beautiful	Wearier More (or less) beautiful	Weariest Most (or least) beautiful
Adverbs	Soon Neatly	Sooner More (or less) neatly	Soonest Most (or least) neatly

Other adjectives and adverbs have irregular comparative and superlative forms. Look at the examples below.

	Positive	Comparative	Superlative
Adjectives	Good	Better	Best
Adverbs	Badly	Worse	Worst

Incorrect: They flew to the farther planet from Earth.
Correct: They flew to the farthest planet from Earth.

Incorrect: Her suitcase was more heavy than the other on the cart.
Correct: Her suitcase was the heavier of the two on the cart.

STEP 5 PRESENTING

Here are two ideas for presenting your poem.

- Form a circle with a group of classmates and read your poems aloud. After each person has read, discuss images you thought were effective.

- Collect all the poems in the class and bind them into a classroom poetry anthology. You might divide the volume into different sections, such as "Incredible Journeys," "Journeys to Adventure," or "Journeys Around the World." Illustrate your anthology and make it available for your class and others to read.

STEP 6 LOOKING BACK

Self-evaluate. What grade would you give your poem? Look back at the Writer's Blueprint and evaluate yourself on each point, from 6 (superior) down to 1 (weak).

Reflect. Think about what you learned from writing this poem as you write answers to these questions.

✔ How did your view of the journey you described change after writing your poem?

✔ How did you use punctuation in your poem to help communicate ideas for your readers?

For Your Working Portfolio: Add your poem, self-evaluation, and reflection responses to your working portfolio.

Beyond Print

Looking at Advertising

Some of the challenges you read about in this unit were foot races. Today when athletes race, one of the most important factors is wearing the right shoes. At least that's what advertisers and shoe manufacturers would like us to believe. A sporting goods store has shoes for every event: tennis shoes, racquetball shoes, basketball shoes, soccer shoes, running shoes, and so on.

What Makes a Shoe?

Comfort • Cost •
Fit • Durability •
Competitiveness •
Appearance • Color

Activity: Building a Better Shoe

If you could design a running shoe, what would it look like? How would it differ from shoes already being sold? The list at the left names some things you should consider in your design. Write a description and draw a picture of your shoe.

Activity Option

A. Develop a plan for selling the shoe. Follow these steps.

1. Name your shoe.

2. Decide how you will sell it. Choose one of the selling techniques at the left or make up one of your own.

3. Write a slogan for the shoe, based on how you will sell it. Try to use words from selections in this unit.

4. Draw an advertisement for your shoe. Be sure to include a picture, a description, and the cost of the shoe.

5. Present your ideas to your classmates. Ask for opinions and suggestions. Then decide what changes you will make in your shoe based on their feedback.

Testimonial

A celebrity recommends the shoe.

Bandwagon

Everyone is buying the shoe.

Emotional Appeal

Be a winner. Be popular. Buy this shoe.

B. Look at several shoe advertisements and compare them to your own selling plan. What characteristics of the shoe does each ad emphasize? Which of the selling techniques described at the left does each advertisement use?

Projects for Collaborative Study

Theme Connection

Moving Hassles Have you ever faced the challenge of having to move to a new state or country? Every year thousands of people immigrate to the United States from other nations. To find out what these immigrants face, invite several speakers to come to your class and describe their biggest challenges in adjusting to a new life.

■ To prepare, brainstorm the names of possible speakers and make a list of questions to ask. Speakers could even be some of your classmates.

■ Based on what you learn, make a list of suggestions that could help the immigrants overcome their challenges.

Literature Connection

Time and Place In this unit, the **setting**— the time and place of the story—has a major influence on the actions and emotions of the characters. In "The King of Mazy May," for example, Walt has to conquer his snowy environment to escape from claim jumpers. Choose two or three selections in the unit and, in a small group, discuss how the main character in each selection responds to the setting.

■ As a group, choose a character from this unit and together write a story in which you place that character in a new setting—a different time or place. Discuss: How would the character react? What would he or she say, do, and feel?

Life Skills Connection

Imagining Success Each of us faces challenges every day regardless of who we are. A common challenge people face is improving their performance. If your challenge is to become a better student, athlete, or musician, what could you do to improve?

One special technique that people have used to improve their performance is visualization. Professional athletes, actors, and musicians use this technique. Prior to an event, they close their eyes and imagine themselves performing perfectly from the beginning of their performance to the end.

Think about an area where you would like to improve your performance:

■ Now close your eyes and imagine yourself performing the task and being a success!

■ Repeat the visualization prior to an upcoming performance.

Multicultural Connection

Working Together Individuality includes facing challenges of many types. Challenges that relate to working and interacting with others can be overcome through more effective **communication.**

With your classmates, prepare a set of suggestions for working with others in small groups.

■ Include suggestions that will enable individuals to feel more comfortable expressing their opinions.

■ Include rules that will allow members of the group to make decisions or reach compromises on important issues.

Read More About Challenges

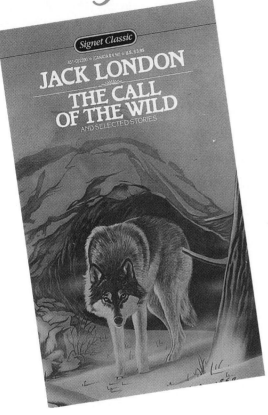

The Call of the Wild (1903) by Jack London. Buck, the dog hero, is forced to work pulling dogsleds. After his master dies, he returns to the wild to lead a pack of wolves.

The Incredible Journey (1961) by Sheila Burnford. Two dogs and a cat face many challenges as they travel 250 miles across the Canadian wilderness to find their owners.

More Good Books

Those Who Love the Game (1994) by Glenn Rivers and Bruce Brooks. With the help of a writer, a professional basketball player describes the lessons he learned about teamwork and family as he worked toward his goal.

The Phantom Tollbooth (1961) by Philip Norton Juster. A bored boy makes an imaginary journey through a tollbooth.

The Great American Elephant Chase (1993) by Gillian Cross. Tad accidentally embarks on an incredible journey with an elephant across the American West.

The Hobbit (1966) by J.R.R. Tolkien. In a fantasy land, a hobbit joins a group of dwarfs in their quest for fabled treasure.

They Shaped the Game (1994) by William Jay Jacobs. This series of biographies focuses on three major players who made their mark in professional baseball.

THE DINNER QUILT

Every Christmas since I can remember we had dinner at Aunt Connie's and Uncle Bates' house in St. Albans, Long Island. Aunt Connie had a little boy my age named Lonnie. I was in love with him. Ever seen a little black boy with red hair and green eyes? That's Lonnie. We used to play Doctor under the piano. One year Lonnie didn't want to play anymore. I tried to pull him under the piano but he ran away from me into the bathroom. I ran after him. Uncle Bates was in there. I turned to leave but Uncle Bates grabbed my pigtail and shook me. "You listen to me, little gal, better learn to let the boys run after you some or you ain't gonna catch none. You hear me?" he said. I shook loose and ran out of the bathroom. That was the end of me and Lonnie playing Doctor. Thereafter, some of Lonnie's boyfriends would come over after dinner and we would all play with his toys in the yard. That was fun too but not nearly as much as before.

1.

Aunt Connie was a fabulous woman. Uncle Bates was crazy about her. "Ain't nothing too good for Connie," he used to say. She was into women's lib back then when nobody even knew what it was all about. One year she embroidered the names of famous black women on her place-mats. Then directed each one of us where to sit. "Mama you and Papa sit over there with Mary McLeod Bethune and Augusta Savage. Dee Dee, you and your handsome young actor go sit with Dorothy Dandridge and Zora Neal Hurston. Miss Vi, you and MC Winston sit with Maria Stewart and Bessie Smith. Lonnie you sit with Harriet Tubman. Melody (that was me) you sit with Sojourner Truth and your ma and Pa next to you with Fannie Lou Hamer and Marian Anderson. Bates and me gonna sit with Billie Holiday and Madame Walker." But she did it eloquently like a lecture with anecdotes on each of the women. By the time we all sat down and Lonnie said a prayer in some foreign language he learned special for the occasion we were all have for the food which was great and enough to feed an army.

2.

Relationships

Keeping Traditions
Part One, pages 220–271

What Really Matters
Part Two, pages 272–337

217

Talking About
RELATIONSHIPS

Relationships with families, friends, and other people we meet are important to us. In the course of daily life, everyone deals with other people. How we act toward others is based in part on our own traditions and cultural backgrounds. How we treat others also shows what really matters to us.

Young people from across the country talk about relationships in their lives. Notice how their comments match ideas from the literature you will be reading.

"Why did some divorced people get married in the first place?"

Derek—Melbourne, FL

I thought that if Mom hadn't asked for the divorce, this wouldn't be happening. Especially then, I was angry at her for messing up my life, and I was mad at Dad for not coming to see me enough.

from "Keri" by Maxine B. Rosenberg, pages 286-287

Family Group, by Henry Moore, 1948-1949, bronze.

"What could we do to relate better to each other?"

Ahmed—Topeka, KS

But nobody believes in that kind of thing anymore, . . . And even if people did, I couldn't run and hit my enemy with the stick and get away with it.

from "Thunder Butte" by Virginia Driving Hawk Sneve, page 227

"Why do people hurt each other?"

Charlotte—Saginaw, MI

It's not convenient, and it's not fair. If I was to deduct half a crown from your salary for it, you'd think yourself ill-used, wouldn't you? Still you expect me to pay a day's wage for a day of no work.

from A Christmas Carol by Charles Dickens, page 239

"Friends and family offer valuable support when we need it."

Karin—Boulder, CO

In the middle of the Depression, for instance, he paid cash for a piano, of all things, and insisted that my twin sisters, Yolande and Yvette, take lessons once a week.

from "President Cleveland, Where Are You?" by Robert Cormier, page 276

" A relationship that is good for one person may be bad for another. "

Joy—Corpus Christi, TX

219

Part One

Keeping Traditions

On your birthday, do you get presents and a cake with candles on it? On Thanksgiving, do you sit down to a big meal featuring a turkey, cranberry sauce, and other delicious foods? If so, you are following some of the common traditions observed by many American families.

 Multicultural Connection Belonging to **groups** involves making, keeping, and changing cultural traditions. Within every group, individuals respond in different ways to these traditions. How do the characters in "Thunder Butte" and *A Christmas Carol* react to the traditions of their cultures? Think about how their traditions are different from yours.

Before Reading

Thunder Butte

by Virginia Driving Hawk Sneve

Virginia Driving Hawk Sneve
born 1933

Whatever your ancestry or religion, at some time in your life, you've probably run into stereotypes that hurt you or made you angry. As a member of the Rosebud Sioux tribe, Virginia Driving Hawk Sneve (snē′vē) noticed many stereotypes about her people when she read books by non-Indian authors. She decided to write her own stories about Native Americans. With her books, she hoped "to correct the many misconceptions and untruths [about Native Americans] which have been too long perpetrated [spread]" by other writers.

Building Background

Buttes In some areas of the southwestern United States, large flat-topped hills rise suddenly out of the surrounding level plains. These striking landforms are known as buttes. Buttes are the remains of what once was a plateau—an extensive high plain. The top of the butte was originally ground level. Over time, wind and water eroded the entire plateau, except for places where the rock was extremely hard. These hard parts became isolated buttes. The painting on page 223 shows a butte. Lightning often strikes buttes, as they are the highest points in relatively flat regions.

Getting into the Story

Discussion What are some traditions in your family or your culture? Do you know where some of these traditions came from? Have you started any traditions in your family? Which traditions are most meaningful to you and why? Are there any traditions with which you are not completely comfortable? What could you do or how could you change the tradition so that it would be more enjoyable?

Reading Tip

Old and New Ways The characters in the story are Native Americans of Sioux ancestry. They have held on to some of their Sioux traditions and adopted some modern ways of doing things. As you read the story, chart differences in the old and new ways of doing things. Consider food, housing, occupations, clothing, habits, and traditions. Classify each item listed in the chart as a Native American tradition, a modern way of doing something, or a combination of the two.

What Character Does	Native way or modern way
Matt Two Bull sleeps in a tent.	Combination

THUNDER BUTTE

Virginia Driving Hawk Sneve

The sun was just beginning to rise when John woke Norman the next morning.

"You must get an early start if you are going to go to the west side of the butte and return by supper," John said to the sleepy boy. "If you are not home by the time I get back from work, I'll come looking for you."

Norman reluctantly rose. Last night he had accepted his grandfather's command to go to the Thunder Butte without too many doubts. Yet now in the morning's chill light the boy wondered if his grandfather's dreams were the meaningless meanderings[1] of an old mind, or if his grandfather was really worthy of the tribe's respect as one of the few remaining wise elders who understood the ancient ways.

Norman dressed in his oldest clothes and pulled on worn and scuffed boots to protect his feet from the rocks and snakes of the butte. He heard his parents talking in the other room and knew his father was telling his mother where Norman was going.

As the boy entered the room, which was kitchen and living room as well as his parents' bedroom, he heard his mother say, "What if there is a rock slide and Norman is hurt or buried on the butte? We won't know anything until you get home from work, John. I don't want Norman to go."

"The boy is old enough to have learned to be careful on the butte. He'll be all right," John answered as he tried to reassure Sarah. "Besides," he added, "my father dreamed of this happening."

Sarah grunted scornfully. "No one believes in dreams or in any of those old superstitious ways anymore."

"I'll be okay, Mom," Norman said as he sat

---

1. **meandering** (mē an′dər ing), *n.* aimless wandering.

down at the table. "I should be able to find lots of agates on the west side where there is all that loose rock. Maybe I can talk the trader into giving me money for them after all." He spoke bravely despite his own inner misgivings about going to the butte.

Sarah protested no more. Norman looked at her, but she lowered her head as she set a plate of pancakes in front of him. He knew she was hiding the worry she felt for him.

John put on his hat and went to the door. "Don't forget to take the willow branch with you," he said to Norman, "and be careful."

Norman nodded and ate his breakfast. When he was finished he stood up. "Guess I'll go," he said to his mother, who was pouring hot water from the tea kettle into her dish pan. When she didn't speak Norman took the willow cane from where he had propped it by the door and his hat from the nail above it.

"Wait," Sarah called and handed him a paper bag. "Here is a lunch for you. You'll need something to eat since you'll be gone all day." She gave him an affectionate shove. "Oh, go on. I know you'll be all right. Like your dad said, you're old enough to be careful."

Thunder Butte **223**

Norman smiled at his mother. "Thanks," he said as he tucked the lunch into his shirt. He checked his back pocket to see if he'd remembered the salt bag to put the agates in.

He walked briskly across the open prairie and turned to wave at his mother, who had come outside to watch him leave. She waved back and Norman quickened his pace. He whistled, trying to echo the meadowlarks who were greeting the day with their happy song. He swiped the willow cane at the bushy sage[2] and practiced spearing the pear cactus[3] that dotted his path. The early morning air was cool, but the sun soon warmed the back of his neck and he knew it would be a hot day.

He crossed the creek south of where Matt Two Bull's tent was pitched and then he was climbing the gentle beginning slope of the butte. He stopped and studied the way before him and wondered if it wouldn't be easier to reach the west side by walking around the base of the butte even though it would be longer. Then Norman smiled as he remembered his grandfather's command to climb the south trail that wound to the top. He decided to do what the old man wanted.

The ascent[4] sharply steepened and the sun rose with him as Norman climbed. What looked like a smooth path from the prairie floor was rough rocky terrain.[5] The trail spiraled[6] up a sharp incline and Norman had to detour around fallen rocks. He paused to rest about half way up and then saw how sharply the overhanging ledge of the butte protruded.[7] Getting to the top of it was going to be a difficult struggle. He climbed on. His foot slipped and his ankle twisted painfully. Small pebbles bounced down the slope and he saw a rattlesnake slither out of the way. He tightly clutched the willow branch and leaned panting against the butte. He sighed with relief as the snake crawled out of sight. He wiggled his foot until the pain left his ankle. Then he started to trudge up the incline again.

At last only the ledge of the butte loomed over him. There appeared to be no way up. Disgusted that his laborious climb seemed dead-ended he stubbornly tried to reach the top. Remembering the courage of the ancient young men who had struggled in this same place to gain the summit and seek their visions, he was determined not to go back. His fingers found tiny cracks to hold on to. The cane was cumbersome and in the way. He was tempted to drop it, but he thought of the snake he'd seen and struggled on with it awkwardly under his arm.

Finally Norman spied a narrow opening in the ledge which tapered down to only a few feet from where he clung. He inched his way up until he reached the base of the opening and then he found a use for the cane. He jammed the stout branch high into the boulders above him. Cautiously he pulled to see if it would hold his weight. It held. Using the cane as a lever he pulled himself to the top.

This final exertion winded the boy and he lay exhausted on the summit, boots hanging over the edge. Cautiously he pulled his feet under him, stood and looked around.

He gazed at a new world. The sun bathed the eastern valley in pale yellow which was spotted with dark clumps of sage. The creek was a green and silver serpent winding its way to the southeast. His grandfather's tent was a white shoe box in its clearing, and beside it stood a diminutive form waving a red flag. It was Matt

---

2. **bushy sage**, sagebrush; a bush with gray-green, aromatic leaves that grows on the dry plains of North America.
3. **pear cactus**, the edible fruit of the prickly pear cactus or other American cactus.
4. ascent (ə sent′), *n.* upward slope.
5. **terrain** (te rān′), *n.* tract of land, especially considered with respect to its natural features and extent.
6. **spiral** (spī′rəl), *v.* form a winding path.
7. protrude (prō trüd′), *v.* stick out.

Two Bull signaling with his shirt, and Norman knew that his grandfather had been watching him climb. He waved his hat in reply and then walked to the outer edge of the butte.

The summit was not as smoothly flat as it looked from below. Norman stepped warily over the many cracks and holes that pitted the surface. He was elated that he had successfully made the difficult ascent, but now as he surveyed the butte top he had a sense of discomfort.

There were burn scars on the rough summit, and Norman wondered if these spots were where the lightning had struck, or were they evidence of ancient man-made fires? He remembered that this was a sacred place to the old ones and his uneasiness increased. He longed to be back on the secure level of the plains.

On the west edge he saw that the butte cast a sharp shadow below because the rim protruded as sharply as it had on the slope he'd climbed. Two flat rocks jutted up on either side of a narrow opening, and Norman saw shallow steps hewn into the space between. This must be the trail of which his grandfather had spoken.

Norman stepped down and then quickly turned to hug the butte face as the steps ended abruptly in space. The rest of the rocky staircase lay broken and crumbled below. The only way down was to jump.

He cautiously let go of the willow branch and watched how it landed and bounced against the rocks. He took a deep breath as if to draw courage from the air. He lowered himself so that he was hanging by his fingertips to the last rough step, closed his eyes and dropped.

The impact[8] of his landing stung the soles of his feet. He stumbled and felt the cut of the sharp rocks against one knee as he struggled to retain his balance. He did not fall and finally stood upright breathing deeply until the wild pounding of his heart slowed. "Wow," he said softly as he looked back up at the ledge, "that must have been at least a twenty foot drop."

He picked up the willow branch and started walking slowly down the steep slope. The trail Matt Two Bull had told him about

He took a deep breath as if to draw courage from the air.

had been obliterated[9] by years of falling rock. Loose shale and gravel shifted under Norman's feet, and he probed cautiously ahead with the cane to test the firmness of each step.

He soon found stones which he thought were agates. He identified them by spitting on each rock and rubbing the wet spot with his finger. The dull rock seemed to come alive! Variegated hues of brown and gray glowed as if polished. They were agates all right. Quickly he had his salt bag half full.

It was almost noon and his stomach growled. He stopped to rest against a large boulder and pulled out his lunch from his shirt. But his mouth was too dry to chew the cheese sandwich. He couldn't swallow without water.

Thirsty and hungry, Norman decided to go straight down the butte and head for home.

Walking more confidently as the slope leveled out he thrust the pointed cane carelessly into the ground. He suddenly fell as the cane went deep into the soft shale.[10]

Norman slid several feet. Loose rocks rolled around him as he came to rest against

---

8. **impact** (im′pakt), *n.* force due to the striking of one thing against another.
9. **obliterate** (ə blit′ə rāt′), *v.* wipe out, remove all traces.
10. shale (shāl), *n.* rock formed from hardened clay or mud in thin layers which split easily.

a boulder. He lay still for a long time fearing that his tumble might cause a rock fall. But no thundering slide came, so he cautiously climbed back to where the tip of the willow branch protruded from the ground.

Norman shivered at the thought that he may have disturbed a grave, . . .

He was afraid that the cane may have plunged into a rattlesnake den. Carefully he pulled at the stout branch, wiggling it this way and that with one hand while he dug with the other. It came loose, sending a shower of rocks down the hill, and Norman saw that something else was sticking up in the hole he had uncovered.

Curious, and seeing no sign of snakes, he kept digging and soon found the tip of a leather-covered stick. Bits of leather and wood fell off in his hand as he gently pulled. The stick, almost as long as he was tall and curved on one end, emerged as he tugged. Holding it before him, his heart pounding with excitement, he realized that he had found a thing that once belonged to the old ones.

Norman shivered at the thought that he may have disturbed a grave, which was *tehinda*,[11] forbidden. He cleared more dirt away but saw no bones nor other sign that this was a burial place. Quickly he picked up the stick and his willow cane and hurried down the hill. When he reached the bottom he discovered that in his fall the salt bag of agates had pulled loose from his belt. But he did not return to search for it. It would take most of the afternoon to travel around the base of the butte to the east side.

The creek was in the deep shade of the butte when he reached it and thirstily flopped down and drank. He crossed the shallow stream and walked to his grandfather's tent.

"You have been gone a long time," Matt Two Bull greeted as Norman walked into the clearing where the old man was seated.

"I have come from the west side of the butte, Grandpa," Norman said wearily. He sat down on the ground and examined a tear in his jeans and the bruise on his knee.

"Was it difficult?" the old man asked.

"Yes," Norman nodded. He told of the rough climb up the south slope, the jump down and finally of his fall which led him to discover the long leather-covered stick. He held the stick out to his grandfather who took it and examined it carefully.

"Are you sure there was no body in the place where you found this?"

Norman shook his head. "No, I found nothing else but the stick. Do you know what it is, Grandpa?"

"You have found a *coup*[12] stick which belonged to the old ones."

"I know that it is old because the wood is brittle and the leather is peeling, but what is—was a *coup* stick?" Norman asked.

"In the days when the old ones roamed all of the plains," the old man swept his hand in a circle, "a courageous act of valor[13] was thought to be more important than killing an enemy. When a warrior rode or ran up to his enemy, close enough to touch the man with a stick, without killing or being killed, the action was called *coup*.

"The French, the first white men in this part of the land, named the brave deed *coup*. In their language the word meant 'hit' or

---

11. *tehinda* (tā hin′ dā).

12 *coup* (kü).

13. valor (val′ər), *n.* bravery; courage.

Pueblo Boy was painted in 1920 by Gerald Cassidy. How does this boy's expression reinforce the struggle of the climb?

'strike.' The special stick which was used to strike with came to be known as a *coup* stick.

"Some sticks were long like this one," Matt Two Bull held the stick upright. "Some were straight, and others had a curve on the end like the sheep herder's crook," he pointed to the curving end of the stick.

"The sticks were decorated with fur or painted leather strips. A warrior kept count of his *coups* by tying an eagle feather to the crook for each brave deed. See," he pointed to the staff end, "here is a remnant of a tie thong which must have once held a feather."

The old man and boy closely examined the *coup* stick. Matt Two Bull traced with his finger the faint zig zag design painted on the stick. "See," he said, "it is the thunderbolt."

"What does that mean?" Norman asked.

"The Thunders favored a certain few of the young men who sought their vision on the butte. The thunderbolt may have been part of a sacred dream sent as a token of the Thunders' favor. If this was so, the young man could use the thunderbolt symbol on his possessions."

"How do you suppose the stick came to be on the butte?" Norman asked.

His grandfather shook his head. "No one can say. Usually such a thing was buried with a dead warrior as were his weapons and other prized belongings."

"Is the *coup* stick what you dreamed about, Grandpa?"

"No. In my dream I only knew that you were to find a *Wakan*,[14] a holy thing. But I did not know what it would be."

Norman laughed nervously. "What do you mean, *Wakan?* Is this stick haunted?"

Matt Two Bull smiled. "No, not like you mean in a fearful way. But in a sacred manner because it once had great meaning to the old ones."

"But why should I have been the one to find it?" Norman questioned.

His grandfather shrugged. "Perhaps to help you understand the ways—the values of the old ones."

"But nobody believes in that kind of thing anymore," Norman scoffed. "And even if people did, I couldn't run out and hit my enemy with the stick and get away with it." He smiled thinking of Mr. Brannon. "No one would think I was brave. I'd probably just get thrown in jail."

Suddenly Norman felt compelled to stop talking. In the distance he heard a gentle rumble which seemed to come from the butte. He glanced up at the hill looming high above and saw that it was capped with dark, low-hanging clouds.

Matt Two Bull looked too and smiled. "The Thunders are displeased with your

---

14. *Wakan* (wä´ kän).

▲ What does the number of feathers tell you about the owner of this coup stick?

"No," murmured Matt Two Bull, "no rain will come. It is just the Thunders speaking." There was another spark of lightning and an explosive reverberation sounded as if in agreement with the old man.

Norman jumped to his feet. "Well, I'm going home. Mom will be worried because I'm late now." He turned to leave.

"Wait!" Matt Two Bull commanded. "Take the *coup* stick with you."

Norman backed away. "No, I don't want it. You can have it."

The old man rose swiftly despite the stiffness of his years and sternly held out the stick to the boy. "You found it. It belongs to you. Take it!"

Norman slowly reached out his hands and took the stick.

"Even if you think the old ways are only superstition and the stick no longer has meaning, it is all that remains of an old life and must be treated with respect." Matt Two Bull smiled at the boy. "Take it," he repeated gently, "and hang it in the house where it will not be handled."

Norman hurried home as fast as he could carrying the long stick in one hand and the willow cane in the other. He felt vaguely uneasy and somehow a little frightened. It was only when he reached the security of his home that he realized the thunder had stopped and there had been no storm.

"Mom," he called as he went into the house. "I'm home."

His mother was standing at the stove. "Oh, Norman," she greeted him smiling. "I'm glad you're back. I was beginning to worry." Her welcoming smile turned to a frown as she saw the *coup* stick in Norman's hand. "What is that?"

"Grandpa says it's a *coup* stick. Here," Norman handed it to her "take a look at it. It's interesting the way it is made and decor—"

"No," Sarah interrupted and backed away

thoughts," he said to Norman. "Listen to their message."

A sharp streak of lightning split the clouds and the thunder cracked and echoed over the plains.

Norman was frightened but he answered with bravado. "The message I get is that a storm is coming," but his voice betrayed him by quavering. "Maybe you'd better come home with me, Grandpa. Your tent will get soaked through if it rains hard."

from him. "I won't touch that heathen thing no matter what it is! Get it out of the house!"

"What?" Norman asked, surprised and puzzled. "There is nothing wrong with it. It's just an old stick I found up on the butte."

"I don't care," Sarah insisted. "I won't have such a thing in the house!"

"But, Mom," Norman protested, "it's not like we believe in those old ways the way Grandpa does."

But Sarah was adamant. "Take it out of the house!" she ordered, pointing to the door. "We'll talk about it when your dad gets home."

Reluctantly Norman took the *coup* stick outside and gently propped it against the house and sat on the steps to wait for his father. He was confused. First by his grandfather's reverent treatment of the *coup* stick as if it were a sacred object and then by Sarah's rejection of it as a heathen symbol.

He looked at the stick where it leaned against the wall and shook his head. So much fuss over a brittle, rotten length of wood. Even though he had gone through a lot of hard, even dangerous, effort to get it he was now tempted to heave it out on the trash pile.

Norman wearily leaned his head against the house. He suddenly felt tired and his knee ached. As he sat wearily rubbing the bruise John Two Bull rode the old mare into the yard. Norman got up and walked back to the shed to help unsaddle the horse.

John climbed stiffly out of the saddle. His faded blue work shirt and jeans were stained with perspiration and dirt. His boots were worn and scuffed.

"Hard day, Dad?" Norman asked.

"Yeah," John answered, slipping the bridle over the mare's head. "Rustlers got away with twenty steers last night. I spent the day counting head and mending fences. Whoever the thief was cut the fence, drove a truck right onto the range and loaded the cattle without being seen." He began rubbing the mare down as she munched the hay in her manger.

"How did your day on the butte go?" John asked.

"Rough." Norman answered. "I'm beat too. The climb up the butte was tough and coming down was bad too." He told his father all that had happened on the butte, winding up with the climax of his falling and finding the old *coup* stick.

John listened attentively and did not interrupt until Norman told of Matt Two Bull's reaction to the stick. "I think Grandpa's mind has gotten weak," Norman said. "He really believes that the *coup* stick has some sort of mysterious power and that the Thunders were talking."

"Don't make fun of your grandfather," John reprimanded, "or of the old ways he believes in."

"I won't touch that heathen thing no matter what it is! Get it out of the house!"

"Okay, okay," Norman said quickly, not wanting another scolding. "But Mom is just the opposite from Grandpa," he went on. "She doesn't want the *coup* stick in the house. Says it's heathen."

He walked to the house and handed the stick to his father. John examined it and then carried it into the house.

"John!" Sarah exclaimed as she saw her husband bring the stick into the room. "I told Norman, and I tell you, that I won't have that heathenish thing in the house!"

But John ignored her and propped the stick against the door while he pulled his tool box out from under the washstand to look for a hammer and nails.

"John," Sarah persisted, "did you hear me?"

"I heard," John answered quietly, but Norman knew his father was angry. "And I don't want to hear anymore."

Norman was surprised to hear his father speak in such a fashion. John was slow to anger, usually spoke quietly and tried to avoid conflict of any kind, but now he went on.

"This," he said holding the *coup* stick upright, "is a relic of our people's past glory when it was a good thing to be an Indian. It is a symbol of something that shall never be again."

Sarah gasped and stepped in front of her husband as he started to climb a chair to pound the nails in the wall above the window. "But that's what I mean," she said. "Those old ways were just superstition. They don't mean anything now—they can't because such a way of life can't be anymore. We don't need to have those old symbols of heathen ways hanging in the house!" She grabbed at the *coup* stick, but John jerked it out of her reach.

"Don't touch it!" he shouted and Sarah fell back against the table in shocked surprise. Norman took a step forward as if to protect his mother. The boy had never seen his father so angry.

John shook his head as if to clear it. "Sarah. I'm sorry. I didn't mean to yell. It's just that the old ones would not permit a woman to touch such a thing as this." He handed Norman the stick to hold while he hammered the nails in the wall. Then he hung the stick above the window.

"Sarah," he said as he put the tools away, "think of the stick as an object that could be in a museum, a part of history. It's not like we were going to fall down on our knees and pray to it." His voice was light and teasing as he tried to make peace.

But Sarah stood stiffly at the stove preparing supper and would not answer. Norman felt sick. His appetite was gone. When his mother set a plate of food before him he excused himself saying, "I guess I'm too tired to eat," and went to his room.

But after he had undressed and crawled into bed he couldn't sleep. His mind whirled with the angry words his parents had spoken. They had never argued in such a way before. "I wish I had never brought that old stick home," he whispered and then pulled the pillow over his head to shut out the sound of the low rumble of thunder that came from the west.

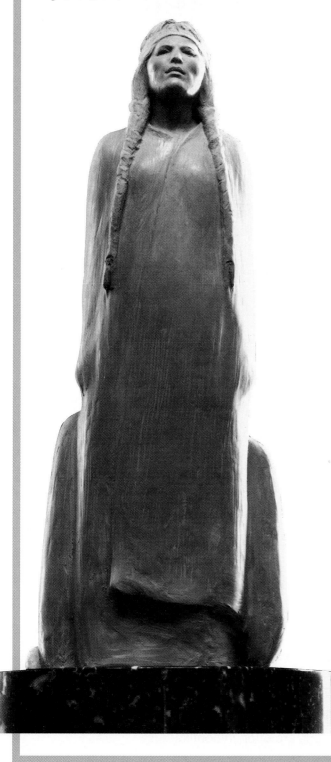

Gifts

Michelle Whatoname

My grandma gave
me her little
dress that she used

5 to wear when she was
little. My grandpa
gave me the part

of land that he
owned. My father
gave me his best horse

10 before he passed away.
Now I still have the
horse. Whenever I feed

or ride the horse, I think
of my father. When I
15 wear the dress my grandma

gave to me I think of
her. My grandpa gave me
part of his land. I always

clean and plant on it.
20 These things were blessed first.

◄ *Earth Song* was cast in bronze by Edward J.
Fraughton in 1993. How does this sculpture
reflect the poet's feelings about keeping
traditions?

After Reading

Making Connections

1. If you could talk to Norman at the end of the story, what would you say to him?

2. Of all the characters in this story, whose views of traditions are closest to your own? Explain.

3. What do you think was the **author's purpose** in ending the story with the rumble of thunder?

4. What evidence does the author provide that tells you Norman's family is keeping some traditional Native American ways of life and changing or dropping others? Refer to the chart that you made while you were reading the story.

5. If the choice were yours, what would you do with the coup stick?

6. The author of the poem "Gifts" is also a Native American. What kind of advice do you think she would give Norman?

7. ☙ Do you think different **groups** in the United States should keep their own tradition and ways of communicating or should they adopt American ways? Explain.

Literary Focus: Theme

Did you find yourself wondering why Norman had to climb the butte and why the discovery of a coup stick was so important? Then you were thinking about the theme of the story. The **theme** is the meaning behind the things that happen in a selection. You usually won't find a sentence that actually states the theme. You have to discover what it is from the events in the story. A story can even have several themes. A theme can be a comment on life—a description of how people act and the effect of their actions on themselves and others.

   Read the statements below. Choose the one that best tells the theme of the story. You may want to write your own statement. Use specific events from the story to support the theme you choose.

1. Traditions are important because they help to establish who you are.

2. Traditions are not important in the modern world.

3. Old and new traditions are often in conflict.

Vocabulary Study

Read the following pieces of advice that Norman gives about climbing the butte. For each piece of advice, write the missing vocabulary word on a sheet of paper.

ascent
impact
obliterate
protrude
valor

1. The ___ to the top of Thunder Butte will not be easy! Be careful.

2. Place your walking stick softly. The ____ of the stick against the ground could cause a rock slide.

3. Watch for objects that ____ from the ground. A piece of wood poking out of some shale turned out to be a coup stick.

4. When you come down the butte, you may not have any trail to follow. As rocks tumble down the butte, they ____ most of the old paths.

5. After I climbed the butte, I thought about the ____ of the ancient warriors. I realized that it was bravery that motivated me to climb the butte.

Expressing Your Ideas

Writing Choices

A Hard Day's Night Pretend you are Norman. Instead of going to bed after excusing yourself from supper, imagine you stay up for a little while. Write an entry in your **journal** telling about your day. Describe your hike to the butte and back, the coup stick, and the feelings you have about the different things that happened.

More on the Coup Stick Do library research to find out more about the coup stick. You may want to use online resources. What groups of Native Americans made coup sticks? How and when did a warrior receive his coup stick? How long were they? What did they look like? What different symbols were carved or painted on the side? Where can you find them today? Organize your information and write an illustrated **report** to share what you learned.

Other Options

View of the Butte Make a **diorama** to show a butte and the land surrounding it. You can use information from reference books, pictures from travel magazines, and descriptions from "Thunder Butte" to help you envision what a butte looks like. Explain the different elements in your diorama to your classmates.

Objects Can Speak Imagine you are a grandparent. Choose an object from your childhood that represents something important about your life. Bring your object to school and give a show-and-tell **presentation** about your object, its importance, and why and how you hope to share it with grandchildren someday. You can also bring an object that has stayed in your family as a reminder of the past.

Before Reading

A Christmas Carol

by Charles Dickens, dramatized by Frederick Gaines

Charles Dickens
1812–1870

Charles Dickens was a person of outstanding talents. Many enjoyed his amateur performances on the stage. When he was twenty-four, he turned to writing. Almost overnight, Dickens became the most popular author of his time and is still considered by many to be one of the greatest writers of all time.

His stories appeared in installments in monthly magazines. They were also adapted and performed as plays. Dickens toured Great Britain and America to read his works aloud. His readings were so vivid and inspiring that fellow British author Thomas Carlyle considered Dickens more than a great actor. "Why, the man's a whole theater," Carlyle is said to have exclaimed.

Building Background

Dickens's London In many ways, Christmas Eve in nineteenth-century London was similar to Christmas Eve in America today. Yet there were some striking differences. There were no cars in London in the mid-1800s; people relied on horse-drawn carriages. Once the sun went down, gaslights burned along the streets, and people carried candles in lanterns. As you read, look closely for other details that help you picture what life was like.

Getting into the Play

Writer's Notebook Most Americans, whether they celebrate Christmas or not, are aware of the holiday and its traditions. How do you feel as the Christmas season approaches? What kinds of traditions related to the holiday do you look forward to? What kinds of traditions do you wish you could avoid? Write your thoughts in your notebook.

Reading Tip

Reading a Play Charles Dickens published *A Christmas Carol* as a novel in 1843. He often read it in public performances that were very popular. It's not surprising that the story has since been adapted as a play.

Reading a play differs from reading other works of fiction. Most plays start with a list of characters. The body of the play consists mainly of dialogue, but the dialogue isn't marked by quotation marks and the words *she said* or *he said*. Instead, the character speaking is listed at the beginning of the line and the words spoken follow immediately. Descriptions are given as stage directions, which are printed in *italics*.

A CHRISTMAS CAROL

FREDERICK GAINES
ADAPTED FROM
CHARLES DICKENS'S NOVEL

CHARACTERS

CAROLERS, FAMILIES, DANCERS

FIRST BOY

SECOND BOY

THIRD BOY

LITTLE GIRL *with a doll*

EBENEZER[1] SCROOGE

FRED, *Scrooge's nephew*

BOB CRATCHIT, *Scrooge's clerk*

GENTLEMAN VISITOR

WARDER AND RESIDENTS OF THE POORHOUSE

SPARSIT, *Scrooge's servant*

COOK

CHARWOMAN

JACOB MARLEY

LEPER

FIRST SPIRIT (*the Spirit of Christmas Past*)

JACK WALTON

BEN BENJAMIN

CHILD SCROOGE

FAN, *Scrooge's sister*

FEZZIWIG

DICK WILKINS

YOUNG EBENEZER

SWEETHEART OF YOUNG EBENEZER

SECOND SPIRIT (*the Spirit of Christmas Present*)

MRS. CRATCHIT

SEVERAL CRATCHIT CHILDREN

TINY TIM

HUNGER AND IGNORANCE, *the beggar children*

PETER

THIRD SPIRIT (*the Spirit of Christmas Yet to Come*)

BUTCHER

COACHMAN

PROLOGUE

The play begins amid a swirl of street life in Victorian London. Happy groups pass; brightly costumed CAROLERS *and* FAMILIES *call out to one another and sing. Three* BOYS *and a* GIRL *are grouped about a glowing mound of coal. As the* CAROLERS *leave the stage, the lights dim and the focus shifts to the mound of coals, bright against the dark. Slowly, the children begin to respond to the warmth. A piano plays softly as the children talk.*

---

1. **Ebenezer** (əb′ə nē′ zər).

◄ What can you tell about Scrooge's personality from this photograph?

SECOND BOY. We're going up onto the roof. *(The boys look at him quizzically.)* My father has a glass. Telescope. A brass one. It opens up and it has twists on it and an eye-piece that you put up to look through. We can see all the way to the park with it.

THIRD BOY. Could I look through it?

SECOND BOY. Maybe . . . where would you look? *(The* THIRD BOY *points straight up.)* Why there?

THIRD BOY. I'd like to see the moon. *(The* BOYS *stand and look upward as the* GIRL *sings to her doll. One of the* BOYS *makes a snow angel on the ground. As snow starts to fall, he stands up and reaches out to catch a single flake.)*

SCENE ONE
Scrooge in His Shop

The percussion thunders. SCROOGE *hurls himself through the descending snowflakes and sends the children scattering. They retreat, watching.* CRATCHIT *comes in. He takes some coal from the mound and puts it into a small bucket; as he carries it to a corner of the stage, the stage area is transformed from street to office.* SCROOGE's *nephew* FRED *enters, talks with the children, gives them coins, and sends them away with a "Merry Christmas."*

FRED. A Merry Christmas, Uncle! God save you!

SCROOGE. Bah! Humbug!²

FRED. Christmas a humbug, Uncle? I hope that's meant as a joke.

SCROOGE. Well, it's not. Come, come, what is it

FIRST BOY. I saw a horse in a window. *(Pause)* A dapple . . . gray and white. And a saddle, too . . . red. And a strawberry mane down to here. All new. Golden stirrups. *(People pass by the children, muttering greetings to one another.)*

SECOND BOY. Christmas Eve.

THIRD BOY. Wish we could go.

FIRST BOY. So do I.

THIRD BOY. I think I'd like it.

FIRST BOY. Oh, wouldn't I . . . wouldn't I!

---

2. **Humbug** (hum′bug′), *n.* word used to indicate disbelief or disgust.

you want? Don't waste all the day, Nephew.

FRED. I want only to wish you a Merry Christmas, Uncle. Don't be cross.

SCROOGE. What else can I be when I live in such a world of fools as this? Merry Christmas! Out with Merry Christmas! What's Christmas to you but a time for finding yourself a year older and not an hour richer? If I could work my will, every idiot who goes about with "Merry Christmas" on his lips should be boiled with his own pudding[3] and buried with a stake of holly through his heart.

FRED. Uncle!

SCROOGE. Nephew, keep Christmas in your own way and let me keep it in mine.

FRED. But you don't keep it.

SCROOGE. Let me leave it alone then. Much good may it do you. Much good it has ever done you.

FRED. There are many things from which I might have derived[4] good by which I have not profited, I daresay,[5] Christmas among the rest. And though it has never put a scrap of gold in my pocket, I believe it has done me good and will do me good, and I say, God bless it!

SCROOGE. Bah!

FRED. Don't be angry, Uncle. Come! Dine with us tomorrow.

SCROOGE. I'll dine alone, thank you.

FRED. But why?

SCROOGE. Why? Why did you get married?

FRED. Why, because I fell in love with a wonderful girl.

SCROOGE. And I with solitude.[6] Good afternoon.

FRED. Nay, Uncle, but you never came to see me before I was married. Why give it as a reason for not coming now?

SCROOGE. Good afternoon.

FRED. I am sorry with all my heart to find you

so determined;[7] but I have made the attempt in homage to Christmas, and I'll keep that good spirit to the last. So, a Merry Christmas, Uncle.

SCROOGE. Good afternoon!

FRED. And a Happy New Year!

SCROOGE. Good afternoon! (FRED *hesitates as if to say something more. He sees that* SCROOGE *has gone to get a volume down from the shelf, and so he starts to leave. As he leaves, the doorbell rings.*) Bells. Is it necessary to always have bells? (*The* GENTLEMAN VISITOR *enters, causing the doorbell to ring again.*) Cratchit!

CRATCHIT. Yes, sir?

SCROOGE. The bell, fool! See to it!

CRATCHIT. Yes, sir. (*He goes to the entrance.*)

SCROOGE (*muttering*). Merry Christmas . . . Wolves howling and a Merry Christmas . . .

CRATCHIT. It's for you, sir.

SCROOGE. Of course, it's for me. You're not receiving callers, are you? Show them in.

CRATCHIT. Right this way, sir. (*The* GENTLEMAN VISITOR *approaches* SCROOGE.)

SCROOGE. Yes, yes?

GENTLEMAN VISITOR. Scrooge and Marley's, I believe. Have I the pleasure of addressing Mr. Scrooge or Mr. Marley?

SCROOGE. Marley's dead. Seven years tonight. What is it you want?

GENTLEMAN VISITOR. I have no doubt that his liberality is well represented by his surviving partner. Here, sir, my card. (*He hands* SCROOGE *his business card.*)

SCROOGE. Liberality? No doubt of it? All right,

---

3. **boiled with his own pudding**, puddings are traditional English desserts very similar to fruit cakes; they are poured into a dish which is placed in a pot of boiling water and steamed.

4. **derive** (di rīv′), *v.* get from a source or origin; receive.

5. **daresay** (der′sā′), *v.* believe.

6. **solitude** (sol′ə tüd), *n.* the state of being alone.

7. **determined** (di tèr′mənd), *adj.* firm.

◄ Do you think Bob Cratchit is too willing to obey Scrooge's orders?

all right, I can read. What is it you want? (*He returns to his work.*)

GENTLEMAN VISITOR. At this festive season of the year . . .

SCROOGE. It's winter and cold. (*He continues his work and ignores the* GENTLEMAN VISITOR.)

GENTLEMAN VISITOR. Yes . . . yes, it is, and the more reason for my visit. At this time of the year it is more than usually desirable to make some slight provision for the poor and destitute who suffer greatly from the cold. Many thousands are in want of common necessaries; hundreds of thousands are in want of common comforts, sir.

SCROOGE. Are there no prisons?[8]

GENTLEMAN VISITOR. Many, sir.

SCROOGE. And the workhouse?[9] Is it still in operation?

GENTLEMAN VISITOR. It is; still, I wish I could say it was not.

SCROOGE. The poor law[10] is still in full vigor then?

GENTLEMAN VISITOR. Yes, sir.

SCROOGE. I'm glad to hear it. From what you said, I was afraid someone had stopped its operation.

GENTLEMAN VISITOR. Under the impression that they scarcely furnish cheer of mind or body to the multitude, a few of us are endeavoring to raise a fund to buy the poor some meat and drink and means of warmth. We choose this time because it is the time, of all others, when want is keenly felt and abundance[11] rejoices. May I put you down for something, sir?

SCROOGE (*retreating into the darkness temporarily*). Nothing.

GENTLEMAN VISITOR. You wish to be anonymous?[12]

SCROOGE. I wish to be left alone. Since you ask me what I wish, sir, that is my answer. I don't make merry myself at Christmas and I can't afford to make idle people merry. I help support the establishments I have mentioned . . . they cost enough . . . and those who are poorly off must go there.

GENTLEMAN VISITOR. Many can't go there, and many would rather die.

SCROOGE. If they would rather die, they had better do it and decrease the surplus population. That is not my affair. My business is. It occupies me constantly. (*He talks both to the* GENTLEMAN VISITOR *and to himself while he thumbs through his books.*) Ask a man to

---

8. **prison** (priz′n), *n.* in Great Britain in the mid-1800s, people who could not pay their debts went to debtor's prison.
9. **workhouse** (wėrk′hous′), *n.* from the 1600s through the 1800s in Great Britain, a house where very poor people were lodged and given work.
10. **poor law,** The Poor Law of 1834 provided ways to help the needy in workhouses.
11. **abundance** (ə bun′dəns), *n.* great plenty.
12. **anonymous** (ə non′ə məs), *adj.* unnamed; from a person whose name is not given.

give up life and means . . . fine thing. What is it, I want to know? Charity? *(His nose deep in his books, he vaguely hears the dinner bell being rung in the workhouse; he looks up as if he has heard it but never focuses on the actual scene. The* WARDER *of the poorhouse stands in a pool of light at the far left, slowly ringing a bell.)*

WARDER. Dinner. All right. Line up. *(The poorly clad, dirty* RESIDENTS *of the poorhouse line up and file by to get their evening dish of gruel, wordlessly accepting it and going back to eat listlessly in the gloom.* SCROOGE *returns to the business of his office. The procession continues for a moment, then the image of the poorhouse is obscured by darkness. The* <u>dejected</u>¹³ GENTLEMAN VISITOR *exits.)*

SCROOGE. Latch the door, Cratchit. Firmly, firmly. Draft as cold as Christmas blowing in here. Charity! (CRATCHIT *goes to the door, starts to close it, then sees the little* GIRL *with the doll. She seems to beckon to him; he moves slowly toward her, and they dance together for a moment.* SCROOGE *continues to work. Suddenly* CAROLERS *appear on the platform, and a few phrases of their carol are heard.* SCROOGE *looks up.)* Cratchit! *(As soon as* SCROOGE *shouts, the* GIRL *and the* CAROLERS *vanish and* CRATCHIT *begins to close up the shop.)* Cratchit!

CRATCHIT. Yes, sir.

SCROOGE. Well, to work then!

CRATCHIT. It's evening, sir.

SCROOGE. Is it?

CRATCHIT. Christmas evening, sir.

SCROOGE. Oh, you'll want all day tomorrow off, I suppose.

CRATCHIT. If it's quite convenient, sir.

SCROOGE. It's not convenient, and it's not fair. If I was to deduct half a crown¹⁴ from your salary for it, you'd think yourself ill-used, wouldn't you? Still you expect me to pay a day's wage for a day of no work.

CRATCHIT. It's only once a year, sir.

SCROOGE. Be here all the earlier the next morning.

CRATCHIT. I will, sir.

SCROOGE. Then off, off.

CRATCHIT. Yes, sir! Merry Christmas, sir!

SCROOGE. Bah! *(As soon as* CRATCHIT *opens the door, the sounds of the street begin, very bright and loud.* CRATCHIT *is caught up in a swell of people hurrying through the street. Children pull him along to the top of an ice slide, and he runs and slides down it, disappearing in darkness as the stage suddenly is left almost empty.* SCROOGE *goes around the room blowing out the candles, talking to himself.)* Christmas Eve. Carolers! Bah! There. Another day. *(He opens his door and peers out.)* Black, very black. Now where are they? *(The children are heard singing carols for a moment.)* Begging pennies for their songs, are they? Oh, boy! Here, boy! *(The little* GIRL *emerges from the shadows.* SCROOGE *hands her a dark lantern and she holds it while he lights it with an ember from the pile of coals.)*

Making Connections

1. Do you think all the characters that appear in this scene are supposed to be part of the real world that Scrooge lives in? Explain your answer.

2. If you could pick one word to describe Scrooge's character, what word would you choose? Give reasons for your choice.

3. How do the **mood**, **setting**, and **action** of the Prologue differ from the mood, setting, and action at the beginning of Scene One?

4. Think about the value systems represented by Scrooge and Fred. Which of these set of values is closest to yours?

---

13. dejected (di jek′tid), *adj.* in low spirits; discouraged.
14. **half a crown**, a coin equal to 1/8th of a British pound.

SCENE TWO
Scrooge Goes Home

SCROOGE (*talking to the little* GIRL). Hold it quiet! There. Off now. That's it. High. Black as pitch. Light the street, that's it. You're a bright lad! Good to see that. Earn your supper, boy. You'll not go hungry this night. Home. You know the way, do you? Yes, that's the way. The house of Ebenezer Scrooge. (*As the two find their way to* SCROOGE'*s house, the audience sees and hears a brief image of a cathedral interior and a large choir singing; the image ends in a blackout. The lights come up immediately, and* SCROOGE *is at his door.*) Hold the light up, boy, up. (*The* GIRL *with the lantern disappears.*) Where did he go? Boy? No matter. There's a penny saved. Lantern's gone out. No matter. A candle saved. Yes, here's the key. (*He turns with the key toward the door, and* MARLEY'*s face swims out of the darkness.* SCROOGE *watches, unable to speak. He fumbles for a match, lights the lantern, and swings it toward the figure, which melts away. Pause.* SCROOGE *fits the key in the lock and turns it as the door suddenly is opened from the inside by the porter,* SPARSIT. SCROOGE *is startled, then recovers.*) Sparsit?

SPARSIT. Yes, sir?

SCROOGE. Hurry, hurry. The door . . . close it.

SPARSIT. Did you knock, sir?

SCROOGE. Knock? What matter? Here, light me up the stairs.

SPARSIT. Yes, sir. (*He leads* SCROOGE *up the stairs. They pass the* COOK *on the way.* SCROOGE *brushes by her, stops, looks back, and she leans towards him.*)

COOK Something to warm you, sir? Porridge?

SCROOGE. Wha . . . ? No. No, nothing.

COOK (*waiting for her Christmas coin*). Merry Christmas, sir. (SCROOGE *ignores the request and the* COOK *disappears. Mumbling,* SCROOGE *follows* SPARSIT.)

SCROOGE (*looking back after the* COOK *is gone*): Fright a man nearly out of his life . . .

Merry Christmas . . . bah!

SPARSIT. Your room, sir.

SCROOGE. Hmmm? Oh, yes, yes. And good night.

SPARSIT (*extending his hand for his coin*). Merry Christmas, sir.

SCROOGE. Yes, yes . . . (*He sees the outstretched hand; he knows what* SPARSIT *wants and is infuriated.*[15]) Out! Out! (*He closes the door after* SPARSIT, *turns toward his chamber, and discovers the* CHARWOMAN *directly behind him.*)

CHARWOMAN. Warm your bed for you, sir?

SCROOGE. What? Out! Out!

CHARWOMAN. Aye, sir. (*She starts for the door.* MARLEY'*s voice is heard mumbling something unintelligible.*)

SCROOGE. What's that?

CHARWOMAN. Me, sir? Not a thing, sir.

SCROOGE. Then, good night.

CHARWOMAN. Good night. (*She exits and* SCROOGE *pantomimes shutting the door behind her. The voice of* MARLEY *over an offstage microphone whispers and reverberates: "Merry Christmas, Scrooge!" Silence.* SCROOGE *hears the voice but cannot account for it. He climbs up to open a window and looks down. A cathedral choir is heard in the distance.* SCROOGE *listens a moment, shuts the window, and prepares for bed. As he pulls his nightcap from a chair, a small handbell tumbles off onto the floor. Startled, he picks it up and rings it for reassurance; an echo answers it. He turns and sees the little* GIRL *on the street; she is swinging her doll, which produces the echo of his bell.* SCROOGE *escapes to his bed; the* GIRL *is swallowed up in the darkness. The bell sounds grow to a din, incoherent as in a dream, then suddenly fall silent.* SCROOGE *sits up in bed, listens, and hears the chains of* MARLEY *coming up the stairs.* SCROOGE *reaches for the bellpull to summon* SPARSIT. *The bell responds with a gong, and*

---

15. **infuriated** (in fyúr′ē ā tid), *adj.* filled with wild rage; furious; enraged.

How does the lighting of the stage add to the mood of this scene?

MARLEY *appears. He and* SCROOGE *face one another.)*

SCROOGE. What do you want with me?

MARLEY *(in a ghostly, unreal voice).* Much.

SCROOGE. Who are you?

MARLEY. Ask who I was.

SCROOGE. Who were you?

MARLEY. In life, I was your partner, Jacob Marley.

SCROOGE. He's dead.

MARLEY. Seven years this night, Ebenezer Scrooge.

SCROOGE. Why do you come here?

MARLEY. I must. It is commanded me. I must wander the world and see what I can no longer share, what I would not share when I walked where you do.

SCROOGE. And must go thus?

MARLEY. The chains? Look at it, Ebenezer, study it. Locks and vaults and golden coins. I forged it, each link, each day when I sat in these chairs, commanded these rooms. Greed, Ebenezer Scrooge, wealth. Feel them, know them. Yours was as heavy as this I wear seven years ago and you have labored to build it since.

SCROOGE. If you're here to lecture, I have no time for it. It is late, the night is cold. I want comfort now.

MARLEY. I have none to give. I know not how you see me this night. I did not ask it. I

A Christmas Carol—Scene Two   **241**

have sat invisible beside you many and many a day. I am commanded to bring you a chance, Ebenezer. Heed it!

SCROOGE. Quickly then, quickly.

MARLEY. You will be haunted by three spirits.

SCROOGE (*scoffing*). Is that the chance?

MARLEY. Mark it.

SCROOGE. I do not choose to.

MARLEY (*ominously*). Then you will walk where I do, burdened by your riches, your greed.

SCROOGE. Spirits mean nothing to me.

MARLEY (*slowly leaving*). Expect the first tomorrow, when the bell tolls one, the second on the next night at the same hour, the third upon the next night when the last stroke of twelve has ended. Look to see me no more. I must wander. Look that, for your own sake, you remember what has passed between us.

SCROOGE. Jacob . . . Don't leave me! . . . Jacob! Jacob!

MARLEY. Adieu,[16] Ebenezer (*At* MARLEY'*s last words a funeral procession begins to move across the stage.* SCROOGE *calls out, "Jacob, don't leave me!" as if talking in the midst of a bad dream. At the end of the procession is the little* GIRL *swinging her doll and singing softly.*)

GIRL. Hushabye, don't you cry,
Go to sleep, little baby.
When you wake, you shall have
All the pretty little horses,
Blacks and bays, dapples and grays,
All the pretty little horses.

(*She stops singing and looks up at* SCROOGE; *their eyes meet and she solemnly rings the doll in greeting.* SCROOGE *pulls shut the bed curtains and the* GIRL *exits. The bell sounds are picked up by the bells of a* LEPER *who enters, dragging himself along.*)

LEPER (*calling out*). Leper! Leper! Stay the way! Leper! Leper! Keep away! (*He exits and the clock begins to chime, ringing the hours.* SCROOGE *sits up in bed and begins to count the chimes.*)

SCROOGE. Eight . . . nine . . . ten . . . eleven . . . it can't be . . . twelve. Midnight? No. Not twelve. It can't be. I haven't slept the whole day through. Twelve? Yes, yes, twelve noon (*He hurries to the window and looks out.*) Black. Twelve midnight (*Pause*) I must get up. A day wasted. I must get down to the office (*Two small chimes are heard.*) Quarter past. But it just rang twelve. Fifteen minutes haven't gone past, not so quickly (*Again two small chimes are heard.*) A quarter to one. The spirit . . . It's to come at one (*He hurries to his bed as the chimes ring again.*) One.

Making Connections

1. What do you think will happen in Scene Three?

2. Has your opinion of Scrooge changed in any way between Scene One and Scene Two? Explain.

3. If you were working for Scrooge, what would you do if he refused to give you a Christmas bonus?

4. Do you think the ghost's prediction for Scrooge's future is reasonable? Explain your answer.

---

16. **adieu** (ə dü′), *n.* French word meaning "good-by."

SCENE THREE

The Spirit of Christmas Past

The hour is struck again by a large street clock and the FIRST SPIRIT *appears. It is a figure dressed to look like the little* GIRL*'s doll.*

SCROOGE. Are you the spirit whose coming was foretold to me?

FIRST SPIRIT. I am.

SCROOGE. Who and what are you?

FIRST SPIRIT. I am the Ghost of Christmas Past.

SCROOGE. Long past?

FIRST SPIRIT. Your past.

SCROOGE. Why are you here?

FIRST SPIRIT. Your welfare. Rise. Walk with me.

SCROOGE. I am mortal still. I cannot pass through air.

FIRST SPIRIT. My hand (SCROOGE *grasps the* SPIRIT*'s hand tightly, and the doll's bell rings softly.* SCROOGE *remembers a scene from his past in which two boys greet each other in the street.*)

FIRST VOICE. Halloo, Jack!

SECOND VOICE. Ben! Merry Christmas, Ben!

SCROOGE. Jack Walton. Young Jack Walton. Spirits . . . ?

FIRST VOICE. Have a good holiday, Jack.

SCROOGE. Yes, yes, I remember him. Both of them. Little Ben Benjamin. He used to . . .

FIRST VOICE. See you next term, Jack. Next . . . term . . .

SCROOGE. They . . . they're off for the holidays and going home from school. It's Christmas time . . . all of the children off home now . . . No . . . no, not all . . . there was one . . (*The* SPIRIT *motions for* SCROOGE *to turn, and he sees a young boy playing with a teddy bear and talking to it.*) Yes . . . reading . . . poor boy.

FIRST SPIRIT. What, I wonder?

SCROOGE. Reading? Oh, it was nothing. Fancy, all fancy and make-believe and take-me-away. All of it. Yes, nonsense.

CHILD SCROOGE. Ali Baba.[17]

SCROOGE. Yes . . . that was it.

CHILD SCROOGE. Yes, and remember . . . and remember . . . remember Robinson Crusoe?[18]

SCROOGE. And the parrot!

CHILD SCROOGE. Yes, the parrot! I love him best.

SCROOGE (*imitating the parrot*). With his stripey green body and yellow tail drooping along and couldn't sing—awk—but could talk, and a thing like a lettuce growing out the top of his head . . . and he used to sit on the very top of the tree—up there.

CHILD SCROOGE. And Robinson Crusoe sailed around the island and he thought he had escaped the island and the parrot said, the parrot said . . .

SCROOGE (*imitating the parrot*). Robinson Crusoe, where you been? Awk! Robinson Crusoe, where you been?

CHILD SCROOGE. And Robinson Crusoe looked up in the tree and saw the parrot and knew he hadn't escaped and he was still there, still all alone there.

SCROOGE. Poor Robinson Crusoe.

CHILD SCROOGE (*sadly replacing the teddy bear*). Poor Robinson Crusoe.

SCROOGE. Poor child. Poor child.

FIRST SPIRIT. Why poor?

SCROOGE. Fancy . . . fancy . . (*He tries to mask his feelings by being brusque.*) It's his way, a child's way to . . . to lose being alone in . . . in dreams, dreams . . . Never matter if they are all nonsense, yes, nonsense. But he'll be all right, grow out of it. Yes. Yes, he did outgrow it, the nonsense. Became a man and left there and he became, yes, he became a man and . . . yes, success-ful . . . rich! (*The sadness returns.*) Never

---

17. **Ali Baba** (ä′lē bä′bə), a character in the book *The Arabian Nights*
18. **Robinson Crusoe**, a sailor shipwrecked on a desert island.

matter . . . never matter (FAN *runs in and goes to* CHILD SCROOGE.)

FAN. Brother, dear brother (*She kisses* CHILD SCROOGE.)

CHILD SCROOGE. Dear, dear Fan.

FAN. I've come to bring you home, home for good and ever. Come with me, come now (*She takes his hand and they start to run off, but the* SPIRIT *stops them and signals for the light on them to fade. They look at the* SPIRIT, *aware of their role in the* SPIRIT's *"education" of* SCROOGE.)

SCROOGE. Let me watch them go? Let them be happy for a moment! (*The* SPIRIT *says nothing.* SCROOGE *turns away from them and the light goes out.*) A delicate, delicate child. A breath might have withered her.

FIRST SPIRIT. She died a woman and had, as I remember, children.

SCROOGE. One child.

FIRST SPIRIT. Your nephew.

SCROOGE. Yes, yes, Fred, my nephew (SCROOGE *pauses, then tries to bluster through.*) Well? Well, all of us have that, haven't we? Childhoods? Sadnesses? But we grow and we become men, masters of ourselves (*The* SPIRIT *gestures for music to begin. It is heard first as from a great distance, then* SCROOGE *becomes aware of it.*) I've no time for it, Spirit. Music and all of your Christmas falderal. Yes, yes, I've learnt what you have to show me (FEZZIWIG, YOUNG EBENEZER, *and* DICK *appear, busily preparing for the party.*)

FEZZIWIG. Yo ho, there! Ebenezer! Dick!

SCROOGE. Fezziwig! It's old Fezziwig that I 'prenticed[19] under.

FIRST SPIRIT. Your master?

SCROOGE. Oh, aye, and the best that any boy could have. There's Dick Wilkins! Bless me. He was very much attached to me was Dick. Poor Dick. Dear, dear.

FEZZIWIG. Yo ho, my boys! No more work tonight. Christmas Eve, Dick! Christmas, Ebenezer! Let's have the shutters up before a man can say Jack Robinson! (*The music continues. Chandeliers are pulled into position, and mistletoe, holly, and ivy are draped over everything by bustling servants.* DANCERS *fill the stage for* FEZZIWIG's *wonderful Christmas party. In the midst of the dancing and the gaiety servants pass back and forth through the crowd with huge platters of food. At a pause in the music,* YOUNG EBENEZER, *who is dancing, calls out.*)

YOUNG EBENEZER. Mr. Fezziwig, sir, you're a wonderful master!

SCROOGE and YOUNG EBENEZER. A wonderful master!

SCROOGE (*echoing the phrase*). A wonderful master! (*The music changes suddenly and the* DANCERS *jerk into distorted postures and then begin to move in slow motion. The celebrants slowly exit, performing a macabre dance to discordant sounds.*)

FIRST SPIRIT. Just because he gave a party? It was very small.

SCROOGE. Small!

FIRST SPIRIT. He spent a few pounds[20] of your "mortal" money, three, four at the most. Is that so much that he deserves this praise?

SCROOGE. But it wasn't the money. He had the power to make us happy, to make our service light or burdensome. The happiness he gives is quite as great as if it cost a fortune. That's what . . . a good master is.

FIRST SPIRIT. Yes?

SCROOGE. No, no, nothing.

FIRST SPIRIT. Something, I think.

SCROOGE. I should like to be able to say a word or two to my clerk just now, that's all.

---

19. **'prentice** (´pren´tis), *v.* shortened form of *apprentice;* learn, work for an employer for free or for low wages or room and board in return for instruction.

20. **pound** (pound), *n.* unit of money in Great Britain.

FIRST SPIRIT. But this is all past. Your clerk Cratchit couldn't be here.

SCROOGE. No, no, of course not, an idle thought. Are we done?

FIRST SPIRIT (*monitoring for the waltz music to begin*). Nearly.

SCROOGE (*hearing the waltz and remembering it*). Surely it's enough. Haven't you tormented me enough? (YOUNG EBENEZER *is seen waltzing with his* SWEETHEART.)

FIRST SPIRIT. I only show the past, what it promised you. Look. Another promise.

SCROOGE. Oh. Oh, yes. I had forgotten . . . her. Don't they dance beautifully? So young, so young. I would have married her if only . . .

SWEETHEART. Can you love me, Ebenezer? I bring no dowry to my marriage, only me, only love. It is no currency that you can buy and sell with, but we can live with it. Can you? (*She pauses, then returns the ring* SCROOGE *gave her as his pledge.*) I release you, Ebenezer, for the love of the man you once were. Will that man win me again, now that he is free?

SCROOGE (*trying to speak to her*). If only you had held me to it. You should not have let me go. I was young, I did love you.

SWEETHEART (*speaking to* YOUNG EBENEZER). We have never lied to one another. May you be happy in the life you have chosen. Good-bye (*She runs out.* YOUNG EBENEZER *slowly leaves.*)

SCROOGE. No, no, it was not meant that way . . . !

FIRST SPIRIT. You cannot change now what you would not change then. I am your mistakes, Ebenezer Scrooge, all of the things you could have done and did not.

SCROOGE. Then leave me! I have done them. I shall live with them. As I have, as I do; as I will.

FIRST SPIRIT. There is another Christmas, seven years ago, when Marley died.

SCROOGE. No! I will not see it. I will not! He died. I could not prevent it. I did not choose for him to die on Christmas Day.

FIRST SPIRIT. And when his day was chosen, what did you do then?

SCROOGE. I looked after his affairs.

FIRST SPIRIT. His business.

SCROOGE. Yes! His business! Mine! It was all that I had, all that I could do in this world. I have nothing to do with the world to come after.

FIRST SPIRIT. Then I will leave you.

SCROOGE. Not yet! Don't leave me here! Tell me what I must do! What of the other spirits?

FIRST SPIRIT. They will come.

SCROOGE. And you? What of you?

FIRST SPIRIT. I am always with you (*The little* GIRL *appears with her doll; she takes* SCROOGE's *hand and gently leads him to bed. Numbed, he follows her. She leans against the foot of the bed, ringing the doll and singing. The* FIRST SPIRIT *exits as she sings.*)

GIRL. When you wake, you shall have
All the pretty little horses,
Blacks and bays, dapples and grays,
All the pretty little horses.

(*She rings the doll and the ringing becomes the chiming of* SCROOGE's *bell. The* GIRL *exits.* SCROOGE *sits upright in bed as he hears the chimes.*)

SCROOGE. A minute until one. No one here. No one's coming (*A larger clock strikes one o'clock.*)

▲ What details in this photograph made the mood different from the one on page 241?

Making Connections

1. Review your prediction about what would happen in Scene Three. Was your prediction accurate?

2. What do you like best about this play so far? least?

3. Do you see any changes in Scrooge's character in this scene? Explain your answer.

4. What inference do you think the author wants you to make about the reason that Scrooge never married?

5. Scrooge thinks he is happier as an adult than he was as a child. Do you think people are happier when they are children or when they are adults? Explain.

SCENE FOUR
The Spirit of Christmas Present

A light comes on. SCROOGE *becomes aware of it and goes slowly to it. He sees the* SECOND SPIRIT, *the Spirit of Christmas Present, who looks like* FEZZIWIG.

SCROOGE. Fezziwig!

SECOND SPIRIT. Hello, Scrooge.

SCROOGE. But you can't be . . . not Fezziwig.

SECOND SPIRIT. Do you see me as him?

SCROOGE. I do.

SECOND SPIRIT. And hear me as him?

SCROOGE. I do.

SECOND SPIRIT. I wish I were the gentleman, so as not to disappoint you.

SCROOGE. But you're not . . . ?

SECOND SPIRIT. No, Mr. Scrooge. You have never seen the like of me before. I am the Ghost of Christmas Present.

SCROOGE. But . . .

SECOND SPIRIT. You see what you will see, Scrooge, no more. Will you walk out with me this Christmas Eve?

SCROOGE. But I am not yet dressed.

SECOND SPIRIT. Take my tails, dear boy, we're leaving.

SCROOGE. Wait!

SECOND SPIRIT. What is it now?

SCROOGE. Christmas Present, did you say?

SECOND SPIRIT. I did.

SCROOGE. Then we are traveling here? In this town? London? Just down there?

SECOND SPIRIT. Yes, yes, of course.

SCROOGE. Then we could walk? Your flying is . . . well, too sudden for an old man. Well?

SECOND SPIRIT. It's your Christmas, Scrooge; I am only the guide.

SCROOGE (*puzzled*). Then we can walk? (*The* SPIRIT *nods.*) Where are you guiding me to?

SECOND SPIRIT. Bob Cratchit's.

SCROOGE. My clerk?

SECOND SPIRIT. You did want to talk to him? (SCROOGE *pauses, uncertain how to answer.*) Don't worry, Scrooge, you won't have to.

SCROOGE (*trying to change the subject, to cover his error*). Shouldn't be much of a trip. With fifteen bob[21] a week, how far off can it be?

SECOND SPIRIT. A world away, Scrooge, at least that far (SCROOGE *and the* SPIRIT *start to step off a curb when a funeral procession enters with a child's coffin, followed by the* POORHOUSE CHILDREN, *who are singing. Seated on top of the coffin is the little* GIRL. *She and* SCROOGE *look at one another.*) That is the way to it, Scrooge (*The procession follows the coffin off-stage;* SCROOGE *and the* SPIRIT *exit after the procession. As they leave, the lights focus on* MRS. CRATCHIT *and her* CHILDREN. MRS. CRATCHIT *sings as she puts* TINY TIM *and the other* CHILDREN *to bed, all in one bed. She pulls a dark blanket over them.*)

MRS. CRATCHIT (*singing*).
When you wake, you shall have
All the pretty little horses, Blacks and bays, dapples and grays,
All the pretty little horses.
To sleep now, all of you. Christmas tomorrow
(*She kisses them and goes to* BOB CRATCHIT, *who is by the hearth.*) How did our little Tiny Tim behave?

BOB CRATCHIT. As good as gold and better.

MRS. CRATCHIT. He's a good boy (*The* SECOND SPIRIT *and* SCROOGE *enter.* MRS. CRATCHIT *feels a sudden draft.*) Oh, the wind (*She gets up to shut the door.*)

SECOND SPIRIT. Hurry (*He nudges* SCROOGE *in before* MRS. CRATCHIT *shuts the door.*)

SCROOGE. Hardly hospitable is what I'd say.

SECOND SPIRIT. Oh, they'd say a great deal more, Scrooge, if they could see you.

SCROOGE. Oh, they should, should they?

SECOND SPIRIT. Oh yes, I'd think they might.

SCROOGE. Well, I might have a word for them . . .

SECOND SPIRIT. You're here to listen.

SCROOGE. Oh. Oh yes, all right. By the fire?

SECOND SPIRIT. But not a word.

BOB CRATCHIT (*raising his glass*). My dear, to Mr. Scrooge. I give you Mr. Scrooge, the founder of the feast.

MRS. CRATCHIT. The founder of the feast indeed! I wish I had him here! I'd give him a piece of my mind to feast upon, and I hope he'd have a good appetite for it.

BOB CRATCHIT. My dear, Christmas Eve.

MRS. CRATCHIT. It should be Christmas Eve, I'm sure, when one drinks the health of such an odious, stingy, hard, unfeeling man as Mr. Scrooge. You know he is, Robert! Nobody knows it better than you

---

21. **bob** (bob), *n.* British slang for *shilling,*

do, poor dear.

BOB CRATCHIT. I only know one thing on Christmas: one must be charitable.[22]

MRS. CRATCHIT. I'll drink to his health for your sake and the day's, not for his. Long life to him! A Merry Christmas and a Happy New Year. He'll be very merry and very happy, I have no doubt.

BOB CRATCHIT. If he cannot be, we must be happy for him. A song is what is needed. Tim!

MRS. CRATCHIT. Shush! I've just gotten him down and he needs all the sleep he can get.

BOB CRATCHIT. If he's asleep on Christmas Eve, I'll be much mistaken. Tim! He must sing, dear, there is nothing else that might make him well.

TINY TIM. Yes, Father?

BOB CRATCHIT. Are you awake?

TINY TIM. Just a little.

BOB CRATCHIT. A song then! *(The* CHILDREN *awaken and, led by* TINY TIM, *sit up to sing. As they sing,* SCROOGE *speaks.)*

SCROOGE. Spirit *(He holds up his hand; all stop singing and look at him.)* I . . . I have seen enough *(When the* SPIRIT *signals to the* CHILDREN *they leave the stage, singing quietly.* TINY TIM *remains, covered completely by the dark blanket, disappearing against the black.)* Tiny Tim . . . will he live?

SECOND SPIRIT. He is very ill. Even song cannot keep him whole through a cold winter.

SCROOGE. But you haven't told me!

SECOND SPIRIT *(imitating* SCROOGE). If he be like to die, he had better do it and decrease the surplus population *(*SCROOGE *turns away.)* Erase, Scrooge, those words from your thoughts. You are not the judge. Do not judge, then. It may be that in the sight of heaven you are more worthless and less fit to live than millions like this poor man's child. To hear an insect on a leaf pronouncing that there is too much

life among his hungry brothers in the dust. Good-bye, Scrooge.

SCROOGE. But is there no happiness in Christmas Present?

SECOND SPIRIT. There is.

SCROOGE. Take me there.

SECOND SPIRIT. It is at the home of your nephew . . .

SCROOGE. No!

SECOND SPIRIT *(disgusted with* SCROOGE). Then there is none.

SCROOGE. But that isn't enough . . . You must teach me!

SECOND SPIRIT. Would you have a teacher, Scrooge? Look at your own words.

SCROOGE. But the first spirit gave me more . . . !

SECOND SPIRIT. He was Christmas Past. There was a lifetime he could choose from. I have only this day, one day, and you, Scrooge. I have nearly lived my fill of both. Christmas Present must be gone at midnight. That is near now *(He speaks to two beggar* CHILDREN *who pause shyly at the far side of the stage. The* CHILDREN *are thin and wan; they are barefoot and wear filthy rags.)* Come *(They go to him.)*

SCROOGE. Is this the last spirit who is to come to me?

SECOND SPIRIT. They are no spirits. They are real. Hunger, Ignorance. Not spirits, Scrooge, passing dreams. They are real. They walk your streets, look to you for comfort. And you deny them. Deny them not too long, Scrooge. They will grow and multiply and they will not remain children.

SCROOGE. Have they no refuge, no resource?

SECOND SPIRIT *(again imitating* SCROOGE). Are there no prisons? Are there no workhouses? *(Tenderly to the* CHILDREN) Come. It's Christmas Eve *(He leads them off-stage.)*

---

22. **charitable** (char′ə tə bəl), *adj.* kindly in judging people and their actions.

Making Connections

1. Make a list of three questions you would ask Dickens if you could.

2. Do you agree with the way the Spirit of Christmas Present judges Scrooge? Why or why not?

3. Why do you think the Spirit of Christmas Present appears to Scrooge as Fezziwig?

4. What do you think Dickens was trying to say by presenting Hunger and Ignorance as children?

5. In order for Scrooge to change his ways would he have to be part of the group celebrating Christmas?

SCENE FIVE
The Spirit of Chistmas Yet to Come

SCROOGE is entirely alone for a long moment. He is frightened by the darkness and feels it approaching him. Suddenly he stops, senses the presence of the THIRD SPIRIT, *turns toward him, and sees him. The* SPIRIT *is bent and cloaked. No physical features are distinguishable.*

SCROOGE. You are the third (*The* SPIRIT *says nothing.*) The Ghost of Christmas Yet to Come (*The* SPIRIT *says nothing.*) Speak to me. Tell me what is to happen—to me, to all of us (*The* SPIRIT *says nothing.*) Then show me what I must see (*The* SPIRIT *points. Light illumines the shadowy recesses of* SCROOGE's *house.*) I know it. I know it too well, cold and cheerless. It is mine (*The* COOK *and the* CHARWOMAN *are dimly visible in* SCROOGE's *house.*) What is . . . ? There are . . . thieves! There are thieves in my rooms! (*He starts forward to accost them, but the* SPIRIT *beckons for him to stop.*) I cannot. You cannot tell me that I must watch them and do nothing. I will not. It is mine still (*He rushes into the house to claim his belongings and to protect them. The two women do not notice his presence.*)

COOK. He ain't about, is he? (*The* CHARWOMAN *laughs.*) Poor ol' Scrooge 'as met 'is end (*She laughs with the* CHARWOMAN.)

CHARWOMAN. An' time for it, too; ain't been alive in deed for half his life.

COOK. But the Sparsit's nowhere, is he . . . ?

SPARSIT (*emerging from the blackness*). Lookin' for someone, ladies? (*The* COOK *shrieks, but the* CHARWOMAN *treats the matter more practically, anticipating*[23] *competition from* SPARSIT.)

CHARWOMAN. There ain't enough but for the two of us!

SPARSIT. More 'an enough . . . if you know where to look.

---

23. **anticipate** (an tis′ə pāt), *v.* expect.

◄ Although the Third Spirit doesn't speak, his presence is very powerful. How is this accomplished?

COOK (*snatching the cuff links from the shirt* SCROOGE *wears*). They're gold, ain't they?

SPARSIT. The purest, madam.

CHARWOMAN. I always had a fancy for that nightcap of his. My old man could use it (*She takes the nightcap from* SCROOGE's *head.* SPARSIT *playfully removes* SCROOGE's *outer garment, the coat or cloak that he has worn in the previous scenes.*)

SPARSIT. Bein' a man of more practical tastes, I'll go for the worsted and hope the smell ain't permanent (*The three laugh.*) Cook, we go round again.

COOK. Do you think that little bell he's always ringing at me is silver enough to sell? (*The three of them move toward the nightstand and* SCROOGE *cries out.*)

SCROOGE. No more! No more! (*As the* SPIRIT *directs* SCROOGE's *attention to the tableau of the three thieves standing poised over the silver bell,* SCROOGE *bursts out of the house, clad only in his nightshirt.*) I cannot. I cannot. The room is . . . too like a cheerless place that is familiar. I won't see it. Let us go from here. Anywhere (*The* SPIRIT *directs his attention to the* CRATCHIT *house; the* CHILDREN *are sitting together near* MRS. CRATCHIT, *who is sewing a coat.* PETER *reads by the light of the coals.*)

PETER. "And he took a child and set him in the midst of them."

MRS. CRATCHIT (*putting her hand to her face*). The light tires my eyes so (*Pause*) They're better now. It makes them tired to try to see by firelight, and I wouldn't show reddened

COOK. Hardly decent is what I'd say, hardly decent, the poor old fella hardly cold and you're thievin' his wardrobe.

SPARSIT. You're here out of love, are ya?

CHARWOMAN. There's no time for that (SPARSIT *acknowledges* SCROOGE *for the first time, gesturing toward him as if the living* SCROOGE *were the corpse.* SCROOGE *stands as if rooted to the spot, held there by the power of the* SPIRIT.)

SPARSIT. He ain't about to bother us, is he?

CHARWOMAN. Ain't he a picture?

COOK. If he is, it ain't a happy one (*They laugh.*)

SPARSIT. Ladies, shall we start? (*The three of them grin and advance on* SCROOGE.) Cook?

eyes to your father when he comes home for the world. It must be near his time now.

PETER. Past it, I think, but he walks slower than he used to, these last few days, Mother.

MRS. CRATCHIT. I have known him to walk with . . . I have known him to walk with Tiny Tim upon his shoulder very fast indeed (*She catches herself, then hurries on.*) But he was very light to carry and his father loved him so that it was no trouble, no trouble (*She hears* BOB CRATCHIT *approaching.*) Smiles, everyone, smiles.

BOB CRATCHIT (*entering*). My dear, Peter . . . (*He greets the other* CHILDREN *by their real names.*) How is it coming?

MRS. CRATCHIT (*handing him the coat*). Nearly done.

BOB CRATCHIT. Yes, good, I'm sure that it will be done long before Sunday.

MRS. CRATCHIT. Sunday! You went today then, Robert?

BOB CRATCHIT. Yes. It's . . . it's all ready. Two o'clock. And a nice place. It would have done you good to see how green it is. But you'll see it often. I promised him that, that I would walk there on Sunday . . . often.

MRS. CRATCHIT. We mustn't hurt ourselves for it, Robert.

BOB CRATCHIT. No. No, he wouldn't have wanted that. Come now. You won't guess who I've seen. Scrooge's nephew Fred. And he asked after us and said he was heartily sorry and to give his respect to my good wife. How he ever knew that, I don't know.

MRS. CRATCHIT. Knew what, my dear?

BOB CRATCHIT. Why, that you were a good wife.

PETER. Everybody knows that.

BOB CRATCHIT. I hope that they do. "Heartily sorry," he said, "for your good wife, and if I can be of service to you in any way—" and he gave me his card—"that's where I live"—and Peter, I shouldn't be at all surprised if he got you a position.

MRS. CRATCHIT. Only hear that, Peter!

BOB CRATCHIT. And then you'll be keeping company with some young girl and setting up for yourself.

PETER. Oh, go on.

BOB CRATCHIT. Well, it will happen, one day, but remember, when that day does come—as it must—we must none of us forget poor Tiny Tim and this first parting in our family.

SCROOGE. He died! No, no! (*He steps back and the scene disappears; he moves away from the* SPIRIT.)

Making Connections

1. Do you think that Scrooge has changed since the beginning of the play? Explain your answer.

2. How did you feel after reading about the way Scrooge's servants reacted to their boss's death?

3. Why do you think the author made the features of the Spirit of Christmas Future difficult to recognize?

4. If you could know your future, would you choose to do so? Explain.

5. Scrooge was given a chance to change. What would you change from your past that would make you a better person?

SCENE SIX
Scrooge's Conversion

SCROOGE. Because he would not . . . no! You cannot tell me that he has died, for that Christmas has not come! I will not let it come! I will be there . . . It was me. Yes, yes, and I knew it and couldn't look. I won't be able to help. I won't *(Pause)* Spirit, hear me. I am not the man I was. I will not be that man that I have been for so many years. Why show me all of this if I am past all hope? Assure[24] me that I yet may change these shadows you have shown me. Let the boy live! I will honor Christmas in my heart and try to keep it all the year. I will live in the Past, the Present, and the Future. The spirits of all three shall strive within me. I will not shut out the lessons that they teach. Oh, tell me that I am not too late! *(A single light focuses on the little* GIRL, *dressed in a blue cloak. She looks up, and from above a dove is slowly lowered in silence to her; she takes it and encloses it within her cloak, covering it. As soon as she does this, a large choir is heard and the bells begin to ring. Blackout. When the lights come up again,* SCROOGE *is in bed.* SCROOGE *awakens and looks around his room.)* The curtains! They are mine and they are real. They are not sold. They are here. I am here, the shadows to come may be dispelled. They will be. I know they will be *(He dresses himself hurriedly.)* I don't know what to do. I'm as light as a feather, merry as a boy again. Merry Christmas! Merry Christmas! A Happy New Year to all the world! Hello there! Whoop! Hallo! What day of the month is it? How long did the spirits keep me? Never mind. I don't care *(He opens the window and calls to a* BOY *in the street below.)* What's today?

BOY. Eh?

SCROOGE. What's the day, my fine fellow?

BOY. Today? Why, Christmas Day!

SCROOGE. It's Christmas Day! I haven't missed it! The spirits have done it all in one night. They can do anything they like. Of course they can. Of course they can save Tim. Hallo, my fine fellow!

BOY. Hallo!

SCROOGE. Do you know the poulterers in the next street at the corner?

BOY. I should hope I do.

SCROOGE. An intelligent boy. A remarkable boy. Do you know whether they've sold the prize turkey that was hanging up there? Not the little prize; the big one.

BOY. What, the one as big as me?

SCROOGE. What a delightful boy! Yes, my bucko![25]

BOY. It's hanging there now.

SCROOGE. It is? Go and buy it.

BOY. G'wan!

SCROOGE. I'm in earnest! Go and buy it and tell 'em to bring it here that I may give them the directions where to take it. Come back with the butcher and I'll give you a shilling.[26] Come back in less than two minutes and give you half a crown.

BOY. Right, guv! *(He exits.)*

SCROOGE. I'll send it to Bob Cratchit's. He shan't know who sends it. It's twice the size of Tiny Tim and such a Christmas dinner it will make (CAROLERS *suddenly appear.* SCROOGE *leans out the window and joins them in the song.)* I must dress, I must. It's Christmas Day! I must be all in my best for such a day. Where is my China silk shirt? *(The* BOY *and the* BUTCHER *run in with the turkey.)* What? Back already? And such a turkey. Why, you can't carry that all the way

---

24. **assure** (ə shür′), *v.* tell positively.
25. **bucko** (buk′o), *n.* an Irish term for "lad" or "young man."
26. **shilling** (shil′ing), *n.* a coin worth 1/20th of a British pound.

◄ 🐾 How does this picture show that Scrooge is willing to accept the traditions of a certain **group?**

GENTLEMAN VISITOR. I will.

SCROOGE. Thank 'ee. I am much obliged to you. I thank you fifty times. God bless you and Merry Christmas!

GENTLEMAN VISITOR. Merry Christmas to you, sir!

SCROOGE (*running downstairs, out of his house, and onto the street*). Now which is the way to that nephew's house. Girl! Girl!

GIRL (*appearing immediately*). Yes, sir?

SCROOGE. Can you find me a taxi,[28] miss?

GIRL. I can, sir (*She rings her doll and a* COACHMAN *appears.*)

SCROOGE (*handing the* COACHMAN *a card*). Can you show me the way to this house?

COACHMAN. I can, sir.

SCROOGE. Good man. Come up, girl (*They mount to the top of the taxi. This action may be stylistically suggested.*) Would you be an old man's guide to a Christmas dinner?

GIRL. I would, sir, and God bless you!

SCROOGE. Yes, God bless us every one! (*Raising his voice almost in song*) Driver, to Christmas! (*They exit, all three singing. Blackout. The lights come up for the finale at* FRED'*s house. The* CRATCHIT*s are there with* TINY TIM. *All stop moving and talking when they see* SCROOGE *standing in the center, embarrassed and humble.*) Well, I'm very glad to be here at my nephew's house! (*He starts to cry.*) Merry Christmas! Merry Christmas! ̄

ALL (*softly*). Merry Christmas (SCROOGE *puts* TINY TIM *on his shoulders.*)

TINY TIM. God bless us every one!

SCROOGE (*to the audience*). Oh, yes! God bless us every one!

to Cratchit's. Here, boy, here is your half a crown and here an address in Camden town.[27] See that it gets there. Here, money for the cab, for the turkey, and for you, good man! (*The* BOY *and the* BUTCHER, *delighted, catch the money and run out.* SCROOGE *sees the* GENTLEMAN VISITOR *walking by the window.*) Halloo, sir!

GENTLEMAN VISITOR (*looking up sadly, less than festive*). Hello, sir.

SCROOGE. My dear sir, how do you do? I hope you succeeded yesterday. It was very kind of you to stop by to see me.

GENTLEMAN VISITOR (*in disbelief*). Mr. Scrooge?

SCROOGE. Yes, that is my name and I fear it may not be pleasant to you. Allow me to ask your pardon, and will you have the goodness to add this (*Throwing him a purse*) to your good work!

GENTLEMAN VISITOR. My dear Mr. Scrooge, are you serious?

SCROOGE. If you please, not a penny less. A great many back payments are included in it, I assure you. Will you do me that favor?

GENTLEMAN VISITOR. My dear sir, I don't know what I can say to such generosity.

SCROOGE. Say nothing! Accept it. Come and see me. Will you come and see me?

---

27. **Camden town**, a section of London.
28. **taxi** (tak′sē), *n.* before the use of automobiles, a horse-drawn carriage driven by a coachman.

After Reading

Making Connections

1. The name Scrooge has come to mean a miserly and heartless person. Explain why the name does not fit the main character at the end of the play.

2. Most of Scene Three of this play takes the reader back to Scrooge's past. What do you learn about Scrooge from his past?

3. ☙ Dickens used Christmas traditions to make his point about the importance of generosity and warmth between **groups** of people. What other traditions could you use to make the same point?

4. Discuss the significance of the little girl in the play and Scrooge's response to her.

5. Think of another **title** for this play.

6. Why do you think this story continues to be popular even though it was written in the 1800s?

7. Scrooge makes dramatic changes in his behavior because of his experiences. In real life, do you think it is possible for someone to change so completely? Why or why not? Tell about any examples you know of.

Literary Focus: Symbolism

Did you notice that throughout *A Christmas Carol,* certain objects showed up again and again and certain events were also repeated? These objects and events are **symbols**—things that have meaning themselves but also suggest other, deeper meanings as well. Many of the symbols are props or actions that can be used to make a strong impact on the audience watching the play.

Choose an event or object below. Trace its use in the different scenes of the play. Tell how the object or event is used and its real meaning.

the bell	doors
carols or songs	the doll
candles	fireplace or hearth
the clock	funeral processions
coins, gold	the lullaby

Vocabulary Study

Following are sentences from an imaginary toast Scrooge might have given the year after the action of the play. Write the words from the list that best complete the paragraph.

abundance
anticipate
anonymous
assure
charitable
dejected
derive
determined
infuriated
solitude

I wish you all a healthy and hearty Merry Christmas during this festive season of __(1)__ . I have made many adjustments and I __(2)__ many more. Among the most important, I have transformed my love of __(3)__ to a love of company. And you, my dear friends and family, have helped me stop being __(4)__ and angry and helped me experience the joy and happiness of life. I __(5)__ much comfort from your merry songs, your conversations, and your advice. But personal matters aside, this is also the season when we must look beyond our own small circle of warmth to the neglected and __(6)__ of our society. I know that each of you will be __(7)__ and contribute to the poor. I __(8)__ you that your contribution will remain __(9)__ . I am __(10)__ that this Christmas be the warmest and most blessed ever. Here's to you, my fine friends.

Expressing Your Ideas

Writing Choices

This Time Next Year Write an **epilogue** for *A Christmas Carol.* This is a final speech or poem addressed to the audience by one of the actors or actresses. Often the epilogue aids in the interpretation of the play. You might focus your epilogue on some of the changes Scrooge made during the upcoming year or how he celebrated the following Christmas. Decide which character will present the epilogue, and write it to match the style of dialogue of the play.

Pick the Cast Think of all the actors and actresses you know and make up a **cast list** for *A Christmas Carol.* After each person named, write a sentence or two telling why you think he or she would be good for the part. Compare your list with those of your classmates.

Other Options

Up on Mike 1 Select a scene from *A Christmas Carol,* and with a group of students, present it as a **radio drama**. Assign parts and practice reading them aloud. Let some people work on sound effects and music. So that the audience will understand the action, write an introduction and conclusion for a narrator to read. After you rehearse a few times, tape your presentation and play it for your class or for another class.

Ghostly Images Ignore the illustrations in the text and create a set of **paintings** or **drawings** of all the ghosts in the play as you imagine them.

Before Reading

From Raisin Pudding to Oysters and Champagne

by Kathleen Krull

Kathleen Krull
born 1952

Dickens might well have agreed with writer Kathleen Krull when she said, "Writing books for children, like any other kind of writing, is a *craft*." Krull has devoted her career to writing, editing, and producing high-quality children's books. Music is also an important part of Krull's life, and she has published collections of her piano arrangements. Dickens probably would have loved one of her music books, *The Christmas Carol Sampler*.

Building Background

Working Day and Night Can you imagine working from eleven to sixteen hours a day in a dimly lit, overheated room, with rats scurrying under your feet, as you carried heavy molds of breakable pottery to and from the ovens? This is one of the many terrible jobs you could have had if you were a child of a poor family in England during the 1800s.

When he was about your age, Charles Dickens worked in such a factory. As an adult, he helped champion child labor reform by making his middle- and upper-class reading audiences aware of the plight of poor, working children in England.

Getting into the Selection

Discussion Did reading the play *A Christmas Carol* make you curious about the world-famous author of the original story? Pretend Charles Dickens's ghost could visit your classroom. What questions would you ask the spirit? What would you hope to find out about his life? Make a class list of questions about Dickens and his work.

Reading Tip

Keeping Track of Chronology "From Raisin Pudding to Oysters and Champagne" is a brief biography of British author Charles Dickens. It paints a portrait of the famous writer and tells some of the major events of his life. This biography is very descriptive and doesn't rely on dates. You can keep track of chronology—when events occurred—to get a better overview of Dickens's life. The biographer gives Dickens's age when various events occurred. Take note of this information as you read, and use it to figure out the year that specific events in Dickens's life occurred. Record the events and the dates on a time line like the one below.

Dickens born	Dickens worked in factory	Dickens died

From Raisin Pudding to Oysters and Champagne

Kathleen Krull

A caricature of Charles Dickens.

Two days after his twelfth birthday, in a damp factory overrun with rats, Charles Dickens went to work to support his family. All day, with two meal breaks (often raisin pudding with a penny loaf of bread), he pasted labels on bottles of black shoe polish. Though his parents were very much alive (his father was in prison for debt—at the time, a crime), he never forgot his feeling of being orphaned.

Dickens eventually returned for two more years to school, where he wrote stories on scraps of paper and sold them to schoolmates for marbles. He later became a law clerk, a court reporter, a journalist—and with the publication of *The Pickwick Papers*[1] when he was twenty-four, he was set for life.

As each new novel was published, Dickens became not only one of the most popular writers of all time but also the most popular public speaker of his day. He entertained people in an age without TV, radio, or movies, and his reading tours earned him pots of money. Audiences treated him as fans do rock stars now, mobbing him, ripping his clothes, lionizing[2] him. His final home, a three-story house called Gad's Hill Place, was the very estate his father had often pointed out years before as the place Dickens might live "if he would only work hard enough."

Dickens did work hard. When he wasn't on tour, he got up at seven o'clock, bathed in cold water, and wrote until lunch. He wrote neatly in blue ink with a goose-quill pen on blue-gray paper, completing two to four pages a day. If his writing wasn't going well, he doodled or picked fights with his wife, his ten children, or his servants. In the afternoon he tried to spend as many hours walking as he had writing—he would often walk twenty or thirty miles at a time, his dogs trotting behind him. He spent the evenings playing twenty questions and charades,[3] and went to bed at midnight.

---

1. *The Pickwick Papers*, Dickens's first novel, published in 1836.
2. **lionize** (lī′ə nīz), *v.* treat someone as very important.
3. **charade** (shə rād′), *n.* game in which one player acts out a word or phrase and the others try to guess what it is.

The objects on his desk had to be in exactly the same position each day before he could begin work, and his bed had to be set in a north-south direction before he could sleep. He touched certain objects three times for luck and thought of Friday as his lucky day. He was fascinated by ghosts, and he attended séances,[4] murder trials, and public hangings whenever he could.

He was also fascinated by his own hair—if he thought a hair was out of place, he'd pull out a comb, even if he was at a dinner party. Notoriously[5] vain, Dickens surrounded himself with mirrors. He wore flashy clothes: red velvet waistcoats, rings on his fingers, and a diamond stickpin on his vest.

For someone whose books were stuffed with descriptions of meals, Dickens drank and ate little—perhaps ham for breakfast and toasted cheese for dinner. In breaks during public readings, he would eat a dozen oysters and sip a little champagne.

His wife, in one of the most famous marriages of his century, was Catherine Hogarth. He called her Mouse and Dearest Pig, and later, when they were not getting along so well, Donkey. He grew impatient with her, and after sixteen years of marriage and amid much gossip from the neighbors, they separated. He kept custody[6] of the children and became obsessed with an actress, Ellen Ternan.

All his life, Dickens was troubled by a pain in his side, an inflamed kidney that caused a fatal stroke at age fifty-eight. He was buried in Westminister Abbey,[7] and thousands of people came for months afterward to pay their respects.

---

4. **séance** (sā′äns), *n.* a meeting of people trying to communicate with spirits of the dead by the help of a medium.
5. **notoriously** (nō tôr′ē əs lē), *adv.* in a well-known or commonly known manner, especially because of something bad.
6. **custody** (kus′tə dē), *n.* watchful keeping or charge, in a legal sense.
7. **Westminster Abbey**, church in London where the kings and queens of Great Britain are crowned and in which many English monarchs and famous people are buried.

Bookmarks

Although Dickens wrote *A Christmas Carol* (an immediate bestseller) mostly for money, the success of the novel helped to create something spiritual—the modern concept of the "Christmas spirit." Dickens was keenly aware of the security that money could bring, and it is said that Ebenezer Scrooge, the most famous miser in fiction, is partly based on himself.

■ *Oliver Twist,* a novel about how poverty can breed crime, was the first book in the English language with a child as its hero; Oliver is still one of the most famous orphans in literature. No matter how rich Dickens became, he always had tremendous empathy for the children of his day, who often had hard lives.

■ The death of Little Nell in *The Old Curiosity Shop* aroused unparalleled public response. Dickens's novels were published in installments, and crowds of Americans awaiting the next episode from overseas would gather at the New York harbor to ask English travelers tearfully, "Is Little Nell dead?"

■ Dickens called *David Copperfield,* the novel that contains the most elements from his own life, his favorite of all his books.

After Reading

Making Connections

1. Was Dickens the type of person you would want to be friends with? Why or why not?

2. Imagine that Kathleen Krull needed to expand her biography by three pages. What other types of information about Dickens would you want her to include?

3. 🐾 Belonging to a **group** often involves keeping cultural traditions. As shown in this biography, what kind of traditions were important to Dickens?

4. Like Scrooge, Dickens felt that money was very important. Do you agree with him? Why or why not?

Literary Focus: Biography

A **biography** is a written account of the life of a real person, composed by someone other than the person himself or herself. When writing about someone who has died, a biographer has to depend on historical documents for most or all information. Charles Dickens died in 1870, so he didn't get to read Kathleen Krull's biography of him. If Dickens could read "From Raisin Pudding to Oysters and Champagne," do you think he would approve of it? Reread the selection. Pick out at least three pieces of information Dickens might find flattering. Then pick out three more pieces of information he might be upset about.

Expressing Your Ideas

What? Where? When? If you made a time line of events in Dickens's life based on the information in the selection, you probably noticed that your time line has very few dates. Use an encyclopedia to find more information on the life of Charles Dickens. Make a new **time line** or add more information to your original time line using facts from the encyclopedia.

More on the Subject Do research to find out more about Dickens. How does he compare to Scrooge? Give an **oral report**.

The Write Stuff Dickens had a certain process that he went through when he wrote. Write a **list** of steps that describe how you prepare to write and what you do while you write.

Before Reading

The Fox and the Grapes by Aesop

The Country Mouse and the City Mouse by Aesop

Aesop

The compiler of Aesop's fables was reputed to be a Greek named Aesop who supposedly lived in the sixth century B.C. This man himself was a figure of fable. Aesop was said to have been a crippled slave living in Greece. Somehow he gained his freedom, and many say he went on to be a favorite adviser to Croesus, king of Lydia, valued for his keen wisdom. Others say that he became a riddle solver for the Babylonian king, Lycurgus. No one will ever know for sure whether a fable collector named Aesop ever existed. The picture above shows how an artist thought Aesop might have looked. The original versions of his fables did not survive. The fables, however, are real enough. Their longevity is a tribute to Aesop or whomever actually did first write them down.

Building Background

Keeping Traditions Aesop's fables are a collection of several hundred ancient tales of which the stories "The Fox and the Grapes" and "The Country Mouse and the City Mouse" are two. The first known set of Aesop's fables was put down in writing in the fourth century B.C. Other written versions were produced in Rome in the second century. They were translated into English in the late 1400s. Since then, Aesop's fables, both in written and spoken form, have become incorporated into the literature of cultures all over the world. By telling and retelling these fables, people have kept alive a tradition that has roots in the earliest eras of civilization.

Getting into the Stories

Discussion In many tales, animals are given human characteristics. Think about what you already know about foxes and mice. What are some of the characteristics of these animals? Which of these animals do you think is the smartest? Do you think of these animals as being urban or rural?

Reading Tip

Cause-and-Effect Relationships Writers often use cause-and-effect relationships, which show how something makes something else happen. A cause brings about a result, or an effect. As you read, write a cause and effect for each character on a chart, such as the one below.

Character	Cause	Effect
City Mouse	Sees how poorly Country Mouse lives	Invites Country Mouse to see her home in the city

The Fox and the Grapes

Aesop

There was a time when a fox would have searched as diligently[1] for a bunch of grapes as for a shoulder of mutton.[2] And so it was that a hungry Fox stole[3] one day into a vineyard where bunches of grapes hung ripe and ready for eating. But as the Fox stood licking his chops under an especially juicy cluster of grapes, he realized that they were all fastened high upon a tall trellis. He jumped, and paused, and jumped again, but the grapes remained out of his reach. At last, weary and still hungry, he turned and trotted away. Looking back at the vineyard, he said to himself: "The grapes are sour!"

There are those who pretend to despise what they cannot obtain.

---

1. **diligently** (dil′ə jənt lē), *adv.* in a hard-working manner.
2. **shoulder of mutton**, meat from the shoulder of a sheep.
3. **steal** (stēl), v. move secretly or quietly.

◄ A screen panel from Savonnerie Tapestry done in the mid eighteenth century depicting "The Fox and the Grapes"

The Country Mouse and the City Mouse
Aesop

An honest, plain, sensible Country Mouse invited her city friend for a visit. When the City Mouse arrived, the Country Mouse opened her heart and hearth in honor of her old friend. There was not a morsel that she did not bring forth out of her larder[1]—peas and barley, cheese parings and nuts—hoping by quantity to make up for what she feared was wanting in quality, eating nothing herself, lest her guest should not have enough. The City Mouse, condescending[2] to pick a bit here and a bit there, at length exclaimed, "My dear, please let me speak freely to you. How can you endure the dullness of your life here, with nothing but woods and meadows, mountains and brooks about? You can't really prefer these empty fields to streets teeming with carriages and men! Do you not long for the conversation of the world instead of the chirping of birds? I promise you will find the city a change for the better. Let's away this moment!"

Overpowered with such fine words and so polished a manner, the Country Mouse agreed, and they set out on their journey. About midnight they entered a great house, where the City Mouse lived. Here were couches of crimson velvet, ivory carvings, and on the table were the remains of a splendid banquet. The Country Mouse was placed in the midst of a rich Persian carpet, and it was now the turn of the City Mouse to play hostess. She ran to and fro to supply all her guest's wants, serving dish upon dish and dainty[3] upon dainty. The Country Mouse sat and enjoyed herself, delighted with this new turn of affairs. Just as she was thinking with contempt of the poor life she had forsaken,[4] the door flew open and a noisy party burst into the room. The frightened friends scurried for the first corner they could find. No sooner did they peek out than the barking of dogs drove them back in greater terror than before. At length, when things seemed quiet, the Country Mouse stole from her hiding place and bade her friend good-bye, whispering, "Oh, my dear, this fine mode of living may do for you, but I prefer my poor barley in peace and quiet to dining at the richest feast where Fear and Danger lie waiting."

A simple life in peace and safety is preferable to a life of luxury tortured by fear.

---

1. **larder** (lär′der), *n.* place where food is kept; pantry.
2. **condescend** (kon′di send′), *v.* grant a favor with a haughty or patronizing attitude.
3. **dainty** (dān′tē), *n.* something very good to eat; delicious bit of food.
4. **foresake** (fôr′sāk′), *v.* leave or give up something.

The Town Mouse and The Country Mouse was painted by E. J. Detmold. ➤

After Reading

Making Connections

1. Whom do you identify with most—the country mouse or the city mouse?

2. Do you think the fox will ever try to eat grapes again? Why or why not?

3. Why do you think the writer used old-fashioned phrases, such as *lest* and *let's away?*

4. Have you ever been in a situation where you thought the benefits of a particular action were not worth the adjustments you would have to make to get them? Explain.

Literary Focus: Fables

From ancient times, **fables** have been a part of literature from many parts of the world. Storytellers and other public speakers have always been fond of fables because they are short, are to the point, and have a clear message. Whether a fable is Greek or Native American in origin, it will have these characteristics. For each fable, describe all of the following.

- the human characteristics of the animals

- the conflict

- the lesson or moral in your own words

Expressing Your Ideas —
Writing Choices

Sweet and Sour Grapes Rewrite the **fable** "The Fox and the Grapes" to show a different cause and effect. Change the action and the ending, and state your moral clearly. Share your fable with your classmates. Discuss how your moral illustrates a different truth about human nature than the original fable.

From the Lap of Luxury Imagine you are the Country Mouse. Write a **postcard** to a friend about your visit to the City Mouse's home. Tell your favorite and least favorite thing about the trip.

City *vs.* Country Would you rather live in the country or the city? Divide into two teams and hold a formal **debate** on the subject. Make sure each team has a chance to rebut the statements of the other side. Let a panel of judges decide who won the debate and explain their reasons for their decisions.

Language Mini-Lesson

Subject-Verb Agreement

Recognizing Agreement Problems Good writers make sure that the subjects of sentences agree in number with the verbs. For example, the sentence *The boys plays ball* is incorrect because the subject, *boys,* is plural but the verb, *plays,* is singular. With correct agreement the sentence would read *The boys play ball.*

Agreement problems can be more difficult to notice in sentences in which the subject and verb are separated by modifying phrases:

- The dogs in the backyard was covered with mud.

- The award-winning band from Grant Middle School are touring the United States.

- One of the car's headlights are broken.

Did you identify the agreement problems? If so, how?

Writing Strategy To check for agreement problems, first identify the subject and verb. Then, read the sentence with only those parts. For example, in this sentence all but the subject and verb have been blocked out. Is it easier to see the agreement problem?

The dogs ~~in the backyard~~ *were* ~~was~~ covered ~~with mud.~~

Activity Options

1. Copy the other two example sentences from above on a sheet of paper. Then cross out all but the subject and verb and correct the agreement problems.

2. Complete the following sentences paying special attention to subject and verb agreement. Have a friend check your work.

- A box of marbles
- A pair of goldfish
- Monkeys in the jungle
- The lights of the city
- The bananas Mary bought

3. How many agreement problems can you find in your portfolio? Give yourself a star for every problem you fix.

For Reference

For more rules on subject and verb agreement, see the Language and Grammar Handbook.

Keeping Traditions

Festive Times

Festivals

History Connection

Festivals are important traditions that have been celebrated around the world since ancient times. Some of the most important festivals take place during planting and harvest seasons. Many also celebrate winter events—some to honor special days, and others to break the tedium of a long, cold season.

A Buddhist family celebrates *Chusok*, a Korean harvest festival also known as Autumn Night. Families enjoy outdoor activities and give thanks for good harvests.

Dragon dancing is one of the traditional activities that mark the Vietnamese Tet (New Year). Public displays including parades and fireworks are customary. Also at this time, everyone makes a great effort to spend time with family members.

Around the World

Id-ul-Fitr is a day of rejoicing for Muslims as they welcome the new month. Here men and boys pray at Badshahi Mosque in Lahore, Pakistan. Later they will visit relatives and perhaps exchange presents.

In Nepal and India, *Diwali* is spectacular. This festival of lights honors the goddess Lakshmi. Before the holiday, every Hindu home is cleaned. Then, on the evening of Diwali, people light their houses, gardens, yards, and gates with oil-filled lamps, candles, or electric lights. The city seems to be ablaze.

A family in traditional dress celebrates the African American festival of *Kwanzaa*. A Swahili word meaning "first fruits of harvest," Kwanzaa is a commemoration of African ancestry. It is celebrated from December 26 through January 1.

A family member helps a young girl light the menora candles during the Jewish *Chanukah*, or *Hanukka*, celebration. Also called the Feast of Lights, Chanukah lasts for eight days. Gifts are exchanged during this commemoration of the rebuilding of the Temple of Jerusalem.

Responding

What winter festivals do you celebrate in your family or in your city? Bring to class one item used in the celebration of a winter festival. With other classmates, set up a display area for winter festival artifacts.

History Connection

Traditions are strong links in the chain of family relationships. Keeping traditions gives a family history, a feeling for the past, and a framework for the future. Guadalupe discovers strength and pride in her name and heritage with the celebration of her name day.

How I Celebrate My Name Day

by Guadalupe V. Lopez

When I was in 7th grade, I didn't like my name. So I told everyone my name was *María*. My father had said that all women were *Marías*, referring to the Virgin Mary, so I wasn't completely lying. My parents found out about my new name at the end-of-year conference with Sister Lorraine. My report cards and other papers said *Guadalupe*, but everyone at school called me *María*.

"*¡Pero ése no es tu nombre!* That is not your name! Your name is *Guadalupe*," said my mother. Then she told me of her grief at having lost her first-born, and of how, while pregnant with me, she had made a solemn promise to Our Lady of Guadalupe that if I were born alive and healthy, I would be named after her. "I even went to the *Basílica* to make this promise," she added. Although I secretly wished she would have made this promise to St. Ann or St. Susan, I felt a deep sense of obligation to carry out my mother's promise, and by the time I entered high school, only Tommy Puchalski still called me *María*.

Several years later, I married a López, which is an inoffensive name, but when paired with *Lupe* sounds a bit like the cartoon character Pepe LePieu. The year we were married, we visited my husband's family in Mexico around the time of my saint's day. On December 12, the house was filled with a flurry of activity as we prepared for the festivities in honor of the Feast Day of Our Lady of Guadalupe: shucking the corn for the *tamales*, winding the wire around the last of the huge colorful paper flowers that would decorate the exterior of the house, stringing the *piñatas* from balcony to balcony, as neighborhood children speculated which *piñata* was the dud that would shower them with flour or water when broken. As we women were nestling the last batch of *tamales* in the pot, we were surprised by a boy at the door with an armful of pink and white carnations. "They're for Lupita," he announced. My mother-in-law, sister-in-law, and I, all named Lupe, stepped forward to accept them, and I offered a few of mine to Lupita, my 4-year-old niece, who giggled shyly. They were from my husband.

In the evening, when it was time to head out to church, we made our 40-minute trek with the other townspeople up a steep, steep hill to *la Capillita*, a church where the special mariachi mass in honor of Our Lady was to be celebrated. After mass, we gathered in the *plaza* to watch the fireworks display and sample some holiday street fare before starting our journey back to the town. It was close to midnight when we settled in to sleep, and I was drifting off when I was pulled out of it by the sound of *canciones Guadalupanas* (songs in honor of Our Lady of Guadalupe) being sung in a familiar off-key voice outside my window. We let the trio and my husband into the house, and mamá Lupe, my mother-in-law, instinctively began preparing the hot chocolate, using the fresh milk from her cows, and heating up the *tamales*.

The trio knew every song I had heard from my father's collection of *música de trío*. They played every song ever written about women named Lupe. They even played *El Chubasco*, the song my father always requests when a mariachi is present, our song: *At 11:00 my Lupita will leave on a steam ship. If I could only create a downpour and delay her departure. . . .*

When I was expecting my daughter, I briefly considered naming her after an Aztec goddess, or after a Mayan flower whose name starts with *X* and ends in -tl. Then I thought about how she would feel when she was 12, cringing as her teacher stopped in her tracks while reading the attendance list on the first day of school. Then I thought about how there wouldn't be any special songs to request when the mariachi came around. So I decided on Julia, the name of a beautiful waltz that is part of the repertoire of any good mariachi.

Responding

1. Why do you think Guadalupe called herself *María* as a young girl?

2. Take a poll in your class. How many students have names that reflect their ethnic background? For those who do have a name of ethnic origin, do you like your given name, or would you change it if you could? Explain your answer.

Reading Mini-Lesson

Cause-and-Effect Relationships

Writers often use cause-and-effect relationships to show how something makes something else happen. A **cause** brings about a result, or **effect.** Sometimes there is a chain reaction of effects, with one effect causing another effect. For example, a law might be passed to protect an endangered species. The effect of this law would increase the population of that species. The effect of the increase in population might cause a food shortage. The effect of the food shortage might cause some animals to die of starvation.

However, you must be careful. Don't assume that just because one event happened *before* another, that the first event *caused* the second one. For example, if there is an earthquake on your birthday, you shouldn't assume your birthday caused the earthquake.

Many events occur in "How I Celebrate My Name Day." Let's say that the first cause in the chain of events is "Lupe's mother's first-born child dies." The last effect is "Lupe decides to name her own child Julia." A diagram like the one below can help you understand how each effect can also be a cause.

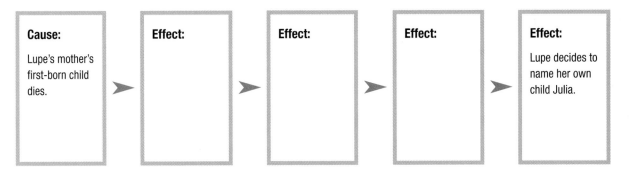

| **Cause:** Lupe's mother's first-born child dies. | **Effect:** | **Effect:** | **Effect:** | **Effect:** Lupe decides to name her own child Julia. |

Activity Options

1. Copy the diagram above and complete it after rereading the selection. Be sure that each effect is the cause of the next effect.

2. In your science book, find one important cycle, such as the food chain or the water cycle. Pick one point in the cycle and make a change at that point. Continue through the cycle and show how one change will cause other changes. Use a diagram like the one above.

Reading Mini-Lesson **271**

Part Two

What Really Matters

Imagine this: A TV reporter holds a microphone under your nose and says, "Channel 25 is doing a survey. We'd like to know: What really matters to you?"

You gulp. You shrug. Finally, you blurt out, "Doing well in school. Or maybe getting a new bike. Or maybe world peace."

Watching yourself on TV that night, you feel kind of silly. Sure, the things you mentioned matter to you—but not as much as the people you care about. As you read, you'll also find out how much others matter to the characters in the following selections.

🐾 Multicultural Connection People are influenced by their relationships with their families and friends. People show **individuality** in how they respond to responsibilities, pressures, and the needs of others.

Before Reading

President Cleveland, Where Are You?

by Robert Cormier

Robert Cormier
born 1925

Robert Cormier has been a journalist and a writer of novels for adults. However, he is best known for his award-winning stories for young people. Cormier often draws inspiration from his experiences growing up in Leominster, Massachusetts, which is the model for Monument City in his stories and also the place where he still lives. Of his boyhood, Cormier says, "I wasn't the physical type, the ball-playing type, and I never got chosen for the team. I was out under a tree reading a book, probably. The streets were terrible. It was the Depression and it was bleak, but home was warm."

Building Background

Great Depression "President Cleveland, Where Are You?" takes place in the 1930s, during the Great Depression. Thousands of banks, factories, stores, and other businesses closed. Millions of people lost their jobs and couldn't find new ones. When they fell behind in their rent or mortgage payments, they lost their homes too. What else do you know about the Depression?

Getting into the Story

Discussion Like many Depression-era children, the characters in "President Cleveland, Where Are You?" collect and trade different kinds of cards. Talk about collections that you or others have. How did the collections get started? What are the most special items in the collections, and what makes them so special?

Reading Tip

Getting to Know a Character The narrator of this story doesn't come right out and say, "This is what I'm like." Still, he reveals a lot about himself and about some of the other characters. Copy the character trait web shown below. As you read, use it to make notes about Jerry's character.

- Write Jerry's name in the center circle.
- Describe what he's like on the lines coming out of the center circle.
- In the outer circles, add examples that illustrate each character trait.

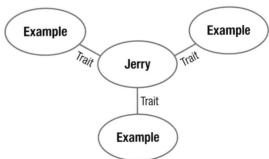

President Cleveland, Where Are You?

Robert Cormier

That was the autumn of the cowboy cards—Buck Jones and Tom Tyler and Hoot Gibson and especially Ken Maynard.[1] The cards were available in those five-cent packages of gum: pink sticks, three together, covered with a sweet white powder. You couldn't blow bubbles with that particular gum, but it couldn't have mattered less. The cowboy cards were important—the pictures of those rock-faced men with eyes of blue steel.

On those windswept, leaf-tumbling afternoons we gathered after school on the sidewalk in front of Lemire's Drugstore, across from St. Jude's Parochial School, and we swapped and bargained and matched for the cards. Because a Ken Maynard serial[2] was playing at the Globe every Saturday afternoon, he was the most popular cowboy of all, and one of his cards was worth at least ten of any other kind. Rollie Tremaine had a treasure of thirty or so, and he guarded them jealously. He'd match you for the other cards, but he risked his Ken Maynards only when the other kids threatened to leave him out of the competition altogether.

You could almost hate Rollie Tremaine. In the first place, he was the only son of Auguste Tremaine, who operated the Uptown Dry Goods Store, and he did not live in a tenement but in a big white birthday cake of a house on Laurel Street. He was too fat to be effective in the football games between the Frenchtown Tigers and the North Side Knights, and he made us constantly aware of the jingle of coins in his pockets. He was able to stroll into Lemire's and casually select a quarter's worth of cowboy cards while the rest of us watched, aching with envy.

Once in a while I earned a nickel or dime by running errands or washing windows for blind old Mrs. Belander, or by finding pieces of copper, brass, and other valuable metals at the dump and selling them to the junkman. The coins clutched in my hand, I would race to Lemire's to buy a cowboy card or two, hoping that Ken Maynard would stare

---

1. **Buck Jones,** 1889–1942, real name Charles Gebhart; **Tom Tyler** 1903–1954, real name Vincent Markowski; **Hoot Gibson** 1892–1962, real name Edmund Gibson; **Ken Maynard** 1895–1973, popular stars of movie westerns in the 1930s.
2. **serial** (sir′ē əl), *n.* story that is published in newspapers or magazines, broadcast on radio or television, or shown at movie theaters one part at a time.

Does *Bat Boys* painted by Lance Richbourg strengthen the descriptions of Jerry, Rollie, and Roger?

boldly out at me as I opened the pack. At one time, before a disastrous matching session with Roger Lussier (my best friend, except where the cards were involved), I owned five Ken Maynards and considered myself a millionaire, of sorts.

One week I was particularly lucky; I had spent two afternoons washing floors for Mrs. Belander and received a quarter. Because my father had worked a full week at the shop, where a rush order for fancy combs had been received, he allotted my brothers and sisters and me an extra dime along with the usual ten cents for the Saturday-afternoon movie.

Setting aside the movie fare, I found myself with a bonus of thirty-five cents, and I then planned to put Rollie Tremaine to shame the following Monday afternoon.

Monday was the best day to buy the cards because the candy man stopped at Lemire's every Monday morning to deliver the new assortments. There was nothing more exciting in the world than a fresh batch of card boxes. I rushed home from school that day and hurriedly changed my clothes, eager to set off for the store. As I burst through the doorway, letting the screen door slam behind me, my brother Armand blocked my way.

President Cleveland, Where Are You?   **275**

He was fourteen, three years older than I, and a freshman at Monument High School. He had recently become a stranger to me in many ways—indifferent to such matters as cowboy cards and the Frenchtown Tigers—and he carried himself with a mysterious dignity that was fractured now and then when his voice began shooting off in all directions like some kind of vocal fireworks.

"Wait a minute, Jerry," he said. "I want to talk to you." He motioned me out of earshot of my mother, who was busy supervising the usual after-school skirmish in the kitchen.

QUESTION: What picture does "the usual after-school skirmish" bring to your mind?

I sighed with impatience. In recent months Armand had become a figure of authority, siding with my father and mother occasionally. As the oldest son he sometimes took advantage of his age and experience to issue rules and regulations.

"How much money have you got?" he whispered.

"You in some kind of trouble?" I asked, excitement rising in me as I remembered the blackmail[3] plot of a movie at the Globe a month before.

He shook his head in annoyance. "Look," he said, "it's Pa's birthday tomorrow. I think we ought to chip in and buy him something . . ."

I reached into my pocket and caressed the coins. "Here," I said carefully, pulling out a nickel. "If we all give a nickel we should have enough to buy him something pretty nice."

He regarded me with contempt.[4] "Rita already gave me fifteen cents, and I'm throwing in a quarter. Albert handed over a dime—all that's left of his birthday money. Is that all you can do—a nickel?"

"Aw, come on," I protested. "I haven't got a single Ken Maynard left, and I was going to buy some cards this afternoon." "Ken Maynard!" he snorted. "Who's more important—him or your father?"

His question was unfair because he knew that there was no possible choice—"my father" had to be the only answer. My father was a huge man who believed in the things of the spirit,[5] although my mother often maintained that the spirits[6] he believed in came in bottles. He had worked at the Monument Comb Shop since the age of fourteen; his booming laugh—or grumble—greeted us each night when he returned from the factory. A steady worker when the shop had enough work, he quickened with gaiety on Friday nights and weekends, a bottle of beer at his elbow, and he was fond of making long speeches about the good things in life. In the middle of the Depression, for instance, he paid cash for a piano, of all things, and insisted that my twin sisters, Yolande and Yvette, take lessons once a week.

I took a dime from my pocket and handed it to Armand.

"Thanks, Jerry," he said. "I hate to take your last cent."

"That's all right," I replied, turning away and consoling myself with the thought that twenty cents was better than nothing at all.

When I arrived at Lemire's I sensed disaster in the air. Roger Lussier was kicking disconsolately at a tin can in the gutter, and Rollie Tremaine sat sullenly on the steps in front of the store.

"Save your money," Roger said. He had known about my plans to splurge on the cards.

---

3. **blackmail** (blak′māl′), *n.* an attempt to get money from someone by threatening to tell or reveal something bad about him or her.

4. contempt (kən tempt′), *n.* the feeling that a person, act, or thing is mean, low, or worthless.

5. **spirit** (spir′it), *n.* the immaterial part of human beings; soul.

6. **spirits**, *n. pl.* strong alcholic liquor.

"What's the matter?" I asked.

"There's no more cowboy cards," Rollie Tremaine said. "The company's not making any more."

"They're going to have President cards," Roger said, his face twisting with disgust. He pointed to the store window. "Look!"

A placard in the window announced: "Attention, Boys. Watch for the New Series. Presidents of the United States. Free in Each 5-Cent Package of Caramel Chew."

"President cards?" I asked, dismayed.

I read on: "Collect a Complete Set and Receive an Official Imitation Major League Baseball Glove, Embossed with Lefty Grove's[7] Autograph."

Glove or no glove, who could become excited about Presidents, of all things?

Rollie Tremaine stared at the sign. "Benjamin Harrison, for crying out loud," he said. "Why would I want Benjamin Harrison when I've got twenty-two Ken Maynards?"

I felt the warmth of guilt creep over me. I jingled the coins in my pocket, but the sound was hollow. No more Ken Maynards to buy.

"I'm going to buy a Mr. Goodbar," Rollie Tremaine decided.

I was without appetite, indifferent even to a Baby Ruth, which was my favorite. I thought of how I had betrayed Armand and, worst of all, my father.

"I'll see you after supper," I called over my shoulder to Roger as I hurried away toward home. I took the shortcut behind the church, although it involved leaping over a tall wooden fence, and I zigzagged recklessly through Mr. Thibodeau's garden, trying to outrace my guilt. I pounded up the steps and into the house, only to learn that Armand had already taken Yolande and Yvette uptown to shop for the birthday present.

I pedaled my bike furiously through the streets, ignoring the indignant[8] horns of automobiles as I sliced through the traffic. Finally I saw Armand and my sisters emerge from the Monument Men's Shop. My heart sank when I spied the long, slim package that Armand was holding.

"Did you buy the present yet?" I asked, although I knew it was too late.

"Just now. A blue tie," Armand said. "What's the matter?"

"Nothing," I replied, my chest hurting.

He looked at me for a long moment. At first his eyes were hard, but then they softened. He smiled at me, almost sadly, and touched my arm. I turned away from him because I felt naked and exposed.

"It's all right," he said gently. "Maybe you've learned something." The words were gentle, but they held a curious dignity, the dignity remaining even when his voice suddenly cracked on the last syllable.

I wondered what was happening to me, because I did not know whether to laugh or cry.

EVALUATE: What do you think is happening to Jerry?

Sister Angela was amazed when, a week before Christmas vacation, everybody in the class submitted a history essay worthy of a high mark—in some cases as high as A-minus. (Sister Angela did not believe that anyone in the world ever deserved an A.) She never learned—or at least she never let on that she knew—we all had become experts on the Presidents because of the cards we purchased at Lemire's. Each card contained a picture of a President, and on the reverse side, a summary of his career. We looked at those cards so often that the biographies imprinted them-

---

7. **Lefty Grove** 1900–1975, real name Robert Moses Grove; left-handed baseball pitcher known for his brilliant performances with the Philadelphia Athletics (1925–1933) and the Boston Red Sox (1934–1941).

8. **indignant** (in dig′nənt) *adj.* angry at something unworthy, unjust, unfair, or mean.

selves on our minds without effort. Even our street-corner conversations were filled with such information as the fact that James Madison was called "The Father of the Constitution," or that John Adams had intended to become a minister.

The President cards were a roaring success and the cowboy cards were quickly forgotten. In the first place we did not receive gum with the cards but a kind of chewy caramel. The caramel could be tucked into a corner of your mouth, bulging your cheek in much the same manner as wads of tobacco bulged the mouths of baseball stars. In the second place the competition for collecting the cards was fierce and frustrating—fierce because everyone was intent on being the first to send away for a baseball glove and frustrating because although there were only thirty-two Presidents, including Franklin Delano Roosevelt, the variety at Lemire's was at a minimum. When the deliveryman left the boxes of cards at the store each Monday, we often discovered that one entire box was devoted to a single President—two weeks in a row the boxes contained nothing but Abraham Lincolns. One week Roger Lussier and I were the heroes of Frenchtown. We journeyed on our bicycles to the North Side, engaged three boys in a matching bout and returned with five new Presidents, including Chester Alan Arthur, who up to that time had been missing.

Perhaps to sharpen our desire, the card company sent a sample glove to Mr. Lemire, and it dangled, orange and sleek, in the window. I was half sick with longing, thinking of my old glove at home, which I had inherited from Armand. But Rollie Tremaine's desire for the glove outdistanced my own. He even got Mr. Lemire to agree to give the glove in the window to the first person to get a complete set of cards, so that precious time wouldn't be wasted waiting for the postman.

We were delighted at Rollie Tremaine's frustration, especially since he was only a substitute player for the Tigers. Once after spending fifty cents on cards—all of which turned out to be Calvin Coolidge—he threw them to the ground, pulled some dollar bills out of his pocket and said, "The heck with it. I'm going to buy a glove!"

"Not that glove," Roger Lussier said. "Not a glove with Lefty Grove's autograph. Look what it says at the bottom of the sign."

We all looked, although we knew the words by heart: "This Glove Is Not For Sale Anywhere."

Rollie Tremaine scrambled to pick up the cards from the sidewalk, pouting more than ever. After that he was quietly obsessed[9] with the Presidents, hugging the cards close to his chest and refusing to tell us how many more he needed to complete his set.

I too was obsessed with the cards, because they had become things of comfort in a world that had suddenly grown dismal. After Christmas a layoff at the shop had thrown my father out of work. He received no paycheck for four weeks, and the only income we had was from Armand's after-school job at the Blue and White Grocery Store—a job he lost finally when business dwindled as the layoff continued.

Although we had enough food and clothing—my father's credit had always been good, a matter of pride with him—the inactivity made my father restless and irritable. He did not drink any beer at all, and laughed loudly, but not convincingly, after gulping down a glass a water and saying, "Lent[10] came early this year." The twins fell sick and went to the hospital to have their tonsils removed. My

---

9. obsessed (əb sest′), *adj.* having one's mind filled with a feeling or idea.
10. **Lent** (lent), *n.* the forty weekdays between Ash Wednesday and Easter, observed in many Christian churches as a time for fasting and repenting of sins.

HOOT GIBSON

BUCK JONES

GROVER CLEVELAND

KEN MAYNARD

TOM TYLER

How do these cards compare with ones that are traded today?

father was confident that he would return to work eventually and pay off his debts, but he seemed to age before our eyes.

When orders again were received at the comb shop and he returned to work, another disaster occurred, although I was the only one aware of it. Armand fell in love.

I discovered his situation by accident, when I happened to pick up a piece of paper that had fallen to the floor in the bedroom he and I shared. I frowned at the paper, puzzled.

"Dear Sally, When I look into your eyes the world stands still . . ."

The letter was snatched from my hands before I finished reading it.

"What's the big idea, snooping around?" Armand asked, his face crimson. "Can't a guy have any privacy?"

He had never mentioned privacy before. "It was on the floor," I said. "I didn't know it was a letter. Who's Sally?"

He flung himself across the bed. "You tell anybody and I'll muckalize you," he threatened. "Sally Knowlton."

Nobody in Frenchtown had a name like Knowlton.

"A girl from the North Side?" I asked, incredulous.

He rolled over and faced me, anger in his eyes, and a kind of despair too.

"What's the matter with that? Think she's too good for me?" he asked. "I'm warning you, Jerry, if you tell anybody . . ."

"Don't worry," I said. Love had no particular place in my life; it seemed an unnecessary waste of time. And a girl from the North Side was so remote that for all practical purposes she did not exist. But I was curious. "What are you writing her a letter for? Did you leave town, or something?"

"She hasn't left town," he answered. "I

"You tell anybody and I'll muckalize you," he threatened.

wasn't going to send it. I just felt like writing to her."

I was glad that I had never become involved with love—love that brought desperation to your eyes, that caused you to write letters you did not plan to send. Shrugging with indifference, I began to search in the closet for the old baseball glove. I found it on the shelf, under some old sneakers. The webbing was torn and the padding gone. I thought of the sting I would feel when a sharp grounder[11] slapped into the glove, and I winced.

"You tell anybody about me and Sally and I'll—"

"I know. You'll muckalize me."

I did not divulge[12] his secret and often shared his agony, particularly when he sat at the supper table and left my mother's special butterscotch pie untouched. I had never realized before how terrible love could be. But my compassion was short-lived because I had other things to worry about: report cards due at Eastertime; the loss of income from old Mrs. Belander, who had gone to live with a daughter in Boston; and, of course, the Presidents.

Because a stalemate[13] had been reached, the President cards were the dominant force in our lives—mine, Roger Lussier's and Rollie Tremaine's. For three weeks, as the baseball season approached, each of us had a complete set—complete except for one President, Grover Cleveland. Each time a box of cards arrived at the store we hurriedly bought them (as hurriedly as our funds allowed) and tore off the wrappers, only to be confronted by

---

11. **grounder** (groun′dər), *n.* baseball hit so as to bounce or roll along the ground.
12. **divulge** (də vulj′), *v.* make known; tell; reveal.
13. **stalemate** (stāl′māt′), *n.* any position in which no action can be taken; complete standstill.

James Monroe or Martin Van Buren or someone else. But never Grover Cleveland, never the man who had been the twenty-second *and* the twenty-fourth President of the United States. We argued about Grover Cleveland. Should he be placed between Chester Alan Arthur and Benjamin Harrison as the twenty-second President or did he belong between Benjamin Harrison and William McKinley as the twenty-fourth President? Was the card company playing fair? Roger Lussier brought up a horrifying possibility—did we need *two* Grover Clevelands to complete the set?

Indignant, we stormed Lemire's and protested to the harassed store owner, who had long since vowed never to stock a new series. Muttering angrily, he searched his bills and receipts for a list of rules.

"All right," he announced. "Says here you only need one Grover Cleveland to finish the set. Now get out, all of you, unless you've got money to spend."

Outside the store, Rollie Tremaine picked up an empty tobacco tin and scaled[14] it across the street. "Boy," he said. "I'd give five dollars for a Grover Cleveland."

When I returned home I found Armand sitting on the piazza steps, his chin in his hands. His mood of dejection[15] mirrored my own, and I sat down beside him. We did not say anything for a while.

"Want to throw the ball around?" I asked.

He sighed, not bothering to answer.

"You sick?" I asked.

He stood up and hitched up his trousers, pulled at his ear and finally told me what the matter was—there was a big dance next week at the high school, the Spring Promenade, and Sally had asked him to be her escort.

I shook my head at the folly of love. "Well, what's so bad about that?"

"How can I take Sally to a fancy dance?" he asked desperately. "I'd have to buy her a corsage . . . And my shoes are practically falling apart. Pa's got too many worries now to buy me new shoes or give me money for flowers for a girl."

I nodded in sympathy. "Yeah," I said. "Look at me. Baseball time is almost here, and all I've got is that old glove. And no Grover Cleveland card yet . . ."

"Grover Cleveland?" he asked. "They've got some of those up on the North Side. Some kid was telling me there's a store that's got them. He says they're looking for Warren G. Harding."

"Holy Smoke!" I said. "I've got an extra Warren G. Harding!" Pure joy sang in my veins. I ran to my bicycle, swung into the seat—and found that the front tire was flat.

"I'll help you fix it," Armand said.

Within half an hour I was at the North Side Drugstore, where several boys were matching cards on the sidewalk. Silently but blissfully I shouted: President Grover Cleveland, here I come!

After Armand had left for the dance, all dressed up as if it were Sunday, the small green box containing the corsage under his arm, I sat on the railing of the piazza, letting my feet dangle. The neighborhood was quiet because the Frenchtown Tigers were at Daggett's Field, practicing for the first baseball game of the season.

I thought of Armand and the ridiculous expression on his face when he'd stood before the mirror in the bedroom. I'd avoided looking at his new black shoes. "Love," I muttered.

Spring had arrived in a sudden stampede of apple blossoms and fragrant breezes. Windows had been thrown open and dust mops had banged on the sills all day long as the women busied themselves with house-

---

14. **scale** (skāl), *v.* throw (a thin flat object) so that it moves edgewise.
15. **dejection** (di jek′shən), *n.* lowness of spirits; sadness; discouragement.

cleaning. I was puzzled by my lethargy.[16] Wasn't spring supposed to make everything bright and gay?

PREDICT: Who will be the first to get a Grover Cleveland card?

I turned at the sound of footsteps on the stairs. Roger Lussier greeted me with a sour face.

"I thought you were practicing with the Tigers," I said.

"Rollie Tremaine," he said. "I just couldn't stand him." He slammed his fist against the railing. "Jeez, why did *he* have to be the one to get a Grover Cleveland? You should see him showing off. He won't let anybody even touch that glove . . ."

I felt like Benedict Arnold[17] and knew that I had to confess what I had done.

"Roger," I said, "I got a Grover Cleveland card up on the North Side. I sold it to Rollie Tremaine for five dollars."

"Are you crazy?" he asked.

"I needed that five dollars. It was an—an emergency."

"Boy!" he said, looking down at the ground and shaking his head. "What did you have to do a thing like that for?"

I watched him as he turned away and began walking down the stairs.

"Hey, Roger!" I called.

He squinted up at me as if I were a stranger, someone he'd never seen before.

"What?" he asked, his voice flat.

"I had to do it," I said. "Honest."

He didn't answer. He headed toward the fence, searching for the board we had loosened to give us a secret passage.

I thought of my father and Armand and Rollie Tremaine and Grover Cleveland and wished that I could go away someplace far away. But there was no place to go.

Roger found the loose slat in the fence and slipped through. I felt betrayed; weren't you supposed to feel good when you did something fine and noble?

A moment later two hands gripped the top of the fence and Roger's face appeared. "Was it a real emergency?" he yelled.

"A real one!" I called. "Something important!"

His face dropped from sight and his voice reached me across the yard: "All right."

"See you tomorrow!" I yelled.

I swung my legs over the railing again. The gathering dusk began to soften the sharp edges of the fence, the rooftops, the distant church steeple. I sat there a long time, waiting for the good feeling to come.

---

16. lethargy (leth′ər jē), *n.* drowsy dullness; lack of energy; sluggish inactivity.

17. **Benedict Arnold** (1741–1801), American general in the Revolutionary War who became a traitor.

After Reading

Making Connections

1. What do you suppose Jerry will be like when he is Armand's age? Explain.

2. How long do you think it took for "the good feeling to come" at the end of the story?

3. What parts of the story were easy for you to relate to? difficult for you to relate to? Explain.

4. Girls and women are barely mentioned in the story. Why do you suppose the author wrote the story this way?

5. Do you think buying and trading cards—or any other collectibles—is a good use of money? Why or why not?

6. Jerry and his friends imitated the tobacco-chewing habit of base-ball stars. Young people today also imitate sports stars. Do you think imitation is a healthy or an unhealthy practice? Explain.

7. 👣 Jerry's **individuality** helped him overlook pressure from his friends. How did his actions reveal what really mattered to him?

Literary Focus: Tone

An author's attitude toward a subject is called **tone.** Tone in writing is like tone in speaking. When you speak, people can tell whether you feel happy or sad by your facial expressions and the sound of your voice. An author shows feelings about a subject with words, treatment of characters, and imagery. Tone will tell you whether the author feels sympathy, disapproval, affection, or humor toward a subject.

The author's tone in "President Cleveland, Where Are You?" is informal and lighthearted and sometimes serious as well. To see how he creates this tone, fill in a chart like the one below. Find examples from the story for each category.

Slang	Jokes/Humor	Exaggeration
I'll muckalize you.	His voice began shooting off in all directions like some kind of vocal fireworks.	Rock-faced men with eyes of blue steel

Vocabulary Study

The list contains vocabulary words that are used to describe traits or feelings. Decide if the following pairs of words are synonyms or antonyms. On your paper, write *S* for synonym or *A* for antonym.

contempt
dejection
indignant
lethargy
obsessed

1. obsessed-uncaring
2. dejection-downheartedness
3. lethargy-alertness
4. contempt-admiration
5. indignant-displeased

Expressing Your Ideas

Writing Choices

Competition Versus Cooperation This story is about both competition and cooperation. What is the value of competition? What is the value of cooperation? Is one "better" than the other? Write an **essay** in which you answer those questions, based on the story and on your own experiences.

Space Jerry and his friends traded cards in a lot like the one pictured below. Write a **description** of what you and your friends might do in this vacant lot.

Other Options

Collectible Count Make a **graph** that shows the different kinds of collections you and your classmates have. For example, you might make a bar graph like the one below.

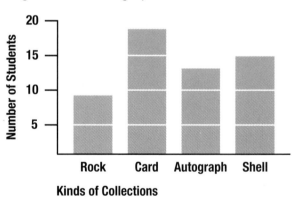

Kinds of Collections

What a Card! Why shouldn't there be a **trading card** featuring you? Make that card. Draw a picture of yourself on the front. On the back, show your **individuality** by listing the important facts and highlights of your life.

◄ *Vacant Lot* was painted by Ben Shahn in 1939.

Before Reading

Keri

by Maxine B. Rosenberg

Maxine B. Rosenberg
born 1939

Most of Maxine B. Rosenberg's books deal with young people in special situations. She has written about what it's like to be disabled, adopted, a twin, and a newcomer to the United States. To prepare a book, Rosenberg researches the subject thoroughly and then interviews young people and their parents. Rosenberg says she often worries about how unhappy the young people might be. But, she says, "Over and over again, I am proven wrong—happily! I love hearing the laughter and joy of kids who with patience, time, and hard work have found happiness where they never dreamed it existed."

Building Background

Divorce When two people get married, everyone hopes they'll live "happily ever after." However, many marriages end in divorce. In the United States, children under age eighteen are affected by over half of all divorces. Usually, the children end up living with one of the parents. Of course, the story may not end there. A divorced person may remarry. The person's children then have a new stepparent, and possibly stepbrothers or stepsisters. Any family that includes a stepparent and/or stepchildren is called a stepfamily.

Getting into the Selection

Discussion In a small group, talk about the ways stepparents and stepfamilies are portrayed in fictional stories, TV shows, and movies. What stereotypes do stories like "Cinderella" present? Why do you think those stereotypes are so common in old stories? Do you think modern stories, TV shows, and movies portray stepfamilies more realistically and fairly—or not?

Reading Tip

Interview Style As soon as you start reading "Keri," you'll notice that it is a mixture of Keri's and the author's words. Sentences and paragraphs that are in quotation marks are things that Keri told the author in an interview. Sentences and paragraphs that are not in quotation marks are things that the author is telling you, the reader, to fill in the gaps between Keri's statements. Both Keri and the author go back and forth between past and present tense. This isn't as confusing as it sounds! As you read, just take your time, and make mental notes of who's speaking and whether they're speaking about then or now.

KERI

Maxine B. Rosenberg

"My friend Mary and I started at a new school at around the same time. Since we didn't know many kids, we hung out together. Mary told me she moved to the neighborhood because her mom had died and her father had just remarried. When I said that my mom had just remarried too, we had a lot to talk about."

Keri still remembers the day her parents separated. "I was six then and had just come home from my friend Candace's house. Mom took me aside and explained that Dad was moving out. As soon as I saw Dad getting ready to go, I ran up to my room, shut the door, and cried. Even though my parents fought so much, I still didn't want their marriage to end."

For the next three years, Keri's father lived with his mother, Keri's grandma, while Keri and her mom stayed in their old house. "In the beginning, it felt weird[1] when Dad didn't come home at night. Worse, it seemed like he hardly visited me. I thought that if Mom hadn't asked for the divorce, this wouldn't be happening. Especially then, I was angry

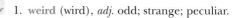

1. **weird** (wird), *adj.* odd; strange; peculiar.

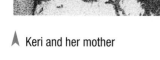

Keri and her mother

at her for messing up my life, and I was mad at Dad for not coming to see me enough.

"Even when I did spend the weekends with Dad, it wasn't much fun. He used to say bad things about Mom and tell me that he was against getting divorced. Finally Mom took me to a therapist[2] a few times, where I learned how to express my feelings to Dad. After that, I started enjoying the visits more.

"Some days Dad and I went to the movies or bowling. Other times we just hung out at Grandma's. If it was warm enough, we fed the birds and ducks at the nearby lake, which we still do today."

Even while she missed her father, Keri admits she liked having her mother to herself. "As soon as Mom got home from work, we'd eat dinner together and then talk or watch TV. It was great, just the two of us. But Mom started dating Tom when I was seven, and when he came over, everything changed."

Tom, a lawyer, was also divorced. He had two daughters, Erin and Megan, who were older than Keri. "In the beginning, Mom saw Tom when I was on weekend visits with Dad. But pretty soon she invited him to dinner. He was pretty nice—always in a good mood, joking around. Soon I realized, though, that Mom was serious about him. That made me mad, because I knew Mom would now have less time for me.

"From then on, I made up my mind that I didn't like Tom. If he talked about boring subjects at the dinner table, I made a face. When he asked me questions, I'd give one word answers or ignore him completely. As soon as he was gone, Mom would say to me, 'You know, you could have been more polite to Tom,' and I'd reply, 'Why should I be? He's not my father.'"

> "From then on, I made up my mind that I didn't like Tom."

After they'd known each other for a year and a half, Keri's mom and Tom made plans to marry. "Mom announced their plans while we were at Tom's house. Erin and Megan were there, too, and my cousin Stephanie. When I heard the news, I started crying in front of everyone. 'No! No!' I kept saying.

"I didn't want Mom to marry, and I didn't want it to be Tom—especially because I knew we'd have to move into his new home. For me, that meant going to another school and leaving my friends."

Now Keri tried harder than ever to get her parents back together again. "Whenever Dad called to talk to me, I'd tell him Mom wanted to speak to him, too, and quickly put her on the phone. My plan never worked. Almost as soon as they started speaking to each other, the conversation ended in a fight. Finally, I gave up trying.

"But then I became angrier at Mom. I kept thinking, If she hadn't wanted a divorce, I wouldn't be going through this. Every day I told her I didn't like Tom, and every day she'd try to convince me that he was a nice man. When I said I felt miserable[3] about leaving my friends, Mom said that I'd make new ones and things would be okay. But I didn't believe her.

"At the wedding, when the priest said to Tom, 'You may now kiss the bride,' I'm the only one in the pictures with a sour face."

When Keri and her mom moved into Tom's place, Keri distanced herself even more from the adults. "If Mom came home from

2. **therapist** (ther′ə pist), *n.* person who specializes in the treatment of diseases or disorders; in this case, someone who helps people deal with emotional or social problems.
3. miserable (miz′ər ə bəl), *adj.* very unhappy or unfortunate; wretched.

work and talked to Tom first, I sulked.[4] If I saw them sitting together on the couch, I walked around the house with a frown, refusing to tell Mom what was bothering me. How could I tell her I didn't want a stepfather—*any* stepfather.

"Mom tried ways to set up situations where Tom and I would be alone together, like suggesting we buy some stuff at the bakery. Immediately, I'd say, 'I'm not going,' but when Tom would start to leave without me, I'd change my mind. Those trips weren't great, but they weren't awful, either."

At least Keri had her stepsisters to look forward to. Although they lived with their mother, they visited their dad a lot. "Megan stayed over about once a month. And Erin spent her college vacations with us."

"From the beginning, I liked both of them. A few weeks before our parents' wedding, the three of us flew to Florida to vacation with their grandparents. While I felt strange being with people I hardly knew, I still had fun with the girls.

"I get along best with Megan, maybe because she's younger. When she comes over, we go ice-skating, to the movies, or to McDonald's. At night, if the parents go out, we stay home and kid around."

During vacations, when Erin lives with Keri's family, she and Keri share the same room. "You'd think that Erin would choose to sleep alone, since there's an empty bedroom with Megan not always here. But my room has the stereo, so that's why she crowds in with me. In the end, it's not so bad. We've learned to work things out. The last time she came home, we made a deal: She promised to keep her belongings on one side of the room if I kept mine on the other. The only time we run into big problems is when our parents get involved in our arguments."

Arguing and fighting are sore points with Keri. She can still remember the quarrels that went on between her mother and father. "Mostly Mom and Dad fought after I had gone to bed, thinking I was asleep. But I heard the yelling and hated it. Even today, I can't stand when people raise their voices, especially when it's Tom arguing with Mom.

"He doesn't do it that often, but when he does I try to get him to stop. It bothers me when he or anyone else yells at my mother. Mom tells me it's natural for people to have disagreements. She says it's more important that they make up and forgive. Still, I don't like it when parents raise their voices."

For a long time after the remarriage, Keri avoided Tom. "But no matter how awful I acted toward him, he never said anything nasty to me or got mean. Mostly he tried to be a friend. One time I needed to make a pillow for Home Economics, and Tom, knowing I'm not great in art, drew the cat I wanted on it. If I got stuck on a homework problem, he helped me, too. Sometimes, though, he made me angry. Once when I asked him to correct my spelling for a book report, he wrote comments up and down the side of my paper. Then I told him he was acting like a teacher.

"I know Tom wants me to do better in school and thinks he can get me to improve. He acts the same with Megan. If *I'm* satisfied with how I'm doing, that's all that's important. I wish Tom could understand that."

Despite her two-year resistance[5] to Tom, Keri has recently begun to mellow.[6] "I've

> # Arguing and fighting are sore points with Keri.

---

4. **sulk** (sulk), *v.* hold (oneself) aloof in a sullen manner; be silent and bad-humored because of resentment.
5. **resistance** (ri zis′təns), *n.* acting against; striving against; opposition.
6. **mellow** (mel′ō), *v.* soften or become wiser through age or experience.

been thinking, If I have to live with Tom, I might as well make the best of things. Besides, he isn't all that bad. He'll drive my friends and me to the movies and not even complain about it. The other day, he surprised me with a tape by my favorite group. I guess he heard me talk about them at the dinner table.

"The best thing about my stepfather is that he sticks up for me when Mom can't see my point. Last Halloween, I got to stay out an hour later because of him. Luckily, Mom doesn't mind if Tom takes my side on small stuff, because she knows he won't interfere if big things about me come up. Then, she and Dad make the decisions. Now that my parents are apart, they agree on most things, especially when it comes to my safety. I'm glad they get along that way.

"Although I wish my parents hadn't divorced, I remember how they argued, and I know that if they had stayed together there would be more problems for me today."

Since her mother's remarriage, Keri's relationship with her father has also changed (although one thing had nothing to do with the other). "Dad recently moved into his own house, which is nice, but now he has a girlfriend, Laura, who's usually there when I visit. That means I don't get to be alone with him

▲ Keri and her stepsisters

as much. Also, Laura's very young—twenty-five—although she looks and acts older. Sometimes I get embarrassed thinking about Dad being with someone almost the same age as my stepsister Erin.

"Despite all these changes in my life, I'm sure that anyone meeting me today would say I have it good. Truthfully, I like things the way they are now—at least most of the time. Some days I'm an only child who gets spoiled a lot. But other days I have Erin and Megan to tell my secrets to. My stepsisters are the best part of Mom's remarriage.

"Even in school I'm happy, and I wouldn't want to be any other place. Although it was hard adjusting at first, I like my friends, and now I'm popular with the cool group.

"As for having Mom all to myself, that's something that can't be. We still play cards together and watch TV, but now Mom sits in the middle, between Tom and me.

"The most important thing is that I have a family with a mother and a father. It doesn't matter if the father is a stepdad. I'm more interested in everyone being kind to one another, and that's what it's finally like in my house."

After Reading

Making Connections

1. Did reading about Keri change any of your ideas about stepfamilies, or not? Explain.

2. Do you think Keri's mother and Tom could have done something more to improve the situation with Keri? Explain.

3. What do you think Keri's life will be like five years from now?

4. ✿ How did Keri's **individuality** affect her relationships with the new members of her family?

5. Suppose you had been the one interviewing Keri. List three questions you would have asked to get more information about her situation and opinions.

6. In the last paragraph of the selection, Keri sums up her opinion about what really matters in family life. Do you agree with her ideas? Why or why not?

Literary Focus: Author's Purpose

Authors have **purposes** for writing the things they do. Three common purposes authors have are to entertain, to inform, and to persuade the reader. Authors often have more than one purpose in a single piece of writing. For example, an author may want to provide information in a way that is interesting, if not entertaining. Usually, though, one purpose outweighs the others.

Decide what the author's main purpose was in writing about Keri. Choose from the following. Support your choice with examples from "Keri."

- The author wanted to entertain.

- The author wanted to inform the readers what life in a stepfamily is really like.

- The author wanted to persuade the readers that life in a stepfamily is great.

Vocabulary Study

Choose the word from the list that most closely relates to the situation described.

mellow
miserable
resistance
sulk
weird

1. When Jamie's grandfather moved in, Jamie had to give up his room and share a room with his brother. The first couple of weeks Grandpa was there, Jamie would ____ and not talk to him.

2. When David's parents were divorced, he was sent to live with an aunt and uncle for the summer. When he woke up the first morning, everything in the unfamiliar room looked ____.

3. Steve's dad has a new wife. Steve shows his ____ to the situation by not doing his chores when his stepmother asks him.

4. Sarah's parents always got into arguments during car trips. In the back seat, Sarah felt ____ and wished she could be somewhere else.

5. Recently, Jennifer found the diary she kept ten years ago, when she was eleven. She couldn't believe all the mean things she wrote about her stepbrother back then. These days, she's much more ____ toward him.

Expressing Your Ideas

Writing Choices

Their Turn Imagine you are either Keri's mom or Tom. Write two **diary entries.** The first entry should focus on a day soon after your wedding, when Keri was nine. The second entry should focus on Keri's eleventh birthday. In both entries, tell what's going on in the family and how you feel about it.

Advice from Keri You are Keri, grown up. Your job is writing a column about personal and family issues for a magazine aimed at young people. Use Keri's prior experiences as well as your own to write this month's **column**, titled "Coping with Your Parents' Divorce."

Other Options

Family Hour With a group of classmates, plan a new TV series about a fictional American family, and make an **oral presentation** of your plan to the rest of the class. In your presentation, answer these questions:

- Who are the members of this family? Where do they live? How do they spend their time?

- How will the series entertain its audience?

- What values will the series reflect?

Room for Improvement What suggestions do you have for ways to improve family relationships? Use drawings and pictures from newspapers and magazines to make a **collage** that gets your ideas across.

Writing mini-Lesson

Maintaining Your Working Portfolio

Looking Over What You Have Whether you have been keeping your working portfolio or your teacher has been keeping it, now is the time to take it out and review it.

- First, review your statement of your goals. Do you have pieces in your portfolio that show that you are working toward or have met each goal? If not, what kinds of writing do you need?

- Next, look at your writing samples. Do you have all your planning pieces, your first drafts, your revised and edited drafts, and the final copies for all your samples? Do you have many different kinds of writing—critical writing, reports, narratives, poems, etc.?

- Finally, is there anything in your portfolio that you don't think should be there? What pieces do you really like? What pieces are not good examples of your best work? Make a list of items that you need to add or remove before you prepare your presentation portfolio at the end of the year.

Making a Mid-Course Correction What about the goals themselves? Look over your goal statement and decide whether these goals are still the ones that you want to reach. Also, think about your progress in reaching the goals. Did you take on more than you can accomplish, or did you underestimate yourself? You might ask a partner for a second opinion on your goals and the written pieces you have produced.

Take some time to rewrite your goals. If you have already met your goals, then set some new ones. Be sure to include the changes you want to make in your portfolio and what you plan to accomplish for the next grading period.

Before Reading

Andre by Gwendolyn Brooks

Common Bond by Kimi Narimatsu

Gwendolyn Brooks
born 1917

Gwendolyn Brooks says, "I loved poetry very early and began to put rhymes together at about seven, at which time my parents expressed most earnest confidence that I would one day be a writer." They were right; Brooks's first poem was published when she was only thirteen, and she won the Pulitzer Prize when she was thirty-three. Many of Brooks's poems are written for young people, and even her poems for adults often center on children's feelings, experiences, hopes, and dreams. To her own children, Brooks once wrote, "Rejoice in many people. But never let your delight in any one prevent you from doing what you know is right for you." Brooks still lives in Chicago, where she grew up. She is the poet laureate (official poet) of Illinois.

Building Background

What Is a Poem? Many people have tried to define poetry, and most have found it a difficult task. Still, we *can* say that poems share certain qualities. For example, almost all poems present feelings that the poet has. A poet may be writing in response to a beautiful scene, an unusual experience, or a caring relationship. Of course, the poet hopes you will read those words and experience the same feelings.

Getting into the Poems

Writer's Notebook A role model is a person whose way of behaving influences someone else's actions and beliefs. Parents are role models for their children in "Andre" and "Common Bond." Who is the most important role model in your life? In your notebook, make a word web like the one below. Write the name of your role model in the center circle. In the outer circles, write words and phrases that tell what the person is like and why he or she is your role model. Add as many circles as you need to.

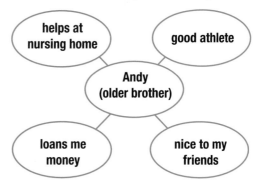

Reading Tip

Structures of Poems You already know that poems can have a wide variety of forms. As you read "Andre" and "Common Bond," take note of their forms. Notice, for example, whether each poem uses rhyme and, if so, what the pattern is. Notice what the rhythm is like in each poem: is it regular or varied? Notice, too, the effects produced by the spaces between certain lines in "Andre" and the indentation of some lines in "Common Bond."

ANDRE

Gwendolyn Brooks

I had a dream last night. I dreamed
I had to pick a Mother out.
I had to choose a Father too.
At first, I wondered what to do,
5 There were so many there, it seemed,
Short and tall and thin and stout.

But just before I sprang awake,
I knew what parents I would take.

And *this* surprised and made me glad:
10 They were the ones I always had!

COMMON BOND

Kimi Narimatsu

My mother,
not so close are we,
yet we share a common bond,
    a goal,
5   a unity.
Not because she is my mother,
and I her daughter
But because we are both Asian,
in a world of prejudices and hate.
10 We need to stay together as one,
to survive,
    to love,
    to live.
We need to fight for our rights.
15 My mother,
she lives in a world as a person.
She fights for what she knows is right.
She works so hard to give me what I need.
    I give her in return what she needs,
20   love,
        peace,
        understanding,
        and the will to live as an Asian
           and person.
Together, my mother and I are one.

▲ *Family Group* is a bronze sculpture that was created by Henry Moore in 1948-1949. What does this sculpture say to you about families?

After Reading

Making Connections

1. Why do you suppose the speaker in the first poem is surprised by his discovery?

2. How old do you think the speaker of each poem is? Why do you think so?

3. Which poem says more to you? Explain why. Be sure to tell whether the **rhyme** pattern or the **rhythm** influenced your choice.

4. How do you think each poem relates to the theme, "What Really Matters"?

5. What common bond do you have with the person who means the most to you?

Literary Focus: Tone

On page 283, you learned that **tone** is an author's attitude toward a subject. With a partner, take turns reading each poem aloud. As you listen to your partner read, write down your ideas about the tone. Your partner should do the same while you read. Then compare your ideas and write a description of the tone of each poem. Compare the similarities and differences in their tones. Decide, too, how each poet created the particular tone that she did. Consider word choice, punctuation, rhyme, rhythm, and other features.

Expressing Your Ideas

Your Own Poetry Write a **poem** about a family member or friend who is important to you. Express your feelings about the person and your relationship with him or her. For example, if the person is a role model for you, you might tell why. Or you might write about something the two of you have in common.

Add One Cup of Love Write a **recipe** for getting along with parents. Use a real food recipe as your model.

Picture This Draw or paint a **picture** to illustrate each of the poems. Make sure each picture reflects not only the content but the tone of the poem.

Poems and More Poems Collect other poems for an **anthology** on the theme of "What Really Matters." Your librarian can help you find a variety of possibilities. Once your collection is complete, share it with your classmates.

Before Reading

The Dog of Pompeii

by Louis Untermeyer

Louis Untermeyer
1885–1977

"Fantasy was the most important part of my boyhood," Louis Untermeyer once said. "At ten I fancied myself a storyteller; my brother was a rewarding listener." Still, Untermeyer admitted, "Until I was eighteen it never occurred to me that I might be a writer." For years, he wrote poems on the side while working in his family's jewelry business. "Increasingly dissatisfied with business routine," he eventually quit in order to write full-time. His numerous works include poetry for young people and adults, retellings of old tales, and original fiction and nonfiction. One of the archaeological finds at Pompeii inspired Untermeyer to write "The Dog of Pompeii."

Building Background

Pompeii Buried In ancient times, Pompeii (pom pā′) was a thriving seaport in the Roman Empire. Then, one day in A.D. 79, a nearby volcano named Mount Vesuvius (və sü′vē əs) erupted. The top of the volcano collapsed during the explosion. Pompeii disappeared under a thick layer of ashes and stones. For centuries, the city lay buried. Today, much of the city has been uncovered by archaeologists. Visitors can wander through the same streets and buildings as the characters in "The Dog of Pompeii."

Getting into the Story

Discussion Talk about the kinds of pets you've had and your relationships with them. Also talk about animals that perform tasks for people, such as dog guides. Whether pets or helpers, what do animals give to their owners?

Reading Tip

Historical Fiction "The Dog of Pompeii" is a work of historical fiction, in which invented characters are placed in a historically factual setting to act out a fictional **plot**. As you read "The Dog of Pompeii," look for details that help you form a mental picture of ancient Pompeii and its people. You might want to keep track of some of the details in lists with headings like *Buildings, Foods, Occupations,* and *Leisure Activities.*

▲ Does this painting fit your image of Pompeii?

THE DOG OF POMPEII

Louis Untermeyer

Tito and his dog Bimbo lived (if you could call it living) under the wall where it joined the inner gate. They really didn't live there; they just slept there. They lived anywhere. Pompeii was one of the gayest of the old Latin towns, but although Tito was never an unhappy boy, he was not exactly a merry one. The streets were always lively with shining chariots and bright red trappings;[1] the open-air theaters rocked with laughing crowds; <u>sham</u>[2] battles and athletic sports were free for the asking in the great stadium. Once a year the Caesar[3] visited the pleasure city and the fireworks lasted for days, the sacrifices in the Forum[4] were better than a show. But Tito saw none of these things. He was blind—had been blind from birth. He was known to everyone in the poorer quarters. But no one could say how old he was, no one remembered his parents, no one could tell where he came from. Bimbo was another mystery. As long as people could remember seeing Tito—about twelve or thirteen years—they had seen Bimbo, Bimbo had never left his side. He was not only dog, but nurse, pillow, playmate, mother and father to Tito.

Did I say Bimbo never left his master? (Perhaps I had better say comrade, for if any one was the master, it was Bimbo.) I was wrong. Bimbo did trust Tito alone exactly three times a day. It was a fixed routine, a custom

---

1. **trappings** (trap′ingz), *n.* ornamental coverings.
2. sham (sham), *adj.* false; pretended; imitation.
3. **Caesar** (sē′zər), title of the ancient Roman emperors.
4. **forum** (fôr′əm), *n.* the public square or market place of an ancient Roman city.

understood between boy and dog since the beginning of their friendship, and the way it worked was this: Early in the morning, shortly after dawn, while Tito was still dreaming, Bimbo would disappear. When Tito woke, Bimbo would be sitting quietly at his side, his ears cocked, his stump of a tail tapping the ground, and a fresh-baked bread—more like a large round roll—at his feet. Tito would stretch himself: Bimbo would yawn; then they would breakfast. At noon, no matter where they happened to be, Bimbo would put his paw on Tito's knee and the two of them would return to the inner gate. Tito would curl up in the corner (almost like a dog) and go to sleep, while Bimbo, looking quite important (almost like a boy) would disappear again. In half an hour he'd be back with their lunch. Sometimes it would be a piece of fruit or a scrap of meat, often it was nothing but a dry crust. But sometimes there would be one of those flat rich cakes, sprinkled with raisins and sugar, that Tito liked so much. At supper time the same thing happened, although there was a little less of everything, for things were hard to snatch in the evening with the streets full of people. Besides, Bimbo didn't approve of too much food before going to sleep. A heavy supper made boys too restless and dogs too stodgy—and it was the business of a dog to sleep lightly with one ear open and muscles ready for action.

But, whether there was much or little, hot or cold, fresh or dry, food was always there. Tito never asked where it came from and Bimbo never told him. There was plenty of rainwater in the hollows of soft stones; the old egg-woman at the corner sometimes gave him a cupful of strong goat's milk; in the grape season the fat wine-maker let him have drippings of the mild juice. So there was no danger of going hungry or thirsty. There was plenty of everything in Pompeii, if you knew where to find it—and if you had a dog like Bimbo.

As I said before, Tito was not the merriest boy in Pompeii. He could not romp with the other youngsters and play Hare-and-Hounds and I-spy and Follow-your-Master and Ball-against-the-Building and Jack-stones and Kings-and-Robbers with them. But that did not make him sorry for himself. If he could not see the sights that delighted the lads of Pompeii he could hear and smell things they never noticed. He could really see more with his ears and nose than they could with their eyes. When he and Bimbo went out walking he knew just where they were going and exactly what was happening.

"Ah," he'd sniff and say, as they passed a handsome villa, "Glaucus Pansa is giving a grand dinner tonight. They're going to have three kinds of bread, and roast pigling, and stuffed goose, and a great stew—I think bear stew—and a fig pie." And Bimbo would note that this would be a good place to visit tomorrow.

Or, "H'm," Tito would murmur, half through his lips, half through his nostrils. "The wife of Marcus Lucretius is expecting her mother. She's shaking out every piece of goods in the house; she's going to use the best clothes—the ones she's been keeping in pine needles and camphor[5]—and there's an extra girl in the kitchen. Come, Bimbo, let's get out of the dust!"

Or, as they passed a small but elegant dwelling opposite the public baths, "Too bad! The tragic poet is ill again. It must be a bad fever this time, for they're trying smoke fumes instead of medicine. Whew! I'm glad I'm not a tragic poet!"

Or, as they neared the Forum, "Mm-m! What good things they have in the Macellum

---

5. **camphor** (kam′fər), *n.* a white, crystalline substance with a strong odor, used in medicine and to protect clothes from moths.

today!" (It really was a sort of butcher-grocer-market-place, but Tito didn't know any better. He called it the Macellum.) "Dates from Africa, and salt oysters from sea caves, and cuttle-fish, and new honey, and sweet onions, and—ugh!—water-buffalo steaks. Come, let's see what's what in the Forum." And Bimbo, just as curious as his comrade, hurried on. Being a dog, he trusted his ears and nose (like Tito) more than his eyes. And so the two of them entered the center of Pompeii.

This mosaic is from the National Archaeological Museum in Naples, Italy. Do you think the dog represented in this mosaic could have done the things that Bimbo did?

The Forum was the part of the town to which everybody came at least once during each day. It was the Central Square and everything happened here. There were no private houses; all was public—the chief temples, the gold and red bazaars,[6] the silk shops, the town hall, the booths belonging to the weavers and jewel merchants, the wealthy woolen market, the Shrine of the Household Gods.[7] Everything glittered here. The buildings looked as if they were new—which, in a sense, they were. The earthquake of twelve years ago had brought down all the old structures and, since the citizens of Pompeii were ambitious to rival Naples and even Rome, they had seized the opportunity to rebuild the whole town. And they had done it all within a dozen years. There was scarcely a building that was older than Tito.

Tito had heard a great deal about the earthquake though, being about a year old at the time, he could scarcely remember it. This particular quake had been a light one—as earthquakes go. The weaker houses had been shaken down, parts of the outworn wall had been wrecked; but there was little loss of life, and the brilliant new Pompeii had taken the place of the old. No one knew what caused these earthquakes. Records showed they had happened in the neighborhood since the beginning of time. Sailors said that it was to teach the lazy city folk a lesson and make them appreciate those who risked the dangers of the sea to bring them luxuries and protect their town from invaders. The priests said that the gods took this way of showing their anger to those who refused to worship properly and who failed to bring enough sacrifices to the altars and (though they didn't say it in so many words) presents to the priests. The tradesmen said that the foreign merchants had corrupted[8] the ground and it was no

6. **bazaar** (bə zär′), *n.* street or streets full of small shops and booths where things are sold.
7. **Shrine of the Household Gods,** place dedicated to the gods that were believed to protect the hearth, crops, livestock, and so on.
8. **corrupt** (kə rupt′), *v.* make evil or wicked; make rotten, spoiled, or decayed.

longer safe to traffic[9] in imported goods that came from strange places and carried a curse with them. Everyone had a different explanation—and everyone's explanation was louder and sillier than his neighbor's.

They were talking about it this afternoon as Tito and Bimbo came out of the side street into the public square. The Forum was the favorite promenade for rich and poor. What with the priests arguing with the politicians, servants doing the day's shopping, tradesmen crying their wares,[10] women displaying the latest fashions from Greece and Egypt, children playing hide-and-seek among the marble columns, knots[11] of soldiers, sailors, peasants from the provinces—to say nothing of those who merely came to lounge and look on—the square was crowded to its last inch. His ears even more than his nose guided Tito to the place where the talk was loudest. It was in front of the Shrine of the Household Gods that, naturally enough, the householders were arguing.

"I tell you," rumbled a voice which Tito recognized as bathmaster Rufus's, "there won't be another earthquake in my lifetime or yours. There may be a tremble or two, but earthquakes, like lightnings, never strike twice in the same place."

"Do they not?" asked a thin voice Tito had never heard. It had a high, sharp ring to it and Tito knew it as the accent of a stranger. "How about the two towns of Sicily that have been ruined three times within fifteen years by the eruptions of Mount Etna? And were they not warned? And does that column of smoke above Vesuvius mean nothing?"

"That?" Tito could hear the grunt with which one question answered another. "That's always there. We use it for our weather guide. When the smoke stands up straight we know we'll have fair weather when it flattens out it's sure to be foggy when it drifts to the east—"

"Yes, yes," cut in the edged voice. "I've heard about your mountain barometer.[12] But the column of smoke seems hundreds of feet higher than usual and it's thickening and spreading like a shadowy tree. They say in Naples—"

"Oh, Naples!" Tito knew this voice by the little squeak that went with it. It was Attilio, the cameo-cutter. "They talk while we suffer. Little help we got from them last time. Naples commits the crimes and Pompeii pays the price. It's become a proverb[13] with us. Let them mind their own business."

"Yes," grumbled Rufus, "and others, too."

"Very well, my confident friends," responded the thin voice which now sounded curiously flat. "We also have a proverb—and it is this: Those who will not listen to men must be taught by the gods. I say no more. But I leave a last warning. Remember the holy ones. Look to your temples. And when the smoke tree above Vesuvius grows to the shape of an umbrella pine, look to your lives."

Tito could hear the air whistle as the speaker drew his toga[14] about him and the quick shuffle of feet told him the stranger had gone.

"Now what," said the cameo-cutter, "did he mean by that?"

"I wonder," grunted Rufus, "I wonder."

Tito wondered, too. And Bimbo, his head at a thoughtful angle, looked as if he had been doing a heavy piece of pondering. By nightfall the argument had been forgotten. If the smoke had increased

---

9. **traffic** (traf′ik), *v.* carry on trade; buy; sell; exchange.
10. **crying their wares**, advertising items for sale by calling out.
11. **knot** (not), *n.* group; cluster.
12. **barometer** (bə rom′ə tər), *n.* something that forecasts the weather.
13. **proverb** (prov′ėrb′), *n.* a short, wise saying used for a long time by many people.
14. **toga** (tō′gə), *n.* a loose, outer garment worn in public by citizens of ancient Rome.

no one saw it in the dark. Besides, it was Caesar's birthday and the town was in holiday mood. Tito and Bimbo were among the merry-makers, dodging the charioteers who shouted at them. A dozen times they almost upset baskets of sweets and jars of Vesuvian wine, said to be as fiery as the streams inside the volcano, and a dozen times they were cursed and cuffed. But Tito never missed his footing. He was thankful for his keen ears and quick instinct—most thankful of all for Bimbo.

They visited the uncovered theater and, though Tito could not see the faces of the

The air was hot. And heavy. So heavy that he could taste it.

actors, he could follow the play better than most of the audience, for their attention wandered—they were distracted by the scenery, the costumes, the byplay, even by themselves—while Tito's whole attention was centered in what he heard. Then to the city walls, where the people of Pompeii watched a mock naval battle in which the city was attacked by the sea and saved after thousands of flaming arrows had been exchanged and countless colored torches had been burned. Though the thrill of flaring ships and lighted skies was lost to Tito, the shouts and cheers excited him as much as any and he cried out with the loudest of them.

The next morning there were *two* of the beloved raisin and sugar cakes for his breakfast. Bimbo was unusually active and thumped his bit of a tail until Tito was afraid he would wear it out. The boy could not imagine whether Bimbo was urging him to some sort of game or was trying to tell something. After a while, he ceased to notice Bimbo. He felt

drowsy. Last night's late hours had tired him. Besides, there was a heavy mist in the air—no, a thick fog rather than a mist—a fog that got into his throat and scraped it and made him cough. He walked as far as the marine gate to get a breath of the sea. But the blanket of haze had spread all over the bay and even the salt air seemed smoky.

He went to bed before dusk and slept. But he did not sleep well. He had too many dreams—dreams of ships lurching in the Forum, of losing his way in a screaming crowd, of armies marching across his chest, of being pulled over every rough pavement of Pompeii.

He woke early. Or, rather, he was pulled awake. Bimbo was doing the pulling. The dog had dragged Tito to his feet and was urging the boy along. Somewhere. Where, Tito did not know. His feet stumbled uncertainly; he was still half asleep. For a while he noticed nothing except the fact that it was hard to breathe. The air was hot. And heavy. So heavy that he could taste it. The air it seemed, had turned to powder, a warm powder that stung his nostrils and burned his sightless eyes.

Then he began to hear sounds. Peculiar sounds. Like animals under the earth. Hissings and groanings and muffled cries that a dying creature might make dislodging the stones of his underground cave. There was no doubt of it now. The noises came from underneath. He not only heard them—he could feel them. The earth twitched; the twitching changed to an uneven shrugging of the soil. Then, as Bimbo half pulled, half coaxed him across, the ground jerked away from his feet and he was thrown against a stone fountain.

The water—hot water—splashing in his face revived[15] him. He got to his feet, Bimbo

---

15. **revive** (ri vīv′), *v.* bring back to consciousness; bring back to a fresh, lively condition; refresh; restore.

The Dog of Pompeii   **303**

steadying him, helping him on again. The noises grew louder; they came closer. The cries were even more animal-like than before, but now they came from human throats. A few people, quicker of foot and more hurried by fear, began to rush by. A family or two—then a section—then, it seemed, an army broken out of bounds.[16] Tito bewildered though he was, could recognize Rufus as he bellowed past him, like a water buffalo gone mad. Time was lost in a nightmare.

It was then the crashing began. First a sharp crackling, like a monstrous snapping of twigs; then a roar like the fall of a whole forest of trees; then an explosion that tore earth and sky. The heavens, though Tito could not see them, were shot through with continual flickerings of fire. Lightnings above were answered by thunders beneath. A house fell. Then another. By a miracle the two companions had escaped the dangerous side streets and were in a more open space. It was the Forum. They rested here awhile—how long he did not know.

Tito had no idea of the time of day. He could feel it was black—an unnatural blackness. Something inside—perhaps the lack of breakfast and lunch—told him it was past noon. But it didn't matter. Nothing seemed to matter. He was getting drowsy, too drowsy to walk. But walk he must. He knew it. And Bimbo knew it; the sharp tugs told him so. Nor was it a moment too soon. The sacred ground of the Forum was safe no longer. It was beginning to rock, then to pitch, then to split. As they stumbled out of the square, the earth wriggled like a caught snake and all the columns of the temple of Jupiter[17] came down. It was the end of the world—or so it seemed.

To walk was not enough now. They must run. Tito was too frightened to know what to do or where to go. He had lost all sense of direction. He started to go back to the inner gate, but Bimbo, straining his back to the last inch, almost pulled his clothes from him. What did the creature want? Had the dog gone mad?

Then, suddenly, he understood. Bimbo was telling him the way out—urging him there. The sea gate of course. The sea gate— and then the sea. Far from falling buildings, heaving ground. He turned, Bimbo guiding him across open pits and dangerous pools of bubbling mud, away from buildings that had caught fire and were dropping their burning beams. Tito could no longer tell whether the noises were made by the shrieking sky or the agonized[18] people. He and Bimbo ran on— the only silent beings in a howling world.

New dangers threatened. All Pompeii seemed to be thronging toward the marine gate and, squeezing among the crowds, there was the chance of being trampled to death. But the chance had to be taken. It was growing harder and harder to breathe. What air there was choked him. It was all dust now—dust and pebbles, pebbles as large as beans. They fell on his head, his hands—pumice[19] stones from the black heart of Vesuvius. The mountain was turning itself inside out. Tito remembered a phrase that the stranger had said in the Forum two days ago: "Those who will not listen to men must be taught by the gods." The people of Pompeii had refused to heed the warnings; they were being taught now—if it was not too late.

Suddenly it seemed too late for Tito. The red hot ashes blistered his skin, the stinging vapors tore his throat. He could not go on. He staggered toward a small tree at the side of the

---

16. **out of bounds**, in this case, out of proper formation.
17. **Jupiter** (jü′pə tər), king of Roman gods.
18. agonized (ag′ə nīzd), *adj.* painfully suffering; greatly anguished.
19. **pumice** (pum′is), *n.* a light, porous, glassy rock formed by the cooling of melted rock flowing from a volcano.

How would you have reacted to this scene?

road and fell. In a moment Bimbo was beside him. He coaxed. But there was no answer. He licked Tito's hands, his feet, his face. The boy did not stir. Then Bimbo did the last thing he could—the last thing he wanted to do. He bit his comrade, bit him deep in the arm. With a cry of pain, Tito jumped to his feet, Bimbo after him. Tito was in despair, but Bimbo was determined. He drove the boy on, snapping at his heels, worrying[20] his way through the crowd; barking, baring his teeth, heedless of kicks or falling stones. Sick with hunger, half dead with fear and sulfur[21] fumes, Tito pounded on, pursued by Bimbo. How long he never knew. At last he staggered through

the marine gate and felt soft sand under him. Then Tito fainted. . . .

Someone was dashing sea water over him. Someone was carrying him toward a boat.

"Bimbo," he called. And then louder, "Bimbo!" But Bimbo had disappeared.

Voices jarred against each other. "Hurry—hurry!" "To the boats!" "Can't you see the child's frightened and starving!" "He keeps calling for someone!" "Poor boy, he's out of his mind." "Here, child—take this!"

---

20. **worry** (wėr′ē), *v.* move by persistent, nagging effort.
21. **sulfur** (sul′fər), *n.* a light-yellow nonmetallic element that burns easily, producing a stifling odor. Sulfur is found in volcanoes.

▲ The ashes of a dog found in the ruins.

They tucked him in among them. The oar-locks creaked; the oars splashed; the boat rode over toppling waves. Tito was safe. But he wept continually.

"Bimbo!" he wailed. "Bimbo! Bimbo!"

He could not be comforted.

Eighteen hundred years passed. Scientists were restoring the ancient city; excavators were working their way thorough the stones and trash that had buried the entire town. Much had already been brought to light—statues, bronze instruments, bright mosaics,[22] household articles; even delicate paintings had been preserved by the fall of ashes that had taken over two thousand lives. Columns were dug up and the Forum was beginning to emerge.

It was at a place where the ruins lay deepest that the Director paused.

"Come here," he called to his assistant. "I think we've discovered the remains of a building in good shape. Here are four huge mill-stones that were most likely turned by slaves or mules—and here is a whole wall standing with shelves inside it. Why! It must have been a bakery. And here's a curious thing. What do you think I found under this heap where the ashes were thickest? The skeleton of a dog!"

"Amazing!" gasped his assistant. "You'd think a dog would have had sense enough to run away at the time. And what is that flat thing he's holding between his teeth? It can't be a stone."

"No. It must have come from this bakery. You know it looks to me like some sort of cake hardened with the years. And, bless me, if those little black pebbles aren't raisins. A raisin cake almost two thousand years old! I wonder what made him want it at such a moment?"

"I wonder," murmured the assistant.

---

22. **mosaic** (mō zā′ik), *n.* picture or design made by inlaying small pieces of colored stone in mortar.

After Reading

Making Connections

1. How did this story make you feel? List three words that describe your feelings.

2. How might the relationship between Tito and Bimbo have been different if Tito had been able to see?

3. How do you suppose Tito managed without Bimbo for the rest of his life?

4. Did the author make you believe a dog like Bimbo could really exist, or did Bimbo seem like some kind of superdog? Explain.

5. Compare and contrast your own relationship with a pet to Tito's relationship with Bimbo.

Literary Focus: Setting

The author portrays the **setting** of the story—Pompeii in A.D. 79—so vividly that you can almost see it, hear it, and smell it. Compare and contrast that setting with the setting of your own community. Copy the diagram below, leaving plenty of room for writing. On the left side, write details from the story. On the right side, write details about your own community. What differences and similarities do you see?

Pompeii in A.D. 79   **My Community Today**

Pompeii in A.D. 79	My Community Today
Public Buildings and Places	**Public Buildings and Places**
↓	↓
Things to Buy in Shops	**Things to Buy in Shops**
↓	↓
Occupations	**Occupations**
↓	↓
Leisure Activities	**Leisure Activities**

The Dog of Pompeii   **307**

Vocabulary Study

Use your understanding of the meaning of the boldfaced word to complete each of the following sentences about Pompeii. Write the letter of the phrase that best completes the sentence.

agonized
corrupt
proverb
revive
sham

1. When **sham** battles took place,
   a. many people died.   c. no one was hurt.
   b. the city was conquered.

2. Those who thought foreign merchants would **corrupt** the ground
   a. feared the foreign merchants.   c. liked foreign ideas.
   b. wanted imports to increase.

3. When the stranger recited his **proverb** at the Forum, he was giving
   a. a recipe for raisin cakes.   c. directions to Naples.
   b. advice based on others' experience.

4. To **revive** Tito after the escape from Pompeii, rescuers probably
   a. left him alone.   c. gave him food and water.
   b. put him to work.

5. The **agonized** victims of Vesuvius
   a. were angry.   c. were unaware of
   b. suffered greatly.   what was happening.

Expressing Your Ideas _____

Writing Choices

In the Year 4000 Two thousand years from now, an archaeologist discovers something of yours. A writer hears about the object and writes a story about it. Decide what the object is, and write a **summary** of the story. Remember, the author knows nothing about you except what he or she imagines from the object!

Tito's Feelings Several days have passed since the eruption of Mount Vesuvius and the destruction of Pompeii. Write a **description** of Tito's feelings about what happened that awful day, especially his feelings about the loss of Bimbo.

Other Options

Drawing the City That Was Use your diagram about life in Pompeii to draw the city as it looked before the eruption. Include as many features from the story as you can.

What Else Have They Found? Archaeologists have found many objects, ranging from works of art to ordinary household items, in the ruins of Pompeii. Do library research to find out more about what the scientists have uncovered. Present your findings in a **bulletin-board display** that includes pictures of the items and brief explanatory captions.

The Princess and the Tin Box

by James Thurber

James Thurber
1894–1961
James Thurber was one of
America's most popular
humorists, as well as being
known for his cartoons, witty
stories, essays, and plays.
Although he made a career of
being funny, Thurber was not
a particularly cheerful or optimistic person. He considered
himself typical of humorists in
that way, saying that "the
notion that such persons
are . . . carefree is curiously
untrue. . . . The little wheels of
their invention are set in
motion by the damp hand of
melancholy." Thurber also
disputed a commonly held
view of his humor: "I'm always
astounded when my humor is
described as gentle," he said
in his joking-yet-serious way
the year before he died. "It's
anything but that, and I intend
to beat up the next person
who says that about me."

Building Background

Fabulous Jewels Jewels are also called gems. Most gems,
including diamonds, are minerals that are dug out of the earth and
then cut and polished until they sparkle. Some gems come from
other sources in nature. For example, pearls form inside the shells
of oysters. In general, the more rare and beautiful a gem is, the
higher its value in dollars. In the past, the most valuable gems, like
diamonds, were called *precious*, while less valuable gems, like
garnets, were called *semiprecious*. Experts no longer use those
terms, because a fine and rare garnet can be more valuable than a
diamond.

Getting into the Story

Discussion It's the birthday of your dreams. You've just received
three fantastic presents. They may even contain gems like those
described above. However, there's a catch. You can open and
keep only one of them. How will you decide which one to open?
Will you be swayed by the givers of the presents? Think about the
problem, and then share your ideas in a small group.

Reading Tip

Understanding a Modern Fable Traditionally, a **fable** is a short
tale that teaches a clear lesson. Usually, the characters are
animals that act like humans, and the lesson is stated as a moral
at the end of the story. "The Princess and the Tin Box" is a
modern fable—a fable with a twist or two. As you read it, look for
ways in which the story is similar to and different from other fables
you know about. You may want to review the characteristics of
fables on page 264 before you start.

The Princess and the Tin Box

James Thurber

Once upon a time, in a far country, there lived a king whose daughter was the prettiest princess in the world. Her eyes were like the cornflower, her hair was sweeter than the hyacinth, and her throat made the swan look dusty.

From the time she was a year old, the princess had been showered with presents. Her nursery looked like Cartier's[1] window. Her toys were all made of gold or platinum or diamonds or emeralds. She was not permitted to have wooden blocks or china dolls or rubber dogs or linen books, because such materials were considered cheap for the daughter of a king.

When she was seven, she was allowed to attend the wedding of her brother and throw real pearls at the bride instead of rice. Only the nightingale, with his lyre[2] of gold, was permitted to sing for the princess. The common blackbird, with his boxwood flute, was kept out of the palace grounds. She walked in silver-and-samite slippers to a sapphire-and-topaz bathroom and slept in an ivory bed inlaid with rubies.

On the day the princess was eighteen, the king sent a royal ambassador to the courts of five neighboring kingdoms to announce that he would give his daughter's hand in marriage to the prince who brought her the gift she liked the most.

The first prince to arrive at the palace rode a swift white stallion and laid at the feet of the princess an enormous apple made of solid gold which he had taken from a dragon who had guarded it for a thousand years. It was placed on a long ebony table set up to hold the gifts of the princess's suitors. The second prince, who came on a gray charger,[3] brought her a nightingale made of a thousand dia-

---

1. **Cartier's** (kär tyāz′), a famous jewelry store.
2. **lyre** (līr), *n.* an ancient stringed musical instrument somewhat like a small harp.
3. **charger** (chär′jər), *n.* a war horse.

▲ *The Royal Music Barque* was painted by James Christensen. Do you think the princess in this painting reinforces the description of the princess in the story?

monds, and it was placed beside the golden apple. The third prince, riding on a black horse, carried a great jewel box made of platinum and sapphires, and it was placed next to the diamond nightingale. The fourth prince, astride a fiery yellow horse, gave the princess a gigantic heart made of rubies and pierced by an emerald arrow. It was placed next to the platinum-and-sapphire jewel box.

Now the fifth prince was the strongest and handsomest of all the five suitors, but he was the son of a poor king whose realm had been overrun by mice and locusts and wizards and mining engineers so that there was nothing much of value left in it. He came plodding up to the palace of the princess on a plow horse and he brought her a small tin box filled with mica and feldspar and hornblende which he had picked up on the way.

The other princes roared with disdainful laughter when they saw the tawdry⁴ gift the fifth prince had brought to the princess. But she examined it with great interest and squealed with delight, for all her life she had been glutted⁵ with precious stones and priceless metals, but she had never seen tin before or mica or feldspar or hornblende. The tin box was placed next to the ruby heart pierced with an emerald arrow.

"Now," the king said to his daughter, "you must select the gift you like best and marry the prince that brought it."

The princess smiled and walked up to the table and picked up the present she liked the most. It was the platinum-and-sapphire jewel box, the gift of the third prince.

"The way I figure it," she said, "is this. It is a very large and expensive box, and when I am married, I will meet many admirers who will give me precious gems with which to fill it to the top. Therefore, it is the most valuable of all the gifts my suitors have brought me and I like it the best."

The princess married the third prince that very day in the midst of great merriment and high revelry. More than a hundred thousand pearls were thrown at her and she loved it.

Moral: All those who thought the princess was going to select the tin box filled with worthless stones instead of one of the other gifts will kindly stay after class and write one hundred times on the blackboard "I would rather have a hunk of aluminum silicate than a diamond necklace."

---

4. **tawdry** (tô′drē), *adj.* showy and cheap; gaudy.
5. **glut** (glut), *v.* feed or satisfy fully.

After Reading

Making Connections

1. Were you surprised by the story's ending? Why or why not?

2. How did you like the **moral** of the story? Explain.

3. Do you suppose the princess will ever regret her choice? Explain.

4. Tell how you think the author would answer this question: How does this story fit into the **theme** "What Really Matters"?

5. If you were the princess, which box would you choose? Why?

Literary Focus: Author's Purpose

After reading "Keri," page 290, you learned that authors have three main purposes for writing: to entertain, to inform, and to persuade. Clearly, James Thurber wanted "The Princess and the Tin Box" to be entertaining. However, was that his only purpose in writing the story?

Arrange the purposes listed below in order of their importance. Write a paragraph in which you support Thurber's **purposes** in writing the story. Give specific examples for each purpose.

- One purpose was to entertain.

- One purpose was to make a particular point about human attitudes and behavior.

- One purpose was to poke fun at a traditional story form.

Expressing Your Ideas

Now, *That's* a Fable You are the editor to whom Thurber sent "The Princess and the Tin Box." Being a traditional sort of person, you say to yourself, This is *not* a fable! Do a **rewrite** of the ending and the moral to make the story end the way you might expect a traditional fable to end.

What a Gem! Do a **research report** on the gems mentioned in the story. Include the mineral name of each gem, its colors, and its special features. Include pictures if possible.

Was She Right, or Not? With a partner, choose roles: One of you is a member of the princess's court and the other is a member of the fifth prince's court. In front of the rest of the class, **debate** whether or not the princess made the right choice.

Before Reading

Damon and Pythias

by Fan Kissen

Fan Kissen
born 1904

Fan Kissen has made a career of turning stories from other times and places into plays that young people can perform and enjoy. Formerly an elementary school teacher in New York City, Kissen devoted seventeen years to writing a popular educational radio series called "Tales from the Four Winds." Her books of plays make use of her skill in radio scriptwriting and her interest in history and faraway places. Kissen also has written biographies for young people.

Building Background

Ancient Legend *Damon and Pythias* is based on a legend of ancient Greece. According to the story, Damon (dā′mən) and Pythias (pith′ē əs) were two young men who lived in Syracuse (sir′ə kyüz), an important city on the island of Sicily in the Mediterranean Sea. By the time Pompeii was destroyed in A.D. 79, Syracuse was part of the Roman Empire. However, in the days of Damon and Pythias—the 300s B.C.—Syracuse was part of the Greek world.

Getting into the Play

Writer's Notebook The main characters in *Damon and Pythias* are best friends. In your notebook, make a chart like the one below and fill it in. When you've finished, consider these questions. Do your lists describe the friends you actually have? Do the lists describe the kind of friend you are?

Qualities a Friend Should Have	What Friends Should Be Willing to Do
sense of humor	

Reading Tip

Reading a Play *Damon and Pythias* is written as a play. Stage directions, which often appear in *italic* type within parentheses, give instructions for performing the play. Because *Damon and Pythias* was written as a radio play, its stage directions also involve sound. Notice the stage directions as you read the play, and try to "hear" the sounds. Also notice the characters called Narrator, First Voice, Second Voice, and Third Voice. What function, or purpose, do they serve?

DAMON AND PYTHIAS

Fan Kissen

CAST

DAMON

FIRST ROBBER

FIRST VOICE

PYTHIAS

SECOND ROBBER

SECOND VOICE

KING

MOTHER

THIRD VOICE

SOLDIER

NARRATOR

(Sound: Iron door opens and shuts. Key in lock.)

(Music: Up full and out.)

NARRATOR. Long, long ago there lived on the island of Sicily two young men named Damon and Pythias. They were known far and wide for the strong friendship each had for the other. Their names have come down to our own times to mean true friendship. You may hear it said of two persons:

FIRST VOICE. Those two? Why, they're like Damon and Pythias!

NARRATOR. The king of that country was a cruel tyrant. He made cruel laws, and he showed no mercy toward anyone who broke his laws. Now, you might very well wonder:

SECOND VOICE. Why didn't the people rebel?[1]

NARRATOR. Well, the people didn't dare rebel because they feared the king's great and powerful army. No one dared say a word against the king or his laws—except Damon and Pythias speaking against a new law the king had proclaimed.[2]

SOLDIER. Ho, there! Who are you that dares to speak so about our king?

PYTHIAS *(unafraid).* I am called Pythias.

SOLDIER. Don't you know it is a crime to speak against the king or his laws? You are under arrest! Come and tell this opinion of yours to the king's face!

(Music: A few short bars in and out.)

NARRATOR. When Pythias was brought before the king, he showed no fear. He stood straight and quiet before the throne.

KING *(hard, cruel).* So, Pythias! They tell me you do not approve of the laws I make.

PYTHIAS. I am not alone, your Majesty, in thinking your laws are cruel. But you rule the people with such an iron hand that they dare not complain.

KING *(angry).* But *you* have the daring to complain *for* them! Have they appointed you

---

1. **rebel** (ri bel′), *v.* resist or fight against law or authority; (reb′əl), *n.* person who resists or fights against authority instead of obeying.

2. **proclaim** (prə klām′), *v.* make known publicly and officially; declare publicly.

This mosaic shows an acting troupe that might have performed this play in ancient Greece.

their champion?³

PYTHIAS. No, your Majesty. I speak for myself alone. I have no wish to make trouble for anyone. But I am not afraid to tell you that the people are suffering under your rule. They want to have a voice in making the laws for themselves. You do not allow them to speak up for themselves.

KING. In other words, you are calling me a tyrant! Well, you shall learn for yourself how a tyrant treats a rebel! Soldier! Throw this man into prison!

SOLDIER. At once, your Majesty! Don't try to resist, Pythias!

PYTHIAS. I know better than to try to resist a soldier of the king! and for how long am I to remain in prison, your Majesty, merely for speaking out for the people?

KING *(cruel)*. Not for very long, Pythias. Two weeks from today at noon, you shall be put to death in the public square as an example to anyone else who may dare to question my laws or acts. Off to prison with him, soldier!

(Music: In briefly and out.)

NARRATOR. When Damon heard that his friend Pythias had been thrown into prison, and about the severe punishment that was to follow, he was heartbroken. He rushed to the prison and persuaded the guard to let him speak to his friend.

DAMON. Oh, Pythias! How terrible to find you here! I wish I could do something to save you!

PYTHIAS. Nothing can save me, Damon, my

---

3. **champion** (cham′pē ən), *n.* person who fights or speaks for another; person who defends a cause.

dear friend. I am prepared to die. But there is one thought that troubles me greatly.

DAMON. What is it? I will do anything to help you.

PYTHIAS. I'm worried about what will happen to my mother and my sister when I'm gone.

DAMON. I'll take care of them, Pythias, as if they were my own mother and sister.

PYTHIAS. Thank you, Damon. I have money to leave them. But there are other things I must arrange. If only I could go see them before I die! But they live two days' journey from here, you know.

DAMON. I'll go to the King and beg him to give you your freedom for a few days. You'll give your word to return at the end of that time. Everyone in Sicily knows you for a man who has never broken his word.

PYTHIAS. Do you believe for one moment that the king would let me leave this prison, no matter how good my word may have been all my life?

DAMON. I'll tell him that *I* shall take your place in the prison cell. I'll tell him that if you do not return by the appointed day, he may kill *me* in your place!

PYTHIAS. No, no, Damon! You must not do such a foolish thing! I cannot—I will not—let you do this! Damon! Damon! Don't go! *(to himself)* Damon, my friend! You may find yourself in a cell beside me!

(Music: In briefly and out.)

DAMON *(begging)*. Your Majesty! I beg of you! Let Pythias go home for a few days to bid farewell to his mother and sister. He gives his word that he will return at your appointed time. Everyone knows that his word can be trusted.

KING. In ordinary business affairs—perhaps. But he is now a man under sentence of death. To free him even for a few days

would strain his honesty—*any* man's honesty—too far. Pythias would never return here! I consider him a traitor,[4] but I'm certain he's no fool.

DAMON. Your Majesty! I will take his place in the prison until he comes back. If he does not return, then you may take *my* life in his place.

KING *(astonished)*. What did you say, Damon?

DAMON. I'm so certain of Pythias that I am offering to die in his place if he fails to return on time.

KING. I can't believe you mean it!

DAMON. I do mean it, your Majesty.

KING. You make me very curious, Damon, so curious that I'm willing to put you and Pythias to the test. This exchange of prisoners will be made. But Pythias must be back two weeks from today, at noon.

DAMON. Thank you, your Majesty!

KING. The order with my official seal[5] shall go by your own hand,[6] Damon. But I warn you, if your friend does not return on time, you shall surely die in his place! I shall show no mercy.

(Music: In briefly and out.)

NARRATOR. Pythias did not like the king's bargain with Damon. He did not like to leave his friend in prison with the chance that he might lose his life if something went wrong. But at last Damon persuaded him to leave and Pythias set out for his home. More than a week went by. The day set for the death sentence drew near. Pythias did not return. Everyone in the city knew of the condition on which the king had permitted Pythias to go home. Everywhere people met, the talk was sure to turn to the

---

4. **traitor** (trā′tər), *n.* person who betrays his or her country or ruler.
5. **seal** (sēl), *n.* design stamped on a piece of wax or other soft material to show ownership or authenticity.
6. **go by your own hand**, be carried by you.

two friends.

FIRST VOICE. Do you suppose Pythias will come back?

SECOND VOICE. Why should he stick his head under the king's ax once he has escaped?

THIRD VOICE. Still would an honorable man like Pythias let such a good friend die for him?

FIRST VOICE. There's no telling what a man will do when it's a question of his own life against another's.

SECOND VOICE. But if Pythias doesn't come back before the time is up, he will be killing his friend.

THIRD VOICE. Well, there's still a few days' time. I, for one, am certain that Pythias *will* return in time.

SECOND VOICE. And *I* am just as certain that he will *not.* Friendship is friendship, but a man's own life is something stronger. *I* say!

NARRATOR. Two days before the time was up, the king himself visited Damon in his prison cell.

(Sound: Iron door unlocked and opened.)

KING *(mocking).* You see now, Damon, that you were a fool to make this bargain. Your friend has tricked you! He will not come back here to be killed! He has deserted[7] you.

DAMON *(calm and firm).* I have faith in my friend. I know he will return.

KING *(mocking).* We shall see!

(Sound: Iron door shut and locked.)

NARRATOR. Meanwhile, when Pythias reached the home of his family, he arranged his business affairs so that his mother and sister would be able to live comfortably for the rest of their years. Then he said a last farewell to them before starting back to the city.

MOTHER *(in tears).* Pythias, it will take you two days to get back. Stay another day, I beg you!

PYTHIAS. I dare not stay longer, Mother. Remember, Damon is locked up in my prison cell while I'm gone. Please don't weep for me. My death may help bring better days for all our people.

NARRATOR. So Pythias began his journey in plenty of time. But bad luck struck him on the very first day. At twilight, as he walked along a lonely stretch of woodland, a rough voice called:

FIRST ROBBER. Not so fast there, young man! Stop!

PYTHIAS *(startled).* Oh! What is it? What do you want?

SECOND ROBBER. Your money bags.

PYTHIAS. My money bags? I have only this small bag of coins. I shall need them for some favors, perhaps, before I die.

FIRST ROBBER. What do you mean, before you die? We don't mean to kill you, only take your money.

PYTHIAS. I'll give you my money, only don't delay me any longer. I am to die by the king's order three days from now. If I don't return on time, my friend must die in my place.

FIRST ROBBER. A likely story! What man would be fool enough to go back to prison ready to die?

SECOND ROBBER. And what man would be fool enough to die *for* you?

FIRST ROBBER. We'll take your money, all right. And we'll tie you up while we get away.

PYTHIAS *(begging).* No! No! I must get back to free my friend! *(fade)* I must go back!

NARRATOR. But the two robbers took Pythias's money, tied him to a tree, and went off as fast as they could. Pythias struggled to free himself. He cried out for a long time. But no one traveled through that lonesome

---

7. **desert** (di zėrt′), *v.* go away and leave a person or a place, especially one that should not be left; forsake.

woodland after dark. The sun had been up for many hours before he finally managed to free himself from the ropes that had tied him to the tree. He lay on the ground, hardly able to breathe.

(Music: In briefly and out.)

NARRATOR. After a while Pythias got to his feet. Weak and dizzy from hunger and thirst and his struggle to free himself, he set off again. Day and night he traveled without stopping, desperately trying to reach the city in time to save Damon's life.

(Music: Up and out.)

NARRATOR. On the last day, half an hour before noon, Damon's hands were tied behind his back, and he was taken into the public square. The people muttered angrily as Damon was led in by the jailer. Then the king entered and seated himself on a high platform.

(Sound: Crowd voices in and hold under single voices.)

SOLDIER *(loud).* Long live the king!

FIRST VOICE *(low).* The longer he lives, the more miserable our lives will be!

KING *(loud, mocking).* Well, Damon, your lifetime is nearly up. Where is your good friend Pythias now?

DAMON *(firm).* I have faith in my friend. If he has not returned, I'm certain it is through no fault of his own.

KING *(mocking).* The sun is almost overhead. The shadow is almost at the noon mark.[8] And still your friend has not returned to give back your life!

DAMON *(quiet).* I am ready and happy to die in his place.

KING *(harsh).* And you shall, Damon! Jailer, lead the prisoner to the—

(Sound: Crowd voices up to a roar, then under.)

FIRST VOICE *(over noise).* Look! It's Pythias!

SECOND VOICE *(over noise).* Pythias has come back!

PYTHIAS *(breathless).* Let me through! Damon!

DAMON. Pythias!

PYTHIAS. Thank the gods I'm not too late!

DAMON *(quiet, sincere).* I would have died for you gladly, my friend.

CROWD VOICES *(loud, demanding).* Set them free! Set them both free!

KING *(loud).* People of the city! *(crowd voices out)* Never in all my life have I seen such faith and friendship, such loyalty between men. There are many among you who call me harsh and cruel. But I cannot kill *any* man who proves such strong and true friendship for another. Damon and Pythias, I set you both free. *(roar of approval from crowd)* I am king. I command a great army. I have stores of gold and precious jewels. But I would give all my money and power for one friend like Damon or Pythias.

(Sound: Roar of approval from crowd up briefly and out.)

(Music: Up and out.)

---

8. **the shadow is almost at the noon mark,** reference to a sundial, which is an instrument for telling time by the position of a shadow cast by the sun as it strikes an upright pointer.

After Reading

Making Connections

1. Did you find this story believable? Why or why not?

2. Suppose Pythias had not been able to return in time. Describe how the story could still have had a happy ending.

3. If the author had not included the characters of the Narrator and the Voices, would the play be better or not as good? Why?

4. Do you think death is a fair and appropriate punishment for disloyalty to a leader or a country? Explain.

5. Imagine you are a parent or a teacher. How would you punish various acts of wrongdoing by your child or a student?

6. 🐾 **Individuality** doesn't stand in the way of a true friendship. How much would you be willing to do for a friend? Explain.

Literary Focus: Plot

Below are the elements of a **plot**.

- A problem is presented.
- A number of events occur (rising action).
- A climax, or turning point, is reached.
- One or more additional events occur (falling action).
- The problem is resolved.

Trace the plot of *Damon and Pythias*. Copy the headings below and fill in the chart. Keep in mind that the problem is not necessarily presented at the start of the play, and so there may be some events from the beginning of the play that don't fit anywhere in the chart. Compare your completed chart with those of your classmates.

Problem	Rising Action	Climax	Falling Action	Resolution
	the king's visit to Damon			

Vocabulary Study

Number a sheet of paper from 1 to 5. For each group of words, write the letter of the word that is not related in meaning to the other words.

champion
desert
proclaim
rebel
traitor

1. **a.** resist   **b.** oppose   **c.** obey   **d.** rebel
2. **a.** proclaim   **b.** whisper   **c.** declare **d.** announce
3. **a.** defender   **b.** listener   **c.** champion **d.** fighter
4. **a.** traitor   **b.** loyalist   **c.** supporter **d.** patriot
5. **a.** support   **b.** forsake   **c.** abandon **d.** desert

Expressing Your Ideas

Writing Choices

A Prisoner's Thoughts Imagine you are Damon waiting in prison for the return of Pythias. Write a **diary entry** for the day before the appointed date of your death. How do you feel? What last words would you like to leave for Pythias? For the king?

What Next? What happened to Damon and Pythias after they were set free? Write another **scene** of the play in which you answer that question. Use the same style the author did, including stage directions involving sound.

The Play Today You are a stage actor (male or female) with ideas for a modern-day version of *Damon and Pythias*. Of course, you would be the star! Write a **letter** to your favorite director, in which you present your ideas for the modern setting, situation, and characters.

Other Options

Posters of Protest Work with a partner to make at least three **posters** protesting the punishment that the king plans for Pythias— or for Damon, if Pythias does not return.

This Just In You are a TV reporter in ancient Syracuse, broadcasting live from the public square on the day Damon is to die. It is just before noon, and you have two minutes to give your report. Present your **newscast** to the class.

Plan for Change You and a small group of classmates are citizens of ancient Syracuse. You feel the government must change for the good of the people. Create a **plan** for a fairer city government. Will you have to overthrow the king? Or might you persuade him to work with a council of elected representatives? Or what? Share your plan with the rest of the class.

What Really Matters

Links to the Roman Empire

History Connection

The importance of the family unit links the ancient Roman Empire to our modern world. We are separated from Roman families by thousands of years. Yet, they treasured family relationships just as we do.

Only wealthy Roman families could afford to live in a *domus,* a private townhouse, such as this.

Food for the family was prepared by slaves. The kitchen was separated from the dining area and the other parts of the house.

The table of a wealthy Roman family might include delicacies such as ostrich, flamingo with dates, and roast parrot. Family members reclined on couches while they ate.

FAMILY LIFE IN ROME

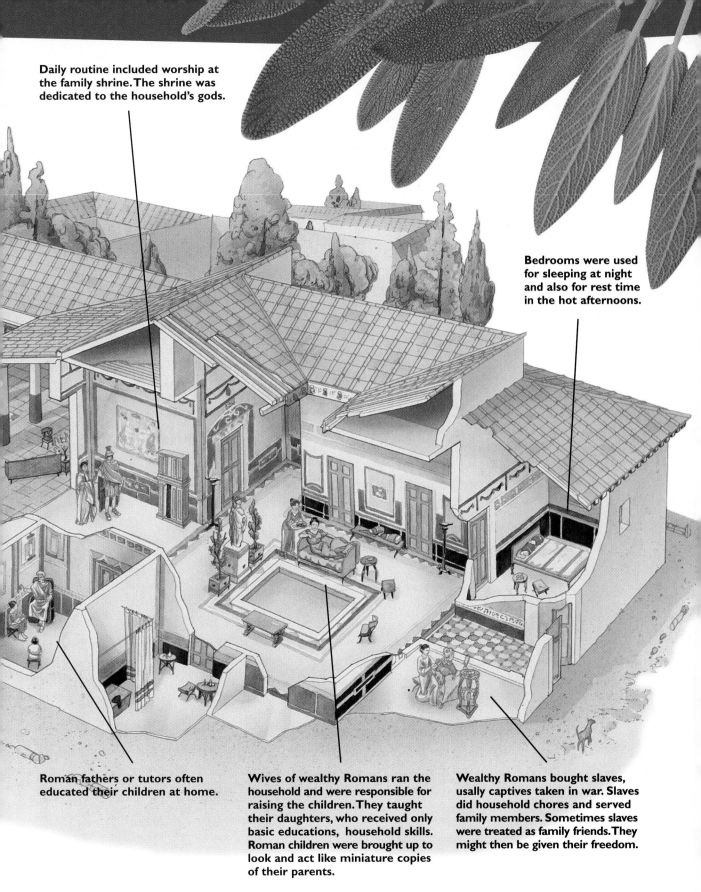

Daily routine included worship at the family shrine. The shrine was dedicated to the household's gods.

Bedrooms were used for sleeping at night and also for rest time in the hot afternoons.

Roman fathers or tutors often educated their children at home.

Wives of wealthy Romans ran the household and were responsible for raising the children. They taught their daughters, who received only basic educations, household skills. Roman children were brought up to look and act like miniature copies of their parents.

Wealthy Romans bought slaves, usally captives taken in war. Slaves did household chores and served family members. Sometimes slaves were treated as family friends. They might then be given their freedom.

Interdisciplinary Study   **323**

This mosaic shows an important male activity—hunting hares for meat. Notice the man's clothing.

ROMANVS·

Gaul

Spain

Illyricum

Rome

Africa

This colored wax picture clearly shows how a wealthy Roman woman looked—her hairstyle, clothing, and jewelry.

Responding
Discuss with the class how your life is both like that of ancient Roman children and different from it.

Anthropology Connection

In A.D. 79, life came to an abrupt end for the people of Herculaneum. The wealthy and poor, free and slaves, died in a molten river of lava from Mt. Vesuvius. In the end, we see what really mattered—not money or possessions—but family, friends, relationships, and life.

THE PEOPLE ON THE BEACH

by Sara C. Bisel with Jane Bisel and Shelley Tanaka

Herculaneum, June, 1982

It was quiet on Herculaneum's ancient beach.

Today this beach is just a narrow dirt corridor that lies several feet below sea level. But thousands of years ago, the waves of the Mediterranean would have lapped where I now stood.

To one side of me stood the arched entryways of the boat chambers, most of them still plugged by volcanic rock, their secrets locked inside. Only one chamber had been opened so far, and its contents were now hidden behind a padlocked plywood door.

Inside, I knew, was the only group of Roman skeletons that had ever been found— the twelve people who had huddled in the shelter and died together when the volcanic avalanches poured down the mountainside into the sea.

The plywood door seemed flimsy as it was pulled open. From inside the chamber came the dank smell of damp earth.

A shiver crept up my neck. We were opening a 2,000-year-old grave. What would we find?

As I entered the cave-like boat chamber, I could barely see, even though the sun flooded through the door. Someone handed me a flashlight, but its light cast greenish shadows, making it feel even more spooky.

The light played over the back of the shelter, no bigger than a single garage and still crusted over with volcanic rock. I saw an oddly shaped, lumpy mound halfway back. I took several steps into the chamber and pointed the light at the mound.

The narrow beam found a skull, the pale face a grimace of death. As my eyes grew accustomed to the dim light, I soon realized there were bones and skulls everywhere. They were all tangled together—clinging to each other for comfort in their final moments—and it was hard to distinguish one from another. But I knew that twelve skeletons had been found in all—three men, four women, and five children. One child had an iron house key near him. Did he think he would be going back home?

I took another step into the cave. At my feet was a skeleton that was almost entirely

The skeleton of a young slave girl was found cradling the tiny, fragile skull of an infant.

uncovered. From the pelvis I could see it was a female, a girl, lying face down. Beneath her, we could just see the top of another small skull.

It was a baby.

I knelt down and gently touched the tiny skull. My throat felt tight as I thought about this girl, this baby, and what it must have been like for them in this dark cave in the moments before they died.

I struggled to free a bronze cupid pin and two little bells from the baby's bones. Whoever the child was, it had been rich enough to wear expensive ornaments.

Later, in the laboratory, I gained enough information to put together a more likely background for the skeleton of the young girl.

Unlike the baby, she had not come from a wealthy family. She had been about fourteen, and from the shape of her skull I knew she had probably been pretty. When I examined her teeth I could tell that she had been starved or quite ill for a time when she was a baby. She had also had two teeth removed about one or two weeks before she died, probably giving her a fair bit of pain. And her life had been very hard. She had done a lot of running up and down stairs or hills, as well as having to lift objects too heavy for her delicate frame.

This girl could not have been the child of a wealthy family, like the baby. She had probably been a slave who died trying to

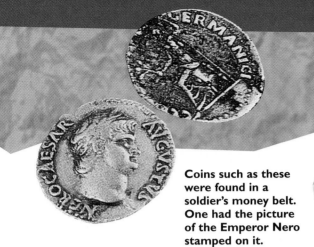

Coins such as these were found in a soldier's money belt. One had the picture of the Emperor Nero stamped on it.

Wealthy Romans used glass drinking cups like this one.

protect the baby of the family she worked for.

And there were many others. Near the slave girl lay the skeleton of a seven-year-old girl whose bones also showed that she had done work far too heavy for a child so young.

We found a sixteen-year-old fisherman, his upper body well developed from rowing boats, his teeth worn from holding cord while he repaired his fishing nets.

Particularly heartbreaking were the two pregnant women I examined, for we were also able to recover their tiny unborn babies, their bones as fragile as eggshells. One woman had been only about sixteen years old.

During the next few months we opened two more boat chambers. In one we discovered forty tangled human skeletons and one of a horse; in another we found twenty-six skeletons creepily lined up like a row of dominoes, as if heading in single file for the back of the chamber.

Responding

Mount Vesuvius created an unfortunate time capsule when it erupted two thousand years ago. Scientists know what life was like for these people by what they left behind. If you were to make a time capsule, what would you include? List ten items that would give a clear picture of your life.

327

Reading Mini-Lesson

Drawing Conclusions

If you were a defense lawyer in a jury trial, it would be your job to present evidence that would help the jury draw this conclusion: Your client is not guilty.

Let's say there is evidence to show the crime was committed in Denver at 10:00 A.M. on Tuesday. You can prove that your client was making a speech in Boston at that time. To help prove your client not guilty, you might use *If . . . then . . .* reasoning. The series of conclusions goes like this.

- *If* your client is in Boston, *then* he cannot be in Denver at the same time.
- *If* he wasn't in Denver, *then* he couldn't have committed the crime.
- *If* he couldn't have committed the crime, *then* he must be found "not guilty."

Archaeologists also study evidence and make use of *If . . . then . . .* reasoning to draw conclusions about the people and cultures that existed in the past. In the second paragraph of "The People on the Beach" on page 325, the narrator concludes that the "narrow dirt corridor" would have been covered by water 2,000 years ago. Perhaps the reasoning went like this: *If* there are boat chambers at this level, *then* the water level must have been high enough for the boats to float into the chambers. *If* the water was that high, *then* the narrow dirt corridor would have been underwater.

Activity Options

1. In "The People on the Beach," the narrator constructed a background for the young girl found with the baby. Complete the sentences below to show the three conclusions that can be drawn about the young girl's life. With each conclusion, give the evidence upon which it is based.
   A. *If*_____, *then*_____.
   B. *If*_____, *then*_____.
   C. *If*_____, *then*_____.

2. Find real-life examples of *if . . . then . . .* in newspaper articles. Then share your findings with your classmates.

Writing Workshop

Person-of-the-Year Speech

Assignment You've read selections about special family members. Think about a special person in your life—a family member or a friend. Nominate this person in a speech for Person of the Year. See the Writer's Blueprint for details.

WRITER'S BLUEPRINT

Product	An essay and a speech
Purpose	To explain why someone is special to you
Audience	Contest judges
Specs	To write a successful essay and speech, you should:

❑ Start with a lively introduction that hooks your audience and makes them want to hear more about your Person of the Year.

❑ Go on to clearly describe the person and provide examples of the personal qualities and/or actions that make him or her special to you.

❑ End with a strong conclusion that brings your important points together and leaves a memorable impression of this individual in the minds of the audience.

❑ Organize your ideas effectively.

❑ Make note cards from your essay and use them to deliver your speech.

❑ Follow the rules of grammar, usage, spelling, and mechanics. Make sure your pronoun reference is clear.

The instructions that follow are designed to help you write an award-winning speech.

Brainstorm a list of special people that you might want to write about. Try to think of people you've known at different times in your life, including family, friends, teachers, and neighbors. Choose one of these people to be the topic of your writing. Note that you will first write an essay about this person and then take notes from the essay to create your speech.

Make a web of personality traits for the person you've chosen. Picture the person and think about times you spent together to get ideas for your web. Include actions or examples to illustrate each of the traits you list. Refer to the Literary Source as an example of how actions can show personality traits. This example shows that Armand is loyal and generous because he would rather buy a gift for his father than buy something for himself.

LITERARY SOURCE
"'Look,' he said, 'it's Pa's birthday tomorrow. I think we ought to chip in and buy him something. . . .'"
from "President Cleveland, Where Are You?" by Robert Cormier

Quickwrite about the person you've chosen for the subject of your speech. Focus on a special time you spent together or one of the actions you listed in your web. Write for three or four minutes about your subject.

Plan your essay. Decide which characteristics you will include in your essay by making a chart similar to the one shown. Then, number your main points in the order that you think will be most convincing to the contest judges.

Armand is . . .	You can tell this about him because . . .
Loyal	He thinks it is more important to buy a birthday gift for their father than to get something he might want for himself.
Thoughtful	When Jerry's bike has a flat tire, Armand helps him fix it.

STEP 2 DRAFTING

Before you write, review the Writer's Blueprint and your Prewriting steps. Good speeches focus on specific ideas and present these clearly. You might want to look ahead to the Revising Strategy for suggestions on how to arrange ideas effectively.

As you draft, don't worry about mistakes in spelling and punctuation. Concentrate on getting the information about your subject down on paper. Here are some ideas for hooking your audience with your opening remarks.

- Open with a moving or exciting experience you shared with this person.

- Start by asking a question for which the judges will want to find out an answer.

- Paint an image of your person in the judges' minds using colorful and precise adjectives.

OR . . .
Draw an illustration of a key scene you want to include in your essay. Use the sketch as a basis for writing.

STEP 3 REVISING

Ask your partner for comments on your draft before you revise it.

✔ Have I followed the specs in the Writer's Blueprint?

✔ Do I interest my audience with a lively introduction?

✔ Do I support descriptions with examples that help the audience get to know this person?

✔ Do I conclude by bringing my major points together?

✔ Do I arrange my ideas effectively?

Revising Strategy

Arranging Ideas Effectively

When deciding how to arrange ideas in their writing, writers often choose one of the following ways.

- Chronological—Begin with the first event of an episode and end with the last.

- Degree of importance—Begin with the most important idea and end with the least important, or begin with the least important and end with the most important.

- Similarity—Group similar ideas together to make a point.

In the Literary Source, Robert Cormier uses chronological arrangement to present ideas.

Notice how the writer of the passage below revised a paragraph to present events in the right sequence.

LITERARY SOURCE

"We journeyed on our bicycles to the North Side, engaged three boys in a matching bout and returned with five new Presidents, including Chester Alan Arthur, who up to that time had been missing."

from "President Cleveland, Where Are You?" by Robert Cormier

○　　At first when I visited my Dad, my brothers and I had to go to

his house. There was no room for me and my brothers to stay. *Put this first.* My

○　　parents got divorced when I was seven years old. He moved to North

Carolina when I was ten. Now I fly on a plane to visit him.

STUDENT MODEL

4 EDITING

Ask a partner to review your revised draft before you edit. When you edit, watch for errors in grammar, usage, spelling, and mechanics. Pay special attention to errors with pronoun reference.

FOR REFERENCE . . .
More rules for pronoun and antecedent reference are listed in the Language and Grammar Handbook.

Editing Strategy

Clear Pronoun Reference

Pronouns always refer to a noun or another pronoun called an antecedent. Make sure that the references between the pronouns and their antecedents are clear. Here are two causes of unclear pronoun reference.

- Sometimes there could be more than one possible antecedent.

Confusing: Ms. Kelly read Clare's essay to the class because she said she had addressed an important issue.
Clear: Because Clare addressed an important issue in her essay, Ms. Kelly read it to the class.

- Sometimes the antecedent is too far away from its pronoun.

Confusing: Students should consult with their teachers who need extra help with their work.
Clear: Students who need extra help with their work should consult with their teachers.

Notice how the writer of this draft corrected a pronoun reference that wasn't clear.

○
　　　　My mother teaches me ways to understand life and how
○
things change. Mom, shows me and my sister all the wonderful

places in our home town who has lived here all her life. She makes

me feel good about myself. That is why I think she should be
○
person of the year.

STUDENT MODEL

5 PRESENTING

Make the note cards you'll use to deliver your speech. Review your essay and list each main idea and the details that support it. Then, rather than simply reading your essay, use these note cards when you give your speech.

When you deliver your speech, you'll want to use these tips.

- **Rehearse your speech.** Become familiar with your material and try out different gestures and vocal expressions.

- **Stand up straight,** but don't be rigid like a stick.

- **Maintain eye contact,** and don't stare at your notes. If all your audience sees is the top of your head, they'll tune out quickly. Pick out different people and direct a sentence or two to each one.

- **Speak loudly and clearly.** Don't shout, but keep in mind that your speech is worthless if no one can hear it.

6 LOOKING BACK

Self-evaluate. What grade would you give your speech? Look back at the Writer's Blueprint and evaluate yourself on each point, from 6 (superior) down to 1 (weak).

Reflect. Think about what you learned from writing this speech as you write answers to these questions.

✔ If someone were to nominate you for Person of the Year, what traits or actions would you want them to include?

✔ Look back at a piece of writing. Check the way you use pronouns in the piece. Are you more aware of how to make pronoun references clear?

For Your Working Portfolio: Add your essay, speech notes, and reflection responses to your working portfolio.

Beyond Print

Looking at Movies

Charles Dickens's story *A Christmas Carol* has so much appeal that it has been made into many movies. You may remember the Muppet version where Kermit the Frog played Bob Cratchit, and Michael Caine played Scrooge. The writers for this movie made some changes in Dickens's words and plot.

Create a Box Office Hit

Now it's your turn to plan a movie scene for *A Christmas Carol*. You can make some changes in Dickens's story.

Activity: Storyboard Your Scenes

Filmmakers plan their scenes by drawing storyboards, panels that show the action in a scene, much like a comic strip. Storyboards do not have to be works of art. Stick figures will do. It is important that the storyboards tell the camera operators how to film the scene. To plan your scene, draw panels to show the following.

- What the camera will show in the scene—people and objects.

- How the camera will show it. For instance, will Scrooge be a large figure towering over a small Bob Cratchit?

- How the camera moves from one panel to the next.

- How the people or things move while the camera films them.

- Anything else you can imagine that will help in filming the movie.

Draw Your Characters

Make detailed sketches of your characters for the makeup people and the wardrobe staff. Show how the characters should look.

Activity Option

Ask classmates to act out your scene and videotape it. Show it to the class. Compare your film with your storyboards.

Projects for Collaborative Study

Theme Connection

Oral Traditions Stories are passed down from one generation to the next as a part of Native American culture. To understand the importance of oral traditions, invite a Native American storyteller to visit your class.

■ To prepare, contact the American Indian Urban and/or Reservation Centers in your area for a list of tribal storytellers. If there are none in your area, contact others in your community with interesting stories to tell about their cultural heritage. Make a list of questions to ask. For example, you may be interested in what kinds of stories are told and what kinds of characters are usually included.

■ As a group, make up a story about traditions in your school that you want to pass on to future students. Then tell your story to another class.

Literature Connection

A New Attitude In this unit, how the author feels about the subject has a major influence on what happens in each selection. The author's attitude toward the subject or toward the audience is called **tone.** Tone in writing is like tone in speaking. When you speak, people can tell whether you feel happy or sad by your facial expressions and the sound of your voice. An author shows feelings about a subject with words, treatment of characters, and imagery.

■ In a small group, present parts of several selections as skits to show what tone is. Select the speeches of different characters and perform them as you think the author intended.

Life Skills Connection

Reflections of You When you look at yourself in the mirror, what do you see? Now look deeper. What other attributes are there about you that your reflection reveals? What about you is hidden from view?

Your physical reflection gives the world only a glimpse of who you really are. Beneath the surface you carry your thoughts, feelings, experiences, hopes, and dreams.

Before you even knew what a mirror was, you became aware of yourself. In time and with experience your awareness has grown and developed. As you have come to know yourself, you have formed a relationship with yourself.

In the following activity you can explore how you view yourself.

■ Using a pencil, paper, and a hand mirror, draw a self-portrait.

■ Write a description about the you in the portrait.

Multicultural Connection

School Culture Your school is like a culture with its special traditions and customs. What things do you do because you're part of this cultural **group?** What things do you do because of your **individuality?**

■ With a group of your classmates, prepare a list of customs and traditions that you associate with being in school. For example, do you carry your books in a special kind of backpack?

■ Then make your own list of things you do to show your individuality in school. Compare your list with others.

Read More About Relationships

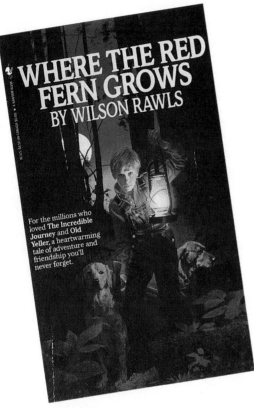

Where the Red Fern Grows (1961) by Wilson Rawls. A boy recalls how he became the owner of two hounds, how he trained them as hunters, and how they became champion coon hunters.

Toning the Sweep (1993) by Angela Johnson. In this novel, Emily enjoys one last summer with her dying grandmother.

More Good Books

Child of the Owl (1977) by Laurence Yep. Casey, a Chinese American girl, learns of her heritage and comes of age in this novel when she goes to live with her grandmother in San Francisco's Chinatown.

Cave Under the City (1986) by Harry Mazer. Twelve-year-old Tolly and his younger brother live on the streets after their father leaves home to find work and their mother becomes ill.

Journey (1991) by Patricia MacLachlan. This novel describes a family's struggle to fill a void left by the loss of their mother.

Jericho (1994) by Janet Hickman. This story explores the connections between four generations of women beginning with twelve-year-old Angela.

He Noticed I'm Alive—And Other Hopeful Signs (1984) by Marjorie W. Sharmat. Jody's adjustment to her father's dating takes a new turn when she is attracted to his girlfriend's son.

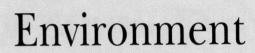

Environment

Appreciating Your World

Protecting Your World

Talking About the
ENVIRONMENT

The earth's environment is made up of its land and water. Throughout history, people have used and misused the environment. Most people appreciate the world's resources, but they do not always agree how to use them. Since the earth's environment is fragile, it is up to all of us to make choices that will preserve it for the future.

As you read these two pages, notice that the authors of the literature you are about to read and many young people share the same concerns about the world's environment.

"What can one person do?"

Reiko—Muncie, IN

He saw this as the chance to turn his pleasure in the care of land into a way of making a living while doing something for the enjoyment of the public.

from "People's Gardens"
by Milton Meltzer,
page 355

...all manufacturing of ozone-depleting chemicals was banned worldwide—the scientists were saying that the sun, the global problem, would begin to get better.

from "The Sand Castle" by Alma Luz Villanueva, page 346

"How can we stop people from taking advantage of the environment?"

Danica–Fairfield, IA

You gotta speak up against what's wrong and bad, or you can't ever stop it.

from Let Me Hear You Whisper by Paul Zindel, page 402

"Is it possible to improve the environment?"

Terrence–Reading, PA

Joel figured the U.S. companies who bought the tuna were deserving targets. After all, they had the power to refuse to buy tuna caught in drift nets.

from "Joel Rubin" by Phillip Hoose, page 384

"The way we live now will affect the way we live in the future."

Robert–Beaufort, SC

341

Part One

Appreciating Your World

I walk in beauty.
Beauty is before me.
Beauty is behind me,
Above and below me.

This poem is a translation of a Navajo chant that captures a deep feeling of appreciation of the world. Where and how do you find beauty in your world? What do you appreciate most about your world?

Multicultural Connection People see the world from different **perspectives,** or points of view. The way you see the world may reflect the experiences you have had. The selections that follow may give you surprising glimpses of beauty and help you come to appreciate your world in new ways.

Before Reading

The Sand Castle

by Alma Luz Villanueva

Alma Luz Villanueva
born 1944

In "The Sand Castle," Alma Luz Villanueva explores a favorite theme of her stories and poems: that women have a special ability to preserve hope in apparently hopeless situations. Villanueva's writing has been influenced by the stories and poems her grandmother taught her. Another influence was a four-year stay in the Sierra Nevada mountains, which brought Villanueva close to nature. When a reader sent a letter thanking Villanueva for her writing, she said: "Writing takes all your courage—to stand by your work and see it through to publication—courage and luck (and discipline, discipline, discipline). But, imagine, someone understanding what you meant to say . . . someone saying thank you."

Building Background

Too Much Sun Could the sun become the earth's enemy? Many scientists fear it could, because they have detected a growing hole in the ozone layer above Antarctica. **Ozone** is a form of oxygen. High in the atmosphere, a natural layer of ozone absorbs most of the sun's ultraviolet rays before they can reach the earth. In this way, the ozone shields living things from the harmful effects of the rays, such as a greater possibility of developing skin cancer.

Getting into the Story

Discussion In a small group, share what you know about environmental problems. What are they called? How are they caused? As you talk, fill in a web like the one shown below. Add as many circles as you need.

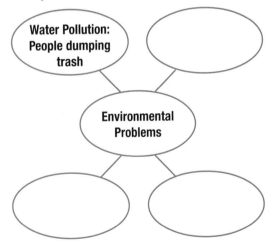

Reading Tip

Order of Events This story switches from the present to the past and back again. To complicate things even more, the "present" is actually some unknown time in the future! The author does provide some hints about the order of events. As you read, be alert to phrases like "She remembered" and other clues. You may want to keep two lists of events in your Writer's Notebook—one titled *Past Events* and one titled *Present Events*.

▲ *Winter Surf (Self-Portrait)* was painted by Victor Kerpel in 1993. Why do you think the person in this painting is wearing such a heavy robe? Predict what this might have to do with the story.

THE SAND CASTLE

Alma Luz Villanueva

"Have you dressed yet?" their grandmother called. "Once a month in the sun and they must almost be forced," she muttered. "Well, poor things, they've forgotten the warmth of the sun on their little bodies, what it is to play in the sea, yes. . . ." Mrs. Pavloff[1] reached for her protective sun goggles that covered most of her face. It screened[2] all ultraviolet light from the once life-giving sun; now, it, the sun, scorched[3] the Earth, killing whatever it touched. The sea, the continents, had changed. The weather, as they'd called it in the last century, was entirely predictable now: warming.

Mrs. Pavloff slipped on the thick, metallic gloves, listening to her grandchildren squabble[4] and she

---

1. **Pavloff** (pav′lov).
2. **screen** (skrēn), *v.* eliminate; close off or out.
3. scorch (skôrch), *v.* burn; dry up; wither.
4. squabble (skwob′əl), *v.* take part in a petty, noisy quarrel or argument.

heard her mother's voice calling her, "Masha,[5] put your bathing suit under your clothes. It's so much easier that way without having to go to the bathhouse[6] first. Hurry! Father's waiting!" She remembered the ride to the sea, the silence when the first shimmers of water became visible. Her father had always been first into the chilly water. "Good for the health!" he'd yell as he dove into it, swimming as far as he could, then back. Then he'd lie exhausted on the sand, stretched to the sun. Such happiness to be warmed by the sun.

Those who emerged during the day wore protective clothing.

Then the picnic. She could hear her mother's voice, "Stay to your knees, Masha! Only to your knees!" To herself: "She'd be a mermaid if I didn't watch," and she'd laugh. Masha would lie belly down, facing the sea, and let the last of the waves roll over her. She hadn't even been aware of the sun, only that she'd been warm or, if a cloud covered it, cold. It was always there, the sun: its light, its warmth. But the sea—they travelled to it. So, she'd given all of her attention to the beautiful sea.

She saw her father kneeling next to her, building the sand castle they always built when they went to the sea. Her job was to find seashells, bird feathers, and strips of seaweed to decorate it. How proud she'd felt as she placed her seashells where she chose, where they seemed most beautiful. Only then was the sand castle complete. She heard her father's voice, "The Princess's castle is ready, now, for her Prince! Come and look, Anna! What do you think?" She saw herself beaming with pride, and she heard her mother's laugh. "Fit for a queen, I'd say! Can I live in your castle, too, Masha? Please,

Princess Masha?" "Of course, Mother! You can live with me always. . . ." She remembered her mother's laughing face, her auburn hair lit up by the sun, making her look bright and beautiful.

The sun, the sun, the sun. The scientists were saying that with the remedies they were employing now and the remedies begun twenty years ago—they'd stopped all nuclear testing[7] and all manufacturing of ozone-depleting chemicals was banned worldwide—the scientists were saying that the sun, the global problem, would begin to get better. Perhaps for her grandchildren's children. Perhaps they would feel the sun on their unprotected bodies. Perhaps they would feel the delicious warmth of the sun.

All vehicles were solar powered. The populations took buses when they needed transportation and people emerged mainly at night. So, most human activity was conducted after the sun was gone from the sky. Those who emerged during the day wore protective clothing. Everything was built to screen the sun's light. Sometimes she missed the natural light of her childhood streaming through the windows so intensely the urge to just run outside would overtake her. She missed the birds, the wild birds.

But today they were going out, outside in the daytime, when the sun was still in the sky. Masha knew they were squabbling because they hated to dress up to go outside. The clothing, the gloves, the goggles, were uncomfortable and cumbersome.[8] She sighed, tears coming to her eyes. Well, they're coming,

---

5. **Masha** (mäsh′ə).
6. **bathhouse**, building containing dressing rooms for swimmers.
7. **nuclear testing**, testing of atomic weapons.
8. cumbersome (kum′bər səm), *adj.* hard to manage; clumsy or burdensome.

What do you think is Masha's **perspective** of *Beach Umbrella* painted by David Hockney in 1971? Is it a sign of hope or just a memory?

sea, didn't seem real to them. What was it: a mass of undrinkable, hostile water. Hostile[9] like the sun. They'd taken no delight, no pleasure, in their journey to the sea.

But today, yes, today we will build a sand castle. Masha smiled at her secret. She'd packed everything late last night to surprise them at the sea.

Why haven't I thought of it before? Masha asked herself, and then she remembered the dream, months ago, of building a sand castle with her father at the sea. It made her want to weep because she'd forgotten. She'd actually forgotten one of the most joyful times of her girlhood. When the sea was still alive with life.

Today we will build a sand castle.

They trudged[10] on the thick, dense sand toward the hiss of pale blue. Only the older people picked up their step, excited by the smell of salt in the air. Masha's grandchildren knew they'd be here for two hours and then trudge all the way back to the bus. The darkened goggles made the sunlight bearable. They hated this forlorn place where the sun had obviously drained the life out of everything. They were

Masha decided. They can remove their goggles and gloves on the bus.

The sea was closer now and the bus ride was comfortable within the temperature controlled interior. Those with memories of the sea signed up, bringing grandchildren, children, friends, or just went alone. Masha had taken her grandchildren before, but they'd sat on the sand, listlessly, sifting it through their gloved hands with bored little faces. She'd tried to interest them in the sea with stories of her father swimming in it as far as he could. But they couldn't touch it, so it, the

9. **hostile** (hos′tl), *adj.* opposed; unfriendly; unfavorable.
10. **trudge** (truj), *v.* walk wearily or with effort.

The Sand Castle   **347**

too young to express it, but they felt it as they walked, with bored effort, beside their grandmother.

"We're going to build a sand castle today—what do you think of that?" Masha beamed, squinting to see their faces.

"What's a sand castle?" the boy mumbled.

"You'll see, I'll show you. . . ."

"Is it fun, Grandmama?" the girl smiled, taking her grandmother's hand.

"Yes, it's so much fun. I've brought different sized containers to mold the sand, and, oh, you'll see!"

The boy gave an awkward skip and nearly shouted, "Show us, Grandmama, show us what you mean!"

Masha laughed, sounding almost like a girl. "We're almost there, yes, we're almost there!"

The first circle of sandy shapes was complete, and the children were so excited by what they were building they forgot about their protective gloves.

"Now, we'll put a pile of wet sand in the middle and build it up with our hands and then we'll do another circle, yes, children?"

The children rushed back and forth from the tide line carrying the dark, wet sand. They only had an hour left. Their eyes, beneath the goggles, darted with excitement.

"Just don't get your gloves in the water, a little wet sand won't hurt, don't worry, children. When I was a girl there were so many birds at the sea we'd scare them off because they'd try to steal our food. Seagulls, they were, big white birds that liked to scream at the sea, they sounded like eagles to me. . . ."

"You used to eat at the sea, Grandmama?" the girl asked incredulously.

"We used to call them picnics. . . ."

"What are eagles, Grandmama?" the boy wanted to know, shaping the dark sand with his gloved hands.

"They used to be one of the largest, most beautiful wild birds in the world. My grandfather pointed them out to me once. . . ." Until that moment, she'd forgotten that memory of nearly sixty years ago. They'd gone on a train, then a bus, to the village where he'd been born. She remembered her grandfather looking up toward a shrill, piercing cry that seemed to come from the sky. She'd seen the tears in her grandfather's eyes and on his cheeks. He'd pointed up to a large, dark flying-thing in the summer blue sky: "That's an eagle, my girl, the spirit of the people."

Sadness overtook Masha, but she refused to acknowledge its presence. The sand castle, Masha told herself sternly—the sand castle is what is important now. "I've brought a wonderful surprise, something to decorate the sand castle with when we're through building it."

"Show us, Grandmama, please?"

"Yes, please, please show us now!"

Masha sighed with a terrible, sudden happiness as she brought out the plastic bag. Quickly, she removed each precious shell from its protective cotton: eight perfect shells from all over the world.

"But grandmama, these are your special shells! You said the sea doesn't make them anymore. . . ."

"It will, Anna, it will." Masha hugged her granddaughter and made her voice brighten with laughter. "Today we will decorate our sand castle with the most beautiful shells in the world, yes!"

And They Lived Happily Ever After for a While

John Ciardi

⋀ How does this picture add to the humor of the poem?

It was down by the Dirty River
    As the Smog was beginning to thin
Because we had been so busy
    Breathing the worst of it in,

5 That the worst remained inside us
    And whatever we breathed back
Was only—sort of—grayish,
    Or at least not entirely black.

It was down by the Dirty River
10   That flows to the Sticky Sea
I gave my heart to my Bonnie,
    And she gave hers to me.

I coughed: "I love you, Bonnie
    And do you love me true?"
15 The tears of joy flowed from my eyes
    When she sneezed back: "Yes-Achoo!"

It was high in the Garbage Mountains,
    In Saint Snivens by the Scent,
I married my darling Bonnie
20   And we built our Oxygen Tent.

And here till the tanks are empty
    We sit and watch TV
And dream of the Dirty River
    On its way to the Sticky Sea.

25 Here till the needles quiver
    Shut on the zero mark
We sit hand in hand while the TV screen
    Shines like a moon in the dark.

I cough: "I love you, Bonnie.
30   And do you love me true?"
And tears of joy flow from our eyes
    When she sneezes: "Yes—Achoo!"

After Reading

Making Connections

1. Did this story seem real to you as you were reading it? Why or why not?

2. If you were to draw or paint your response to the story, what color or colors would you use? Why?

3. Suppose the author had written the story with the sequence of events occurring in their actual order. Would the story be more or less effective than it is? Explain.

4. What do you think the **author's purpose** in writing the story was?

5. John Ciardi uses humor to write about environmental issues in "And They Lived Happily Ever After for a While" on page 349. Compare his purpose for writing with that of Villanueva.

6. 👆 Think about your own **perspective** of the world's environment today. How do you think the environment will change in the future?

Literary Focus: Setting

You've learned that **setting** is the time and place in which the events of a story occur. The setting of "The Sand Castle" is vital to the characters' actions and feelings, and yet we know few facts about it. No dates are given; no cities, landforms, or bodies of water are named. The author seems to want us to imagine the details of the setting for ourselves.

What do you imagine the setting of "The Sand Castle" to be? Write a descriptive paragraph in which you answer that question. Include a specific date, the country and the city or town in which the characters live, and the sea that they visit. (You may want to look at an atlas first.) The idea is not to give a "right" answer, because there is no such thing. However, you should base your ideas about the setting on clues you find in the story and mention those clues in your paragraph.

Vocabulary Study

The sentences below come from a diary entry that might have been written by Mrs. Pavloff's grandson. For each underlined word or phrase, write the word from the list that is closest in meaning.

cumbersome
hostile
scorch
squabble
trudge

1. Grandmama wanted to take us to the beach. My sister and I had to <u>walk wearily</u> with her to the bus.

2. I hated that we had to put on <u>clumsy</u> equipment just to go outside.

3. Grandmama said that if we didn't put on special suits, the sun would <u>burn</u> our skin.

4. On the bus, we heard some other kids <u>argue</u> about who was going to sit next to the window—as if it mattered, when you couldn't see anything out of it.

5. I gave those dumb kids my most <u>unfriendly</u> look, but Grandmama frowned at me, so I stopped.

Expressing Your Ideas

Writing Choices

Sand Castle Contest Imagine that you have made the sand castle below. Write a **persuasive paragraph** telling judges why it should win a sand castle contest.

Where It Stands Look back at your web of environmental problems. Find up-to-date information about one of the problems in magazines or newspapers. Write a brief **status report** about the problem.

Other Options

For Better or for Worse Plan and conduct an **interview** with an older person about environmental changes he or she has experienced during his or her lifetime. Be sure to ask about positive changes as well as negative ones, and ask for the person's ideas as to the causes of the various changes. Share the results of the interview with the class.

A Castle of Your Own Build a **miniature castle** out of sand or papier-mâché. Form the parts of the castle with your hands, or use containers of different sizes and shapes to mold the parts. Decorate your castle with seashells, beads, or other objects you have handy.

Before Reading

People's Gardens: Frederick Law Olmsted and the First Public Parks by Milton Meltzer

Milton Meltzer
born 1915

Meltzer started college during the Great Depression. After attending college, he got a job as a writer for a government project. This experience made him aware of deep struggles going on within American society.

As a writer, Meltzer produced many biographies for young readers. He made this generalization about his subjects: "My subjects choose action. They show the will to do something about what troubles them. Action takes commitment, the commitment of dedicated, optimistic individuals. Our American past is full of examples of people . . . who sometimes understood that they could not manage their own life without seeking to change society, without trying to reshape the world they lived in."

Building Background

Park Place Parks come in many sizes, from a city block to thousands of acres. Most of them are for the public to enjoy. Urban parks often have playground equipment, basketball and tennis courts, and picnic tables. At lakeside parks, people can swim and sail. Throughout the United States, there are state and national parks. Here people can enjoy spectacular scenery and unusual wildlife.

Getting into the Selection

Writer's Notebook Before you read "People's Gardens," make your own K-W-L chart in your notebook. Fill in the first two columns with what you know and what you want to know about public parks. Look for answers to your questions while you read. After you are done with the story, complete the last column of your chart. Share your chart with your classmates.

What I **K**now	What I **W**ant to Know	What I **L**earned
Parks are fun.	When were parks first developed?	

Reading Tip

Subjects and Verbs The author uses a variety of types of sentences. Although this style makes the writing interesting, the construction of some sentences may make them difficult to understand. If you have trouble understanding a complex sentence, look for the **subject** and **verb** of that sentence. You can usually get the main idea by identifying the actor and the action of the sentence. Once you understand these parts of the sentence, see how the other parts of the sentence add to your knowledge.

PEOPLE'S GARDENS

Frederick Law Olmsted and the First Public Parks

MILTON MELTZER

What would America's cities be like without their public parks?

I try to imagine my town, New York. No Central Park? No Prospect Park? No Riverside Park? Think of your own city with its high buildings, crowded streets, noisy traffic eating up every foot of ground. And not a patch of quiet for relief, not a grove of trees, a stretch of meadow, a bed of flowers, a playground or bicycle path or walkway . . .

Today, however, there's scarcely a city that lacks a public park. But none of them just grew. They had to be created. And one man was responsible for discovering the need, designing the space to fulfill that need, and organizing the huge effort to get the job done.

His name was Frederick Law Olmsted [see portrait above]. To him and his partner, Calvert Vaux, America owes many of the parks across the country that have offered us pleasure and beauty for the last one hundred and fifty years.

Where did the idea of a park come from?

In the early 1800s New York was already a "tumultuous and brutal city," packed into the lower part of the island of Manhattan. Businessmen were bent on buying up and making a profit from every square foot of the city's tight space. If this kept on, some feared, masses of New Yorkers would be crowded to death. It was a few thoughtful people, led by the poet and newspaper editor William Cullen Bryant[1] and the writer Washington Irving,[2] who imagined what a great open space could do to bring light and air and peace and quiet to the harried souls of the great city. And especially to the children.

For ten years such public-minded citizens campaigned for the city to acquire a large tract as yet untouched by greedy hands. It was hard going. The rich New Yorkers didn't

---

1. **William Cullen Bryant**, (1794–1878) poet and long-time editor of the New York newspaper the *Evening Post*.
2. **Washington Irving**, (1783–1859) well-known American writer best known for stories such as "The Legend of Sleepy Hollow" and "Rip Van Winkle."

think the city needed a park. (They could go to the mountains or seashore for escape.) And the poor, they said, didn't even know they needed a park. Finally, against great resistance, in 1856 the land was bought by the city for five million dollars.

The area was a series of such rocky ledges that no developer wanted to invest the money to improve even a small part of it. The only people living there were bands of squatters whose shanties[3] clustered under the shelter of the barren rocks. Unfit for farming, the lower parts were swamped in the overflow of pigsties and slaughterhouses; the stench was sickening.

To prepare the ground for construction of the park a superintendent was needed. Olmsted applied for the position. At thirty-five, he had already tried clerking, farming, sailoring, editing, and publishing. But nothing had brought him great success. He knew something about topographical engineering, had studied scientific farming, and had read widely in the theory of landscape design. On visits to Europe and the British Isles he had seen public parks he admired for the way "art had been employed to obtain from nature such beauty." He had to admit there was nothing in democratic America to compare with these "people's gardens."

Olmsted's open opposition to slavery had led the *New York Times* to send him to the South for two years to report on how slavery affected the region's economy and culture. He concluded that the system of slavery perpetuated[4] crude and harsh frontier conditions lacking in the values of community. But the great Eastern cities, too, bursting with immigrants from rural America and immigrants from Europe, were a raw frontier that needed the humanizing influence of parks. Olmsted's work on a book about his recent

---

3. **shanty** (shan′te), *n.* a roughly built hut or cabin.
4. **perpetuate** (pər pech′ü āt), *v.* prolong the existence of.

Southern experience had just been finished when the Central Park job opened up.

Seeking the influence of prominent citizens, Olmsted managed to win the job. His prospects[5] were not promising. The city's politics were corrupt, the economy seemed headed for trouble, he would be poorly paid, and who knew if he could handle such a job? Only himself. He saw this as the chance to turn his pleasure in the care of land into a way of making a living while doing something for the enjoyment of the public.

At the time, Olmsted did not expect to have a hand in the design of the park. He plunged into the daily round of overseeing the seven hundred men hired to build walls, clear brush, and fill in swamps. The site was so rugged, there was scarcely an acre of level ground. His workers—desperate for jobs because the Panic of 1857[6] had thrown thousands on the street—had been hired by politicians not for their skills but for their votes at the next election. But Olmsted had a gift for matching men to jobs and organizing team effort. He made the work so interesting and important in their eyes that they gave him their best.

With the ground-clearing work under way, the Park Commission announced a contest for the park's design. Olmsted and his friend Calvert Vaux decided to enter the contest. And they won. They were a great team. Vaux, an architectural planner from England, was more highly trained, but Olmsted had the surveyor's[7] skills and an intimate knowledge of every hollow in the rocks, every open space, every rock ledge.

The two young men tramped the park together, seeing and measuring, dreaming

THE CITY'S POLITICS WERE CORRUPT...

and thinking, visualizing how this wasteland could be transformed into lakes, ponds, meadows, woods. The area the partners had to plan for was already determined. It was a rectangle two and a half miles long (between 59th Street on the south end and 110th Street on the north) and half a mile wide (between Central Park West and Fifth Avenue), a total of eight hundred and forty-three acres. Looking at Central Park today, you would think that its designers had found a beautiful landscape and had luckily preserved[8] it for us. But what they really did was to create scenery in so natural a way that most users of the park believe it was always like that.

They not only accomplished this amazing feat but did it in the most practical and economic way. They brought in gravel cheaply by boat from the upper Hudson, let trees of any size remain, took rock for boardbed from the excavations[9] in the park itself. The overflow from the site's old slaughterhouses made the nearby soil organically rich, and they used it to improve the thinner soil, enhancing the beauty of grass and trees.

They could foresee how swiftly the city would surround the park. People would need it for recreation, for exercise, for socializing. But above all, it was to be scenery, whose charm would gradually and silently come over the city dwellers, whose beauty would enter their souls without their knowing exactly how or when, but when

◄ Site on which Central Park was developed, as it looked in 1850.

---

5. **prospect** (pros′pekt), *n.* thing expected.
6. **Panic of 1857**, financial disturbance that occurred in the United States in 1857 that caused bank failures, a climate of fear, and widespread unemployment.
7. **surveyor** (sər vā′ər), *n.* person who measures the size, shape, position, and boundaries of land.
8. **preserve** (pri zėrv′), *v.* keep from change or harm.
9. **excavation** (ek′skə vā′shən), *n.* a digging out.

▲ *Skating in Central Park* was painted by Agnes Tait in 1934. Look back at the photograph on 354. Does this painting show that Olmsted accomplished his goal?

going away, they would remember it with a tender joy.

Olmsted gave special attention to children's needs. As well as shelters, arbors, benches, and pavilions that everyone could use, he placed rustic rest houses in several locations especially for mothers with young children. Sheep and lambs were pastured nearby for the children's amusement. Besides the lake for skating, he created ponds for children's boats and ponds for wading.

The park area originally contained small reservoirs[10] for water from the Catskill Mountains. The partners converted them into lawns and built a large new reservoir. They designed curving drives in a north and south circular flow, masking them with trees. They added a long, broad tree-lined promenade,[11] or mall, with a fountain and terrace at one end. From the terrace one could view the lake and the Ramble[12] beyond. One of the ingenious[13] ideas was the design of four trans-

10. **reservoir** (rez′ər vwär), *n.* place where water is collected and stored for use. Reservoirs often form beautiful lakes.
11. **promenade** (prom′ə nād′), *n.* a public place for a pleasurable walk.
12. **the Ramble** (ram′bəl), a wooded, hilly part of Central Park that was known as an excellent place for bird-watching.
13. **ingenious** (in jē′nyəs), *adj.* showing skill in planning or making; clever.

verse roads to carry city traffic rapidly across the park. The partners had them built below park level in open cuts and tunnels so that they would not spoil the scenery.

In the twenty years of his direct connection to Central Park, "Olmsted was probably never happier and never more himself," wrote his biographer. He personally supervised every bit of work on every foot of ground. Without waiting for the park to be completed, the public began to enjoy it. By the winter of 1858–1859 skaters were waltzing and racing over the frozen lake. And in the spring thousands were strolling the park's paths, boating on the lake, and riding on horseback or in carriages along the bridle paths and roads. In June the Ramble was opened, and in July the first concert was performed. By this time Olmsted had nearly four thousand men at work. They built many viaduct[14] arches and seven miles of walk, laid ten miles of drainage pipe, and planted over seventeen thousand trees and shrubs. Olmsted later figured that nearly five million cubic yards of earth and stone had been handled in constructing the park, much of it moved from one part of the site to another.

WITH VAUX, OLMSTED HAD FOUNDED A NEW AMERICAN PROFESSION.

That fall the Park Commission sent Olmsted abroad to study the design of parks in Europe's great cities. Welcomed as a master of landscape planning, he returned home to be hailed as "the only American expert of the first class on parks." He was confident that what he and Vaux had done equaled or surpassed Europe's parks, and he was brimming with ideas of what more might be done.

With Vaux, Olmsted had founded a new American profession. In years to come the partners would plan several more parks in New York and would be commissioned to design parks in Philadelphia, Boston, Washington, D.C., Detroit, Chicago, and California. To Olmsted we also owe measures taken to preserve the natural settings at Niagara Falls, at Yosemite, and in the Adirondacks. He died in 1903, at the age of eighty-one. But his thoughts on the beauty of the wild and the necessity to preserve it still resonate in the actions of today's environmentalists.

---

14. **viaduct** (vī′ə dukt), *n.* a bridge for carrying a road or railway over a valley or other low-lying area.

After Reading

Making Connections

1. Complete your K-W-L chart and make **generalizations** about parks.

2. What do you think was the **author's main purpose** in writing this essay? Explain.

3. Why do you think the author used sentences of varying complexity and length?

4. What do you think was the most important element of Olmsted's background or personality that allowed him to succeed in his job as superintendent of Central Park? Explain.

5. 👣 Olmsted believed that parks had a humanizing effect on cities. What is your **perspective**? Can you imagine a place or situation where parks might need to be sacrificed for other needs such as housing or food production?

Literary Focus: Author's Viewpoint

Whether they state a **viewpoint** openly or not, all authors have opinions, and these opinions usually make their way into an author's work. An author shows bias by presenting a particular point of view. It is important for readers to recognize the author's viewpoint in order to better evaluate what they are reading. In this selection, Meltzer celebrates Olmsted's work and shows him in a very positive light.

One way Meltzer shows his bias is by using **loaded words.** Loaded words don't just present facts, they introduce strong feelings or opinions. In the sentence below, *bent on* is a loaded term. It implies that the businessmen were so determined to reach their goal, they didn't care about anything else. If Meltzer had used the word *considering,* the sentence would be a fact instead of an opinion.

considering
"Businessmen were ~~bent on~~ buying up and making a profit from every square foot of the city's tight space."

Find five other examples of bias through the use of loaded words in this selection. For each word, copy the sentence and list other word choices the author could have made.

Vocabulary Study

Following is part of a speech Olmsted might have made at the dedication of Central Park. For each underlined word or phrase, choose the vocabulary term that is closest in meaning.

**excavation
ingenious
preserve
prospect
reservoir**

1. In New York, the apartments and streets are jammed full. With all the noise, dirt, toil, and trouble, how can we New Yorkers <u>keep a hold on</u> our sanity?

2. The <u>large lake where water is stored</u> gives us a peaceful view to gaze on.

3. To the many hundreds who helped in the <u>digging out of the land</u> to build the park, your hard work benefits us all.

4. To my <u>clever</u> partner, Calvert Vaux, your insight into landscape design is our delight.

5. The <u>expectation</u> that we will have many years and many more parks to plan makes me very, very happy.

Expressing Your Ideas

Writing Choices

Olmsted's the Man Pretend you are a member of the commission to appoint a superintendent to oversee the building of Central Park. Write a **persuasive letter** to the other members of the commission to convince them that Olmsted is the right person for the job. Try using loaded words to support your viewpoint.

Why the Ramble? Imagine you could interview Olmsted. What would you ask him? Write six or more **interview questions** about Olmsted's career, the parks he designed, how he worked with people, his philosophy, what he was proudest of, or any other thing you wish to know about him. Use your school or local library to locate a biography of Olmsted and read it to see if you can find the answers to your questions.

Other Options

Grand Opening Design a **banner** announcing the opening of Central Park. Then draw that image on a banner made of paper or fabric. Include a short slogan. Display it in your classroom.

Parks or Not? How important are parks? Conduct a **debate** between a group of students who want to develop a shopping mall on a piece of land and another group who want to develop a park in the same space.

The Perfect Park Draw a **picture** of the perfect park for a character from a selection you have read in this book. Choose from the narrator of "Stolen Day," Hamlet from "The Dandelion Garden," or the children in "The Sand Castle." Use details about the characters and the setting to help you.

Language Mini-Lesson

Spelling Contractions and Possessives

When to Use Apostrophes You use apostrophes in both contractions and possessives but for different reasons.

In contractions, an apostrophe signals that at least two words are combined, and letters are left out of the new word. What letters are left out in the following examples?

do not → **don't**	she is → **she's**
I will → **I'll**	we are → **we're**

In possessives, an apostrophe signals ownership. Possessives are formed according to the following rules:

- If the noun is singular, add -'s.
  skater's award   **class's** trip   **James's** decision

- If the noun is plural and ends in -s, add only an apostrophe.
  players' awards   **classes'** trip   the **Carrs'** house

- If the noun is plural and does not end in -s, add -'s.
  women's victory   **children's** toys   **mice's** squeaks

Writing Strategy Double-check contractions by reminding yourself which two words were combined and making sure you inserted an apostrophe where letters were left out. For possessives, determine which rule applies by checking first whether the noun ends in -s, and then whether it is singular or plural.

Activity Options

1. Work with a partner to create a crossword puzzle that features contractions and possessives. Trade with another set of partners and try to solve each other's puzzles.

2. Skim newspapers or magazines to find examples of contractions and possessives. Write down at least five examples of each. For the contractions, write down the words that are being combined. For the possessives, write down the rule that is being followed.

3. Make a list of ten nouns. Trade with a partner and then, for each word, write a possessive phrase like those shown above.

Before Reading

April Rain Song by Langston Hughes

I'll tell you how the sun rose by Emily Dickinson

Langston Hughes
1902–1967

Hughes once worked at a restaurant where the famous poet Vachel Lindsay dined. Boldly, Hughes put three of his poems beside Lindsay's plate one evening. Lindsay was so impressed that he helped launch Hughes in his writing career.

Emily Dickinson
1830–1886

Although Emily Dickinson wrote more than 1,700 poems, less than ten were published during her lifetime. Years after her death, her sister collected and published many of her poems.

Building Background

Big Things Come in Small Packages One of the defining features of poetry is its compactness. Compared with prose selections, poems usually have few words. Each word in a poem packs in a lot of meaning on a lot of different levels when compared with a single word of prose. The two poems that follow are very short and compact. However, each shows a different way of appreciating nature.

Getting into the Poems

Writer's Notebook Think about something you appreciate about the world or find especially beautiful. Write it in the center circle of a word web like the one below. Fill in the other circles with words or phrases to describe the thing you find beautiful. Use the web as the outline for a simple poem that conveys your personal sense of beauty.

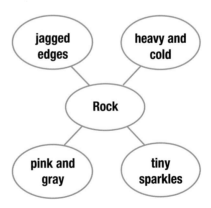

Reading Tip

Sound and Rhythm Some poems rhyme. Others do not. Nevertheless, **sound and rhythm** are very important in almost all poems. The best way to notice these patterns is to read the poems aloud a few times. Listen for sounds that remind you of the subject of the poem. Listen for repeated rhythms that link one part of the poem to another. Poets use these subtle patterns of sound and rhythm to paint appealing pictures with words.

April Rain Song

Langston Hughes

Let the rain kiss you.
Let the rain beat upon your head with silver liquid drops.
Let the rain sing you a lullaby.

The rain makes still pools on the sidewalk.
5 The rain makes running pools in the gutter.
The rain plays a little sleep-song on our roof at night—

And I love the rain.

I'll tell you how the sun rose

Emily Dickinson

I'll tell you how the sun rose,—
A ribbon at a time.
The steeples swam in amethyst,
The news like squirrels ran.

5 The hills untied their bonnets,
The bobolinks begun.
Then I said softly to myself,
"That must have been the sun!"

▲ What words from the poems can you use to describe *Springtime Rainbow* painted by
Jozef Bakos in 1923?

After Reading

Making Connections

1. Think about how you feel about rain and sun. To which of your senses does each of the poems appeal most strongly?

2. How does Hughes use **sound** and **rhythm** in "April Rain Song"?

3. Each of these poems captures a moment of beauty. How do you capture moments of beauty?

Literary Focus: Lyric Poetry

The word *lyric* comes from the name of a musical instrument—the lyre. In ancient times, this stringed instrument was played to accompany poets at a poetry reading.

These two poems are typical of **lyric poetry**. They deal with subjects in nature and create for the reader a single, strong impression. Make a chart like the one below. Reread the poems. Write a word or phrase that describes the impression you get from each poem. Then list any words and describe any rhythms or sound patterns the poet uses to create that impression.

Poem	Impression	Words or Rhythms
April Rain Song	peaceful	lullaby
I'll tell you how the sun rose		

Expressing Your Ideas

Beauty Is . . . Write your own **poem** about what beauty is from your **perspective**. Use any of the forms, structures, or sound devices found in these poems. You can also refer to the poetry web you made before you read the poems. Compare your perspective of beauty with the perspective of others in the class.

Paint Your Poem Pick your favorite poem and make a **painting** that brings out the same feelings as the poem. You may choose a poem from this book or any other poem you have read or written.

Before Reading

Why the Rooster Crows at Sunrise

by Lynette Dyer Vuong

Lynette Dyer Vuong
born 1938

Lynette Dyer Vuong (vōng) grew up in Michigan and began writing "little books of fabulous adventures" as a young child. Although one teacher criticized Vuong's subject matter, she continued writing for herself and "from my heart, pursuing interests that have not changed much over the years: interests in folklore and mythology and in people throughout the world and through the ages."

While working as a nurse, Dyer met Ti Quang Vuong, a student from Vietnam. They married and then lived in Vietnam from 1962 to 1975. Vuong began collecting and adapting Vietnamese stories for American readers. Vuong now lives in Texas with her husband and children.

Building Background

In the Beginning "Why the Rooster Crows at Sunrise" is a **folk tale**. Folk tales are old stories that have been passed from generation to generation by word of mouth. Some folk tales, like "The Rooster Crows at Sunrise," are **origin tales** that seek to explain why certain natural events happen.

Getting into the Story

Discussion All life on earth—people, animals, and plants—depends on the sun's energy. Not only is the sun necessary for survival, but it can also make you feel good. How do you feel when you wake up and see the sun shining brightly? How might you feel if you had to go for weeks or even months without seeing the sun shine?

Reading Tip

Cause and Effect Whether it's fiction or nonfiction, you'll get more out of what you read if you see the relationships between ideas. Writers often use **cause-and-effect relationships,** which show how something makes something else happen. A cause brings about a result, or effect. Remember that one cause can have more than one effect, and one effect can have more than one cause.

Make a chart like the one below. As you read the story, list as many causes and effects as you can.

Cause	Effect
People never gave the sun any respect.	The sun was unhappy.

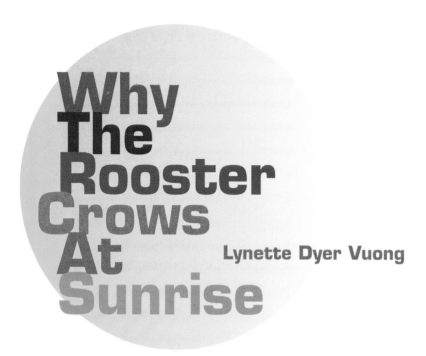

Why The Rooster Crows At Sunrise

Lynette Dyer Vuong

Long ago the sun lived close to the earth. She spent her days just above the tree-tops, shining down on the fields and houses below. But as day followed day, she grew more and more unhappy with her lot. The people who owed her their light and warmth neither gave her thanks nor showed her any respect. Housewives hung their laundry in front of her face and dumped their garbage right under her nose. Men and women alike burned wood and trash, choking her with the smoke, until one day her father, Ngoc Hoang[1]—Jade Emperor, the king of heaven—took pity on her and carried her away from the polluted atmosphere.[2]

"The people don't deserve you," Jade Emperor said as he set her down in a safe place on the other side of the Eastern Sea. "If I had left you there, they would have poisoned you with their filth."

Now day was no different from night. People shivered in their houses and could not recognize each other even when they stood side by side.

In the forest the animals could not see to hunt, and day by day they grew hungrier. At last they gathered to discuss the situation.

The rooster spoke first. "If only we could go to the sun and appeal to her in person, perhaps she would take pity on us and give us a little light."

The duck nodded. "We could try. If only we knew where to find her."

"I've heard she lives across the Eastern Sea," the bluebird chirped. "I'd be willing to lead you there if you'd do the talking."

"I'd do the talking," the rooster offered, "if

---

1. **Ngoc Hoang** (ngk′ hwng′), or Jade Emperor. He appears in many Vietnamese folk tales as the supreme being among spirits.
2. **polluted atmosphere**, usually, dirtied, fouled, or contaminated air. In this case, atmosphere is being used in a broader sense, to mean the general character of the surroundings.

If you were the Sun, would you have listened to this rooster? ➤

I had a way to get there. But you know I can't swim. How could I get across the Eastern Sea?"

The duck smiled. "On my back, of course. No one's a better swimmer than I am."

The three friends set off at once, the bluebird leading the way and the rooster riding on the duck's back. At last they reached the other side of the sea, where they found the sun taking her ease.[3]

"Please come back, sister sun," they begged as they told her of the plight[4] the world was in. "Come back and stay with us the way you did before."

But the sun shook her head. "How can you ask me to come back? You know I had to leave for my health's sake. Why, my very life was in danger in that polluted atmosphere."

"We are starving to death because we can't see to find food. Won't you take pity on us and give us a little light before we all die?" the rooster pleaded.

The sun was silent for a long moment. Finally she sighed. "I know you must be desperate, or you wouldn't have come all this way to see me." She sighed again. "I can't live with you as I used to; but if you'll call me when you need light, I'll come and shine for you for a few hours."

The rooster nodded eagerly. "My voice is loud, so I'll do the calling. When you hear me crowing, you'll know it's time to wake up and get ready to cross the sea."

"I can help too." The bluebird stepped forward. "My voice may not be as loud as brother rooster's; but once he wakes you, you'll be able to hear me, and you'll know it's time to leave your home and start your journey."

The sun agreed. And from then on, the sun, the rooster, and the bluebird have kept their bargain. When the rooster crows, the sun knows it's time to get ready for her day's work; and just as the birds begin their chirping, she appears over the eastern horizon.

---

3. **taking her ease**, relaxing; resting.
4. **plight** (plīt), *n.* condition or situation, usually bad.

After Reading

Making Connections

1. What message did you get from the story?

2. The story explains more than why the rooster crows at sunrise. Invent another title for the story that begins with the word *Why*.

3. What value, if any, do you think a story like this has for people who no longer believe it to be true?

4. In "The Sand Castle," people lived in a world where they had to wear special clothing and goggles to protect themselves from the sun. Would you rather live in that world or in a world in which the sun did not shine at all? Explain.

Literary Focus: Personification

Writers of folk tales often give human traits to animals or objects. This type of literary device is known as **personification**. Copy the chart. Look back through the story and complete the chart.

Animal or Object	Human Characteristics
sun	feels unhappy has a nose
rooster	
bluebird	
duck	

Expressing Your Ideas

Give It to Me Straight For a friend who is too impatient to read the story, write a brief **summary** of why the rooster crows at sunrise.

Thank You, Ms. Sun Imagine you are one of the people mentioned in "Why the Rooster Crows at Sunrise." Write a **thank-you note** to the sun. Be sure to apologize for driving her away in the first place, and tell her how you will "do better" from now on.

What Happened and Why Draw or paint an **illustration** of a scene from the story. The scene should be one that shows a cause-and-effect relationship.

I'll Be the Sun . . . With three classmates, prepare and present a short **play** based on the story. Make simple costumes.

Time Flies The story doesn't specify how much time passes between events. Decide for yourself, and make a **time line** showing the main events of the story and the length of time between them.

Before Reading

Persephone

by Alice Low

Alice Low
born 1926

Alice Low is a successful writer of children's books. She has had several careers—writer and producer of educational filmstrips, teacher, and editor, but writing books comes naturally "because my mother wrote children's books and many of her friends were in the arts and publishing." Of her writing, Low once said, "Travel stimulates and many a line has come to me on a . . . walk."

Building Background

Old Stories Greek myths were told for hundreds of years before they were written down around 800 B.C. During the Middle Ages and the Renaissance in Europe, people read them in Latin. Later, people translated the Greek myths into English and other languages.

Getting into the Story

Discussion Why does the moon change shape? What causes leaves to change color in the fall? These are questions about nature that many people ask. Make a list of your own questions about things in nature. Where would you look to find the answers to these questions? Do you think you could find the kind of answer you are looking for in a story?

Reading Tip

Greek Gods and Goddesses The ancient Greeks worshipped gods and goddesses that ruled over different aspects of nature. The chart below lists some of them and their domains.

Although Greek gods had magical powers and lived forever, they often seemed more human than divine. As you read "Persephone," write down examples of the human characteristics that each god or goddess shows.

Name	Pronunciation	Domain
Zeus	(züs)	ruler of the gods; ruler over the sky and weather
Hades	(hā′dēz′)	god of the dead (the underworld) and earth's fertility
Demeter	(di mē′tər)	goddess of the harvest
Persephone	(pər sef′ə nē)	queen of the underworld
Hermes	(hėr′mēz)	messenger of the gods

Persephone

Alice Low

Persephone was a high-spirited, sunny girl who loved springtime and flowers and running outdoors with her friends. She was the daughter of Demeter, goddess of the harvest, and she and her mother spent more time on earth than on Mount Olympus.

One bright day on earth Persephone was picking lilies and violets with her friends. She could not gather enough of them, though her basket was overflowing.

"Persephone, it is time to go home," called her friends.

"Just one minute longer," she called back. "I see the sweetest flower of all—a narcissus, I think. I must have one." She wandered into a far corner of the meadow, and just as she was about to pick the narcissus, she heard a deafening noise. Suddenly the earth split open at her feet. Out dashed a golden chariot pulled by black horses and driven by a stern-faced man in black armor.

Persephone dropped her basket and started to run, but the driver grabbed her by the wrist. He pulled her into his chariot, which descended back into the earth as quickly as it had risen. Then the earth closed up after it.

Persephone screamed and wept, but her friends could not hear her. Though they searched for her everywhere, all they found was her basket, with a few crushed flowers lying next to it.

Down into the earth the chariot sped, through dark caverns and underground tunnels, while Persephone cried, "Who are you? Where are you taking me?"

"I am Hades, king of the underworld, and I am taking you there to be my bride."

"Take me back to my mother," screamed Persephone. "Take me back."

"Never!" said Hades. "For I have fallen in love with you. Your sunny face and golden hair will light up my dark palace."

The chariot flew over the river Styx[1] where Charon,[2] the boatman, was ferrying ghostly souls across the water. "Now we are at the gate to my kingdom," said Hades, as they landed next to the huge three-headed dog who guarded it.

Persephone shivered, and Hades said, "Oh, that is Cerberus.[3] He guards the gate so that no live mortals enter and no souls of the dead escape. Nobody escapes from the underworld."

Persephone became speechless. Never escape from this terrible place full of pale, shadowy ghosts, wandering through stony fields full of pale, ghostly flowers!

Beautiful Persephone, who loved sunshine, became Hades' queen and sat on a cold throne in his cold palace. Hades gave her a gold crown and bright jewels, but her heart was like ice and she neither talked nor ate nor drank.

---

1. **Styx** (stiks).
2. **Charon** (ker′ən).
3. **Cerberus** (sèr′bər əs).

▲ *Purity and Passion* was painted by Franz Dvorak. How does this image of Persephone compare and contrast with the description of her in the story?

Persephone's mother, Demeter, knew that something terrible had happened to her daughter. She alone had heard Persephone's screams, which had echoed through the mountains and over the sea.

Demeter left Olympus, disguised as an old woman, and wandered the earth for nine days and nine nights, searching for her daughter. She called to the mountains and rivers and sea, "Persephone, where are you? Come back. Come back." But there was never an answer. She did not weep, for goddesses do not cry, but her heart was heavy. She could not eat or drink or rest, so deep was her grief.

Finally she reached a place called Eleusis, not far from the spot where Persephone had disappeared. There a prince named Triptolemus[4] recognized her and told her this story: "Over a week ago, my brother was taking care of the royal pigs. He heard a thundering noise, and the earth opened up. Out rushed a chariot, driven by a grim-faced man. He grabbed a beautiful young girl, and down into the earth they went. They were swallowed up, along with the pigs."

"That man must have been Hades," cried Demeter. "I fear that he has kidnapped my daughter."

---

4. **Triptolemus** (trip′təl ə məs).

Demeter hurried to the sun, Helios,[5] who sees everything. And the sun confirmed Demeter's fears. Demeter cried, "Persephone, my gay lovely daughter, is imprisoned in the underworld, never again to see the light of day or the flowers of spring."

Then Demeter became stony and angry, and she caused the earth to suffer with her. The earth became cold and barren. Trees did not bear fruit, the grass withered and did not grow again, and the cattle died from hunger. A few men succeeded in plowing the hard earth and sowing seeds, but no shoots sprouted from them. It was a cruel year for mankind. If Demeter continued to withhold her blessings from the earth, people would perish from hunger.

Zeus begged Demeter to let the earth bear fruit again, but Demeter said, "The earth will never be green again. Not unless my daughter returns!"

Then Zeus knew what he must take action to save people from starvation. "I will see that Persephone returns," he told Demeter, "but only on one condition. She must not have eaten any of the food of the dead."

Zeus sent Hermes, messenger of the gods, down to the underworld to ask Hades for Persephone's release. When Persephone saw that Hermes had come to her home, she became lively and smiled and talked for the first time that year.

To her delight, Hades did not protest but said, "Go, my child. Although I love you, I cannot keep you here against Zeus's will. But you must eat a little something before you leave, to give you strength for your journey." Then he gave Persephone several seeds from a red pomegranate,[6] which was the fruit eaten by the dead. He knew that if she ate even one, she would have to return to him.

Persephone ate four seeds quickly. Then she climbed into the golden chariot and waved good-by. Hermes drove her to earth, to the temple where Demeter waited, and mother and daughter hugged and laughed and said they would never be parted again. Then Demeter remembered Zeus's warning and said, "I hope you did not eat anything while you were in the underworld."

"I was too sad to eat," said Persephone. "I didn't eat or drink all year."

"Not anything at all?" said Demeter.

"Oh, just a few little pomegranate seeds before I left," said Persephone. "Why do you ask?"

"Because, my dearest," cried Demeter, "if you have eaten any of the food of the dead, you must return to Hades."

Zeus heard the loud wails of Demeter and her daughter, and he decided to compromise. Persephone must spend just four months of each year in the underworld, one for each of the seeds she had eaten. The rest of the year she could be with her mother on earth.

That is why every year, for four months, the earth becomes cold and barren. Persephone is in the dark underworld and Demeter is overcome with grief.

And every year, when Persephone returns to earth, she brings spring with her. The earth is filled with flowers and fruits and grasses. And summer and fall, the seasons of growth and harvest, follow in their natural order. Every year Demeter and the whole earth rejoice that Persephone has returned.

---

5. **Helios** (hē′lē os).
6. **pomegranate** (pom′gran′it), *n.* a reddish-yellow fruit with a thick skin and many seeds.

After Reading

Making Connections

1. Do you think Zeus's judgment at the end of the myth was a fair one? State your reasons.

2. Hades assumes that a gold crown and bright jewels will make Persephone happy. Do you think people can "buy" love or friendship? Explain.

3. 🖋 Based on your interpretation of this story, in what respects did the ancient Greeks have a different **perspective** about their world than you do about your world? Explain.

Literary Focus: Myths

A **myth** is a very old tale, usually involving gods or other supernatural beings. Make a checklist like the one below of the characteristics of myths. Reread "Persephone" and "The Quest for the Golden Apples" on pages 370 and 144 to determine which characteristics each myth has.

Characteristics of a Myth	Persephone	The Quest for the Golden Apples
Includes gods and goddesses		
Has simple setting		
Explains something in nature		
Has serious tone		
Point is clearly stated at end		

Expressing Your Ideas

I, Persephone . . . Pretend you are one of the main characters of the myth "Persephone." Write your **autobiography** based on the information given in the myth. Describe how you felt about each of the main events of your life.

The Greek Inquirer Suppose this story had happened today. Write a sensational **headline** to create interest, such as, "Local Beauty Kidnapped by Underworld King," and a **news article**.

Missing Child Pretend you are Demeter. Draw a **missing-person poster** for your daughter, Persephone. Include a physical description of her, where she was last seen, and what she was doing.

Ancient Calendars

History Connection
Checking the time seems to be a very simple matter. Clocks, watches, TV, radio, and even the computer can instantly give the correct time. This has not always been the case. For ancient societies, tracking time was a complicated affair. See how they relied on clues in their environment to establish working calendars.

Aztec

From the fourteenth to the sixteenth centuries, the Aztec nation ruled much of what is now Central America. Their calendar was based on the movement of the sun, moon and stars. The Aztec calendar had a total of 365 days divided into 18 months with 20 days each. An extra five days completed the calendar year. This system worked for 52 years before the seasons no longer matched. Then the Aztecs started a new 52-year calendar.

Hebrew

The Hebrew, or Jewish calendar, has as its first year the estimated date of the creation of the world. According to Hebrew tradition, the creation took place 3,760 years and 3 months before the first year of the calendar based on the birth of Jesus Christ, or the Gregorian calendar. To find the year in the Hebrew calendar, add 3,760 to the date in the Gregorian calendar. The year 1997 in the Gregorian calendar is the year 5757 according to the Hebrew calendar.

The Hebrew year is based on the moon and usually has twelve months. To keep the calendar in line with the seasons, seven times during each nineteen-year period an extra month is added. This calendar is used today in Israel and by many of the world's Jews.

Egyptian

To grow their crops and protect their families, ancient Nile Valley farmers had to know when the Nile River would flood each year. The flooding always began when the brightest fixed star, Sirius, rose in the east. The Egyptians began their lunar calendar with the first full moon following the appearance of Sirius. This lunar calendar was divided into 12 months of 29 1/2 days each. The total 354 days was 11 short of the 365–day solar cycle. To match the calendar date with the flooding, an extra 11 days was sometimes added.

Mayan

Mayan Indians ruled the Yucatan Peninsula of Mexico and the area that is now Guatemala and Honduras. About 2,300 years ago, Mayan priests/astronomers developed an exact numbering system. By the year 300, they had used this system to create an accurate solar calendar. The Mayan calendar was actually two separate calendars, one civil and one religious, which worked together in 52–year cycles. The 365–day civil calendar had 18 months, each with 20 days, and a 5–day month. The religious calendar had 260 sacred days.

Responding

1. What similarities do you see among all of the ancient calendars?

2. Research one of the following calendars: Sumerian, Babylonian, Greek, Roman, Gregorian, Jewish, Muslim, or Inca. Report to the class on your findings.

INTERDISCIPLINARY STUDY

Environment Connection

All living creatures, from the smallest bacteria to humans, must learn to adapt to their environments in order to survive. When we examine just how difficult and treacherous this process can be for some creatures, appreciating our world suddenly becomes easier.

Choose to be an animal, plant, or insect listed below. The object of the game is to survive a whole year as you battle the seasons. Up to six people can play. Cut out rectangles of cardboard, one inch by one-half inch, to make a counter for each player. Write (or draw) on each counter one of these names: Oak, Poppy Seed, Thrush, Swallow, Dragonfly Nymph, Badger. On the reverse of the poppy seed counter write Poppy Flower. You will be instructed when to turn the counter over to show when the seed has grown and flowered; and when to turn it back again to show when the flower has made seeds. On the reverse of the dragonfly-nymph counter write Dragonfly Adult. You will be instructed when the dragonfly changes from one stage of its life cycle to another. All pieces start at the beginning of spring. Put three coins in a jar. Take turns to shake out the coins. For each coin that turns up "heads," move one square. For example, if you score two heads and one tail, you move two squares. If you score three tails, you stay where you are! Read the square and follow instructions that apply to your piece. If you move forward or back, read the instructions on that square as well. If the instruction is in CAPITAL LETTERS, your animal, plant, or insect has been killed. Start again, with a new piece if you like. See which piece is the first to complete a whole year, and which one goes around the most times.

Mild days, frosty nights
Dragonfly nymphs and poppy seeds are well-suited to winter survival.
Dragonfly adults and **poppy flowers**: DIE.
Swallows: any left will STARVE.

Harsh frost
Poppy flower, dragonfly adult, and **swallow**: DIE.
Badger and thrush: *Move back 1 space.*

Deep snow
Food is covered.
Thrush, dragonfly (adult only), **poppy** (flower only): DIE.
Swallow: all swallows should have migrated. Any left will STARVE.

Winter

Hedge cut
Hedges provide food for animal life.
Oak: new growth is cut back. *Move back 2 spaces.*
Thrush: STARVE. There are no berries to eat.
Badger: food shortage. *Move back 2 spaces.*

Humans provide food
Thrush and **badger**: *move 3 spaces.*

Early frost
Plants and insects are affected.
Poppy, dragonfly (adult only): KILLED.
Swallow: migrate to Africa for winter.
Leave the game for 3 turns until spring arrives. Then rejoin at the start point.

Sunshine and showers
Good growing conditions.
Poppy: if at flower stage, makes seed. *Turn counter over.*
Dragonfly: adult lays egg to make nymphs. *Turn counter over.*

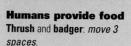

Snow thaws
Rest here before the seasonal cycle continues.

Start point
Fine spring weather

Nature Reserve
All wildlife is protected here.
Move 2 spaces.

Shooters and trappers
Animal life is at risk.
Thrush SHOT
Swallow SHOT
Badger TRAPPED

Spring

Warm sunny weather
Plants and animals grow quickly.
Poppy seed grows into flower.
Turn the counter over.
Dragonfly nymph hatches into adultdragonfly.
Turn the counter over.

Surviving the Seasons

Summer

Late frost
Insects and plants may die.
Swallow: no insects to feed on,so you STARVE.
Poppy: if you are at the flower stage, you are KILLED. If you are a seed, you survive.
Badger: delay breeding.
Move back 1 space.

Continuous wet weather
This affects animal life.
Thrush: DIE of cold if this is your first circuit of the board. Most birds die in their first year.
Dragonfly: DIE if adult. Dragonfly; nymph survives.

Autumn

Drought
If water is short, wildlife suffers.
Thrush and **swallow:** *move back 1 space*
Oak: *move back one space if on first round.* Young trees need water.
Dragonfly nymph: DIES when the pond dries out.

Warm showery weather
Poppy: seed grows into flower.
Turn counter over. Or: flower makes seed. Turn counter over.
Dragonfly: nymph hatches into adult.
Turn counter over. Or: adult lays egg.
Turn counter over.

Poison sprayed on gardens and fields
Thrush, swallow, and **badger** become ill.
Move back 1 space and miss a turn in the wildlife area.
Oak: POISONED if on first circuit. Young trees are easily killed.
Dragonfly (adult or nymph): POISONED.

Wildlife area made at school
Wildlife flourishes.
Move 2 spaces.

Responding
1. Based on the game you just played, which creatures have the most difficult time surviving the elements?

2. Research one of the insects, plants, or animals in this game. What, if anything, is being done to help them survive in their natural environments?

Physical Science Connection

Are you ever frustrated because the clock seems to rule your life? Do you ever wish that a quiet lazy summer day could stand still? Tracking time does have some drawbacks, but without the ability to synchronize time, the modern world would cease to function as it now does.

ABOUT TIME

Linda Allison

An hour can seem like forever when you are at the dentist. But an hour is no time at all when you are having fun with your best friend.

People have been thinking about time and ways to keep track of it throughout most of history. At the dawn of humanity (and even now in remote areas of the world) there were no hours and certainly no minutes or seconds. These measures of time had not yet been invented—and there was no need for them.

Simple-living folk measure time in cycles. They observe sunrise and moon rise, daytime and night-time. They measure time in cycles of the moon, seasons, growth, and birth and death. Their sense of time is an unhurried, eternal one.

There are other ways to think of time. Historians think of time as a series of events. Politicians think of time in terms of five-year plans and future elections. In school kids think of time as periods—math periods, reading periods, and lunch periods, not to mention recess and vacation.

Scientists think of time as intervals. Time to them is a precise and measurable unit of length, whether in microseconds or in light years.

People have been marking time by the sun for many millennia. Gradually, after careful observation, they worked out ways to divide days using shadow devices. But no matter how ingenious they were, people still had to adjust their timekeeping for longer days in the summer and shorter days in winter. And there were also cloudy days when there was no sunshine.

The earliest timekeeping methods were pretty tiresome on a day-to-day basis. They were also rather inaccurate.

The present-day clock has undergone many refinements since early-day devices. Archimedes is said to have used a falling weight to measure time. But a falling weight needs a brake, so various kinds of regulators and gear systems were invented.

Galileo's work with pendulums was applied to timekeeping by a Dutchman named Christian Huyghens. The balance wheel later made time measurable in even smaller intervals.

The alternating electric current was applied to clock knowledge and now even the rate of radioactive decay has been used to make an all-time, super accurate atomic clock which is able to measure the most minute amounts of time.

So when you call the time lady and she says, "The time is four twenty-two, exactly," you'll appreciate how right she is.

Responding

Imagine what the world would be like with no clocks. Consider business, education, sports, transportation, entertainment, and other areas of your environment. Write a one-page description of a clock-less world. Share your ideas with your classmates.

Reading Mini-Lesson

Recalling Details

Did this ever happen to you? You're asked to run an errand. You get halfway there and forget what you were supposed to do. Where did that piece of information go? Why didn't your memory do its job?

When you read, you will be able to recall details easier if you set a purpose. Here are some good questions to ask.

- What do I need to be able to do after I read this? (write a general summary, or list eight specific details)

- When and where will I have to do it? (during five minutes in class tomorrow, or at my own speed at home)

- What kind of container should I use to package this information?

You might not think of containers when you think of recalling details, but "packaging" details makes recall easier. Just as it is easier to find things in an organized desk, it is easier to "find" things in your memory if you organize details carefully.

If you are listing the similarities and differences of various characters in a story, a good container for recall is a chart. If you are reading a chapter in social studies to study for a quiz on dates the next day, a good container for recall is a time line.

Activity Options

Person or Group	Ways to Think of Time
Simple-living folk	cycles (sun, moon, seasons)
Historian	significant dates, eras

1. The first half of the article "About Time" on page 378 shows how different people think of time. Work with a small group of classmates to make a chart like the one at the left that shows ways to think of time.

2. The second half of the article shows the progression of timekeeping from its early days to present time. With a partner, create a time line. Even if you don't have dates for each step on the time line, the time line will help you keep steps in order. The first and last steps on the time line are marked for you. You mark the rest and write in the significant development at each step.

Archimedes   **atomic clock**

Part Two

Protecting Your World

Years ago, there was a popular musical play called *Stop the World—I Want to Get Off.* You may feel that way when you think about all the things that are wrong with the world. Dirty air and water, mountains of trash, ruined rain forests—it's almost enough to make you give up hope. Of course, except for astronauts, none of us can leave. Would we really want to? After all, the world can be a beautiful place, if we'll only allow it to be.

The selections that follow describe some of the ways people hurt the world and some of the ways they can help it. Which will you do? It's your world; it's your choice.

Multicultural Connection Choice involves considering options, weighing pressures, making decisions, and accepting consequences. The characters in these selections all make choices that have important consequences.

Joel Rubin

by Phillip Hoose

Phillip Hoose
born 1947

Concern about the environment is a big part of Phillip Hoose's life. He has a master's degree in environmental science and works for the Nature Conservancy, an organization that identifies and protects the habitats of endangered species. But Hoose firmly believes people don't need a degree or professional experience to make a difference in the world. At the beginning of *It's Our World, Too!,* Hoose says this to young people: "Though your generation is facing some new and very hard challenges . . . there's plenty you can do. . . . You can gain from [other young people's] courage, caring, and shrewdness, and then take your own steps to change things for the better."

Building Background

Dolphins of the Deep Dolphins play a major role in the environmental issue presented in "Joel Rubin." Did you know that, even though they live in the water, dolphins are *not* fish? They're mammals. Like other mammals, dolphins are warm-blooded and feed their young with milk produced in the mother's body. Dolphins also have lungs. A dolphin comes to the water's surface once or twice a minute and breathes through a blowhole at the top of its head.

Getting into the Selection

Writer's Notebook Think about a time when you did something to make a difference. Maybe you took a stand on an environmental issue by signing a petition or writing a letter to a government official. Whatever you did, write about it in your notebook. How did it make you feel? Would you do it again? Why or why not?

Reading Tip

Facts and Opinions Environmental issues often stir up strong feelings in people. Don't be surprised to find **opinions**, as well as **facts**, throughout the selection. Keep in mind that statements of fact can be proved to be either true or false. Statements of opinion can not be proved true or false, because they express personal feelings, beliefs, or evaluations. Any statement about a future event is also an opinion, because it can not be proved now. As you read, look for facts and opinions. Keep track of them in a chart like the one that's been started for you below.

Statements of Fact	Statements of Opinion
The net full of fish and dolphins landed with a crash.	"It was the most disgusting thing I had ever seen," Joel said later.

Joel Rubin

Phillip Hoose

Joel Rubin, fifteen, found a way to influence a huge multinational corporation[1] to change the way it catches tuna in the Pacific Ocean in order to keep dolphins from being killed. His strategy[2] was direct, personal, and hardhitting. As he put it, "You don't always have to be polite."

▲ Dolphin caught in a net intended for tuna.

One Sunday afternoon, Joel Rubin, a fifteen-year-old tenth-grader from Cape Elizabeth, Maine, slumped into a chair in the family rec room[3] and snapped on the TV. He flipped around on the cable channels for a while, then locked onto a show about dolphins.

At first there were scenes of dolphins in family groups. They seemed amazingly like humans: intelligent, friendly, and playful. Through something like radar,[4] they beamed out sounds that let them talk to one another.

Then the scene changed to a large tuna fishing boat in the eastern Pacific. The boat was specially equipped with large drift nets to haul in hundreds of tuna at once. The narrator said that dolphins and yellowfin tuna swim together. The dolphins swim above the tuna, leaping out of the water from time to time to breathe. That makes them perfect markers for tuna fishers.

"The tuna ship sent out helicopters to spot[5] dolphins," Joel remembers. "Then the pilot would radio back to the ship, and suddenly speed-boats would zoom out to surround the dolphins. They wanted to make the dolphins stay in one place so the tuna below wouldn't move. That way they could get nets around all the tuna."

As Joel watched, horrified, boat pilots hurled small bombs at the male dolphins who led the group and tried to run over them with their boat propellers. The sea was soon smeared with blood. The tuna ship steamed into the picture, and fishermen on deck hurriedly cast out a mile-long net. One edge was held up on the sur-

---

1. **multinational corporation**, corporation with branches in many nations.
2. **strategy** (strat′ə jē), *n.* careful plan or method.
3. **rec room**, abbreviation for recreation room, also called a family room.
4. **radar** (rā′där), instrument for locating unseen objects by sending out radio waves that are then reflected, or bounced back, by the objects.
5. **spot** (spot), *v.* pick out; find out; recognize.

face by a line of floats,[6] while the other edge sunk down several hundred feet into the water.

The workers on the tuna boat closed up the net by cranking cables,[7] as if they were

. . . .HE WAS NEARLY PARALYZED WITH SHOCK.

pulling the drawstrings on a giant purse. Underwater cameras showed dolphins, trapped among hundreds of tuna, frantically trying to thrash[8] their way out of the net before they ran out of oxygen. Then the giant net, bulging with writhing[9] fish and dolphins, was hoisted[10] high above the ship and dropped about forty feet down onto the deck. It landed with a crash that shook the camera.

Joel sank back into his chair. He had never been an emotional person, but now he was nearly paralyzed[11] with shock. "Those pictures did something to me," he remembers. "I had never felt that way before. It was the most disgusting thing I had ever seen. I had never tried to change anything before, but I had to do something about this."

WHAT COULD ONE STUDENT DO?

In the winter of 1990, many students throughout the U.S. were feeling the same way Joel did. They were forming environmental action groups and writing to their political representatives, demanding laws to save the dolphins.

Some were boycotting[12] the companies who bought tuna that had been captured in drift nets. Thousands of students were refusing to pack tuna fish sandwiches in their lunch boxes. Others protested against tuna in their school cafeterias. One Colorado high school student named Tami Norton organized a boycott that forced her entire school

system to remove tuna from lunchroom menus.

But Joel Rubin didn't know about the tuna boycotts that were going on elsewhere. He kept asking himself, what can I do? He called the producers of the TV show, the Earth Island Institute, and asked for more information. When a package arrived, the information made him even angrier: he learned that ten million dolphins had died at the hands of tuna fishers since 1960.

He also learned that the tuna fishers didn't have to use the drift nets; there were nets available that could open to release dolphins trapped inside.

Joel went to Dr. Hackett, his biology teacher, and told him about the show. Dr. Hackett was Joel's favorite teacher, an energetic, fast-talking man who seemed to spill over with ideas. They brainstormed together each day after class. After about two weeks, an idea began to take form. "We came up with the idea of starting a message-writing campaign[13] aimed at a big company that buys tuna from the fishing boats using the drift nets. It started out really loose, but each day we worked out more details."

---

6. **float** (flōt), anything that stays up or holds up something else in water. A cork on a fishline is a float.
7. **cable** (kā′bəl), a strong, thick rope, usually made of wires twisted together.
8. **thrash** (thrash), *v.* move, swing, or beat vigorously.
9. **writhing** (rīтн′ing), *adj.* twisting and turning.
10. **hoist** (hoist), *v.* raise on high; lift up.
11. **paralyze** (par′ə līz), *v.* affect with a lessening or loss of ability to move, feel, or function; make powerless.
12. **boycott** (boi′kot), *v.* join together against and agree not to buy from, sell to, or associate with a business in order to force a change.
13. **campaign** (kam pān′), *n.* series of connected activities to do or get something.

Joel figured the U.S. companies who bought the tuna were deserving[14] targets. After all, they had the power to refuse to buy tuna caught in drift nets. If they did, the people who caught the fish would have to change their ways or lose business.

Joel decided to try to convince his schoolmates to write hundreds of messages to the H. J. Heinz Company. Joel had always thought of Heinz as a ketchup maker, but he had learned that Heinz also owned the world's biggest tuna company, Star-Kist. At the time, Star-Kist bought some of its tuna from fishers like those in the TV show.

Joel made a presentation to every science class in his school. "I asked their teachers to let me talk to the students. I needed their help. I told them what was going on with the dolphins and the facts I had learned. It was the first time most of them had heard about it. Most were as disgusted as I was."

Joel asked for volunteers[15] to write personal messages to the Heinz Company. "I told them I didn't want anyone who didn't honestly want to work on this to be in on it. It had to be honest. Not a single student turned me down."

GETTING PERSONAL

After talking more with Dr. Hackett, Joel decided the best strategy would be to send postcards to the homes of the H. J. Heinz Company's executives.[16] Postcards would work better than letters, he thought, since family members would notice them and read the messages. "I imagined the kids of these people showing the cards to their parents when they came home from work and asking, 'What's this?' I thought that would help make the executives think about what they were doing."

And home was more personal than the office. "If we just wrote letters to the company," says Joel, "they would just get thrown in a pile by a secretary. We wanted to have the

postcards waiting at home each night after a day at the office."

How many executives should they send cards to? Not just one, since one could just throw all the cards away and no one else in the company would know. Not too many, either, since they wanted a few targeted individuals to feel responsible. Three sounded about right.

> *I understand you buy tuna from dolphin killers. I feel that until you stop doing that murderous act, I will stop eating tuna and urge other people to do the same.*

> *I hope to understand to the fullest, what you are doing to these helpless dolphins. There is other ways of catching your tuna, either you're just to lazy or you just don't care!*

▲ Two of the postcards sent to carefully selected executives of the H. J. Heinz Company.

Next Joel and Dr. Hackett went to the library to try to find out whom to send the cards to. The reference librarian brought out a book called Standard and Poor's Register of Corporations, Directors and Executives. It listed the names of the top executives in most of the big companies in America. Volume Two: Directors and Executives told a little bit about each boss.

They picked the president of the company, the head of the fish division, and the head of public relations—the person who is responsible for the company's public image.[17]

---

14. **deserving** (di zėr′ving), *adj.* fit or suitable for.
15. **volunteer** (vol′ən tir′), *n.* a person who offers services of his or her own free will.
16. **executive** (eg zek′yə tiv), person who carries out or manages affairs. In a business, executives run departments and supervise the work of other people.
17. **public image**, impression that a person, group, or organization presents to the public.

▲ Joel Rubin enjoys a swim with a friend.

Now they needed to find home addresses. The company headquarters was in Pittsburgh, so they found a copy of the Pittsburgh telephone directory in the library. They found addresses for three people with the right names, including their middle initials.

Dr. Hackett had a friend who lived in Pittsburgh. The friend called the three houses and asked if there was someone there who worked for the Heinz Company. Bingo.[18]

They bought postcards of Maine, and the next day at school Joel passed them out in the science classes. He asked each student to write three postcards, one to each executive's address, and return them to him. He hadn't decided yet whether to send them all at once or a few each day.

And just to be fair, before he sent them, Joel wrote a letter to Anthony O'Reilly, the president of the Heinz Company asking him to stop buying tuna caught in drift nets. "I explained to him what we were prepared to do and why," Joel says. "I didn't give away the details. I gave him two weeks to reply. He never answered."

Joel decided to mail six cards a day to each of the three executives. He figured that was just about the right amount so that each card would get read. When O'Reilly's deadline passed, Joel took the first six to the mailbox and dropped them in.

Two weeks later, Joel received an angry reply from one of the executives. "He was really upset," Joel says. "He wrote: 'I believe it is inappropriate[19] to be mailing business

---

18. **bingo** (bing′gō), an exclamation that indicates something has been achieved or accomplished. It comes from a game of chance in which the winning player calls out "Bingo."

19. **inappropriate** (in′ə prō′prē it), *adj.* not suitable; not fitting.

Joel Rubin **385**

correspondence[20] to people's homes. I resent this as it crosses the border from professional to personal life. . . . I expect that I will not be hearing from you again."

Joel took the letter to school and passed it around the science classes. "We had a little celebration in class that day," Joel says, "because it showed we were getting somewhere. As for getting too personal, we felt very personally about the death of thousands of dolphins. We kept right on mailing to his home."

About a month later, in April of 1990, Heinz suddenly gave in. Anthony O'Reilly announced at a press conference[21] that Heinz would start buying only tuna that were caught in nets that allowed dolphins to escape. Star-Kist tuna cans would say "Dolphin Safe" so that shoppers would know that no dolphins had been killed.

On the same day, two other big tuna companies, Bumble Bee and Van Camp, announced that they would do the same. Together, those three companies bought about seven out of every ten cans of tuna sold in the United States. It was an amazing victory.

In explaining why Star-Kist was making the change, Mr. O'Reilly held up several postcards from high school students in Cape Elizabeth, Maine. One read: "How can you sleep at night knowing your company is doing this?" O'Reilly said that even his own children had been urging him to stop killing dolphins.

Joel Rubin was on vacation with his family in California while O'Reilly was speaking. He happened to be at the Earth Island Institute, hoping to get more information, when he heard the news. The staff gathered around to congratulate him for inspiring[22] the powerful postcards. In its own way, the news was almost as shocking as the television show had been a

few months before. "It was an unbelievable feeling to know that I had something to do with helping to solve a big environmental problem," he says.

What was it that made the postcard campaign so effective? Joel believes several factors[23] were key:

- *We believed deeply in what we were doing. It really came from our hearts.*

- *We made the campaign personal. We tried to find the people most responsible for the problem and tell them we expected them to change it.*

- *The messages were very simple. Some of the best postcards just said, "Why are you doing this?" or "How can you sleep at night?" They got right to the point.*

- *We weren't scared of a big company. I learned that you don't always have to be polite. The company wasn't polite to dolphins, so why should we beg, "Oh, please, please, would you stop doing that?"*

- *We assumed we would succeed. We didn't even think about failing.*

- *We took chances and were ready to change plans.*

- *We gave our target a chance to do the right thing before we started. We tried to be fair.*

"What happened is amazing," Joel says. "It just goes to show that if you really try, and plan, you can make a difference."

---

20. **correspondence** (kôr′ə spon′dəns), *n.* letters; an exchange of letters.
21. **press conference**, meeting arranged by a person or group with reporters for the purpose of releasing some news or submitting to an interview.
22. **inspire** (in spīr′), *v.* bring something about; cause something to happen.
23. **factor** (fak′tər), *n.* a cause that help brings about a result; an element in a situation.

ALMOST HUMAN

Pat Moon

Come and see the people, dear.
Oh, look how they sit!
Aren't they sweet
The way they laugh?
5 I really must admit
That they seem quite intelligent.
Just hear the sound they make;
You could almost believe

They're trying to communicate.
10 They're very easily trained
And respond to simple rules.
Just watch how they point and wave
As we swim around the pool.
See how they stand and clap
15 When we dive through the hoop?
And the noise they make
When we walk on our trails
Or leap the bar in one swoop!

Just watch how they jump and shout
20 In my favourite part of the shows
When we dive and splash the water
All over the front few rows.

It's time to leave them now, dear,
They've had enough for one day.
25 It's quite amazing what people can do
If you treat them in the right way.

▲ Is your **perspective** of these dolphins similar to the dolphins' perspective of humans?

After Reading

Making Connections

1. How did you feel after you read the selection? List three words that describe your feelings, and tell why you felt the way you did.

2. Do you think Joel's strategy would work just as well in other situations, such as protesting against companies that are polluting the air? Explain.

3. Think of another real-life protest action that you have seen or heard about, past or present. Did the protesters act appropriately, or did they go too far? Explain your answer.

4. Do you think the author approves of Joel and what he did, or not? Give your reasons.

5. The author of "Almost Human" tells how dolphins feel about humans. Do you agree with the dolphins' perspective? Why or why not?

6. Some people would say that Joel and the students should have been as concerned about the tuna as they were about the dolphins. If you were going to help in this situation, what choice would you have made? Why?

Literary Focus: Cause and Effect

Which of the following sentences is the **cause**? Which is the **effect**?

- Joel saw a TV show about dolphins caught in drift nets.
- Joel decided to help save the dolphins.

In this case, the first sentence describes the cause—something that made something else happen. The second sentence describes the effect—the thing that happened as a result of the cause. However, cause and effect relationships are not always so simple. For example, a cause may have more than one effect, and an effect may have more than one cause. Also, any event may be both an effect and a cause.

Whether you're reading fiction or nonfiction, seeing cause and effect relationships can help you understand why people act as they do and why events happen. Reread "Joel Rubin," and list as many pairs of causes and effects as you can. Repeat events as you need to, in order to show the various cause-and-effect relationships in the selection.

Saving dolphins is only one concern of environmental activists. Below is part of a TV reporter's account of an anti-fur protest. Write the word from the list that best completes each unfinished sentence.

boycott
paralyze
spot
strategy
thrash

Today, anti-fur protests continued, as more than five hundred protestors marched outside the Fashion Fur Company. This reporter was able to __(1)__ Sam Vege, head of the organization "Down with Fur." Vege told me that marching is just one part of his group's __(2)__ for ending the use of animals for fur. Of course, Down with Fur members will continue to __(3)__ stores that sell fur coats.

Fashion Fur is predicting a severe loss in earnings for the coming year if the warm weather continues. However, the anti-fur forces feel the loss is due to their ability to __(4)__ the fur industry by their actions. One of these actions was showing a TV program on trapped animals. Seeing a young fox repeatedly __(5)__ its bleeding foot to escape from the trap apparently affected many viewers. The next day, Fashion Fur was flooded with angry phone calls.

Expressing Your Ideas

Writing Choices

Sincerely, You Suppose Joel had tried to convince you to write to executives of the Heinz Company about the dolphins. Decide what your reaction would be. Write a short **note**. It can be either a protest note to a Heinz executive or a note to Joel explaining why you don't want to take part in the protest.

Think Like a Dolphin Imagine yourself as a dolphin who has narrowly escaped a drift net or one who must live in captivity. Write the **story** of your experience as you might tell it to the other members of your family group. Use any ideas you get from the selection and the poem.

Other Options

Free the Dolphins? Through the years, dolphins have been captured and put on display in zoos and aquariums. They've been studied. They've even been trained to carry out military tasks. Work with a partner to carry out a **debate** on the subject of whether dolphins should be captured for such uses. Plan to present both facts and opinions. You may want to do some research first.

Plan to Make a Difference In a small group, think of an environmental cause involving animals that you would like to work for. Brainstorm strategy ideas. Then choose one strategy and develop an **action plan** to carry out the strategy. Present your group's plan to the rest of the class.

Before Reading

Let Me Hear You Whisper

by Paul Zindel

Paul Zindel
born 1936

Paul Zindel majored in chemistry in college and taught chemistry and physics for ten years before deciding to pursue a full-time writing career.

Zindel remembers a childhood a surrounded by animals and little else. "We had no books in the house," he says. He entertained himself by putting together aquariums and other miniature environments and observing the animals and plants in them. He also began to write, and he had completed two plays by the time he saw his first professional theater production at the age of twenty-three. In addition to his stage, screen, and TV plays, Zindel has written many young-adult novels with intriguing titles like *The Pigman* and *Confessions of a Teenage Baboon*.

Building Background

Animal Research Animal experimentation has resulted in important medical advances and the saving of human lives. However, some people criticize the use of animals in research. They point out that the animals often suffer physical pain. Opponents believe greater use of computers and other methods could produce medical benefits for humans without harming or killing animals.

Getting into the Play

Discussion Scientists often perform experiments in which they try to communicate with animals. Have you ever had an experience in which you felt you communicated with an animal? If so, what was it like? Do you think it's possible for humans and animals to communicate with one another as equals? Why or why not? As you read, compare your experience with that of the main character in the play.

Reading Tip

Scientific Terms *Let Me Hear You Whisper* contains many scientific terms that may be unfamiliar to you. The chart below explains some of them. To avoid interrupting your reading, study the chart before you begin. You may have to look up other terms.

Scientific Terms	Meanings
formaldehyde bath	a solution containing the colorless gas formaldehyde, used as a preservative
electrode implanting	the insertion of devices that measure electrical activity
nicotine mustard	a colorless poison derived from tobacco
encephalogram	a recording, usually on chart paper, of the electrical activity of a human or animal brain
psychotic	of, having, or caused by a psychosis, which is any severe form of mental disorder that seriously disrupts normal behavior and social functioning

Let Me Hear You Whisper

Paul Zindel

CHARACTERS

HELEN *A little old cleaning lady who lives alone in a one-room apartment and spends most of her spare time feeding stray cats and dogs. She has just been hired to scrub floors in a laboratory that performs rather strange experiments with dolphins.*

MISS MORAY *A briskly efficient custodial supervisor who has to break Helen in to her new duties at the laboratory. She has a face that is so uptight she looks like she either throws stones at pigeons or teaches Latin.*

DR. CROCUS *The dedicated man of science who devises and presides over the weird experiments.*

MR. FRIDGE *Assistant to Dr. Crocus. He is so loyal and uncreative that if Dr. Crocus told him to stick his head in the mouth of a shark, he'd do it.*

DAN *A talky janitor, also under Miss Moray's control, who at every chance ducks out of the Manhattan laboratory for a beer at the corner bar.*

A DOLPHIN *The subject of an experiment being performed by Dr. Crocus.*

SETTING: *The action takes place in the hallway, laboratory and specimen room of a biology experimentation association located in Manhattan near the Hudson River.*

TIME: *The action begins with the night shift on a Monday and ends the following Friday.*

ACT ONE

SCENE ONE

DR. CROCUS *and* MR. FRIDGE *are leaving the laboratory where they have completed their latest experimental tinkering with a dolphin, and they head down a corridor to the elevator. The elevator door opens and* MISS MORAY *emerges with* HELEN.

MISS MORAY. Dr. Crocus. Mr. Fridge. I'm so glad we've run into you. I want you to meet Helen.

HELEN. Hello.

(DR. CROCUS *and* MR. FRIDGE *nod and get on elevator.*)

MISS MORAY. Helen is the newest member of our Custodial Engineering Team.

(MISS MORAY *and* HELEN *start down the hall.*)

MISS MORAY. Dr. Crocus is the guiding heart here at the American Biological Association Development for the Advancement of Brain Analysis.[1] For short, we call it "Abadaba."

HELEN. I guess you have to.

(*They stop at a metal locker at the end of the hall.*)

---

1. analysis (ə nal′ə sis), *n.* separation of anything into its parts or elements to find out what it is made of; also, an examining carefully and in detail.

MISS MORAY. This will be your locker and your key. Your equipment is in this closet.

HELEN. I have to bring in my own hangers, I suppose.

MISS MORAY. Didn't you find Personnel pleasant?

HELEN. They asked a lot of crazy questions.

MISS MORAY. Oh, I'm sorry. *(Pause)* For instance.

HELEN. They wanted to know what went on in my head when I'm watching television in my living room and the audience laughs. They asked if I ever thought the audience was laughing at *me.*

MISS MORAY *(laughing).* My, oh, my! *(Pause)* What did you tell them?

HELEN. I don't have a TV.

MISS MORAY. I'm sorry.

HELEN. I'm not.

MISS MORAY. Yes. Now, it's really quite simple. That's our special soap solution. One tablespoon to a gallon of hot water, if I may suggest.

(Helen is busy running water into a pail which fits into a metal stand on wheels.)

MISS MORAY. I'll start you in the laboratory. We like it done first. The specimen room is next, and finally the hallway. By that time we'll be well toward morning, and if there are a few minutes left, you can polish the brass strip. *(She points to brass strip which runs around the corridor, halfway between ceiling and floor.)* Ready? Fine.

(They start down the hall, MISS MORAY thumbing through papers on a clipboard.)

MISS MORAY. You were with one concern[2] for fourteen years, weren't you? Fourteen years with Metal Climax Building. That's next to the Radio City Music Hall,[3] isn't it, dear?

HELEN. Uh-huh.

MISS MORAY. They sent a marvelous letter of recommendation. My! Fourteen years on the seventeenth floor. You must be very proud. Why did you leave?

HELEN. They put in a rug.

(MISS MORAY leads HELEN into the laboratory, where DAN is picking up.)

MISS MORAY. Dan, Helen will be taking Marguerita's place. Dan is the night porter[4] for the fifth through ninth floors.

DAN. Hiya!

HELEN. Hello. *(She looks around.)*

MISS MORAY. There's a crock on nine you missed, and the technicians on that floor have complained about the odor.

(HELEN notices what appears to be a large tank of water with a curtain concealing its contents.)

HELEN. What's that?

MISS MORAY. What? Oh, that's a dolphin, dear. But don't worry about anything except the floor. Dr. Crocus prefers us not to touch either the equipment or the animals.

HELEN. Do you keep him cramped up in that all the time?

MISS MORAY. We have a natatorium for it to exercise in, at Dr. Crocus's discretion.[5]

HELEN. He looks really cramped.

(MISS MORAY closes a curtain which hides the tank.)

MISS MORAY. Well, you must be anxious to begin. I'll make myself available at the reception desk in the hall for a few nights in case any questions arise. Coffee break at two and six A.M. Lunch at four A.M. All clear?

HELEN. I don't need a coffee break.

MISS MORAY. Helen, we all need Perk-You-Ups. All of us.

HELEN. I don't want one.

---

2. **concern** (ken sėrn′), *n.* a business company; firm.
3. **Radio City Music Hall,** theater in New York City, famous for lavish stage shows.
4. **porter** (pôr′tər), *n.* janitor.
5. discretion (dis kresh′ən), *n.* freedom to decide or choose.

▲ *Proletarian* was painted by Gordon Samstag in 1934. How do you think Helen feels about her discovery?

MISS MORAY. They're compulsory.[6] *(Pause)* Oh, Helen, I know you're going to fit right in with our little family. You're such a nice person. *(She exits.)* (HELEN *immediately gets to work, moving her equipment into place and getting down on her hands and knees to scrub the floor.* DAN *exits.* HELEN *gets in a few more rubs, glances at the silhouette of the dolphin's tank behind the curtain, and then continues. After a pause, a record begins to play.)*

RECORD. "Let me call you sweetheart,
I'm in love with you.
Let me hear you whisper
That you love me, too."

(HELEN's *curiosity makes her open the curtain and look at the dolphin. He looks right back at her. She returns to her work, singing "Let Me Call You Sweetheart" to herself, missing a word here and there; but her eyes return to the dolphin. She becomes uncomfortable under his stare and tries to ease her discomfort by playing peek-a-boo with him. There is no response and she resumes scrubbing and humming. The dolphin lets out a bubble or two and moves in the tank to bring his blowhole to the surface.)*

DOLPHIN. Youuuuuuuuuuuu.

(HELEN *hears the sound, assumes she is mistaken, and goes on with her work.)*

DOLPHIN. Youuuuuuuuuuuu.

(HELEN *has heard the sound more clearly this time. She is puzzled, contemplates a moment, and then decides to get up off the floor. She closes the curtain on the dolphin's tank and leaves the laboratory. She walks the length of the hall to* MISS MORAY, *who is sitting at a reception desk near the elevator.)*

MISS MORAY. What is it, Helen?

HELEN. The fish is making some kinda funny noise.

MISS MORAY. Mammal, Helen. It's a mammal.

HELEN. The mammal's making some kinda funny noise.

MISS MORAY. Mammals are supposed to make funny noises.

HELEN. Yes, Miss Moray.

(HELEN *goes back to the lab. She continues scrubbing.)*

DOLPHIN. Youuuuuuuuuuuu.

(She *apprehensively*[7] *approaches the curtain and opens it. Just then* DAN *barges in. He goes to get his reaching pole, and* HELEN *hurriedly returns to scrubbing the floor.)*

DAN. Bulb out on seven.

HELEN. What do they have that thing for?

DAN. What thing?

HELEN. That.

DAN. Yeah, he's something, ain't he? *(Pause)* They're tryin' to get it to talk.

HELEN. Talk?

DAN. Uh-huh, but he don't say nothing. They had one last year that used to laugh. It'd go "heh heh heh heh heh heh heh." Then they got another one that used to say, "Yeah, it's four o'clock." Everybody took pictures of that one. All the magazines and newspapers.

HELEN. It just kept saying "Yeah, it's four o'clock"?

DAN. Until it died of pneumonia. They talk outta their blowholes, when they can talk, that is. Did you see the blowhole?

HELEN. No.

DAN. Come on and take a look.

HELEN. I don't want to look at any blowhole.

DAN. Miss Moray's at the desk. She won't see anything.

(HELEN *and* DAN *go to the tank. Their backs are to the lab door and they don't see* MISS MORAY *open the door and watch them.)*

DAN. This one don't say anything at all. They been playing the record every seven minutes for months, and it can't even learn a single word. Don't even say "Polly want a

---

6. **compulsory** (kəm pul′ sər ē), *adj.* compelled; required.
7. **apprehensively** (ap′ri hen′siv lē), *adv.* in a way that indicates alarm, fear, anxiety, or worry.

cracker."

MISS MORAY. Helen?

(HELEN *and* DAN *turn around.*)

MISS MORAY. Helen, would you mind stepping outside a moment?

HELEN. Yes, Miss Moray.

DAN. I was just showing her something.

MISS MORAY. Hadn't we better get on with our duties?

DAN. All right, Miss Moray.

(MISS MORAY *guides* HELEN *out into the hall, and puts her arm around her as though taking her into her confidence.*)

MISS MORAY. Helen, I called you out here because . . . well, frankly, I need your help.

HELEN. He was just showing me . . .

MISS MORAY. Dan is an idle-chatter breeder. How many times we've told him, "Dan, this is a scientific atmosphere you're employed in and we would appreciate a minimum of subjective[8] communication." So—if you can help, Helen—and I'm sure you can, enormously—we'd be so grateful.

HELEN. Yes, Miss Moray.

(MISS MORAY *leads* HELEN *back to the lab.*)

MISS MORAY. Now, we'll just move directly into the specimen room. The working conditions will be ideal for you in here.

(HELEN *looks ready to gag as she looks around the specimen room. It is packed with specimen jars of all sizes. Various animals and parts of animals are visible in their formaldehyde baths.*)

MISS MORAY. Now, you will be responsible not only for the floor area but the jars as well. A feather duster—here—is marvelous.

(MISS MORAY *smiles and exits. The sound of music and voice from beyond the walls floats over.*)

RECORD. "Let me call you sweetheart . . ."

(HELEN *gasps as her eyes fall upon one particular jar in which is floating a preserved human brain. The lights go down, ending Act One, Scene 1.*)

SCENE TWO

It is the next evening. HELEN *pushes her equipment into the lab. She opens the curtain so she can watch the dolphin as she works. She and the dolphin stare at each other.*

HELEN. Youuuuuuuuuuuu. (*She pauses, watches for a response.*) Youuuuuuuuuuuu (*Still no response. She turns her attention to her scrubbing for a moment.*) Polly want a cracker? Polly want a cracker? (*She wrings out a rag and resumes work.*) Yeah, it's four o'clock. Yeah, it's four o'clock. Polly want a cracker at four o'clock?

(*She laughs at her own joke, then goes to the dolphin's tank and notices how sad he looks. She reaches her hand in and just touches the top of his head. He squirms and likes it.*)

HELEN. Heh heh heh heh heh heh heh heh heh.

(MISS MORAY *gets off the elevator and hears the peculiar sounds coming from the laboratory. She puts her ear against the door.*)

HELEN. Heh heh heh heh heh . . .

MISS MORAY (*entering*). Look how nicely the floor's coming along! You must have a special rinsing technique.[9]

HELEN. Just a little vinegar in the rinse water.

MISS MORAY. You brought the vinegar yourself. Just so the floors . . . they are sparkling, Helen. Sparkling! (*She pauses—looks at the dolphin, then at* HELEN.) It's marvelous, Helen, how well you've adjusted.

HELEN. Thank you, Miss Moray.

MISS MORAY. Helen, the animals here are used for experimentation, and . . . . Well, take Marguerita. She had fallen in love with the mice. All three hundred of them. She seemed shocked when she found out Dr.

---

8. subjective (səb jek′tiv), *adj.* about the thoughts, feelings, and experiences of the speaker; personal.
9. technique (tek nēk′), *n.* a special method or system used to accomplish something.

Crocus was . . . using . . . them at the rate of twenty or so a day in connection with electrode implanting. She noticed them missing after a while and when I told her they'd been decapitated,[10] she seemed terribly upset.

HELEN. What do you want with the fish—mammal?

MISS MORAY. Well, dolphins may have an intelligence equal to our own. And if we can teach them our language—or learn theirs—we'll be able to communicate.

HELEN. I can't understand you.

MISS MORAY (louder). Communicate! Wouldn't it be wonderful?

HELEN. Oh, yeah. . . . They chopped the heads off three hundred mice? That's horrible.

MISS MORAY. You're so sensitive, Helen. Every laboratory in the country is doing this type of work. It's quite accepted.

HELEN. Every laboratory cutting off mouse heads!

MISS MORAY. Virtually. . . .

HELEN. How many laboratories are there?

MISS MORAY. I don't know. I suppose at least five thousand.

HELEN. Five thousand times three hundred . . . that's a lot of mouse heads. Can't you just have one lab chop off a couple and then spread the word?

MISS MORAY. Now, Helen—this is exactly what I mean. You will do best not to become fond of the subject animals. When you're here a little longer you'll learn . . . well . . . there are some things you just have to accept on faith.

(MISS MORAY exits, leaving the lab door open for HELEN to move her equipment out.)

DOLPHIN. Whisper. . . . (HELEN pauses a moment.) Whisper to me. (She exits as the lights go down, ending the scene.)

SCENE THREE

It is the next evening. HELEN *goes from her locker to the laboratory.*

DOLPHIN. Hear . . . .

HELEN. What?

DOLPHIN. Hear me . . . .

(DAN *barges in with his hamper, almost frightening* HELEN *to death. He goes to dolphin's tank.*)

DAN. Hiya, fella! How are ya? That reminds me. Gotta get some formaldehyde jars set up by Friday. If you want anything just whistle.

(*He exits.* HELEN *goes to the tank and reaches her hand out to pet the dolphin.*)

HELEN. Hear. (*Pause*) Hear.

DOLPHIN. Hear.

HELEN. Hear me.

DOLPHIN. Hear me.

HELEN. That's a good boy.

DOLPHIN. Hear me . . . .

HELEN. Oh, what a pretty fellow. Such a pretty fellow.

(MISS MORAY *enters.*)

MISS MORAY. What are you doing, Helen?

HELEN. I . . . uh . . . .

MISS MORAY. Never mind. Go on with your work.

(MISS MORAY *surveys*[11] *everything, then sits on a stool.* DAN *rushes in with large jars on a wheeled table.*

DAN. Scuse me, but I figure I'll get the formaldehyde set up tonight.

MISS MORAY. Very good, Dan.

HELEN (*noticing the dolphin is stirring*). What's the formaldehyde for?

MISS MORAY. The experiment series on . . . the dolphin will . . . terminate[12] on Friday. That's why it has concerned me that

---

10. **decapitate** (di kap′ə tāt), *v.* cut off the head of; behead.
11. **survey** (sər vā′), *v.* look over; view; examine.
12. **terminate** (tėr′mə nāt), *v.* come to an end.

About 1,600 B.C. the Minoans of ancient Greece created this tribute to dolphins by painting their images on plaster. How does this perspective of dolphins differ from the one held by Miss Moray?

you've apparently grown . . . fond . . . of the mammal.

HELEN. They're gonna kill it?

DAN. Gonna sharpen the handsaws now. Won't have any trouble getting through the skull on this one, no, sir. *(He exits.)*

HELEN. What for? Because it didn't say anything? Is that what they're killing it for?

MISS MORAY. Helen, no matter how lovely our intentions, no matter how lonely we are and how much we want people or animals . . . to like us . . . we have no right to endanger the genius about us. Now, we've spoken about this before.

(HELEN is dumfounded as MISS MORAY exits. HELEN gathers her equipment and looks at the dolphin, which is staring desperately at her.)

DOLPHIN. Help. *(Pause)* Please help me.

(HELEN is so moved by the cries of the dolphin she looks ready to burst into tears as the lights go down, ending Act One.)

ACT TWO

The hall. It is the night that the dolphin is to be dissected. Elevator doors open and HELEN *gets off, nods, and starts down the hall.* MISS MORAY *comes to* HELEN *at closet.*

MISS MORAY. I hope you're well this evening.

HELEN. When they gonna kill it?

MISS MORAY. Don't say kill, Helen. You make it sound like murder. Besides, you won't have to go into the laboratory at all this evening.

HELEN. How do they kill it?

MISS MORAY. Nicotine mustard, Helen. It's very humane. They inject it.

HELEN. Maybe he's a mute.[13]

MISS MORAY. Do you have all your paraphernalia?[14]

HELEN. Some human beings are mute, you know. Just because they can't talk we don't kill them.

MISS MORAY. It looks like you're ready to open a new box of steel wool.

HELEN. Maybe he can type with his nose. Did they try that?

---

13. **mute** (myüt), *n.* person (or in this case, animal) who cannot speak.

14. **paraphernalia** (par/ə fər nā′lyə), *n.* equipment.

MISS MORAY. Now, now, Helen—

HELEN. Miss Moray, I don't mind doing the lab.

MISS MORAY. Absolutely not! I'm placing it off limits for your own good. You're too emotionally involved.

HELEN. I can do the lab, honest. I'm not emotionally involved.

MISS MORAY (*motioning her to the specimen-room door*). Trust me, Helen. Trust me.

HELEN (*reluctantly disappearing through the door*). Yes, Miss Moray.

(MISS MORAY *stations herself at the desk near the elevator and begins reading her charts.* HELEN *slips out of the specimen room and into the laboratory without being seen. The lights in the lab are out and moonlight from the window casts eerie shadows.*)

DOLPHIN. Help.

(HELEN *opens the curtain. The dolphin and she look at each other.*)

DOLPHIN. Help me.

HELEN. You don't need me. Just say something to them. Anything. They just need to hear you say something. . . . You want me to tell 'em? I'll tell them. I'll just say I heard you say "Help." (*Pauses, then speaks with feigned cheerfulness*) I'll go tell them.

DOLPHIN. Nooooooooooooooo.

(HELEN *stops. Moves back toward tank.*)

HELEN. They're gonna kill you!

DOLPHIN. Plaaaaan.

HELEN. What?

DOLPHIN. Plaaaaaaaaan.

HELEN. Plan? What plan?

(DAN *charges through the door and snaps on the light.*)

DAN. Uh-oh. Miss Moray said she don't want you in here.

(HELEN *goes to* DR. CROCUS's *desk and begins to look at various books on it.*)

HELEN. Do you know anything about a plan?

DAN. She's gonna be mad. What plan?

HELEN. Something to do with . . . . (*She indicates the dolphin.*)

DAN. Hiya, fella!

HELEN. About the dolphin . . . .

DAN. They got an experiment book they write in.

HELEN. Where?

DAN. I don't know.

HELEN. Find it and bring it to me in the animals' morgue.[15] Please.

DAN. I'll try. I'll try, but I got other things to do, you know.

(HELEN *slips out the door and makes it safely back into the specimen room.* DAN *rummages through the desk and finally finds the folder. He is able to sneak into the specimen room.*)

DAN. Here.

(HELEN *grabs the folder and starts going through it.* DAN *turns and is about to go back out into the hall when he sees that* MISS MORAY *has stopped reading.* HELEN *skims through more of the folder. It is a bulky affair. She stops at a page discussing uses of dolphins.* MISS MORAY *gets up from the desk and heads for the specimen-room door.*)

DAN. She's coming.

HELEN. Maybe you'd better hide. Get behind the table. Here, take the book. (DAN *ducks down behind one of the specimen tables, and* HELEN *starts scrubbing away.* MISS MORAY *opens the door.*)

MISS MORAY. Perk-You-Up time, Helen. Tell Dan, please. He's in the laboratory.

(HELEN *moves to the lab door, opens it, and calls into the empty room.*)

HELEN. Perk-You-Up time.

MISS MORAY. Tell him we have ladyfingers.[16]

---

15. **morgue** (môrg), *n.* usually, a place in which the bodies of unknown persons found dead are kept until they can be identified and claimed. In this case, Helen uses the term to refer to the specimen room.

16. **ladyfinger** (lā′dē fing′gər), *n.* a small sponge cake shaped somewhat like a finger.

HELEN. We have ladyfingers.

MISS MORAY. Such a strange thing to call a confectionery,[17] isn't it? It's almost macabre.

HELEN. Miss Moray . . . .

MISS MORAY. Yes, Helen?

HELEN. I was wondering why they wanna talk with . . . .

MISS MORAY. Now now now!

HELEN. I mean, supposing dolphins *did* talk?

MISS MORAY. Well, like fishing, Helen. If we could communicate with dolphins, they might be willing to herd fish for us. The fishing industry would be revolutionized.

HELEN. Is that all?

MISS MORAY. All? Heavens, no. They'd be a blessing to the human race. A blessing. They would be worshipped in oceanography. Checking the Gulf Stream[18] . . . taking water temperatures, depth, salinity readings. To say nothing of the contributions they could make in marine biology, navigation,[19] linguistics![20] Oh, Helen, it gives me the chills.

HELEN. It'd be good if they talked.

MISS MORAY. God's own blessing.

(DAN *opens the lab doors and yells over* HELEN*'s head to* MISS MORAY.)

DAN. I got everything except the head vise. They can't saw through the skull bone without the head vise.

MISS MORAY. Did you look on five? They had it there last week for . . . what they did to the St. Bernard.

(*From the laboratory, music drifts out. They try to talk over it.*)

DAN. I looked on five.

MISS MORAY. You come with me. It must have been staring you in the face.

(DAN *and* MISS MORAY *get on the elevator.*)

MISS MORAY. We'll be right back, Helen.

(*The doors close and* HELEN *hurries into the laboratory. She stops just inside the door, and it is obvi-ous that she is angry.*)

DOLPHIN. Booooooooook.

HELEN. I looked at your book. I looked at your book all right!

DOLPHIN. Booooooooook.

HELEN. And you want to know what I think? I don't think much of you, that's what I think.

DOLPHIN. Booooooooook.

HELEN. Oh, shut up. Book book book book book. I'm not interested. You eat yourself silly—but to get a little fish for hungry humans is just too much for you. Well. I'm going to tell 'em you can talk.

(*The dolphin moves in the tank, lets out a few warning bubbles.*)

HELEN. You don't like that, eh? Well, I don't like lazy selfish people, mammals or animals.

(*The dolphin looks increasingly desperate and begins to make loud blatt and beep sounds. He struggles in the tank.*)

HELEN. Cut it out—you're getting water all over the floor.

DOLPHIN. Booooooooook!

(HELEN *looks at the folder on the desk. She picks it up, opens it, closes it, and sets it down again.*)

HELEN. I guess you don't like us. I guess you'd die rather than help us . . . .

DOLPHIN. Hate.

HELEN. I guess you do hate us . . . .

(*She returns to the folder.*)

---

17. **confectionery** (kən fek′shə ner′ē), *n.* candy, pastry, or other sweet food.
18. **Gulf Stream**, current of warm water that begins in the Caribbean Sea. It flows through the Gulf of Mexico, north along the east coast of the United States, and then heads northeast across the Atlantic Ocean.
19. **navigation** (nav′ə gā′shən), *n.* art or science of finding a ship's or an aircraft's position and course.
20. **linguistics** (ling gwis′tiks), *n.* science of language; comparative study of languages.

HELEN (reading). Military implications[21] . . . war . . . plant mines in enemy waters . . . deliver atomic warheads . . . war . . . nuclear torpedoes . . . attach bombs to sub-marines . . . terrorize enemy waters . . . war . . . . They're already thinking about ways to use you for war. Is that why you can't talk to them? (Pause) What did you talk to me for? (Pause) You won't talk to them, but you . . . you talk to me because . . . you want something . . . there's something . . . I can do?

DOLPHIN. Hamm . . . .

HELEN. What?

DOLPHIN. Hamm . . . .

HELEN. Ham? I thought you ate fish.

DOLPHIN (moving with annoyance). Ham . . . purrrr.

HELEN. Ham . . . purrrr? I don't know what you're talking about.

DOLPHIN (even more annoyed). Ham . . . purrrr.

HELEN. Ham . . . purrrr. What's a purrrr?

(Confused and scared, she returns to scrubbing the hall floor just as the doors of the elevator open, revealing MISS MORAY, DAN, and MR. FRIDGE. DAN pushes a dissection table loaded with shiny instruments toward the lab.)

MISS MORAY. Is the good doctor in yet?

MR. FRIDGE. He's getting the nicotine mustard on nine. I'll see if he needs assistance.

MISS MORAY. I'll come with you. You'd better leave now, Helen. It's time. (She smiles and the elevator doors close.)

DAN (pushing the dissection table through the lab doors). I never left a dirty head vise. She's trying to say I left it like that.

HELEN. Would you listen a minute? Ham . . . purrrr. Do you know what a ham . . . purrrr is?

DAN. The only hamper I ever heard of is out in the hall. (HELEN darts to the door, opens it, and sees the hamper at the end of the hall.)

HELEN. The hamper!

▲ Suppose animals were superior to humans. How would you feel about being experimented on by this surgeon in order to make medical advances for dolphins?

DAN. Kazinski left the high-altitude chamber dirty once, and I got blamed for that, too. (He exits.)

HELEN (rushing to the dolphin). You want me to do something with the hamper. What? To get it? To put . . . you want me to put you in it? But what'll I do with you? Where can I take you?

DOLPHIN. Sea . . . .

HELEN. See? See what?

DOLPHIN. Sea . . . .

HELEN. I don't know what you're talking about. They'll be back in a minute. I don't

21. **implication** (im′plə kā′shən), n. a possible significance.

know what to do!

DOLPHIN. Sea . . . sea . . . .

HELEN. See? . . . The sea! That's what you're talking about! The river . . . to the sea!

(She darts into the hall and heads for the hamper. Quickly she pushes it into the lab, and just as she gets through the doors unseen, MISS MORAY gets off the elevator.)

MISS MORAY. Helen?

(She starts down the hall. Enters the lab. The curtain is closed in front of the tank.)

MISS MORAY. Helen? Are you here? Helen?

(She sees nothing and is about to leave when she hears a movement behind the curtain. She looks down and sees HELEN's shoes. MISS MORAY moves to the curtain and pulls it open. There is HELEN with her arms around the front part of the dolphin, lifting it a good part of the way out of the water.)

MISS MORAY. Helen, what do you think you're hugging?

(HELEN drops the dolphin back into the tank.)

MR. FRIDGE (entering). Is anything wrong, Miss Moray?

MISS MORAY. No . . . nothing wrong. Nothing at all. Just a little spilled water.

(HELEN and MISS MORAY grab sponges from the lab sink and begin to wipe up the water around the tank. DR. CROCUS enters and begins to fill a hypodermic syringe while MR. FRIDGE expertly gets all equipment into place. DAN enters.)

MR. FRIDGE. Would you like to get an encephalogram during the death process, Dr. Crocus?

DR. CROCUS. Why not?

(MR. FRIDGE begins to implant electrodes in the dolphin's head. The dolphin commences making high-pitched distress signals.)

MISS MORAY. Come, Helen. I'll see you to the elevator.

(MISS MORAY leads her out to the hall. HELEN gets on her coat and kerchief.)

MISS MORAY. Frankly, Helen, I'm deeply disap-

pointed. I'd hoped that by being lenient[22] with you—and heaven knows I have been—you'd develop a heightened loyalty to our team.

HELEN (bursting into tears and going to the elevator). Leave me alone.

MISS MORAY (softening as she catches up to her). You really are a nice person, Helen. A very nice person. But to be simple and nice in a world where great minds are giant-stepping the micro- and macrocosms, well—one would expect you'd have the humility[23] to yield in unquestioning awe. I truly am very fond of you, Helen, but you're fired. Call Personnel after nine A.M.

(As MISS MORAY disappears into the laboratory, the record starts to play.)

RECORD. "Let me call you sweetheart, I'm in love with you. Let me hear you whisper. . . ."

(The record is roughly interrupted. Instead of getting on the elevator, HELEN whirls around and barges into the lab.)

HELEN. Who do you think you are? (Pause) Who do you think you are? (Pause) I think you're a pack of killers, that's what I think.

MISS MORAY. Doctor. I assure you this is the first psychotic outbreak she's made. She did the entire brass strip . . . .

HELEN. I'm tired a being a nice person, Miss Moray. I'm going to report you to the ASPCA,[24] or somebody, because . . . I've decided I don't like you cutting the heads off mice and sawing through skulls of St. Bernards . . . and if being a nice person is just not saying anything and letting you pack of butchers run around doing what-

---

22. lenient (lē′nyənt), adj. mild or gentle; not harsh or stern; merciful.
23. humility (hyŭ mil′ə tē), n. humbleness of mind; lack of pride; meekness.
24. ASPCA, American Society for the Prevention of Cruelty to Animals.

ever you want, then I don't want to be nice anymore. *(Pause)* You gotta be very stupid people to need an animal to talk before you know just from looking at it that it's saying something . . . that it knows what pain feels like. I'd like to see you all with a few electrodes in your heads. Being nice isn't any good. *(Looking at dolphin)* They just kill you off if you do that. And that's being a coward. You gotta talk back. You gotta speak up against what's wrong and bad, or you can't ever stop it. At least you've gotta try. *(She bursts into tears.)*

MISS MORAY. Nothing like this has ever happened with a member of the Custodial Engineering . . . . Helen, dear . . . .

HELEN. Get your hands off me. *(Yelling at the dolphin)* You're a coward, that's what you are. I'm going.

DOLPHIN. Loooooooooveeeeeeeee.

(Everyone turns to stare at the dolphin.)

DOLPHIN. Love.

DR. CROCUS. Get the recorder going.

(HELEN pats the dolphin, exits. The laboratory becomes a bustle of activity)

DOLPHIN. Love . . . .

DR. CROCUS. Is the tape going?

MR. FRIDGE. Yes, Doctor.

DOLPHIN. Love.

DR. CROCUS. I think that woman's got something to do with this. Get her back in here.

MISS MORAY. Oh, I fired her. She was hugging the mammal . . . and . . . .

DOLPHIN. Love . . . .

DR. CROCUS. Just get her. *(To* MR. FRIDGE *)* You're sure the machine's recording?

MISS MORAY. Doctor, I'm afraid you don't understand. That woman was hugging the mammal . . . .

DR. CROCUS. Try to get another word out of it. One more word . . . .

MISS MORAY. The last thing in the world I want is for our problem in Custodial Engineering to . . . .

DR. CROCUS *(furious).* Will you shut up and get that washwoman back in here?

MISS MORAY. Immediately, Doctor.

(She hurries out of the lab. HELEN *is at the end of the hall waiting for the elevator.)*

MISS MORAY. Helen? Oh, Helen? Don't you want to hear what the dolphin has to say? He's so cute! Dr. Crocus thinks that his talking might have something to do with you. Wouldn't that be exciting? *(Pause)* Please, Helen. The doctor . . . .

HELEN. Don't talk to me, do you mind?

MISS MORAY. It was only in the heat of argument that I . . . of course, you won't be discharged. All right? Please, Helen, you'll embarrass me . . . .

(The elevator doors open and HELEN *gets on to face* MISS MORAY. *She looks at her a moment and then lifts her hand to press the button for the ground floor.)*

MISS MORAY. Don't you dare . . . Helen, the team needs you, don't you see? You've done so well—the brass strip, the floors. The floors have never looked so good. Ever. Helen, please. What will I do if you leave?

HELEN. Why don't you get a rug?

(HELEN helps slam the elevator doors in MISS MORAY'*s face as the lights go down, ending the play.)*

After Reading

Making Connections

1. If you were Helen, what choice would you have made in the final scene?

2. Helen thinks the dolphin is a coward for not speaking to save itself. But some might say the dolphin's refusal to speak is braver than speaking. What do you think?

3. The subject of the play is serious, and yet the play contains many instances of humor. Why do you suppose the author included so much humor?

4. What **purpose** or purposes for writing the play do you think the author had? Support your answer with examples from the play.

5. In what ways are Helen the fictional character and Joel Rubin the real person similar? In what ways are they different?

6. After reading the play, how do you feel about the use of animals in scientific experiments? Explain.

Literary Focus: Characterization

Many authors use dialogue to make their characters come alive. This is especially true in a play. After reading *Let Me Hear You Whisper,* you probably have definite ideas about what the characters are like, and most of those ideas are based on what they say.

To get a better understanding of how dialogue reveals what characters are like, copy the chart below, leaving plenty of room to write in the second and third columns. Then complete the chart with descriptions and dialogue for each character.

Character	Words or Phrases That I Think Describe the Character	Dialogue That Supports My Descriptions
Helen		
Miss Moray		

Vocabulary Study

Match each event of a day at an animal research laboratory with the word from the list that is most closely related.

analysis
apprehensively
compulsory
discretion
humility
lenient
subjective
survey
technique
terminate

1. a sign in the locker room reminding workers they must wash their hands before entering the laboratory

2. the laboratory supervisor demonstrating the correct method of injecting chimpanzees with drugs to relieve pain

3. a scientist carefully examining the organs of a dead chimpanzee to determine the cause of death

4. a chimpanzee backing up in its cage as a scientist approaches

5. government investigators touring the laboratory and taking notes about what they see

6. the supervisor giving only a mild warning to a new worker who failed to do an assigned task before the investigators arrived

7. the worker hanging his head and apologizing to the supervisor

8. a passer by telling an activist her experience of having a daughter whose illness was cured as a result of experimentation and the activist describing how her dog ended up in a research laboratory

9. the laboratory supervisor announcing that the experiments involving chimpanzees will end

10. the supervisor deciding to let all the workers go home early

Expressing Your Ideas

Writing Choices

The Next Monday The play ends on Friday. What happened the next Monday? Did Helen call the ASPCA, and if so, what was the result? Was Miss Moray still in trouble with Dr. Crocus? There are lots of possibilities. Write an **outline** for Act Three that tells what you think happened on Monday.

We, the Undersigned Write an **opening statement for a petition** on the issue of animal experimentation. The petition can be one that opposes or supports such experiments.

Other Options

A Different Kind of Animal Research Choose one of the topics below to research and present an **oral report** to the class.

• How animals are used in scientific experimentation and how they are treated

• How dolphins and/or other animals communicate with one another

Dolphin Art Using papier-mâché or other materials, work in small groups to make a **sculpture** of a dolphin.

Writing Mini-Lesson

Choosing and Narrowing a Topic

Writing a research paper does not have to be boring and tedious! It can be fun and rewarding, especially if you plan carefully and work steadily. The most important step in a successful research paper is to choose a topic you are interested in and narrow the topic so you can describe a few aspects of the topic well.

The cluster diagram shows how one student began to narrow the topic high school sports.

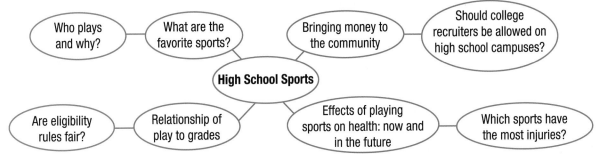

Writing Strategy Ask yourself these questions after you have narrowed your topic:

- Am I really interested in this topic?

- Will I find information about this topic? (Remember, it will be difficult to find information on very recent topics or on topics that are too narrow. For example, you will find more information on the general topic of sports injuries than on a specific injury.)

- Will I find data and facts as well as opinions on the topic?

Activity Options

1. Narrow one of the following topics to three subtopics.

   Dance in America   Vegetarianism   Teen Employment

2. Write three topics of your own and have a partner narrow them to three or more subtopics.

3. Review something you have written that involved research. How did you decide on a topic? How did you narrow it?

Before Reading

The Departure of the Giants

by Harold Courlander

Harold Courlander
born 1908

Harold Courlander was born in Indiana and was once a farmer in Michigan. However, for most of his life, he has worked at researching, collecting, and retelling folk tales from various countries and cultures of the world. His special interest in African folklore is reflected in collections like *The Crest and the Hide and Other African Stories,* which includes "The Departure of the Giants." Courlander says, "Although my work has been both fiction and nonfiction, I think of myself primarily as a narrator." Courlander is interested in folk tales that communicate values and reflect cultural heritage, and he considers folklore one way "to bridge communications between other cultures and our own."

Building Background

Hand-Me-Downs "The Departure of the Giants," like "Why the Rooster Crows at Sunrise" on page 366, is a **folk tale**. "The Departure of the Giants" is similar to an **origin tale** because it seeks to explain how something began. The author wrote it down after hearing it told in northeastern Africa. As with other folk tales, slightly different versions of this same story are told by various cultural groups.

Getting into the Story

Discussion "It was too much of a good thing." "It's bad when things are too good." Have you ever heard people use those expressions, or others like them? What do you think they mean? Do you think they're true? Why or why not? Discuss your ideas with a small group of classmates.

Reading Tip

Author's Purpose One way to get more enjoyment from a story is to think about why the author wrote it. You already know that the author wrote this story to explain something. However, an author can have more than one purpose in a single piece of writing. Authors may also write to entertain or persuade. As you read, think about the different purposes the author may have had in writing this story. Copy the chart below in your notebook. Write details from the story that support each purpose.

To Explain Something	To Entertain	To Teach a Lesson
This story is about how the giants disappeared.		

HAROLD COURLANDER

THE DEPARTURE OF THE GIANTS

Before the first Mensa, Habab, Beni-Amer, and Cunama[1] people arrived, a tribe of giants was living in the land. It is said by some that God created the giants first, and that later he made people in the size they are today. The giants were truly giants. They used water skins[2] made of whole elephant hides. Their spears were as tall as euphorbia trees,[3] and the stones they threw from their slings were not pebbles but large boulders. They roasted whole cows over their fires for a single meal, and drank milk from great wooden tubs. When other tribes came into the country looking for water for their cattle and goats, the giants killed them or drove them away. Many courageous Mensa, Beni-Amer, and Habab warriors[4] died trying to hold watering places against the giants.

Today the giants are gone, but you may still see the great stones they used for foundations of their houses, and here or there people find the remains of the enormous tombs[5] in which the giants were buried. This story is about how the giants finally disappeared. It is told by the old people of the tribes.

---

1. **Mensa** (men′sə), **Habab** (hab′ab), **Beni-Amer** (be′nī ə mer′), **Cunama** (kun′ə mä), four ethnic groups of Eritrea, a country on the northeastern coast of Africa that was once part of Ethiopia.
2. **water skin**, container made of animal skins used for drinking water.
3. **euphorbia tree** (yŭ fôr′bē ə), cactus like tree that grows in eastern Africa.
4. **warrior** (wôr′ē ər), *n.* person experienced in fighting battles.
5. **tomb** (tŭm), *n.* grave, vault, mausoleum, etc., for a dead body, often above ground.

God concluded that things were not peaceful because of the giants. The world was out of balance. So he sent for the chief of the giants and said to him: "It is time for your tribe to leave the world." The chief of the giants said: "Master, how have we offended[6] you that we should have to leave?" God replied: "Your tribe has been too hard with the small people. You have forgotten that water holes were given to all the tribes for their cattle. You drive the people away, though they have done you no harm." The chief of the giants said: "Master, all tribes guard their wells. All tribes fight to protect their land. What have we done that is different?" God said: "Because you are so large and the others so small, everything is out of balance. Your tribe consumes everything. While you eat a whole cow for your dinner, the other tribes stand on a hilltop watching you swallow down enough to keep them alive for a month."

The giant chief said: "Master, it was you who created us as we are. Is the fault ours?" God said: "No, the fault is not yours, yet I have to send your tribe out of this world. Therefore I will be as kind as I can. I will give you a choice. I will let you choose how to depart. You may disappear with my curse[7] or my blessings."[8]

The chief of the giants said: "Who would want to receive God's curse? If we must go, send us on our way with your blessings." God answered: "Good. Let it be that way. I will lay blessings on you. Because sons are a blessing to all families, henceforth all your children to come will be sons. Because cows are a blessing on account of the calves they bear[9] and the milk they give, henceforth all calves that are born will be females."

The chief of the giants returned to his tribe. He told the people of the blessings God had given them, and they were happy. Things came to pass as God had promised. Women gave birth only to sons, and cows gave birth only to female calves. The sons grew up. It was time for them to marry, but there were no young women to be their wives. The female calves matured, but there were no bulls for them to mate with. So in time no more children were born to the giants, and no more calves were born to the cattle. People grew old and died. Cattle grew old and died. The tribe of giants withered.[10]

At last the chief called a council of the old people who were still alive. He said to them: "As all men can see, we are dying out from our blessings. Let us not linger here any more, waiting for the end. Let every person build a tomb for himself and cover it with a roof of stones. Let each one enter his tomb and close up the entrance. In this way we will finally depart from the world." So every person built himself a tomb and covered it with a roof of stones, after which he entered, closed up the opening, and remained there until he died. Thus the giants perished[11] and disappeared from the face of the land.

The roofs of the tombs fell long ago, and all that remain are piles of stones. Because they remember what happened to the giants, people of the tribes sometimes say when life seems too generous to them:

"Take care, let us not die from blessings like the giants did."

---

6. **offend** (ə fend′), v. make angry; hurt the feelings of.
7. **curse** (kėrs), n. harm or evil.
8. **blessing** (bles′ing), n. a gift of kindness; benefit.
9. **bear** (ber), v. give birth to.
10. **wither** (wiŦH′ər), v. shrink (become fewer) in number; dry up.
11. **perish** (per′ish), v. die.

After Reading

Making Connections

1. Suppose the giants had chosen to receive God's curse. What do you suppose the curse might have been? Explain the effect caused by the curse.

2. Can you think of a solution to the problem presented in the story that would have allowed both the giants and the people to go on living? If so, describe it. If not, tell why you think no such solution would be possible.

3. Look back at the chart you made in your notebook for **author's purpose**. Which purpose do you think is the strongest? Explain your answer with examples from the story.

4. Do the giants remind you of modern-day people? Explain.

5. What message about the environment do you get from this story?

Literary Focus: Setting and Mood

The time and place of the events in a story is called the **setting**. The author of "The Departure of the Giants" uses some powerful visual images to transport you to a faraway place and time. The details that the author uses for the setting also establish the **mood**, or the feeling within the folk tale.

What kind of mood do you think this folk tale has? Write a description of it. Include details about the setting that help create that mood.

Expressing Your Ideas

Who Left This Mess? The story is just one possible explanation for the piles of stones that are found in the African landscape. Think of another **explanation,** and write it. Don't worry too much about being scientifically or historically accurate.

The Day After Yesterday, the last of the giants went into their tombs and closed themselves in. Write a **news report** in which you describe how people are reacting to this major event. Include their ideas about how life is going to be different from now on.

Tourist Attraction Imagine that you're a tour guide who shows visitors the tombs of the giants. Prepare your **presentation,** using both details of setting from the story and your own imagination to make the story exciting for the tourists.

Protecting Your World

It's Your World Too

History Connection

To prehistoric peoples, animals were more than pets, or curiosities in zoos, or part of a balanced diet. They were life. Without game, especially in colder environments, prehistoric societies could not have survived.

Cave Art

These paintings of bison were found in the Altamira Caves in Santillana del Mar, Spain. The images are about 15,000 years old.

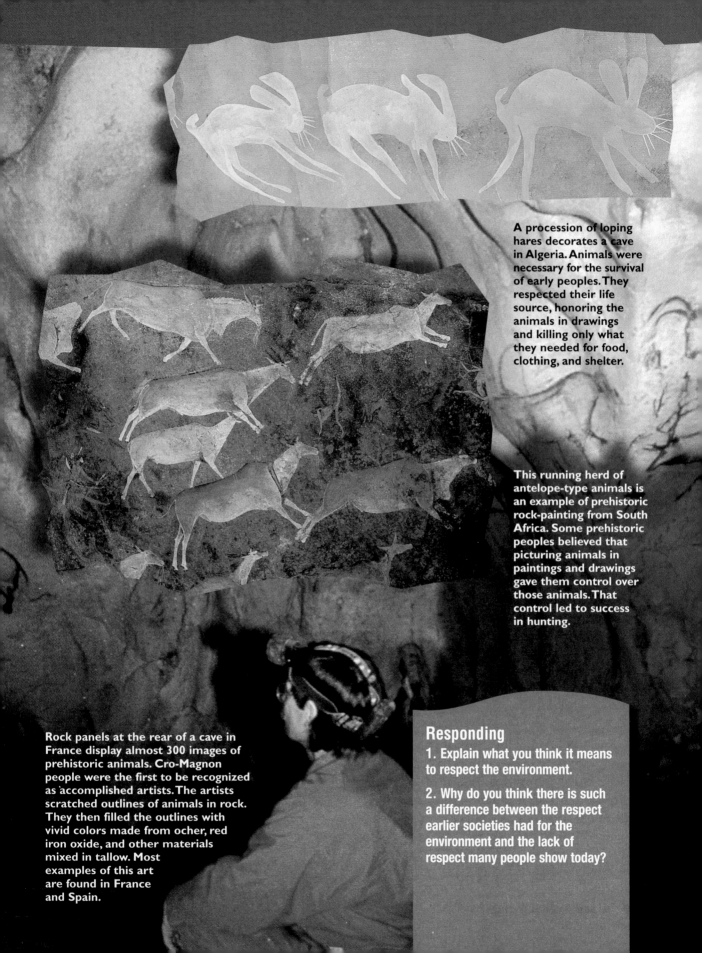

A procession of loping hares decorates a cave in Algeria. Animals were necessary for the survival of early peoples. They respected their life source, honoring the animals in drawings and killing only what they needed for food, clothing, and shelter.

This running herd of antelope-type animals is an example of prehistoric rock-painting from South Africa. Some prehistoric peoples believed that picturing animals in paintings and drawings gave them control over those animals. That control led to success in hunting.

Rock panels at the rear of a cave in France display almost 300 images of prehistoric animals. Cro-Magnon people were the first to be recognized as accomplished artists. The artists scratched outlines of animals in rock. They then filled the outlines with vivid colors made from ocher, red iron oxide, and other materials mixed in tallow. Most examples of this art are found in France and Spain.

Responding

1. Explain what you think it means to respect the environment.

2. Why do you think there is such a difference between the respect earlier societies had for the environment and the lack of respect many people show today?

Environment Connection

Why do people buy products made from endangered species? Sometimes they just don't care. Most of the time, they don't know the effect they have on the environment when they do it. It's up to all of us to spread the word—protect our world.

BLOW THE HORN
on Wildlife Trade

Why would anyone want a pair of snakeskin cowboy boots if they knew an endangered snake was killed to make them? Maybe because of fashion, or because they meant something special to the wearer. Even though laws now protect many endangered animals, hunters still kill them and illegally sell fashionable or special body parts to eager buyers.

Wildlife Close-up: The Elephant

Since 1981, the number of elephants left in the wild has been cut in half. Three hundred are killed every day. Several are destroyed by angry farmers whose crops are trampled by browsing herds. A few are hunted for sport. But most are shot for their tusks. African elephant tusks are ivory, which is used in carvings, piano keys, even billiard balls.

Ivory has been called "white gold." The value of two tusks is equal to what the average African earns in one year. Governments try to limit the number of elephants killed and use some of the money from ivory sales to pay for conservation projects. But the temptation to kill elephants illegally is great. The only solution seems to be to stop the sale of all ivory.

Like people, elephants are social creatures. They live in large, close, family groups. The death of an elephant affects the entire family. If a mother is killed, the young perish. The older, large-tusked males take with them unborn offspring.

The killing of elephants also affects other wildlife. Elephants are giant seed-dispersal machines; they eat plants and disperse the seeds in their excrement. If they become extinct, plants that depend on them will be threatened, too.

Is it too late to save the elephants? Pessimists say they will be extinct in the wild by 2030. Maybe. Then again, maybe not. People can help stop the slaughter by refusing to buy ivory. Consumers have power. People's anger over the disappearance of the whales and big spotted cats has nearly stopped trade in whale products and coats made from big-cat fur.

Traditions are important but attitudes can be changed. A poacher (illegal hunter) can earn money as a tourist guide, and it's legal. With luck, conservation, and wildlife management, we can save the elephant from becoming a memory.

Wildlife Close-up: The Rhinoceros

Pity the poor rhinoceros. Rhino horn is used in Yemen to make dagger handles that are given to boys at the age they become men. Even though all five kinds of rhinos are classified as endangered and protected by law, poachers shoot them for their horns. Plastic dagger handles won't do and it's the rhino who pays—with its life.

A recent drastic experiment involved trapping and drugging rhinos, sawing off and destroying their horns, and then releasing the beasts again into the wild. This foiled poachers, but proved disastrous for the rhino. Without his horn, a male rhino can't find a mate. He becomes an outcast.

Success Stories

Sure there are lots of sad stories about wildlife, but there are successes, too. People have identified species that are near extinction and have found ways to help them. With care and a bit of luck, a number of once-endangered animals are now able to make a go of survival.

The Muskox in Canada

A hundred years ago, people wanted muskox rugs in their sleighs, so hunters went out and shot the animals. Muskoxen are easy marks for hunters because when danger approaches, the slow-moving adults form a defensive ring around their young. This circling works well against wolves, but it only makes it easier for people to shoot whole herds at a time.

In 1917, the Canadian government outlawed all muskox hunting. By 1990, the muskox had recovered from a low of 2000 to a population of 50,000 in northern Canada. Now that's a success story!

Responding

1. Why do you feel it is important to save endangered animals from extinction?

2. Two more endangered species success stories are the tiger in India and the sea otter of the Pacific coast. Research one of these animals or another endangered species to see what is being done to save it from extinction. Share your findings with the class.

Environment Connection

Much has already been done to save animal and plant species—by people just like you. But there is much more that needs to be done. It's your world, too. Help save the environment for yourself and for your grandchildren.

What can YOU DO?

Build bird houses. Set out bird feeders. Grow flowers in window boxes to provide food for insects and birds.

Read all you can about endangered species.

Ask your parents to use natural pesticides on garden plants and crops. Dispose of anti-freeze and oil properly.

Respect the land and animals.

Leave plants in the wild. If you pick or dig them, rare plants will become endangered plants.

Cut plastic rings on six-packs before discarding them so birds and animals don't get caught in them.

Plant a tree. Trees help filter out pollution. They also provide homes and food for many animals.

Walk, ride a bike, or take a bus when you can to cut down on the pollution from exhaust fumes.

Write to your state representatives and let them know that you support the Endangered Species Act.

Support breeding programs in zoos by visiting the zoos. Your entrance fee helps. Join zoo clubs and "adopt" an animal.

Spread the word. Tell people about the importance of saving our wildlife.

Join organizations that are active in conservation, such as Wildlife Conservation Society, Earth Force, Greenpeace, Save the Manatee Club, and others.

A Select List of North American Endangered Species

Mammals
Gray Bat
Grizzly Bear
Wood Bison
Black-footed Ferret
West Indian Manatee
Red Wolf

Birds
California Condor
Whooping Crane
Peregrine Falcon

Reptiles
American Crocodile
Iguana (13 species)

Fish
Short-nose Sturgeon
Trout (1 species)

Invertebrates
Snails (13 species)
Mussels (53 species)
Butterflies (16 species)

Source: U.S. Fish and Wildlife Service, Wash., D.C.

Responding

1. Choose one of the organizations listed on the previous page or any other you know about. Find its address at your public library and write to the organization. Ask for information about its role in wildlife preservation.

2. Choose at least two of the other activities listed on the previous page. Make a plan to carry them out. In two weeks, report to the class on your progress.

Reading Mini-Lesson

Skimming and Scanning

Just as it is unwise to begin exercising without warming up, it does not make sense to begin reading without warming up, or previewing. Like a movie preview, a preview of a reading selection gives a glimpse of what is coming.

Previewing sometimes includes the rapid reading technique of **skimming.** You can use skimming to see how an article is organized before you ever read a sentence. This technique lets you create a mental map of your reading that will help you know what to expect and how to find your way around the article.

By skimming the article, "Blow the Horn on Wildlife Trade," you can see that the headings are:

> Wildlife Close-up: The Elephant
> Wildlife Close-up: The Rhinoceros
> Success Stories
> The Muskox in Canada

Therefore, you know that, in general, the article is about the wildlife trade. More specifically, since certain animals—the elephant, the rhinoceros, and the muskox—are mentioned, you can predict that they are important in the wildlife trade. The "Success Stories" heading suggests there might be "failure stories" somewhere in the article, also.

Scanning is a similar, but more specific, rapid-reading technique. You can use it to find a specific piece of information or specific kinds of information. If you scan the same article, you'll find the dates 1981, 2030, 1917, and 1990. You may want to make a time line and add the dates. Then as you read the article, write the significance of each date.

Activity Options

1. Find another article that has headings, make a list of the headings, and predict what the article will be about.

2. Find an article that does not have headings and skim through it. Write the headings that you think would help a reader get the main ideas of the article. Let a friend read only the headings to see if you have been successful. Your friend should be able to predict some of the ideas in the article if you have done a good job.

Writing Workshop

Personalized Research Paper

Assignment The selections you've read raise issues about the impact that humans have on the environment. Now is your chance to investigate an environmental issue in a personal research paper. Topics you might investigate include deforestation, the greenhouse effect, toxic waste, recycling, and endangered species.

WRITER'S BLUEPRINT

Product	A personalized research paper
Purpose	To investigate an environmental issue of concern to you
Audience	A congressional committee looking for information about this issue
Specs	To write a successful personalized research paper, you should:

❑ Begin by describing the environmental issue you'll research. Use the first-person ("I") point of view to summarize what you already know about this issue and to identify questions you have.

❑ Research your topic thoroughly. Use primary sources such as interviews with experts, information from environmental organizations, and field trips, as well as secondary sources such as books, newspaper and magazine articles, and videos.

❑ Go on to write an explanation of the process you went through to gather your information. Where did you go? Whom did you speak with? What did you observe? Include anything that was part of your information-gathering process.

❑ Next write your report in which you present the information you've gathered.

❑ Conclude by describing what you believe are your three most important discoveries.

❑ Vary sentence structure throughout to make your writing lively and more interesting.

❑ Document the sources you used in a Works Cited list, using the correct format. Follow the rules of grammar, usage, spelling, and mechanics.

The following instructions should help you write a successful personalized research paper.

List environmental topics. Working in a group, review the selections and list the environmental issue presented in each. Brainstorm other environmental issues and add these to the list.

Brainstorm an issue web. Choose a topic from your list and, working on your own, brainstorm a web of details related to that topic. You might end up with a web similar to the one below.

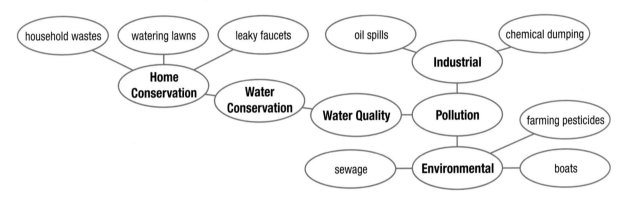

Narrow your research topic. Select the portion of your web you want to research and write about. Make your topic as narrow as possible. Look at the web in the previous step. The topic **Water Quality** is too broad, and there would be far too much information. If **Water Quality** is narrowed to **Water Conservation** and then narrowed even more to **Home Conservation,** the information will be more focused, and so will the final report.

Ask yourself: *What do I want to find out about my topic?* Make a list of questions and use them to guide your research. Use your web to prompt questions about your topic. Number your questions. The numbers will help you code your research later on.

Do your research. Use your questions to guide your research. Look for primary sources and secondary sources as suggested in the Writer's Blueprint. Write the name of each source on a 3x5 note card and then number the card. You will use these numbers to code your information and identify your sources for a citation later. These cards are your source cards.

1

Bailey, Donna. Wasting Water.

New York: Watts, 1991.

Number of source

Source as it will appear in Works Cited list

Make note cards on which you write information you find while reading about your subject. The information should answer your questions about the subject. Be sure to add other questions that come up as you work with your sources. Write the number of your source in the upper right corner of the card. In the upper left corner, write the number of the question.

Number of question	Number of source
3	1

On the average, each American uses about 80 gallons of water every day. A bath uses about 20 gallons. A shower uses about 6 gallons. An average toilet flushes about 3.5 gallons of water, and a dishwasher uses about 13 gallons each time it runs.

Plan your paper. Begin organizing your ideas by creating an outline. This outline was done by a student who chose to write about how we can conserve water.

I. Why I chose this topic
   A. What I know about it
   B. Questions I have about it
II. Resources I used in my research
   A. Library information
   B. People I spoke with
   C. Other sources of information
III. How people waste water every day
IV. Ideas for conserving water

Arrange your note cards into stacks that correspond with your outline. After you and your partner have reviewed each other's plans, revise your plan to reflect the most useful comments from the review.

STEP 2 DRAFTING

Draft your paper in three parts. In part one, describe the environmental issue you've researched. In part two, describe how you gathered information during your research process. In part three, the main part of your paper, explain what you learned about your topic and, if there is a problem associated with the issue, what you think can be done to help solve it.

To keep your writing interesting, you'll want to vary your sentence structure. Look ahead to the Revising Strategy for tips on this.

Ask your partner for comments on your draft before you revise it.

✔ Have I followed the specs in the Writer's Blueprint?

✔ Have I explained the issue and my questions about it?

✔ Have I explained how I did my research?

✔ Have I described my discoveries to the committee?

✔ Have I varied my sentence structure?

Revising Strategy

LITERARY SOURCE

"At first there were scenes of dolphins in family groups. They seemed amazingly like humans: intelligent, friendly, and playful. Through something like radar, they beamed out sounds that let them talk to one another."

from "Joel Rubin" by Phillip Hoose

Varied Sentence Structure

To make your writing more interesting, add variety to your sentence structure. Here are some ways to vary sentence structure.

- Vary the length of your sentences so your reader can focus on the important ideas.

- Avoid writing strings of short, simple sentences.

- Vary your sentence beginnings. Begin sentences with modifying words and phrases.

Look at the Literary Source from "Joel Rubin" by Phillip Hoose. How did the author vary sentence structure? How would the passage sound if every sentence began with a subject and a verb?

Notice how the writer of this draft revised to vary sentence structure.

○ First I went to the public library. ~~Then I~~ *and* looked for all the information I could get. I took notes. *Using my notes,* I wrote down some questions

○ for an interview. I interviewed the manager of a nuclear power plant. *Following the interview,* ~~Then~~ I typed up a rough draft.

STUDENT MODEL

Ask a partner to review your revised draft before you edit. When you edit, watch for errors in grammar, usage, spelling, and mechanics. Pay special attention to the correct form for your Works Cited list.

Editing Strategy

Works Cited List

Every research paper includes a list called *Works Cited* or *Bibliography*. This list tells the reader what sources you used in your research.

- Begin the list on a new page following the last page of your paper.

- List all the sources from which you actually took information.

- List each entry in alphabetical order, beginning with the author's last name. If you don't know the author, begin the entry with the title.

- If the entry is more than one line, indent all lines after the first line.

- Double space between entries.

The form changes somewhat for different kinds of sources. Look at the examples below for differences.

For a first-hand interview:
Frey, Burt; interview by author, tape recording, Chicago, IL, 1996.

For a book:
Bailey, Donna. *Wasting Water*. New York: Watts, 1991.

For a magazine article:
"Excellent Water Tips." *National Geographic World*, vol. 219 (November, 1993), pp. 28–29.

STEP 5 PRESENTING

Here are two ideas for presenting your paper.

- As each student presents his or her paper, the other members should act as a congressional committee. After each paper is read aloud, the "committee" should discuss the three most important discoveries each writer made and how these can affect the lives of the American people.

- Convert your paper to a script for a documentary on your particular issue. Present some of the scripts as radio presentations, complete with sound effects.

STEP 6 LOOKING BACK

Self-evaluate. What grade would you give your paper? Look back at the Writer's Blueprint and evaluate yourself on each point, from 6 (superior) down to 1 (weak).

Reflect. Think about what you learned from writing your research paper as you write answers to these questions.

✔ Why is it important that all writers be able to do and report research? Why is accurate research and information so necessary to our society today?

✔ What do you feel was the most valuable piece of information you uncovered about your topic in your research process?

For Your Working Portfolio: Add your research paper and your reflection responses to your working portfolio.

Beyond Print

Debating Animal Rights

People often debate issues about the care of animals. The dolphin is an animal that generates strong feelings. Some people feel that no dolphins should be in captivity. Others believe dolphins are treated very well in most seaquariums and ocean exhibits.

Activity

Debate this issue: Dolphins should live in the ocean. Your class can separate into two teams. Write the words *Argue For* and *Argue Against* on separate pieces of paper. Place the papers in a bag. A person from each group should pick a piece of paper.

Your team will argue for or against the issue, depending on the paper you selected. Even though you may not agree with this position, you must try to debate persuasively.

Brainstorm Make a list of at least five reasons for your position. You may have to do some research. Then place these reasons in order from most persuasive to least persuasive.

Get organized Decide on who will actually present the arguments. Help the speaker create two-minute speeches.

Prepare questions Try to guess how the other team will argue. Practice asking questions. Brainstorm answers that the other team may give.

Prepare answers. Try to guess what the other team will ask you.

Debating

Presentation of the issue Each team should state its position and arguments. One or more people can participate.

Questions and answers After both presentations are given, each team should be given five minutes to ask questions.

Closing arguments After questions, each team should present a closing argument that disputes the other team's position.

Activity Option

Debate another issue such as year-round school.

Debating Tips

Maintain eye contact.

Speak clearly.

Use effective hand gestures.

Evaluating the Debate

Have the teacher or a team of judges (classmates if possible) evaluate your debate, using the criteria below. If you wish, use a five-point scale for each of these points, with five being high.

- quality of arguments
- quality of answers
- quality of summary
- speaking ability

Projects for Collaborative Study

Theme Connection

Keep It Beautiful In order to appreciate what we have in nature, we may need to see what the world would be like if we do not take care of the earth's resources.

■ Work in small groups to collect or draw pictures showing nature is beautiful and pictures illustrating how the natural world has been damaged by humans.

■ As a class, use the pictures to create two large collages—one showing a beautiful environment and one showing a polluted environment.

■ Get permission from the principal to display the collages in a prominent place in your school.

Literature Connection

Personification In this unit, **personification** is used to make selections more lively. In "Why the Rooster Crows at Sunrise," the sun is given human traits so that it can dramatically and forcefully tell people to clean up the environment. Choose two or three selections in the unit and, in a small group, discuss the human traits that are given to animals or inanimate objects.

■ As a group, choose an animal or inanimate object from a selection in this unit and give it another set of human traits. How will these new traits affect the story? Present an oral description of the animal and its new character traits to the class.

Life Skills Connection

Areas for Improvement As you look around your home, school, and community you can see opportunities to improve "what is" with "what could be."

Start with your room at home. What is it like now? What could it be like? What could you do to improve the setting? Can you make the changes alone? If you need someone else's help, how can you get it?

As a class, identify five areas in your school or community that could use some improvements. What improvements or changes would you make in these areas? Whom would you ask for help? What could your class do to make these improvements happen? How would these improvements benefit people?

Multicultural Connection

Space Wise Imagine that a room has just become available in the school and it does not have to be used for a classroom. Students are being asked how the room should be used. A **choice** will have to be made. Your own choice is based upon your **perspective** and that perspective may differ from that of others.

■ Working in small groups, prepare a list of possible uses. Then decide on the one you like best. Be prepared to support your choice with facts or research. Finally, present the class your proposal, or suggestion, for how the room should be used. After each group has made a presentation, vote for the proposal you like best.

Read More About Environment

Hatchet (1987) by Gary Paulsen. After a plane crash, thirteen-year-old Brian survives in the wilderness for 54 days with the aid of a hatchet. He also learns he will be able to survive his parents' divorce.

Island of the Blue Dolphins (1960) by Scott O'Dell. A fact-based novel about an Indian girl's account of eighteen years alone on an island off the California coast during the early 1800s.

More Good Books

The Cay (1987) by Theodore Taylor. During World War II, young Phillip and old Timothy are stranded on a Caribbean island after the ship is sunk by a German torpedo. They must survive by living off the land.

Rascal (1963) by Sterling North. In an autobiographical memoir, the author shares his enjoyment of the great outdoors with his pet raccoon.

Keepers of Life: Discovering Plants Through Native American Stories and Earth Activities for Children (1994) by Michael J. Caduto and Joseph Bruchac. Learn about environmental awareness through Native American stories and activities.

Rama: A Legend (1994) by Jamake Highwater. This Hindu legend has all the ingredients of a action-packed adventure story—hideous monsters, enchanted creatures, magical powers, and extraordinary battles.

Justice

Facing Prejudice
Part One, pages 430–464

What's Fair, What's Not
Part Two, pages 465–519

Talking About
JUSTICE

"What is the right thing to do when people or animals are treated unjustly?"

Alicia–Bethesda, MD

Y ou may be familiar with the words "liberty and justice for all" from the Pledge of Allegiance. However, from some people's perspectives, these words are not always true.

One of the reasons justice fails is that people are often prejudiced against others with different backgrounds. As people interact, they sometimes treat others unfairly.

On these two pages, sixthgraders talk about justice. Match their comments with passages from selections you are about to read.

You had to give that innocent animal, who never harmed you, something that would kill her, on spite! And you knew it—you knew it!

from "Princess" by Nicholasa Mohr, page 475

"**What exactly does justice mean?**"

Fernando—San Juan, PR

If I'm not good enough to play on your team, I'm not good enough to be friends with.

from "Southpaw" by Judith Viorst, page 432

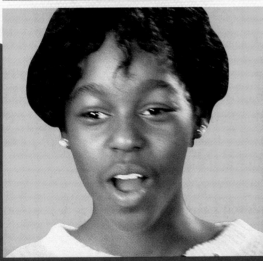

Ibrahima was an African who loved freedom no less than other beings on earth. And he was denied that freedom.

from "Ibrahima" by Walter Dean Myers, page 498

"**Life would be easier if we could learn to treat all people the same.**"

Shanice—Augusta, GA

Part One

Facing Prejudice

When we prejudge something, we form an opinion about it before we find out all the facts. That opinion—hastily and unfairly formed—is a *prejudice*. Some prejudices are mild, harmless, or both. "Isn't my new grandchild the cutest baby you've ever seen?" a grandparent may say. Most prejudice, though, is far from cute. Prejudice can hurt. Prejudice can make people feel like failures. At its worst, prejudice can ruin lives.

In the selections that follow, you'll read about fictional characters and real people who face prejudice and fight it. Their weapons? Courage, desire for justice, determination, and something you might not expect: a sharp sense of humor.

Multicultural Connection **Interactions** between people of different backgrounds cause conflicts when one person or group treats another as inferior or as an outsider. How do the characters in the following selections handle such situations?

Southpaw

by Judith Viorst

Judith Viorst
born 1931

Judith Viorst (vē′orst) doesn't believe in rigidly defined roles. The mother of three sons, she understands and cares about girls too, and she often challenges traditional roles for boys and girls in her writing. Viorst doesn't stick to one kind of writing, either. She's perhaps best known for her humorous, yet sensitive, poems about everyday life. However, her magazine articles, short stories, and books for young people and adults also have contributed to her popularity. There's one thing Viorst is quite definite about, though. "I always, always, always wanted to be a writer," she says. "I never wanted to be anything else— never."

Building Background

Play Ball! "Southpaw" is about a girl who wants to play baseball. It may seem strange now to think of baseball as being only for boys, but that's the way it used to be. Little League baseball was closed to girls for thirty-five years after it was founded in 1939. It wasn't until 1974—the same year "Southpaw" was published— that girls were allowed play on Little League teams with boys. And that only happened because some girls and their parents took the matter all the way to the State Superior Court of New Jersey.

Getting into the Story

Discussion Baseball as well as other sports and leisure activities, school subjects, and household chores are just some of the things people may label *Girls Only* or *Boys Only*. On the chalkboard, copy the diagram below. In a small group, brainstorm items for each part of the diagram as one student records them. About which items does the group disagree? On which items can you all agree? Discuss your reasons for disagreeing or agreeing.

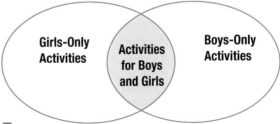

Reading Tip

A Story Told Through Letters In most short stories, the plot unfolds through a series of paragraphs. The author of "Southpaw" presents the story through a series of letters. Many of the letters include a P.S., which stands for "postscript." A postscript is an addition to a letter or note.

Because the story is told through letters, neither the characters nor the plot are developed in detail. As you read "Southpaw," use your imagination to form opinions about the characters and to predict what is going to happen next.

Southpaw

Judith Viorst

Dear Richard,

Don't invite me to your birthday party because I'm not coming. And give back the Disneyland sweat shirt I said you could wear. If I'm not good enough to play on your team, I'm not good enough to be friends with.

Your former friend,
Janet

P.S. I hope when you go to the dentist he finds twenty cavities.[1]

Dear Janet,

Here is your stupid Disneyland sweat shirt, if that's how you're going to be. I want my comic books now—finished or not. No girl has ever played on the Mapes Street baseball team, and as long as I'm captain, no girl ever will.

Your former friend,
Richard

P.S. I hope when you go for your checkup you need a tetanus shot.

Dear Richard,

I'm changing my goldfish's name from Richard to Stanley. Don't count on my vote for class president next year. Just because I'm a member of the ballet[2] club doesn't mean I'm not a terrific ballplayer.

Your former friend,
Janet

P.S. I see you lost your first game, 28–0.

Dear Janet,

I'm not saving any more seats for you on the bus. For all I care you can stand the whole way to school. Why don't you forget about baseball and learn something nice like knitting?

Your former friend,
Richard

P.S. Wait until Wednesday.

Dear Richard,

My father said I could call someone to go with us for a ride and hot-fudge sundaes. In case you didn't notice, I didn't call you.

Your former friend,
Janet

P.S. I see you lost your second game, 34–0.

Dear Janet,

Remember when I took the laces out of my blue-and-white sneakers and gave them to you? I want them back.

Your former friend,
Richard

P.S. Wait until Friday.

---

1. **cavity** (kav′ə tē), *n.* hollow place; hole. Cavities in teeth are caused by decay.
2. **ballet** (bal′ā), *adj.* having to do with a type of dancing performed on a stage.

Dear Richard,

Congratulations on your unbroken record. Eight straight losses, wow! I understand you're the laughingstock[3] of New Jersey.

Your former friend,
Janet

P.S. Why don't you and your team forget about baseball and learn something nice like knitting, maybe?

> Dear Janet,
> Here's the silver horseback-riding trophy[4] that you gave me. I don't think I want to keep it anymore.
>
> Your former friend,
> Richard
>
> P.S. I didn't think you'd be the kind who'd kick a man when he's down.[5]

Dear Richard,

I wasn't kicking exactly. I was kicking back.

Your former friend,
Janet

P.S. In case you were wondering my batting average is .345.

> Dear Janet,
> Alfie is having his tonsils out tomorrow. We might be able to let you catch next week.
> Richard

Dear Richard,

I pitch.

Janet

> Dear Janet,
> Joel is moving to Kansas and Danny sprained his wrist. How about a permanent[6] place in the outfield?
> Richard

Dear Richard,

I pitch.

Janet

> Dear Janet,
> Ronnie caught the chicken pox and Leo broke his toe and Elwood has these stupid violin lessons. I'll give you first base. That's my final offer.
> Richard

Dear Richard,

Susan Reilly plays first base, Marilyn Jackson catches, Ethel Kahn plays center field, I pitch. It's a package deal.[7]

Janet

P.S. Sorry about your 12-game losing streak.

> Dear Janet,
> Please! Not Marilyn Jackson.
> Richard

Dear Richard,

Nobody ever said that I was unreasonable. How about Lizzie Martindale instead?

Janet

> Dear Janet,
> At least could you call your goldfish Richard again?
>
> Your friend,
> Richard

---

3. **laughingstock** (laf′ing stok′), *n.* person or thing that is made fun of.
4. **trophy** (trō′fē), *n.* any prize, cup, etc., awarded to a victorious person or team.
5. **kick a man when he's down**, be unkind to someone who already has problems.
6. **permanent** (pėr′mə nənt), *adj.* intended to last.
7. **package deal**, an offer involving a number of elements or items grouped as a unit.

Louisa's Liberation

Jean Little

Emily and I got talking and we decided
It was up to us to make sure Louisa grew up liberated.
"They start teaching them sex stereotypes
           in Nursery School, my mother read," I said.
5 "Well, there's no time like the present," said Emily.
"Let's find her and *do* something."

We went in search of Louisa.
She was in the backyard with all her toys laid out in a row.
She was trundling around, as busy as a bee,
10   so involved she didn't even notice us arriving.

"Louisa, what are you doing?" Emily asked.
Louisa, still preoccupied, answered, "This is my hospital.
These need operations. Those are dying."

Emily and I exchanged looks as Louisa went back to work.
15 "Isn't that great!" murmured Emily.
"She's not stuck in a kitchen, playing house; she's a nurse!"

Louisa glanced up.
"No, I'm not," she said, "I'm a doctor."

After Reading

Making Connections

1. Think about these jobs or activities—class president, doctor, nurse, ballet, knitting. In which category would you list each one in the diagram on page 431? Explain.

2. 🐾 You learn a lot about the **interaction** between Janet and Richard through their notes. Who do you think handled the situation better? Explain.

3. How angry do you think Richard and Janet really were? Explain.

4. Did Richard change his mind about whether girls should play baseball, or did he only agree to let girls join his team out of desperation? Give a reason for your answer.

5. Do you think it was a good idea for the author to write the story as a series of letters rather than as a "regular" short story? Explain.

6. Do you think the author of "Louisa's Liberation" is effective in delivering her message? Explain.

7. Has being a girl or a boy ever kept you from doing something you wanted to do? Explain.

Literary Focus: Exaggeration

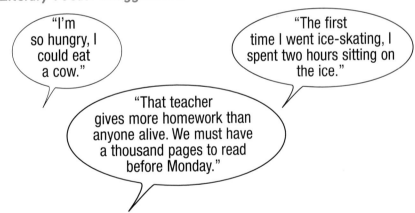

"I'm so hungry, I could eat a cow."

"The first time I went ice-skating, I spent two hours sitting on the ice."

"That teacher gives more homework than anyone alive. We must have a thousand pages to read before Monday."

People's everyday conversations often contain **exaggerations**, or overstatements, such as the ones above. Authors also exaggerate to make their readers laugh. Find examples of humorous exaggeration in "Southpaw." Think about what makes each example funny. Then write a funny, exaggerated diary entry based on your own experience. For example, you might write about a day when the weather was extremely cold or hot. When you've finished, exchange diary entries with a partner. What ideas do the two of you have for making each other's entries even funnier?

Vocabulary Study

A. Match each vocabulary word in the second column with the book in which you would expect to find that word. Write the letter of the matching word.

ballet
cavity
laughingstock
permanent
trophy

1. *History of Dance in America*
2. *The Joke Was on Me*
3. *Tales from the Dentist's Chair*
4. *How to Have a Lasting Marriage*
5. *The Winning Team*

  a. trophy
  b. cavity
  c. ballet
  d. permanent
  e. laughingstock

B. Now create your own book title for each of the vocabulary words.

Expressing Your Ideas

Writing Choices

Sum It Up A friend of yours sees you reading "Southpaw" and asks, "What's that story about, anyway?" Write a one-paragraph **summary** of the story for your friend.

On Another Note Take "Southpaw" a little further. Add four **notes** to the story, beginning with a note from Janet and ending with a note from Richard. Write the notes in such a way that a reader could believe they were part of the original story.

I Can *Do* This! Imagine a situation in which you want to perform a task that is usually done by members of the opposite sex. Write a **letter** in which you try to persuade a person in authority that you can perform the task just as well as anyone else.

Other Options

Janet and Richard: The Interview With two classmates, carry out a TV **interview** with Janet and Richard five years after the events described in "Southpaw." Make sure the interview includes discussion of what Janet and Richard are like today and of how the "Southpaw" incident affected their lives.

Taking Sides With a partner, plan and carry out a **debate** on one of these questions:

• Should people be discouraged from doing certain jobs because they are most often done by males or females?

• Should male and female athletes play on the same teams and take part in the same competitions?

Try to make a convincing case for your side, even if you don't personally agree with it. Afterwards, poll your classmates. Which side do they think won the debate?

Before Reading

The Noble Experiment

by Jackie Robinson as told to Alfred Duckett

Jackie Robinson
1919–1972

Jackie Robinson's athletic career began in college, where he excelled in four sports. In baseball, he helped the Brooklyn Dodgers win six National League pennants and the World Series in 1955.

Alfred Duckett
1917–1984

In creating his autobiography, Robinson sought help from a professional writer. That writer was Alfred Duckett. Although he was a poet, journalist, and lecturer in his own right, Duckett enjoyed collaborating. He also worked with Martin Luther King, Jr., on the famous "I Have a Dream" speech.

Building Background

Separate, Not Equal When future baseball great Jackie Robinson was born in 1919, racial segregation was a fact of life in the United States. The Southern states passed laws that separated blacks and whites. Under these laws, African Americans had to attend separate schools, ride in separate railroad cars, and use separate drinking fountains and restrooms in public places. Almost always, the facilities set aside for African Americans were inferior to those reserved for whites.

Baseball was no exception. Prohibited from playing in the major leagues, African American players competed in separate leagues known as the Negro leagues.

Getting into the Selection

Writer's Notebook Segregation grew out of white Americans' prejudice against African Americans. Any group of people can be prejudiced against another group, just as any group can be victims of prejudice. In your notebook, write about a time when you observed or experienced the effects of prejudice. What happened? How did it make you feel?

Reading Tip

Pros and Cons In "The Noble Experiment," Jackie Robinson had to make a difficult choice. Often, when people are faced with tough decisions, they make a list of "pros and cons"—reasons for and against taking a particular action. Copy the chart below. As you read the selection, list Robinson's pros and cons as well as any ideas of your own.

Pros (Reasons for Robinson to Join the Major Leagues)	Cons (Reasons for Robinson Not to Join the Major Leagues)
to pave the way for others	

The Noble Experiment

Jackie Robinson as told to Alfred Duckett

In 1910 Branch Rickey was a coach for Ohio Wesleyan. The team went to South Bend, Indiana, for a game. The hotel management registered the coach and team but refused to assign a room to a black player named Charley Thomas. In those days college ball had a few black players. Mr. Rickey took the manager aside and said he would move the entire team to another hotel unless the black athlete was accepted. The threat was a bluff because he knew the other hotels also would have refused accommodations to a black man. While the hotel manager was thinking about the threat, Mr. Rickey came up with a compromise. He suggested a cot be put in his own room, which he would share with the unwanted guest. The hotel manager wasn't happy about the idea, but he gave in.

Years later Branch Rickey told the story of the misery of that black player to whom he had given a place to sleep. He remembered that Thomas couldn't sleep.

"He sat on that cot," Mr. Rickey said, "and was silent for a long time. Then he began to cry, tears he couldn't hold back. His whole body shook with emotion. I sat and watched him, not knowing what to do until he began tearing at one hand with the other—just as if he were trying to scratch the skin off his hands with his fingernails. I was alarmed. I asked him what he was trying to do to himself.

"Charley," Mr. Rickey said, "the day will come when they won't have to be white."

"'It's my hands,' he sobbed. 'They're black. If only they were white, I'd be as good as anybody then, wouldn't I, Mr. Rickey? If only they were white.'"

Thirty-five years later, while I was lying awake nights, frustrated, unable to see a future, Mr. Rickey, by now the president of the Dodgers, was also lying awake at night, trying to make up his mind about a new experiment.

He had never forgotten the agony of that black athlete. When he became a front-office executive in St. Louis, he had fought, behind the scenes, against the custom that consigned[1] black spectators to the Jim Crow section of the Sportsman's Park, later to become Busch Memorial Stadium. His pleas to change the rules were in vain. Those in power argued that if blacks were allowed a free choice of seating, white business would suffer.

Branch Rickey lost that fight, but when he became the boss of the Brooklyn Dodgers in 1943, he felt the time for equality in baseball

---

1. **consign** (kən sīn′), *v.* set apart; assign.

▲ As a tribute to Jackie Robinson, Karen Felicity Berkenfeld made *Jack of Diamonds,* a quilt with printed, painted, and stenciled images.

had come. He knew that achieving it would be terribly difficult. There would be deep resentment, determined opposition, and perhaps even racial violence. He was convinced he was morally right, and he shrewdly[2] sensed that making the game a truly national one would have healthy financial results. He took his case before the startled directors of the club, and using persuasive eloquence, he won the first battle in what would be a long and bitter campaign. He was voted permission to make the Brooklyn club the pioneer in bringing blacks into baseball.

SUMMARIZE: How would you describe Branch Rickey at this point?

Winning his directors' approval was almost insignificant in contrast to the task which now lay ahead of the Dodger president. He made certain that word of his plans did not leak out, particularly to the press. Next, he had to find the ideal player for his project, which came to be called "Rickey's noble experiment." This player had to be one who could take abuse, name-calling, rejection by fans and sportswriters and by fellow players not only on opposing teams but on his own. He had to be able to stand up in the face of merciless persecution and not retaliate. On the other hand, he had to be a contradiction in human terms; he still had to have spirit. He could not be an Uncle Tom.[3] His ability to turn the other cheek had to be predicated on his determination to gain acceptance. Once having proven his ability as player, teammate, and man, he had to be able to cast off humbleness and stand up as a full-fledged participant whose triumph did not carry the poison of bitterness.

Unknown to most people and certainly to me, after launching a major scouting program, Branch Rickey had picked me as that

player. The Rickey talent hunt went beyond national borders. Cuba, Mexico, Puerto Rico, Venezuela, and other countries where dark-skinned people lived had been checked out. Mr. Rickey had learned that there were a number of black players, war veterans mainly, who had gone to these countries, despairing of finding an opportunity in their own country. The manhunt had to be camouflaged.[4] If it became known he was looking for a black recruit for the Dodgers, there would have been all kinds of trouble. The gimmick he used as a coverup was to make the world believe that he was about to establish a new Negro league. In the spring of 1945 he called a press conference and announced that the Dodgers were organizing the United States League, composed of all black teams. This, of course, made blacks and prointegration whites indignant. He was accused of trying to uphold the existing segregation and, at the same time, capitalize on black players. Cleverly, Mr. Rickey replied that his league would be better organized than the current ones. He said its main purpose, eventually, was to be absorbed into the majors. It is ironic that by coming very close to telling the truth, he was able to conceal that truth from the enemies of integrated baseball. Most people assumed that when he spoke of some distant goal of integration, Mr. Rickey was being a hypocrite[5] on this issue as so many of baseball's leaders had been.

Black players were familiar with this kind of hypocrisy. When I was with the Monarchs,

---

2. **shrewdly** (shrŭd′lē), *adv.* in a way that shows a sharp mind; cleverly.
3. **Uncle Tom,** an African American person who tries overly hard to please white people: from the main character of Harriet Beecher Stowe's 1852 novel, *Uncle Tom's Cabin.*
4. **camouflage** (kam′ə fläzh), *v.* give a false appearance in order to conceal; disguise.
5. **hypocrite** (hip′ə krit), *n.* person who is not sincere; pretender.

shortly before I met Mr. Rickey, Wendell Smith, then sports editor of the black, weekly Pittsburgh *Courier,* had arranged for me and two other players from the Negro league to go to a tryout with the Boston Red Sox. The tryout had been brought about because a Boston city councilman had frightened the Red Sox management. Councilman Isadore Muchneck threatened to push a bill through banning Sunday baseball unless the Red Sox hired black players. Sam Jethroe of the Cleveland Buckeyes, Marvin Williams of the Philadelphia Stars, and I had been grateful to Wendell for getting us a chance in the Red Sox tryout, and we put our best efforts into it. However, not for one minute did we believe the tryout was sincere. The Boston club officials praised our performance, let us fill out application cards, and said "So long." We were fairly certain they wouldn't call us, and we had no intention of calling them.

Incidents like this made Wendell Smith as cynical[6] as we were. He didn't accept Branch Rickey's new league as a genuine project, and he frankly told him so. During this conversation, the Dodger boss asked Wendell whether any of the three of us who had gone to Boston was really good major league material. Wendell said I was. I will be forever indebted to Wendell because, without his even knowing it, his recommendation was in the end partly responsible for my career. At the time, it started a thorough investigation of my background.

In August 1945, at Comiskey Park in Chicago, I was approached by Clyde Sukeforth, the Dodger scout. Blacks have had to learn to protect themselves by being cynical but not cynical enough to slam the door on potential opportunities. We go through life walking a tightrope to prevent too much disillusionment. I was out on the field when Sukeforth called my name and beckoned. He told me the Brown Dodgers were looking for top ballplayers, that Branch Rickey had heard about me and sent him to watch me throw from the hole.[7] He had come at an unfortunate time. I had hurt my shoulder a couple of days before that, and I wouldn't be doing any throwing for at least a week.

Sukeforth said he'd like to talk with me anyhow. He asked me to come to see him after the game at the Stevens Hotel.

Here we go again, I thought. Another time-wasting experience. But Sukeforth looked like a sincere person, and I thought I might as well listen. I agreed to meet him that night. When we met, Sukeforth got right to the point. Mr. Rickey wanted to talk to me about the possibility of becoming a Brown Dodger. If I could get a few days off and go to Brooklyn, my fare and expenses would be paid. At first I said that I couldn't leave my team and go to Brooklyn just like that. Sukeforth wouldn't take no for an answer. He pointed out that I couldn't play for a few days anyhow because of my bum arm. Why should my team object?

I continued to hold out and demanded to know what would happen if the Monarchs fired me. The Dodger scout replied quietly that he didn't believe that would happen.

I shrugged and said I'd make the trip. I figured I had nothing to lose.

Branch Rickey was an impressive-looking man. He had a classic face, an air of command, a deep, booming voice, and a way of cutting through red tape and getting down to basics. He shook my hand vigorously and, after a brief conversation, sprang the first question.

"You got a girl?" he demanded.

It was a heck of a question. I had two reactions: why should he be concerned about my

---

6. cynical (sin′ə kəl), *adj.* doubting the sincerity and goodness of others.

7. **throw from the hole,** throw a baseball from deep in the infield to first base.

relationship with a girl; and, second, while I thought, hoped, and prayed I had a girl, the way things had been going, I was afraid she might have begun to consider me a hopeless case. I explained this to Mr. Rickey and Clyde.

Mr. Rickey wanted to know all about Rachel. I told him of our hopes and plans.

"You know, you *have* a girl," he said heartily. "When we get through today, you may want to call her up because there are times when a man needs a woman by his side."

My heart began racing a little faster again as I sat there speculating.[8] First he asked me if I really understood why he had sent for me. I told him what Clyde Sukeforth had told me.

"That's what he was supposed to tell you," Mr. Rickey said. "The truth is you are not a candidate for the Brooklyn Brown Dodgers. I've sent for you because I'm interested in you as a candidate for the Brooklyn National League Club. I think you can play in the major leagues. How do you feel about it?"

My reactions seemed like some kind of weird mixture churning in a blender. I was thrilled, scared, and excited. I was incredulous. Most of all, I was speechless.

"You think you can play for Montreal?" he demanded.

I got my tongue back. "Yes," I answered.

Montreal was the Brooklyn Dodgers' top farm club. The players who went there and made it had an excellent chance at the big time.

I was busy reorganizing my thoughts while Mr. Rickey and Clyde Sukeforth discussed me briefly, almost as if I weren't there. Mr. Rickey was questioning Clyde. Could I make the grade?

Abruptly, Mr. Rickey swung his swivel chair in my direction. He was a man who conducted himself with great drama. He pointed a finger at me.

"I know you're a good ballplayer," he barked. "What I don't know is whether you have the guts."

EVALUATE: What do you think Rickey is getting at with this statement?

I knew it was all too good to be true. Here was a guy questioning my courage. That virtually amounted to him asking me if I was a coward. Mr. Rickey or no Mr. Rickey, that was an insinuation hard to take. I felt the heat coming up into my cheeks.

Before I could react to what he had said, he leaned forward in his chair and explained.

I wasn't just another athlete being hired by a ball club. We were playing for big stakes.[9] This was the reason Branch Rickey's search had been so exhaustive. The search had spanned the globe and narrowed down to a few candidates, then finally to me. When it looked as though I might be the number-one choice, the investigation of my life, my habits, my reputation, and my character had become an intensified study.

"I've investigated you thoroughly, Robinson," Mr. Rickey said.

One of the results of this thorough screening were reports from California athletic circles that I had been a "racial agitator"[10] at UCLA. Mr. Rickey had not accepted these criticisms on face value. He had demanded and received more information and came to the conclusion that if I had been white, people would have said, "Here's a guy who's a contender, a competitor."

After that he had some grim words of

---

8. **speculating** (spek′yə lā′ting), *adj.* guessing; conjecturing; wondering.

9. **playing for big stakes**, idiom meaning taking a large risk or making a large bet; also, *playing for high stakes.*

10. **racial agitator** (rā′shəl aj′ə tā′tər), a negative term for someone who tries to stir up trouble between people of different races.

warning. "We can't fight our way through this, Robinson. We've got no army. There's virtually nobody on our side. No owners, no umpires, very few newspapermen. And I'm afraid that many fans will be hostile. We'll be in a tough position. We can win only if we can convince the world that I'm doing this because you're a great ballplayer and a fine gentleman."

He had me transfixed as he spoke. I could feel his sincerity, and I began to get

⋀ Jackie Robinson and Branch Rickey seal the deal on October 23, 1945.

a sense of how much this major step meant to him. Because of his nature and his passion for justice, he had to do what he was doing. He continued. The rumbling voice, the theatrical gestures, were gone. He was speaking from a deep, quiet strength.

"So there's more than just playing," he said. "I wish it meant only hits, runs, and errors—only the things they put in the box score. Because you know—yes, you would know, Robinson, that a baseball box score is a democratic thing. It doesn't tell how big you are, what church you attend, what color you are, or how your father voted in the last election. It just tells what kind of baseball player you were on that particular day."

I interrupted. "But it's the box score that really counts—that and that alone, isn't it?"

"It's all that *ought* to count," he replied. "But it isn't. Maybe one of these days it *will* be all that counts. That is one of the reasons I've got you here, Robinson. If you're a good enough man, we can make this a start in the right direction. But let me tell you, it's going to take an awful lot of courage."

He was back to the crossroads question that made me start to get angry minutes earlier. He asked it slowly and with great care.

"Have you got the guts to play the game no matter what happens?"

"I think I can play the game, Mr. Rickey," I said.

The next few minutes were tough. Branch Rickey had to make absolutely sure that I knew what I would face. Beanballs[11] would be thrown at me. I would be called the kind of names which would hurt and infuriate any man. I would be physically attacked. Could I take all of this and control my temper, remain steadfastly[12] loyal to our ultimate[13] aim?

---

11. **beanball** (bēn′bôl′), *n.* a baseball thrown deliberately by the pitcher near or at a batter's head.
12. **steadfastly** (sted′fast′lē), *adv.* showing firmness of purpose; loyally and unwaveringly.
13. **ultimate** (ul′tə mit), *adj.* greatest possible; highest.

Jackie Robinson appears positive as he begins his journey to the major leagues.

He knew I would have terrible problems and wanted me to know the extent of them before I agreed to the plan. I was twenty-six years old, and all my life I had believed in payback, retaliation. The most luxurious possession, the richest treasure anybody has, is his personal dignity.[14] I looked at Mr. Rickey guardedly, and in that second I was looking at him not as a partner in a great experiment, but as the enemy—a white man. I had a question, and it was the age-old one about whether or not you sell your birthright.

"Mr. Rickey," I asked, "are you looking for a Negro who is afraid to fight back?"

I will never forget the way he exploded.

"Robinson," he said, "I'm looking for a ballplayer with guts enough not to fight back."

After that, Mr. Rickey continued his lecture on the kind of thing I'd be facing.

He not only told me about it, but he acted out the part of a white player charging into me, blaming me for the "accident" and calling me all kinds of foul racial names. He talked about my race, my parents, in language that was almost unendurable.

"They'll taunt[15] and goad you," Mr. Rickey said. "They'll do anything to make you react. They'll try to provoke a race riot in the ballpark. This is the way to prove to the public that a Negro should not be allowed in the major league. This is the way to frighten the fans and make them afraid to attend the games."

If hundreds of black people wanted to come to the ballpark to watch me play and Mr. Rickey tried to discourage them, would I understand that he was doing it because the emotional enthusiasm of my people could harm the experiment? That kind of enthusiasm would be as bad as the emotional opposition of prejudiced white fans.

Suppose I was at shortstop. Another player comes down from first, stealing, flying in with spikes high, and cuts me on the leg. As I feel the blood running down my leg, the white player laughs in my face.

"How do you like that, boy?" he sneers.

Could I turn the other cheek? I didn't know how I would do it. Yet I knew that I must. I had to do it for so many reasons. For black youth, for my mother, for Rae, for myself. I had already begun to feel I had to do it for Branch Rickey.

I was offered, and agreed to sign later, a contract with a $3,500 bonus and $600-a-month salary. I was officially a Montreal Royal. I must not tell anyone except Rae and my mother.

_____

14. **dignity** (dig′nə tē), *n.* proud and self-respecting character or manner; stateliness.
15. **taunt** (tônt), *v.* jeer at; mock; reproach.

After Reading

Making Connections

1. Do you think money or morals was the stronger motivation for Jackie Robinson? for Branch Rickey? Explain.

2. Look at the pros and cons you listed for Jackie Robinson to join the major leagues. Based on your lists, did Robinson make the right choice? Explain.

3. If you had been in Robinson's place, would you have accepted Rickey's offer? Why or why not?

4. Suppose Robinson had refused to take part in the experiment. What do you suppose might have happened to him?

5. 👆 Rickey depended on Robinson not to have any negative **interaction** with his teammates and fans and to still play ball well. Did Rickey have reasonable expectations?

6. Robinson was expected to be an almost-perfect human being, a role model for other people. Is it fair to expect an athlete to be a role model? Explain.

Literary Focus: Autobiography

Like a biography, an **autobiography** is the story of a real person's life. The difference is that an autobiography is written by the person who lived the life, while a biography is written by someone else. An autobiography is written in the first person, and it often reveals a great deal about the subject's thoughts and feelings.

Look back at "The Noble Experiment." How closely does it fit the above description of an autobiography? In what ways does it differ from that description? Now, imagine you are Branch Rickey, and rewrite paragraphs seven through thirteen on page 442 for your autobiography.

Vocabulary Study

Choose the vocabulary word from the list that completes each sentence.

camouflage
consign
cynical
dignity
hypocrite
shrewdly
speculating
steadfastly
taunt
ultimate

1. After years of being passed over for promotions, a woman was ____ when her boss promised that things would change.

2. A new civil rights group declared that its ____ goal was to achieve equal opportunity for all races.

3. Jackie Robinson often had to ____ his true feelings when he first played in the major leagues.

4. Despite threats against their lives, civil rights activists ____ continued to hold rallies and conduct protest marches.

5. Business leaders ____ realized that working with schools to ensure education for all students would result in better employees.

6. Whites would often ____ African Americans as they stood in line to vote.

7. A young Hispanic girl displayed ____ as she walked with her head held high through a hostile crowd on her first day at a formerly all-white school.

8. Fearfully ____ about the consequences, passers-by watched as an African American drank from a water fountain, labeled *Whites Only.*

9. African Americans who rode on buses were expected to ____ themselves to seats in the last few rows.

10. A politician who voted against civil rights legislation was labeled a ____ after he told disabled voters that he was on their side.

Expressing Your Ideas

Writing Choices

First Major-League Game Write a **newspaper article** about Jackie Robinson's first game with the Brooklyn Dodgers.

Your Own Story Think about an important or interesting experience in your life—preferably one that marked a turning point of some kind. Write an **autobiographical sketch** about the experience.

Other Options

Jackie Robinson's Life and Times With a group of classmates, prepare the Jackie Robinson **exhibit** for the National Baseball Hall of Fame.

Rickey Meets Robinson With a partner, prepare and present a **short play** based on the conversation between Branch Rickey and Jackie Robinson in "The Noble Experiment."

Before Reading

No Irish Need Apply

by J. F. Poole and Pete Seeger

Pete Seeger
born 1919

Pete Seeger, who wrote the musical arrangement for "No Irish Need Apply," fell in love with folk music as a teenager in the mid-1930s, when he attended a square dance festival in North Carolina. Within a few years, Seeger began his career of collecting, singing, playing, and writing the kind of music that deals with "the meat of human life," as he calls it. Although he is one of the most influential folk artists in the United States, Seeger says, "I'm still learning. I've found out that some of the simplest music is some of the most difficult to do. I've also found, of course, that America has in it as many different kinds of folk music as there are folks. We have strains from Ireland and Scotland, Africa and Mexico, France and Germany, and a hundred other countries."

Building Background

Yes, We Have No Potatoes Can you imagine eating the same food for every meal, day after day? In the early 1840s, the people of Ireland grew and ate potatoes—and almost nothing else. Then, in 1845, a plant disease attacked and wiped out the potato crop. During the next several years, more than 750,000 Irish men, women, and children died of starvation. About a million fled their homeland. Most headed to the United States.

Many Americans saw the Irish immigrants as a potential threat to their jobs. The Irish were ridiculed and discriminated against. The song "No Irish Need Apply," written in the late 1840s, is one immigrant's response to what he encountered in the United States.

Getting into the Song

Discussion In a small group, talk about stereotypes and prejudices. How are they different? How are they similar? Does one naturally lead to the other?

Reading Tip

Songs "No Irish Need Apply" contains several terms, some Irish in origin, that may be unfamiliar to you. However, the unusual terms are explained in the footnotes. First read the footnotes, and then read the song's words. Think of the words as a poem, and read them as you would any poem, paying attention to punctuation, rhyme, and rhythm. You may want to work with a partner and take turns reading aloud until you get a feel for how the song should move along.

J.F. POOLE and PETE SEEGER

I'm a decent boy just landed from the
   town of Ballyfad;
I want a situation and I want it very bad.
I've seen employment advertised, "It's
   just the thing," says I,
But the dirty spalpeen [rascal] ended
   with "No Irish Need Apply."
5 "Who," says I, "that is an insult, but to
   get the place I'll try,"
So I went there to see the blackguard[1]
   with his "No Irish Need Apply."

Chorus:
Some do think it is a misfortune to be
   christened Pat or Dan,
But to me it is an honor to be born an
   Irishman.

I started out to find the house, I got
   there mighty soon;
10 I found the old chap seated—he was
   reading the *Tribune*.
I told him what I came for, when he in a
   rage did fly;
"No!" he says, "You are a Paddy,[2] and No
   Irish Need Apply."
Then I gets my dander[3] rising, and I'd
   like to black his eye

For to tell an Irish gentleman "No Irish
   Need Apply."
15 I couldn't stand it longer so a-hold of
   him I took,
And I gave him such a welting[4] as he'd
   get at Donnybrook.[5]
He hollered "Milia Murther," and to get
   away did try,
And swore he'd never write again "No
   Irish Need Apply."
Well, he made a big apology; I told him
   then goodbye,
20 Saying, "When next you want a beating,
   write 'No Irish Need Apply.'"

---

1. **blackguard** (blag′ärd), *n.* a low, contemptible person; scoundrel.
2. **Paddy** (pad′ē), *n.* slang term for Irish person, based on the name Patrick.
3. **dander** (dan′dər), *n.* anger; temper.
4. **welting** (welt′ing), *n.* beating; whipping.
5. **Donnybrook** (don′nē brük), a town in Ireland where an annual fair was suppressed in 1855 because of its wild brawls. The word *donnybrook*, meaning a riot or brawl, comes from the town name.

▲ *The Emigrants* was painted by Hans Baluschek in 1925. How does this painting illustrate the loneliness and prejudice the Irish faced in the words from the song?

After Reading

Making Connections

1. ✋ Think about the Irish boy's **interaction** with the "old chap." What is your opinion of the way the boy reacts to prejudice?

2. The "old chap" apologizes at the end of the song. Do you suppose his attitude toward Irish people really changed? Explain. Consider stereotypes about Irish people he may have held.

3. Should employers be free to refuse to hire people of a particular gender, race, or ethnic group? Why or why not?

Literary Focus: Songs About Issues

Every culture has **songs** and songwriters. People write and sing songs for many reasons. Expressing religious beliefs, glorifying heroes, and declaring love are a few common ones. Sometimes, songwriters compose songs to express their thoughts and feelings about political and social issues. These songs are often called *protest songs*. Such songs have been around a long time. For example, during the American Revolution, patriots wrote and sang songs that criticized the British king and expressed support for the Revolutionary cause.

Imagine you could ask the man who wrote the words to "No Irish Need Apply" why he did so. Write a paragraph that expresses what you think his answer would be. Include examples from the song.

Expressing Your Ideas

A Kinder, Gentler Song Imagine yourself as an Irish immigrant of the mid-1800s. You want to create a song that will persuade Americans to treat Irish people better—without threatening the Americans with a beating! Write the **lyrics** to your song.

To Emigrate or Not to Emigrate You are the boy from Ballyfad. Write a **letter** to your best friend back in Ireland, telling about your experiences in the United States and giving advice as to whether he or she should join you here.

Sing, Sing a Song Look for the music for "No Irish Need Apply" in the library. Then work with a partner or small group to give a **performance** of the song for the class. One of you should sing the words; the others can sing and/or play the music on a guitar, piano, or other instrument. If none of you can read music, get help from a teacher. You may be able to find a recording of the song to give you ideas.

Before Reading

Lewis Hine and the Crusade Against Child Labor

by Russell Freedman

Russell Freedman
born 1929

A glance at the titles of Freedman's many books tells you that one of his interests is history and the role that young people have played in it. Freedman's books include *Kids at Work, Teenagers Who Made History, Immigrant Kids,* and *Children of the Wild West.*

As a boy, two of Freedman's favorite books were the adventure novel *Treasure Island* and a natural history book called *Wild Animals I Have Known.* Freedman says, "In those innocent days I didn't worry about distinctions like fiction and nonfiction. . . . I did know that I was thrilled by both of those books. . . . I read *Wild Animals I Have Known* with as much pleasure and satisfaction as I have any novel or story."

Building Background

A Need for Change The progressive movement, a campaign for reform in government, business, and society, swept the United States in the early 1900s. The progressive movement had its roots in a depression that began in 1893 and lasted for several years.

As people lost their jobs, their homes, and their hope, progressives began to demand change. They pushed for laws to end corruption and waste in government, improve the living and working conditions of poor people, and extend voting rights to women. The progressive movement ended in 1917, when the United States entered World War I.

Getting into the Selection

Discussion By the early 1900s photography had already become an important profession and an exciting hobby in the United States. Today, inexpensive, easy-to-use cameras make it possible for almost anyone to take photographs. In a small group, share your experiences with photography. Do you or other members of your family take photographs? If so, do you try to capture everyday moments on film, or just vacations, holidays, and birthdays?

Reading Tip

Previewing "Lewis Hine and the Crusade Against Child Labor" is a photographic essay. It presents information about a real-life situation through a combination of photographs and text. To get the most out of the selection, preview it by studying the photographs. Look carefully at the settings, clothing, and expressions on the children's faces. What do you learn? What questions come to your mind? Next, read the text. As you read, look for the answers to your questions. Finally, return to the photographs. Use them, along with what you've read, to visualize the life of a child laborer in the early 1900s. What does the child see, hear, smell, and feel as he or she struggles through another workday?

Lewis Hine and the Crusade Against Child Labor

A Crusader with a Camera

Russell Freedman

Sadie cleaning lint from a cotton spinning machine in 1908.

Manuel, a Mississippi shrimp-picker.

Manuel is five years old but big for his age. When the whistle blows at 3 o'clock in the morning, he pulls on his clothes and hurries to the shrimp and oyster cannery where he spends the day peeling the shells off iced shrimp. He has been working as a shrimp-picker since he was four.

Manuel posed for his picture on a February morning in 1911 at a seafood cannery in Biloxi,[1] Mississippi—a shrimp pail in each hand, a mountain of oyster shells behind his back. This spunky little boy was one of thousands of working children who were photographed by Lewis Hine in the years before the First World War.

America's army of child laborers had been growing steadily for the past century. The nation's economy[2] was expanding. Factories, mines, and mills needed plenty of cheap labor. When Manuel's picture was taken, more than two million American children under sixteen years of age were a regular part of the work force. Many of them worked twelve hours or more a day, six days a week, for pitiful wages under unhealthy and hazardous conditions.

---

1. **Biloxi** (bi luk′sē).
2. economy (i kon′ə mē), *n.* system of managing the production, distribution, and consumption of goods and services.

Lewis Hine and the Crusade Against Child Labor   **453**

⋀ This young girl has to stand on a box to do work that is intended for adults.

Thousands of young boys descended into dark and dangerous coal mines every day, or worked aboveground in the stifling dust of the coal breakers, picking slate from coal with torn bleeding fingers. Small girls tended noisy machines in the spinning rooms of cotton mills, where the humid, lint-filled air made breathing difficult. They were kept awake by having cold water thrown in their faces. Three-year-olds could be found in the cotton fields, twelve-year-olds on factory night shifts. Across the country, children who should have been in school or at play had to work for a living.

By the early 1900s, many Americans were calling child labor "child slavery" and were demanding an end to it. They argued that long hours of work deprived children of an education and robbed them of their chance for a better future. Instead of preparing youngsters for useful lives as productive adults, child labor promised a future of illiteracy,[3] poverty, and continuing misery.

Besides, the reformers said, children have certain rights. Above all, they have the right to be children and not breadwinners.[4]

Lewis Hine, a New York City schoolteacher and photographer, was one of those early reformers. He knew that a picture can tell a powerful story. He felt so strongly about the

---

3. **illiteracy** (i lit′ər ə sē), *n.* inability to read and write.
4. **breadwinner** (bred′win′ər), *n.* person who earns a living and supports a family.

Breaker boys at a Pennsylvania coal mine.

use of children as industrial[5] workers that he quit his teaching job to become an investigative[6] photographer for the National Child Labor Committee (NCLC).

Hine traveled around the country with an old-fashioned box camera, taking pictures of kids at work. It took courage to get those pictures. Factory owners did not want photographers nosing around their plants, aiming cameras at underage workers. In the past, child-labor investigators had been harassed, jailed, and run out of town.

Hine was clever enough to bluff his way into many plants. He searched where he was not welcome, snapped scenes that were meant to be hidden from the public. At times, he was in real danger, risking physical attack when factory managers realized what he was up to. A slender, birdlike man who was usually retiring and shy, he put his life on the line in order to record a truthful picture of working children in early-twentieth-century America.

Seeing is believing, said Hine. If people could see for themselves the abuses and injustice[7] of child labor, surely they would demand laws to end those evils. His pictures of sooty-faced boys in coal mines and small girls tending giant machines revealed a shocking reality that most Americans had never seen before.

---

5. **industrial** (in dus′trē əl), *adj.* engaged in or connected with business, trade, or manufacturing.
6. **investigative** (in ves′tə gā′tiv), *adj.* of or having to do with careful and systematic searching for facts.
7. **injustice** (in jus′tis), *n.* unfairness; wrongfulness.

Lewis Hine and the Crusade Against Child Labor **455**

The Children's Hour

Henry Wadsworth Longfellow

Between the dark and the daylight,
    When the night is beginning to
        lower,
Comes a pause in the day's
        occupations,
That is known as the Children's Hour.

5 I hear in the chamber above me
    The patter of little feet,
The sound of a door that is opened,
    And voices soft and sweet.

From my study I see in the lamplight,
10   Descending the broad hall stair,
Grave Alice, and laughing Allegra,
    And Edith with golden hair.

A whisper, and then a silence:
    Yet I know by their merry eyes
15 They are plotting and planning
        together
    To take me by surprise.

A sudden rush from the stairway,
    A sudden raid from the hall!
By three doors left unguarded
20   They enter my castle wall!

They climb up into my turret
    O'er the arms and back of my
        chair;
If I try to escape, they surround me;
    They seem to be everywhere.

25 They almost devour me with kisses,
    Their arms about me entwine,
Till I think of the Bishop of Bingen
    In his Mouse-Tower on the
        Rhine!

Do you think O blue-eyed banditti,
30   Because you have scaled the
        wall,
Such an old moustache as I am
    Is not a match for you all!

I have you fast in my fortress,
    And will not let you depart,
35 But put you down into the dungeon
    In the round-tower of my heart.

And there will I keep you forever,
    Yes, forever and a day,
Till the walls shall crumble to ruin,
40   And molder in dust away!

After Reading

Making Connections

1. Were you surprised by what you learned in "Lewis Hine and the Crusade Against Child Labor?" Explain.

2. An argument that was sometimes made for child labor was that families desperately needed the money their children earned. What might be Lewis Hine's response to that argument?

3. Russell Freedman could have written this selection without including any of Hine's photographs. Why do you suppose he wanted to include them, and do you agree with his decision?

4. Compare and contrast the lives of one of the children in the selection with a child in the poem, "The Children's Hour."

5. All factory workers received pitifully low wages in the early 1900s, but children generally received much less than adults for the same jobs. Do you think young people who work at part-time and summer jobs today are paid fairly compared with adult workers? Why or why not?

6. Child labor is still controversial, with some people arguing that the laws should be relaxed to allow more young people to work longer hours at a wider variety of jobs. What rules do you think there should be regarding child labor? Explain your thinking.

Literary Focus: Mood

The atmosphere or feeling of a selection is called its **mood**. There are as many possible moods in selections as there are emotions in people. In a selection like "Lewis Hine and the Crusade Against Child Labor," the mood is created not only by the author's choice of subject and the words used to describe it, but also by the illustrations—in this case, Lewis Hine's photographs.

Talk about the mood of this selection with a partner. If you had to choose one word to describe the mood, what would it be? What has the author done to create that mood? How do the photographs contribute to that mood? Considering the subject matter, do you think any other mood would have been possible? Explain.

Vocabulary Study

Write the letter of the correct answer to each question.

economy
illiteracy
industrial
injustice
investigative

1. Which word describes a problem that results from a lack of education?

   a. economy   **b.** ability   **c.** illiteracy

2. Which word describes a job that involves uncovering hidden facts?

   a. investigative   **b.** photographic   **c.** pitiful

3. Which word describes a situation in which a person is sentenced to jail for a crime he did not commit?

   a. illiteracy   **b.** injustice   **c.** fairness

4. Which word describes all the banks, businesses, and stores of a country?

   a. geography   **b.** economy   **c.** poverty

5. Which word describes workers whose jobs involve manufacturing goods?

   a. agricultural   **b.** industrial   **c.** underage

Expressing Your Ideas

Writing Choices

Young People's Bill of Rights What rights do you think all young people—let's say, people under age eighteen—should have? Make a **list**, and show it to your classmates and your family. What do they think?

Learn the Law Do library research to find out what child labor laws affect you. Keep in mind that there are federal and state child-labor laws, and your community may have additional laws. Write a **report** on what you learn.

Other Options

Protest Poster You are an artist living in the early 1900s. You believe in the progressive movement, and you want to do your part to end the abuses of child labor. Draw a **poster** to help accomplish that.

Follow in Hine's Footsteps Think of a situation in your own community that you would like to see improved. Take **photographs** that you could use to convince other people that change is needed. Try to create a particular mood with your photographs.

Writing Mini-Lesson

Writing and Supporting Assertions

Use facts and examples. An assertion is a positive statement that can be supported. Read the following assertions.

- Jackie Robinson displayed courage when he signed a contract to play with the Brooklyn Dodgers.

- Lewis Hine's work was very important to children.

Both assertions make positive statements. The following passages provide facts and examples to support each assertion.

- Jackie Robinson displayed courage when he signed a contract to play with the Brooklyn Dodgers. He was the first African American to play major league baseball in a time when racial prejudice was openly displayed. He was treated unfairly, and was even injured because of the color of his skin.

- Lewis Hine's work was very important to children. Through Hine's photographs, people were able to see the poor and dirty conditions in which children were forced to work to help support their families. Hine's photos turned public opinion against child labor, and laws were established to end the practice.

Writing Strategy Be sure you have evidence to back up your assertions. Use facts and quotations from reliable sources.

Activity Options

1. Locate an editorial from your local newspaper and bring it to class. Working with a partner, underline the assertions. Circle the supporting evidence. Can the evidence be verified? How?

2. Think of a topic that involves your school or community. Write an assertion based on the topic. Trade papers with a partner and locate evidence for the assertion. Write your supporting facts or quotations under the assertion.

3. Review some of your previous work in your writing portfolio. Check for general statements that need facts or quotations for support. Revise your work to support your assertions.

History Connection

Religion is more than attending a church, synagogue, or temple. It is more than rites and ceremonies. From religion people develop a source of ethics—a sense of right and wrong. There are so many religions that seem so different from one another, but take a closer look. Most are based on some very basic and similar precepts of justice, beginning with "Do unto others as you would have them do unto you."

Hindu

Do good and not evil.
From delusion lead me to Truth.
From darkness lead me to Light.
From death lead me to immortality.
Grihad–Aranyaka Upanishad 1, 3, 28

Represented here is a Hindu deity. There are two principal gods of Hinduism—Vishnu and Shiva.

RELIGIONS:
Our
Source
of
Ethics

Buddhism

The Five Precepts

Not to harm any living thing.

Not to take what is not given.

Not to live in an over excited way.

Not to say unkind things.

Not to take drugs or drink that will cloud the mind.

Those living beings whose acts are sinful pass to the sphere of misery.

Those who act well win a place in heaven.

The title *Buddha*, meaning "Enlightened One," was given to Siddhartha Gautama, the founder of Buddhism, by his followers. He lived sometime in the 500s and 400s B.C. Buddha taught that people could find release from physical suffering in nirvana, a state of complete peace and contentment. In order to reach nirvana, one had to be free of all attachments to worldly goods and desires.

Islam

The Muslim should seek for knowledge from the cradle to the grave.

Hadith

And whosoever is given knowledge is given indeed abundant wealth.

Sura II, the Cow

The Lord hath decreed that ye worship none save him and (that ye show) kindness to parents. If one of them, or both of them attain old age with thee, say not Fie unto them nor repulse them but speak unto them a gracious word.

Sura XVII, the Children of Israel

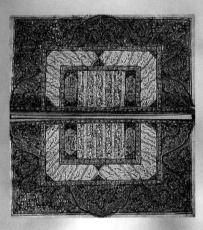

The holy book of Islam is the Koran. For Muslims, this book is eternal and infallible. It contains all truths and is the final authority for all religious, social, and legal issues. The message of the Koran was delivered by Allah (God) to his prophet Muhammad. It is both a warning to those who refuse to believe in the true God, and a promise of eternal happiness to those who do His will.

Confucius

Let young people show filial piety at home, respectfulness towards their elders when away from home; let them be circumspect, be truthful; their love going out freely towards all, cultivating good will to men. And if; in such a walk, there be time or energy left for other things, let them employ it in the acquisition of literary or artistic accomplishments.

Do not do unto others that which you do not wish them to do unto you.

Confucius, who lived from about 551 to 479 B.C., was the most influential Chinese philosopher of all time. From about 100 B.C. to the revolution of 1911, the teachings of Confucius were the strongest single influence on all aspects of Chinese society. The importance of moral character and responsibility are at the heart of the teachings of Confucius.

Christianity/ Judaism

The Ten Commandments

I am the Lord thy God, who brought thee out of the land of Egypt, out of the house of bondage.

Thou shalt have no other gods before Me.

Thou shalt not make unto thee a graven image, not any likeness of anything that is in heaven above, or that is in the earth beneath, or that is in the water under the earth.

Thou shalt not take the name of the Lord thy God in Vain.

Remember the sabbath day, to keep it holy. . . .

Honor thy father and thy mother.

Thou shalt not kill.

Thou shalt not commit adultery.

Thou shalt not steal.

Thou shalt not bear false witness against thy neighbor.

Thou shalt not covet [desire] thy neighbor's wife, nor his manservant, nor his maidservant, nor his ox, nor his ass, nor anything that is thy neighbor's.

Exodus 20: 2–17

Therefore all things whatsoever ye would that men should do to you, do ye even so to them.

Matthew 7:12

He has shown you, O Man, what is good; and what does the Lord require of you but to do justice, and to love kindness, and to walk humbly with your God.

Prophet Micah

The Hebrew word *Torah* means "to teach" or "to show the way." In this way, it is found throughout the Hebrew Bible in reference to teachings from God, moral teachings by religious leaders, and the written laws of the books of Moses. In a narrower sense, the Torah refers to the first five books of the Hebrew Bible, which are usually credited to Moses.

The heart of the law of Moses is perhaps the best known of all ancient codes of behavior—the Ten Commandments. God is believed to have presented these laws to Moses, who in turn gave them to his people.

Responding

Which of the religious precepts listed on these pages have Americans accepted into daily life? To answer this question, ask yourself which have been written into law and which are considered common courtesy. Are there any that you think are not at all part of the American culture? Explain your answer.

Mathematics Connection

What do you believe? Is your sense of justice based on a solid religious background, or do you have another basis for your ethics? Take a look at how you compare with other teens.

What Do You Believe?

Religions

Religious preferences of teenagers:

Protestant	47%
None	13%
Other	5%
Jewish	2%
Mormon	3%
Roman Catholic	30%

Source: America's Youth in the 1990s, *George H. Gallup International Institute,* 1993.

Beliefs

Percent of teens who:

Believe in God or a universal spirit 95%

Believe there is heaven 91%

Believe there is a hell 76%

Believe in life after death 67%

Have confidence in organized religion 52%

Consider their own religious beliefs very important 39%

Believe religion can answer today's problems 25%

Source: America's Youth in the 1990s, *George H. Gallup International Institute.* 1993.

Materialism

Percent of teenagers who agree very much with these statements:

Personal happiness is more important than being rich 67%

I want to help those less fortunate than myself 58%

Making money is what it's all about. 25%

Source: America's Youth in the 1990s, *George H. Gallup International Institute,* poll of 13- to 17-year-olds, summer 1992.

Responding

Take an anonymous poll in your classroom. First, write down your religious affiliation. If your choice is not listed in the chart above, write *Other* or *None*. Next, list each of the items in the second and third charts on your paper. After each item, write Yes or No. Have two or three students tally all the responses. Determine the percentage for each item in a chart. Compare the percentages tallied for your class to those listed in the polls on this page. To what can you attribute any major differences?

Reading Mini-Lesson

Using Graphic Aids

You have probably noticed that this book includes many charts, diagrams, graphs, and maps. They are called *graphic aids*. They help the reader make connections between pieces of information.

Now let's take a look at the article "What Do You Believe?" on page 463. You can see that the page is almost entirely made up of graphic aids. If all this information had been presented in paragraphs, it would be harder to pick out the facts that you should remember.

Charts organize information in columns. This makes it easy to make comparisons. For example, the "Beliefs" chart is a simple list of percentages of teens who respond to questions in certain ways. You can see, for example, that about twice as many teens (52%) have confidence in organized religion as believe that religion can answer today's problems (25%).

Pie graphs show divisions that add up to 100 percent. The pie graph on "Religion" shows you that almost half of the teens surveyed selected "Protestant" as their religious preference.

Activity Options

1. Look at the chart on "Materialism." Working with a partner, write a paragraph about the information presented. When you are finished, decide which way is better for showing the information.

2. Take a class survey on the major problems facing the United States today. Ask each student to select the biggest problem on the following list and tally the responses. Then make a chart or a pie graph of the results.

   Prejudice and racism
   Violence
   AIDS
   National economy
   Pollution
   Homelessness and poverty
   Other _____

Part Two

What's Fair, What's Not

If you are like most people, you probably have had experiences in which you have been treated in a way you consider terribly unfair. But what's fair? What might seem unfair to you might seem quite fair to the person whose actions you are evaluating.

Multicultural Connection People who have different **perspectives** see things from different points of view. The way you see things comes from the experiences you have. As you read the following selections, you'll discover your own perspectives on fairness as well as those of the characters.

Before Reading

Princess

by Nicholasa Mohr

Nicholasa Mohr
born 1935

A successful painter, Nicholasa Mohr started writing in response to a customer's request for her to write about her life. During her youth, she experienced poverty, alienation, and prejudice. As an avid reader, she knew there were no stories for or about young people of Puerto Rican descent and therefore decided to write them herself.

Mohr considers story-telling, whether it is in pictures or in words, to be a magic gift. She dedicated the book in which the story "Princess" appears to her mother: "To the memory of my mother, for those days of despair when she shared her magic gift of storytelling, making all things right."

Building Background

Cash or Charge Before computers, many stores kept their records of merchandise and sales in a record book called a ledger. The store owner in "Princess" used a ledger to keep track of his sales. Some of his customers were credit customers—people who buy things without paying for them right away. Instead, they promise to pay at some later date. By selling groceries on credit, the store owner was making personal loans to his customers. Today, many people use credit cards to make purchases instead of relying on merchants to lend them money. Credit card companies lend money to people and make a profit on the interest they charge for the loans.

Getting into the Story

Discussion The story "Princess" involves a beloved pet. Discuss how you feel about pets with your classmates. Why do people value their pets? Do you think it's right for pet owners to value their pets more than they do people? Why or why not? Discuss your answers with your classmates.

Reading Tip

Recognizing Values The issue of fairness comes up in many different ways in the story "Princess." Make a chart like the one below. As you read the story, fill in the chart with more issues.

Fairness Chart		
Issue	**What Does the Story Imply About the Issue**	**What Do You Think?**
Is it fair for pet owners to treat their pets better than they do people?	People should treat other people at least as well as they treat their pets.	

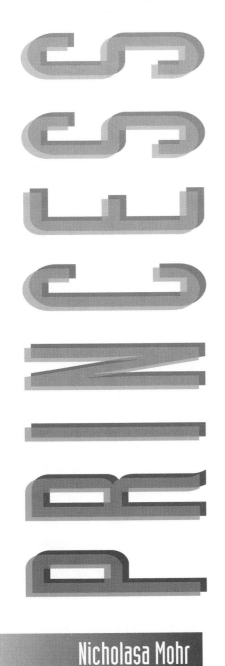

PRINCESS

Nicholasa Mohr

"Can I take Princess for a walk later?" Judy asked. "Please, Don Osvaldo?"[1]

"We'll see . . . later," Don Osvaldo said. "Let me finish now with your order." He checked the handwritten list of groceries against the items stacked on the counter. "A quarter pound of salt, butter, fifteen cents' worth of fatback, two pounds of dried red beans. . . ."

Judy played with Princess as she waited for him to pack the groceries. "Sit . . . sit up, Princess. That's a good girl. Nice. Now shake hands. Give me your paw. Right paw! Left paw! Good. Good." The little dog wagged her tail and licked Judy's hand.

"O.K., Judy, I got everything your Mama ordered here in the bag."

"Thank you, Don Osvaldo; put it on our bill."

"I already did," he said, closing a large thick ledger. The grey binding on the ledger was worn, frayed, and filthy with grease spots from constant use. Don Osvaldo would jot down whatever his credit customers bought, including how much it cost. Every name was there in the book in alphabetical order; a clear record for all to see. At the end of each month, before any more credit was extended, customers were obliged to settle accounts according to the ledger.

"Can I come back and take Princess for a walk?" Judy asked again.

"All right," he said.

"I'm coming back to take you for a walk later," she said to the little dog, and patted her on the head.

Princess began to whine and bark after Judy. Don Osvaldo looked at the dog and smiled. "Nereida, Nereida,"[2] he called into the back of the store.

"What is it?" his wife asked.

---

1. **Osvaldo** (ōz bäl′do).
2. **Nereida** (nā re′i dä).

"Princess is crying—she wants to go with Judy for a walk."

"She's too smart for her own good," his wife said, coming into the store. "Give her something to make her feel better. . . . Go on."

Don Osvaldo went over to the meat counter and removed a hunk of boiled ham. Taking a sharp knife, he cut off a small piece and fed it to the dog. Amused, they watched Princess as she chewed the piece of ham, then sat up begging for more.

"She's so clever," said Doña Nereida, and patted the dog affectionately.

"I wish my kids ate as well as that mutt."

Five years ago a customer had given them the white fluffy-haired puppy, which Doña Nereida had decided to call Princess. Princess was loving and friendly, and showed her gratitude by being obedient. Osvaldo and Nereida Negrón lavished all their affection on the little dog and doted on her. They had no children, hobbies, or interests other than their store, Bodega Borinquén,[3] a grocery specializing in tropical foods, which they kept open seven days a week, and Princess. The dog shared the small sparsely furnished living quarters in the back of the store with her owners. There, she had her own bed and some toys to play with. Doña Nereida knitted sweaters for Princess and shopped for the fanciest collars and leashes she could find. A child's wardrobe unit had been purchased especially for her.

Customers would comment among themselves:

"That dog eats steak and they only eat tuna fish."

"Princess has better furniture than they have."

"I wish my kids ate as well as that mutt. It's not right, you know. God cannot justify this." And so on.

Despite all the gossip and complaints about the dog, no one dared say anything openly to Don Osvaldo or Doña Nereida.

Customers had to agree that Princess herself was a friendly little animal, and pleasant to look at. When children came into the store to shop they would pet her, and she was gentle with them, accepting their attention joyfully.

Princess was especially fond of Judy, who frequently took her out and taught her tricks. At first, Don Osvaldo and Doña Nereida were worried about letting Judy take Princess for walks. "Hold on to that leash. You mustn't let her get near other dogs; especially those male dogs," they warned. But several months had gone by and Judy and the dog always returned safe and sound. Actually, neither owner liked to leave the store, and they were silently grateful that Judy could take Princess out for some air.

"Mami, can I go back downstairs and take Princess for a walk?" Judy asked her mother.

Her mother had emptied the brown grocery bag and was checking the items.

"Look at that! Fifteen cents' worth of fatback and look at the tiny piece he sends. Bendito!"[4] She shook her head. "I have to watch that man, and she's no better. Didn't I tell you to check anything that he has to weigh?" Judy looked at her mother, expecting her to complain as always about Don Osvaldo and Doña Nereida. "Because we have to buy on credit, they think they can cheat us. When I have cash I will not buy there. I cannot trust them. They charge much more than any other store, but they can get away with it because we buy on credit. I would like to see him charge a cash-paying customer what he does me!"

---

3. **Bodega Borinquén** (bō′ reng ken′).
4. **Bendito** (ben dē′ tō).

▲ *Woman with a Dog* was painted by Pablo Picasso in 1962. How does this painting compare to the descriptions of Doña Nereida and Princess?

"Mami, can I go to walk Princess now?" Judy asked again.

"Why do you want to walk that dog? You are always walking that dog. What are you, their servant girl, to walk that stupid dog?"

"I'm the one who wants to walk her. . . . I love Princess. Please may I—"

"Go on!" her mother interrupted, waving her hands in a gesture of annoyance.

EVALUATE: Why do you think Judy's mother is so annoyed with Judy's request to walk Princess?

Before her mother could change her mind, Judy quickly left the apartment. Her little brother, Angel, had had another asthma attack today, and she knew her mother was in a lousy mood. After her father's death, Judy had moved into this neighborhood with her family: her mother, older sister Blanca, older brother William, and little brother Angel. That was three years ago, when she was just eight. The family had been on public assistance since almost immediately after her father had died. Her mother was always worried about making ends meet, but she was especially hard to live with whenever Angel got sick.

She ran toward the grocery store, anxious to take Princess for her walk. Judy had wanted to have a pet ever since she could remember. It was the one thing that she had always prayed for at Christmas and on her birthday, but her mother absolutely refused. Once she had brought home a stray cat and her little brother Angel had had a severe asthma attack. After that, she was positive that she could never ever have a pet. No matter how she had reasoned, her mother could not be persuaded to change her mind.

"I could give the cat my food, Mami. You don't have to spend no money. And during the day I could find a place to keep it until I got home from school."

"No. We cannot make ends meet to feed human beings, and I am not going to worry about animals. Besides, there's Angel and his allergies."[5] Her mother always won out.

If Papi had lived, maybe things could be different, Judy often thought. But since she could play with Princess and take her out, that was almost like having her own dog, and she had learned to be content with that much.

When Judy arrived at the store Doña Nereida had Princess all ready.

"See, Judy," Doña Nereida said, "she's got a new leash—pale-blue with tiny silver studs. She looks good in blue, don't you think so?" she asked. "It goes with her coloring. Her fur is so nice and white."

The little dog ran, tugging at the leash, and Judy followed, laughing.

Outside in the street, Judy shouted, "Ready, get set . . . go!" Quickly, Judy and Princess began to run, as usual, in the direction of the schoolyard. Once they got there, Judy unleashed Princess and she ran freely, chasing her and some of the other children.

They were all used to Princess, and would pet her, run with her, and sometimes even play a game of ball with the little dog. They watched as Princess followed Judy's commands: She could sit up, roll over, play dead, retrieve, and shake hands. Everyone at the schoolyard treated Princess as if she belonged to Judy and asked her permission[6] first before they played or ran with the little dog. And Princess behaved as if she were Judy's dog. She listened and came obediently when Judy called her. After they had finished playing, Judy leashed Princess and they walked back to the store.

---

5. allergy (al′ər jē), n. an unusual reaction of the body to certain substances, such as particular kinds of pollen, pet hair, food, or cloth.
6. permission (pər mish′ən), n. consent; agreement to allow or permit something.

"Did you have a good time?" Doña Nereida asked when they returned. "Come inside with Mama. . . . She has a little something for you," she said to Princess.

Judy handed the leash to Doña Nereida. She had never been invited inside where Princess lived. Whenever she came back from her walks she waited around, hoping they would ask her in as well, but they never did. No one was invited into the back rooms where Don Osvaldo, Doña Nereida, and Princess lived.

"Before you leave—Judy, here, have a piece of candy." Doña Nereida opened the cover of a glass display case and removed a small piece of coconut candy that sold for two cents apiece or three for a nickel. She handed it to Judy.

"Thank you," Judy said, taking the candy. She didn't much like it, but she ate it anyway.

"Osvaldo . . . Osvaldo," Doña Nereida called, "come out here, I have to take Princess inside." Turning to Judy, she said, "Good-bye, Judy, see you later."

Judy smiled and left the store. She wished she could see where Princess lived. Shrugging her shoulders, she said to herself, Maybe tomorrow they'll ask me in.

"It's not funny," her mother said. "If these beans are rotten we could die."

"There's something wrong with these beans. Smell!" her mother said, handing the can of pork and beans to her children.

"Whew, yeah!" said Blanca. "They smell funny." She handed the can to William, who agreed, and then to Judy.

"They smell funny," Judy nodded.

"Can I smell too?" asked Angel. Judy handed him the can.

"Peeoowee . . ." he said, making a face. They all laughed.

"It's not funny," her mother said. "If these beans are rotten we could die." She held up the can. "Look—see that? The can is dented and swollen. Sure, he always gives us inferior merchandise.[7] That no-good louse!" She shook her head. "We have to return them, that's all. You go, Judy, bring them back and tell him we want another can that's not spoiled."

"I have to walk Princess, Mami; send somebody else."

"You have to walk to the store and back here. Never mind Princess. Go on!"

"But I'll be too late then," Judy protested, thinking about her friends in the schoolyard.

"How would you like not to walk that mutt at all? What if I say that you cannot walk her any more," her mother said, looking severely at Judy.

Quietly, Judy got up and took the can of beans. "Mami, they are already opened."

"Of course. How would I know otherwise if they are rotten? Here is the cover—just place it on top." She put the tin lid back on the opened can. "There . . . don't spill them and come right back here. I have to start supper."

"Can I walk Princess after I come back?"

"Yes," her mother said with exasperation.[8] "Just come back with another can of beans!"

Judy rushed as quickly as she could, at the same time making sure that she did not spill the contents of the can.

"Here she is," said Doña Nereida when she saw Judy, "ready to take you out, Princess." As she fastened the leash, the dog barked and jumped, anxious to go out.

"Doña Nereida, I have to give you something first," Judy said.

"What?"

"Here is a can of beans that my brother

---

7. **merchandise** (mèr′chən dīz), *n.* goods for sale.
8. **exasperation** (eg zas′pə rā′shən), *n.* anger; extreme annoyance.

Head of a Woman was painted by Alexej Jawlensky around 1910. Do you think this painting represents Doña Nereida or Judy's mother?

William brought home before, and they are rotten." She put the can on the counter. "So my mother says could you please give us another can that is not spoiled."

Doña Nereida picked up the can and lifted the lid, sniffing the contents. "What's wrong with them?" she asked.

"They are rotten."

"Who says? They smell just fine to me. Wait a minute. Osvaldo! Osvaldo, come out here please!" Doña Nereida called loudly.

"What do you want? I'm busy." Don Osvaldo came out.

"Smell these beans. Go on." She handed her husband the opened can.

Don Osvaldo sniffed the contents and said, "They are fine. What's wrong?"

"Judy brought them—her mother wants another can. She says they are spoiled, that they are rotten."

"Tsk . . ." Don Osvaldo sighed and shook his head. "They are fine. They don't smell spoiled to me, or rotten. Besides, the can is opened. I can't exchange them if she opened the can already." He put the can back on the counter and covered it with the lid. "Here, take it back to your mother and tell her that there is nothing wrong with those beans. I can't exchange them."

Judy stood there and looked at the couple. She wanted to say that they smelled bad to her, too, but instead she said, "O.K., I'll tell her." She picked up the can of beans and returned home.

"What? Do you mean to tell me that he told you that there is nothing wrong with this can of beans?" Her mother's voice was loud and angry. "I don't believe it! Did he smell them?" she asked Judy.

"Yes," Judy said. "They both did."

Her mother shook her head. "I'm not putting up with this any more. This is the last time that thieving couple do this to me. Come on, Judy. You come with me. I'm taking back the beans myself. Let's see what he will tell me. You too, William; you come with us, since you were the one that bought the beans."

"Can I come too?" asked Angel.

"No," his mother answered, "stay with Blanca till I get back. I don't want you going up and down the stairs. And you, Blanca, start the rice. I'll be back in a little while."

Her mother walked in first, holding the can of beans. Judy and William followed.

"Don Osvaldo, I would like to return this can of beans," her mother said. Don Osvaldo was seated behind the counter, looking through his ledger. He put the book down.

"Mrs. Morales,[9] there is nothing wrong with them beans," he said.

"Did you take a good smell? I sent Judy down before; and I cannot believe that after smelling them, you could refuse to exchange them for another can that is not spoiled!" She put the can on the counter.

Doña Nereida walked in, followed by Princess. When the dog saw Judy, she began to bark and jump up. "Shh . . ." said Doña Nereida. "Down! Get down, Princess, you are not going out right now. Maybe later. Down!" Princess sat down obediently, wagging her tail and looking at Judy. "What's happening here, Mrs. Morales?" she asked.

"It's about these beans. I refuse to accept them. That can is dented and swollen, that's how it got spoiled. Surely you don't expect me to feed this to my children."

"Why not?" said Doña Nereida. "They smell and look perfectly fine to me."

"Look, Mrs. Morales," said Don Osvaldo, "you probably opened the can and left it open a long time, and that's why they smell funny to you. But they are not spoiled, and I cannot give you another one or any credit for this."

"How could I know they are rotten unless I open up the can? Besides I did not leave them open a long time. William just bought it here this afternoon," Mrs. Morales said and turned to her son. "Isn't that so, William?"

"Yes. I got them here and the can was already dented," said William.

"That doesn't mean anything," said Don Osvaldo. "You people opened them. There's nothing we can do."

Mrs. Morales looked at Don Osvaldo and Doña Nereida and smiled, remaining silent. After a moment, she asked, "You expect me to eat this and to feed this to my children?"

"You can do what you want with those beans," said Don Osvaldo. "It's not my affair."

"Will you at least give us some credit?" asked Mrs. Morales.

"We already told you, no!" said Doña Nereida. "Listen, you are making a big thing over a can of beans when there is nothing wrong with them"

"Would you eat this, then?" asked Mrs. Morales.

"Of course," said Don Osvaldo.

"Certainly!" Doña Nereida nodded in agreement.

"O.K.," said Mrs. Morales, smiling, "I'll tell you what: You take them. A present from me to you. Eat them and enjoy them."

"All right." Don Osvaldo shrugged his shoulders. "If that's how you feel. It will be your loss. This can is not spoiled."

"Well then, I'll tell you what," said Mrs. Morales. "Why don't you feed it to Princess? Let Judy give it to her—a little present from us."

Don Osvaldo looked at his wife and she returned his glance, shrugging her shoulders.

"We are not going to eat them anyway, so why should they go to waste?" said Mrs. Morales. "Go on, Judy, take the beans and feed them to Princess." Turning toward Doña Nereida, she asked, "Perhaps you could give Judy a little dish?"

Doña Nereida did not answer, and looked with uncertainty at her husband. Mrs. Morales continued; this time she spoke to Don Osvaldo. "Why not? Don Osvaldo, if there is nothing wrong with the beans, then let's give them to Princess. She would probably enjoy them. It would be a treat."

EVALUATE: Why do you think Doña Nereida is uncertain at this moment?

---

9. **Morales** (mō rä′ läs).

"O.K.," he nodded, "sure. Nereida, get her blue dish from inside. If there is something wrong with the beans, Princess will not eat them."

His wife went into the back and returned, holding a bright-blue bowl with a happy white poodle on it.

"Here, Judy, you do it," said Mrs. Morales, looking at her daughter. "You give it to the dog. She'll take it from you."

Doña Nereida emptied the contents of the can into the bowl and gave it to Judy. Judy set it down on the floor near Princess.

"Here, girl, here's some beans for you," she said. Quickly, the little dog went over to the bowl and began to eat the beans, wagging her tail.

"See? Mrs. Morales, Princess is eating them beans. . . . There! Nothing was wrong with them. So you gave them away for nothing."

"That's all right, Don Osvaldo," Mrs. Morales responded. "It's not for nothing. Princess is enjoying the beans."

"Do you want another can of pork and beans?" asked Don Osvaldo, laughing. "I'm afraid I'll have to charge you, though!" His wife joined him in laughter as they both watched Princess finish the beans.

"No, thanks. I'll make do with what I have at home." Mrs. Morales turned to leave the store.

"Mami," said Judy, "can I walk Princess now?"

"No," her mother said, "you may not walk her now or later." As Judy followed her mother and brother out of the store, Don Osvaldo and Doña Nereida could still be heard laughing and commenting.

"How about tomorrow, Mami? Can I walk Princess tomorrow?" Judy persisted.

"We'll see . . . tomorrow," her mother answered.

At two the next morning, Osvaldo and Nereida Negrón were awakened by low whining sounds and grunts. When they got up to investigate, they found that Princess was having convulsions. Frightened, they tried to comfort the little dog by giving her water and then warm milk to drink. They even placed a hot-water bottle in her bed, but nothing seemed to help. The whining became softer and lower, until there was no sound at all. Princess lay in her small bed quietly, her eyes wide open, staring. The only visible sign of life was when her body jumped involuntarily, as if she had hiccups.

Don Osvaldo tried to calm his wife; she cried and wrung her hands, on the verge of hysteria.[10] After a while, they decided the best thing to do was to take Princess to a veterinarian. Don Osvaldo found the names of several animal hospitals in the Yellow Pages, and after some telephone calls found one that would take Princess at this time of the morning. They wrapped the dog in a blanket and took a cab to the animal hospital. The doctor examined Princess and told them that her chances of surviving were slim. Whatever she had eaten was already digested and in her bloodstream. However, he promised to do his best and call them no matter what happened.

The Negróns returned to their store at six A.M., and at six thirty A.M. they received a phone call from the hospital informing them that Princess was dead. For a small fee they offered to dispose of the remains, and Don Osvaldo agreed.

Doña Nereida took to her bed, refusing to get up. Don Osvaldo opened his store a little late that day. Many of his credit customers had been patiently waiting outside; they had no place else to shop.

No one seemed to notice that Princess was not in the store. Don Osvaldo waited on his customers in silence, checking the back

---

10. **hysteria** (hi stir′ē ə), *n.* uncontrollable excitement or emotion.

rooms every once in a while to see how his wife was. She remained in her bed, moaning softly and crying quietly.

As usual, that afternoon Judy went to the store to see Princess before going home. She entered and looked around for the little dog. Don Osvaldo was working behind the meat counter.

"Hi, Don Osvaldo," she said. "Where's Princess?"

"She's not here."

"You killed her, that's what you did. You, too, Judy, both of you . . . all of you."

"Is she inside with Doña Nereida?" Judy asked and waited for a response. Don Osvaldo continued his work behind the meat counter, not speaking. Judy felt awkward and stepped up a little closer to the counter so that she could see Don Osvaldo. He was carefully cutting small, neat slices from a large side of beef and stacking them evenly on the other side of the chopping block.

After a short while, she said, "I'll be back, then, to walk her later. Good-bye, see you later," and turned to leave.

"Judy," Don Osvaldo said, "please tell your mother that when she sends for her groceries today, she should come herself." He paused. "Did you hear? Tell your mother to come for her groceries herself!"

"Yes," Judy replied, and went home.

Mrs. Morales entered Don Osvaldo's store accompanied by William and Judy.

"Be right with you, Mrs. Morales," Don Osvaldo said, and continued his work on the ledger.

The store was empty, and Judy looked around for Princess. In spite of her concern, she dared not ask Don Osvaldo about the little dog. Her mother's solemn attitude and Don Osvaldo's request this afternoon frightened her. For once, she wished her mother had not asked her to come along.

Don Osvaldo closed the ledger and looked at Mrs. Morales, staring at her without speaking. Finally, he asked, "Do you want anything? Can I get you something?"

"No, thank you," Mrs. Morales answered.

"Nothing?" he asked. "How about you, Judy? Do you want to take Princess for a walk?"

Judy looked at her mother, who reached out and pulled her daughter close to her.

"Do you want me to get her for you, Judy?" Don Osvaldo continued, raising his voice loudly. "Do you want to take Princess for a little stroll? Well, answer! Answer!" he yelled.

Judy could feel her mother's body tensing up and trembling slightly.

"What do you want? You sent for me— what is it?" her mother asked.

"Do you know where she is? Where Princess is? She's dead. Dead. You killed her, that's what you did. You, too, Judy, both of you . . . all of you." Don Osvaldo's voice was angry. "She never did anything to you, to any of you. But you!" He pointed at Mrs. Morales. "You had to give that innocent animal, who never harmed you, something that would kill her, on spite! And you knew it—you knew it!"

"What do you want?" Mrs. Morales asked in a loud voice. "You have business with me? Tell me, or I'll leave!"

"Here . . ." Don Osvaldo said and pushed a white sheet of paper across the counter. "I don't want to touch you. Here is your bill. Pay up by the end of the week, or I'll take you to court. You get no more credit here!"

Mrs. Morales picked up the bill and examined it carefully. "I see, Don Osvaldo, that you have charged me for the beans." Her voice was shaking and she paused, clearing her throat. "I'm glad, real glad you did. It's a small price to pay for the life of my children. As God will judge!" Mrs. Morales made the sign of the cross. "You will get your money, don't worry, Don Osvaldo. It will be my pleasure."

In a moment, Mrs. Morales and her two children left the store.

Judy cried that night and on many other nights whenever she remembered Princess. She wished she had never given the beans to Princess. She stopped going to the schoolyard; she didn't know what to tell the kids there.

Her mother found a grocery store that sold to credit customers. It was farther away—an extra fifteen-minute walk. They had two cats that Judy enjoyed playing with, but it was not the same.

Very often, she would pass by Don Osvaldo's grocery and glance inside, wondering if it had all been a dream and Princess were really in there waiting for her to come and play. She had spoken to several of the kids that shopped there, and all of them told her that the little dog was definitely not in the store. Still, there were times she would walk by and imagine Princess barking and wagging her tail, asking to be taken out to the schoolyard.

Two months went by, and one day, as Judy walked by Don Osvaldo's store on the way home, she heard someone call her name.

"Judy . . . psst, Judy . . . come over here."

She saw Doña Nereida calling her. "Come over here, Judy. . . . I want to talk to you." Judy moved slowly, with some trepidation. "Come on," Doña Nereida insisted. "I just want to see you a minute."

She followed the woman into the store. It was the first time she had set foot inside since the day that Don Osvaldo had spoken to her mother. She could hear her heart pounding and she wondered what they wanted.

Don Osvaldo was busy waiting on a customer, and did not look in her direction.

"Come on with me," Doña Nereida whispered. "Come on!" Judy followed as she led her behind the counter and over to the back of the store.

They entered a medium-sized room with an old gas stove, a sink, a small refrigerator, and several kitchen cabinets. The room was furnished with an old armchair in need of upholstering and a kitchen table with four chairs.

"Sit . . . sit down, Judy." They both sat down.

"I suppose you are wondering why I asked you in," she said. Judy nodded. "It's that . . . I just want to talk to you. About . . . Princess." Doña Nereida lowered her eyes and sighed. "You miss her too, I'll bet." Judy blushed. Being here with Doña Nereida embarrassed her. "Don't you?"

"Yes . . ." Judy said.

"She was so good; such a fine little dog. Almost like a person. We had her five years. She was so obedient." Doña Nereida paused and, choking back the tears, wiped her eyes. "It's not the same any more, you know. And he . . ." She gestured into the store. "He doesn't understand and expects me to forget! I can't. You understand, don't you?"

Judy nodded.

"See—I knew it. I told him. Judy—Judy knows. She loved Princess. She'll understand. I don't want another dog. You see, it wouldn't be fair to Princess. I have all her things, and he wants me to give them away!" She paused. "Would you like to see them? Would you?"

Judy shrugged her shoulders, feeling uncomfortable.

"Don't be shy. I know you want to see where Princess slept. Come on now." Doña Nereida stood up and took Judy into a small adjoining room. It had a large double bed and a dresser. Over in a corner was a child's colorful yellow-and-blue wardrobe unit. Next to it, on the floor, was what appeared to Judy to be a flat kind of wicker basket with a pillow. Inside was a rubber ball, a teething ring, and a toy telephone. "That's her little bed. We bought it at the pet shop on Third Avenue."

The room was stuffy and unkempt. Judy tried not to show her displeasure at the way the room smelled.

"It's been very hard on me." Judy wished that Doña Nereida would stop talking.

"Doña Nereida," Judy said, "I have to go home now. My mother is waiting."

"Of course. What will you think of me?" She led Judy back out through the front. Don Osvaldo was busy looking at his ledger. "Here, Judy. . . ." Doña Nereida reached into the glass display case and took a piece of white coconut candy. "Here."

"Thank you," said Judy.

"I know how you used to like this candy." She smiled.

"Good-bye," said Judy.

"Tomorrow. Come back tomorrow, Judy, and we'll talk some more!" She smiled.

"O.K.," Judy said, leaving the store. She put the candy in her mouth and decided that she definitely did not like it.

As she walked home, she felt strange about what had just happened. The back of the store didn't seem to have anything to do with the Princess she remembered—barking wildly, jumping, running, playing in the schoolyard, and chasing all the kids.

Judy made sure that on her way home from school, she did not pass by Don Osvaldo's store the next day, or any other day.

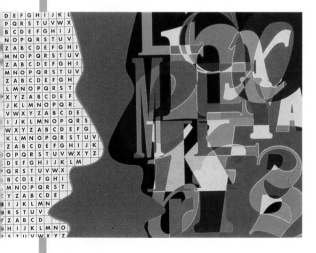

▲ How does this painting by Frank Collyer reinforce the subject of the poem?

Words
Pauli Murray

We are spendthrifts with words,
We squander them,
Toss them like pennies in the air—
Arrogant words,
5 Angry words,
Cruel words,
Comradely words,
Shy words tiptoeing from mouth to ear.

But the slowly wrought words of love
10 And the thunderous words of heartbreak—
These we hoard.

After Reading

Making Connections

1. Who do you think suffered the biggest loss after Princess died: Mrs. Morales, Judy, Don Osvaldo, or Doña Nereida? Why?

2. Look back at the chart you completed as you read the story. Which issue do you feel was most important? Why?

3. How do you think the author's cultural background contributed to this story?

4. What do you think is the **theme** or the author's main message in this story? Explain.

5. How does the poem "Words" relate to the conflict between Mrs. Morales and Don Osvaldo?

6. 🐾 Think about your own **perspective** on pets. Do you think what happened to Princess was fair? Why or why not?

Literary Focus: Dialogue

The conversation of two or more characters as written in a story is called **dialogue.** It is one of the main literary devices that the author uses in "Princess." Dialogue is distinguished from other writing by the use of quotation marks around sentences or phrases. Also, a change in speaker is usually signaled by a new paragraph.

Dialogue can serve many important functions in a story. Study the checklist below. Then, read through "Princess" again and decide which of the functions of dialogue Mohr used in this story. For each function you choose, give an example from the story.

Different Functions of Dialogue
✓ It moves the action along.
✓ It reveals the personality of the characters.
✓ It shows how different characters relate to one another.
✓ It shows the cultural background, social position, education, and special interests of different characters.
✓ It helps define the setting through dialect and vocabulary.
✓ It makes the story seem realistic.
✓ It presents opinions and ideas.
✓ It helps to set the mood of the story.
✓ It can be used to display humor or sadness.

Vocabulary Study

Below is an imaginary dialogue between Judy and her brother after Judy visited Doña Nereida in the back of the store. Select the vocabulary word that best completes each incomplete sentence.

allergy
exasperation
hysteria
merchandise
permission

"Doña Nereida invited me to the rooms behind the store last week. Even though I didn't have Mom's __(1)__ I went anyway."

"Is their home as inferior as the __(2)__ that they sell?" William echoed the scorn of his mother. "I bet I know why they don't have much furniture." William laughed loudly and meanly, almost with __(3)__ .

"William, it's not funny," Judy whispered in __(4)__ . "What really got to me was the smell, dusty and moldy. It would it have been more than enough to aggravate your __(5)__ . And Princess's things are still in place in their bedroom!"

Expressing Your Ideas

Writing Choices

Rotten Beans, Rotten Day Pretend you are Judy. Write a **diary** entry about the day you found out that Princess had died. Include your feelings about your mother, Mr. and Mrs. Negrón, and Princess.

To the Inspector Most cities have regulations involving the sale of spoiled merchandise. Write a **letter** to your city, county, or state health department to find out how they would deal with an incident like the one that occurred in "Princess." In your letter, ask what the penalty is, if any, for selling spoiled or damaged merchandise.

Other Options

Portrait of a Puppy To help Doña Negrón get over her grief, Don Osvaldo has commissioned you to paint a **portrait** of Princess in the family home. Use details from the story to help you sketch out and paint the portrait. Display your painting in the classroom and tell your classmates why you chose to include particular details.

Take to the Stage With all the dialogue, "Princess" is a good story to make into a **play.** Work in small groups on the script, stage design and props, direction, music, and lighting for the play. Assign roles and practice the lines. Then, perform your play for another class or for your school.

Before Reading

Ghost Town

by Jack Schaefer

Jack Schaefer
1907–1991

Jack Schaefer was a newspaper editor turned writer. His first book, *Shane,* was hailed as the best western novel ever written. The curious thing about Schaefer is that he had never been west of Ohio when the book was published. His reading of American history helped capture the drama of the West. After *Shane,* Schaefer wrote many other western short stories and novels. A number of them have been made into movies. He explained that he liked writing about characters "conditioned by the wide open spaces of the old West, in which the energies and capabilities of men and women, for good or for evil, were unleashed . . . as they rarely had been before or elsewhere in human history."

Building Background

Boom or Bust Many gold rushes occurred across the American west in the mid- and late-1800s. Thousands of people went to search for gold and other minerals in isolated areas in the present-day states of California, Alaska, Arizona, Colorado, Idaho, Wyoming, Nevada, Montana, New Mexico, South Dakota, and Utah. If riches were found, a boom town would spring up. As more people arrived, stores, restaurants, and hotels were opened to serve the miners. When the mines closed, people left the area. Most of the mining towns were abandoned as quickly as they had been built. The boom towns became ghost towns.

Getting into the Story

Writer's Notebook You probably wouldn't want the place where you live to become a ghost town. Think about the things that make a place important to you. What is important about your home, street, neighborhood, or city? Make a list in your notebook.

Reading Tip

Sequence of Events The narrator of "Ghost Town" sets his story completely in the past. As he describes the ghost town and tells about his adventures there, he moves forward and backward in time. Make a time line, like the one below, to keep track of the **sequence** of events in this story. The dates are estimates, based on the general history of the American West. Use clues from the story to help you figure out other dates. Then fill in the time line with other important events of the story as you read.

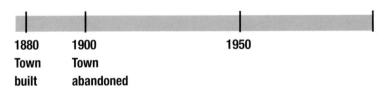

Ghost TOWN

Jack Schaefer

I owned a whole town once. What was left of it anyway. A ghost town. One of the mining camps back in the hills that must have been quite a place when the gold rush was on. Then the diggings there petered out and people began moving on and the flimsy houses started collapsing after everyone was gone.

You can find traces of plenty of those old towns scattered up the back creeks. But this one was better than most. Some of the men there knew how to build a kiln[1] and fire it and there was a clay bank nearby. A half dozen buildings were made of brick and these stood solid enough through the years. The roofs had fallen in, and the windows and doors were missing, but the walls were still standing. You could even figure out what they had been: a general store; a post office and stage station; a blacksmith shop; a two-room jail; a small saloon; another saloon with space for dancing or gambling tables and some rooms on a second floor.

This old town of mine was up a narrow gulch[2] that wasn't good for a thing once the gold was gone. But it was only about a half mile from a modern main highway and the old dirt road leading to it was still passable. I drove in there one day and was poking around when another car loaded with tourists pulled up and the people piled out and wandered around with the women oh-ing and ah-ing as if they were seeing something wonderful.

That's when I had my idea.

It took time but I ran that town down on the tax books and found out all about it. The county had taken title to the whole place for back taxes maybe fifty years before—so long before, it had been written off the accounts as a dead loss and just about forgotten. When I offered to buy it the county officials thought I was crazy and jumped to make a deal. They hadn't expected ever to get another nickel out of the place. I paid $800 and I owned a town.

I cleaned out the old buildings enough so you could walk around inside them. I painted names on them telling what they had been. I fixed a few bad spots in the dirt road. I plas-

---

1. **kiln** (kiln), *n.* furnace or oven for burning, baking, or drying something. Bricks are baked in a kiln.
2. **gulch** (gulch), *n.* a very deep, narrow ravine with steep sides, especially one marking the course of a stream.

Ghost Town **481**

tered signs along the highway for maybe five miles in each direction and a big one where the dirt road turned off. I roofed over one room of the old jail for my own quarters. I charged fifty cents a head for a look-see through the old place—and I was in business.

EVALUATE: What do you think [rator's business? Does it see] [honest way to make a living?]

It was a good business. No[t] course, and slow in the spri[ng] good all summer—enough to carry me comfortably all year. During the rough months I'd stay at a rooming house in the live town that was the county seat and as soon as the weather was right I'd move out and start collecting my half dollars.

Sometimes I'd have four or five cars at a time parked by the entrance and a dozen or more people listening to my talk. I'd check the license plates and temper[3] the talk accordingly. If they were from the home state or one nearby, I'd go easy on the fancy trimmings. Those people might know too much real history. But if they were from far states, maybe eastern ones, I'd let loose and make it strong. I'd tell about fights in the saloons—shootings and knifings and big brawls with bottles flying. I'd tell about road agents stopping stages carrying gold and getting caught and being locked up in the jail and maybe a daring escape or two. I'd make it good and the eastern tourists lapped it up. What if all of it happened only in my head? Such things could of happened and maybe did. What if I did get a couple of complaints from the state historical society? There wasn't anything anyone could do so long as I made up the names too. The town belonged to me.

It was a good business. For three years.

Then it collapsed just the way the old town itself did 'way back when. The state started straightening the highway and knocked off the loop that came near my ghost town. That put the main route about seven miles away. I slapped up more signs but not many people would bother to turn off onto the old route

[handwritten notes: reason 2nd col in business unloa soc]

summer season started and I was lucky to average a single car a day. I was figuring I'd have to swallow the loss and move on when this pink-cheeked young fellow came along. It was late one afternoon and he was pink-cheeked like a boy with maybe a little fuzz on his chin that hadn't begun to be whiskers yet. He drove up in an old car that had lost its color in dust and he paid his fifty cents and started poking around. I was so lonesome for customers, or just anyone to talk to, that I stuck close and kept words bouncing back and forth with him. He looked so young and innocent I figured he was a college kid seeing some of the country on vacation time.

PREDICT: Do you think the author will trust his first impression of this visitor? Why or why not?

But no. He said he'd had all the college he could absorb. He was a mining engineer by profession but there wasn't much professing to be done in that field about then, so he was knocking around looking over the old camps. He liked to see how they did things in the old

---

3. **temper** (tem′pər), *v.* moderate; adjust.

▲ *The Last Stage* was painted by Ernest Berke in 1964. Why do you think the visitor is interested in a town like this?

days. Maybe he'd write a book on it some time.

"Mighty interesting town you have here," he said. "Those buildings. Brick. Don't see much brick in the old camps. They haul them in here?"

"Why no," I said. "They had a kiln right here—you can see where it was behind the blacksmith shop. They dug the clay out of the bank over there." And right away this young fellow had to see that too.

"Mighty interesting," he said. "Found the clay right here. Don't often come on good brick clay in these parts. But you can see the

cleaned out this streak in the bank. They sure liked bricks. If they hadn't run out of the clay they might still be making them."

"That'd be a darn fool stunt," I said. "Who'd be wanting bricks around here now?"

"Yes," he said. "Yes, it would. A darn fool stunt." And he wandered on, me with him and him talking more about what sturdy buildings these bricks had made and other things like that.

"Mighty interesting business you're in," he _____ to an old town like _____ pay to look it over. _____e." _____ other idea.

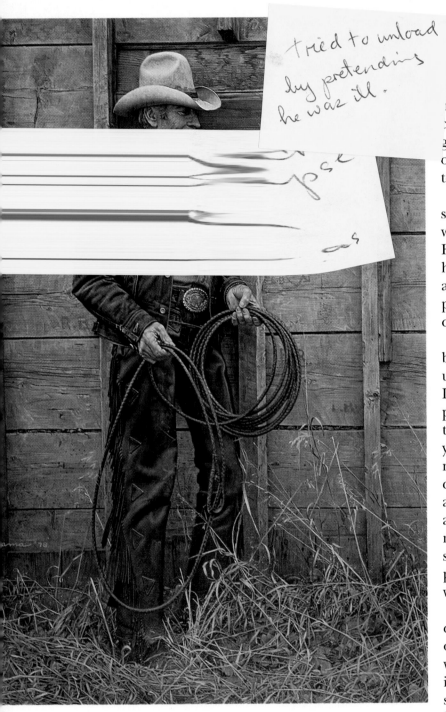

tried to unload by pretending he was ill.

◄ *Slim Warren, the Old Cowboy* was painted by James Bama, an artist known for his realistic portrayals of the Western experience.

leaving such a nice life in such an interesting business. I played it clever with indirect questions and got out of him the fact he had a bit of cash to invest. Then I really went to work on him.

"Stay here tonight," I said, "and stick around tomorrow. You'll see what a good business this really is." He said he would and I worked on him some more and after a while I asked him to keep an eye on the place while I drove over to the county seat to tend to a few things.

I tended to the things all right but not at the county seat. I burned up the roads getting to various men I knew around about. Each stop I put the same proposition.[5] "There's ten dollars in it for you," I said, "if you'll take time tomorrow to put the missus and anyone else handy in the car and drive over to the old town and make like a tourist gawking around some." I covered a lot of miles and I was turned down at a few stops, but at last I had eleven cars promised and with the extras that would run to about forty people.

When I got back, my pink-cheeked baby was sleeping like one on the cot I'd fixed up for him. He woke long enough to grunt a greeting, then rolled over and went to sleep again. But I could tell he'd been snooping in the last summer's tally-book I'd left out on purpose where he

I took that pink-cheeked young fellow into my jail-room and persuaded him to stay for supper. I began coughing at strategic[4] intervals during the meal and I told him my health was bad and the climate bothered me, otherwise I wouldn't even be thinking of maybe

---

4. **strategic** (strə tē′jik), *adj.* based on a preconceived plan.
5. **proposition** (prop′ə zish′ən), *n.* scheme.

would see it. The highway change hadn't been finished then and that had been a good summer.

Come morning everything clicked just right. My homegrown tourists started coming and kept coming at about the times I'd suggested all the way through the morning and early afternoon. I was worried that my young visitor might get to talking with them and sniff some suspicions but he didn't bother with them at all. He just watched what was going on and wandered around by himself and spent some time poking in what was left of the old kiln. I worked on him a bit during lunch and about the middle of the afternoon, when the last of the cars had left, I figured it was time to hook him.

"Not bad," I said. "Eleven cars and forty-one people. Twenty dollars and a fifty cent piece over. And all I did was just sit here and let them come."

"Mighty interesting," he said. "That's more people than I expected."

"That?" I said. "Just a low average. Good enough for a weekday but you should see the weekends. Saturdays double it. And Sundays? Why, Sundays triple it."

"You don't say?" he said. "Too bad about your health. Didn't you mention something about wanting to sell out?"

And right then I knew I had him.

It was just a matter of price after that and on price I always was a tough one. When I chucked my things in my car so I could turn the place over to him that same day and led the way to the county seat with him following so we could find a notary[6] and sign the papers, I'd pushed him up to a thousand bucks. He looked so young and innocent tagging after me into the notary's that I was almost ashamed of myself . . .

PREDICT: What do you think is going to happen with the business deal?

Brother, let me tell you something. When a pink-cheeked young tenderfoot[7] with maybe some fuzz on his chin that hasn't even begun to be real whiskers comes your way, just watch your step. Watch it close. That's the kind will take you for anything you've got worth taking—while you're still wondering whether he's been weaned. It wasn't a week later I saw this baby-faced sucker I thought I'd trimmed coming toward me along a street and I ducked quick into a bar. He followed me in and cornered me.

"How's business?" I said, hoping to get any unpleasantness over with fast.

"Business?" he said. "Now that's mighty interesting. Do you really think you fooled me with those fake tourists? The license plates tipped me right away. All from this state. All from this county." He grinned—the same innocent grin he had the first time I saw him. "Let me buy you a drink. No hard feelings. Your so-called business didn't interest me at all. It was the buildings. I've a crew out there now tearing them down."

"Tearing them down?" I said.

"Certainly," he said. "Those bricks. That clay was the best pocket of pay dirt in the whole gulch—only those old-time miners didn't know it. There was gold dust in that clay and it's right there in the bricks. I'm having them crushed and washing the gold out. There's close to a hundred tons of those bricks and they're panning about eight hundred dollars to the ton."

---

6. notary (nō′tər ē), *n.* a public official authorized to certify deeds and contracts and to attend to other legal matters.

7. **tenderfoot** (ten′dər fut′), *n.* an inexperienced person; beginner.

Vacant House

Jeanne DeL. Bonnette

Beside the old earth-colored
adobe house haphazard on the ground
whose doors have vanished
and whose window frames are empty
5 wherein tumbleweeds have hidden at last
from the wind in corners

the rusty upside-down cars
lie like dark wing-folded shells
of beetles on the dry earth.

10 Majestic cottonwoods
rise above the corral
with no boy to throw a rope
over a low-hanging branch,
no man to lean
15 against the grea
no woman to sta
her apron flutte
a hand over her
against the brilli

20 The echo of hors
has long ago fade
and now only the
perch high in the
to scold the ghosts
25 of those who once were here
working, belonging.

▲ *The Blue Portal* was painted by Freemont Ellis. Is your perspective of this vacant house the same as the poet's or do you have other feelings?

After Reading

Making Connections

1. How do you think the narrator felt when he heard what the mining engineer was doing with his town? Why do you think he felt this

   what do you see in the illustration?

   d what's not in this story—what the narrator
   g engineer did.

   e line you made. Choose the ever
   nt. Do you think the narrator is te
   pened, a few years after it happe
   ppened? Explain.

4. The author creates the character of the mining engineer
   giving you information that is the opposite of the way he
   Why do you think the author uses this technique?

5. A scam artist is a person who takes advantage of others through unscrupulous business deals. Which character or characters, if any, do you think are scam artists? Explain.

6. You may have heard the saying "Honesty is the best policy." What do you think might have happened if both characters had followed this advice?

7. The narrator, the mining engineer, and the author of the poem "Vacant House" each have a different **perspective** a place. How do their perspectives co value of an important place in you

Literary Focus: Informal

People often use **informal la
fragments, and colorful expres
The author uses informal langua
the story seem more real. Make a
go through the story and list examp
informal language listed. Exchange c
look over some of the different example round. Then, discuss how you might change some of t anguage if the story were set in different location, such as your own town.

Informal Language		
Slang Terms	**Colorful Expressions**	**Sentence Fragments**
diggings	dead loss	what was left of it anyway

Vocabulary Study

Following are some signs you might see in the narrator's ghost town. For each underlined word or phrase, choose the vocabulary term that is closest in meaning.

gulch
kiln
notary
proposition
strategic

1. Warning! No off-road travel. <u>Narrow ravine</u> with steep, slippery sides ahead.

2. Welcome to Ghostville. There's still gold in these hills. Look around and stake your claim. You can file it with the <u>public official that records deeds</u> in the courthouse on Main Street.

3. This is the bank. When the town was in its heyday, armed guards were posted in <u>prime</u> places to prevent robberies.

4. This is the <u>oven where the town's bricks were baked</u>. The clay was gathered from the bank of the stream and formed into bricks.

5. A business <u>proposal</u>: If you would like to set up a concession stand for this town, please see the Town Manager in Room 102 of the old city hall.

Expressing Your Ideas

Writing Choices

The Joke's on You Pretend you are the narrator. Continue the **dialogue.** Will you pretend you are doing as well as the engineer, or will you say how you really feel about the deal?

Sham "Historical" Town Run by Fake Historian Imagine you are a historian in the state where the ghost town in the story is located. You visit the ghost town and are appalled at the liberty the owner is taking with the local history. Write an **editorial** explaining why you are upset and tell what you think should be done about the situation.

What's So Funny? Write an **anecdote** or paragraph about a scam or practical joke you have heard about. If you wish, turn your idea into a **story.**

Other Options

Now It's Gone The mining engineer tore down the ghost town. But you can use the descriptions in this story to make a **model** of the town. Include the streambed and the area where the clay was dug out for the town's bricks. Show all the different buildings and the room in the jail that the narrator fixed up for himself.

Be a Real Historian Do research on a genuine old mining town and on the different people who lived there. You might consider such places as Sutter's Mill in California or Silverton, Colorado. Work with a group to create a **brochure** that would to attract tourists to the town. Mention any events that actually took place. Use photocopies of old photographs to create interest.

Before Reading

Ibrahima
by Walter Dean Myers

Walter Dean Myers
born 1937

From reading the biographical account "Ibrahima," you might think that Walter Dean Myers prefers to write nonfiction. However, Myers is best known for the novels he writes for young adults. He often writes about young African Americans who live in inner-city neighborhoods. Myers has always felt that the challenge of writing fiction was to portray "the nuances of value, of religion, of dreams. It meant capturing the subtle rhythms of language and movement and weaving it all, the sound and the gestures, the sweat and the prayers, into the recognizable fabric of black life."

Building Background

Ancient West Africa Part of "Ibrahima" is set in the western part of Africa in the late 1700s. This part of Africa was home to the Fula, or Fulani, a people who followed the Muslim religion and traditionally herded cattle. The main character of this story was a Fulani. The Mandingo are another West African group represented in this selection.

Getting into the Selection

Writer's Notebook This selection deals with slavery. Make a K-W-L chart like the one below about slavery. In the first column, list what you already know about slavery. In the second column, write down what you'd like to learn about slavery. After you finish reading, complete the third column.

What I **K**now	What I **W**ant to Know	What I **L**earned
Many Africans were sold into slavery.		

Reading Tip

Adjusting Your Reading Rate While you may read some selections with great speed, you may read other selections at a slower pace and with more concentration. "Ibrahima" includes names and places that probably will be unfamiliar to you. Therefore, you will have to slow down your reading rate, to understand all of the information.

As you read the selection, refer to the footnotes or look up unfamiliar terms in a dictionary or encyclopedia. Reread paragraphs to see if they make more sense to you. After each page, stop to summarize what has happened. Reading this way is slower, but it can increase your understanding.

IBRAHIMA

WALTER DEAN MYERS

Who were these Africans being brought to the New World?
What was their African world like? There is no single answer. The
Africans came from many countries, and from many cultures. Like
the Native Americans, they established their territories based on
centuries of tradition. Most, but not all, of the Africans who were
brought to the colonies came from central and west Africa. Among
them was a man named Abd al-Rahman Ibrahima.[1]

The European invaders, along with those Africans who cooperated with them, had made the times dangerous. African nations that had lived peacefully together for centuries now eyed each other warily. Slight insults led to major battles. Bands of outlaws roamed the countryside attacking the small villages, kidnapping those unfortunate enough to have wandered from the protection of their people. The stories that came from the coast were frightening. Those kidnapped were taken to the sea and sold to whites, put on boats, and taken across the sea. No one knew what happened then.

Abd al-Rahman Ibrahima was born in 1762 in Fouta Djallon,[2] a district of the present country of Guinea.[3] It is a beautiful land of green mountains rising majestically from grassy plains, a land rich with minerals, especially bauxite.

Ibrahima was a member of the powerful and influential Fula people and a son of one

of their chieftains. The religion of Islam had swept across Africa centuries before, and the young Ibrahima was raised in the tradition of the Moslems.

The Fula were taller and lighter in complexion than the other inhabitants of Africa's west coast; they had silky hair, which they often wore long. A pastoral people, the Fula had a complex system of government, with the state divided into nine provinces and each province divided again into smaller districts. Each province had its chief and its subchiefs.

As the son of a chief, Ibrahima was expected to assume a role of political leadership when he came of age. He would also be expected to set a moral example, and to be

---

1. **Abd al-Rahman Ibrahima** (əb dùl ra män′ ib′ rä hē′ mä).
2. **Fouta Djallon** (fü tä′ jä lôn′), a mountainous region in West Africa.
3. **Guinea** (gin′ē).

⋀ The city of Timbuktu

well versed in his religion. When he reached twelve he was sent to Timbuktu[4] to study.

Under the Songhai[5] dynasty leader Askia the Great, Timbuktu had become a center of learning and one of the largest cities in the Songhai Empire. The young Ibrahima knew he was privileged to attend the best-known school in west Africa. Large and sophisticated, with wide, tree-lined streets, the city attracted scholars from Africa, Europe, and Asia. Islamic law, medicine, and mathematics were taught to the young men destined to become the leaders of their nations. It was a good place for a young man to be. The city was well guarded, too. It had to be, to prevent the chaos that, more and more, dominated African life nearer the coast.

Ibrahima learned first to recite from the Koran, the Moslem holy book, and then to read it in Arabic. From the Koran, it was felt, came all other knowledge. After Ibrahima had finished his studies in Timbuktu, he returned to Fouta Djallon to continue to prepare himself to be a chief.

---

4. **Timbuktu** (tim′buk tū′).
5. **Songhai** (song hi′), an empire that flourished in West Africa from 1468 to 1590.

▲ *Cinque* was painted by Nathaniel Jocelyn around 1840.

and brought to the Fula chiefs, he was more dead than alive.

Dr. Cox, an Irishman, told of being separated from a hunting party that had left from a ship on which he had sailed as ship's surgeon. The Fula chief decided that he would help Cox. He was taken into a hut, and a healer was assigned the task of curing his infected leg.

During the months Dr. Cox stayed with the Fula, he met Ibrahima, now a tall, brown-skinned youth who had reached manhood. His bearing reflected his status as the son of a major chief. Dr. Cox had learned some Fulani, the Fula language, and the two men spoke. Ibrahima was doubtless curious about the white man's world, and Dr. Cox was as impressed by Ibrahima's education as he had been by the kindness of his people.

The Fula had little contact with whites, and what little contact they did have was filled with danger. So when, in 1781, a white man claiming to be a ship's surgeon stumbled into one of their villages, they were greatly surprised. John Coates Cox hardly appeared to be a threat. A slight man, blind in one eye, he had been lost for days in the forested regions bordering the mountains. He had injured his leg, and it had become badly infected as he tried to find help. By the time he was found

When Dr. Cox was well enough to leave, he was provided with a guard; but before he left, he warned the Fula about the danger of venturing too near the ships that docked off the coast of Guinea. The white doctor knew that the ships were there to take captives.

Cox and Ibrahima embraced fondly and said their goodbyes, thinking they would never meet again.

Ibrahima married and became the father of several children. He was in his mid-twenties when he found himself leading the Fula cavalry in their war with the Mandingo.

The first battles went well, with the enemy retreating before the advancing Fula. The foot warriors attacked first, breaking the enemy's ranks and making them easy prey for the well-trained Fula cavalry. With the enemy in full rout, the infantry returned to their towns while the horsemen, led by Ibrahima, chased the remaining stragglers. The Fula fought their enemies with spears, bows, slings, swords, and courage.

The path of pursuit led along a path that narrowed sharply as the forests thickened. The fleeing warriors disappeared into the forest that covered a sharply rising mountain. Thinking the enemy had gone for good, Ibrahima felt it would be useless to chase them further.

"We could not see them," he would write later.

But against his better judgment, he decided to look for them. The horsemen dismounted at the foot of a hill and began the steep climb on foot. Halfway up the hill the Fula realized they had been lured into a trap! Ibrahima heard the rifles firing, saw the smoke from the powder and the men about him falling to the ground, screaming in agony. Some died instantly. Many horses, hit by the gunfire, thrashed about in pain and panic. The firing was coming from both sides, and Ibrahima ordered his men to the top of the hill, where they could, if time and Allah permitted it, try a charge using the speed and momentum of their remaining horses.

Ibrahima was among the first to mount and urge his animal onward. The enemy warriors came out of the forests, some with bows and arrows, others with muskets that he knew they had obtained from the Europeans. The courage of the Fula could not match the fury of the guns. Ibrahima called out to his men to save themselves, to flee as they could. Many tried to escape, rushing madly past the guns. Few survived.

Those who did clustered about their young leader, determined to make one last, desperate stand. Ibrahima was hit in the back by an arrow, but the aim was not true and the arrow merely cut his broad shoulder. Then something smashed against his head from the rear.

IBRAHIMA SENSED THAT THINGS WOULD NOT GO WELL FOR HIM.

The next thing Ibrahima knew was that he was choking. Then he felt himself being lifted from water. He tried to move his arms, but they had been fastened securely behind his back. He had been captured.

When he came to his full senses, he looked around him. Those of his noble cavalry who had not been captured were already dead. Ibrahima was unsteady on his legs as his clothes and sandals were stripped from him. The victorious Mandingo warriors now pushed him roughly into file with his men. They began the long trek that would lead them to the sea.

In Fouta Djallon, being captured by the enemy meant being forced to do someone else's bidding, sometimes for years. If you could get a message to your people, you could, perhaps, buy your freedom. Otherwise, it was only if you were well liked or if you married one of your captor's women that you would be allowed to go free or to live like a free person.

Ibrahima sensed that things would not go well for him.

The journey to the sea took weeks. Ibrahima was tied to other men, with ropes around their necks. Each day they walked from dawn to dusk. Those who were slow were knocked brutally to the ground. Some of those who could no longer walk were speared and left to die in agony. It was the lucky ones who were killed outright if they fell.

When they reached the sea, they remained bound hand and foot. There were men and women tied together. Small children clung to their mothers as they waited for the boats to come and the bargaining to begin.

BUT IT DIDN'T MATTER WHO WAS EVIL AND WHO WAS GOOD. IT ONLY MATTERED WHO HELD THE GUN.

Ibrahima, listening to the conversations of the men who held him captive, could understand those who spoke Arabic. These Africans were a low class of men, made powerful by the guns they had been given, made evil by the white man's goods. But it didn't matter who was evil and who was good. It only mattered who held the gun.

Ibrahima was inspected on the shore, then put into irons and herded into a small boat that took him out to a ship that was larger than any he had ever seen.

The ship onto which Ibrahima was taken was already crowded with black captives. Some shook in fear; others, still tied, fought by hurling their bodies at their captors.[6] The beating and the killing continued until the ones who were left knew that their lot was hopeless.

On board the ship there were more whites with guns, who shoved them toward the open hatch. Some of the Africans hesitated at the hatch, and were clubbed down and pushed below decks.

It was dark beneath the deck, and difficult to breathe. Bodies were pressed close against other bodies. In the section of the ship he was in, men prayed to various gods in various languages. It seemed that the whites would never stop pushing men into the already crowded space. Two sailors pushed the Africans into position so that each would lie in the smallest space possible. The sailors panted and sweated as they untied the men and then chained them to a railing that ran the length of the ship.

The ship rolled against its mooring as the anchor was lifted, and the journey began. The boards of the ship creaked and moaned as it lifted and fell in the sea. Some of the men got sick, vomiting upon themselves in the wretched darkness. They lay cramped, muscles aching, irons cutting into their legs and wrists, gasping for air.

Once a day they would be brought out on deck and made to jump about for exercise. They were each given a handful of either beans or rice cooked with yams, and water from a cask. The white sailors looked hardly better than the Africans, but it was they who held the guns.

Illness and the stifling conditions on the ships caused many deaths. How many depended largely on how fast the ships could be loaded with Africans and how long the voyage from Africa took. It was not unusual for 10 percent of the Africans to die if the trip took longer than the usual twenty-five to thirty-five days.

Ibrahima, now twenty-six years old, reached Mississippi in 1788. As the ship approached land, the Africans were brought onto the deck and fed. Some had oil put on their skins so they would look better; their sores were treated or covered with pitch.[7] Then they were given garments to wear in an obvious effort to improve their appearance.

Although Ibrahima could not speak English, he understood he was being bargained for. The white man who stood on the

---

6. **captor** (kap′tər), *n.* person who takes or holds a prisoner.

7. **pitch** (pich), *n.* thick, black, sticky substance made from tar or turpentine.

platform with him made him turn around, and several other white men neared him, touched his limbs, examined his teeth, looked into his eyes, and made him move about.

Thomas Foster, a tobacco grower and a hard-working man, had come from South Carolina with his family and had settled on the rich lands that took their minerals from the Mississippi River. He already held one captive, a young boy. In August 1788 he bought two more. One of them was named Sambo, which means "second son." The other was Ibrahima.

Foster agreed to pay $930 for the two Africans. He paid $150 down and signed an agreement to pay another $250 the following January and the remaining $530 in January of the following year.

When Ibrahima arrived at Foster's farm, he tried to find someone who could explain to the white man who he was—the son of a chief. He wanted to offer a ransom[8] for his own release, but Foster wasn't interested. He understood, perhaps from the boy whom he had purchased previously, that this new African was claiming to be an important person. Foster had probably never heard of the Fula or their culture; he had paid good money for the African, and wasn't about to give him up. Foster gave Ibrahima a new name: He called him Prince.

For Ibrahima there was confusion and pain. What was he to do? A few months before, he had been a learned man and a leader among his people. Now he was a captive in a strange land where he neither spoke the language nor understood the customs. Was he never to see him family again? Were his sons forever lost to him?

As a Fula, Ibrahima wore his hair long; Foster insisted that it be cut. Ibrahima's clothing had been taken from him, and his sandals. Now the last remaining symbol of his people, his long hair, had been taken as well.

He was told to work in the fields. He refused, and he was tied and whipped. The sting of the whip across his naked flesh was terribly painful, but it was nothing like the pain he felt within. The whippings forced him to work.

For Ibrahima this was not life, but a mockery of life. There was the waking in the morning and the sleeping at night; he worked, he ate, but this was not life. What was more, he could not see an end to it. It was this feeling that made him attempt to escape.

Ibrahima escaped to the backwoods regions of Natchez. He hid there, eating wild berries and fruit, not daring to show his face to any man, white or black. There was no telling who could be trusted. Sometimes he saw men with dogs and knew they were searching for runaways, perhaps him.

Where was he to run? What was he to do? He didn't know the country, he didn't know how far it was from Fouta Djallon or how to get back to his homeland. He could tell that this place was ruled by white men who held him in captivity. The other blacks he had seen were from all parts of Africa. Some he recognized by their tribal markings, some he did not. None were allowed to speak their native tongues around the white men. Some already knew nothing of the languages of their people.

As time passed, Ibrahima's despair deepened. His choices were simple. He could stay in the woods and probably die, or he could submit his body back into bondage.[9] There is no place in Islamic law for a man to take his own life. Ibrahima returned to Thomas Foster.

Foster still owed money to the man from whom he had purchased Ibrahima. The debt

---

8. **ransom** (ran′səm), *n.* price paid for a captive to be set free.
9. **bondage** (bon′dij), *n.* slavery; a being held against one's will under the control of another person.

⋀ *From the Fields* was painted by Anna Belle Lee Washington. What does this painting show about slavery?

would remain whether he still possessed the African or not. Foster was undoubtedly glad to see that the African had returned. Thin, nearly starving, Ibrahima was put to work.

Ibrahima submitted himself to the will of Thomas Foster. He was a captive, held in bondage not only by Foster but by the society in which he found himself. Ibrahima main-

tained his beliefs in the religion of Islam and kept its rituals as best he could. He was determined to be the same person he had always been: Abd al-Rahman Ibrahima of Fouta Djallon and of the proud Fula people.

By 1807 the area had become the Mississippi Territory. Ibrahima was forty-five and had been in bondage for twenty years.

During those years he met and married a woman whom Foster had purchased, and they began to raise a family. Fouta Djallon was more and more distant, and he had become resigned[10] to the idea that he would never see it or his family again.

Thomas Foster had grown wealthy and had become an important man in the territory. At forty-five Ibrahima was considered old. He was less useful to Foster, who now let the tall African grow a few vegetables on a side plot and sell them in town, since there was nowhere in the territory that the black man could go where he would not be captured by some other white man and returned.

It was during one of these visits to town that Ibrahima saw a white man who looked familiar. The smallish man walked slowly and with a limp. Ibrahima cautiously approached the man and spoke to him. The man looked closely at Ibrahima then spoke his name. It was Dr. Cox.

The two men shook hands, and Dr. Cox, who now lived in the territory, took Ibrahima to his home. John Cox had not prospered over the years, but he was still hopeful. He listened carefully as Ibrahima told his story— the battle near Fouta Djallon, the defeat, the long journey across the Atlantic Ocean, and finally his sale to Thomas Foster and the years of labor.

Dr. Cox and Ibrahima went to the Foster plantation. Meeting with Foster, he explained how he had met the tall black man. Surely, he reasoned, knowing that Ibrahima was of royal blood, Foster would free him? The answer was a firm but polite no. No amount of pleading would make Foster change his mind. It didn't matter that Dr. Cox had supported what Ibrahima had told Foster so many years before, that he was a prince. To Foster the man was merely his property.

Dr. Cox had to leave the man whose people had saved his life, but he told Ibrahima that he would never stop working for his freedom.

Andrew Marschalk, the son of a Dutch baker, was a printer, a pioneer in his field, and a man of great curiosity. By the time Marschalk heard about it, Cox had told a great many people in the Natchez district the story of African royalty being held in slavery in America. Marschalk was fascinated. He suggested that Ibrahima write a letter to his people, telling them of his whereabouts and asking them to ransom him. But Ibrahima had not been to his homeland in twenty years. The people there were still being captured by slave traders. He would have to send a messenger who knew the countryside and who knew the Fula. Where would he find such a man?

For a long time Ibrahima did nothing. Finally, some time after the death of Dr. Cox in 1816, Ibrahima wrote the letter that Marschalk suggested. He had little faith in the procedure but felt he had nothing to lose. Marschalk was surprised when Ibrahima appeared with the letter written neatly in Arabic. Since one place in Africa was the same as the next to Marschalk, he sent the letter not to Fouta Djallon but to Morocco.[11]

The government of Morocco did not know Ibrahima but understood from his letter that he was a Moslem. Moroccan officials, in a letter to President James Monroe, pleaded for the release of Ibrahima. The letter reached Henry Clay, the American secretary of state.

The United States had recently ended a bitter war with Tripoli[12] in North Africa and welcomed the idea of establishing good relations with Morocco, another North African country. Clay wrote to Foster about Ibrahima.

Foster resented the idea of releasing Ibrahima. The very idea that the government of Morocco had written to Clay and discussed a religion that Ibrahima shared with other

---

10. resigned (ri zīnd′), *adj.* accepting what comes without complaint.
11. **Morocco** (mə rok′ō).
12. **Tripoli** (trip′ə lē).

Africans gave Ibrahima a past that Foster had long denied, a past as honorable as Foster's. This idea challenged a basic premise[13] of slavery—a premise that Foster must have believed without reservation: that the Africans had been nothing but savages, with no humanity or human feelings, and therefore it was all right to enslave them. But after more letters and pressure from the State Department, Foster agreed to release Ibrahima if he could be assured that Ibrahima would leave the country and return to Fouta Djallon.

Many people who believed that slavery was wrong also believed that Africans could not live among white Americans. The American Colonization Society had been formed expressly to send freed Africans back to Africa. The society bought land, and a colony called Liberia[14] was established on the west coast of Africa. Foster was assured that Ibrahima would be sent there.

By then Ibrahima's cause had been taken up by a number of abolitionist[15] groups in the North as well as by many free Africans. They raised money to buy his wife's freedom as well.

On February 7, 1829, Ibrahima and his wife sailed on the ship *Harriet* for Africa. The ship reached Liberia, and Ibrahima now had to find a way to reach his people again. He never found that way. Abd al-Rahman Ibrahima died in Liberia in July 1829.

Who was Ibrahima? He was one of millions of Africans taken by force from their native lands. He was the son of a chief, a warrior, and a scholar. But to Ibrahima the only thing that mattered was that he had lost his freedom. If he had been a herder in Fouta Djallon, or an artist in Benin,[16] or a farmer along the Gambia,[17] it would have been same. Ibrahima was an African who loved freedom no less than other beings on earth. And he was denied that freedom.

---

13. premise (prem′is), *n.* a statement assumed to be true and used to draw a conclusion.
14. **Liberia** (lī bir′ē ə).
15. **abolitionist** (ab′ə lish′ə nist), *adj.* related to people or groups that favored the end of slavery.
16. **Benin** (be nēn′).
17. **Gambia** (gam′bē ə), a river that flows through West Africa.

After Reading

Making Connections

1. What words would you use to describe Ibrahima?

2. Fill in the last column of your K-W-L chart. What did you learn about Africa and slavery from reading this selection?

3. Do you agree with Ibrahima that his life in bondage was "but a mockery of life"? Explain.

4. Which parts of this selection did you think were most difficult to read? What did you do to help increase your understanding of these parts?

5. The author never called Ibrahima a slave. Why do you think he avoided using this word?

6. 👁 From Dr. Cox's **perspective,** slavery was unfair for Ibrahima because of his royal background. Do you think Ibrahima's bondage was more unfair than that of other slaves?

7. Reread the description of slavery in Fouta Djallon on page 493. How does this form of slavery compare with slavery in America? Do you think any form of slavery is fair? Explain.

Literary Focus: Theme

As you read "Ibrahima," you probably identified slavery as a central issue in the selection. What do you think was the author's message about slavery? The central message of a piece of writing is its **theme.** The theme is not usually directly stated in the selection itself. There is almost always more than one way to state the theme of a piece of writing.

Work with a partner to state the theme of "Ibrahima." Then share your theme statements with your class.

Vocabulary Study

The sentences below tell the story of another African. Choose the vocabulary word that best completes each sentence.

bondage
captor
premise
ransom
resigned

1. I based the ＿＿＿ that I would always have a comfortable life on the fact that my family was rich with cattle.

2. One day, an enemy of my father kidnapped me while I was washing clothes at the river. My ＿＿＿ took me far away to his village.

3. I pleaded that he ask my father to pay a ＿＿＿ for my release.

4. He handcuffed me and brought me to a ship, where I was placed in ＿＿＿ and forced to cook for the crew.

5. We sailed to a strange land with strange people, speaking a strange language. I was ＿＿＿ to the fact that I would never see my family or friends again.

Expressing Your Ideas

Writing Choices

My Fellow Countrymen Imagine you are Ibrahima about to write a **letter** to your countrymen announcing your arrival in Liberia. You haven't seen or heard from them and they have known nothing of you for the past thirty years. What will you share of your experience?

Here Lies Ibrahima Ibrahima died in Liberia in 1829 at sixty-seven years of age. Write an **epitaph** for Ibrahima—a brief summary of something important about his life, which you think he would most want to be remembered for. Write it as if it were for his tombstone, including the dates and places of his birth and death.

Other Options

This Is Your Life Make an illustrated **time line** that shows the events in the life of Ibrahima. Use the selection to find the dates when certain events occurred, including Ibrahima's birth, his capture, his arrival in North America, his meeting Dr. Cox, his leaving for Liberia, and his death. Use your time line to make a bulletin board display.

So, We Meet Again Work together with a group to create a **dialogue** between Ibrahima and Dr. Cox, when they said goodbye to one another in Africa and when they met again in Mississippi. Two different pairs of people can be actors, one pair acting out the scene in Africa and another pair acting out the scene in Mississippi. Perform your dialogue for the class.

Before Reading

Turtle's Race with Bear

as told by Joseph Bruchac

Joseph Bruchac
born 1942

Teaching English in West Africa, teaching creative writing to prison inmates in the United States, and writing poetry in his home in upstate New York are some of the experiences that have enriched Joseph Bruchac's life. He says that his goal in writing is to "share my insights into the beautiful and all too fragile world of human life and living things we have been granted." Of Native American ancestry, Bruchac has published several collections of Native American stories. One is *Iroquois Stories: Heroes and Heroines, Monsters and Magic,* from which "Turtle's Race with Bear" is taken.

Building Background

The Iroquois About 500 years ago, five Native American groups who lived in what is now upper New York State got together and made a pact to work together and form a common government. They were known as the Iroquois League. All the groups spoke related languages of the Iroquois-language family.

The Iroquois were hunters, gatherers, fishers, and farmers who paid close attention to nature. The stories they told often included animals of the lakes and forest. "Turtle's Race with Bear" is just one of many Iroquois folk tales.

Getting into the Story

Discussion As you can tell from the title, this folk tale has two main characters, a turtle and a bear. Based on what you know about these animals, what do you think these characters will be like? What do you think will happen in the race? Share your predictions with your classmates.

Reading Tip

Vivid Verbs In "Turtle's Race with Bear," the author develops the characters and the plot in just a few pages. He does this by using very descriptive verbs. These action words show not only what the characters are doing, but also what they are thinking, feeling, and wishing. Make a chart like the one below. As you read this story, write the information you get from the verbs the author chose.

Verb	What You Learn About the Character or Plot from This Verb
grumbled	the bear was cranky or unhappy

Turtle's Race with Bear **501**

Turtle's Race

Joseph Bruchac

It was an early winter, cold enough so that the ice had frozen on all the ponds and Bear, who had not yet learned in those days that it was wiser to sleep through the White Season, grumbled as he walked through the woods. Perhaps he was remembering a trick another animal had played on him; perhaps he was just not in a good mood.

It happened that he came to the edge of a great pond and saw Turtle there with his head sticking out of the ice.

"Hah," shouted Bear, not even giving his old friend a greeting. "What are you looking at, Slow One?"

Turtle looked at Bear. "Why do you call me slow?"

Bear snorted. "You are the slowest of the animals. If I were to race you, I would leave you far behind." Perhaps Bear did not remember that Turtle, like Coyote, is an animal whose greatest speed is in his wits.

"My friend," Turtle

with Bear

said, "let's have a race to see who is the swiftest."

"All right," said Bear. "Where will we race?"

"We will race here at this pond and the race will be tomorrow morning when the sun is the width of one hand above the horizon. You will run along the banks of the pond and I will swim in the water."

"How can that be?" Bear said. "There is ice all over the pond."

"We will do it this way," said Turtle. "I will make holes in the ice along the side of the pond and swim under the water to each hole and stick my head out when I reach it."

"I agree," said Bear. "Tomorrow we will race."

When the next day came, many of the other animals had gathered to watch. They lined the banks of the great pond and watched Bear as he rolled in the snow and jumped up and down making himself ready.

Finally, just as the sun was a hand's width in the sky, Turtle's head popped out of the hole in the ice at the starting line. "Bear," he called, "I am ready."

Bear walked quickly to the starting place and as soon as the signal was given, he rushed forward, snow flying from his feet and his breath making great white clouds above his head. Turtle's head disappeared in the first hole and then in almost no time at all reappeared from the next hole, far ahead of Bear.

"Here I am, Bear," Turtle called. "Catch up to me!" And then he was gone again. Bear was astonished and ran even faster. But before he could reach the next hole, he saw Turtle's green head pop out of it.

"Here I am, Bear," Turtle called again. "Catch up to me!" Now bear began to run in earnest. His sides were puffing in and out as he ran and his eyes were becoming bloodshot, but it was no use. Each time, long before he would reach each of the holes, the ugly green head of Turtle would be there ahead of him, calling out to him to catch up!

When Bear finally reached the finish line, he was barely able to crawl. Turtle was waiting there for him, surrounded by all the other animals. Bear had lost the race. He dragged himself home in disgrace, so tired that he fell asleep as soon as he reached his home. He was so tired that he slept until the warm breath of Spring came to the woods again.

It was not long after Bear and all the other animals had left the pond that Turtle tapped on the ice with one long claw. At his signal a dozen ugly heads just like his popped up from the holes all along the edge of the pond. It was Turtle's cousins and brothers, all of whom looked just like him!

"My relatives," Turtle said, "I wish to thank you. Today we have shown Bear that it does not pay to call other people names. We have taught him a good lesson."

Turtle smiled and a dozen other turtles, all just like him, smiled back. "And we have shown the other animals," Turtle said, "that Turtles are not the slowest of the animals."

◄ *Daydreamer—Grizzly Bear* was sculpted by Dan Ostermiller. Predict what a sleeping bear might have to do with the story.

After Reading

Making Connections

1. Were your predictions about the characters and the race correct? Explain.

2. How do the verbs the author uses give you information about each of the characters?

3. Suppose you were judging the race. Would you allow turtle to win? Explain.

Literary Focus: Blending Folk Tales and Fables

"Turtle's Race with Bear" is an Iroquois folk tale. However, it also includes elements of a fable. Read the characteristics of each kind of story shown in the diagram below. Then, reread "Turtle's Race with Bear." What characteristics of folk tales does this story have? What characteristics of fables does it have? Copy the diagram and fill in the middle section.

Folk Tales
- Are traditional tales that have been passed down within a culture for centuries
- Have very fast-moving plots
- Have simple characters that are animal or human
- Are usually told by a narrator who is not one of the characters
- Often explain something in nature

Turtle's Race with Bear

Fables
- Are short, simple stories
- Have animal characters with human traits
- Are usually told by a narrator who is not one of the characters
- Have conflicts that are resolved quickly
- Usually teach a lesson
- Have a moral that is clearly stated at the end

Expressing Your Ideas

Retelling for Children Imagine that you are a children's book writer. Rewrite "Turtle's Race with Bear" in simple language for young children. Prepare your story as a **picture book** with one or two sentences on each page and lots of room for a large picture. Then illustrate each page.

Scandal Uncovered Bear awoke in the spring and discovered how Turtle was able to win. Interview Bear about the race. Conduct a talk show kind of **interview** with another student acting as Bear before a "studio audience" of your classmates.

Language Mini-Lesson

Varying Sentence Structure

Using Phrases and Subordinate Clauses You can make your writing more interesting by varying sentence structure. One way to do this is by using phrases and clauses in different positions.

Notice how the structure of these sentences changes when phrases and subordinate clauses are moved.

- Three shops were having sidewalk sales **across the street.**

- **Across the street,** three shops were having sidewalk sales.

- Three shops **across the street** were having sidewalk sales.

- **When the storm hit,** we all took shelter in the basement.

- We all took shelter in the basement **when the storm hit.**

Writing Strategy If you notice that all of your sentences have the same structure, you can vary them by moving phrases or subordinate clauses to different positions.

Activity Options

1. Review the selections to find examples of sentences with phrases and clauses. Copy at least three examples of each and keep this list in your writing portfolio.

2. Look over your past writing assignments to find paragraphs you could improve by varying the sentence structure. Rewrite one or two of these paragraphs and keep the new versions in your working portfolio.

3. On separate slips of paper, write at least five sentences that have a phrase or subordinate clause. Mix your slips of paper with those of some classmates. Take turns drawing sentences out of the pile, and reading them aloud both as they appear on the slips of paper and with the phrase or clause moved to a different position.

What's Fair, What's Not

Within the Law

History Connection

Societies have always needed laws to determine what is fair and what is not. Justice and peace result when people learn to live within the law. The development of writing systems for the first time enabled people to assemble formal codes of law. The earliest known examples were written by ancient societies in the Middle East.

HOW THE LAW CAME ABOUT

This Babylonian cuneiform from Istanbul, Turkey, recorded Hammurabi's Code in 1790 B.C. Hammurabi's Code is one of the earliest written collections of laws. King Hammurabi based his code of laws on some earlier Sumerian and Akkadian laws, but he added his own interpretation. The Babylonian king stressed justice for all, including conquered nations. He promised that "the strong shall not oppress the weak."

Solomon, who lived around 960 B.C., is known as Israel's wisest king. According to the Bible, God appeared to the young king at the beginning of his reign and asked Solomon what he wanted. Solomon replied that he wanted only an understanding heart so that he would rule with wisdom and justice. Solomon was consulted on matters of law and justice not only by his own people, but by rulers from distant lands.

The imperial dynastic system of Chinese government and law began in 221 B.C. and remained intact until it was overthrown in 1911. In the more than two thousand years of its existence, specific dynasties were overturned and at times foreign invaders ruled, but the imperial dynastic system remained strong. Even invaders such as the fourteenth-century Mongols were largely absorbed into the Chinese system of culture and law.

The most thorough and complex system of law in the ancient world was created by the Romans. Developed over a period of several centuries, the Romans held their legal system in high esteem. Here the great conquering ruler, Emperor Trajan, who reigned from A.D. 98 to 117, accompanies his troops to war. Copies of Roman laws were taken into battle so that the Romans could impose their system on conquered peoples.

Members of the English upper class forced King John to sign the *Magna Carta*, or Great Charter, in 1215. Although the upper classes gained many rights, the Magna Carta did little to better the lives of the common people. However, in later years, the document became a model for countries, including the United States and Canada, that wanted to create a democratic government with rights for all.

A French court, *Cour de Comptes*, sits in session. Under the Emperor Napoleon, a civil code of law was created in 1804. It has been adapted and used as the basis for law in most European countries and in Latin America. Under Napoleon's law, for the first time, all people were judged as equal, and all class privileges were eliminated.

Responding

Does your school have a code of law—a set of rules and guidelines that all students must follow? Find a copy of those laws. They may be in a student handbook. Review the laws. Do they seem reasonable and fair? If some do not, discuss how you might work within the school system to make changes.

Health Connection

Justice is an issue in all walks of life. What's fair and what's not is as important to you as it is to a judge and jury. There are some ways you can take control of your situation. You can work toward making a just environment for you and your classmates.

Talk It

Mediation Referral Form

Date _____

Name of Disputant _____

Name of Disputant _____

Type of dispute:
- ☐ Fight
- ☐ Rumor
- ☐ Harassment
- ☐ Boyfriend-girlfriend
- ☐ Racial
- ☐ Other

Referral Source:
- ☐ Teacher
- ☐ Counselor
- ☐ Administrator
- ☐ Student
- ☐ Self

Comments:
_____
_____
_____
_____
_____
_____
_____
_____

* TURN IN TO SECRETARY IN N
* A MEDIATION SESSION WILL

Talking to others about your feelings is a good idea—not just at home or with your family. Mediation centers are popping up all over. Adults who are having problems with each other can come and talk with someone who will listen and help them work out an answer.

Many schools—elementary, middle, and high—are doing the same thing. Students at the school volunteer to become mediators. They are taught good communication and listening skills. Then they practice with each other, learning how to help settle problems. The students learn to work together in pairs when mediating a problem.

If two students are having a problem with each other, they can fill out a form to set up a time to meet with the student mediators. Sometimes a teacher or another friend may suggest they talk with a mediator. At the meeting, the student mediators will let both persons take turns telling their side of the problem. The mediators will ask questions

Peer Mediation Application

Name

Advisory Teach   rade   Date

I think me

Mediation Contract

Date

_____

dent

dent

iation:
lem

ent

to try to help the students say how they feel so the other person will better understand them. Finally, the mediators help the students think of ways to fix the problem. They write down the ideas in a contract that says exactly what each person agrees to do, and everybody signs it. Sometimes there will be another meeting with the mediators to see how things worked out.

Lots of students think this is a great idea. They find it easier to talk to other kids than to adults and feel that kids like them can better understand how they feel. Many say that they like the feeling that they can handle problems on their own without adults stepping in. With a little bit of help, they find ways to understand another person's point of view—and learn that they can find ways to satisfy both people. Most important, through mediation students have a chance to put angry feelings into words rather than fighting—and that's good for everyone.

Responding
Discuss the situation in your school. Does mediation sound like a good idea? Do you think it would work? Why or why not? If you think it is a good idea, bring up the issue at your next class or student council meeting.

Reading Mini-Lesson

Summarizing

Let's say you are the architect hired to design a new school. You need to make drawings and construct a model of what the new building will look like. Since your drawings and model can't be the actual size of the building you design, you will have to make *scale* drawings and build a *scale* model. A scale model is a miniature that shows length and width and height in the same proportions as will be found in the actual building.

When you write a summary of an article, you are making a scale model of the ideas of the article. The summary can't be as long as the article, but it should include the same ideas as the article, only in a shorter form.

A summary must include the main idea—the most important point the writer makes about the topic. A summary should also include all important details in the selection. Nothing else should be included. If the summary is only 10 percent of the original, it needs to be the most essential 10 percent.

Below are some steps to take in constructing a summary.

- Get firmly in mind the topic—what the selection is *about*. For example, in the article "Talk It Out" on page 508, "Mediation" is the main topic.

- Find and list the main points the author makes about the topic. For example, "Mediation works for adults." "Mediation works for students."

- Look back at your list of main points. Write a summary of two or three sentences that include all the main points.

Activity Options

1. Working with a partner, follow the steps above and write a summary of the article on page 508.

2. Working with a partner, follow the steps above and write a summary of a newspaper article.

Writing Workshop

Convincing the Jury

Assignment You've read selections that deal with fair and unfair treatment. Imagine that one of these characters is being tried by a jury for his or her actions. Write the final argument in which you try to convince the jury of the character's guilt or innocence. See the Writer's Blueprint for details.

WRITER'S BLUEPRINT

Product	A persuasive essay
Purpose	To convince a jury a character is guilty or innocent
Audience	The jury
Specs	As the writer of a successful essay, you should:

❑ Begin by stating what the character is accused of and hooking the jury.

❑ Go on to clearly state your position.

❑ Then discuss point by point how the character's actions in the story support your opinion.

❑ Next, discuss other factors which you think will convince the jury, such as the actions of other characters in the story.

❑ Conclude by restating your position and the main points of the argument.

❑ Follow the rules for correct grammar, usage, spelling, and mechanics. Be careful not to confuse adjectives and adverbs.

The instructions that follow should lead you to a successful essay.

STEP **1** PREWRITING

Chart characters' actions. At least one character in each selection could be charged with a crime and tried in court. Determine who these characters are and the crimes they could be charged with by completing a chart similar to this one.

Character	Actions	Possible Crime
Mrs. Morales	Suggests that spoiled food be fed to a dog	Cruelty to animals

In the Literary Source, Nicholasa Mohr shows the results of Mrs. Morales's actions.

Choose a character to defend or prosecute. Review your chart and select the character who most interests you. Review the actions of that character. Do you believe he or she is innocent or guilty? Cluster details about the character's actions and how he or she acted afterward. Your cluster might be similar to this one.

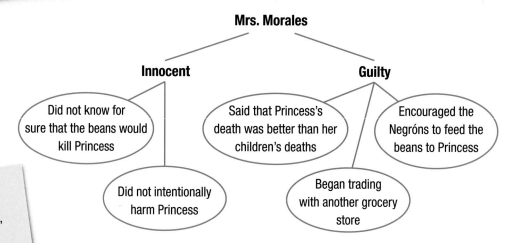

Mrs. Morales

Innocent
- Did not know for sure that the beans would kill Princess
- Did not intentionally harm Princess

Guilty
- Said that Princess's death was better than her children's deaths
- Encouraged the Negróns to feed the beans to Princess
- Began trading with another grocery store

OR . . .
Instead of doing a chart to clarify your argument, you might want to skip ahead to "Try a quickwrite."

Try a quickwrite. After you have added to your chart, take a few minutes to write down details about the guilt or innocence of your character. How do the character's actions in the story support your opinion? How do the actions of the other characters influence your opinion? Here is part of one student's quickwrite.

It's completely unfair that Don Osvaldo blamed Mrs. Morales for Princess's death. He and his wife knew those beans were bad, but they were too cheap to give Mrs. Morales another can. Feeding them to Princess was just stupid. Don Osvaldo and his wife should have admitted they were wrong and given Mrs. Morales another can.

STUDENT MODEL

Plan your argument. Use your quickwrite and your charts to help you organize your argument. You might use a chart similar to this one.

Introductory statement:
Paragraph A Main Idea: Evidence: My Thoughts: This thought leads to the next main idea because:
Paragraph B Main Idea: Evidence: My Thoughts: This thought leads to the next main idea because:
Paragraph C Main Idea: Evidence: My Thoughts: This thought leads to the next main idea because:
Conclusion:

Ask a partner: *How is my plan working?*

✔ Do I state my opinion clearly?

✔ Is my argument for guilt or innocence convincing?

Use your partner's comments to help you revise your plan.

STEP **2** DRAFTING

Before you write, review your quickwrite, charts, cluster, and any other notes you have made. Remember that you are addressing the jury. Think of yourself as the defense attorney or the prosecuting attorney. What tone will you use with the jury?

As you draft, concentrate on getting your ideas on paper. Look ahead to the Revising Strategy for ways to get your reader's attention immediately. Here are some ideas for getting started.

• Begin with a quick review of the alleged crime.

• Ask whether the jury believes in your client's guilt or innocence.

• Begin with your opinion and set about to support it.

Ask your partner for comments on your draft before you revise it.

✔ Does my opener draw my reader into the argument?

✔ Have I followed the specs in the Writer's Blueprint?

✔ Have I clearly stated why the jury should find the character guilty or innocent?

✔ Have I fully supported my claim of guilt or innocence with ample evidence?

Revising Strategy

Hooking the Jury

There are many ways to hook your audience at the very beginning of a piece of writing. You might try one of the following.

- Begin with an unusual statement.

- Begin with a question that is later answered in the writing.

- Begin with an exciting moment that makes the reader want to continue reading.

In the Literary Source, which method does Nicholasa Mohr use to hook her readers?

Notice how the writer of the passage below revised to include an unusual statement and a question as hooks.

> **LITERARY SOURCE**
> "'Can I take Princess for a walk later?' Judy asked. 'Please, Don Osvaldo?'
> 'We'll see . . . later,' Don Osvaldo said. 'Let me finish now with your order.'"
> from "Princess" by Nicholasa Mohr

Shouldn't a grocer know when a can of beans has spoiled?
~~Mrs. Morales is innocent in the death of Don Osvaldo's dog, Princess,~~
~~and the charges against her should be dropped.~~ *for Princess's death* If anyone is to blame, it is

Don Osvaldo and Doña Nereida. When food is spoiled, it smells. Yet these

two chose to ignore that and feed spoiled beans to an innocent dog.

Ask a partner to review your revised draft before you edit. When you edit, watch for errors in grammar, usage, spelling, and mechanics. Pay special attention to confusing adjectives and adverbs.

Editing Strategy

Confusing Adjectives and Adverbs

Do you sometimes confuse adjectives and adverbs in your writing? Adjectives modify nouns and pronouns. Adverbs modify verbs, adjectives, and other adverbs. Below are pairs of easily confused adjectives and adverbs. To use them correctly, be sure you know what kind of word you want to modify.

FOR REFERENCE . . .
More rules for adjectives and adverbs are listed in the Language and Grammar Handbook.

Adjective	Adverb
good	well
bad	badly
scarce	scarcely
slow	slowly
quick	quickly
sure	surely
real	really
lone	lonely

Notice how the writer of the draft below paid attention to correct use of adjectives and adverbs.

It's obvious that Mrs. Morales is not to blame. She knew that the beans were spoiled. The can was dented and swollen and the beans smelled ~~badly~~ *bad*. Don Osvaldo and his wife were ~~real~~ *really* stupid to feed them to their dog. They had to know the beans would make her sick.

STUDENT MODEL

5 PRESENTING

Here are two ideas for presenting your essay.

- Have a mock trial. Locate a student who wrote an opposing view of the same character. Present your arguments to the class as if they were closing arguments in a trial. Ask the jury to decide whether the character is guilty or innocent.

- Ask a family member to read the selection your essay is based on. Then share your essay. Do you agree or disagree?

6 LOOKING BACK

Self-evaluate. What grade would you give your paper? Look back at the Writer's Blueprint and evaluate yourself on each point, from 6 (superior) down to 1 (weak).

Reflect. Think about what you learned from writing your persuasive essay as you write answers to these questions.

✔ Do you still believe your character is guilty or innocent? Why or why not?

✔ Do you think the language used by an attorney can lead the jury to agree with him or her? Explain.

For Your Working Portfolio: Add your argument and your reflection responses to your working portfolio.

Beyond Print

Looking at Images

Many people say "A picture is worth a thousand words." Pictures can reveal emotions and situations that are hard to put in words. Look at the picture below. You may already have ideas about what has happened. Do any of the questions at the left come to mind?

Questions

Why is one girl crying?

Was she teased?

Did she miss a very important shot?

Is the basketball important?

Are the girls friends?

Are the girls helping each other?

Is one girl physically hurt or emotionally hurt?

Turning Pictures into Words

Make up a story about the picture. You can tell the story from the point of view of one of the girls in the picture. Or you can use a narrator. You can use the picture as the first scene in your story or as the last scene. You may want to use answers to some of the questions at the left to shape your story.

Activities

1. Draw several scenes from your story. Which do you think tells the story better—your words or your pictures?

2. Look at the picture again. If you think someone was cruel to one of the girls, what could she or the other girl do to get justice? Draw a picture of the solution.

Projects for Collaborative Study

Theme Connection

Why Us? Almost everyone is prejudiced against something. Suppose all of the sixth graders in your school were bullied and humiliated by seventh and eighth graders What would you do to fight that prejudice? How would you prove that you were the same as everyone else?

■ Make a list of things that might happen to you. For example, you might have to wait until all the upperclassmen got water before you could use the drinking fountain.

■ As a group, decide how you would fight this type of prejudice. Write a plan showing the steps you would take.

Literature Connection

The Plot Thickens In this unit, many selections contain a **plot**, which is a series of events selected by the author to present and bring about the resolution of some conflict. In "Southpaw," the conflict of Janet not playing baseball is resolved when a series of mishaps leaves Richard without a baseball team. Choose two or three selections in the unit and, in a small group, discuss what series of events led to the resolution of each conflict.

■ As a group, choose a selection from this unit and together write a new series of events but keep the resolution the same.

Life Skills Connection

Responsibilities and Privileges When you were three years old, there were many things you were not allowed to do. As your abilities increased, you were given certain personal and household responsibilities. Imagine you are back in the first grade. What are you expected to do in your home and school on a regular basis? What rewards do you receive for doing these things?

■ Now move forward in time to the present. What new responsibilities do you have at school, home, or elsewhere?

■ Now, project yourself into the future as a senior in high school. What new responsibilities do you have at school, home, or elsewhere? What privileges do you have?

■ As a class, discuss the connection between responsibilities and privileges.

ℰ Multicultural Connection

Seeing Eye to Eye In your **interactions** with friends, classmates, and family members, you have probably discovered that others do not have the same **perspective** or point of view that you have on certain topics.

■ With your classmates, look at local newspapers for situations in your community in which two people or groups have different perspectives on an issue. The editorial page is a good place to start. Some students should study one perspective while others study another perspective. Discuss the differences in opinions and whether compromises can be made.

Read More About Justice

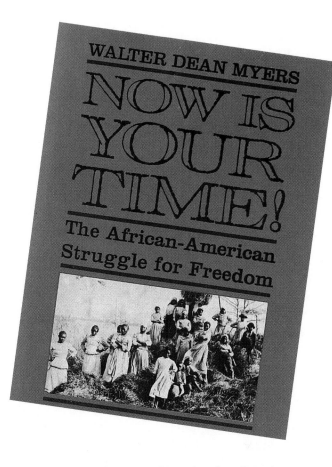

Number the Stars (1989) by Lois Lowry. During World War II, Annemarie's quick thinking saves her family and friends from being captured by the Nazis.

Now Is Your Time!: The African-American Struggle for Freedom (1991) by Walter Dean Myers. Through biographical and narrative accounts, Myers shows how African Americans were instrumental in shaping the history of the United States.

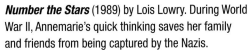

More Good Books

The Well (1995) by Mildred D. Taylor. Tensions between a white teenager and a black teenager run high when they both have to share water from the well of the black teenager's family.

Listen for the Singing (1977) by Jean Little. After Anna and her family moved to Canada from Germany at the beginning of World War II, she experienced prejudice because of her impaired vision and her German heritage.

I Have a Dream: The Life and Words of Martin Luther King, Jr. (1992) by Jim Haskins. This biography is set apart from many others because it includes mostly King's own words.

Untold Tales (1992) by William J. Brooke. Justice, often the theme in fairy tales, takes on new meaning with this collection of contemporary retellings of such classics as "Beauty and the Beast" and "Snow White."

Conflict and Resolution

Facing the Problem Head-On
Part One, pages 524–568

Finding Solutions
Part Two, pages 569–623

"Serenade" (detail), by Christian Pierre.

Talking About
CONFLICT
AND
RESOLUTION

People encounter problems every day. Some problems are more difficult to solve than others. To face a problem head on usually involves a difficult choice. However, finding a solution to a problem is better than leaving it unresolved.

Notice how the comments from students across the country match the ideas in the literature you are about to read.

> 66 **I wish my parents and I could agree.** 99
>
> Lars–
> Parkersburg, WV

"You can't go out in public like that!"

from "The All-American Slurp" by Lensey Namioka, page 583

"Problems sometimes occur when you don't tell the truth."

Rebecca–Asland, KY

Fausto looked at the bill and knew he was in trouble. . . . How could he have been so deceitful?

from "The No-Guitar Blues" by Gary Soto, page 575

This is my last warning that if you don't immediately send a tadpole in a bottle kit to our home, I shall contact the Better Business Bureau.

from "The Empty Box" by Johanna Hurwitz, page 528

"Can a conflict be completely resolved?"

Dillon–Cranston, RI

Arabian Manuscript (detail, A.D. 1350)

"Parents often know best even when we don't want to admit it."

Mei–Sandy, VT

I'm not going to punish you, . . . This is too bad for a whipping to settle. But I want you to think about today.

from "Christmas Hunt" by Borden Deal, page 542

Part One

Facing the Problem Head-On

Everyone has problems, but people handle them in different ways. Some people close their eyes, and hope that the problem will just go away. Most of the time, though, problems have to be solved.

In the selections that follow, characters charge head-on into their problems. Unfortunately the problem is not always solved. Sometimes the would-be problem solver has nothing to show for the effort except the satisfaction of having made a valiant try.

Multicultural Connection When people attempt to solve problems, they are hoping to bring about **change** in a situation. As you read these selections, look for changes that occur when people of different backgrounds come to understand each other better.

Before Reading

The Empty Box

by Johanna Hurwitz

Johanna Hurwitz
born 1937

By age ten, Johanna Hurwitz knew she wanted to be both a librarian and a writer. Her love of books and writing inspired her to create about forty books for young people—and hundreds of letters addressed to friends and relatives. "When I write a letter," she says, "it is usually long and has bits of conversation and perhaps a humorous incident or two recorded in it. I am sure the letter writing that I do has been the best type of training for my book writing."

Building Background

Sincerely Yours Why do people write letters? In general, letter writers have the same purposes that book authors do: to inform, to persuade, and/or to entertain. The letters you write to keep in touch with friends and family are personal, or informal, letters. The letters written by people in business, government, and other organizations are business, or formal, letters. Individuals write business letters too: for example, to ask for information, to offer an opinion or suggestion, or to make a complaint about a product, service, or situation.

Getting into the Story

Discussion In a small group, talk about times when you were a dissatisfied customer. Why were you dissatisfied? What did you do to express your dissatisfaction to someone who could do something about it? What were the results? If you had it to do over again, what might you do differently?

Reading Tip

Charting Events "The Empty Box" is actually a series of thirteen letters written by six different people. To keep from getting confused, copy the chart below. As you read each letter in the story, record the appropriate information under the headings. Then use the chart to remind yourself of previous events.

Date of letter	Who wrote the letter	Summary or purpose of the letter
February 17	Mrs. Peacock	

The Empty Box

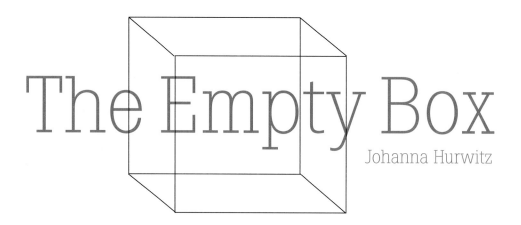

Johanna Hurwitz

February 17

Natures Wonder & Co.
To Whom It May Concern:

Two weeks ago I ordered the "tadpole in a bottle" kit advertised in your catalog. The package arrived yesterday, just in time for my son Jason's twelfth birthday, which was today. I didn't open your package to check it. Why should I? I had no reason to suspect that the tadpole wouldn't be inside. I covered your brown cardboard box with gift wrap and presented it to Jason this morning.

Jason ripped the paper off the box with great anticipation. He pulled out all the Styrofoam popcorn that was inside. The kitchen floor was covered with that awful stuff, but as it was Jason's birthday, I didn't scold him. However, within a minute the whole family stood ankle deep in the Styrofoam, and it was clear that there had been a packing error on your part. There was no bottle, with or without a tadpole, inside the package. You sent an empty box!

Of course Jason was very disappointed. It's a mean trick to give an empty box to a child on his birthday. I've explained to Jason that you must have accidentally forgotten to include his bottle and that you will ship it to him immediately. I tried phoning your 800 number all afternoon, but the line has been busy. I assume that this means your business is booming and not that your phone was off the hook. I would never have guessed so many people wanted to own tadpoles. Jason is anxiously awaiting his bottle.

Sincerely,
Lillian Peacock
(Jason's mother)

February 22

Dear Valued Customer:
  We regret the slight delay in sending the article you ordered.
  Please expect it within the next four to six weeks.

Natures Wonder & Co.

February 23

Natures Wonder & Company

Dear Sirs:

Re: Tadpole in a bottle kit #574-10937

Some time ago, my wife ordered a tadpole kit from your firm. Your company sent an empty box to our home. It had been ordered for our son's birthday, and we shared his upset that he had been given an empty box on this special occasion.

On February 17th, my wife wrote to complain about this error. Today, another package came from your company. Jason opened it

▲ Do you think the Assistant Sales Manager of Natures Wonder & Company felt like the man in this picture?

eagerly. We were both distressed[1] that he was faced with a second disappointment. You sent him an empty bottle! Had there been liquid in the bottle, we might have suspected that the infant tadpole was so tiny that the human eye could not yet see it. However, the bottle was totally empty. No tadpole could have existed in it.

I insist that you air-express a replacement kit to our address at once.

Yours truly,
A. Peacock

February 28

Dear Sir:

I regret to inform you that Natures Wonder & Company cannot supply you with a peacock or its eggs. However, if you consult the enclosed catalog you will see that we have chicken and duck eggs at very reasonable prices. In fact, there is an *early spring special* of twelve fertilized chicken eggs at half the usual cost.

Please fill out the enclosed order form or place your order by calling our 800 number.

We are glad to be of service to you.

Sincerely,
Ellen George
Asst. Sales Manager

P.S. We are <u>negotiating</u>[2] with a new <u>distributor</u>[3] and hope in the future to also be able to supply turtle eggs.

---

1. distressed (distrest′), *adj.* sad or anxious.
2. negotiate (ni gō′shē āt), *v.* talk over and arrange terms; consult.
3. distributor (dis trib′yə tər), *n.* person or company that sells goods to a particular market, usually other companies.

March 1

Natures Wonder & Co.
Dear Mr. Natures,

When my class studied about writing letters, I told my teacher Mrs. Shea that all my friends lived nearby. I didn't think I would ever have to bother writing a real letter. Mrs. Shea said everyone needs to write a letter at some time or other. I guess she is right because now I am writing to you.

My birthday was on February 17. It was a pretty good day. I got some neat stuff, and Mom made my favorite dinner, which is sloppy joes. The present I most wanted and kept talking about was a tadpole in a bottle kit. I really was hoping to get it. When I opened my presents I saved the biggest package for last, because I was sure that the tadpole in a bottle would be inside.

Well guess what? The box was empty (unless you count all that junk you put in a package to keep the stuff inside from breaking). My dog got sick eating all that plastic stuff. But that's not the worst thing. I am worried about my tadpole. Where is it? It wasn't in the empty bottle you sent either.

Please look for it at your company and send it to my home right away. I want to watch the tadpole turn into a frog. If you don't hurry it will be too late.

Your friend,
Jason Peacock

March 2

Natures Wonder & Company
To Whom It May Concern:

Since you have still not sent the "tadpole in a bottle" kit that I ordered more than a month ago, I am forced to write to you again. Let me remind you, I am the mother of the twelve-year-old boy who thought he was getting a "tadpole in a bottle" for his birthday. My son has been very disappointed, not only because he did not receive this gift but because of your carelessness—sending an empty package to our home.

Jason is quite mature for his age, and he understands that no one is perfect. I told him that his frog, I mean tadpole, will be arriving any day now. But am I right? Please don't make a liar out of me. Restore a young boy's faith, and send the "tadpole in a bottle" kit to our home at once.

Thank you for taking care of this.

Sincerely,
Lillian Peacock
(Mrs. Andrew Peacock)

March 5

Natures Wonder & Co.
Dear Ms. Ellen George:
Re: Tadpole in a bottle kit #574-10937

This is my last warning that if you don't immediately send a tadpole in a bottle kit to our home, I shall contact the Better Business Bureau.[4] I hate to think how many other people, in addition to my young son, have been disappointed by the inefficient[5] packaging done by your company. I don't know why you think I would want to order chicken eggs from you. They are easily available by the dozen at my local supermarket.

Yours truly,
A. Peacock

March 7

Dear Valued Customer:
    We regret the slight delay in sending the article you ordered.
    Please expect it within the next four to six weeks.

Natures Wonder & Co.

---

4. **Better Business Bureau**, a nonprofit corporation organized by businesses to protect the public from unfair advertising and business practices.

5. inefficient (in′ə fish′ənt), *adj.* wasteful; incompetent.

March 8

Dear Mr. Peacock:

I am responding to your letter of March 5th, which was addressed to Ms. Ellen George. Unfortunately, Ms. George no longer works here at Natures Wonder & Company. I have been promoted to her job and hope that I will be able to take care of any problems that you have.

As you know, the goal of Natures Wonder & Company is to bring the wealth and glory of the natural world into the average home. Our company specializes[6] in selling live animals, as well as numerous products such as jewelry and clothing that take their design from the animal form.

I understand that you are interested in frogs. To this end, I have underlined in red ink all those items in our catalog that were inspired by these charming creatures. You may be especially interested in the pair of coffee mugs shaped like frogs on page 17 of our catalog. The mugs come in frog green or toad brown and hold eight ounces of beverage. The ceramic exteriors of the mugs resemble the scales on the skin of these wonderful amphibians.

In view of the problems you seem to have had when ordering from our company in the past, I wish to extend to you a one-time-only discount of 10% when you order these mugs.

> Sincerely,
> Marilyn Pippin
> Asst. Sales Manager
> Natures Wonder & Company

March 10

Natures Wonder & Co.

Dear Mr. Wonder:

I was supposed to get a tadpole in a bottle kit for my birthday last month. I have been waiting for it for a long time. I'm worried that if you don't hurry and send it to my home, the tadpole will already be a frog. Then I won't be able to watch how it grows. I heard it was a very educational experience and I don't want to miss it.

Please hurry and send my tadpole.

> Your friend,
> Jason Peacock

P.S. How does the frog get out of the bottle?

March 11

Natures Wonder & Company

Attention: Marilyn Pippin

Congratulations on your promotion. However, if I were you, I'd look for a job at another company. For the past month, my wife and I have written to your company repeatedly. We are not interested in peacock, chicken, or duck eggs. We certainly do not want drinking mugs that resemble frogs or toads.

On February 2nd, my wife ordered a "tadpole in a bottle" kit for our son as a birthday present. First we received an empty box. Then we received an empty bottle. Is it too much to expect a box with a tadpole in a bottle to arrive before our son's next birthday?

I have threatened before to inform the Better Business Bureau about the sloppy manner in which your firm conducts its operation. Please know that I am sending them a duplicate copy of this letter. I do not want other children to have the same disappointment on their birthday that my son had.

> Yours truly,
> A. Peacock

---

6. **specialize** (spesh′ə līz), *v.* pursue some special branch of work, study, etc.

How would you feel if you received these frogs in the mail?

March 18

Dear Mr. Peacock,

I know you will be disappointed to hear that Natures Wonder & Company has decided to discontinue shipping live tadpoles in bottles to its customers. We now plan to limit our stock to stuffed frogs (made out of cloth, not real frog), ceramic frogs, frog posters, and a large and unusual stone frog, which can be used as a garden seat.

In view of the problems you have had in the past weeks in trying to obtain a "tadpole in a bottle" kit for your son, I have arranged that the company ship all remaining stock of such bottles to your address. I'm sorry they won't arrive in time for your son's birthday—either this year's or next—but I know that young boys are delighted to get gifts at any time of the year.

Most sincerely,
Marilyn Pippin
Sales Manager
Natures Wonder

April 1

Natures Wonder & Co.

Dear Mr. Natures Wonder,

This has been the best day of my life. It's spring break so I was home from school when the United Parcel truck came to my house this morning. The driver brought two big boxes, and they were addressed to *me*. Then he went back to his truck and brought two more. All together there were twenty-four boxes!

Underneath those plastic pieces that you put in the boxes to keep the stuff inside from breaking was a tadpole in the bottle kit in each box. I never dreamed I would ever own twenty-four tadpoles. The tadpoles were pretty big. In fact, they were practically frogs. They had legs and feet and only the tiniest bit of tail left. It's too bad that I missed watching them grow up, but I don't care. It's great to have twenty-four frogs.

My friend Allan came over to my house, and very, very carefully, we broke the bottles so that the frogs could get out. At the moment they are all in my bathtub hopping about. I'm not sure how we are going to get washed. I think if we all took showers without using any soap it will work out fine.

Thanks a lot for sending all the frogs. I know I'm going to learn a lot just watching them.

Your friend,

Jason Peacock

P.S. Do dogs eat frogs? I hope not.
P.P.S. If my mother says I can't keep them all, I'm going to give them to my friends as birthday surprises.

Good morning.
          Hmm.
Nice day.
          Dim.
Sorry.
          Glad.
Hadn't.
          Had.
Go.
          Stay.
          Work.
Play.

Pro.
          Con.
Off.
          On.
Front.
          Back.
          Taut.
Slack.
Open.
          Shut.
And.
          But.

Over.
          Under.
Cloudless.
          Thunder.
Detour.
          Highway.
New way.
          Thruway.
Byway . . . ?
          MY WAY!

Eve Merriam

After Reading

Making Connections

1. Would you say this story has a happy ending? Explain your answer.

2. Did Mr. and Mrs. Peacock deal with the problem in the best possible way? Explain.

3. 👣 What other things could the Peacock family and Natures Wonder & Company have said or done to bring about a **change** in the situation and better understand each other?

4. What do you think was the **author's purpose** in writing this story? Keep in mind that she might have had more than one purpose.

5. Has reading this story changed the way you feel about ordering products from catalogs? Explain.

6. Compare the dispute in "The Empty Box" with the one in the poem "Argument."

7. Some people might say that only top executives with a company have important jobs. What do you say? Why?

Literary Focus: Diction

Even without signatures, you could probably guess that the letters in "The Empty Box" were written by several people. One reason is that each writer chose different words and a different style to express his or her ideas. Sometimes the style is conversational and sometimes it is formal.

Work with three classmates to study the **diction,** or writing style and word choice, used by the main characters in "The Empty Box." Each of you should take a character's letters to study. How would you describe the diction in your character's first letter? Does the diction change in the letter or letters that follow? If so, how?

Vocabulary Study

On the next page is a letter sent by a dissatisfied customer to a catalog company. Choose the vocabulary word from the list that best completes each sentence.

August 15

President
A Better You Company

Dear Sir or Madam:

distressed
distributor
inefficient
negotiate
specialize

I've become increasingly __(1)__ in dealing with your customer service department. I finally decided to bypass your incompetent, __(2)__ employees and write directly to you.

I was impressed that you __(3)__ in helping people create better lives through self-improvement videotapes. I ordered the video titled "Sixty Steps to Happiness" from your catalog.

Three months went by. I called your customer service department and was repeatedly told the video would arrive "any day." Finally, it did. Well, the video turned out to be an old Three Stooges movie! I called your customer service department—again. The representative blamed the problem on Red Tape Co., Inc., the __(4)__ that sells tapes to *your* company.

I finally received the tape. Of course, I returned the Three Stooges video. However, I was charged for *two* videos on my credit card bill! The credit card company says I need to __(5)__ with your company to work out a settlement. That's why I'm writing to you.

Sincerely,

A. Grump

Expressing Your Ideas

Writing Choices

It's Not Over Yet "The Empty Box" had to end somewhere, but Marilyn Pippin must have received at least one more letter after April 1. Imagine you're Mr. or Mrs. Peacock, and write that **letter.**

What's the Right Way? Contact the Better Business Bureau nearest you to find out the procedure for filing a complaint against a company. Based on what you learn, write a **list** of steps to follow.

Other Options

Consumer Study Conduct a **survey** of classmates, teachers, and family members to find out how satisfied they were with mail-order experiences they've had in the last three months. What conclusions can you draw from your survey?

Finding Frog Facts Research different kinds of frogs: where they live, how they grow, and so on. The library, a science teacher, or a science museum is a good place to start. Give a **speech** to the class about what you've learned.

Before Reading

The Christmas Hunt

by Borden Deal

Borden Deal
1922–1985

When Borden Deal was born in Pontotoc, Mississippi, his farming parents probably did not expect him to turn out to be an author. But he did. In his thirty-year writing career, Deal drew on his experiences growing up in the rural South during the Great Depression to create a large number of novels, short stories, and other works. Much of Deal's writing explores people's attachment to the land and the struggles involved in growing up. Deal once said he wanted his books to be a "panorama of the New South," and he proudly noted that his fictional characters "live and work in real time in real places."

Building Background

Hunting "The Christmas Hunt" is about hunting game—that is, searching for and killing wild animals. In this case, the animals are quail, small birds that belong to the same family as pheasants and turkeys. In many places in the United States, it is legal to hunt quail for food or sport.

Quail hunters often use trained dogs to help them. The dog uses its sense of scent to search the ground for birds. This searching is called quartering. When the dog locates the quails, it alerts the hunter by pointing: holding up a front paw and staring toward the birds while standing perfectly still. The dog then startles the birds so they fly up suddenly. The hunter shoots. If a bird falls, the dog finds the dead bird and brings it back to the hunter.

Getting into the Story

Writer's Notebook The main character in "The Christmas Hunt" thinks he is old enough to go on his first hunt. In your notebook, write about a time when you thought you were old enough to take a big step in life. What was it that you wanted to do? How old were you? Did your parents agree that you were old enough?

Reading Tip

Making and Checking Predictions As you read "The Christmas Hunt," you'll encounter questions that ask you to make a prediction. Copy the chart below in your notebook, leaving plenty of room for writing. Each time you come to a "Predict" question, fill in the chart. When you finish the story, review your completed chart. How accurate were your predictions?

"Predict" Question	What I Predict	What Actually Happened
What will Tom's father say when Tom asks to go on the Christmas hunt?		

The Christmas Hunt

Borden Deal

It should have been the best Christmas of them all, that year at Dog Run. It started out to be, anyway. I was so excited, watching my father talking on the telephone, that I couldn't stand still. For I was ten years old, and I had never been on a quail shoot in my whole life. I wanted to go on the big Christmas Day hunt even more than I wanted that bicycle I was supposed to get. And I really needed the bicycle to cover with speed and ease the two miles I had to walk to school.

The Christmas Day hunt was always the biggest and best of the season. It was almost like a field trial; only the best hunters and the finest dogs were invited by my father. All my life I had been hearing tales of past Christmas Day hunts. And now I knew with a great ten-year-old certainty that I was old enough to go.

My father hung up the phone and turned around, grinning. "That was Walter," he said. "There'll be ten of them this year. And Walter is bringing his new dog. If all he claims for that dog is true—"

"Papa," I said.

"Lord," my mother said. "That'll be a houseful to feed."

My father put his arm around her shoulders, hugging her. "Oh, you know you like it," he said. "They come as much for your cooking as they do for the hunting, I think."

My mother pursed her lips in the way she had and then smiled. "Wild turkey," she said. "You think you could shoot me four or five nice fat wild turkeys?"

I wanted to jump up and down to attract attention. But that was kid stuff, a tactic for the five-year-olds, though I had to admit it was effective. But I was ten. So I said, "Papa."

My father laughed. "I think I can," he said. "I'll put in a couple of mornings trying."

"Papa," I said desperately.

"Wild turkey stuffed with wild rice," my mother said quickly, thoughtfully, in her planning voice. "Giblet gravy, mashed potatoes, maybe a nice potato salad—"

"If I don't fail on the turkeys," my father said.

"Papa!" I said.

My father turned to me. "Come on, Tom," he said. "We've got to feed those dogs."

That's the way parents are, even when you're ten years old. They can talk right on and never hear a word you say. I ran after my father as he left the kitchen, hoping for a chance to get my words in edgewise. But my father was walking fast, and already the clamor[1] of the

---

1. **clamor** (klam′ər), *n.* a loud noise, especially of voices; continual uproar.

bird dogs was rising up to cover any speech I might want to make.

The dogs were standing on the wire fence in long, dappled rows, their voices lifted in greeting. Even in my urgent need I had to stop and admire them. There's nothing prettier in the whole world than a good bird dog. There's a nobleness to its head, an intelligence in its eyes, that no other animal has. Just looking at them sent a shiver down my backbone, and the thought of shooting birds over them—well, the shiver just wasn't in my backbone now; I was shaking all over.

All of the dogs except one were in the same big run. But my father kept Calypso Baby in her own regal pen. I went to her and looked into her soft brown eyes. She stood up tall on the fence, her strong, lithe body stretched to its full height, as tall as I was.

"Hello, Baby," I whispered, and she wagged her tail. "You gonna find me some birds this Christmas, Baby? You gonna hunt for me like you do for Papa?"

She lolled her tongue, laughing at me. We were old friends. Calypso Baby was the finest bird dog in that part of the country. My father owned a number of dogs and kept and trained others for his town friends. But Calypso Baby was his personal dog, the one that he took to the field trials, the one he shot over in the big Christmas Day hunt held at Dog Run.

My father was bringing the sack of feed from the shed. I put out my hand, holding it against the wire so Calypso Baby could lick my fingers.

▲ *Prepared for the Season* was painted in 1986 by Terry Redlin. How does this painting help set the mood of the story?

"This year," I whispered to her. "This year I'm going." I left Calypso Baby, went with determination toward my father. "Papa," I said, in a voice not to be denied this time.

PREDICT: What will Tom's father say when Tom asks to go on the Christmas hunt?

My father was busy opening the sack of dog food.

"Papa," I said firmly, "I want to talk to you." It was the tone and the words my father used often toward me, so much of mimicry[2] that my father looked down at me in surprise, at last giving me his attention.

"What is it?" he said. "What do you want?"

"Papa, I'm ten years old," I said.

My father laughed. "Well, what of it?" he said. "Next year you'll be eleven. And the next year twelve."

"I'm old enough to go on the Christmas hunt," I said.

Incredibly, my father laughed. "At ten?" he said. "I'm afraid not."

I stood, stricken.[3] "But—" I said.

"No," my father said, in the voice that meant No, and no more talking about it. He hoisted the sack of feed and took it into the wire dog pen, the bird dogs crowding around him, rearing up on him in their eagerness.

"Well, come on and help me," my father said impatiently. "I've got a lot of things to do."

Usually I enjoyed the daily feeding of the dogs. But not today; I went through the motions dumbly, silently, not paying any attention to the fine dogs crowding around me. I cleaned the watering troughs with my usual care, but my heart was not in it.

After the feeding was over, I scuffed stubbornly about my other tasks and then went up to my room, not even coming down when my father came home at dusk excited with the two wild turkeys he had shot. I could hear him talking to my mother in the kitchen, and the ring of their voices had already the feel of Christmas, a hunting cheer that made them brighter, livelier, than usual. But none of the cheer and the pleasure came into me, even though Christmas was almost upon us and yesterday had been the last day of school.

That night I hunted. In my dreams I was out ahead of all the other men and dogs, Calypso Baby quartering the field in her busy way, doing it so beautifully I ached inside to watch her. All the men and dogs stopped their own hunting to watch us, as though it were a field trial. When Calypso Baby pointed, I raised the twelve-gauge shotgun, moved in on her on the ready, and Calypso Baby flushed the birds in her fine, steady way. They came up in an explosive whir, and I had the gun to my shoulder, squeezing off the shot just the way I'd been told to do. Three quail dropped like stones out of the covey, and I swung the gun, following a single. I brought down the single with the second barrel, and Calypso Baby was already bringing the first bird to me in her soft, unbruising mouth. I knelt to pat her for a moment, and Baby whipped her tail to tell me how fine a shot I was, how much she liked for me to be the one shooting over her today.

Soon there was another covey, and I did even better on this one, and then another and another, and nobody was hunting at all, not even my father, who was laughing and grinning at the other men, knowing this was his boy, Tom, and his dog, Calypso Baby, and just full of pride with it all. When it was over, the men crowded around and patted me on the shoulder, hefting the full game bag in admiration, and then there was my father's face

---

2. **mimicry** (mim′ik rē), *n.* act or practice of imitating.
3. **stricken** (strik′ən), *adj.* hit, wounded, or affected by (a weapon, disease, trouble, sorrow, etc.).

close before me saying, "I was wrong, son, when I said a ten-year-old boy isn't old enough to go bird hunting with the best of us."

Then I was awake, and my father, dressed in his hunting clothes, was shaking me, and it was morning. I looked up dazedly into his face, unable to shake off the dream, and I knew what it was I had to do. I had to show my father. Only then would he believe.

"Are you awake?" my father said. "You'll have to change the water for the dogs. I'm going to see if I can get some more turkeys this morning."

"All right," I said. "I'm awake now."

My father left. I got up and ate breakfast in the kitchen, close to the warm stove. I didn't say anything to my mother about my plans. I went out and watered the dogs as soon as the sun was up, but I didn't take the time, as I usually did, to play with them.

"Me and you are going hunting," I told Calypso Baby as I changed her water. She jumped and quivered all over, knowing the word as well as I did.

I went back into the house, listening for my mother. She was upstairs, making the beds. I went into the spare room where my father kept all the hunting gear. I was trembling, remembering the dream, as I went to the gun rack and touched the cold steel of the double-barreled twelve-gauge. But I knew it would be very heavy for me. I took the single-barrel instead, though I knew that pretty near ruined my chances for a second shot unless I could reload very quickly.

I picked up a full shell bag and hung it under my left arm. I found a game bag and hung it under my right arm. The strap was too long, and the bag dangled emptily to my

"ME AND YOU ARE GOING HUNTING," I TOLD CALYPSO BABY. . .

knees, banging against me as I walked. I tied a knot in the strap so the bag would rest comfortably on my right hip. The gun was heavy in my hands as I walked into the hallway, listening for my mother. She was still upstairs.

"Mamma, I'm gone," I shouted up to her. "I'll be back in a little while." That was so she wouldn't be looking for me.

"All right," she called. "Don't wander far off. Your father will be back in an hour or two and might have something for you to do."

PREDICT: Will Tom be caught in the act of hunting without permission?

I hurried out of the house, straight to Calypso Baby's pen. I did not look up, afraid that my mother might be watching out of the window. That was a danger I could do nothing about, so I just ignored it. I opened the gate to Baby's pen, and she came out, circling and cavorting.[4]

"Come on, Baby," I whispered. "Find me some birds now. Find me a whole lot of birds."

We started off, circling the barn so we would not be seen from the house and going straight away in its shadow as far as we could. Beyond the pasture we crossed a cornfield, Calypso Baby arrowing straight for the patch of sedge grass beyond. Her tail was whiplike in its thrash, her head high as she plunged toward her work, and I had to hurry to keep up. The gun was clumsy

———————————————

4. **cavort** (kə vôrt´), v. prance about; jump around.

in my hands, and the two bags banged against my hips. But I remembered not to run with the gun, remembered to keep the breech[5] open until I was ready to shoot. I knew all about hunting; I just hadn't had a chance to practice what I knew. When I came home with a bag full of fine birds, my father would have to admit that I knew how to hunt, that I was old enough for the big Christmas Day hunt when all the great hunters came out from town for the biggest day of the season.

When I ducked through the barbed-wire fence, Calypso Baby was waiting for me, standing a few steps into the sedge grass, her head up watching me alertly. Her whole body quivered with her eagerness to be off. I swept my arm in the gesture I had seen my father use so many times, and Calypso Baby plunged instantly into the grass. She was a fast worker, quartering back and forth with an economical use of her energy. She could cover a field in half the time it took any other dog. The first field was empty, and we passed on to the second one. Somehow Calypso Baby knew that birds were here. She steadied down, hunting slowly, more thoroughly.

Then, startling me though I had been expecting it, she froze into a point, one foot up, her tail straight back, her head flat with the line of her backbone. I froze too. I couldn't move; I couldn't even remember to breech the gun and raise it to my shoulder. I stood as still as the dog, all of my knowledge flown out of my head, and yet far back under the panic, I knew that the birds weren't going to hold. They were going to rise in just a moment. Calypso Baby, surprised at my inaction, broke her point to look at me in inquiry. Her head turned toward me, and she asked the question as plain as my father's voice: *Well, what are you going to do about these fine birds I found for you?*

I could move then. I took a step or two, fumblingly breeched the gun, raised it to my

Companions was painted by James Charles around 1890. Do you think Tom and Calypso Baby have the same kind of relationship as this boy and dog?

shoulder. The birds rose of their own accord in a sudden wild drum of sound. I yanked at the trigger, unconsciously bracing myself against the blast and the recoil.[6] Nothing happened. Nothing at all happened. I tugged at the trigger wildly, furiously, but it was too late and the birds were gone.

I lowered the gun, looking down at it in bewilderment. I had forgotten to release the safety.[7] I wanted to cry at my own stupidity. I could feel the tears standing in my eyes. This was not at all like my dream of last night, when I and the dog and the birds had all been so perfect.

---

5. **breech** (brēch), *n.* rear part of a gun barrel.
6. **recoil** (ri koil′), *n.* the force with which a gun springs back when it is fired.
7. **safety** (sāf′tē), *n.* device to prevent injury or accident.

Calypso Baby walked back to me and looked up into my face. I could read the puzzled contempt in her eyes. She lay down at my feet, putting her muzzle on her paws. I looked down at her, ashamed of myself and knowing that she was ashamed. She demanded perfection, just as my father did.

"It was my fault, Baby," I told her. I leaned over and patted her on the head. "You didn't do anything wrong. It was me."

I started off then, looking back at the bird dog. She did not follow me. "Come on," I told her. "Hunt."

She got up slowly and went out ahead of me again. But she worked in a puzzled manner, checking back to me frequently. She no longer had the joy, the confidence, with which she had started out.

"Come on, Baby," I coaxed her. "Hunt, Baby. Hunt."

PREDICT: What will happen the next time Calypso Baby points?

We crossed into another field, low grass this time, and when we found the covey, there was very little time for setting myself. Calypso Baby pointed suddenly. I jerked the gun to my shoulder, remembering the safety this time, and then Calypso Baby flushed the birds. They rose up before me, and I pulled the trigger, hearing the blast of the gun, feeling the shock of it into my shoulder knocking me back a step.

But not even one bird dropped like a fateful stone out of the covey. The covey had gone off low and hard on an angle to the left, and I had completely missed the shot, aiming straight ahead instead of swinging with the birds. Calypso Baby did not even attempt to point singles. She dropped her head and her tail and started away from me, going back toward the house.

I ran after her, calling her, crying now but with anger rather than hurt. Baby would never like me again. She would hold me in the indifference she felt toward any person who was not a bird hunter. She would tolerate me as she tolerated my mother and the men who came out with shiny new hunting clothes and walked all over the land talking about how the dogs didn't hold the birds properly so you could get a decent shot.

I couldn't be one of those. I ran after the dog, calling her, until at last she suffered me to come near. I knelt, fondling her head, talking to her, begging her for another chance.

"I'll get some birds next time," I told her. "You just watch. You hear?"

At last, reluctantly, she consented to hunt again. I followed her, my hands gripping the heavy gun, determined this time. I knew it was my last chance; she would not give me another. I could not miss this time.

We hunted for an hour before we found another covey of birds. I was tired, the gun and the frustration heavier with every step. But, holding only last night's dream in my mind, I refused to quit. At last Calypso Baby froze into a beautiful point. I could feel myself sweating, my teeth gritted hard. I had to bring down a bird this time.

It seemed to be perfect. I had plenty of time, but I hurried anyway, just to be sure. Then the birds were rising in a tight cluster, and I was pulling the trigger before I had the heavy gun lined up—and in the midst of the thundering blast, I heard Calypso Baby yell with pain as the random shot tore into her hip.

I threw down the gun and ran toward her, seeing the blood streaking down her leg as she staggered away from me, whimpering. I knelt, trying to coax her to me, but she was afraid. I was crying, feeling the full weight of the disaster. I had committed the worst crime of any bird hunter; I had shot my own dog.

Calypso Baby was trying to hide in a clump of bushes. She snapped at me in her fear when

I reached in after her, but I did not feel the pain in my hand. I knelt over her, looking at the shredded hip. It was a terrible wound. I could see only blood and raw flesh. I snatched off the empty hunting bag I had donned so optimistically, the shell bag, and took off my coat. I wrapped her in the coat and picked her up in my arms. She was very heavy, hurting, whining with each jolting step as I ran toward the house.

PREDICT: What will happen when Tom takes Calypso Baby home?

I came into the yard doubled over with the catch in my side from the running, and my legs were trembling. My father was sitting on the back porch with three wild turkeys beside him, cleaning his gun. He jumped to his feet when he saw the wounded dog.

"What happened?" he said. "Did some fool hunter shoot her?"

I stopped, standing before my father and holding the wounded dog. I looked into his angry face. They were the most terrible words I ever had to say. "I shot her, Papa," I said.

My father stood very still. I did not know what would happen. I had never done anything so bad in my whole life, and I could not even guess how my father would react. The only thing justified would be to wipe me off the face of the earth with one irate gesture of his hand.

I gulped, trying to move the pain in my throat out of the way of the words. "I took her out bird hunting," I said. "I wanted to show you—if I got a full bag of birds, I thought you'd let me go on the Christmas Day hunt—"

"I'll talk to you later," my father said grimly,

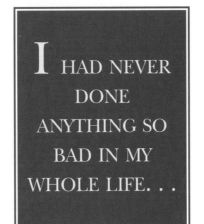

I HAD NEVER DONE ANYTHING SO BAD IN MY WHOLE LIFE. . .

taking the dog from me and starting into the kitchen. "I've got to try to save this dog's life now."

I started into the kitchen behind my father. He turned. "Where's the gun you shot her with?" he said.

"I—left it."

"Don't leave it lying out there in the field," my father said in a stern voice.

I wanted very badly to go into the kitchen, find out that the dog would live. But I turned, instead, and went back the way I had come, walking with my head down, feeling shrunken inside myself. I had overreached. I had risen up today full of pride beyond my ability, and in the stubbornness of the pride, I had been blind until the terrible accident had opened my eyes so that I could see myself clearly—too clearly. I found the gun, the two bags, where I had dropped them. I picked them up without looking at the smear of blood where Calypso had lain. I went back to the house slowly, not wanting to face it, reluctant to see the damage I had wrought.

When I came into the kitchen, my father had the dog stretched out on the kitchen table. My mother stood by his side with bandages and ointment in her hands. The wound was cleaned of the bird shot and dirt and blood. Calypso Baby whined when she saw me, and I felt my heart cringe with the rejection.

My father looked at me across the dog. The anger was gone out of him; his voice was slow and searching and not to be denied. "Now I want to know why you took my gun and my dog without permission," he said.

"David," my mother said to him.

My father ignored her, kept his eyes hard on my face. I knew it wouldn't do any good to look toward my mother. This was between me and my father, and there was no refuge[8] for me anywhere in the world. I didn't want a refuge. I knew I had to face not only my father but myself.

"I—I wanted to go on the Christmas Day hunt," I said again. "I thought if I—" I stopped. It was all that I had to say. It seemed pretty flimsy to me now.

My father looked down at the dog. I was surprised at the lack of anger in him. I could read only sadness in his voice. "She may be ruined for hunting," he said. "Even if the wound heals good, if she doesn't lose the use of her leg, she may be gun-shy for the rest of her life. At best, I'll never be able to show her in field trials again. You understand what you've done?"

Woodland Walk was painted by Burt Silverman in 1989. Imagine that these two people are Tom and his father. What might they be talking about?

"Yes, sir," I said. I wanted to cry. But that would not help, any more than anger from my father would help.

"You see now why I said you weren't old enough?" my father said. "You've got to be trained for hunting, just like a dog is trained. Suppose other men had been out there; suppose you had shot a human being?"

"David!" my mother said.

My father turned angrily toward her. "He's got to learn!" he said. "There's too many people in this world trying to do things without learning how to do them first. I don't want my boy to be one of them."

"Papa," I said. "I'm—I'm sorry. I wouldn't have hurt Calypso Baby for anything in the world."

"I'm not going to punish you," my father said. He looked down at the dog. "This is too bad for a whipping to settle. But I want you to think about today. I don't want you to put it out of your mind. You knew that when the time came ripe for it, I intended to teach you, take you out like I'd take a puppy, and hunt with you. After a while, you could hunt by yourself. Then if you were good enough—and only if you were good enough—you could go on the Christmas Day hunt. The Christmas Day hunt is the place you come to, not the place you start out from. Do you understand?"

"Yes, sir," I said. I would have been glad to settle for a whipping. But I knew that a mere dusting of the breeches would be inadequate for my brashness, my overconfidence, for the

_____

8. **refuge** (ref′yüj), *n.* shelter or protection from danger or trouble; safety; security.

hurt I had given not only to the fine bird dog but also to my father—and to myself.

"You've got to take special care of Calypso Baby," my father said. "Maybe if you take care of her yourself while she's hurt, she'll decide to be your friend again."

PREDICT: Will Calypso Baby be all right, and will she and Tom be friends again?

~

I looked at the dog, and I could feel the need of her confidence and trust. "Yes, sir," I said. Then I said humbly, "I hope she will be friends with me again."

I went toward the hall, needing to be alone in my room. I stopped at the kitchen doorway, looking back at my father and mother watching me. I had to say it in a hurry if I was going to say it at all.

"Papa," I said, the words rushing softly in my throat, threatening to gag there before I could get them out. "I—I don't think I deserve that bicycle this Christmas. I don't deserve it at all."

My father nodded his head. "All right, son," he said gravely. "This is your own punishment for yourself."

"Yes," I said, forcing the word, the loss empty inside me, and yet feeling better too. I turned and ran out of the room and up the stairs.

Christmas came, but without any help from me at all. I went to bed on Christmas Eve heavy with the knowledge that tomorrow morning there would be no shiny new bicycle under the tree; there would be no Christmas Day hunt for me. I couldn't prevent myself from waking up at the usual excited time, but I made myself turn over and go back to sleep. When I did, reluctantly, go downstairs, the Christmas tree did not excite me, nor the usual gifts I received every year: the heavy sweater, the gloves, the scarf, the two new pairs of blue jeans. I just wouldn't let myself think about the bicycle.

After my father had gone outside, my mother hugged me to her in a sudden rush of affection. "He would have given you the bicycle anyway," she said, "if you hadn't told him you didn't want it."

I looked up at her. "I didn't deserve it," I said. "Maybe next year I will."

She surprised me then by holding me and crying. I heard the first car arrive outside, the voices of the men excited with the promise of hunting. My mother stood up and said briskly, "Well, this is not getting that big dinner cooked," and went into the kitchen without looking back.

I went out on the front porch. It was perfect quail-hunting weather, cold but not too cold, with a smoky haze lying over the earth. The dogs knew that today was for hunting. I could hear them from around behind the house, standing on the wire fence in broad-shouldered rows, their voices yelping and calling. All except Calypso Baby. All except me.

I stood aside, watching the men arrive in their cars, my father greeting them. Their breaths hung cloudy in the air, and they moved with a sharp movement to their bodies. These were the best hunters in the whole countryside, and today would be a great comradeship and competition. Any man invited on this hunt could be proud of the invitation alone.

I felt almost remote as I watched, as I went with them around the side of the house to the dogs. They all went to examine Calypso Baby, and I felt a freezing inside; but my father only said, "She got shot by accident," and did not tell the whole terrible story.

Then my father looked at his watch and said, "Let's wait for a few more minutes. Walter ought to be here soon. Hate to start without him."

One of the men called, "Here he comes now," and Walter drove up in his battered car.

"Come here, son," my father said, speaking to me for the first time this morning, and I went reluctantly to his side. I was afraid it was coming now, the whole story, and all the men would look at me in the same way that Calypso Baby had after I had shot her. My father drew me to the side of Walter's car, reached in, and brought out a basket. "You wanted a bicycle," he said. "Then you decided yourself you should wait. Because you made the decision yourself, I decided you were old enough for this."

I looked at the bird-dog puppy in the basket. All of a sudden Christmas burst inside me like a skyrocket, out of the place where I had kept it suppressed all this time.

"Papa," I said. "Papa—"

"Take him," my father said.

I reached into the basket and took out the puppy. The puppy licked my chin with his harsh, warm tongue. He was long, gangly, his feet and head too big for his body—but absolutely beautiful.

My father knelt beside me, one hand on the puppy. "I told Walter to bring me the finest bird-dog puppy he could find," he said. "He's kin to Calypso Baby. He's got good blood."

"Thank you, Papa," I said in a choking voice. "I—I'd rather have him than the bicycle. I'll name him Calypso Boy. I'll—"

"When this puppy is ready for birds, we'll train him," my father said. "While we train the puppy, we'll train you too. When the time comes, you can both go on the Christmas Day hunt—if you're good enough."

"We'll be good enough," I said. "Both of us will be good enough."

"I hope so," my father said. He stood up and looked at the men standing around us, all of them smiling down at me and Calypso Boy. "Let's go," he said. "Those birds are going to get tired of waiting on us."

They laughed and hollered, and the dogs moiled and sounded[9] in the excitement as they were let out of the pen. They fanned out across the pasture, each man or two men taking a dog. I stood watching, holding the puppy warm in my arms. I looked at Calypso Baby, standing crippled in her pen looking longingly after the hunters. I went over and spoke to her. She whined; then for the first time since the accident, she wagged her tail at me.

I looked down at the puppy in my arms. "We'll be going," I told him, as he licked at my chin. "One of these days, when you're a dog and I'm a man, we'll be right out there with the best of them."

It was three years more before I got to go on my first Christmas hunt. Papa had been right, of course. In the time between, I had learned a great deal myself while training Calypso Boy to hunt. With the good blood in him, he turned out to be a great bird dog—second only, I guess, to Calypso Baby, who recovered well from her wound and was Papa's dog the day Calypso Boy and I made our first Christmas hunt.

But of all the Christmases, before and since, I guess I remember best the one when Calypso Baby was hurt—and Calypso Boy first came to me.

---

9. **moil and sound**, run about and howl.

After Reading

Making Connections

1. Did the story end the way you thought it would? Explain.

2. Describe your reaction to Tom's decision to refuse a bicycle for Christmas.

3. Why do you think Tom was surprised when his mother held him and cried?

4. ☺ The solution to the problem in the story helped bridge a gap between childhood and adulthood. Summarize the events that brought about this **change.**

5. How do you think the author's cultural background may have contributed to this story?

6. What do you wish you were "old enough" to do? How do you think you—and your parents—will know when you're "old enough"?

7. Hunting is an accepted part of Tom's family's life. But many people oppose hunting. How do you feel about hunting for food? for fur? for sport? Explain.

Literary Focus: Theme

The central idea or meaning of a story is its **theme.** Sometimes, an author states the theme directly. Most of the time, though, the author only implies, or hints at, the theme. It's up to you, the reader, to discover the theme and state it in your own words. The theme is not a summary of the plot or a lesson on how to live. A theme statement should be a general comment on life, on people, or on nature.

Write a theme statement for "The Christmas Hunt." Then write a brief paragraph in which you tell whether you agree or disagree with the theme. In other words, do you think the theme reveals something true about life, or not? Explain why you think as you do.

Vocabulary Study

Match each phrase with the word from the list that best relates to it.

cavort
clamor
mimicry
refuge
stricken

1. a toddler pretending to steer while sitting in her car seat

2. running and splashing through puddles on the way home from school

3. a family sitting in their basement after hearing that a tornado is nearby

4. nine cats surrounding their owner as she opens their food bag

5. a person learning that a favorite relative has died

Expressing Your Ideas

Writing Choices

A Punishment to Fit the Crime Suppose you did something as terrible as what Tom did to Calypso Baby. Make a **list** of five possible punishments to give yourself that would have as much impact on you as Tom's refusal of the bicycle had on him.

How Could You? Did you visualize Calypso Baby's reaction to being shot? Write a **comparison** of the way Calypso Baby felt toward Tom at that moment and the feelings of the dog in the painting below.

Other Options

Working Dogs Hunting is just one way dogs have helped humans through the centuries. Research other ways dogs work for and with people, and present an **oral report** on your findings. Conclude your report with your opinion as to whether people should or should not put animals to work, and why you think as you do.

Handle with Care Find out about how guns can and should be handled for safety. Create a **poster** that includes artwork and tips for gun safety.

Gun Control: Yes or No? With a partner, carry out a **debate** about gun control. You might debate the general issue of whether the government should or should not regulate gun ownership and use. Or you might debate a more specific aspect of the gun control issue—perhaps one that is currently in the news. Keep in mind that you don't have to agree with the side that you present, but you do need to present it convincingly.

Before Reading

What Stumped the Blue Jays

by Mark Twain

Mark Twain
1835–1910

Mark Twain was America's first literary "superstar." Twain (who was born Samuel Clemens) was a novelist, short-story writer, journalist, lecturer, and household name during his lifetime. A number of his books, including *The Adventures of Tom Sawyer* and *The Adventures of Huckleberry Finn,* are considered classics. Twain might not have liked that idea, however. He once defined a classic as "something that everybody wants to have read and nobody wants to read."

Twain loved to poke fun at false pride, self-satisfaction, and other unattractive traits of the human race. His attitude is expressed in one of his most famous quotations: "Man is the only animal that blushes. Or needs to."

Building Background

A Jay by Any Other Name Blue jays are attractive birds with blue, black, and white coloring. However, they are very bold. Jays commonly take and eat eggs and young birds from other birds' nests, and they don't make up for their behavior with lovely songs. Blue jays have loud, harsh voices. When jays get together, the screeching could hurt your ears!

Getting into the Selection

Writer's Notebook Have you ever noticed that some pets and their owners seem to belong together and even look alike? Think of an animal that resembles humans in one or more ways. In your notebook, write about the similarities you observe between that animal and humans. As you read "What Stumped the Blue Jays," look for similarities between the birds and people.

Reading Tip

Dialect Dialect is the special way a language is spoken by a certain group of people. People who live in the same geographical area, for example, may speak the same dialect. In "What Stumped the Blue Jays," Twain reproduced the pronunciation and vocabulary he heard when he lived among western miners in the middle 1800s. The chart below gives the meanings of some of the special words and phrases Twain used in the story.

Words and Phrases in Story	Meanings
get to pulling fur	start fighting
in a measure	in a way
lay over	be better than; surpass
this ain't no fat thing	this isn't any foolish thing
I never struck no such hole as this	I've never seen a hole like this
jawing	scolding; lecturing
ripping	violent speaking

What Stumped the Blue Jays

Mark Twain

Animals talk to each other, of course. There can be no question about that; but I suppose there are very few people who can understand them. I never knew but one man who could. I knew he could, however, because he told me so himself. He was a middle-aged, simple-hearted miner who had lived in a lonely corner of California, among the woods and mountains, a good many years, and had studied the ways of his only neighbors, the beasts and the birds, until he believed he could accurately translate any remark which they made. This was Jim Baker. According to Jim Baker, some animals have only a limited education, and use only very simple words, and scarcely ever a comparison or a flowery figure; whereas, certain other animals have a large vocabulary, a fine command of language and a ready and fluent delivery; consequently these latter talk a great deal; they like it; they are conscious of their talent, and they enjoy "showing off." Baker said, that after long and careful observation, he had come to the conclusion that the bluejays were the best talkers he had found among birds and beasts. Said he:

There's more *to* a bluejay than any other creature. He has got more moods, and more different kinds of feelings than other creatures; and, mind you, whatever a bluejay feels, he can put into language. And no mere commonplace language, either, but rattling, out-and-out book-talk—and bristling with metaphor, too—just bristling! And as for command of language—why *you* never see a bluejay get stuck for a word. No man ever did. They just boil out of him! And another thing: I've noticed a good deal, and there's no bird, or cow, or anything that uses as good grammar as a bluejay. You may say a cat uses good grammar. Well, a cat does—but you let a cat get excited once; you let a cat get to pulling fur with another cat on a shed, nights, and you'll hear grammar that will give you the lockjaw. Ignorant people think it's the *noise* which fighting cats make that is so aggravating,[1] but it ain't so; it's the sickening grammar they use. Now I've never heard a jay use bad grammar but very seldom; and when they do, they are as ashamed as a human; they shut right down and leave.

You may call a jay a bird. Well, so he is, in a measure—because he's got feathers on him, and don't belong to no church, perhaps; but otherwise he is just as much a human as you be. And

---

1. **aggravating** (ag′rə vāt ing), *adj.* annoying; irritating; exasperating.

I'll tell you for why. A jay's gifts, and instincts,[2] and feelings, and interests, cover the whole ground. A jay hasn't got any more principle than a Congressman. A jay will lie, a jay will steal, a jay will deceive, a jay will betray; and four times out of five, a jay will go back on his solemnest promise. The sacredness of an obligation is a thing which you can't cram into no bluejay's head. Now, on top of all this, there's another thing; a jay can out-swear any gentleman in the mines. You think a cat can swear. Well, a cat can; but you give a bluejay a subject that calls for his reserve pow-ers, and where is your cat? Don't talk to *me*—I know too much about this thing. And there's yet another thing; in the one little particular of scolding—just good, clean, out-and-out scolding—a bluejay can lay over any-thing, human or divine. Yes, sir, a jay is everything that a man is. A jay can cry, a jay can laugh, a jay can feel shame, a jay can reason and plan and discuss, a jay likes gossip and scandal, a jay has got a sense of humor. If a jay ain't human, he better take in his sign, that's all. Now I'm going to tell you a perfectly true fact about some bluejays. When I first begun to under-stand jay language correctly, there was a little incident happened here. Seven years ago, the last man in this region but me moved away. There stands his house—been empty ever since; a log house, with a plank roof—just one big room, and no more; no ceiling—nothing

Do you think this blue jay painted by Halstead Craig Hannah matches Twain's description?

between the rafters and the floor. Well, one Sunday morning I was sitting out here in front of my cabin, with my cat, taking the sun, and looking at the blue hills, and listening to the leaves rustling so lonely in the trees, and thinking of the home away yonder in the

2. **instinct** (in′stingkt), *n.* a natural feeling, knowledge, or power, such as that which guides animals; inborn tendency to act in a certain way.

states, that I hadn't heard from in thirteen years, when a bluejay lit on that house, with an acorn in his mouth, and says, "Hello, I've reckon I've struck something." When he spoke, the acorn dropped out of his mouth

"I've shoveled acorns enough in there to keep the family thirty years!"

and rolled down the roof, of course, but he didn't care; his mind was all on the thing he had struck. It was a knot-hole in the roof. He cocked his head to one side, shut one eye and put the other one to the hole, like a possum looking down a jug; then he glanced up with his bright eyes, gave a wink or two with his wings—which signifies gratification,[3] you understand—and says, "It looks like a hole, it's located like a hole—blamed if I don't believe it *is* a hole!"

Then he cocked his head down and took another look; he glances up perfectly joyful, this time; winks his wings and his tail both, and says, "Oh, no, this ain't no fat thing, I reckon! If I ain't in luck!—why it's a perfectly elegant hole!" So he flew down and got that acorn, and fetched it up and dropped it in, and was just tilting his head back, with the heavenliest smile on his face, when all of a sudden he was paralyzed into a listening attitude and that smile faded gradually out of his countenance[4] like breath off'n a razor, and the queerest look of surprise took its place. Then he says, "Why, I didn't hear it fall!" He cocked his eye at the hole again, and took a long look; raised up and shook his head; stepped around to the other side of the hole and took another look from that side; shook his head again. He studied a while, then he just went into the details—walked round and round the hole and spied into it from every point of the compass. No use. Now he took a thinking attitude on the comb of the roof and

scratched the back of his head with his right foot a minute, and finally says, "Well, it's too many for *me*, that's certain; must be a mighty long hole; however, I ain't got no time to fool around here, I got to 'tend to business; I reckon it's all right—chance it, anyway."

So he flew off and fetched another acorn and dropped it in, and tried to flirt his eye to the hole quick enough to see what become of it, but he was too late. He held his eye there as much as a minute; then he raised up and sighed, and says, "Confound it, I don't seem to understand this thing, no way; however, I'll tackle her again." He fetched another acorn, and done his level best to see what become of it, but he couldn't. He says, "Well, *I* never struck no such a hole as this before; I'm of the opinion it's a totally new kind of a hole." Then he begun to get mad. He held in for a spell,[5] walking up and down the comb of the roof and shaking his head and muttering to himself; but his feelings got the upper hand of him, presently, and he broke loose and cussed himself black in the face. I never see a bird take on so about a little thing. When he got through he walks to the hole and looks in again for half a minute; then he says, "Well, you're a long hole, and a deep hole, and a mighty singular hole altogether—but I've started in to fill you, and I'm d—d if I *don't* fill you, if it takes a hundred years!"

And with that, away he went. You never see a bird work so since you was born. He laid into his work, and the way he hove acorns into that hole for about two hours and a half was one of the most exciting and astonishing spectacles I ever struck. He never stopped to take a look any more—he just hove 'em in and

---

3. gratification (grat/ə fə kā/shən), *n.* a being pleased or satisfied.
4. countenance (koun/tə nəns), *n.* face; features.
5. spell (spel), *n.* a length of time.

went for more. Well, at last he could hardly flop his wings, he was so tuckered out. He comes a-drooping down, once more, sweating like an ice-pitcher, drops his acorn in and says, "*Now* I guess I've got the bulge on[6] you by this time!" So he bent down for a look. If you'll believe me, when his head come up again he was just pale with rage. He says, "I've shoveled acorns enough in there to keep the family thirty years, and if I can see a sign of one of 'em I wish I may land in a museum with a belly full of sawdust in two minutes!"

He just had strength enough to crawl up on to the comb and lean his back agin the chimbly, and then he collected his impressions and begun to free his mind. I see in a second that what I had mistook for profanity in the mines was only just the rudiments, as you may say.

Another jay was going by, and heard him doing his devotions, and stops to inquire what was up. The sufferer told him the whole circumstance, and says, "Now yonder's the hole, and if you don't believe me, go and look for yourself." So this fellow went and looked, and comes back and says, "How many did you say you put in there?" "Not any less than two tons," says the sufferer. The other jay went and looked again. He couldn't seem to make it out, so he raised a yell, and three more jays come. They all examined the hole, they all made the sufferer tell it over again, then they all discussed it, and got off as many leather-headed opinions about it as an average crowd of humans could have done.

They called in more jays; then more and more, till pretty soon this whole region 'peared to have a blue flush about it. There must have been five thousand of them; and such another jawing and disputing and ripping and cussing, you never heard. Every jay in the whole lot put his eye to the hole and delivered a more chuckle-headed opinion about the mystery than the jay that went there before him. They examined the house all over, too. The door was standing half open, and at last one old jay happened to go and light on it and look in. Of course, that knocked the mystery galley-west in a second. There lay the acorns, scattered all over the floor. He flopped his wings and raised a whoop. "Come here!" he says, "Come here, everybody; hang'd if this fool hasn't been trying to fill up a house with acorns!" They all came a-swooping down like a blue cloud, and as each fellow lit on the door and took a glance, the whole absurdity[7] of the contract that that first jay had tackled hit him home and he fell over backward suffocating with laughter, and the next jay took his place and done the same.

Well, sir, they roosted around here on the housetop and the trees for an hour, and guffawed[8] over that thing like human beings. It ain't any use to tell me a bluejay hasn't got a sense of humor, because I know better. And memory, too. They brought jays here from all over the United States to look down that hole, every summer for three years. Other birds, too. And they could all see the point, except an owl that come from Nova Scotia[9] to visit the Yo Semite, and he took this thing in on his way back. He said he couldn't see anything funny in it. But then he was a good deal disappointed about Yo Semite, too.

---

6. **get the bulge on,** To get something on a person—in this case, "the bulge"—is to get the advantage, or get the upper hand on a person.
7. **absurdity** (ab sėr′də tē), *n.* ridiculous quality or condition; foolishness.
8. **guffaw** (gu fô′), *v.* laugh loudly and coarsely.
9. **Nova Scotia** (nō′və skō′shə), province in southeastern Canada.

After Reading

Making Connections

1. What did you find funny about this selection? Why?

2. Jim Baker praises the blue jay's grammar while criticizing the way cats talk. What do you think of Jim Baker's grammar?

3. Do you suppose Mark Twain really believed blue jays can think and talk the way they do in the story? Give a reason for your answer.

4. What point or points about human nature do you think Twain was trying to make in this story?

5. Twain's opinion of Congressmen could just as easily have come from a modern-day comedian. Does it surprise you that at least some people had a low opinion of political figures in the 1800s? Why or why not?

6. Write a few sentences in which you compare yourself to the blue jay or another animal.

Literary Focus: Similes and Metaphors

To help readers look at things in new and different ways, authors often make comparisons between unlike things. A comparison that uses the word *like* or *as* is called a **simile.** *Her hands were strong as steel* is an example. A comparison that does not use any words of comparison is called a **metaphor.** *Life is a roaring sea* is an example.

The author uses both similes and metaphors in "What Stumped the Blue Jays." He even uses the term *metaphor* as part of a metaphor, when he says the blue jay's language is "bristling with metaphor." What other metaphors and similes you can find in the story? Record your findings in a chart like the one below. Two examples have been done for you.

Example from the Story	Simile or Metaphor	Two Things Being Compared
bristling with metaphor	metaphor	blue jay's language and an animal covered with bristles (hairs)
. . . they [jays] are as ashamed as a human. . .	simile	blue jays and a human

Vocabulary Study

Write the letter of the correct answer to each question.

absurdity
aggravating
countenance
gratification
instinct

1. Which word describes the feeling you get when someone appreciates your hard work?

   a. consciousness   **b.** instinct   **c.** gratification

2. Which word describes a pesky little brother or sister?

   a. aggravating   **b.** absurdity   **c.** flowery

3. Which word describes your eyes, nose, and mouth?

   a. figure   **b.** countenance   **c.** instinct

4. Which word describes a mother cat's urge to protect her kittens?

   a. profanity   **b.** instinct   **c.** gratification

5. Which word describes the idea of electing a horse to Congress?

   a. gratification   **b.** absurdity   **c.** improvement

Expressing Your Ideas

Writing Choices

Animal Behavior, Part One You are a scientist who specializes in animal behavior. Observe an animal for a half hour or so. (The animal can be any type: a pet, a farm animal, a wild animal, or a zoo animal.) Take detailed notes about what the animal does. Then, use your notes to write a straightforward **description** of the animal's behavior.

Animal Behavior, Part Two Write a **short story** about an animal you have observed. Include the animal's "thoughts" and "speech." What was that big squirrel saying to the other squirrels in your backyard? Make your story funny!

Other Options

Lesson in Problem Solving Think about a time when you did what Twain's blue jay did, attacking a problem without really understanding it. What happened? What did you learn from the experience? Share your thoughts in a short **speech** to your classmates.

The Blue Jay Comics Have you ever noticed how many comic strips have animals as characters? Imagine you are the creator of a comic strip called "Life Among the Blue Jays." You plan to tell the story of the jay and the big hole over a period of weeks. Draw one day's **comic strip** in which you tell part of the story.

Language Mini-Lesson

Checking Your Spelling

Recognize spelling problems. Have you ever made such obvious spelling errors that you wondered if you were unconscious when you wrote the words? Sometimes the worst kinds of spelling mistakes we make are the most obvious. Read the passage below.

Last winter we went to Florda to visit are grandparents and see Disneyworld. I got to bring a freind, and we could hardly wait untill we got there.

What four words did the writer of that passage misspell? How do you spell them correctly?

Writing Strategy Make yourself aware of words that are easily misspelled. Here are some tips.

- Know the spellings and definitions for words that sound alike, such as *to* and *too* or *there* and *their*.

- Be alert to silent letters in a word like *building*. If you're not sure of all the letters in a word, look it up in a dictionary.

- Watch for letters you might have accidentally switched. Sometimes *enemy* ends up being spelled *emeny*.

Activity Options

1. How many misspellings can you find in a single day? Keep your eyes open for misspellings you see every day, whether they're done on purpose or not. Write down the incorrect and correct spellings and keep your list handy. Compare lists with other students to see what they found.

2. Write five sentences that include the following words, but use them incorrectly: *too, our, then, which, whole,* and *we're.* Exchange papers with a partner and correct each other's sentences.

3. Keep a "Tricky Words" list of words you have sometimes misspelled because they have silent letters or you've accidentally switched letters. Compare your list with others to see how many words you have in common.

Before Reading

Porcupine and the Sky Mirrors

by Katherine Davison

Katherine Davison
born 1933

"Porcupine and the Sky Mirrors" comes from the book *Moon Magic: Stories from Asia* by Katherine Davison. Like other authors, Davison is deeply in love with the written word. Although *Moon Magic* is her first book, she is involved with words every day in her job as editor and co-owner of a newsletter publishing company.

Building Background

Siberia "Porcupine and the Sky Mirrors" originated in Siberia. Siberia makes up about 75 percent of the land area of Russia; yet only 20 percent of Russia's people live there. Most of the region is covered by ice and snow for half the year, and temperatures sometimes fall as low as –90° F. Knowing these facts will help you appreciate the importance of the sky mirrors to the characters in the story.

Getting into the Story

Discussion An act of hospitality leads to a big problem in "Porcupine and the Sky Mirrors." According to the dictionary, *hospitality* means "generous treatment of guests or strangers." In a small group, share your ideas about hospitality. What do you think being a "good host" means? What are the responsibilities of a "good guest"? Have you ever had a bad experience as a host or as a guest? What happened?

Reading Tip

Examining Consequences The characters in "Porcupine and the Sky Mirrors" all perform actions that have important consequences. Sometimes a consequence for one character will lead to an action and a consequence by another character. As you read, fill in the chart with an action and a consequence for each character.

Character	Action	Consequences
Sky King	He offers his brother anything in his home.	His brother takes the most valuable item.

PORCUPINE and the SKY MIRRORS

Katherine Davison

Long ago, when the world was new, the people of Siberia knew that Porcupine was a wise little fellow who could solve any problem. He was also a good neighbor and a careful farmer.

Because Porcupine was so good-hearted and kind, he had a full social life, as you can imagine. He was even a friend to the Sky King, who lived above the clouds in his Sky House. One day, Porcupine paid his friend a visit.

The Sky House was a splendid place. Its walls were slabs of sparkling ice, and ice bells tinkled cheerfully in every room. The blue floor was covered with fluffy, white rugs, and in the largest room, a great fire was always blazing. But the finest things of all were the two huge mirrors that stood on either side of the fire. One was made of gold and the other of silver, and they reflected the fire's light so brightly that it shone through the walls of ice and lighted the whole earth.

Porcupine and the Sky King enjoyed themselves very much that afternoon. They drank hot, sweet tea poured from a shiny samovar.[1] They ate a great many honey cakes and told funny stories. The king was a very amusing fellow when he could forget he was a king, and of course Porcupine was always good company.

At last, when it was time for Porcupine to go home, the Sky King said, "Friend Porcupine, take something with you so you will think of me and remember this wonderful visit." (It was very polite for a host to give something to his guests as they were leaving.)

"I don't need a gift to remember this enjoyable day," said Porcupine. "You've given me your fine hospitality, and that's enough. Save your gift."

The Sky King tugged at his long mustache and shook his head.

"No, no, I insist!" he said firmly. "I want to give you something from the Sky House. It would be bad manners for you to refuse."

Porcupine said, "Well then, since I live a long way away, I'll take something to eat on the way home. Thank you."

The Sky King was pleased, and he gave Porcupine a leather bag full of delicious black bread. The king even walked part of the way

---

1. **samovar** (sam′ə vär), *n.* a metal urn used for heating water for tea.

home with him, to make the way seem shorter.

On the road, whom should they meet but the Earth King. "Hello, Brother," said the Sky King. "You're a long way from home today."

"I was just coming to visit you, Brother," said the Earth King, "but I got a late start. My goodness, how bright it is up here in the evening sky!"

"You see the light from my fire," answered the Sky King. Then he embraced his brother and said, "I'm delighted that you're here to visit me! Please stay for dinner! And perhaps my good friend Porcupine will come back and join us. It would be like a real party!"

Of course, Porcupine never liked to refuse a friend's request, and he could not resist the idea of a party, so the three of them went back through the cold northern sky to the Sky House.

When they got there, the Sky King laid out more good things to eat and drink. He built up the fire and set candles in every window until the northern lights[2] flickered all over the sky. Everything was so cheerful and beautiful that the Earth King became just a bit envious of his brother. His Earth House was a rather dark place, made of tree trunks and located in a gloomy forest.

In spite of this little stab[3] of envy, the Earth King enjoyed himself very much. He sat beside the warm fire and feasted on tiny salted fish and rich red soup. He ate three kinds of black bread with two kinds of caviar[4] and four kinds of cheese. For dessert there were rosy apples and more honey cakes. He drank many glasses of hot tea and laughed at the funny stories told by Porcupine and the Sky King. He even told some stories of his own. But at the same time, he couldn't help wishing his house was as pretty and cheerful as his brother's.

The Sky King enjoyed the visit too, and when it was time for his guests to go home, he

said, "Please take something to remember me by."

Porcupine answered, "No, nothing for me. I still have that nice black bread you gave me before."

"But you must have something more," said the Sky King. "I insist!"

So Porcupine took a little piece of goat's-milk cheese to go with the bread, and he promised to eat it on the way home.

Then the Sky King turned to the Earth King. "And you, Brother, what will you take to remember our visit?"

Now, all evening, as the Earth King admired the Sky House, the things he liked best of all were the shining mirrors on either side of the fire. More than anything else, the Earth King wanted those mirrors.

"Oh . . . I don't need a gift. Thank you, anyway," he said slowly, looking at the beautiful mirrors.

"But you must take something," the Sky King said. "I insist!"

"Well then, if I have to take something . . . give me those two mirrors. They will look very nice on each side of my own fireplace," said the Earth King.

"Oh," said the Sky King. "Oh, my goodness!"

He really didn't want to part with his sky mirrors. He had expected the Earth King to choose something small, the way Porcupine had done. But it would have been extremely bad manners to refuse, so very sadly he took down the mirrors and gave them to his brother.

The Earth King took the mirrors and went home. Porcupine went home too, but the Sky King didn't walk even a little part of the way

---

2. **northern lights**, streamers or bands of light appearing in the northern sky at night.
3. **stab** (stab), *n.* usually, a thrust or blow made by a pointed weapon, or the wound that results. In this case, the Earth King is experiencing an emotional blow, or an injury to his feelings.
4. **caviar** (kav′ē är), *n.* the salted eggs of sturgeon or of certain other large fish, eaten as an appetizer.

with them. It took a long time to get home, because now that the Sky King had no sky mirrors to reflect the light of his fire onto the earth, it had become very dark, both in the sky and on the earth.

The next day, it was still dark, and the next day too. The Sky King sat by his fire feeling gloomy because his house seemed very dull without his sky mirrors. "Well, anyway, I did the right thing," the king said to himself. He said it several times, because it made him feel a little better to think about his good manners.

On earth, Porcupine's farm was not doing well anymore, and all his neighbors' crops were dying too. "I'm worried about this," he thought to himself. "What if the world is never bright and warm again? The mirrors must be returned to the Sky House where they belong."

Porcupine considered the problem all day long, and the next day he went to pay a visit to his friend the Earth King. When Porcupine got to the Earth House, the Earth King was very glad to see him. "Sit down and have a glass of tea," he said. "How have you been, dear Porcupine?"

"Not as well as usual," Porcupine said truthfully. "It has been pretty dark at my house. Without the sky mirrors, I can no longer see the light of your brother's fire. And because there is no light, all the crops are dying."

QUESTION: What reaction to this statement do you suppose Porcupine is hoping for?

The Earth King didn't like that answer. He pulled crossly on his mustache.

"Where are the mirrors, anyway?" asked Porcupine. "I thought you would have them standing by your fire."

"They are too beautiful to leave lying about. I put them away so nothing would happen to them," said the Earth King. (Really, he was

Provincetown, Sunset and Moonrise (Moonset and Sunrise) was painted by Marguerite Zorach in 1916. Compare the details of this painting to the description of the Sky House on page 556.

afraid that his brother might come and take the mirrors back, so he had hidden them.)

Porcupine looked all around, but he couldn't see the mirrors anywhere.

The Earth King made tea in his big samovar, and he got out some honey cakes. The food was good, but somehow the stories they told each other didn't seem very funny, and the visit was a little sad. To tell the truth, the Earth King felt very sorry that the earth was now so dark and cold, but he couldn't bear to give back those beautiful mirrors.

When it was time for Porcupine to go, the Earth King said politely, "Please take something with you so that you will remember our visit."

"Oh no, nothing," said Porcupine.

"But I insist you take something. Perhaps some nice bread and cheese?"

"No, thank you," said Porcupine slowly. Then, just as he was speaking, he noticed something that gave him a wonderful idea. "But since you insist," Porcupine continued slowly, "I will ask you for a mirage—one of those images in the air that look real, such as a lake in the middle of the desert. May I have one of those?"

The Earth King was surprised and unhappy at this request. "But a mirage is just a reflection of light on the air," he said. "I can't give you that!"

"Well, never mind," said Porcupine, pretending to be disappointed. "You have plenty of echoes in the Earth House. Will you give me an echo instead?"

The Earth King tugged on his mustache so hard that he had to stop very suddenly because he hurt himself. It was terrible manners to refuse something to a guest, but how could he give Porcupine an echo to take with him? "An echo is only a reflection of a sound," he said. "I just can't give you an echo, Porcupine! Ask me for something I can really give to you! Ask me for anything in my house, and it will be yours!"

Porcupine shrugged his shoulders and looked sad. But he was really very happy, because several minutes before, his sharp eyes had noticed something interesting. Beside the front door stood a large, old box. Under the lid, Porcupine could see a tiny sparkle of light. He had guessed that the sky mirrors were in that box, and now that the Earth King had refused him twice, he certainly could not refuse his third request!

"Well then," said Porcupine, "I guess I'll just take whatever is in that old box there—since I must take something."

The Earth King was furious! He pulled on his mustache so hard his eyes watered. How did Porcupine know the mirrors were in that box? The Earth King didn't want to give them back, but he couldn't refuse Porcupine a third time.

"I have good manners! I have very good manners!" he said, chewing on his mustache, his eyes watering terribly. He lifted the box and handed it to Porcupine. "Here, take it!" He tried to sound generous, but he slammed the door when Porcupine went out, and he did not offer to walk him any part of the way home.

EVALUATE: Is the Earth King right—does he indeed have good manners? Give your reasons.

Porcupine didn't go home, anyway. He ran all the way to the Sky House with the box in his arms. He was out of breath when he gave it to the Sky King, saying, "I have brought you (puff-puff) a present (puff-puff), old friend!"

When the Sky King opened the box and saw the mirrors, he was so happy he forgot his manners and didn't even remember to say, "Thank you."

He ran and set the mirrors beside his fire, and at once the firelight flashed all through the Sky House and down over the earth. Only then did the Sky King turn to Porcupine and say, "I thank you, old friend!"

If you look into the sky, you can see that the mirrors stand there still. The gold mirror is the warmest, and we call it the sun. The silver mirror is the moon that lights the night. If you go to the Sky House, you can see them there now.

After Reading

Making Connections

1. Would you recommend this story to a friend? Why or why not?

2. This story has survived for centuries. Why do you suppose that's true?

3. **Origin tales** like "Porcupine and the Sky Mirrors" try to explain natural occurrences. Give the story a new title that reflects what it tries to explain. Begin your title with the word *Why*.

4. Do you think it's possible to be *too* polite? Support your answer with consequences from your chart on page 555 and observations from real life.

5. The Earth King gives Porcupine the mirrors, painful as it is for him. In real life, people often find it painful to do the right thing. What makes people willing to do the right thing despite the pain it might cause them?

6. Suppose your culture has a custom that a host must offer a possession of value to a guest. What is the one thing you could not bear to let a guest have? Why?

Literary Focus: Problems and Solutions

You may have seen a film like this at school: A problem is presented. At a critical point, the film stops. Then the audience is asked to discuss possible solutions to the problem. After the discussion, the film starts up again.

With a group of classmates, imagine "Porcupine and the Sky Mirrors" is such a film. The first time the film stops is just after the Sky King says, "Oh. Oh, my goodness!" on page 557. At this point, your group should talk about what the Sky King could do to be a good host while not giving the Earth King the mirrors. Try to come up with three possible solutions, and write them down.

Of course, the Sky King can't hear you, so he gives the mirrors to the Earth King. The film continues. The next time it stops is right after Porcupine says to the Earth King, "I guess I'll just take whatever is in that old box there—since I must take something" on page 559. Assume that the mirrors are *not* in the old box, and Porcupine leaves the Earth King's home with an old box full of used, crumpled aluminum foil. Talk about what Porcupine might do next to retrieve the mirrors. Try to come up with three possible solutions and write them down.

Expressing Your Ideas

Writing Choices

Move Over, Miss Manners The term *etiquette* refers to the customary rules for polite behavior. Write a **pamphlet** in which you list etiquette rules you think hosts and guests of your age should follow. You might divide your pamphlet into sections dealing with different situations: dinner, sleepovers, birthday parties, and so on.

New Home for the Earth King There's no reason the Earth King should have a dark and gloomy home. The earth has many sunny, attractive places he could live. Think of a real place like that, and write a **description** of it that you could read to the Earth King to help persuade him to move there. Use lots of adjectives, and make the place sound as appealing as you can.

Excuse Me! Have you ever tried to do the right thing but still managed to offend someone anyway? Think of a situation that resulted in the words on the sign below. What did you do to **change** the situation and come to an understanding? Make a **list** of things that you have done or would do to overcome an embarrassing situation.

Other Options

Plan the Movie Imagine you work for a Hollywood studio that plans to make an animated film of "Porcupine and the Sky Mirrors." Your job is to create storyboards: large sketches or drawings that show, in sequence, the actions that will occur in the film. Choose one scene from the story and create the **storyboards** for it. Show your storyboards to your classmates, explaining them as you do so.

Puppets on Stage With at least two classmates, plan and present a **puppet play** based on the story. Create a script, make the puppets, gather or make props, and arrange for sound effects. When you're ready, put on your play, perhaps for a group of younger children at your school.

To Have, or Not to Have In a play, a *soliloquy* is a speech a character says that the other characters do not hear. It's like thinking out loud. Imagine you are either the Sky King at the moment that the Earth King asks for the mirrors, or the Earth King right after you've gotten home with them. Deliver a **soliloquy** to the class that describes what you're thinking. Put some feeling into it!

Facing the Problem Head-On

Skywatching

Stargazers of Old

Science Connection

For thousands of years, people have watched the night sky and wondered about what they saw. However, skywatching was more than a hobby for early societies. The earliest astronomers watched the sky for signs of the changing seasons. On clear nights they looked for familiar patterns and observed the changing stages of the heavens.

In the second century B.C., Egyptian astronomer Ptolemy proposed that the earth was the center of the universe. Also a mathematician and geographer, Ptolemy identified and named forty-eight constellations.

In centuries past, the position of the planets in the sky helped farmers determine when to plant and harvest their crops. This fifteenth century Italian illustration represents farm workers being influenced by the position of the planet Mercury.

This celestial atlas, or map of the sky, drawn by Englishman John Bevis around the year 1750, illustrates his vision of the constellations.

Many constellations can be seen only from the Northern or Southern Hemisphere. The twelve constellations of the zodiac, including Scorpio, shown here in this sixteenth century Turkish work of art, can be seen from both hemispheres. ▼

▲ A medieval astronomer studies the heavens. In the sixteenth century, the astronomer Copernicus theorized that Earth and the other planets revolved around the sun.

◄ A medieval French seaman uses a navigational instrument to determine his course.

Responding

Many folk tales have been written to explain the movement of the sun, stars, and planets. Find and read one of these tales. Then tell the tale to your class.

History Connection

The standing stones at Stonehenge were used to record key celestial events. Survival of entire ancient civilizations rested in part on the ability to accurately predict the changing seasons. The people who built Stonehenge, and many others around the world who built similar structures, faced the problem head on. They developed accurate instruments for recording changing patterns in the sky that related to the changing seasons.

SOLVING
the Mystery of Stonehenge

by Malcolm E. Weiss

In England, on Salisbury Plain, about seventy-five miles from London, stand the ruins of an astronomical tool that was built long ago. This tool is Stonehenge. It is a complicated structure of mammoth stone pillars and slabs. Stonehenge was built in three phases. The building began around 2600 B.C. It was completed in about 1400 B.C.—some twelve hundred years later.

Stonehenge was used for religious ceremonies. But it was more than a temple—it was also a giant calendar.

If you stand in the center of Stonehenge at dawn on June 21, the summer solstice, and look to the east through the center of the opening in the outer ditch, you will be looking at the point where the sun is rising.

This has been known for centuries. But in the mid-1960s, Gerald Hawkins, then an astronomer at Boston University, used a computer to show that the stones and holes at Stonehenge were lined up with certain risings and settings of both moon and sun. These risings and settings marked major dates in the ancient calendar. Hawkins also tried to prove that Stonehenge could have been used to predict eclipses of the sun and moon. Some scientists are still skeptical about this. For one thing, the skeptics point out, the Mayas, who did learn how to predict eclipses, had a well-developed number system. And the Babylonians, who lived thousands of years before the Mayas, also predicted the motions of heavenly bodies and the times of eclipses. Their mathematics were even more advanced than the Mayas'. But at the time Stonehenge was built, the people of Britain did not have a number system.

On the other hand, it is also true that for centuries most scientists thought Stonehenge could not have been built by the early people of Britain. The stones were too carefully smoothed, squared and joined together for that. Stonehenge was believed to be the work of more "civilized" peoples from the area around the Mediterranean Sea.

But now scientists agree that Stonehenge is even older than the Mediterranean civilizations once thought to have designed it. It was in fact the "primitive" natives of ancient Britain who designed and erected this imposing structure.

Besides Stonehenge, there are thousands of other prehistoric monuments scattered over Europe. There are still others in Africa, along the Mediterranean coast, and in the areas that are now Ethiopia and the Sudan.

Monuments have also been found in Palestine, Iran, Pakistan, Tibet, India, Southeast Asia, Japan, and Borneo.

Some of these ancient monuments are great circles of stone like Stonehenge. Others are tall stones set in the earth like pillars. These are called *menhirs*, from a word that means "long stone" in the Breton language. Breton is a dialect spoken in Brittany, a region in northwestern France.

When menhirs are placed in a circle, they are called *cromlechs*. Cromlech is also a Breton word. It means "curved stone." Menhirs are sometimes found in long straight rows called alignments. The most famous of these is at Carnac in Brittany. There, more than ten rows of menhirs stretch out across the countryside over a distance of four miles—three thousand menhirs in all.

Responding
Research one of the other ancient monuments that was built to predict the seasons or mark the passage of time. You may choose a monument from any of the countries mentioned in this reading. Draw a picture and write a short description of the monument. With classmates, make a bulletin board display of your projects.

Science Connection

Skywatching is not for professional astronomers alone. With a little practice you will be able to recognize constellations and planets, too. Watch the sky over the course of a year, and you see patterns that change with the seasons.

TAKING A LOOK AT THE NIGHT SKY

Carole Stott

There are some marvelous sights in the night sky. With a little patience and some good clear skies, you'll soon be familiar with them.

If you have difficulty remembering the constellations, you may find it helps to make your own pictures. Place some tracing paper over one of the star maps in the book. Trace the dots

which represent the stars, but don't trace the lines. Then connect the dots to make your own pictures. You may find that Orion looks more like a robot than a hunter, and Crux looks like a kite rather than a cross.

At first, all the stars look silvery-white. But after a few nights of observing, you will notice that some have a very faint coloring. The color comes from the temperature of the star's surface. The hottest stars are blue, and slightly cooler ones are white. Stars that are cooler still are yellow, and the coolest are red.

There is no need to buy expensive equipment to look at the sky. You can see hundreds of objects just by using your eyes. But, if you have the chance, borrow some binoculars. They are easy to use and show as much as a small telescope. They'll reveal thousands more stars, as well as details on the moon's surface. Try counting

the new stars you can see with the help of the binoculars. You'll find it easier if you support the binoculars to stop them from wobbling around.

Start a diary and sketch-book of your observations. Note down what you saw and the time you saw it. Compare what something looks like from one night to the next. Draw the shape of the moon as it changes through the lunar month.

If you are eager to make a more detailed study of the sky, why not join your local astronomical society? They'll give you helpful advice and information, and may even have a large telescope you can look through. They'll also have up-to-date information on what is happening in the sky.

Responding

Try some of the ideas in this reading. With a friend, do some skywatching for several nights. Record your observations. Report to the class on which constellations you were able to recognize.

Reading Mini-Lesson

Visualizing

"Do you see what I mean?"
"Do you get the picture now?"
"Can you see the big picture?"
"I didn't see that problem coming."

When people ask these questions, they're usually not talking about *seeing* or *pictures*—they're talking about *understanding*. Perhaps this happens because we depend so much on our eyesight to deal with and interpret our environment. When we are reading, we have to visualize the picture suggested by the writer's words.

In "Solving the Mystery of Stonehenge," on page 565, you read that monuments made of huge stones were placed in circles or in rows. The writer's description helps you to picture the arrangements, and picturing the arrangements helps you to understand the explanations of the purposes of these stone monuments.

"Taking a Look at the Night Sky" on page 567 also contains descriptions which help you to visualize. For example, the second paragraph gives you easy-to-see directions for making your own pictures for groups of stars.

Science and social studies textbooks often have photos, diagrams, and illustrations to show structures (a plant cell), landforms (a river delta), or a series of events (a battle). When there is no visual aid to help you to see what is going on, you might have to make one of your own. Use a pencil and try to sketch the object or person or place you need to visualize.

Activity Options

1. Sketch the picture you "see" from the description of Stonehenge. Before you start, think about the best angle or point of view from which to show the monument. Use the clues in the article to visualize what the drawing should look like.

2. In a newspaper, magazine, or book, find another selection that uses a lot of description and visual detail. Working with a partner, make a map or picture that can be used as an illustration with the selection. From the selection, identify 5–10 visual details on which to base your illustration.

Part Two

Finding Solutions

How do you find solutions to problems you face? Do you take a long walk by yourself and think it over? Or call your best friend on the phone and talk? Or get lost in music, a book, or a movie and hope that when you return to your own life you'll know what to do? These are just a few ways that people try to solve their problems.

Multicultural Connection In finding a solution to a problem, people are often faced with making a difficult **choice.** That choice may involve weighing group pressures and accepting the consequences of one's actions. As you read, pay attention to the choices made by the characters in these selections.

Before Reading

The No-Guitar Blues

by Gary Soto

Gary Soto
born 1952

Like the main character in "The No-Guitar Blues," Gary Soto grew up in a poor Mexican American neighborhood in the city of Fresno, California. He draws deeply on his childhood experience in his poetry and his fiction. But his career as a writer, Soto admits, basically came out of thin air. "I don't think I had any literary aspirations when I was a kid." In college, Soto stumbled across a poetry anthology and thought, "This is terrific. I'd like to do something like this." The first books Soto published were poetry. Later, he wrote prose, especially stories for young adult readers. But his prose, too, has lyrical grace. According to one reviewer, each of his stories is "a little treasure of human experience skillfully drawn with poetic sensitivity."

Building Background

Rock and Roll If you like rock and roll music, you would probably enjoy watching reruns of the television show "American Bandstand." Airing nationally from 1957 to 1987, this show featured up-and-coming singers and bands.

Among the groups whose appearance on "American Bandstand" helped lead them to national fame was Los Lobos, a Chicano band from East Los Angeles. They played traditional Mexican music, rock music, and music that blended these two musical styles. Many Mexican American youth were inspired by Los Lobos' success.

Getting into the Story

Writer's Notebook Based on the title, predict what this story will be about. Also make predictions about the setting and the main character. Write your predictions in your notebook.

Reading Tip

Making a Problem/Solution Chart The main character in "The No-Guitar Blues" faces some personal problems. For each one, he comes up with what he thinks is the best solution. Make a chart like the one at the right and fill it in as you read this story. Note how each set of problems and solutions determines the shape of the story.

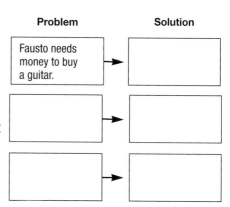

Problem	Solution
Fausto needs money to buy a guitar.	

The No-Guitar Blues

GARY SOTO

The moment Fausto[1] saw the group Los Lobos on "American Bandstand," he knew exactly what he wanted to do with his life—play guitar. His eyes grew large with excitement as Los Lobos ground out a song while teenagers bounced off each other on the crowded dance floor.

He had watched "American Bandstand" for years and had heard Ray Camacho and the Teardrops at Romain Playground, but it had never occurred to him that he too might become a musician. That afternoon Fausto knew his mission in life: to play guitar in his own band; to sweat out his songs and prance around the stage; to make money and dress weird.

Fausto turned off the television set and walked outside, wondering how he could get enough money to buy a guitar. He couldn't ask his parents because they would just say, "Money doesn't grow on trees" or "What do you think we are, bankers?" And besides, they hated rock music. They were into the *conjunto* music[2] of Lydia Mendoza, Flaco Jiménez, and Little Joe and La Familia. And, as Fausto recalled, the last album they bought was *The Chipmunks Sing Christmas Favorites.*

But what the heck, he'd give it a try. He returned inside and watched his mother make tortillas. He leaned against the kitchen counter, trying to work up the nerve to ask her for a guitar. Finally, he couldn't hold back any longer.

"Mom," he said, "I want a guitar for Christmas."

She looked up from rolling tortillas. "Honey, a guitar costs a lot of money."

"How 'bout for my birthday next year," he tried again.

"I can't promise," she said, turning back to her tortillas, "but we'll see."

Fausto walked back outside with a buttered tortilla. He knew his mother was right. His father was a warehouseman at Berven Rugs, where he made good money but not enough to buy everything his children wanted.

PREDICT: What do you think Fausto is planning? Give your evidence.

Fausto decided to mow lawns to earn money, and was pushing the mower down the street before he realized it was winter and no one would hire him. He returned the mower and

---

1. **Fausto** (foust′ô).
2. **conjunto music**, African-Cuban style of music developed in the 1930s that included piano, bongos, conga drums, bass, trumpets, and singers, with a chorus and a lead singer.

picked up a rake. He hopped onto his sister's bike (his had two flat tires) and rode north to the nicer section of Fresno[3] in search of work. He went door-to-door, but after three hours he managed to get only one job, and not to rake leaves. He was asked to hurry down to the store to buy a loaf of bread, for which he received a grimy, dirt-caked quarter.

He also got an orange, which he ate sitting at the curb. While he was eating, a dog walked up and sniffed his leg. Fausto pushed him away and threw an orange peel skyward. The dog caught it and ate it in one gulp. The dog looked at Fausto and wagged his tail for more. Fausto tossed him a slice of orange, and the dog snapped it up and licked his lips.

"How come you like oranges, dog?"

The dog blinked a pair of sad eyes and whined.

"What's the matter? Cat got your tongue?" Fausto laughed at his joke and offered the dog another slice.

At that moment a dim light came on inside Fausto's head. He saw that it was sort of a fancy dog, a terrier or something, with dog tags and a shiny collar. And it looked well fed and healthy. In his neighborhood, the dogs were never licensed,[4] and if they got sick they were placed near the water heater until they got well.

This dog looked like he belonged to rich people. Fausto cleaned his juice-sticky hands on his pants and got to his feet. The light in his head grew brighter. It just might work. He called the dog, patted its muscular back, and bent down to check the license.

"Great," he said, "There's an address."

The dog's name was Roger, which struck Fausto as weird because he'd never heard of a dog with a human name. Dogs should have names like Bomber, Freckles, Queenie, Killer, and Zero.

Fausto planned to take the dog home and collect a reward. He would say he had found Roger near the freeway. That would scare the daylights out of the owners, who would be so happy that they would probably give him a reward. He felt bad about lying, but the dog *was* loose. And it might even really be lost, because the address was six blocks away.

Fausto stashed the rake and his sister's bike behind a bush, and tossing an orange peel every time Roger became distracted,[5] walked the dog to his house. He hesitated on the porch until Roger began to scratch the door with a muddy paw. Fausto had come this far, so he figured he might as well go through with it. He knocked softly. When no one answered, he rang the doorbell. A man in a silky bathrobe and slippers opened the door and seemed confused by the sight of his dog and the boy.

"Sir," Fausto said, gripping Roger by the collar. "I found your dog by the freeway. His dog license says he lives here." Fausto looked down at the dog, then up to the man. "He does, doesn't he?"

The man stared at Fausto a long time before saying in a pleasant voice, "That's right." He pulled his robe tighter around him because of the cold and asked Fausto to come in. "So he was by the freeway?"

"Uh—huh."

"You bad, snoopy dog," said the man, wagging his finger. "You probably knocked over some trash cans, too, didn't you?"

Fausto didn't say anything. He looked around, amazed by this house with its shiny furniture and a television as large as the front window at home. Warm bread smells filled the air and music full of soft tinkling floated in from another room.

---

3. **Fresno** (frez′nō), city in south-central California.
4. license (lī′sns), *v.* give a tag, card, sticker, or certificate to show that something is registered with the city or state.
5. distracted (dis trak′tid), *adj.* having attention drawn away from a given purpose.

▲ Do you think Fausto's dream of owning a guitar will become a reality? Why?

How does this home compare to that of the dog owner's home?

"Helen," the man called to the kitchen. "We have a visitor." His wife came into the living room wiping her hands on a dish towel and smiling. "And who have we here?" she asked in one of the softest voices Fausto had ever heard.

"This young man said he found Roger near the freeway."

Fausto repeated his story to her while staring at a perpetual clock with a bell-shaped glass, the kind his aunt got when she celebrated her twenty-fifth anniversary. The lady frowned and said, wagging a finger at Roger, "Oh, you're a bad boy."

"It was very nice of you to bring Roger home," the man said. "Where do you live?"

"By that vacant lot on Olive," he said. "You know, by Brownie's Flower Place."

The wife looked at her husband, then Fausto. Her eyes twinkled triangles of light as she said, "Well, young man, you're probably hungry. How about a turnover?"

"What do I have to turn over?" Fausto asked, thinking she was talking about yard work or something like turning trays of dried raisins.

"No, no, dear, it's a pastry." She took him by the elbow and guided him to a kitchen that sparkled with copper pans and bright yellow wallpaper. She guided him to the kitchen table and gave him a tall glass of milk and something that looked like an *empanada*.[6] Steamy waves of heat escaped when he tore it in two. He ate with both eyes on the man and woman who stood arm-in-arm smiling at him. They were strange, he thought. But nice.

"That was good," he said after he finished the turnover. "Did you make it, ma'am?"

"Yes, I did. Would you like another?"

"No, thank you. I have to go home now."

As Fausto walked to the door, the man

---

6. *empanada* (em′ pə nä′ də), *n.* a Spanish pastry with a flaky crust and a spicy or sweet filling; similar to a turnover.

opened his wallet and took out a bill. "This is for you," he said. "Roger is special to us, almost like a son."

Fausto looked at the bill and knew he was in trouble. Not with these nice folks or with his parents but with himself. How could he have been so deceitful? The dog wasn't lost. It was just having a fun Saturday walking around.

CONNECT: If you were Fausto, do you think you would have felt the same way? Why or why not?

"I can't take that."

"You have to. You deserve it, believe me," the man said.

"No, I don't."

"Now don't be silly," said the lady. She took the bill from her husband and stuffed it into Fausto's shirt pocket. "You're a lovely child. Your parents are lucky to have you. Be good. And come see us again, please."

Fausto went out, and the lady closed the door. Fausto clutched the bill through his shirt pocket. He felt like ringing the doorbell and begging them to please take the money back, but he knew they would refuse. He hurried away, and at the end of the block, pulled the bill from his shirt pocket: it was a crisp twenty-dollar bill.

"Oh, man, I shouldn't have lied," he said under his breath as he started up the street like a zombie. He wanted to run to church for Saturday confession,[7] but it was past four-thirty, when confession stopped.

He returned to the bush where he had hidden the rake and his sister's bike and rode home slowly, not daring to touch the money in his pocket. At home, in the privacy of his room, he examined the twenty-dollar bill. He had never had so much money. It was probably enough to buy a secondhand guitar. But he felt bad, like the time he stole a dollar from

the secret fold inside his older brother's wallet.

Fausto went outside and sat on the fence. "Yeah," he said. "I can probably get a guitar for twenty. Maybe at a yard sale—things are cheaper."

His mother called him to dinner.

The next day he dressed for church without anyone telling him. He was going to go to eight o'clock mass.

"I'm going to church, Mom," he said. His mother was in the kitchen cooking *papas*[8] and *chorizo con huevos*.[9] A pile of tortillas lay warm under a dishtowel.

"Oh, I'm so proud of you, Son." She beamed, turning over the crackling *papas*.

His older brother, Lawrence, who was at the table reading the funnies, mimicked, "Oh, I'm so proud of you, my son," under his breath.

At Saint Theresa's he sat near the front. When Father Jerry began by saying that we are all sinners, Fausto thought he looked right at him. Could he know? Fausto fidgeted[10] with guilt. No, he thought. I only did it yesterday.

. . . he started up the street like a zombie.

Fausto knelt, prayed, and sang. But he couldn't forget the man and the lady, whose names he didn't even know, and the *empanada* they had given him. It had a strange name but tasted really good. He wondered how they got rich. And how that dome clock worked. He had asked his mother once how

---

7. confession (kən fesh′ən), *n.* a Catholic ritual in which a person tells his or her sins to a priest.
8. *papa* (pä′ pä), Spanish word for potato.
9. *chorizo con huevos* (chō rē′ so kōn wā′ vōs), Spanish for sausage and eggs, a popular breakfast dish for Mexicans and Mexican Americans.
10. fidget (fij′it), *v.* move about restlessly or uneasily.

his aunt's clock worked. She said it just worked, the way the refrigerator works. It just did.

Fausto caught his mind wandering and tried to concentrate on his sins. He said a Hail Mary[11] and sang, and when the wicker basket came his way, he stuck a hand reluctantly in his pocket and pulled out the twenty-dollar bill. He ironed it between his palms, and dropped it into the basket. The grown-ups stared. Here was a kid dropping twenty dollars in the basket while they gave just three or four dollars.

There would be a second collection for Saint Vincent de Paul,[12] the lector announced. The wicker baskets again floated in the pews, and this time the adults around him, given a second chance to show their charity, dug deep into their wallets and purses and dropped in fives and tens. This time Fausto tossed in the grimy quarter.

Fausto felt better after church. He went home and played football in the front yard with his brother and some neighbor kids. He felt cleared of wrongdoing and was so happy that he played one of his best games of football ever. On one play, he tore his good pants, which he knew he shouldn't have been wearing. For a second, while he examined the hole, he wished he hadn't given the twenty dollars away.

Man, I coulda bought me some Levi's, he thought. He pictured his twenty dollars being spent to buy church candles. He pictured a priest buying an armful of flowers with *his* money.

Fausto had to forget about getting a guitar. He spent the next day playing soccer in his good pants, which were now his old pants. But that night during dinner, his mother said she remembered seeing an old bass guitarron[13]

the last time she cleaned out her father's garage.

"It's a little dusty," his mom said, serving his favorite enchiladas, "But I think it works. Grandpa says it works."

Fausto's ears perked up. That was the same kind the guy in Los Lobos played. Instead of asking for the guitar, he waited for his mother to offer it to him. And she did, while gathering the dishes from the table.

"No, Mom, I'll do it," he said, hugging her. "I'll do the dishes forever if you want."

It was the happiest day of his life. No, it was the second-happiest day of his life. The happiest was when his grandfather Lupe placed the guitarron, which was nearly as huge as a washtub, in his arms. Fausto ran a thumb down the strings, which vibrated in his throat and chest. It sounded beautiful, deep, and eerie.[14] A pumpkin smile widened on his face.

"OK, *hijo*, now you put your fingers like this," said his grandfather, smelling of tobacco and aftershave. He took Fausto's fingers and placed them on the strings. Fausto strummed a chord on the guitarron, and the bass resounded in their chests.

The guitarron was more complicated than Fausto imagined. But he was confident that after a few more lessons he could start a band that would someday play on "American Bandstand" for the dancing crowds.

---

11. **Hail Mary**, a Roman Catholic prayer to Mary, the mother of Jesus.
12. **Saint Vincent de Paul**, Roman Catholic charitable organization.
13. **guitarron** (gē′ tä rōn′), a folk guitar that originated in Mexico, used in mariachi bands. Mariachi bands are traditional street bands of Mexico.
14. eerie (ir′ē), *adj.* mysterious or suggesting of the supernatural.

After Reading

Making Connections

1. Look back at your predictions about the story. How close were your predictions to what actually happened? Explain.

2. Look back at your problem/solution chart. Did you agree with Fausto's solution to each problem? Explain what you would have done.

3. Do you think the author should have given more context clues to aid understanding of the story's details or do you think most readers would have enough prior knowledge about both Mexican-American culture and modern culture to enjoy this story? Explain.

4. What clues do you have that the author drew on his own experience to write this story?

5. Do you think people do what they feel is right for its own sake or because they would feel guilty if they did otherwise? Explain.

Literary Focus: The Climax of a Story

The plot of a story consists of the following elements: the presentation of a problem, rising action, a **climax**, falling action, and resolution of the problem. In many stories, the climax is usually the most exciting event. What do you think is the climax of "The No-Guitar Blues"? In your opinion, is the climax the most exciting event of this story? Make a plot structure map, like the one below.

Plot the following events on the map.

- Fausto needs money to buy a guitar.
- Fausto finds a dog.
- Fausto returns the dog to its owners.
- Fausto receives a large reward.
- Fausto feels guilty about the large reward he receives.
- Fausto donates the money to the church.
- Fausto finds an old guitar in his grandfather's garage.

Vocabulary Study

For each of the imaginary song titles listed in Column One, write the letter of the vocabulary word in Column Two that best relates to the title.

license
fidget
eerie
distracted
confession

Column One

____ **1.** "Mysterious Howl at Midnight"

____ **2.** "I Just Have to Tell the Truth: I Love You"

____ **3.** "Why Can't You Keep Your Mind on What You've Got to Do?"

____ **4.** "We Signed that Slip of Paper Down at City Hall"

____ **5.** "I Get Restless Whenever I Talk to You"

Column Two

a. confession

b. distracted

c. eerie

d. fidget

e. license

Expressing Your Ideas

Writing Choices

Forgive Me for I Have Been Bad Imagine you are Fausto. After leaving the house where you delivered the dog, you have just enough time to get to church at Saint Theresa's. What would you say to the priest? Write out your **confession.**

How It All Began Imagine Fausto has become a successful rock star. He has hired you to write a **song** telling the story of how he got started as a musician. Include three or four verses and a chorus that summarizes the main events of "The No-Guitar Blues."

Other Options

"American Bandstand" Live Work with a group to **videotape** your own version of "American Bandstand." One group of students should pose as an up-and-coming rock band; another group should be the audience; one person should take the part of the host and interview the band; and a crew of two or three can film the show for later viewing. Have the band practice lip-synching to several of the group's hits. Encourage the audience to dance their hearts out.

The World of Guitars What does a guitarron look and sound like? Find pictures of the guitarron and taped music, if possible. Look for pictures of other types of guitars and tapes of what each sounds like. Then, put together a **guitar guide** with pictures of different types of guitars. As you share your guitar guide with your classmates, play any taped music you have found.

Before Reading

The All-American Slurp

by Lensey Namioka

Lensey Namioka
born 1929

Lensey Namioka (nä mē ō′kä) is no stranger to the problems, solutions, and humor of the mixing of different cultures. She was born in China; she married a man from Japan; and she has traveled and lived all over the world. Namioka has written one autobiographical book about how her family adjusted to life in America. However, most of her books are adventure stories for young people, set centuries ago in Japan or China. They feature samurai warriors or fierce Mongol invaders on horseback. It might seem surprising, but Lensey Namioka was a math major in college and taught university-level courses for several years. "My long years of training in mathematics had little influence on my writing," Namioka states.

Building Background

Let's Eat! One thing all people have in common is eating. However, people from different cultures around the world have very different styles of eating. Europeans and people from North and South America share the custom of using metal utensils—forks, knives, and spoons—when eating. In India and Ethiopia, people often eat with their hands. They use soft, flat bread for picking up more slippery items of food. In eastern Asia, people use chopsticks and their main food is rice.

Getting into the Story

Discussion The words below all appear in the story "The All-American Slurp." Based on these words and the title, what do you think the story will be about? Do you think the story will be funny or serious? Predict some of the incidents that might occur in the story. Talk over your predictions with your classmates.

celery	dinner party	Americanized
zip	jeans	future perfect tense

Reading Tip

Similarities and Differences "The All-American Slurp" describes many similarities and differences between Chinese and American culture. The narrator actually states some comparisons. Others are hinted at through the incidents and dialogue in the story. As you read "The All-American Slurp," fill in a chart like the one below to help you analyze the similarities and differences between Chinese and American culture. Leave the last column of your chart blank for now.

Similarities	Differences	How Shown in Story	Purpose in Story
	Chinese aren't used to eating raw celery.	The celery strings get caught in the Lin family's teeth.	

The All-American SLURP

Lensey Namioka

The first time our family was invited out to dinner in America, we disgraced ourselves while eating celery. We had emigrated[1] to this country from China, and during our early days here we had a hard time with American table manners.

In China we never ate celery raw, or any other kind of vegetable raw. We always had to disinfect the vegetables in boiling water first. When we were presented with our first relish tray, the raw celery caught us unprepared.

We had been invited to dinner by our neighbors, the Gleasons. After arriving at the house, we shook hands with our hosts and packed ourselves into a sofa. As our family of four sat stiffly in a row, my younger brother and I stole glances at our parents for a clue as to what to do next.

Mrs. Gleason offered the relish tray to Mother. The tray looked pretty, with its tiny red radishes, curly sticks of carrots, and long, slender stalks of pale green celery. "Do try some of the celery, Mrs. Lin," she said. "It's from a local farmer, and it's sweet."

Mother picked up one of the green stalks, and Father followed suit. Then I picked up a stalk, and my brother did too. So there we sat, each with a stalk of celery in our right hand.

Mrs. Gleason kept smiling. "Would you like to try some of the dip, Mrs. Lin? It's my own recipe: sour cream and onion flakes, with a dash of Tabasco sauce."

Most Chinese don't care for dairy products, and in those days I wasn't even ready to drink fresh milk. Sour cream sounded perfectly revolting.[2] Our family shook our heads in unison.

Mrs. Gleason went off with the relish tray to the other guests, and we carefully

---

1. **emigrate** (em′ə grāt), *v.* leave one's country to settle in another.
2. **revolting** (ri vōl′ting), *adj.* disgusting.

watched to see what they did. Everyone seemed to eat the raw vegetables quite happily.

Mother took a bite of her celery. *Crunch.* "It's not bad!" she whispered.

Father took a bite of his celery. *Crunch.* "Yes, it *is* good," he said, looking surprised.

I took a bite, and then my brother. *Crunch, crunch.* It was more than good; it was delicious. Raw celery has a slight sparkle, a zingy taste that you don't get in cooked celery. When Mrs. Gleason came around with the relish tray, we each took another stalk of celery, except my brother. He took two.

There was only one problem: long strings ran through the length of the stalk, and they got caught in my teeth. When I help my mother in the kitchen, I always pull the strings out before slicing celery.

I pulled the strings out of my stalk. *Z-z-zip, z-z-zip.* My brother followed suit. *Z-z-zip, z-z-zip, z-z-zip.* To my left, my parents were taking care of their own stalks. *Z-z-zip, z-z-zip, z-z-zip.*

Suddenly I realized that there was dead silence except for our zipping. Looking up, I saw that the eyes of everyone in the room were on our family. Mr. and Mrs. Gleason, their daughter Meg, who was my friend, and their neighbors the Badels—they were all staring at us as we busily pulled the strings of our celery.

That wasn't the end of it. Mrs. Gleason announced that dinner was served and invited us to the dining table. It was lavishly covered with platters of food, but we couldn't see any chairs around the table. So we helpfully carried over some dining chairs and sat down. All the other guests just stood there.

Mrs. Gleason bent down and whispered to us, "This is a buffet dinner. You help yourselves to some food and eat it in the living room."

Our family beat a retreat back to the sofa as if chased by enemy soldiers. For the rest of the evening, too mortified[3] to go back to the dining table, I nursed a bit of potato salad on my plate.

Next day Meg and I got on the school bus together. I wasn't sure how she would feel about me after the spectacle our family made at the party. But she was just the same as usual, and the only reference she made to the party was, "Hope you and your folks got enough to eat last night. You certainly didn't take very much. Mom never tries to figure out how much food to prepare. She just puts everything on the table and hopes for the best."

CONNECT: If you were in the narrator's place right then, what do you think you would do?

I began to relax. The Gleasons' dinner party wasn't so different from a Chinese meal after all. My mother also puts everything on the table and hopes for the best.

Meg was the first friend I had made after we came to America. I eventually got acquainted with a few other kids in school, but Meg was still the only real friend I had.

My brother didn't have any problems making friends. He spent all his time with some boys who were teaching him baseball, and in no time he could speak English much faster than I could—not better, but faster.

I worried more about making mistakes, and I spoke carefully, making sure I could say everything right before opening my mouth. At least I had a better accent than my parents, who never really got rid of their Chinese accent, even years later. My parents had both studied English in school before coming to

---

3. **mortified** (môr′tə fīd), *adj.* humiliated.

⌃ The girl in this picture appears to be a symbol of America. Do you think the narrator sees herself this way?

America, but what they had studied was mostly written English, not spoken.

Father's approach to English was a scientific one. Since Chinese verbs have no tense, he was fascinated by the way English verbs changed form according to whether they were in the present, past imperfect, perfect, pluperfect, future, or future perfect tense. He was always making diagrams of verbs and their inflections, and he looked for opportunities to show off his mastery of the pluperfect and future perfect tenses, his two favorites. "I shall have finished my project by Monday," he would say smugly.

Mother's approach was to memorize lists of polite phrases that would cover all possible social situations. She was constantly muttering things like "I'm fine, thank you. And you?"

Once she accidentally stepped on someone's foot, and hurriedly blurted, "Oh, that's quite all right!" Embarrassed by her slip, she resolved to do better next time. So when someone stepped on *her* foot, she cried, "You're welcome!"

In our own different ways, we made progress in learning English. But I had another worry, and that was my appearance. My brother didn't have to worry, since Mother bought him blue jeans for school, and he dressed like all the other boys. But she insisted that girls had to wear skirts. By the time she saw that Meg and the other girls were wearing jeans, it was too late. My school clothes were bought already, and we didn't have money left to buy new outfits for me. We had too many other things to buy first, like furniture, pots, and pans.

The first time I visited Meg's house, she took me upstairs to her room, and I wound up trying on her clothes. We were pretty much the same size, since Meg was shorter and thinner than average. Maybe that's how we became friends in the first place. Wearing Meg's jeans and T-shirt, I looked at myself in the mirror. I could almost pass for an American—from the back, anyway. At least the kids in school wouldn't stop and stare at me in the hallways, which was what they did when they saw me in my white blouse and navy blue skirt that went a couple of inches below the knees.

When Meg came to my house, I invited her to try on my Chinese dresses, the ones with a high collar and slits up the sides. Meg's eyes were bright as she looked at herself in the mirror. She struck several sultry poses, and we nearly fell over laughing.

The dinner party at the Gleasons' didn't stop my growing friendship with Meg. Things were getting better for me in other ways too. Mother finally bought me some jeans at the end of the month, when Father got his pay-check. She wasn't in any hurry about buying them at first, until I worked on her. This is what I did. Since we didn't have a car in those days, I often ran down to the neighborhood store to pick up things for her. The groceries cost less at a big supermarket, but the closest one was many blocks away. One day, when she ran out of flour, I offered to borrow a bike from our neighbor's son and buy a ten-pound bag of flour at the big supermarket. I mounted the boy's bike and waved to Mother. "I'll be back in five minutes!"

Before I started pedaling, I heard her voice behind me. "You can't go out in public like that! People can see all the way up to your thighs!"

"I'm sorry," I said innocently. "I thought you were in a hurry to get the flour." For dinner we were going to have pot-stickers (fried Chinese dumplings), and we needed a lot of flour.

"Couldn't you borrow a girl's bicycle?" complained Mother. "That way your skirt won't be pushed up."

"There aren't too many of those around," I said. "Almost all the girls wear jeans while riding a bike, so they don't see any point buying a girl's bike."

We didn't eat pot-stickers that evening, and Mother was thoughtful. Next day we took the bus downtown and she bought me a pair of jeans. In the same week, my brother made the baseball team of his junior high school, Father started taking driving lessons, and Mother discovered rummage sales. We soon got all the furniture we needed, plus a dart board and a 1,000-piece jigsaw puzzle (fourteen hours later, we discovered that it was a 999-piece jigsaw puzzle). There was hope that the Lins might become a normal American family after all.

Then came our dinner at the Lakeview restaurant.

The Lakeview was an expensive restaurant, one of those places where a headwaiter dressed in tails[4] conducted you to your seat, and the only light came from candles and flaming desserts. In one corner of the room a lady harpist played tinkling melodies.

I squirmed and died at least fifty times.

Father wanted to celebrate, because he had just been promoted. He worked for an electronics company, and after his English started improving, his superiors decided to appoint him to a position more suited to his training. The promotion not only brought a higher salary but was also a tremendous boost to his pride.

Up to then we had eaten only in Chinese restaurants. Although my brother and I were becoming fond of hamburgers, my parents didn't care much for western food, other than chow mein.

But this was a special occasion, and Father asked his coworkers to recommend a really elegant restaurant. So there we were at the Lakeview, stumbling after the headwaiter in the murky dining room.

At our table we were handed our menus, and they were so big that to read mine I almost had to stand up again. But why bother? It was mostly in French, anyway.

Father, being an engineer, was always systematic.[5] He took out a pocket French dictionary. "They told me that most of the items would be in French, so I came prepared." He even had a pocket flashlight, the size of a marking pen. While Mother held the flashlight over the menu, he looked up the items that were in French.

"*Pâté en croûte*,"[6] he muttered. "Let's see . . . *pâté* is paste . . . *croûte* is crust . . . hmm . . . a paste in crust."

The waiter stood looking patient. I squirmed and died at least fifty times.

At long last Father gave up. "Why don't we just order four complete dinners at random?" he suggested.

"Isn't that risky?" asked Mother. "The French eat some rather peculiar things, I've heard."

"A Chinese can eat anything a Frenchman can eat," Father declared.

The soup arrived in a plate. How do you get soup up from a plate? I glanced at the other diners, but the ones at the nearby tables were not on their soup course, while the more distant ones were invisible in the darkness.

Fortunately my parents had studied books on western etiquette[7] before they came to America. "Tilt your plate," whispered my mother. "It's easier to spoon the soup up that way."

She was right. Tilting the plate did the trick. But the etiquette book didn't say anything about what you did after the soup reached your lips. As any respectable Chinese knows, the correct way to eat your soup is to slurp. This helps to cool the liquid and prevent you from burning your lips. It also shows your appreciation.

We showed our appreciation. *Shloop*, went my father. *Shloop*, went my mother. *Shloop, shloop*, went my brother, who was the hungriest.

The lady harpist stopped playing to take a rest. And in the silence, our family's consumption of soup suddenly seemed unnaturally loud. You know how it sounds on a rocky beach when the tide goes out and the water drains from all those little pools? They go *shloop, shloop, shloop*. That was the Lin family, eating soup.

At the next table a waiter was pouring

---

4. **tails** (tālz), *n.* a formal evening suit for men.
5. systematic (sis′tə mat′ik), *adj.* in a carefully planned way.
6. **Pâté en croûte** (pä tā′ on krüt′), French phrase meaning seasoned chopped meat in a crust.
7. etiquette (et′ə ket), *n.* manners; the customary rules for behavior in polite society.

wine. When a large *shloop* reached him, he froze. The bottle continued to pour, and red wine flooded the tabletop and into the lap of a customer. Even the customer didn't notice anything at first, being also hypnotized by the *shloop, shloop, shloop.*

It was too much. "I need to go to the toilet," I mumbled, jumping to my feet. A waiter, sensing my urgency, quickly directed me to the ladies' room.

I splashed cold water on my burning face, and as I dried myself with a paper towel, I stared into the mirror. In this perfumed ladies' room, with its pink-and-silver wallpaper and marbled sinks, I looked completely out of place. What was I doing here? What was our family doing in the Lakeview restaurant? In America?

The door to the ladies' room opened. A woman came in and glanced curiously at me. I retreated into one of the toilet cubicles and latched the door.

Time passed—maybe half an hour, maybe an hour. Then I heard the door open again, and my mother's voice. "Are you in there? You're not sick, are you?"

There was real concern in her voice. A girl can't leave her family just because they slurp their soup. Besides, the toilet cubicle had a few drawbacks as a permanent residence. "I'm all right," I said, undoing the latch.

Mother didn't tell me how the rest of the dinner went, and I didn't want to know. In the weeks following, I managed to push the whole thing into the back of my mind, where it jumped out at me only a few times a day. Even now, I turn hot all over when I think of the Lakeview restaurant.

But by the time we had been in this country for three months, our family was definitely making progress toward becoming Americanized. I remember my parents' first PTA meeting.

Father wore a neat suit and tie, and Mother put on her first pair of high heels. She stumbled only once. They met my homeroom teacher and beamed as she told them that I would make honor roll soon at the rate I was going. Of course Chinese etiquette forced Father to say that I was a very stupid girl and Mother to protest that the teacher was showing favoritism toward me. But I could tell they were both very proud.

The day came when my parents announced that they wanted to give a dinner party. We had invited Chinese friends to eat with us before, but this dinner was going to be different. In addition to a Chinese-American family, we were going to invite the Gleasons.

PREDICT: What do you think will happen at the Lin's dinner party?

"Gee, I can hardly wait to have dinner at your house," Meg said to me. "I just *love* Chinese food."

That was a relief. Mother was a good cook, but I wasn't sure if people who ate sour cream would also eat chicken gizzards stewed in soy sauce.

Mother decided not to take a chance with chicken gizzards. Since we had western guests, she set the table with large dinner plates, which we never used in Chinese meals. In fact we didn't use individual plates at all, but picked up food from the platters in the middle of the table and brought it directly to our rice bowls. Following the practice of Chinese-American restaurants, Mother also placed large serving spoons on the platters.

The dinner started well. Mrs. Gleason exclaimed at the beautifully arranged dishes of food: the colorful candied fruit in the sweet-and-sour pork dish, the noodle-thin shreds of chicken meat stir-fried with tiny

peas, and the glistening pink prawns[8] in a ginger sauce.

At first I was too busy enjoying my food to notice how the guests were doing. But soon I remembered my duties. Sometimes guests were too polite to help themselves and you had to serve them with more food.

I glanced at Meg, to see if she needed more food, and my eyes nearly popped out at the sight of her plate. It was piled with food: the sweet-and-sour meat pushed right against the chicken shreds, and the chicken sauce ran into the prawns. She had been taking food from a second dish before she finished eating her helping from the first!

Horrified, I turned to look at Mrs. Gleason. She was dumping rice out of her bowl and putting it on her dinner plate. Then she ladled prawns and gravy on top of the rice and mixed everything together, the way you mix sand, gravel, and cement to make concrete.

I couldn't bear to look any longer, and I turned to Mr. Gleason. He was chasing a pea around his plate. Several times he got it to the edge, but when he tried to pick it up with his chopsticks, it rolled back toward the center of the plate again. Finally he put down his chopsticks and picked up the pea with his fingers. He really did! A grown man!

All of us, our family and the Chinese guests, stopped eating to watch the activities of the Gleasons. I wanted to giggle. Then I caught my mother's eyes on me. She frowned and shook her head slightly, and I understood the message: the Gleasons were not used to Chinese ways, and they were just coping the best they could. For some reason I thought of celery strings.

When the main courses were finished, Mother brought out a platter of fruit. "I hope you weren't expecting a sweet dessert," she said. "Since the Chinese don't eat dessert, I didn't think to prepare any."

"Oh, I couldn't possible eat dessert!" cried Mrs. Gleason. "I'm simply stuffed!"

Meg had different ideas. When the table was cleared, she announced that she and I were going for a walk. "I don't know about you, but I feel like dessert," she told me, when we were outside. "Come on, there's a Dairy Queen down the street. I could use a big chocolate milkshake!"

Although I didn't really want anything more to eat, I insisted on paying for the milkshakes. After all, I was still hostess.

Meg got her large chocolate milkshake and I had a small one. Even so, she was finishing hers while I was only half done. Toward the end she pulled hard on her straws and went *shloop, shloop.*

"Do you always slurp when you eat a milkshake?" I asked, before I could stop myself.

Meg grinned. "Sure. All Americans slurp."

---

8. **prawn** (prôn), *n.* any of several shellfish, such as large shrimp, used for food.

After Reading

Making Connections

1. What was your reaction to the end of the story?

2. How did your prediction compare with what the story was actually about?

3. Look at the chart you made about the similarities and differences between Chinese and American cultures. For each similarity or difference you listed, what do you think is the **author's purpose** for including it in the story? List these reasons in the last column of your chart.

4. Look for three incidents that show different ways the author created humor in "The All-American Slurp." Summarize the humor of each incident you chose.

5. ☺ The narrator faced many problems and **choices** as she adjusted to life in her new home. Which of her solutions was your favorite? Why?

6. If you were a friend of the narrator, what advice would you give her about adjusting to life in the United States?

7. The narrator indicates she thinks that it is an important goal to become Americanized. Do you think this should be an important goal for people who move to the United States from other countries? Why or why not?

Literary Focus: Onomatopoeia

How did the Lins eat their celery? They bit into it and it went crunch. The word *crunch* is an example of **onomatopoeia** (on′ə mat′ə pē′ə)—a word that sounds like what it means. The author uses onomatopoeia throughout "The All-American Slurp" to reinforce meanings, to dramatize events, and to add liveliness to her writing. Look for examples of onomatopoeia in the story. Make a chart like the one below to help you analyze the use of onomatopoeia in the story. Discuss the examples you found with your classmates.

Word	Sentence in which the word is found	Main purpose of the onomatopoeia
crunch	Mother took a bite of her celery. Crunch.	to dramatize events

Vocabulary Study

The following sentences are from an imaginary book the narrator might have written to help Chinese people understand American manners. For each underlined word or phrase, write the vocabulary word that best replaces it in meaning.

mortified
emigrate
revolting
systematic
etiquette

1. When you <u>leave your home country</u>, you may have some embarrassing moments before you learn the customs of living in a new place.

2. Although you feel <u>humiliated</u>, as would any person in a similar situation, you learn how to make jokes about your blunders.

3. Once you learn American <u>manners</u>, you will feel more comfortable.

4. Americans may find some of the things the Chinese eat to be <u>disgusting</u> and likewise, the Chinese may find American dairy products indigestible.

5. The best way to learn about American manners is to watch people in a <u>carefully planned</u> way and take note of their actions.

Expressing Your Ideas

Writing Choices

My Friends, the Lins The Lin family wants to see America; and your relatives in another part of the country have agreed to be their hosts for a few days. Write a **letter of introduction** telling your family about the Lins. Include details that will help your family feel comfortable with the Lins and things that will also help them make the Lins feel comfortable when they visit. Include suggestions for activities that everyone might enjoy.

"The Chinese Pea Chase" Pretend you are Meg and rewrite the **story** from her point of view. What was it like to meet the narrator and have her family over for dinner? What was it like to swap clothes with the narrator? How did you feel about the Chinese dinner at the narrator's house? Use first-person point of view and include some humor.

Other Options

This Is a Fork Give a **how-to speech** on proper dining manners in America. Include a demonstration of how to set the table; how to ask for and serve food onto your plate; what to do with a napkin; and how to use a knife, fork, and spoon. You also might show how to cut meat, how to eat spaghetti, and how to eat soup with a spoon. Explain why manners are important.

Dinner of a Thousand Delights With a group, plan and prepare an authentic **Chinese meal** for your classmates. You might research dishes mentioned in the story or select items from a Chinese cookbook. Find out if any members of your class have food restrictions, and prepare foods that everyone can eat. Serve rice in rice bowls and have everyone eat with chopsticks.

Before Reading

Straight Talk (from a surfer)
74th Street by Myra Cohn Livingston

Myra Cohn Livingston
born 1926

Myra Cohn Livingston has had a long career in the arts. From a young age, she played the French horn professionally. She started writing poetry in her freshman English class in college. She transferred her love of musical sounds and rhythms to the written word: "I think poetry *must* have music," Livingston asserts.

Livingston has published more than thirty books of her own poems and put together just as many collections of poems, all for young readers. She hopes to both inspire people to rejoice in life's simple beauties as well as to work towards improving the world. "I am suggesting to young people that they name, spell out and attack the cankers [diseased parts] of our society, for I harbor the faith that they have the power to do so."

Building Background

On Land or Water The poems you are about to read both involve popular sports. The first poem is about surfing. Surfers paddle a big, long board out from a beach where there are large, consistent waves. As a wave approaches the surfers, they kneel, paddling ahead of it. When they feel the wave begin to lift the board, they stand up and ride the wave toward the shore. Timing and balance are important in surfing.

The second poem is about roller skating. Roller skates were invented in Belgium around 1760. Roller skating requires a smooth hard, surface for a comfortable, stable ride. Modern urban areas, with their miles of sidewalks are ideal for roller skating or in-line skating.

Getting into the Poems

Writer's Notebook When you have a new skill to learn or a problem to solve, how do you work on it? Do you read a book, ask for advice, or just start trying things? Do things seem to work best for you if you do the first thing you think of? Or are you more comfortable if you develop a systematic plan of action to follow before you start? Write about your way of learning or solving problems in your notebook. Give a specific example of your methods.

Reading Tip

Finding Themes in Poetry Even a very short work, such as each of these two poems, can have a powerful theme. As you read these poems, try to figure out the main idea of each one. Write a statement that you feel best conveys the theme of each poem. Are the themes similar?

Straight Talk
(from a surfer)

Myra Cohn Livingston

Now here it is   straight
Get up   get up your way
You've got the hang of it
Get up   keep it going

You only go round once in life   kid

▲ Do you think this is good advice for anyone trying to learn something new? Why?

74th Street

Myra Cohn Livingston

Hey, this little kid gets roller skates.
She puts them on.
She stands up and almost
flops over backwards.
5 She sticks out a foot like
she's going somewhere and
falls down and
smacks her hand. She
grabs hold of a step to get up and
10 sticks out the other foot and
slides about six inches and
falls and
skins her knee.

And then, you know what?
15 She brushes off the dirt and the
blood and puts some
spit on it and then
sticks out the other foot

again.

▲ *Rollerskating* was created by Abastenia St. Leger Eberle before 1909. Do you think this girl is as determined as the one described in the poem?

After Reading

Making Connections

1. What words would you use to describe the girl in "74th Street"? the surfer in "Straight Talk"?

2. Suggest some reasons you think the author chose each title for the poem.

3. What do you think is the theme of each of these poems?

4. How do the ways the subjects of the poems tackle a difficult task compare with the way you do? Explain.

Literary Focus: Appreciating Poetry

Poems are made of words, lines, and spaces. How these elements are arranged in a poem can affect your appreciation and understanding. Study the lines of each poem. Does the spacing make the poem easy or difficult to read? How does the spacing affect the way you read each poem aloud? Listen to a classmate read the poems. Write each poem down the way you hear it. How do your written versions compare with Livingston's poems?

Expressing Your Ideas

Wear It on Your Chest Make up a **slogan** for a T-shirt you might give as a gift to each of the young people in these poems. Your slogan should give encouragement to the person or praise for the person's attitudes or accomplishments. Trade your slogans with your classmates and discuss your ideas.

Straight Talk (from a roller skater) Rewrite one or both of the **poems** from the point of view of the person who is the subject of the poem. Your poem can rhyme or be written in free verse. You might also consider writing the poem as a concrete poem. Share your poem with your friends or family, if you wish.

Do the Wave Make up a **modern dance** to go along with one of the poems. The dance should indicate both the actions and the theme of the poem. You can do the dance to music or to a tape of someone reading the poem aloud. Perform your dance.

Before Reading

Frozen Man

by David Getz

David Getz
Best known for his works of fiction for middle-grade readers, David Getz is an elementary school science teacher by profession. His love of science and the dramatic in literature comes out in "Frozen Man." To write "Frozen Man," Getz conducted personal interviews with many of the scientists and archaeologists who helped solve the mystery of the glacier-locked body. David Getz lives and works in New York City.

Building Background

Hand Me That Wrench! Stone tools have been found at prehistoric sites throughout the world. The oldest are almost two million years old. This period during which people mainly relied on stone tools is known as the Stone Age. People in the Middle East began making copper tools around 6500 B.C. The use of this metal spread to Europe over the next few thousand years. Then, people began mixing copper with tin to make a stronger metal called bronze. The entire period, during which people made copper and then bronze tools is called the Bronze Age. In the Middle East, the Bronze Age lasted until about 1000 B.C., when iron became the metal of choice.

Getting into the Selection

Discussion The selection "Frozen Man" involves a mystery. You may often have mysteries to solve, although probably not as dramatic as the one in "Frozen Man." Where is your cat hiding? Why are you always missing socks after the laundry comes out of the dryer? Think of a mystery you've faced recently and the steps you took to solve it. Discuss the steps with your classmates. Talk about how you looked for clues, analyzed evidence, checked facts, and drew conclusions.

Reading Tip

Setting Purposes for Reading One purpose for reading "Frozen Man" is to solve a mystery. Another purpose may be to find out more about a particular subject or to simply enjoy a piece of writing. Read the first sentence of the selection. Then decide why you want to finish reading it. After reading the selection, compare your purpose for reading with those of your classmates. Was your purpose for reading fulfilled? Were all your questions answered?

FROZEN MAN

David Getz

Nobody knew what stories the body could tell.

On September 19, 1991, German tourists Erika and Helmut Simon had just climbed Finail Peak, the second-highest summit in the Ötztal Alps. Deciding to try something new, they took an unmarked path back down across the Similaun Glacier to their lodge. They spotted the body at an altitude of about 10,500 feet, nearly two miles above sea level. It lay near the border of Italy and Austria.

At first glance they thought they had come upon an abandoned doll. Getting closer, they both realized that the body was an adult man. Still frozen to the glacier, the dead man seemed to have risen from the ice, as if he was getting out of a pool. He appeared to be naked. His face was pressed down into the snow.

The Simons discovered a small hole in the back of the victim's head. Suspicious that the man had been murdered, they rushed to a hiker's shelter to report the crime.

Markus Pirpomer, the owner of the shelter, called both the Italian and the Austrian police. The Italian authorities showed no interest. They assumed the body was simply another victim of a mountaineering accident. The Austrian authorities agreed to send over an officer. That summer they had already retrieved the bodies of eight accident victims from the snow and ice of the Alps.

When Markus Pirpomer reached the body, it struck him as remarkably different from other bodies that had emerged from the glacier.

A glacier is a river of ice. As snow on mountains gets deeper and heavier, it gradually turns into ice that can be hundreds of feet thick. Sometimes glaciers flow slowly down mountains.

Pirpomer knew that it wasn't unusual for a hiker to die in the Alps, get covered by falling snow, and be trapped in a glacier. He knew that as a glacier moves down a mountain, it occasionally reveals a body it captured higher up. These bodies are usually horribly crushed and mangled from being dragged by the massive glacier over rocks and boulders.

Pirpomer noticed that the body the Simons had discovered was remarkably intact. It was in the position of someone who had stretched out to take a nap. How could a man dragged down a mountain under tons of ice appear nearly undamaged?

Just as puzzling to Pirpomer was the body's skin. Being trapped in a glacier prevents oxygen from reaching a body's soft tissues. This turns the skin, muscles, and fat into adipocere, or "grave wax," a creamy or waxy substance that makes these victims appear to be made of soap or plaster.

This man was brown and leathery, as dried out as an Egyptian mummy. How could this happen to a man surrounded by ice and snow? Pirpomer suspected that there was something remarkable about this victim. He guessed that this man had died a long time ago, though how long ago he couldn't be sure.

The Austrian policeman arrived the afternoon of September 20. He had no reason to

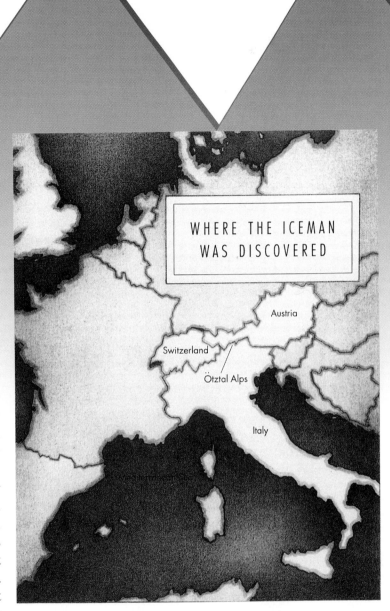

WHERE THE ICEMAN WAS DISCOVERED

Austria

Switzerland

Ötztal Alps

Italy

⋀ What would you have done if you had made this discovery?

believe there was anything special about the body. He had no idea that this "Iceman" had come from a place no one alive had ever seen. He had no idea that the Iceman had brought with him strange tools and clothing from that distant place. They were buried along with him in the ice. The Iceman's body and his clothing and tools were like the pieces of a puzzle, waiting to be put back together.

The policeman nearly destroyed everything. He brought a jackhammer to free the body. He drilled right through the Iceman's hip, shattering the bone. He also ripped to shreds what turned out to be the remains of the Iceman's cloak. By luck, the jackhammer ran out of power before it could do further harm. The officer contacted his superiors. He made plans to resume his efforts the following week. It was the next time a helicopter would be available to return him to the site.

Before he left, the policeman took some photographs. He also discovered a crude hand ax. It consisted of a small, tongue-shaped blade stuck into the end of an L-shaped branch. The policeman removed the ax as possible evidence of a crime.

The policeman removed the ax as possible evidence of a crime.

Word began to spread about the man in ice. The next day, six mountaineers visited the body. They tried to free it but failed. Before leaving, they also took some photographs.

On September 22, the chairman of the Austrian mountain rescue team arrived with a friend. Together they freed the body, using a pickax, then informed the local police it was ready to be retrieved. The two also carried away from the site the remains of the Iceman's clothing, along with what was probably his backpack frame, part of a bow, and some clumps of grass. They left these objects at a local hotel in the Ötz valley.

The following day Rainer Henn found a note on his desk, informing him of this man in ice. Henn, the director of forensic medicine (medicine related to crimes and accidents) at the University of Innsbruck, had already examined six bodies that had emerged from glaciers that year. One of those victims had died in 1934, 57 years ago. Transformed by adipocere and terribly muti-

lated,[1] the victim had resembled a damaged statue. Henn had found railway tickets and a membership card to a mountaineering club in the victim's pockets. But Henn had heard nothing of the condition of this body, the strange ax, or any of the other objects found at the site. Who would this new victim turn out to be?

Each year the Alps prove too treacherous[2] for some skiers or hikers. The weather can change suddenly. Warm sunshine can instantly become a blinding snowstorm. At the altitude, or height, where the body was found, the air is thin. Breathing is difficult. It's easy to become tired and careless, to stumble and fall. Each year about 200 people lose their lives in the Alps from accidents or exposure to the cold.

When Henn arrived by helicopter and the site, he was surprised to discover another helicopter already there. It belonged to an Austrian television crew. The man in ice was making the news. There were rumors that he might be over 500 years old.

Though freed from the ice the previous day, the body had refrozen into the surrounding slush overnight. Not having brought any tools along with him, Henn was forced to borrow an ice pick and some ski poles to chip the body free. Like Pirpomer, Henn was immediately struck by the condition of the body. He wondered why it hadn't developed adipocere. He guessed that somehow the body had completely dried out, or mummified, before it was captured within the glacier. Then he discovered a dagger. It was made with a wooden handle and had a small stone blade.

---

1. **mutilated** (myü′tl ā′tid), *adj.* cut or torn up, sometimes with limbs removed.
2. **treacherous** (trech′ər əs), *adj.* dangerous; marked by unforeseen hazards.

▲ Mountaineers visit the ancient body, still frozen in ice.

What was this twentieth-century hiking victim doing with a tool from the Stone Age?

Henn immediately ordered his helpers to proceed with caution. This body is old, he told them.

With great effort Henn and his helpers removed the body from the ice, wrapped it in plastic, and forced it into a wooden coffin. It was then transported by helicopter and ambulance to the nearest morgue. The objects that had been found alongside the body were gathered and sent along. Henn's next step, by Austrian law, would be to perform an <u>autopsy</u>[3] on the body to determine its cause of death.

The Iceman was about to be cut open and taken apart like a laboratory frog.

Fortunately archaeologist Konrad

---

3. **autopsy** (ô′top sē), *n.* medical examination of a dead body to find the cause of death.

Spindler got to the body first. As dean of the Institute for Pre- and Protohistory at the University of Innsbruck,[4] Konrad Spindler is an expert on life in the Alps. Having heard some of the rumors about the man in ice, Spindler contacted Henn and expressed an interest in seeing the body and the objects found alongside it.

Spindler got his wish the following morning. He was astonished. The objects appeared to be the tools someone would carry if he was wandering around the mountains thousands of years ago! And then there was the body. Though his hip was damaged, the Iceman had arrived from the distant past remarkably whole. Scientists would be able to study his body as well as any doctor studying a patient.

Though brown, leathery, dried out, and somewhat hideous to look at, the Iceman was probably the most magnificent sight Konrad Spindler had ever witnessed.

"I felt like Howard Carter[5] when he opened the coffin of Tutankhamen—King Tut—and saw the golden face of the pharaoh," Spindler said. "From that first moment I saw that we would want to spend a lot of time studying this man and his equipment. This is one of the most remarkable archaeological discoveries of the century."

Helmut and Erika Simon had discovered a prehistoric man, possibly on his way to work. Who was this man? How did he live? How did he die? When did he last walk the paths of the Alps, and what could he tell us about his world? As chief archaeologist at the University of Innsbruck, Spindler would head the team of scientists that would seek to answer those questions.

The first step was to get the Iceman to reveal his secrets. How could scientists learn when he lived?

What clues did the Iceman offer? Simply looking at his body, scientists couldn't tell if he died 2,000 or 8,000 years ago. True, he was brown and leathery and so dried out that he weighed 29 pounds. The dehydration must have taken some time. And the shape of his face had been changed by the weight of the ice continuously pressing down on him. This too must have taken a long time. But how long?

Spindler turned to the Iceman's artifacts for clues. Artifacts are any objects that are made by people. To learn about ancient people, archaeologists study what artifacts are made of, how they are made, and what they were used for. The Iceman's artifacts were particularly fascinating. What was the man in ice doing with a dagger with a stone blade? Why didn't he have a Swiss Army knife with a stainless-steel blade? Daggers with stone blades hadn't been used in Europe for thousands of years!

What was the man in ice doing with a stone blade? Why didn't he have a Swiss Army knife . . .?

Then there was that "murder weapon," the ax. Its shaft was made from an L-shaped branch of a yew tree. Like the dagger blade, that shaft also belonged to a period in Europe called the Stone Age. The Stone Age began in Europe about a million years ago and ended about 5,000 years ago. During this period people used stones, such as flint, for their tools. The Iceman had been found with a stone

---

4. **Innsbruck** (inz′brúk), city in southwest Austria.
5. **Howard Carter**, British archaeologist who discovered the tomb of Pharoah Tutankhamen in 1922.

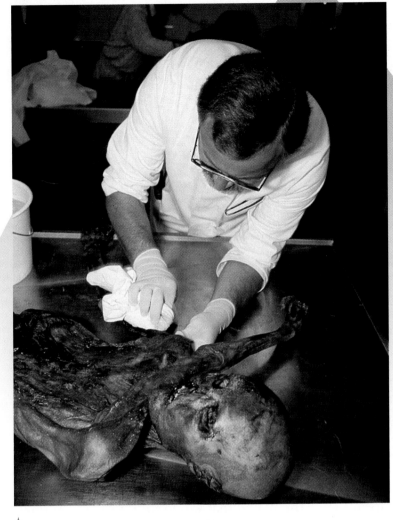
▲ A scientist examines the well-preserved Iceman.

style handle suggested it was made at the beginning of the Bronze Age.

"The archaeological dating can't be wrong," Spindler said. "So the ax dates from approximately 2,000 B.C., or 2,000 years before the birth of Christ."

If the policeman's suspicions were correct, then the ax would be evidence of a crime committed over 4,000 years ago.

The next step was to test Spindler's hypothesis[6] scientifically. The archaeologists working with Spindler returned to the Iceman's body. They removed tiny fragments of the hipbone damaged by the policeman. About an ounce, or the weight of a paper clip, was sent to Robert Hedges at his Oxford University laboratory in England. Hedges would count how many atoms of carbon 14 the bones still contained. This would help him tell when the Iceman died.

All living things take in carbon. Plants absorb it as they "breathe" in carbon dioxide. People absorb it by eating plants or by eating animals that eat plants. A small but constant percentage of that carbon is carbon 14, which is radioactive. It is continually decaying, or coming apart.

If we look at the carbon atoms as marbles, then a sample of something that was once alive, such as a piece of bone, can be compared to a jar filled with trillions of marbles. In that jar are just a handful of strange marbles. While all the other marbles remain the

knife blade and two arrows with stone points. Could he have lived during the Stone Age?

No, he couldn't, was Spindler's first guess. The Iceman's ax appeared to be bronze. Stone Age people didn't have the technology to make bronze tools.

The Bronze Age followed the Stone Age. It began in Europe about 5,000 years ago and lasted for nearly 2,000 years. During this time people in Europe began to master the technique of melting copper in furnaces that reached 1,981 degrees Fahrenheit and alloying it with tin to make bronze.

If the ax's blade was bronze, its Stone-Age-

6. **hypothesis** (hī poth′ə sis), *n.* a tentative explanation that accounts for a set of facts and can be tested by further investigation.

Frozen Man **599**

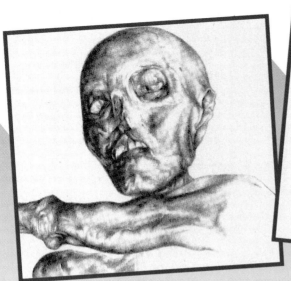

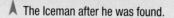
The Iceman after he was found.

An artist's sketch of how the Iceman may have looked when he was alive.

same over thousands of years, the strange ones, the carbon-14 marbles, slowly disappear.

When a person dies, he or she stops taking in carbon. The quantity of regular carbon (carbon 12) stays the same, but the quantity of carbon 14 gets smaller and smaller as the carbon 14 atoms decay. The rate of this decay is as precise as the ticking of a clock. A slow clock! It takes 5,730 years for half the carbon 14 in a sample to tick away and disappear.

After counting the carbon 14 in the sample of bone, Hedges determined that the Iceman died about 5,300 years ago. This placed him more than 1,000 years farther back in time than Spindler's estimate. Hedges's carbon-14 dating pushed the Iceman backward out of the Bronze Age into the end of the Stone Age.

Scientists in Zurich,[7] Switzerland, used another sample of the Iceman for radiocarbon dating. They followed the same procedures as Hedges. They arrived at a similar answer. The Iceman was clearly over 5,000 years old.

But what about that ax? How could a man who lived during the Stone Age carry a bronze tool that wasn't invented for another thousand years or so? That was like finding a computer buried beside a Viking.

Dietrich Ankner, a metallurgist at the Roman-Germanic Museum in Mainz,[8] Germany, analyzed the ax blade. Bronze is an alloy of copper and tin. If Ankner found any tin in the composition of the blade, that would indicate it was bronze. His tests showed no tin. This meant the blade was almost pure copper.

Spindler had made a reasonable mistake. Copper and bronze look the same to the naked eye.

The Iceman lived more than 3,000 years before the invention of gunpowder or paper. Carbon-14 dating placed him in Europe over 3,000 years before Julius Caesar ruled the Roman Empire, 2,000 years before the first Olympic Games in Greece, and more than

---

7. **Zurich** (zur'ik), city in northern Switzerland.
8. **Mainz** (mīnts), a city in the central part of Germany.

700 years before Imhotep[9] designed the first pyramid in Egypt. He roamed the Alps at a time when the wheel was a new invention! His contemporaries[10] in central Europe lived in wooden houses that were built on stilts above the shorelines of lakes. These villages were often surrounded by a fence. Inside, people raised wheat and barley, kept animals in pens, and probably considered cooked dog a pretty good meal. Cheese was also a new invention. They used deer antler and chipped stone for tools. They buried their dead in rows in huge stone tombs. Men were placed on their right side, females on their left side. People were buried with what they would need in the after-life: axes, knives, and beads.

Since the Iceman died on his way to work, he wasn't buried in a tomb. Even so, the Iceman is the oldest, best-preserved body ever discovered.

A number of chance events made the Iceman's trip to the present possible.

Most creatures disappear shortly after they die, especially if they die and are left out in the open, as the Iceman was. Blood stops flowing in their veins, and the body starts to decay. Scavengers, such as vultures, rodents, and insects, dine on the decaying body. Flies lay eggs in its eyes. Microscopic organisms finish off what the bigger animals started. The weather, wind, and rain scatter what's left.

The Iceman avoided disappearing by chance. He died at the bottom of a gap between two large rock formations in the mountains. This shelter probably hid him from most large scavengers, such as vultures. By luck, it probably began to snow right as he died. Soon he was covered in a white blanket. This further helped hide his body from the animals that would make a meal of it.

Somehow, and scientists are still not exactly sure how, his body was mummified. Many archaeologists believe a steadily blowing wind passed through the loosely packed snow,

carrying away the moisture from his body. "He was freeze-dried," said Konrad Spindler. The Iceman was too dry to develop adipocere, or grave wax. Drying is one way to prevent decay. Egyptians mummified their pharaohs' bodies to make sure they would survive into the after-life. More commonly, everyone from Native Americans to European explorers has dried meats and fish over smoky fires to preserve the food for long periods.

Another method to preserve meat, or a human body, is refrigeration. Extreme cold prevents decay. Think of a refrigerator.

But how did the Iceman survive the forces of the glacier? At times the ice towered 100 to 200 feet above his body, the height of a 20-story building. How was he not crushed? And why wasn't he dragged down over the mountain with the movement of the glacier? How did he remain in one piece?

Luck. The Iceman died in a deep, narrow gap between two rocky ridges. These ridges acted like train tracks. The glacier slid down the mountain over these tracks while the Iceman lay safely beneath them.

At last, why did the Iceman suddenly appear?

In 1991 a dust storm in the Sahara Desert sent huge amounts of dust into the atmosphere. Some of this dust traveled over the Alps, where it fell and darkened the snow. Dark colors absorb more heat than light colors. This dust, along with an unusually warm summer, caused the snow to melt rapidly, exposing the Iceman for the first time in over 5,000 years!

---

9. **Imhotep** (im hō′ tep), architect and minister to the Egyptian pharoah Zoser, famed for designing the oldest pyramid in the world, built around 2650 B.C.
10. contemporary (kən tem′pə rer′ē), *n.* person living in the same period of time.

New World

N. Scott Momaday

1.
First Man,
behold:
the earth
glitters
5 with leaves;
the sky
glistens
with rain.
Pollen
10 is borne
on winds
that low
and lean
upon
15 mountains.
Cedars
blacken
the slopes—
and pines.

2.
20 At dawn
eagles
hie and
hover
above
25 the plain
where light
gathers
in pools.
Grasses
30 shimmer
and shine.
Shadows
withdraw
and lie
35 away
like smoke.

3.
At noon
turtles
enter
40 slowly
into
the warm
dark loam.
Bees hold
45 the swarm.
Meadows
recede
through
planes
50 of heat
and pure
distance.

4.
At dusk
the gray
55 foxes
stiffen
in cold;
blackbirds
are fixed
60 in the
branches.
Rivers
follow
the moon,
65 the long
white track
of the
full moon.

After Reading

Making Connections

1. Was your purpose for reading "Frozen Man" satisfied? Explain.

2. Which of the problems faced by the people working with the Iceman do you think was the most difficult to solve? Why?

3. On a scale of 1 to 5, how would you rate the author's ability to explain the mystery of the Iceman? How do you think he could have improved his explanation?

4. Could the person described in the poem "New World" be the same person found in the glacier? Give reasons for your answer.

5. How does this selection show that it is important to consider all possibilities when trying to solve a mystery? Give at least two examples.

6. Which of your own mystery-solving techniques did you find in this selection?

Literary Focus: Narrative and Expository Nonfiction

Although "Frozen Man" unfolds like an exciting mystery story, the selection is actually **narrative nonfiction**—a true story, told basically in chronological order. It also includes elements of **exposition,** writing that gives an explanation of an object or an event. Reread "Frozen Man" and make a time line that shows the events involved in the discovery and study of the Iceman. Also look for examples of exposition—explanations of techniques or methods of doing things. Which example of expository writing do you think is the clearest and most interesting? Share your time line and discuss your examples with your classmates.

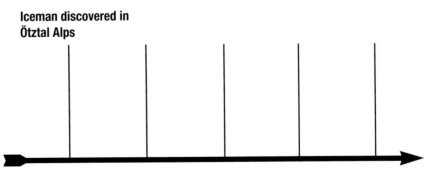

Iceman discovered in Ötztal Alps

Sept. 19, 1991

Vocabulary Study

Below is an account of the discovery of an Inuit woman buried in an ice storm. For each blank, write the vocabulary word that best completes the sentence.

autopsy
contemporary
hypothesis
mutilated
treacherous

The sight of the body would have disturbed most people. It was most hideous. But as an archaeologist working on a dig in Alaska, for me it was a beautiful sight. The face was mangled, but there was no doubt that it was an Inuit woman. Unlike the Alpine Iceman, the woman died in her house, __(1)__ by a heavy timber beam that crushed her chest. The evidence indicates that her home was destroyed by a __(2)__ storm that hurtled boulder-sized blocks of ice on the roof. My __(3)__ is that the roof caved in and the people in the house were crushed. An __(4)__ revealed that the woman was about 40 years old when she died. Tests later done by carbon dating showed that the woman's bones were about 500 years old, making her a __(5)__ of Christopher Columbus!

Expressing Your Ideas

Writing Choices

For Archaeologists Only Articles about scientific discoveries often begin with a short summary. Write a summary of "Frozen Man" for archaeologists who want to know about the discovery and its importance. Include when the discovery was made, what artifacts were found along with it, how it was dated, and why it is significant.

A Day in the Life, 5,000 Years Apart
Imagine you are the Iceman. Write a **journal entry** about your plans for the day. Now, imagine you are Helmut or Erika Simon. Write a journal entry about the day you discovered the Iceman. With your classmates, share your journal entries and talk about the similarities and differences between the life of the Iceman and the lives of the German tourists who lived 5,000 years later.

Other Options

While We're on the Subject The selection "Frozen Man" is from a book of the same title in which you can learn even more about the Iceman. Look for a copy of the book in your school or local library. After you read it, present an oral **summary** of the book to your class.

Dig That! Amazing discoveries have been made at archaeological sites all over the United States. Do research to find out where these sites are and what has been discovered there. Present your findings as a **visual time line** with pictures or photocopies of fossils and artifacts and dates and captions.

Writing Mini-Lesson

Preparing Your Presentation Portfolio

Now is the time to change your **working portfolio** into your **presentation portfolio**. This is the collection of written work that will be presented to others to show how you have met your goals for the year.

Reviewing and Selecting Samples

- Start by checking with your teacher to find out the requirements for the presentation portfolio.

- Next, decide which pieces you will include in your presentation portfolio. Divide your work into three stacks: **definitely use, definitely not use,** and **unsure.** Use your goal statements as a guide to review each piece of work.

Arranging Your Portfolio

How will you arrange your portfolio? Here are some ideas.

- Chronological—Arrange your samples from the beginning of the year to the end. This order will show your progress.

- By Category—Group the same kinds of writing together, such as narratives, essays, reports, and so forth. This arrangement shows your growth on each kind of writing separately.

- By Theme—Sort your pieces by mood or topic. This arrangement highlights the major themes in your writing.

Completing the Package

- Write an introduction to your folder that first explains the entire folder and then each piece. This helps the reader see your work the way you want them to see it. Use your goal statements as a guide.

- Finalize the cover.

- Skim over the portfolio to make sure no pages are missing and that they're ordered the way you'd like.

Before Reading

How the Animals Kept the Lions Away

by Inea Bushnaq

Inea Bushnaq

A scholar of the Arabic language, Inea Bushnaq has collected folk tales not only from Algeria, but from all the Arab countries and published them in a book called *Arab Folktales.* She has made in-depth studies of Arabic poetry as well. She has also translated books from both French and Arabic into English. Born in Jerusalem, she now lives in New York City.

Building Background

Traveling Tales "How the Animals Kept the Lions Away" is an Algerian folk tale. Algeria is a country in North Africa. Most of the land is covered by the Sahara, the world's largest desert. The lack of rainfall in this region prevents people from farming. Instead, people live as nomads, wandering from place to place to find food for cattle. The Bedouins are one group of nomads who have wandered the Sahara for thousands of years.

Most Bedouins are Muslims and speak Arabic. Storytelling has always been an important part of Arabic culture, and the Arabs have preserved and spread numerous stories that have become a treasured part of world literature.

Getting into the Story

Discussion The animals in this folk tale include a rooster, a donkey, a ram, and a dog who all live in the desert. How do you predict the animals in this story will solve the problem of keeping the lions away? Talk about your ideas with your classmates.

Reading Tip

Comparing Characters As in many folk tales, the animals in this story behave like people. As you read, use a chart like the one below to compare the animal characters.

Animal	Appearance	Personality	Role in Keeping Lions Away
Rooster			
Donkey			
Ram			
Dog			

How the Animals Kept the Lions Away

INEA BUSHNAQ

Once when a tribe of Bedouins moved their camp to a new site, they left behind them a lame rooster, a broken-backed donkey, a sick ram, and a desert greyhound suffering from mange.[1] The animals swore brotherhood and determined to live together. They wandered until they came to an unfrequented oasis, where they decided to settle.

One day when the rooster was flying to the top of a tree, he noticed something important: the opening to a grain silo full of barley. The food was wholesome, and he began to visit the place daily. Soon his feathers became glossy as polished silk, and his comb began to glow like the fire inside a ruby. The donkey, observing the improvements, asked his friend, "How is it that your cap has grown so bright?" The rooster feigned[2] surprise and tried to change the subject. But with the perseverance of his race, the donkey continued to pester the fowl until at last he said, "Very well, I shall show you the reason why my cap has grown so bright, but it must remain a secret between us." The donkey promised to be discreet and the rooster led him to the grain silo.

At the sight of the barley the donkey flung himself into the grain and fed until he could eat no more. Brimming with well-being, he danced back to the others and said, "I feel the

---

1. **mange** (mānj), *n.* a skin disease of animals.
2. **feign** (fān), *v.* pretend; put on a false appearance.

urge to sing come upon me. With your permission I shall bray awhile!" The animals objected. "What if a lion should hear you?" they said. "He will surely come and devour us all!" But despite his friends, the donkey could not contain his high spirits. He cantered off by himself and began to bray long and noisily.

Now, a lion did hear the sound and came streaking across the wilderness on his silent feet until he was within one spring of the donkey. Almost too late the donkey became aware of the danger. "Sire," he said. "I see that my fate has been written, but I beg you to do me the favor not to devour me without my friends. It would be more honorable, considering that the animals of this oasis have sworn an oath of brotherhood to live together and die together, if you made an end of us all without exception." The lion conceded[3] the merit of this plea and allowed the donkey to guide him to his friends.

When the other animals saw the donkey leading a lion toward them, they put their heads together and said, "How can we defend ourselves against a lion!" And they made their plans. When the lion came near they all said with one voice, "Greetings and welcome, uncle lion!" Then the ram butted him in his side and knocked the breath out of his lungs, the rooster flew up and pecked at his eyes, and the dog buried his teeth in the lion's throat. The lion died, of course. His flesh was given to the dog to eat, but the animals kept his skin and tanned it.

After that the four friends were able to live in peace for a time. However, soon the donkey was announcing, "I sense that I must bray again!" "Be still, O ill-omened animal!" said the others. But the donkey could not suppress[4] his feelings, and his unmelodious call rang repeatedly in the air.

A second lion prowling that quarter[5] of the desert was attracted to the braying. With water running in his mouth, he hurried to the oasis. Again the donkey invited the lion to kill all the animals of the oasis together, and the lion gladly complied.[6] This time too the rooster, the ram, and the dog put their heads together when they saw the lion approaching and made a plan.

But what they said to the visitor was, "Welcome, may you be a thousand times welcome!" Then the rooster hinted to the ram, "Our guest should be made comfortable and have a carpet to sit on!" The ram trotted into their dwelling and brought out the tanned lion skin. "Be ashamed, O ram!" chided[7] the rooster when he saw him. "Our guest is of a noble tribe. His presence among us is an honor. Do you want to disgrace us by offering him that old, worn-out mat?" Meekly the ram carried the lion skin back into the house and brought it out a second time. This time the dog expressed impatience. "Surely we have a softer carpet than that, O ram! Besides, this one is quite faded." Obediently the ram took the lion skin inside and returned with it a third time. Now the donkey chimed in, "For one of such eminence as the lion, nothing but the finest can serve the occasion! Choose more carefully from among our store!" The ram withdrew into the house, but the lion did not linger further. He jumped to his feet and without bidding his hosts a formal farewell, ran away as fast as he was able.

Although the donkey continued to bray from time to time, no lion was seen near the animals' oasis again.

---

3. **concede** (kən sēd′), *v.* admit as true; acknowledge.
4. **suppress** (sə pres′), *v.* keep in; hold back.
5. **quarter** (kwôr′tər), *n.* region; section.
6. **comply** (kəm plī′), *v.* act in agreement with a request.
7. **chide** (chīd), *v.* scold.

After Reading

Making Connections

1. Do you think it was fair of the donkey to put his friends in danger by bringing the lion to their oasis? Why or why not?

2. Compare the two solutions the animals had for keeping the lions away and your own **prediction.** Which one did you think was the best solution and why?

3. If the **characters** were people, what kind of person would each character be? Refer to the chart you made as you read the story to help you analyze the characters.

4. What message did you get from this story? Is the message relevant to your life or not? Explain.

Literary Focus: Cultural Borrowing in Folk Tales

The Algerian folk tale "How the Animals Kept the Lions Away" actually originated in India. Look at the chart below. Notice that the cultures of both India and Algeria are represented in the folk tale. How would you change each item listed in the chart to make the folk tale represent your own culture? Add your ideas to the chart.

Indian Culture	Algerian Culture	My Culture
grain silo for farming	Bedouins	
ruby, a gem commonly found in India	oasis	
	desert greyhound	
	lack of food for the animals	
	carpets	

Expressing Your Ideas

The Sequel Write your own version of this **folk tale.** Include the same characters, but focus on how the ram and the dog get the rooster and the donkey to share the grain. Refer to the chart you made as you read the story.

Fable in the Funnies Make up a **comic-strip** version of "How the Animals Kept the Lions Away."

Finding Solutions

Serving Your Community

Helping Others

Community Service Connection

Every community has problems large and small. Finding solutions to those problems is everyone's responsibility. Everyone can do something to help—even you.

Our community has seniors who appreciate some extra company. Everyone benefits when we get together.

By helping renovate a building, we take pride in our community.

OUR SCHOOL HAS "ADOPTED" A NEARBY ROAD. IT'S OUR RESPONSIBILITY TO KEEP IT CLEAN.

By collecting newspapers for recycling, we help the environment and make money for our organization.

WE PLANTED TREES TO BEAUTIFY THE CITY.

Responding
Take a look at your community. Are any of the projects pictured on these two pages projects that would improve your world? Are there any other projects that might be more beneficial?

Community Service Connection

Choosing a volunteer activity is a little bit like choosing a career. Select something that suits your personality, your talents, and your interests, and you will likely stick with it. Here are some ideas for deciding which community service projects you might like to try.

Volunteers Wanted

VOLUNTEERS WANTED:

Enthusiastic Young People Willing to Help Others. No Minimum Age. Work in Any Field. Thousands of Positions to Choose From. No Prior Experience Necessary. Rewards Unlimited. Please Hurry. We Can't Get Along Without You.

Does an ad like the one on the left interest you?

Good. But that's not surprising. Thousands of young people all over the country are already actively volunteering in more projects than ever before. From neighborhood clean-up squads in low-income housing developments in Minneapolis to drawing soil test samples on crop lands in Kansas. From digging latrines in Latin America to calling bingo games at nursing homes in suburban New Jersey. From door-to-door canvassing for political candidates in Connecticut to sponsoring a needy child in an Ethiopian village. From providing positive peer pressure to help classmates stay in school in downtown Detroit to cleaning litter from trout streams in Virginia. From raising puppies for Leader Dogs to collecting newspapers and cans for recycling nearly everywhere. And everywhere they go, they are appreciated.

All volunteers share some very special traits. They have energy to spare. They care about the people and world around them. But most of all, they share a willingness to get involved for the good of others, the community in general, and the world at large.

Are you one of them? If not, you could be.

Ten-year-old Teddy Andrews is volunteering his time and energy to a group called Save American Youth—Youth–Advocates for Youth! These young people help other young people who are homeless or disadvantaged.

Taking a Look at Yourself

Never volunteered before? Don't worry, getting involved is easy even for beginners, no matter how old or young they are. All you have to do is be willing to participate.

But before you jump into a project, take a look at yourself. If you have goals you want to accomplish, if you would like to make the world a better place to live in, then do some serious thinking before selecting which volunteer activities you want to be involved in.

The following questions will help you make choices.

- What do I believe in?
- What priority does it have in my life?
- Which causes do I feel strongly about supporting?
- Am I familiar with any current programs or projects that address these issues?
- Do I know any of the people involved? Does it matter?
- What are they doing to help?
- Is it helping?
- Is it something I'd be willing to do?
- Am I currently contributing to this cause in some way?
- Does this project require a long- or short-term commitment?
- Do I have time to make a positive contribution?
- Am I willing to make time?
- Am I interested in developing skills that would help make me a good volunteer for this cause?
- What skills, abilities, or special interests do I currently possess that would be useful to this cause?
- Would it help to know more about the cause itself, the subject matter, and/or the program and people involved?

- Would I rather find a different way to contribute to this cause? What are my choices?
- Are there any reasons to say "no" to this project?
- How would contributing to this cause affect the rest of my life, my friends, or my family?

Once you've analyzed your goals, you can start looking for ways to accomplish them. The easiest way to start may be to join a club or organization that already is involved in volunteer projects that interest you. But you don't have to join a club to become a volunteer. If you want to come up with a volunteer activity on your own, brainstorm with your friends or family, and you're sure to find a worthwhile way to help.

Once you become involved as a volunteer, evaluate your goals occasionally. As you learn and grow and experience new things, your interests and priorities may change. Learning to react positively to it will help keep you in charge of your life. And when you're in charge of your life, there's nothing you can't do. Just ask a successful volunteer!

Responding
Answer the questions in this reading about your interests and goals. Then decide what type of work best fits you. Research clubs and organizations that are related to your interests. Make a commitment to spend some time as a volunteer with the group you choose. If you feel at home in your choice, stick with it. Otherwise, try another direction. There are lots of ways you can contribute.

Reading Mini-Lesson

Distinguishing Between Fact and Opinion

Mrs. Kago receives a progress report from her daughter's social studies teacher: I like Ayanna's attitude toward the class. I'm sure that if she continues to progress, she will do well in this course.

Are there any facts in this report? No. The teacher expresses a positive opinion about Ayanna, but no facts are offered. Here is the report with some facts to back up the opinion.

Ayanna has missed only one day of school, and she has completed every assignment on time. Her current average on tests and quizzes is 85. I like her attitude toward the class. I'm sure that if she continues to progress, she will do well in this course.

If someone else checked the attendance book, Ayanna should have only one absence. If a third person calculated Ayanna's average, it should still be 85.

Opinions, however, are personal views which can change from one person to another. Opinions can differ even when they are based on the same fact. One day, in the swimming pool:

Leslie: *This water is too warm.*
Guin: *I'm so cold my lips are turning blue.*
Ryan: *The pool thermometer reads 84 degrees.*

The same temperature that is too cold for one person is too warm for another. Remember that **facts** can be checked out. They can be demonstrated. **Opinions** are personal views.

Activity Options

1. Assume that the information in "Volunteers Wanted" on page 612 is accurate. In a small group, answer the following questions. Which of the following statements are facts and which are opinions? Explain how you can tell.
   A. Soil test samples were drawn on crop lands in Kansas.
   B. All you have to do is be willing to participate.
   C. When you're in charge of your life, you can do anything.

2. Find a newspaper or magazine *editorial* that expresses the writer's opinions. With a partner, identify the opinion of the article and two facts which support that opinion.

Writing Workshop

Solving a Problem

Assignment In the fable in this part, the animals found a solution to their problem through cooperation. Write a fable of your own in which animal characters find a solution to a problem.

WRITER'S BLUEPRINT

Product   A fable

Purpose   To illustrate a lesson by telling how animal characters solve a problem

Audience   Classmates

Specs   As the writer of a successful fable, you should:

❑ Begin with a title that summarizes what happens, such as "How Rabbit Tricked Otter."

❑ Go on to describe two incidents which illustrate the problem facing the animals.

❑ Continue with a third incident which shows how the animals solve their problem.

❑ Conclude by showing what your audience can learn from your fable by stating the moral.

❑ Use dialogue that reveals the personalities of your characters.

❑ Follow the correct rules for grammar, usage, spelling, and mechanics. Be sure that you use commas correctly.

The instructions that follow should help you write a successful fable.

STEP **1** PREWRITING

Brainstorm sayings that point to a moral. One way to choose a problem to write about is to start with a moral. Many old sayings teach a lesson and one might spark an idea for a fable. Brainstorm to recall sayings such as the following:

A stitch in time saves nine.
Two heads are better than one.
The early bird gets the worm.

Choose one of the sayings and decide what problem it suggests. What animal characters could you use to act out that problem?

Cluster animals and their characteristics. Most fables have animal characters, each of which has a single trait, for example, bravery, cowardice, greed. Cluster several animals that would make interesting characters. Then add one or two words that describe each animal. For your fable, choose the animals that work best with the problem you're writing about.

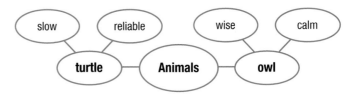

Try a quickwrite. Now you need a plot for your fable. It should be fairly simple, with three main incidents. Do a quickwrite as if you were describing the story to someone. Concentrate on how the animals solve the problem you've given them. Here is part of one student's quickwrite.

> Two groups of cows eat every day in a pasture that is separated by a fence. The cows are very haughty and stuck up. They grumble that the grass on the other side of the fence is better. They decide to switch sides through a hole in the fence.

STUDENT MODEL

Plan the fable with a cartoon strip. Divide your fable into several incidents. Print the title of your fable on a large piece of drawing paper. Draw panels and sketch the main incidents of your plot in the panels. Include dialogue balloons for the characters' speeches. Dialogue should tell the reader something about the character. Look ahead to the Revising Strategy for tips on how to do this. On the back, write notes about the details of each scene. Write the moral and a note about how your fable teaches this moral.

Ask a partner: *How is my plan shaping up?*

✔ Is the problem the characters must solve clearly stated?

✔ Do the animal characters I've chosen fit the story?

✔ Am I following the specs in the Writer's Blueprint?

Use your partner's comments to help you revise your plan.

STEP 2 DRAFTING

Before you write, review your notes from brainstorming, animal cluster, quickwrite, writing plan, and any other notes you've made. Reread the Writer's Blueprint.

As you draft, don't worry about mistakes with spelling and punctuation. Concentrate on getting your story on paper. Here are some ideas for getting started.

• Begin with a statement of the problem.

• Begin with two characters complaining about the problem.

• Begin with a description of all the animals gathered together and tell why they are together.

As you draft, try to create dialogue that reveals the personalities of your characters.

STEP 3 REVISING

Ask your partner for comments on your draft before you revise it.

✔ Have I made it clear what the problem is?

✔ Do the animals solve the problem in a logical way?

✔ Does the moral fit the fable?

✔ Does my dialogue reveal the personalities of the characters?

Revising Strategy

Dialogue that Reveals Personality

The purpose of dialogue, what the characters in a story say, is to help tell the story. However, dialogue can also reveal things about the characters. Think of how your friends express themselves. Do they reveal their personalities by what they say and how they say it?

Here are tips for writing dialogue that reveals personality.

- Different personality types speak at different speeds. An impatient squirrel might say, "Yes, yes, yes, I know." A sleepy bear might say, "Yeah . . . I know . . . Right."
- The size of the words a character uses also reveals character. A wise old owl might say, "I advise you to reconsider," while an alley cat might say, "Think it over, okay?"
- As you write dialogue, make the words fit each character's personality. Here a timid mouse, a confident lion, and a joking hyena have a conversation:

"Maybe we shouldn't disturb that elephant," said the mouse.
"Nonsense," said the lion. "I'm king of the jungle."
"King of the bungle, you mean," laughed the hyena.

What does the dialogue in the Literary Source tell about the characters?

Note how the writer of the passage below revised dialogue.

LITERARY SOURCE

"'Oh, I'm so proud of you, Son.' She beamed, turning over the crackling *papas*. His older brother, Lawrence, who was at the table reading the funnies, mimicked, 'Oh, I'm so proud of you, my son,' under his breath."
from "The No-Guitar Blues" by Gary Soto

His neighbor spoke, "I'm sure ~~you are wrong.~~ *it is only your mind that deceives you.* There is no difference between our pastures. Our farmers ~~take care~~ *tend to each* of the pastures the ~~same.~~ We are ~~pretty much the same.~~ *alike in every aspect.* How could we have something that is so *significantly* different from you?"

STUDENT MODEL

Ask a partner to review your revised draft before you edit. When you edit, pay special attention to how you use commas.

Editing Strategy

FOR REFERENCE . . .
More rules for using commas correctly are listed in the Language and Grammar Handbook.

Using Commas Correctly

Commas help your writing make sense. Here are some important rules for using commas.

- In a series of three or more words, use a comma to set off all but the last word.

  Otter, Beaver, and Grizzly Bear met Fox in the woods.

- Use commas to set off the name of someone being addressed.

  "Fox, could you help me reach these berries?" asked Mouse.

- Use commas to set off words or phrases not necessary to the main idea of the sentence. The use of commas can change meaning.

  Jaguars, who usually are portrayed as cunning, are the villains in fables. *(All jaguars are portrayed as villains.)*
  Jaguars who usually are portrayed as cunning are the villains in fables. *(Only those jaguars who are portrayed as cunning are the villains in fables.)*

- Use a comma before a conjunction that introduces an independent clause.

  Bear waded into the icy water, but he quickly backed out again.

The writer of the passage below edited for correct use of commas.

> Once upon a time in neighboring farms, there were two pastures, side by side. The pastures were separated by a fence. To an observer who would care to notice these pastures seemed identical. Lush in color, each seemed as fertile as the other.

STUDENT MODEL

STEP 5 PRESENTING

Here are two ideas for presenting your fable.

- Read your fable to a younger child or a group of children. Afterward, discuss the moral and how it applies to everyday life.

- Post your fables in the classroom, covering up the moral on each piece. Then, as a class, have a Gallery Walk. Each student reads the fables and decides what the moral could be. He or she writes the moral on a small "sticky note" and attaches it to the fable. Afterwards the author of each fable can share the suggestions.

STEP 6 LOOKING BACK

Self-evaluate. What grade would *you* give your paper? Look back at the Writer's Blueprint and evaluate yourself on each point, from 6 (superior) down to 1 (weak).

Reflect. Think about what you learned from writing your fable as you write answers to these questions.

✔ Have you ever worked with a group of friends or relatives to solve a problem cooperatively? What did you learn from the experience?

✔ Which step did you enjoy most in writing your fable? Which step was hardest?

For Your Working Portfolio: Add your fable and your reflection responses to your working portfolio.

Beyond Print

Computer Terms

Monitor A screen used to project the information from a computer or video player.

Hardware The mechanical parts of a computer.

Software Programs for a computer.

Application A particular computer program, or set of instructions to be followed by the machine.

Document A file that is created by using a computer program or piece of software.

Font A particular character type and size; fonts are grouped into families, such as Geneva, Helvetica, Bookman.

Writing with Computers

Two of the earliest tools for writing were feather quills and scrolls made from the bark of trees. Today writers of all ages depend on computers instead. Software programs allow you to easily write, edit, and proofread using a computer. Here are some tips that will help you conquer the writing process on a computer.

1. Don't worry about mistakes. Just write! You can correct mistakes and check spelling errors later.

2. Avoid just typing a paper that you have already written out entirely by hand. Try using the computer for prewriting activities such as brainstorming. You might even create a rough outline on the computer.

3. Use cut, copy, and paste tools to edit your writing. You can move around words, sentences, and even paragraphs.

4. Software programs usually provide a spelling check to help you edit. However, don't rely on it to find usage mistakes: We went to there house. A spelling check will not tell you that the word *there* is used incorrectly in the sentence. It's a good idea to print a copy of your work and proofread it carefully.

5. Save your work often. A power outage can cause the computer to lose your work.

6. Use the computer to center headings, change typefaces, and show words in boldface and italic type.

Activity Option

Now that you know some strategies for using a word processor, let's put them to work! Use your word processor on your next assignment. If you don't have a computer at home, try to use one at school or at a public library.

- Start by brainstorming your ideas on the screen.
- Now create an outline. Print your outline.
- Start composing your product on screen, using the outline as a guide.
- Proofread your work.

Projects for Collaborative Study

Theme Connection

Rules for Resolving Conflict Work with your classmates to develop a list of rules for clear communication during conflicts. Draw upon what you learned from reading the selections in this unit.

■ In a group, brainstorm what you already know about communicating clearly during conflicts.

■ Invite a school counselor or health teacher to speak to your group about ways that communication can help resolve conflicts.

■ Explore library resources on conflict resolution and communication skills.

■ Create a poster listing your rules and display it in your classroom or school.

Literature Connection

What's the Word? In several of the selections in this unit, words are used to create a humorous tone. In "The All-American Slurp," **onomatopoeia**—words that sound exactly like their meaning—makes situations more humorous. *Crunch* and *slurp* are two examples. **Diction,** the style in which words are spoken or written, adds humor to the letters in "The Empty Box." **Dialect,** the special way a language is spoken by a particular group of people is used in "What Stumped the Blue Jays."

■ As a group, choose a humorous situation from one of the selections in this unit. Rewrite the situation to give it a serious tone. Use diction, dialect, or onomatopoeia.

Life Skills Connection

Getting Help Every day you have problems to solve that challenge you to use your talents and skills. As you gain experience, your knowledge of how to solve problems increases. If you were having difficulty completing a tough math problem or sinking your hook shot, what would you do?

Identify useful ways to attack problems. Discuss these questions.

■ What are some of the most difficult problems you have solved in the past?

■ How did you go about solving them?

■ Did you ask others for help? If not, what stopped you from asking?

Now, in small groups make a chart of:

■ Ten problems sixth graders face.

■ The people who might help you solve each problem.

Share the chart with the class.

Multicultural Connection

Continuing the Fight In the early 1900s many groups sought to bring about **change,** from regulating big business to improving child labor laws. Parties on different sides of an issue had to make important **choices.**

■ With a group of classmates, research a "cause" of the early 20th century. What things were done to promote the cause?

■ Now decide on a cause that you and your group would like to support. Make a list of things that you will do to support your cause. How do your methods compare with those of early groups?

Read More About Conflict and Resolution

Maniac Magee (1990) by Jerry Spinelli. In this Newbery Award winner, a young boy helps break down racial barriers in a small town.

Tuck Everlasting (1975) by Natalie Babbitt. Set in the 1880s, a kidnapping, a murder, and a jailbreak are part of this exciting story about Winnie Foster and her relationship with the Tuck family.

More Good Books

The House of Dies Drear (1968) by Virginia Hamilton. Is Thomas Small's new home haunted? Join him as he tries to solve the mystery of the old house which was once the residence of a murdered abolitionist and a station in the underground railroad.

Who's Hu? (1981) by Lensey Namioka. Emma comes to America with her family in the 1950s. She is constantly faced with having to choose between Chinese customs and culture and the American way.

No Way Out (1988) by I. Ruckman. Amy's ideal weekend of hiking through a canyon with her boyfriend and younger brother is turned into a nightmare of survival by a flash flood.

Trouble's Child (1985) by Mildred Pitts Walter. Martha longs to leave her island home off the Louisisana coast and go to high school where she can find her true place in society.

Some of the Kinder Planets (1995) by Timm Wynee-Jones. In this collection of short stories, seemingly ordinary situations become very strange, as young people try to find their place.

Glossaries, Handbooks, and Indexes

Understanding Fiction

Fiction is writing that comes from an author's imagination. Its purpose is to illustrate some truth about life or to entertain. A **novel** is a long work of fiction dealing with characters, actions, and scenes that copy those of real life in a complex plot. A **short story** is shorter than a novel. It often describes just one event, and the characters are usually fewer in number and not as fully developed as those in a novel. Short stories can usually be read in one sitting.

Fiction shapes our own imaginations because it provides glimpses into the past, ideas about life in the future, and understanding of the world as it is today. Fiction has several important elements.

Characters

The **characters**—the people or animals—are one of the most important elements in fiction. Authors make their characters seem real by describing such things as what they look like (Anna was tall and wore jeans), the way they speak or act (Tony spoke calmly but his hands shook), and sometimes even what they are thinking (Norman wondered why his parents disagreed).

Plot

The **plot**—what happens to the characters—is a second important element in fiction, and it is carefully worked out by the author so that one event flows logically after another. In most fiction, the plot is built around a **conflict,** a problem or struggle of some sort. The conflict may be between characters, between a character and some object or event, or between a character and that character's inner self. The conflict builds to an emotional moment called a **climax,** or turning point, when the main character takes an action to end the conflict, or when the way events are working out causes some important change. Usually the turning point comes close to the end of the story and sometimes it is at the very end. The conclusion of a story, where the complications of the plot are worked out, is called the **resolution.** The events before the climax are often referred to as the *rising action,* while the events after the climax are called the *falling action.*

Setting

The **setting**—when and where the action takes place—is a third important element in fiction. Sometimes the setting is crucial to what happens, and then it is described in detail by the author. If the particular city or town and the exact season or year are important to the action, an author usually states them directly (New York City on a cold December Monday in 1996). Often authors do not need to be so definite. If all that happens occurs in one room and involves a character with an inner conflict, then the setting may not be described in detail because it is irrelevant to the story.

Theme

Another important thing to look for in fiction is **theme,** or underlying meaning. A theme may be directly stated by the author or only implied. Theme is not the same as subject, or topic, in that it involves a statement or an opinion about the topic. Not every work of fiction has a theme, and various readers may discover different themes in the same selection.

Mood/Tone

The author's choice of words and details to describe setting, characters, and events contributes to two additional elements of fiction—mood and tone. **Mood** refers to the atmosphere or feeling created in the reader by the author. **Tone** is the author's attitude toward the subject or toward the reader.

Strategies for Reading Fiction

When reading fiction, it is helpful to consider the following things:

- Think about the **characters.** What happens to each one? Who is your favorite character and why?

- Think about the **events.** What is the central problem or conflict? What is the moment of greatest suspense? Is the order of events important? Do you like the ending?

- Think about when and where the action takes place. Often the **setting** will be explained in the first few paragraphs. What are some of the other things that create a sense of time and place?

As you read, think about what the author suggests as well as what he or she actually states. When the information about the characters, events, and setting is only suggested, rather than stated, you must make **inferences.** An inference is a reasonable conclusion based on clues provided by the author. Looking for clues and making inferences will help you become a better reader.

If a story is not too long, read it through without stopping. What is it about? To become involved, **visualize** the characters and the place. After reading, it is often necessary to go back and reread sections. Try it. Be sure you know who the main characters are and what they are like. Be sure you understand where the action takes place and what the main problem is and how it is solved.

You'll also want to consider the **narrator,** or who is telling the story. Is the narrator a charac-ter participating in the events, or someone out-side the story who is simply observing what hap-pens? The two most common **points of view** are first person (a character in the story) and third person (an outsider). Ask yourself: From whose point of view am I seeing the characters, events, and setting?

As you read, stop occasionally and think about what you are reading.

Question yourself about the characters and events. "Why is this character such a bully? Is she jealous or just plain mean?"

Predict what may happen next. "Will the girl come out of the coma?"

Clarify what is happening by trying to explain things to yourself. "The carpet design helps me understand the game the boy has made up to amuse himself."

Summarize what has happened so far, an espe-cially important step when you are reading a long story or difficult novel.

Evaluate by making judgments about the qual-ity of the author's work. You can also evaluate such elements as a character's actions. "This story seems true to life because I think it's pos-sible for a dog to save a person's life."

Connect the story with your own experiences—do you think the character is doing the right thing? Do you identify with the way the charac-ter feels? "I felt exactly the same way—scared and lonely—when I moved last year."

Understanding Nonfiction

Nonfiction is about real people, real places, and things that actually happened. It includes many kinds of writing but can be divided into two general groups—**informational nonfiction,** such as newspaper articles, and **narrative nonfiction,** such as biography, which has many of the same literary elements as fiction. Although narrative nonfiction may tell a story, the story should be true and based on facts.

Below are descriptions of some of the most common types of nonfiction.

Autobiography

An **autobiography** is an account of all or part of a person's life written by that person. Feelings and observations about life's experiences are often important in an autobiography. Because the author is the narrator, an autobiography is almost always told from the first-person point of view.

Shorter forms of autobiography include **diaries, memoirs,** and **journals.** Today some autobiographies of people noted for contributions in special fields, such as politics or sports, are written with the help of a professional writer. Examples of autobiography included in this book are the selection from *The Diary of Latoya Hunter: My First Year in Junior High* and "The Noble Experiment" by Jackie Robinson as told to Alfred Duckett.

Biography

A **biography** is an account of a real person's life written by another person. Biographers try to learn about a noteworthy person and then help readers get to know that person. A biography can take us back in time or around the world to learn about fascinating people and their remarkable lives. In this book, you will find a short biography of Charles Dickens, "From Raisin Pudding to Oysters and Champagne" by Kathleen Krull.

Doing research is part of a biographer's job, and books, letters, and journals all can be a source of details for a biography. If possible, a biographer interviews the subject of the biography, or people who have known the person. To help readers visualize time periods, places, and people, a biography may have a setting and characterization, just as fiction does. Although the goal of a biographer is to provide a truthful account, sometimes inferred details are drawn from the facts available.

Essay

An **essay** is a discussion about a specific topic, and it often expresses an opinion on the topic. Some essays are primarily expository, or informative. They explain something or give more information about a subject. Essays may be classified as formal or informal. A formal essay has a serious tone and is generally intended to persuade the reader. An informal essay, more concerned with entertaining than persuading, has a personal, friendly tone. Sometimes an informal essay is humorous. "What Stumped the Blue Jays" by Mark Twain is an example of an informal essay.

Speech

A **speech** is written to be given as a public talk, usually for a particular occasion such as a graduation, a memorial service, or a political rally. It may be formal or informal, and the topic will depend upon the intended audience.

Strategies for Reading Nonfiction

When reading nonfiction, it is helpful to consider the following strategies:

• Before you actually begin reading nonfiction, warm-up by **previewing.** Consider the title and read the first paragraph. Also look at any illustrations. What clues to the subject do you find? Knowing what to expect should help you better understand what you read.

• Think about the **facts** and **opinions** presented. Since accuracy is important in nonfiction you'll want to distinguish between statements of fact and statements of opinion. Remember that a statement of fact can be proved while a statement of opinion expresses personal feelings, beliefs, or evaluations. Any statement about a future event is an opinion since it cannot be proved that it will happen.

• Consider the **author's purpose**. Why do you think this author wrote this particular work of nonfiction? Is it simply to inform you by providing facts? Is it to persuade you? Or is the purpose to entertain?

• Consider your own purpose for reading. It can allow you to read with **flexibility.** For example, if you are reading a difficult article about a recent discovery in space in preparation for reporting on it in science class, you will want to slow down and pay careful attention to the details. On the other hand, if you are looking for the name of the scientist who made the discovery, you might skim the article by glancing quickly at the material to find the specific information you want.

• Use the **time-order relationships** in the material. Paying attention to when things happen is particularly important when you read a history textbook, a biography, or an autobiography. Dates and clue words, such as *in 1900,* will help you find the order of events.

• Think about **cause-and-effect relationships.** Noticing how events are linked in a pattern, one event happening as the result of another, will help you follow narrative nonfiction. Using cause-and-effect relationships is also very useful in reading the directions for a science experiment or a history text.

• Looking for the **main idea, topic,** and **details** in nonfiction can be a help in remembering as well as understanding what you read. Recall that the topic is the subject of the selection and the main idea is the "big" idea about that topic. Details are included to support the main idea.

Understanding Poetry

Poetry is a type of literature that creates an emotional response through the imaginative use of words. It helps you experience what you might not otherwise notice. It can surprise or delight you, and it often will suggest some new ideas for thought. Poetry dates back to the beginning of human communities when poetic forms were used in tribal ceremonies. Later, stories were told in verse and passed along from one generation to the next.

Traditional poems are written in **stanzas,** or groups of lines that are set off visually from the other lines in a poem. Many traditional poems are **narrative poems,** poems that tell stories. They have the same literary elements you find in fiction, such as plot, characters, and setting. The **repetition** of sounds is another characteristic of traditional poems.

A modern poem characteristically is written in the language of everyday speech, and it may be about a variety of subjects, from rattlesnakes to homework. Often a modern poem creates a single **image** that appeals to your senses. Many modern poems are written in **free verse,** meaning they are free from any fixed or repeated patterns.

Below are descriptions of several important elements in poetry.

Rhythm

The pattern of sounds that are stressed and not stressed in a poem provides the **rhythm.** As you read the following stanza from Lewis Carroll's "The Walrus and the Carpenter," what syllables do you emphasize, or pronounce louder?

> The sun was shining on the sea,
>   Shining with all his might:
> He did his very best to make
>   The billows smooth and bright—
> And this was odd, because it was
>   The middle of the night.

The pattern of stressed syllables gives you a feeling for the beat of the stanza. Notice that the rhythm is not quite regular. In the first line, every other syllable is stressed: *sun, shin-, on,* and *sea,* but in the second line, there are two unaccented syllables between the stressed syllables *Shin-,* and *all (-ing, with).* Rhythm makes poetry enjoyable to read. It may be regular, or it may be slightly irregular to emphasize certain words.

Rhyme

The repetition of a sound in two or more words is called **rhyme.**

In poetry, the last words of lines often rhyme. In the stanza from "The Walrus and the Carpenter," there is end rhyme in the second, fourth, and sixth lines *(might, bright,* and *night).*

Figurative Language

Figurative language goes beyond the ordinary meanings of words in order to achieve a new effect or to express an idea in a fresh way. Two of the most common figures of speech are **simile** and **metaphor.** The following stanza from the poem "I'll tell you how the sun rose" by Emily Dickinson illustrates figurative language.

> I'll tell you how the sun rose, —
> A ribbon at a time.
> The steeples swam in amethyst,
> The news like squirrels ran.

Notice that the sunrise is described as "a ribbon" and steeples are surrounded by a purple, violet color. "News" is compared to a scurrying squirrel in the simile in the fourth line.

Imagery

When writers help us experience things through our senses of sight, hearing, smell, taste, and touch, they are using images, or

imagery. Imagery is used by many writers of fiction, but it is most commonly found in poetry. Notice how Henry Wadsworth Longfellow communicates images of sound in these lines from "The Children's Hour."

> I hear in the chamber above me
>> The patter of little feet,
> The sound of a door that is opened,
>> And voices soft and sweet.

Alliteration

Sound devices are an important part of poetry. The repetition of consonant sounds at the beginnings of words or within words is called **alliteration,** as shown in these lines from "The Walrus and the Carpenter." Notice the repeat of the sound of *s* in *seven, mops, swept, suppose, Walrus,* and *said.*

> "If seven maids with seven mops
>> Swept it for half a year,
> Do you suppose," the Walrus said,
>> "That they could get it clear?"

Strategies for Reading Poetry

When we read poems, it's important to listen to the words. Often they say more than they directly tells us. Keep in mind the following tips as you read poetry.

- **Use the title** to get a clue to the topic of the poem.

- **Do not pause or stop at the end of a line** unless there is a mark of punctuation indicating that you should do so.

- **Look for the meaning.** One way to do this is to pay attention to the punctuation. Although lines may flow from one to the next, ideas are often expressed as statements or questions.

- **Try to see in your mind the pictures** created by the words.

- In a poem that tells a story, **look for the action and visualize the characters** who determine the action.

- In reading poetry that focuses on an image or an emotion, **listen for the voice of the poem.** Notice how the word choices of the poet help you visualize an object or experience an emotion.

- **Give careful attention to each word in a poem.** Because poets use words precisely and sparingly, each word is significant.

- With any poem, it helps to **try reading aloud.** By listening to the poem's sounds you will get insight into the meaning. Hear the beat of the rhythm, the pattern of rhyme, and the repetition of sounds.

- **Keep in mind that the speaker of a poem is not necessarily the poet** but rather the voice the poet has chosen to communicate the experience.

Understanding Drama

A **drama** is a literary work that is written for presentation to an audience. It tells a story through the speech and actions of the characters. It may be written in verse or in prose. Generally, plays are fictional, but occasionally they are based on true events and real people. Even a play that tells the story of something that actually happened will probably not re-create the exact words that were spoken. This happens because no one may remember just what was said at a particular moment.

As is true for fiction, the **characters** in a drama are developed in several ways. You can learn about them from what the playwright tells you, from what the characters say about themselves, from what others say about the characters, and from what the characters do.

Most plays have the same elements of **plot** that you find in fiction. There will be a problem, a conflict, and a resolution.

Below are descriptions of common forms that drama takes and several important terms to know as you read plays.

Stage Plays

In the nineteenth and early twentieth centuries, the **stage** was seen as a room with one wall removed. The audience viewed all that happened through this invisible "fourth" wall. Before the performance and during intermissions, a curtain replaced the invisible wall. Recently the traditional stage has become less confined, and some theaters have been built with the stage in the center and seating on all sides. Stage plays are acted in front of live audiences.

Television Plays

A **television play** is performed on a stage for broadcast to television viewers. You will see this form of drama most frequently on public or educational television networks.

Movies

Usually filmed at different locations and over a period of time, **movies** can include more action than is possible in a stage or television play. Movies are produced for both large public theaters and for first-time viewing on television.

Radio Plays

The two most significant features of **radio plays** are dialogue between characters and sound effects that add to the drama. Although radio plays are not common today, they were very popular before the days of television.

Cast of Characters

If you go to the performance of a play, you will likely get a program that lists all of the **characters** who have parts in the production. The script for a play you read will have a similar list of characters at the beginning, before the scene is described or the action starts. Sometimes this list not only names the characters in the play but also describes or identifies them for you. Here is the beginning of the cast of characters in a play version of Charles Dickens's *A Christmas Carol*.

CHARACTERS
CAROLERS, FAMILIES, DANCERS
FIRST BOY
SECOND BOY
THIRD BOY
LITTLE GIRL *with a doll*
EBENEZER SCROOGE
FRED, *Scrooge's nephew*

Script

A play, whether it is performed live on stage or filmed by a camera, starts with a **script** made up of the stage directions and dialogue. In a play of more than one scene, the script shows how the play is divided into parts.

Stage Directions

Stage directions are the playwright's instructions to the performers. The setting may be described in detail in stage directions at the beginning of a play. You will notice that stage directions are usually printed in a different type, as in the following example from *A Christmas Carol*.

PROLOGUE

The play begins amid a swirl of street life in Victorian London. Happy groups pass; brightly costumed CAROLERS *and* FAMILIES *call out to one another and sing.*

Stage directions also provide information for the actors on how to interpret lines and how to move. When you read a play, they help you visualize the **characters' actions**. Stage directions may be set apart in parentheses as well as different type. This example is also from *A Christmas Carol*.

SCROOGE *(hearing the waltz and remembering it)*. Surely it's enough. Haven't you tormented me enough? (YOUNG EBENEZER *is seen waltzing with his* SWEETHEART.)

Dialogue

Since the story in the play is revealed through the words of the characters as they perform on stage, **dialogue** makes up most of the text of a play. It is the chief means of moving the plot along in a play and is made up of the lines, or speeches, of the various characters. The following conversation takes place between Scrooge and his nephew, Fred, in *A Christmas Carol*.

FRED. A Merry Christmas, Uncle! God save you!

SCROOGE. Bah! Humbug!

FRED. Christmas a humbug, Uncle? I hope that's meant as a joke.

SCROOGE. Well, it's not. Come, come, what is it you want? Don't waste all the day, Nephew.

Strategies for Reading Drama

Reading a play is different from viewing it because you must picture the scene, imagine the characters, and interpret the actions.

• **Use the stage directions to visualize.** The information the playwright provides in the stage directions will help you picture the **setting** and **actions** of the characters.

• **Read the stage directions carefully.** It's important to read the stage directions carefully because they help you imagine the scene and the action. You may be tempted to skip over the directions and focus on the dialogue, but if you do this you will miss some things you would see or hear if you were viewing the play or movie.

• **Try reading the characters' lines aloud.** Work with a partner or small group of classmates. Choose a scene from a play or movie script and assign individuals to the different parts. Read the dialogue as you imagine the character would say the words. Consider your tone of voice as well as the signals the playwright has included in the punctuation.

• **Be alert to special terms.** A play written for filming will usually include some specific directions for the person doing the camera work. For example, *fade in* means "to become slowly more distinct" and *pan* means "to move horizontally or vertically to take in the larger scene."

Glossary of Literary Terms

Words within entries in SMALL CAPITAL LETTERS refer you to other entries in the Glossary of Literary Terms.

author's purpose The reason an author writes a work. Three common purposes authors have are to entertain, to inform, and to persuade the reader. Authors often have more than one purpose in a single piece of writing.

biography Any account of a real person's life. "Ibrahima" by Walter Dean Myers (page 490) is a biography. An autobiography is the story of part or all of a person's life written by the person who lived it. Jackie Robinson's "The Noble Experiment" (page 438) is an autobiography.

characterization The methods an author uses to acquaint a reader with the characters in a work. An author may develop a character through describing the character's physical appearance, as Robert Cormier does in describing Rollie Tremaine (page 274). A character's speech and behavior may be described, as are those of the the Other June in "Tuesday of the Other June" (page 6). The thoughts and feelings of a character may be told, as are the narrator's in Anderson's "Stolen Day" (page 31). The author may also develop a character by revealing the attitudes and reactions of other characters, as Toshio Mori does in showing the patience of Uncle Hiroshi with Tatsuo by contrasting his actions with those of Tatsuo's father in "The Six Rows of Pompons" (page 23).

dialogue The conversation between two or more people in a literary work. Dialogue can serve to develop CHARACTERIZATION, as in Budge Wilson's "The Dandelion Garden" (page 67), or it can help create the MOOD, as in Lensey Namioka's "The All-American Slurp" (page 580). Dialogue can also advance the PLOT, as it often does in plays, such as *Damon and Pythias* (page 315).

diction The writing style or words used by the author or characters to express ideas. In "The Empty Box" (page 526) several characters write letters to achieve the same goal but each person uses different words to say the same thing.

drama A composition in prose or verse written to be acted on a stage, before motion-picture or television cameras, or in front of a microphone. *A Christmas Carol* (page 235), *Damon and Pythias* (page 315), and *Let Me Hear You Whisper* (page 391) are examples of drama.

end rhyme The rhyming of words at the ends of lines of poetry.

> I hear in the chamber above me
>   The patter of little feet
> The sound of a door that is opened,
>   And voices soft and sweet
> —Henry Wadsworth Longfellow, "The Children's Hour," page 456

essay A brief composition that presents a personal point of view. "What Stumped the Blue Jays" (page 548) is a good example of an essay.

exaggeration An overstatement, sometimes involving FIGURATIVE LANGUAGE, used chiefly to heighten the effect of a statement. An example of exaggeration is, "I hope when you go for your checkup you need a tetanus shot" in "Southpaw" (page 432).

fable A brief tale, in which the characters are often animals, told to point out a moral truth. "The Fox and the Grapes" (page 261) is a fable.

fiction A story, novel, or play about imagined people and events. Examples are "Southpaw" (page 432) and "The No-Guitar Blues" (page 571).

figurative language Language expanded beyond its ordinary literal meaning. It uses comparisons to achieve new effects, to provide fresh insights, or to express a relationship between things that are essentially different. The most common figures of speech are SIMILE, METAPHOR, and EXAGGERATION.

folk tale A traditional story that has been told for centuries before it was written down. Folk tales usually have simple plots, lively action, and characters that are not well developed. "Turtle's Race with Bear" (page 502) is one example.

free verse A type of poetry that is "free" from a fixed pattern of RHYTHM or RHYME. Poems in free verse in this book include "Thinking" (page 14) and "What We Said Sitting Making Fantasies" (page 182).

humor In a literary work, something that is funny or amusing. A joke or a funny story about a character or person are examples of humor. "The Empty Box" (page 526) and "The All-American Slurp" (page 580) are examples of humorous stories.

imagery Concrete words or details that appeal to the senses of sight, sound, touch, smell, taste, and to internal feelings. Lillian Morrison's "The Sprinters" (page 126) is rich in specific, concrete details that appeal to the senses.

legend A story by an unknown author, handed down through the years. A legend may have some basis in historical fact, and usually there are many slightly different versions of it. "Why the Rooster Crows at Sunrise" (page 366) is a Vietnamese legend.

lyrics The words of a song. "No Irish Need Apply" (page 448) is one example.

metaphor A figure of speech that involves an implied comparison between two basically unlike things. In a metaphor there is never a connective such as *like* or *as* to signal a comparison is being made. (See SIMILE.) The comparison may be stated (She was a stone) or implied (Her stony silence filled the room). In "The Dandelion Garden" (page 67), for example, Budge Wilson compares Hamlet's hurt feelings to a punctured balloon.
(See also FIGURATIVE LANGUAGE.)

mood The atmosphere or overall feeling within a work. The choice of setting, objects, details, images, and words all contribute to create a specific mood. The mood can change during the course of a story. In "Lob's Girl" (page 166) for example, the mood can shift suddenly from the happiness of Sandy and Lob's relationship to sadness when an accident threaten's Sandy's life.

moral The lesson or teaching in a FABLE or story. Aesop's fables contain morals that are usually revealed in the last few lines. *A simple life in peace and safety is preferable to a life of luxury tortured by fear* is an example of a moral from "The City Mouse and the Country Mouse" (page 262).

myth A traditional story connected with the religion or beliefs of a people, usually attempting to account for something in nature. "Persephone" (page 370) is a Greek myth.

narrative A story or account of an event or a series of happenings. It may be true or fictional. "Emily" (page 50) and "Princess" (page 467) are both narratives.

narrator The teller of a story. The teller may be a character in the story, as in Jack Shaefer's "Ghost Town" (page 481), an anonymous voice outside the story, as in Dahl's "The Wish" (page 157), or the author, as in Jackie Robinson's "The Noble Experiment" (page 438).
(See also POINT OF VIEW.)

nonfiction Any writing that is not fiction; any type of literature that deals with real people and events. BIOGRAPHY, ESSAY, and speech are types of nonfiction. "From Raisin Pudding to Oysters and Champagne" (page 257), "Lewis Hine and the Crusade Against Child Labor" (page 452), and "Frozen Man" (page 594) are examples of nonfiction.

novel Long works of FICTION dealing with characters, situations, and settings that copy those of real life. *Number the Stars* by Lois Lowry is an example of a novel.

onomatopoeia Words used to imitate the sound of a thing. *Hiss, smack, buzz,* and *hum* are examples of such words. The following example is from "The All-American Slurp" (page 580): Father took a bite of his celery. *Crunch.*

oral history A written version of a taped interview, in which the author recalls personal experiences. "Amitabh" (page 187) by Janet Bode is one example.

personification A figure of speech or FIGURATIVE LANGUAGE in which human characteristics are given to nonhuman things. In "The Circuit" (page 56) Francisco Jiménez personifies a river when he describes it as murmuring a greeting.

play *(See DRAMA.)*

plot In the simplest sense, a series of happenings in a literary work. The term is also used to refer to the action as it is organized around a *conflict* and builds through complication to a *climax* followed by a RESOLUTION.

poetry Composition in verse. The words in poetry are arranged in lines that have RHYTHM and, sometimes, RHYME.

point of view The perspective from which an author presents the actions and characters of a story. The story may be related by a character (the *first-person* point of view), as in "Stolen Day" (page 31) or "The All-American Slurp" (page 580), or the story may be told by a narrator who does not participate in the action (the *third-person* point of view), as in "Princess" (page 467).

(See also NARRATOR.)

resolution The tying up of the PLOT; the conclusion, where the complications in a plot are resolved.

rhyme The repetition of syllable sounds. End words that share a particular sound are called END RHYMES. Rhyming words within a line of poetry are called *internal rhymes.*

rhyme scheme The pattern of END RHYMES in a poem. You can chart a rhyme scheme with letters of the alphabet by using the same letter for end words that rhyme, as in this example:

The sun was shining on the sea,	a
Shining with all his might:	b
He did his very best to make	c
The billows smooth and bright—	b
And this was odd, because it was	d
The middle of the night.	b

rhythm The arrangement of stressed and unstressed sounds in writing and speech. Rhythm may be regular or it may be varied.

setting The time and place in which the events of a narrative occur. The setting may be specific and detailed and introduced at the very beginning of the story, or it may be merely suggested through the use of details scattered throughout the story. In some stories the setting is essential to the narrative: it may have an effect on the events of the PLOT, reveal character, or create a certain MOOD. In other stories the setting is relatively unimportant. The setting is important in *A Christmas Carol* (page 235) and "The Dog of Pompeii" (page 298).

short story A story shorter than a NOVEL. Although it generally describes just one event, it most often has a beginning, a middle, and an end. The characters are usually fewer in number and not as fully developed as those in a novel. "The King of Mazy May" (page 129) and "The Sand Castle" (page 344) are short stories.

simile A comparison in which the word *like* or *as* is used to point out a similarity between two basically unlike things. Jean Craighead George uses a simile in "The Pacing White Mustang" when she describes the mustang as being "wild as the cornflower and as beautiful as snow on the mountains." (page 139).

(See also METAPHOR.)

speaker The same as a NARRATOR. Often the narrator of a poem is called the speaker.

stanza A group of lines set off visually from the other lines in a poem. Charlotte Zolotow's poem "Change " (page 78) has five stanzas.

symbol An object, action, person, or situation that suggests a meaning beyond its obvious meaning. In "The All-American Slurp" (page 580), food is a symbol of cultural differences.

theme The underlying meaning of a literary work. A theme may be directly stated, but more often it is merely implied. In Budge Wilson's short story "The Dandelion Garden" (page 67), the topic or subject of the story is a boy's garden but an important theme is his pride in spite of the lack of encouragement he gets in cultivating it.

tone An author's attitude toward the subject of a literary work or toward the reader. That attitude may be sad, serious, bitter, humorous, sympathetic, or cynical. Tone is conveyed through the author's particular choice of words and details in describing setting, portraying characters, and presenting events. Robert Cormier's tone in "President Cleveland, Where Are You?" (page 274) is both lighthearted and serious. Nicholasa Mohr's tone in "Princess" (page 467) is serious and cynical.

Glossary of Vocabulary Words

a	hat	ī	ice	ü	rule
ā	age	o	hot	ch	child
ä	far	ō	open	ng	long
â	care	ô	order, all	sh	she
e	let	oi	oil	th	thin
ē	equal	ou	out	ŦH	then
ė	term	u	cup	zh	measure
i	it	ù	put		

ə {
a in about
e in taken
i in pencil
o in lemon
u in circus
}

A

absurdity (ab sėr′də tē), *n.* ridiculous quality or condition; foolishness.

abundance (ə bun′dəns), *n.* great plenty.

accurately (ak′yər it lē), *adv.* without errors or mistakes.

adjust (ə just′), *v.* accommodate oneself; get used to something.

aggravating (ag′rə vāt ing), *adj.* annoying; irritating; exasperating.

agonized (ag′ə nīzd), *adj.* painfully suffering; greatly anguished.

allergy (al′ər jē), *n.* an unusual reaction of the body to certain substances, such as particular kinds of pollen, pet hair, food, or cloth.

analysis (ə nal′ə sis), *n.* separation of anything into its parts or elements to find out what it is made of; also, an examining carefully and in detail.

anonymous (ə non′ə məs), *adj.* unnamed; from a person whose name is not given.

anticipate (an tis′ə pāt), *v.* expect.

anticipation (an tis′ə pā′shən), *n.* expectation or a looking forward to something.

apprehensively (ap′ri hen′siv lē), *adv.* in a way that indicates alarm, fear, anxiety, or worry.

ascent (ə sent′), *n.* upward slope.

assure (ə shür′), *v.* tell positively.

astonish (ə ston′ish), *v.* greatly surprise or amaze.

autopsy (ô′top sē), *n.* medical examination of a dead body to find the cause of death.

avert (ə vėrt′), *v.* turn aside.

B

ballet (bal′ā), *adj.* having to do with a type of dancing performed on a stage.

bondage (bon′dij), *n.* slavery; a being held against one's will under the control of another person.

boycott (boi′kot), *v.* join together against and agree not to buy from, sell to, or associate with a business in order to force a change.

C

camouflage (kam′ə fläzh), *v.* give a false appearance to in order to conceal; disguise.

capsize (kap sīz′), *v.* overturn.

captor (kap′tər), *n.* person who takes or holds a prisoner.

catapult (kat′ə pult), *v.* shoot forward or up suddenly; spring.

cavity (kav′ə tē), *n.* hollow place; hole. Cavities in teeth are caused by decay.

cavort (kə vôrt′), *v.* prance about; jump around.

champion (cham′pē ən), *n.* person who fights or speaks for another; person who defends a cause.

channel (chan/l), *n.* usually the bed of a stream, river, etc., but in this case a narrow strip of color in the rug.

charitable (char/ə tə bəl), *adj.* kindly in judging people and their actions.

citizen (sit/ə zən), *n.* a person who is or becomes a member of a nation.

civilization (siv/ə lə zā/shən), *n.* advanced stage in the development of a society.

clamor (klam/ər), *n.* a loud noise, especially of voices; continual uproar.

coma (kō/mə), *n.* prolonged period of unconsciousness often caused by a serious injury.

compel (kəm pel/) *v.* drive or urge with force.

composition (kom/pə zish/ən), *n.* a piece of music made up of different parts, such as a symphony.

compulsory (kəm pul/sər ē), *adj.* compelled; required.

concept (kon/sept), *n.* big idea or general notion.

condition (kən dish/ən), *n.* thing on which something else depends.

confession (kən fesh/ən), *n.* a Catholic ritual in which a person tells his or her sins to God or to a priest.

consign (kən sīn/), *v.* set apart; assign.

contemporary (kən tem/pə rer/ē), *n.* person living in the same period of time.

contempt (kən tempt/), *n.* the feeling that a person, act, or thing is mean, low, or worthless.

corrupt (kə rupt/), *v.* make evil or wicked; make rotten, spoiled, or decayed.

counsel (koun/səl), *n.* advice.

countenance (koun/tə nəns), *n.* face; features.

cultivation (kul/tə vā/shən), *n.* preparing land and growing plants.

cumbersome (kum/bər səm), *adj.* hard to manage; clumsy, or burdensome.

cynical (sin/ə kəl), *adj.* doubting the sincerity and goodness of others.

D

dejected (di jek/tid), *adj.* in low spirits; discouraged.

dejection (di jek/shən), *n.* lowness of spirits; sadness; discouragement.

delicacy (del/ə kə sē), *n.* fineness of feeling for small differences; precision.

derive (di rīv/), *v.* get from a source or origin; receive.

desert (di zėrt/), *v.* go away and leave a person or a place, especially one that should not be left; forsake.

determined (di tėr/mənd), *adj.* firm.

dignity (dig/nə tē), *n.* proud and self-respecting character or manner; stateliness.

discretion (dis kresh/ən), *n.* freedom to decide or choose.

dismal (diz/məl), *adj.* miserable.

distracted (dis trakt/əd), *adj.* having attention drawn away from a given purpose.

distraught (dis trôt), *adj.* very upset.

distressed (dis trest/), *adj.* sad or anxious, as a result of some unfortunate event.

distributor (dis trib/yə tər), *n.* person or company that sells goods to a particular market, usually other companies.

drone (drōn/), *v.* talk or say in a monotonous voice.

E

economy (i kon/ə mē), *n.* system of managing the production, distribution, and consumption of goods and services.

eerie (ir/ē), *adj.* mysterious or suggesting of the supernatural.

emerge (i mėrj/), *v.* come out.

emigrate (em/ə grāt), *v.* leave one's country to settle in another.

etiquette (et/ə ket), *n.* manners; the customary rules for behavior in polite society.

evidently (ev′ə dənt lē), *adv.* plainly; clearly.

exasperation (eg zas′pə rā′shən), *n.* anger; extreme annoyance.

excavation (ek′skə vā′shən), *n.* a digging out.

F

fan (fan), *v.* stir up; arouse.

fidget (fij′it), *v.* move about restlessly or uneasily.

flounder (floun′dər), *v.* struggle awkwardly without making much progress.

fortunately (fôr′chə nit lē), *adv.* luckily.

frantically (fran′tik lē), *adv.* with wild fear.

fringe (frinj), *n.* an edging of hanging threads or cords.

frivolous (friv′ə ləs), *adj.* silly; lacking in seriousness.

G

gingerly (jin′jər lē), *adv.* with extreme care or caution.

gratification (grat′ə fə kā′shən), *n.* a being pleased or satisfied.

gratitude (grat′ə tüd), *n.* thankfulness.

grudgingly (gruj′ing lē), *adv.* unwillingly.

gulch (gulch), *n.* a very deep, narrow ravine with steep sides, especially one marking the course of a stream.

H

hesitantly (hez′ə tənt′lē), *adv.* undecidedly or with uncertainty.

hostile (hos′tl), *adj.* opposed; unfriendly; unfavorable.

humility (hyü mil′ə tē), *n.* humbleness of mind; lack of pride; meekness.

hypocrite (hip′ə krit), *n.* person who is not sincere; pretender.

hypothesis (hī poth′ə sis), *n.* a tentative explanation that accounts for a set of facts and can be tested by further investigation.

hysteria (hi stir′ē ə), *n.* uncontrollable excitement or emotion.

I

illiteracy (i lit′ər ə sē), *n.* inability to read and write.

impact (im′pakt), *n.* force due to the striking of one thing against another.

impressive (im pres′iv), *adj.* having a strong effect on the mind or feelings of others.

indifferent (in dif′ər ənt), *adj.* not caring one way or the other; having or showing no interest.

indignant (in dig′nənt), *adj.* angry at something unworthy, unjust, unfair, or mean.

industrial (in dus′trē əl), *adj.* engaged in or connected with business, trade, or manufacturing.

industrious (in dus′trē əs), *adj.* working hard and steadily; diligent.

inefficient (in′ə fish′ənt), *adj.* wasteful; incompetent.

infuriated (in fyùr′ē ā′tid), *adj.* filled with wild rage; furious; enraged.

ingenious (in jē′ nyəs), *adj.* with skill in planning or making; clever.

injustice (in jus′ tis), *n.* lack of fairness or rightness; being unjust; wrongfulness.

instinct (in′stingkt), *n.* a natural feeling, knowledge, or power, such as that which guides animals; inborn tendency to act in a certain way.

instinctively (in stingk′tiv lē), *adv.* following a natural tendency.

intelligence (in tel′ə jəns), *n.* ability to learn and know; quickness of understanding.

investigative (in ves′tə gā′tiv), *adj.* of or having to do with careful and systematic searching for facts.

K

kiln (kiln), *n.* furnace or oven for burning, baking, or drying something; bricks are baked in a kiln.

L

laboratory (lab′rə tôr′ē), *n.* place where scientific work is done or where drugs, medicines, or other chemicals are manufactured.

laughingstock (laf′ing stok′), *n.* person or thing that is made fun of.

lenient (lē′nyənt), *adj.* mild or gentle; not harsh or stern; merciful.

lethargy (leth′ər jē), *n.* drowsy dullness; lack of energy; sluggish inactivity.

liable (lī′ə bəl), *adj.* likely; unpleasantly likely.

license (lī′sns), *v.* give a tag, card, sticker, or certificate to show that something is registered with the city or state.

M

marvel (mär′vəl), *n.* something wonderful; astonishing thing.

mellow (mel′ō), *v.* soften or become wiser through age or experience.

merchandise (mėr′chən dīz), *n.* goods for sale.

mimicry (mim′ik rē), *n.* act or practice of imitating.

miserable (miz′ər ə bəl), *adj.* very unhappy or unfortunate; wretched.

mock (mok), *v.* make fun of by copying or imitating.

mortified (môr′tə fīd), *adj.* humiliated.

murmur (mėr′mər), *v.* say in a soft, low, indistinct voice.

mutilated (myü′tl ā′tid), *adj.* cut or torn up, sometimes with limbs removed.

N

negotiate (ni gō′shē āt), *v.* talk over and arrange terms; consult.

notary (nō′tər ē), *n.* a public official authorized to certify deeds and contracts and to attend to other legal matters.

O

obliterate (ə blit′ə rāt′), *v.* wipe out, remove all traces.

obsessed (əb sest′), *adj.* having one's mind filled with a feeling or idea.

offender (ə fen′dər), *n.* person who does wrong or offends in some way.

offspring (ôf′spring′), *n.* the young of a person, animal, or plant.

onlooker (ôn′lŭk′ ər), *n.* person who watches without taking part; spectator.

opportunity (op′ər tü′nə tē), *n.* chance for advancing in life.

outstrip (out strip′) *v.* go faster than; leave behind in a race.

P

paralyze (par′ə līz), *v.* affect with a lessening or loss of ability to move, feel, or function; make powerless.

pavilion (pə vil′yən), *n.* a building, for shelter, usually somewhat open.

pawn (pôn), *v.* leave an object with another person as security that borrowed money will be repaid.

pedigreed (ped′ə grēd′), *adj.* said of a purebreed animal whose ancestry is known and recorded.

perilous (per′ə ləs), *n.* dangerous.

perilously (per′ə ləs lē), *adv.* dangerously.

permanent (pėr′mə nənt), *adj.* intended to last.

permission (pər mish′ən), *n.* consent; agreement to allow or permit something.

persist (pər sist′), *v.* continue stubbornly, firmly, or without letting up.

personality (pėr′sə nal′ə tē), *n.* the individual quality that makes one person act differently from another person.

pitch (pich), *v.* fall or plunge forward.

poise (poiz), *v.* balance.

premise (prem′is), *n.* a statement assumed to be true and used to draw a conclusion.

preserve (pri zėrv′), *v.* keep from change or harm.

procession (prə sesh′ən), *n.* a group of persons moving along in a formal, orderly way.

proclaim (prə klām′), *v.* make known publicly and officially; declare publicly.

prodigy (prod′ ə jē), *n.* person with amazing brilliance or talent, especially a remarkably talented child.

proposition (prop′ə zish′ən), *n.* scheme.

prospect (pros′pekt), *n.* thing expected.

protrude (prō trüd′), *v.* stick out.

proverb (prov′ėrb′), *n.* a short, wise saying used for a long time by many people.

pummel (pum′əl), *v.* hit; strike; beat.

R

rampage (ram′pāj), *n.* fit of rushing wildly about; spell of violent behavior.

ransom (ran′səm), *n.* price paid for a captive to be set free.

ration (rash′ən), *n.* a fixed allowance of food.

rebel (ri bel′), *v.* resist or fight against law or authority; (reb′əl), *n.* person who resists or fights against authority instead of obeying.

refuge (ref′yüj), *n.* shelter or protection from danger or trouble; safety; security.

relief (ri lēf′), *n.* the lessening of or freeing from a burden.

reluctant (ri luk′tənt), *adj.* unwilling.

reputation (rep′yə tā′shən), *n.* what people think and say the character of a person is.

reservoir (rez′ər vwär), *n.* place where water is collected and stored for use. Reservoirs often form beautiful lakes.

resigned (ri zīnd′), *adj.* accepting what comes without complaint.

resist (ri zist′), *v.* keep from doing or stop oneself from doing.

resistance (ri zis′təns), *n.* acting against; striving against; opposition.

resolution (rez′ə lü′shən), *n.* vow or thing firmly decided upon.

revive (ri vīv′), *v.* bring back to consciousness; bring back to a fresh, lively condition; refresh; restore.

revolting (ri vōl′ting), *adj.* disgusting.

S

sacred (sāk′rid), *adj.* holy.

savor (sā′vər), *v.* enjoy very much.

scales (skālz), *n.* series of tones arranged according to rising or falling pitch.

scorch (skôrch), *v.* burn; dry up; wither.

scramble (skram′bəl), *v.* climb or walk quickly over rough ground.

sense (sens), *n.* normal, sound condition of mind.

sham (sham), *adj.* false; pretended; imitation.

shrewdly (shrüd′lē), *adv.* in a way that shows a sharp mind; cleverly.

shriveled (shriv′əld), *adj.* dried up; withered.

sidekick (sīd′kik′), *n.* partner or close friend.

slacken (slak′ən), *v.* become less active, vigorous, or brisk; become slower.

smear (smir), *v.* overwhelm; defeat (in this case, bring to the ground by other players).

snag (snag), *v.* catch or obtain by quick action.

solitude (sol′ə tüd), *n.* the state of being alone.

specialize (spesh′ə līz), *v.* pursue some special branch of work, study, etc.

speculating (spek′yə lāt ing), *adj.* guessing; conjecturing; wondering.

spot (spot), *v.* pick out; find out; recognize.

squabble (skwob′əl), *v.* take part in a petty, noisy quarrel or argument.

startled (stär′tld), *adj.* surprised.

static (stat′ik), *n.* noise or other interference with reception on radio or television or in a public address system.

steadfastly (sted′fast′lē), *adv.* showing firmness of purpose; loyally and unwaveringly.

strategic (strə tē′jik), *adj.* based on a preconceived plan.

strategy (strat′ə jē), *n.* careful plan or method.

stricken (strik′ən), *adj.* hit, wounded, or affected by (a weapon, disease, trouble, sorrow, etc.).

subjective (səb jek′tiv), *adj.* about the thoughts, feelings, and experiences of the speaker; personal.

suburb (sub′ėrb′), *n.* smaller town or village just outside or near a city.

sulk (sulk), *v.* hold (oneself) aloof in a sullen manner; be silent and bad-humored because of resentment.

summit (sum′it), *n.* highest point; top.

surge (sėrj), *n.* a swelling wave or something like such a wave.

survey (sər vā′), *v.* look over; examine.

swell (swel), *v.* become larger or thicker.

sympathize (sim′pə thīz), *v.* feel someone else's sorrow or unhappiness.

systematic (sis′tə mat′ik), *adj.* in a carefully planned way.

T

tackle (tak′əl), *v.* seize and stop, or throw to the ground. In football, players try to tackle the opposing player who has the ball.

taunt (tônt), *v.* jeer at; mock; reproach.

technique (tek nēk′), *n.* a special method or system used to accomplish something.

tend (tend), *v.* take care of; look after; attend to.

terminate (tėr′mə nāt), *v.* come to an end.

thrash (thrash), *v.* move, swing, or beat vigorously.

torment (tôr ment′), *v.* worry or annoy very much.

traitor (trā′tər), *n.* person who betrays his or her country or ruler.

treacherous (trech′ər əs), *adj.* dangerous; marked by unforseen hazards.

triumphantly (trī um′fənt lē), *adv.* successfully.

trophy (trō′fē), *n.* any prize, cup, etc. awarded to a victorious person or team.

troubleshooter (trub′ əl shü′tər), *n.* person who discovers and eliminates causes of trouble.

trudge (truj), *v.* walk wearily or with effort.

tutor (tü′tər), *n.* a private teacher.

U

ultimate (ul′tə mit), *adj.* greatest possible; highest.

V

valor (val′ər), *n.* bravery; courage.

W

weird (wird), *adj.* odd; strange; peculiar.

Language and Grammar Handbook

The following **Language and Grammar Handbook** will help you as you edit your writing. It is alphabetically arranged with each entry explaining a certain term or concept. For example, if you can't remember when to use *accept* and *except,* look up the entry **accept, except** and you'll find an explanation of the meaning of each word and a sentence (many from selections in this book) using each word.

a, an The choice between *a* and *an* depends on the beginning sound, not the beginning letter, of the following word. *A* is used before a consonant sound, and *an* is used before a vowel sound.

◆ I want to watch the tadpole turn into *a* frog.
   from "The Empty Box" by Johanna Hurwitz

◆ He had come at *an* unfortunate time.
   from "The Noble Experiment" by Jackie Robinson

accept, except *Accept* means "to take or receive; consent to receive; say yes to." It is always a verb. *Except* is most commonly used as a preposition meaning "but."

◆ "Well, then, Mr. Dodsworth," he said briskly, "we'll *accept* your offer and thank you very much.".
   from "Lob's Girl" by Joan Aiken

◆ All of the dogs *except* one were in the same big run.
   from "The Christmas Hunt" by Borden Deal

adjective Adjectives are modifiers that describe nouns and pronouns. Adjectives tell *what kind, which one,* or *how many.*

What kind:	*red* jacket	*sunny* day	*brick* sidewalk
Which one:	*this* car	*that* truck	*those* keys
How many:	*three* strikes	*several* books	*few* opportunities

See also **comparative forms of adjectives and adverbs.**

adverb Adverbs modify verbs, adjectives, or other adverbs. They tell *how, when,* or *where* about verbs.

How:	confidently	loudly	slowly
When:	today	now	later
Where:	there	near	outside

See also **comparative forms of adjectives and adverbs.**

agreement

1. Subject-verb agreement. When the subject and verb of a sentence are both singular or both plural, they agree in number. This is called subject-verb agreement. Usually, singular verbs in the present tense end in *s*. Plural verbs do not have the *s* ending.

Chris sings. (singular subject; singular verb)

Chris and Pat sing. (plural subject; plural verb)

Pronouns generally follow the same rule. However, the singular pronouns *I* and *you* always take plural verbs.

	Singular	Plural
1st person	I sing	we sing
2nd person	you sing	you sing
3rd person	he/she/it sings	they sing

Changes also occur with the verb *to be* in both the present and past tense.

Present Tense		Past Tense	
I am	we are	I was	we were
you are	you are	you were	you were
he/she/it is	they are	he/she/it was	they were

a. Most compound subjects joined by *and* or *both . . . and* are plural and are followed by plural verbs.

> ◆ And from then on, the sun, the rooster, and the bluebird *have kept* their bargain.
> > from "Why the Rooster Crows at Sunrise" by Lynette Dyer Vuong

b. A compound subject joined by *or, either . . . or,* or *neither . . . nor* is followed by a verb that agrees in number with the closer subject.

Neither *Rollie Tremaine* nor the other *boys own* a Grover Cleveland card.

Problems arise when it isn't obvious what the subject is. The following rules should help you with some of the most troublesome situations.

c. When the subject is a noun, phrases or clauses coming between the subject and the verb do not affect the subject-verb agreement.

A new *box* of cards *is* here.

d. Singular verbs are used with the singular indefinite pronouns *each, either, neither, anyone, anybody, one, everyone, everybody, someone, somebody, nobody,* and *no one.*

e. Plural indefinite pronouns take plural verbs. They are *both, few, many,* and *several.*

      s   v
Many of them *are* for sale.

     s   v
Both enjoy a good joke.

f. The indefinite pronouns *all, any, most, none,* and *some* can be either singular or plural depending on their meaning in a sentence.

Singular	Plural
None of us *was* really sure.	*None* of the postcards *were* mailed.
Some of the music *was* good.	*Some* of the runners *were* exhausted.

g. Unusual word order does not affect agreement; the verb generally agrees with the subject, whether the subject follows or precedes it.

◆ Suddenly, over this snow rim *came* the flying *body* of the Irishman. . . .
    from "The King of Mazy May" by Jack London

NOTE: When writing dialogue, an author may intentionally use *there's* incorrectly for effect.

In informal English you may often hear sentences like "There's a book and some paper for you on my desk." *There's* is a contraction for *There is.* Technically, since the subject is a *book and some paper,* the verb should be plural and the sentence should begin, "There are . . . . " Since this may sound strange, you may want to revise the sentence to something like "A book and some paper are on my desk." Be especially careful of sentences beginning with *There;* be sure the verb agrees with the subject:

◆ There *were* burn *scars* on the rough summit. . . .
    from "Thunder Butte" by Virginia Driving Hawk Sneve

◆ There *was* no *wind,* but the speed at which he traveled created a bitter blast. . . .
    from "The King of Mazy May" by Jack London

2. Pronoun-antecedent agreement.
a. An *antecedent* is a word, clause, or phrase to which a pronoun refers. The pronoun agrees with its antecedent in person, number, and gender.

   antec.   pron.   pron.   pron.
◆ *Norman* nodded and ate *his* breakfast. When *he* was finished *he* stood up.
    from "Thunder Butte" by Virginia Driving Hawk Sneve

b. Singular pronouns are generally used to refer to the indefinite pronouns *one, anyone, each, either, neither, everybody, everyone, somebody, someone, nobody,* and *no one.*

The chief of the giants told *each* to enter *his* tomb and close up the entrance.

Now look at the following sentence:

Everybody wanted to get her program autographed.

This sentence poses problems. First, it is clearly plural in meaning but "everybody" and "her" are singular pronouns; second, "everybody" may not refer to women only. To avoid the latter problem, you could write "Everybody wanted to get his or her program autographed." However, this solution gets clumsy and wordy. Sometimes it is best to revise:

The fans wanted to get their programs autographed.

This sentence is now clear and non-sexist.

all right *All right* is generally used as an adjective and should always be spelled as two words.

 ◆ Then Walt Masters received the news that old Loren was nearly *all right,* again, and about to move on afoot for Dawson. . . .
   from "The King of Mazy May" by Jack London

among, between *Among* implies more than two persons, places, or things. *Between* usually refers to two, followed either by a plural or by two expressions joined by *and*—not by *or:*

 ◆ After talking for a while *among* themselves, they told the children to come back in a week to hear the decision of the Council.
   from "The Ancestor Tree" by T. Obinkaram Echewa

 ◆ We stand there with this big smile of respect *between* us.
   from "Raymond's Run" by Toni Cade Bambara

See also **between you and me.**

apostrophe An apostrophe is used in possessive words and in contractions.

June's radio	Gus's backpack
can't didn't	He got all *A's* and *B's.*

appositive An appositive is a noun or phrase that follows a noun and identifies or explains it. It is usually set off by commas.

 ◆ Ito, the *strawberry sharecropper,* did not smile.
   from "The Circuit" by Francisco Jiménez

 ◆ I try to imagine my town, *New York.*
   from "People's Gardens" by Milton Meltzer

awkward writing A general term (abbreviated *awk*) sometimes used in editing to indicate faults in writing such as inappropriate word choice, unnecessary repetition, clumsy phrasing, confusing word order, or any other weakness or expression that makes reading difficult.

B

bad, badly Be careful in using the modifiers *bad* and *badly. Bad* is an adjective. Use it to modify a noun or a pronoun. Use the adverb *badly* to modify a verb.

♦ "In the end, it's not so *bad.*"
from "Keri" by Maxine B. Rosenberg

♦ I fixed a few *bad* spots in the dirt road.
from "Ghost Town" by Jack Shaefer

♦ "I wanted very *badly* to go into the kitchen, find out that the dog would live."
from "The Christmas Hunt" by Borden Deal

between you and me After prepositions such as *between,* use the objective form of the personal pronouns: *between you and **me**, between you and **her**, between you and **him**, between you and **us**, between you and **them**.*

Let's split this candy bar *between you and me.*

C

capitalization

1. Capitalize all proper nouns and adjectives.

Proper Nouns	Proper Adjectives
China	Chinese
Canada	Canadian
Elizabeth	Elizabethan

NOTE: If an article or possessive pronoun comes before a family title, the title is *not* capitalized: Everyone calls *my cousin* Squirt. *A brother* can be a real bother sometimes.

2. Capitalize people's names and titles.

Justice Clarence Thomas	Uncle Rob
President of the United States	Dr. Amy Kuhns
the Pope	the Secretary of the Treasury

3. Capitalize the names of races, languages, religions, and religious figures and writings. Also capitalize any adjectives made from these names.

NOTE: Do not capitalize *god* when it refers to those found in ancient myths and legends.

Spanish dance	German
English	Roman mythology
the Bible	Biblical prophet
Allah	the Koran

4. Capitalize geographical names (except for articles and prepositions).

NOTE: Do not capitalize directions of the compass or adjectives that indicate direction: The storm is coming from the *east.*

Australia	South America
the Pacific Ocean	Lake Ontario
the Midwest	Vail Valley
Mt. Vernon	Yellowstone National Park

NOTE: *Earth* is capitalized when used with other planet names but *not* when preceded with *the.*

5. Capitalize the names of structures, organizations, and bodies in the universe.

the Washington Memorial	Mars is closer to the sun than Earth.
Democratic Party	The earth orbits the sun.
American Medical Association	Springman Middle School
Venus	the Solar System

6. Capitalize the names of historical events, times, and documents.

the Emancipation Proclamation	the Battle of Waterloo
the Victorian Age	the Bill of Rights

NOTE: Do *not* capitalize the names of the seasons: *spring, summer, fall, winter.*

7. Capitalize the names of months, days, holidays, and time abbreviations.

May	Tuesday
Veteran's Day	A.M. P.M.

8. Capitalize the first words in sentences, lines of poetry, and direct quotations.

◆ He gazed at a new world.
　　from "Thunder Butte" by Virginia Driving Hawk Sneve

◆ I hear in the chamber above me
　The patter of little feet,
　The sound of a door that is opened,
　And voices soft and sweet.
　　from "The Children's Hour" by Henry Wadsworth Longfellow

9. Capitalize certain parts of letters, outlines, and the first, last, and all other important words in titles.

Dear Sir or Madam:	Dear Uncle Joe,
Sincerely yours,	Very truly yours,

I. Movies
　A. Types
　　I. Comedy
　　2. Drama
　　3. Horror
　B. Trends in Movie Making

Book Title	*Water Sky*
Newspaper	*The Wall Street Journal*
Play	*Let Me Hear You Whisper*
Television Show	*Wheel of Fortune*
Short Story	"The King of Mazy May"
Song	"No Irish Need Apply"
Work of Art	*Mona Lisa*
Magazine	*Sports Illustrated*

clause A clause is a group of words that has a subject and a verb. A clause is *independent* when it can stand alone and make sense. A *dependent* clause has a subject and a verb, but it cannot stand alone. The reader is left wondering about the meaning.

          S   V

Independent clause: Branch Rickey hired Jackie Robinson.

          S   V

Dependent clause: Because Branch Rickey hired Jackie Robinson,

colon (:) The colon is used after the greeting of a business letter and between the hour and minutes when you write time in numbers.

Dear Valued Customer: 6:30 A.M.

A colon is also used after phrases that introduce a list or a quotation.

◆ He wore flashy clothes: red velvet waistcoats, rings on his fingers, and a diamond stickpin on his vest.
  from "From Raisin Pudding to Oysters and Champagne" by Kathleen Krull

comma Commas are used to show a pause or separation between words and word groups in sentences, to avoid confusion in sentences, to separate items in addresses and dates, in dialogue, and in figures and friendly letters.

1. Use commas between items in a series. Words, phrases, and clauses in a series are separated by commas.

◆ The tray looked pretty, with its tiny red radishes, curly sticks of carrots, and long, slender stalks of pale green celery.
  from "The All-American Slurp" by Lensey Namioka

◆ Meg got her large chocolate milkshake and I had a small one.
  from "The All-American Slurp" by Lensey Namioka

> NOTE: Some professional writers leave out the comma before the *and*. In general, however, student writers should include this comma unless told otherwise by their teachers.

2. Use a comma after certain introductory words and groups of words such as clauses and prepositional phrases of five words or more.

◆ *"Sure,* he always gives us inferior merchandise."
  from "Princess" by Nicholasa Mohr

◆ *As the son of a chief,* Ibrahima was expected to assume a role of political leadership when he came of age.
  from "Ibrahima" by Walter Dean Myers

3. Use a comma to set off nouns in direct address. The name or title by which persons (or animals) are addressed is called a noun of direct address. It is set off by commas.

◆ "No, Mom, I'll do it," he said, hugging her.
  from "The No-Guitar Blues" by Gary Soto

4. Use commas to set off interrupting words and appositives. Any phrase or clause that interrupts the general flow of a sentence is often set off by commas.

◆ The weather, *as they'd called it in the last century*, was entirely predictable now: warming.
    from "The Sand Castle" by Alma Luz Villanueva

◆ Atalanta, *a great huntress*, was resolved to live unwed after learning that her father abandoned her because she had not been born a boy.
    from "The Quest for the Golden Apples" by Josephine Preston

5. Use a comma before the conjunction in a compound sentence. A comma is generally used before the coordinating conjunction *(and, but, for, or, nor, yet, so)* that joins the parts (independent clauses) of a compound sentence.

◆ Fausto strummed a chord on the guitarron, *and* the bass resounded in their chests.
    from "The No-Guitar Blues" by Gary Soto

NOTE: If the compound parts are very short, no comma is needed.

◆ That dog eats steak and they only eat tuna fish.
    from "Princess" by Nicholasa Mohr

6. Use a comma after a dependent clause that begins a sentence. Do not use a comma before a dependent clause that follows the independent clause.

◆ *When Aaron brought her out on the road to town,* she seemed somewhat astonished.
    from "Zlateh the Goat" by Isaac Bashevis Singer

◆ The populations took buses *when they needed transportation.* . . .
    from "The Sand Castle" by Alma Luz Villanueva

7. Use commas to separate items in a date. If a date is within a sentence, put a comma after the year.

◆ On February 7, 1829, Ibrahima and his wife sailed on the ship *Harriet* for Africa.
    from "Ibrahima" by Walter Dean Myers

8. Use a comma to separate items in an address. The number and street are considered one item. The state and Zip Code are also considered one item. Use a comma after the Zip Code if it is within a sentence.

Jason Peacock	Natures Wonder & Company
724 W. Madison	8246 Camino Real
Green Bay, WI 54301	San Antonio, TX 78200

9. Use a comma to separate numerals greater than three digits.

74,900   1,126,816 $51,000

10. Use a comma after the greeting in a friendly letter and after the closing in all letters.

Dear Larry,   Yours truly,

11. Use commas in punctuating dialogue. *See* **dialogue.**

comma splice *See* **run-on sentence.**

comparative forms of adjectives and adverbs Most adjectives and adverbs have three forms to show comparison. The **positive** form does not make a comparison, the **comparative** form compares two things, and the **superlative** form compares three or more of anything.

Most adjectives and adverbs form the comparative and superlative in regular ways.

NOTE: Slight spelling changes occur with some words.

1. Most one- and two-syllable modifiers add *-er* and *-est* to make the comparative and superlative forms.

Positive	Comparative	Superlative
big	bigger	biggest
cool	cooler	coolest
soon	sooner	soonest
crispy	crispier	crispiest

2. Longer modifiers use *more* and *most* to make comparisons.

Positive	Comparative	Superlative
careful	more careful	most careful
easily	more easily	most easily

3. Some adjectives and adverbs do not follow the usual rules. Their comparative and superlative forms are made differently.

Positive	Comparative	Superlative
good	better	best
well	better	best
badly	worse	worst
much	more	most

conjunction A conjunction is a word that links one part of a sentence to another. It can join words, phrases, or entire sentences.

D

dash (—) The dash is used to show a sudden change in thought or to set off words that interrupt the main thought of a sentence.

◆ As long as people could remember seeing Tito—about twelve or thirteen years—they had seen Bimbo.
from "The Dog of Pompeii" by Louis Untermeyer

◆ He and Bimbo ran on—the only silent beings in a howling world.
from "The Dog of Pompeii" by Louis Untermeyer

dialogue Dialogue is often used to enliven many types of writing. Notice the paragraphing and punctuation of the passage at the top of the next page. *See also* **quotation marks.**

Language and Grammar Handbook   **651**

◆ "How do you suppose the stick came to be on the butte?" Norman asked.

His grandfather shook his head. "No one can say. Usually such a thing was buried with a dead warrior as were his weapons and other prized belongings."

"Is the *coup* stick what you dreamed about, Grandpa?"

"No. In my dream I only knew that you were to find a *Wakan,* a holy thing. But I did not know what it would be."

from "Thunder Butte" by Virginia Driving Hawk Sneve

E

ellipsis (. . .) An ellipsis is used to indicate that words (or sentences or paragraphs) have been omitted. An ellipsis consists of three dots, but if the omitted portion would have completed the sentence, a fourth dot is added for the period:

◆ I resent this as it crosses the border from professional to personal life. . . . I expect that I will not be hearing from you again.

from "Joel Rubin" by Phillip Hoose

exclamation point (!) An exclamation point is used at the end of an exclamatory sentence—one that shows excitement or strong emotion. Exclamation points can also be used with strong interjections. *See also* **quotation marks.**

◆ "The grapes are sour!"

from "The Fox and the Grapes" by Aesop

F

fragment *See* **sentence fragment.**

G

good, well *Good* is used as an adjective to modify a noun or pronoun. Do not use it to modify a verb. Use the adverb *well* to modify a verb.

◆ I sat there a long time, waiting for the *good* feeling to come.

from "President Cleveland, Where Are You?" by Robert Cormier

◆ He must sing, dear, there is nothing else that might make him *well.*

from *A Christmas Carol* by Charles Dickens

It felt good to Lisa to be home from the hospital and in her own bed.

NOTE: When you are referring to health, both *good* and *well* can be used. They mean different things. If the meaning is "not ill," use *well.* If the meaning is "pleasant" or "in good spirits," use *good.*

H

hopefully This is often used to mean "it is hoped" or "I hope," as in the following sentence.

Hopefully, the dentist will find twenty cavities! That's what you deserve!

However, in formal writing, avoid this usage and write the sentence as follows:

◆ I *hope* when you go to the dentist he finds twenty cavities.

from "Southpaw" by Judith Viorst

interjection An interjection is a word or phrase used to express strong emotion.

- ◆ *"Gee!"* Nephew Tatsuo said.
  from "The Six Rows of Pompons" by Toshio Mori

italics Italics are used to indicate titles of whole works such as books, magazines, newspapers, plays, films, and so on. They are also used to indicate foreign words and phrases and to add special emphasis to a word or phrase. *See* **capitalization**, rule 9, for examples of italicized titles.

NOTE: In handwritten or noncomputer writing, underlining takes the place of italics.

- ◆ In the old Chinese tradition, the *ch'i-lin* is the symbol of a promising male offspring.
  from "The Ch'i-lin Purse" by Linda Fang

- ◆ No, old fellow, you can *not* come in. Hospitals are for people, not for dogs.
  from "Lob's Girl" by Joan Aiken

its, it's *Its* is the possessive form of the personal pronoun *it*; *it's* is the contraction meaning "it is."

- ◆ *Its* attendants lifted the child onto a stretcher as carefully as if she were made of fine thistledown.
  from "Lob's Girl" by Joan Aiken

- ◆ *"It's* very rude of him," she said, "To come and spoil the fun!"
  from "The Walrus and the Carpenter" by Lewis Carroll

lay, lie This verb pair presents problems because, in addition to the similarity between the words, the past tense of *lie* is *lay*. The verb *to lay* means "to put or place something somewhere."

Present	Past	Past Participle	Present Participle
lay	laid	(has) laid	(is) laying

- ◆ I will *lay* blessings on you.
  from "The Departure of the Giants" by Harold Courlander

- ◆ She took the purse and *laid* it on her lap.
  from "The Ch'i-lin Purse" by Linda Fang

The verb *to lie* means "to rest in a flat position."

Present	Past	Past Participle	Present Participle
lie	lay	(has) lain	(is) lying

Notice the way the verbs are used in the following sentences:

- ◆ I picked them up without looking at the smear of blood where Calypso *had lain*.
  from "The Christmas Hunt" by Borden Deal

- ◆ She *lay* down at my feet, putting her muzzle on her paws. (past tense)
  from "The Christmas Hunt" by Borden Deal

NOTE: When the meaning you intend is "not to tell the truth," *lie (lied, has lied)* is the verb to use.

The boy *could* not *lie* to his father; he confessed that he had shot Calypso Baby.

Language and Grammar Handbook **653**

M

myself (and himself, herself, etc.) Be careful not to use *myself* and the other reflexive and intensive pronouns when you simply need to use the personal pronoun *I* or its objective form, *me*.

> Incorrect: Karen and myself won the poster contest.
> Correct: Karen and I won the poster contest.

> Incorrect: Carlos asked Susan and myself to his party.
> Correct: Carlos asked Susan and me to his party.

Reflexive pronouns reflect the action of the verb back to the subject. An intensive pronoun adds intensity to the noun or pronoun just named.

> I *myself* would not eat the rotten beans that Don Osvaldo sold to Mrs. Morales. (The reflexive pronoun *myself* refers back to *I*.)

> Don Osvaldo *himself* would not eat the beans, but he let his dog Princess eat them. (The intensive pronoun *himself* refers back to *Don Osvaldo*.)

N

noun A *noun* is a word that names a person, place, thing, or idea. Most nouns are made plural by just adding *-s* or *-es* to the singular. When you are unsure about a plural form, check a dictionary.

P

parentheses ( ) Parentheses have two uses: 1) to enclose words that interrupt the thought of the sentence and 2) to enclose references to page numbers, chapters, or dates.

> ◆ Although his parents were very much alive (his father was in prison for debt—at the time a crime), he never forgot his feeling of being orphaned.
> from "From Raisin Pudding to Oysters and Champagne" by Kathleen Krull

> Charles Dickens (1812–1870) died of a stroke.

possessive case The possessive case is formed in various ways. For singular nouns and indefinite pronouns, add an apostrophe and *s*. *See also* **apostrophe.**

> my brother's bat   somebody's fault   everybody's job

For plural nouns ending in an *s,* add only an apostrophe:

> the dentists' office   the babies' pool   the teachers' lounge

NOTE: Apostrophes are **not** used with personal pronouns to show possession.

However, if the plural is irregular and does not end in *s,* add an apostrophe and then an *s*.

> women's magazines   children's boots   men's hats

preposition Prepositions are words that show the relationship between a noun or pronoun and some other word in a sentence.

Common prepositions include:

about	as	by	into	to
across	at	during	like	under
after	before	for	of	until
against	behind	from	off	up
among	below	in	on	with
around	between	inside	through	without

prepositional phrase Prepositional phrases are groups of words that begin with a preposition and end with a noun or pronoun. These phrases act as modifiers and create more vivid pictures for the reader. Notice the five prepositional phrases marked with parentheses in the following sentence:

◆ She went (through a white gate), (past a row) (of bushes), (up the stairs) (to the front door).
    from "The Circuit" by Francisco Jiménez

pronoun Subject pronouns are used as subjects of sentences. Object pronouns can be used as direct objects, indirect objects, or objects of prepositions.

When a pronoun is used as the subject of a sentence, the pronoun is in the nominative case and is called a *subject pronoun.*

Subject Pronouns

Singular	I	you	he, she, it
Plural	we	you	they

When a pronoun is used as an object, the pronoun is in the objective case and is called an *object pronoun.*

Object Pronouns

Singular	me	you	him, her, it
Plural	us	you	them

NOTE: To check that you are using the correct pronoun in a compound subject or object, say the sentence with just one pronoun. For the compound subject *She and I,* you would say *I went (Not: me went).* In a compound subject with *I,* the *I* is always second.

She went to the mall.

I went to the mall.

She and *I* went to the mall.

The waiter served *me* lunch.

The waiter served *him* lunch.

The waiter served *him* and *me* lunch.

quotation marks Quotation marks enclose a speaker's exact words. They are also used to enclose some titles. When you use someone's exact words in your writing, use these rules.

1. The first word of a direct quotation begins with a capital letter. When a quotation is broken into two parts, use two sets of quotation marks. Use one capital letter if the quote is one sentence. Use two capital letters if it is two sentences.

◆ "All right," Uncle Hiroshi said, "but did you see those holes in the ground with the piled-up mounds of earth?"
    from "The Six Rows of Pompons" by Toshio Mori

◆ "They ought to be bathed," said Jean Pengelly. "Sandy, run a bowl of warm water while I get the disinfectant."
    from "Lob's Girl" by Joan Aiken

2. Use a comma between the words that introduce the speaker and the words that are quoted. Place the end punctuation or the comma that ends the quotation inside the quotation marks. Begin a new paragraph each time the speaker changes.

◆ "If the snow keeps falling like this, we may have to stay here for days," Aaron explained.

"Maaa," Zlateh bleated.

"What does 'Maaa' mean?" Aaron asked. "You'd better speak up clearly."

from "Zlateh the Goat" by Isaac Bashevis Singer

3. Put question marks and exclamation points inside the quotation marks if they are a part of the quotation. Put question marks and exclamation points outside the quotation marks if they are not part of the quotation.

◆ "And someday," said my mother, "you'll have a daughter of your own. What will you name her?"

from "Tuesday of the Other June" by Norma Fox Mazer

◆ Why did the Other June say, "Wrong. Your—name—is—Fish—Eyes"?

See also **dialogue.**

4. Enclose titles of short works such as stories, songs, poems, and book chapters in quotation marks. See capitalization, rule 9 for examples of titles enclosed in quotation marks.

R **raise, rise** Use *raise* to mean "lift up; bring up; grow." Use *rise* to mean "get up":

Present	Past	Past Participle	Present Participle
rise	rose	had risen	is rising
raise	raised	had raised	is raising

◆ *Rising* above them all, flailing his feet as he commanded, was the Pacing White Mustang.

from "The Pacing White Mustang" by Jean Craighead George

run-on sentence This occurs when there is only a comma (known as a comma splice) or no punctuation between two independent clauses. Separate the clauses into two complete sentences, join them with a semicolon, or join them with a comma and a coordinating conjunction (*and, but, or, nor, yet, so, for*).

Run-on: The janitor locked the school door, then he went home.

Correct: The janitor locked the school door. Then he went home.

Correct: The janitor locked the school door; then he went home.

Correct: The janitor locked the school door, and then he went home.

S

semicolon (;) Use this punctuation mark to separate the two parts of a compound sentence when they are not joined by a comma and a conjunction.

◆ She stopped going to the schoolyard; she didn't know what to tell the kids there.
from "Princess" by Nicholasa Mohr

sentence fragment A fragment, like a run-on sentence, should be avoided because it signals an error in the understanding of a sentence. A fragment often occurs when one sentence is finished, but another thought occurs to the writer and that thought is written as a complete thought. A fragment may be missing a subject, a verb, or both.

Fragment: The ending was eerie. Especially when you found out Lob was dead.

Correct: The ending was eerie, especially when you found out Lob was dead.

◆ Nice. Very nice indeed. He rubbed the circle and it didn't hurt.
from "The Wish" by Roald Dahl

NOTE: As with run-ons, fragments are sometimes used by writers for effect or emphasis.

sit, set *Sit* means to "sit down"; *set* means to "put something somewhere."

Present	Past	Past Participle	Present Participle
sit	sat	had sat	is sitting
set	set	had set	is setting

◆ She picks it up, opens it, closes it, and *sets* it down again.
from "Let Me Hear You Whisper" by Paul Zindel

T

their, there, they're *Their* is a possessive, *there* is an introductory word or adverb of place, and *they're* is the contraction for *they are.*

◆ Adults began telling the children to stay away from his door and not to bother him with *their* noise and anxious questions.
from "The Ancestor Tree" by T. Obinkaram Echewa

◆ You may play with him anywhere in the garden, but *there* is one place you must never go.
from "The Ch'i-lin Purse" by Linda Fang

◆ *They're* compulsory. (contraction of *they are*)
from "Let Me Hear You Whisper" by Paul Zindel

to, too, two *To* is a preposition that means "toward, in that direction" or is used in the infinitive form of the verb (e.g., "to follow"); *too* means "also" or "more than enough"; *two* means "one more than one."

◆ The princess smiled and walked up *to* the table and picked the present she liked the most.
from "The Princess and the Tin Box" by James Thurber

◆ If I got stuck on a homework problem, he helped me, *too*.
from "Keri" by Maxine B. Rosenberg

◆ They spotted the body at an altitude of about 10,500 feet, nearly *two* miles above sea level.
from "Frozen Man" by David Getz

V

verb A *verb* is a word that tells about an action or a state of being. The form or *tense* of the verb tells whether the action occurred in the past, the present, or the future. *See also* **agreement 1. Subject-verb agreement.**

verb shifts in tense Use the same tense to show two or more actions that occur at the same time.

Incorrect: April *saw* (past) the twins and *waves* (present) hello.
Correct: April *saw* (past) the twins and *waved* (past) hello.

W

who, whom *Who* is used as a subject. *Whom* is used as a direct object or the object of a preposition.

◆ *Who* was Ibrahima?
from "Ibrahima" by Walter Dean Myers

◆ On the road *whom* should they meet but the Earth King.
from "Porcupine and the Sky Mirrors" by Katherine Davison

who's, whose *Who's* is a contraction meaning "who is;" *whose* is a possessive.

Who's going to teach Nephew Tatsuo how to cultivate pompons?

Whose rows of pompons were full of bugs and weeds?

Y

your, you're *Your* is the possessive form of the personal pronoun *you; you're* is a contraction meaning "you are":

◆ "That new girl should give you a run for *your* money."
from "Raymond's Run" by Toni Cade Bambara

◆ "Well, young man, *you're* probably hungry. How about a turnover?"
from "The No-Guitar Blues" by Gary Soto

Index of Skills and Strategies

Reading/Thinking Strategies

Opinion, 381
Oral reading, 18, 21, 53, 102

Personal response, 5, 15, 21, 28,
35, 41, 53, 64, 74, 80, 88, 95,
120, 136, 146, 153, 162, 176,
185, 191, 193, 200, 232, 239,
242, 251, 259, 264, 268, 270,
283, 285, 290, 293, 296, 305,
307, 309, 320, 350, 364, 368,
373, 388, 400, 403, 427, 429,
435, 445, 450, 457, 487, 499,
504, 532, 545, 552, 560, 587,
592, 613
Predict, 5, 15, 24, 28, 41, 53, 72,
80, 118, 120, 177, 191, 193,
196, 199, 242, 254, 259, 264,
282, 283, 290, 307, 309, 400,
416, 431, 445, 457, 482, 487,
501, 518, 534, 537, 538, 540,
541, 543, 570, 571, 579, 585,
587, 606, 609, 627
Preview, 30, 37, 49, 55, 77, 81,
111, 123, 128, 138, 143, 156,
165, 178, 186, 193, 221, 234,
256, 260, 273, 285, 293, 297,
309, 314, 343, 352, 361, 365,
369, 390, 406, 431, 437, 447,
451, 466, 480, 489, 501, 525,
534, 547, 555, 570, 579, 589,
593, 606, 629
Problem and solution, 409, 560,
570

Question, 146, 204, 242, 276, 296,
368, 427, 462, 487, 558, 627

Reading rate, 489

Scanning techniques, 416
Sequence
keeping track of, 30
time markers in, 96, 480, 629
understanding, 96
Set a purpose for reading, 4, 5, 18,
22, 30, 37, 49, 55, 77, 81, 96,
110, 111, 123, 128, 138, 143,
155, 156, 165, 178, 193, 220,
221, 256, 260, 272, 273, 285,
297, 307, 309, 314, 342, 343,
352, 361, 365, 369, 379, 381,

Set a purpose for reading
(continued)
406, 430, 431, 437, 451, 465,
466, 480, 489, 501, 524, 525,
534, 547, 555, 569, 570, 579,
589, 592, 606
Similarities and differences, 154,
185, 186, 296, 307, 375, 403,
547, 579, 587, 603
Skimming, 360, 416, 605
techniques for, 416
Summarize, 15, 53, 96, 113, 358,
379, 440, 489, 499, 510, 587,
627
Supporting details, 207, 233, 290,
334, 510, 614
recognizing, 47

Topics, recognizing, 47, 629

Use prior knowledge, 5, 18, 22, 30,
37, 49, 55, 65, 77, 81, 88, 103,
104, 111, 123, 128, 138, 143,
156, 162, 165, 178, 186, 191,
193, 221, 234, 254, 260, 273,
284, 285, 293, 297, 307, 314,
342, 343, 352, 361, 365, 369,
381, 390, 406, 431, 435, 437,
447, 451, 466, 480, 489, 501,
518, 525, 534, 547, 553, 555,
589, 592, 603, 622

Visualize, 143, 156, 451, 568, 627

Word choice, context clues.
See Vocabulary and Study Skills
Index.

■

Vocabulary and Study Skills
Antonyms, 284, 321

Charts
action/consequences, 555
adjectives, forms of, 211
advantages/disadvantages, 138
adverbs, forms of, 211
arguments, 513
author's purpose, 406
Briticisms, 165
cause/effect, 260, 365

characters, 98, 606
character's actions, 512
classification, 18, 30, 55, 98,
138, 165, 178, 191, 221, 283,
352, 373, 381
comparison/contrast, 28, 154,
186, 606
cultural elements in folk tales, 609
cultural mores, 201
dialogue, 403
facts/opinions, 381
fairness, 466
first-person point of view, 191
folk tales, cultural elements in, 609
food chain, 271
imagery/sense, 120
informal language, 487
information, 64
K-W-L, 55, 64, 352, 358, 489
letters, 525
main event, 96
meanings of names, 81
metaphors, 74
myth characteristics, 373
old ways/modern ways, 221
onomatopoeia, 587
personal experience, 18
personality traits, 331
personification, 368
plot sequence, 320
poem types, 178
poetry, 364
points of view, 162
predictions, 534
problem/solution, 146, 570
problems sixth graders face, 622
pros/cons, 437
qualities of friends, 314
religious beliefs, 463
report card, 136
scientific terms, 390
sensory details, 209
sequence, 193
similarities/differences, 154,
186, 579
simile or metaphor, 552
similes, 142
study tips, 54
teens' beliefs, 464
time, thinking about, 379
tone, 283

Grammar, Usage, Mechanics, and Spelling

■

Speaking, Listening, and Viewing

Listening, 127
    effective, 103
    hints for, 103
    to a tape, 54
Media literacy, movies, 335. *See also* Media and Technology Index.

Oral history, 103

Speaking
    debating tips, 423
    dialogue, 36, 500
    dramatize a story, 104
    explanation, 588
    newscast, 321
    oral description, 43, 424
    oral presentation, 291
    oral reading, 102, 296
    oral report, 137, 142, 259, 375, 404, 546, 564, 567
    oral summary, 103, 604
    oral traditions, 336
    performing a play, 147, 479
    performing a skit, 16, 201, 336
    play-by-play broadcast, 147
    presentation, 213, 233, 368, 389, 409, 561
    radio drama, 255
    soliloquy, 561
    storytelling, 89, 517
Speech, 121, 533, 553, 588
    tips for delivering, 334

Technology
    computer terms, 621
    videotape, 335, 578
    writing with computers, 51, 99, 554, 621

Viewing
    images, 517
    movies, 335

■
Interdisciplinary Connections

Ancient calendars, 374-375
    Aztec, 374
    Egyptian, 375
    Hebrew, 374

Ancient calendars (continued)
    Mayan, 375
    seasons, 376-377
    time, 378
Anthropology, rites of passage around the world, 42-43
Anthropology connection, Mt. Vesuvius' eruption, 325-327

Art, writing Chinese numbers, 205-206
Art connection, 205
    ancient cave art, 410-411

Banner, 359
Books
    class anthology, 296
    class collection, 103
Brochure, 488
Bulletin boards, 308, 566

Cartoon, 616
Collages, 41, 75, 291, 424
Comic strips, 36, 553, 609
Community service connection
    helping others, 610-613
    volunteering, 612-613

Dance, 127, 592
Diorama, 233
Displays
    festival artifacts, 268
    learning styles, 54
Do Unto Others, 460-463
Drawings, 29, 41, 77, 80, 156, 163, 213, 255, 284, 296, 308, 331, 335, 336, 359, 424, 458, 517, 566

Environmental connection
    endangered species, 415
    surviving the seasons, 376-377
    What can you do?, 414
    wildlife trade, 412-413
Ethics, religion as a source of, 460-463
Exhibits
    baseball, 446,
    museum, 137

Festive times, 266-270

Festive times (continued)
    Chusok, 266
    Diwali, 267
    Feast of Lights, 268
    Il-ul-Fitr, 267
    Kwanzaa, 268
    personal, 269-70
    Vietnamese New Year, 266

Game, create a, 376
Going for It, 148-153

Handbook, 104
Health
    making adjustments, 90-95
    Should I be worried?, 44
    worrywarts, 45
Health connection, 44, 90
    dealing with stress, 94-95
    stress, 90-95
    talking about feelings, 508-509
History, 152, 202
    ancient calendars, 374-375
    family life in Rome, 322-324
    festivals around the world, 266-270
    keeping traditions, 266-270
    Mt. Vesuvius eruption, 325-327
    religions, 460-463
    Stonehenge, 565-566
    tracking time, 374-378
    written law, 506-507

Illustrations, 296, 233, 368, 504
It's Your World Too, 410-415

Law, origins of, 506-507
Links to China's Past, 202-206
    The Silk Road, 202-204
    writing Chinese numbers, 205-206
Links to the Roman Empire, 322-327

Mathematics connection, 148, 463
Meeting challenges, 148-153
    competition, 148-53
Memorial plaque, 89
Mural, 36, 185
Music, 16, 177, 578

■

Media and Technology

■

Multicultural Awareness and Appreciation

■

Life Skills

Index of Fine Art and Artists

Index of Titles and Authors

Acknowledgments

continued from page iv

139 "The Pacing White Mustang" from *Animals Who Have Won Our Hearts* by Jean Craighead George. Text copyright © 1994 by Jean Craighead George. Reprinted by permission of HarperCollins Publishers. **152** From *Wilma* by Wilma Rudolph and Bud Greenspan. Copyright © 1977 by Bud Greenspan. Used by permission of Dutton Signet, a division of Penguin Books USA Inc. **157** "The Wish" from *Someone Like You* by Roald Dahl. Copyright © 1948, 1949, 1950, 1951, 1952, 1953 by Roald Dahl. Reprinted by permission of the author and the Watkins/Loomis Agency. **161** "Halfway Down," from *When We Were Very Young* by A. A. Milne. Copyright 1924 by E. P. Dutton, renewed 1952 by A. A. Milne. Used by permission of Dutton Children's Books, a division of Penguin Books USA Inc. **166,** "Lob's Girl," from *A Whisper in the Night* by Joan Aiken. Copyright © 1984 by Joan Aiken. Used by permission of Delacorte Press, a division of Bantam Doubleday Dell Publishing Group, Inc. **182** "What We Said Sitting Making Fantasies" from *When I Dance,* copyright © 1991, 1988 by James Berry, reprinted by permission of Harcourt Brace & Company. **187** "Amitabh" from *New Kids on the Block* by Janet Bode. Copyright © 1989 by Janet Bode. Reprinted by permission of Franklin Watts, Inc. **194** "The Ch'i-lin Purse" from *The Ch'i-Lin Purse: A Collection of Ancient Chinese Stories* by Linda Fang. Copyright © 1995 by Linda Fang. Reprinted by permission of Farrar, Straus & Giroux, Inc. **205** Adapted from "How to Write Chinese Numbers" from *Understanding Asian Americans*, compiled by Marjorie H. Li and Peter Li. Copyright © 1990 by Marjorie H. Li and Peter Li. Reprinted by permission of Neal Schuman Publishers, Inc. **222** "Thunder Butte" from *When Thunders Spoke* by Virginia Driving Hawk Sneve. Copyright © 1974 by Virginia Driving Hawk Sneve. Reprinted by permission of the author. **231** "Gifts" by Michelle Whatoname from *Rising Voices,* selected by Arlene B. Hirschfelder and Beverly R. Singer, 1992. **235, 632, 633, 652** "A Christmas Carol," adapted by Frederick Gaines, from *Five Plays from the Children's Theatre Company of Minneapolis,* edited by John Clark Donahue and Linda Walsh Jenkins. Minneapolis: The University of Minnesota Press and the Children's Theatre Company. **257** "From Raisin Pudding to Oysters and Champagne: Charles Dickens" from *Lives of the Writers: Comedies, Tragedies (And What the Neighbors Thought),* copyright © 1994 by Kathleen Krull, reprinted by permission of Harcourt Brace & Company. **261** "The Fox and the Grapes," from Aesop's Fables. Copyright © 1981 by Viking Penguin, Inc., text. Used by permission of Viking Penguin, a division of Penguin Books USA Inc. **262** "The Country Mouse and the City Mouse," from *Aesop's Fables.* Copyright © 1981 by Viking Penguin, Inc., text. Used by permission of Viking Penguin, a division of Penguin Books USA Inc. **269** How I Celebrate My Name Day by Guadalupe V. Lopez. Copyright © 1994 Guadalupe V. Lopez. **274** "President Cleveland, Where Are You?" from *Eight Plus One* by Robert Cormier. Copyright © 1965 and renewed 1993 by Robert Cormier. Reprinted by permission of Pantheon Books, a division of Random House, Inc. **286** "Keri Age 11" from *Talking About Stepfamilies* by Maxine B. Rosenberg. Copyright © 1990 by Maxine B. Rosenberg. Reprinted by permission of Simon & Schuster Books for Young Readers. **294** "Andre" from *Bronzeville Boys and Girls* by Gwendolyn Brooks. Copyright © 1956 by Gwendolyn Brooks Blakely. Reprinted by permission of HarperCollins Publishers. **294** "Common Bond" by Kimi Narimatsu. **298** "The Dog of Pompeii" from *Donkey of God* by Louis Untermeyer. Copyright 1932 by Harcourt Brace Jovanovich, Inc. and renewed 1960 by Louis Untermeyer. Reprinted by express permission of Laurence S. Untermeyer. **310** "The Princess and the Tin Box" (text only) by James Thurber. Copyright © 1948 James Thurber. Copyright © 1976 Rosemary A. Thurber. From The Beast in Me and Other Animals, published by Harcourt Brace. Reprinted by permission of James Thurber Literary Properties. **315** "Damon and Pythias" from *The Bag of Fire and Other Plays* by Fan Kissen. Copyright © 1964 by Houghton Mifflin Company, renewed © 1993 by John Kissen Heaslip. Reprinted by permission of Houghton Mifflin Company. All rights reserved. **325** Adapted from "The People on the Beach" from *The Secrets of Vesuvius* Sara C. Bisel. Copyright © by Sara C. Bisel and Family and The Madison Press Limited. Reprinted by permission of Scholastic Inc. **342** "Now I Walk In Beauty" by Greg Smith. Copyright © 1979 by G. Schirmer, Inc. (ASCAP) International Copyright Secured. All Rights Reserved. Reprinted by permission. **344** "The Sand Castle" from *Weeping Woman* by Alma Luz Villanueva. Copyright © 1994 by Alma Luz Villanueva. Reprinted by permission of Bilingual Press/Editorial Bilingüe, Arizona State University, Tempe, AZ. **349** "And They Lived Happily Ever After For a While" from *Fast and Slow.* Copyright © 1975 by John Ciardi. Reprinted by permission of Houghton Mifflin Company. All rights reserved. **353** "People's Gardens: Frederick Law Olmstead and the First Public Parks" by Milton Meltzer. Copyright © 1993 by Milton Meltzer. Reprinted by permission of Harold Ober Associates Incorporated. **362** "April Rain Song" from *The Dream Keeper and Other Poems* by Langston Hughes. Copyright 1932 by Alfred A. Knopf Inc. and renewed 1960 by Langston Hughes. Reprinted by permission of the publisher. **362, 630** Reprinted by permission of the publishers and the Trustees of Amherst College from *The Poems of Emily Dickinson,* Thomas H. Johnson, ed., Cambridge, Mass.: The Belknap Press of Harvard University Press, Copyright © 1951, 1955, 1979, 1983 by the President and Fellows of Harvard College. **366** "Why the Rooster Crows at Sunrise" from *Sky Legends of Vietnam* by Lynette Dyer Vuong. Text Copyright © 1993 by Lynette Dyer Vuong. Reprinted by permission of HarperCollins Publishers. **370** Reprinted with the permission of Simon & Schuster Books for

Young Readers from *The Macmillan Book of Greek Gods and Heroes* by Alice Low. Copyright © 1985 Macmillan Publishing Company. **376–377** From *Fun With Science - The Seasons* by Rosie Harlow & Garth Morgan, published by Kingfisher. Copyright © Grisewood & Dempsey 1991. Reprinted by permission. **378** From *The Reason for the Seasons* by Linda Allison. Copyright © 1975 by the Yolla Bolly Press. By permission of Little, Brown and Company. **382** "Joel Rubin," from *It's Our World Too!* by Phillip Hoose. Copyright © 1993 by Phillip Hoose. By permission of Little, Brown and Company. **387** "Almost Human" from *Earth Lines* by Pat Moon. Copyright © 1993 by Pat Moon. Reprinted by permission of Greenwillow Books, a division of William Morrow & Company, Inc. **391** "Let Me Hear You Whisper" by Paul Zindel. Reprinted by permission of the William Morris Agency, Inc. on behalf of the Author. Copyright © 1970 by Zindel Productions, Inc. **407** "The Departure of the Giants" from *The Crest and the Hide* by Harold Courlander. Copyright © 1982 by Harold Courlander. Reprinted by permission of the author. **412** "Blow the Horn on Wildlife Trade" and "Success Stories" from *Take Action* by Ann Love and Jane Drake. Copyright © 1992 by World Wildlife Fund Canada. Reprinted by permission of Tambourine Books, a division of William Morrow and Company, Inc. and Kids Can Press Ltd., Toronto. **414** Adapted from "How You Can Help," *Kids Discover*, 1995. Copyright © 1995 Kids Discover. Reprinted by permission of the publisher. **432** "Southpaw" from *Free to Be. . .You and Me* by Judith Viorst. Copyright © 1974 by Judith Viorst. Reprinted by permission of Lescher & Lescher, Ltd. **434** "Louisa's Liberation" from *Hey World, Here I Am!* by Jean Little. Text Copyright © 1986 by Jean Little. Reprinted by permission of HarperCollins Publishers and Kids Can Press Ltd., Toronto. **438** "The Noble Experiment," from *I Never Had It Made* by Jackie Robinson with Alfred Duckett. Copyright © 1995 by Rachel Robinson. First published by The Ecco Press in 1995. Reprinted by permission. **452** Excerpt from *Kids at Work: Lewis Hine and the Crusade Against Child Labor.* Text copyright © 1994 by Russell Freedman. Reprinted by permission of Clarion Books/Houghton Mifflin Co. All rights reserved. **463** From *Scholastic Update, T/E* January 14, 1994. Copyright © 1994 by Scholastic Inc. Reproduced by permission. **467** "Princess" from *El Bronx Remembered: A Novella and Stories* by Nicholasa Mohr. Copyright © 1975 by Nicholasa Mohr. Reprinted by permission of HarperCollins Publishers. **477** "Words" from *The Dark Testament and Other Poems* by Pauli Murray. Copyright © 1970 by Pauli Murray. Reprinted by permission of Frances Collin, Literary Agent. **481** "Ghost Town" by Jack Shaefer. Copyright 1953, © renewed 1981 by Jack Shaefer. Reprinted by permission of Harold Matson Company, Inc. **486** "Vacant House" by Jeanne DeL. Bonnette. **490** "Ibrahima" from *Now Is Your Time: The African-American Struggle for Freedom* by Walter Dean Myers. Copyright © 1991 by Walter Dean Myers. Reprinted by permission of HarperCollins Publishers. **502** "Turtle's Race with Bear" from *Iroquois Stories:*

Heroes and Heroines, Monsters and Magic, as told by Joseph Bruchac. Copyright © 1985 by Joseph Bruchac. Reprinted by permission of The Crossing Press. **508** Excerpts from "Talk It Out," from *Current Health 1,* November 1993, Volume 17, No. 3. Reprinted by permission from Weekly Reader Corporation. Copyright © 1993 by Weekly Reader Corporation. All rights reserved. **526** "The Empty Box" from *Birthday Surprises* by Johanna Hurwitz. Copyright © 1995 by Johanna Hurwitz. Reprinted by permission of Morrow Junior Books, a division of William Morrow and Company, Inc. **531** "Argument" from *Out Loud* by Eve Merriam. Copyright © 1973 by Eve Merriam. Reprinted by permission of Marian Reiner. **535** "The Christmas Hunt" by Borden Deal. Reprinted by permission of Ashley Deal Moss on behalf of the Borden Family Trust. **556** "Porcupine and The Sky Mirrors" from *Moon Magic* by Katherine Davison. Text copyright © 1994 by Katherine Davison. Used by permission of the publisher, Carolrhoda Books, Inc. All rights reserved. **565** Adapted from *Sky Watchers of Ages Past.* Copyright © 1982 by Malcolm E. Weiss. Reprinted by permission of Houghton Mifflin Company. All rights reserved. **567** Adapted from *Observing the Sky* by Carole Stott. Copyright © 1991 by Eagle Books Limited. Used by permission of Troll Communications. **571** "The No-Guitar Blues" from *Baseball in April and Other Stories,* copyright © 1990 by Gary Soto, reprinted by permission of Harcourt Brace & Company. **580** "The All-American Slurp," by Lensey Namioka, copyright © 1987, from *Visions,* edited by Donald R. Gallo. All rights reserved by Lensey Namioka. Reprinted by permission of Ruth Cohen, Inc. **590** "Straight Talk (from a surfer)" from *The Malibu and Other Poems* by Myra Cohn Livingston. Copyright © 1972 by Myra Cohn Livingston. Reprinted by permission of Marian Reiner for the author. **591** "74th Street" from *The Malibu and Other Poems* by Myra Cohn Livingston. Copyright © 1972 by Myra Cohn Livingston. Reprinted by permission of Marian Reiner for the author. **594** From *Frozen Man* by David Getz. Copyright © 1994 by David Getz. Reprinted by permission of Henry Holt and Company, Inc. **602** "New World" from *The Gourd Dancer* by N. Scott Momaday. Copyright © 1976 by N. Scott Momaday. Reprinted by permission of the author. **607** "How the Animals Kept the Lions Away," (pp. 555, 556) from *Arab Folktales* by Inea Bushnaq, editor and translator. Copyright © 1986 by Inea Bushnaq. Reprinted by permission of Pantheon Books, a division of Random House, Inc. **612** Excerpt from "Volunteers Wanted" from *What Would We Do Without You?* by Kathy Henderson. Copyright © 1990 by Kathy Henderson. Reprinted by permission of Betterway Publications, Inc.

Illustrations

Unless otherwise acknowldeged, all photographs are the property of Scott, Foresman and Company. Page abbreviations are as follows: (t)top, (c)center, (b)bottom, (l)left, (r)right, (ins)inset.

ii "Ka-tat," 1922, Grace Carpenter Hudson. Courtesy of

the Grace Hudson Museum, City of Ukiah **vii** Andrew Wyeth, "Faraway," 1951. Drybrush watercolor. Private collection. Copyright © 1995 by Andrew Wyeth. **ix** Robert Pummill, "Kickin Up Some Dust" **xi** Faith Ringgold, "The Dinner Quilt," 1986, dyed, painted, pieced fabric with beads, 48½" x 66". Faith Ringgold Inc. copyright, private collection **xiii** Donna Clair, "Wild Asters at Picuris," 1990, oil on canvas **xv** "Liberty in the Form of the Goddess of Youth, giving support to the Bald Eagle in front of the Trenton Arches," c.1800–1815, unknown artist(s) possibly from NY or NJ, silk embroidery, watercolor, sequins and mica on silk. The Daughters of the American Revolution Museum, Washington, D.C., (Gift of New Jersey State Society) **xvii** Henri Rousseau, "Tropical Forest: Battling Tiger and Bull," 1908, oil on canvas, Hermitage State Museum, St. Petersburg/A. Buratouskyl/Superstock, Inc. **xxiv** Christie's London/Superstock, Inc. **0–1** Andrew Wyeth, "Faraway," 1951. Drybrush watercolor. Private collection. Copyright ©1995 by Andrew Wyeth. **1, 4, 17, 42, 47, 48, 76, 90, 96(icon)** Superstock, Inc. **5** Courtesy Bantam Doubleday Dell **7** Andrew Wyeth, "Siri," 1970. Tempera on panel, 30 x 30½ inches. Collection of the Brandywine River Museum, purchased for the museum by John T. Dorrance, Jr., Mr. and Mrs. Felix duPont, Mr and Mrs. James P. Mills, Mr. and Mrs. Bayard Sharp, two anonymous donors, and The Pew Charitable Trust. **11** Four By Five/Superstock, Inc. **18(b)** AP/Wide World **21** Charles White, "Freedom," 1966–67. Collection of African American Museum of Art and Culture, Los Angeles; courtesy Heritage Gallery, Los Angeles **22** Courtesy University of Washington Press **25** Bob Daemmrich Photography **30** UPI/Corbis-Bettmann **32** Adam Emory Albright, *Untitled*, 1906. Oil on canvas, 24 x 30 inches. Private Collection. **36** Lars Topelmann/Graphistock **39** From *The Diary of Latoya Hunter* by Latoya Hunter. Photo copyright © 1992 by Jill LeVine. Published by Crown Publishers, Inc. Used with permission. **42(l)** Stephen Trimble **42(r)** Daniel Laine/Gamma Liaison **43(t)** Raghu Rai/Magnum Photos **46** © 1995 Cindy Lewis **49** Courtesy of the author **50** © 1994 Elena Dorfman **52** Charles Demuth, "I Saw the Figure 5 in Gold", 1928. Oil on composition board, 36 x 29¾ inches. Metropolitan Museum of Art, Alfred Stieglitz Collection, 1949. **55** Courtesy Eugene Louie/*San Jose Mercury News* **56** Ken Danby, "On the Arrowback" 1975. Watercolor, 21 x 27 inches. Used by permission of the artist and Gallery Moos, Toronto **61** Marilyn Levine, "Rick and Margaret's Suitcase", 19776, Ceramic. Courtesy O.K.Harris Works of Art **63** UCLA at the Armand Hammer Museum of Art & Cultural Center **66** Courtesy of the author **68** Bibliotheque Nationale, Paris/Superstock, Inc. **71** Collection of Irwin Goldstein, M.D. **75** Runk/Schoenberger/Grant Heilman **77(t)** Courtesy Harper, Collins Publishers **77(b)** Dartmouth College **78–79** John F. Carlson, "March Thaw," 1936. Oil on canvas, 40 x 52 inches. Photo courtesy Babcock Galleries, New York **81** Courtesy Penguin USA, Photo: Art Smith **84** William Vincent, "Zanzibar, Tanzania," Oil, 30 x 40 inches. © William Vincent **90** Bob Daemmrich

91(all) David Young-Wolff/PhotoEdit **92** Jill Krementz **94** FOXTROT © 1995 Bill Amend. Reprinted with permission of Universal Press Syndicate. All rights reserved. **106–107** Robert Pummill, "Kickin Up Some Dust," Robert Pummill **107, 110, 122, 148, 154(icon)** Superstock, Inc. **107, 155, 164, 202, 207(icon)** Courtesy Erika Hugo **108, 126** Jacob Lawrence, *Munich Olympic Games*, (Study for the Munich Olympic Games Poster)" 1971. Gouache on paper, 35½ x 27 inches. The Seattle Art Museum, purchased with funds from PONCHO. Courtesy of the artist and Francine Seders Gallery, Seattle **111** Photo by Sandra L. Swans/Random House **112** Kay Life © Lifescapes **115** Marilee Whitehouse-Holm, International/ Superstock, Inc. **117** Superstock, Inc. **123(t)** Courtesy of Boyds Mills Press **123(b)** AP/Wide World **124** William Hawkins, "Ohio State University Stadium," 1984. Enamel housepaint on paneling with painted wood frame, 46½" x 48". National Museum of American Art, Smithsonian Institution, gift of Herbert Waide Hemphill, Jr., and museum purchase made possible by Ralph Cross Johnson. 1986.65.118/Art Resource **131** Sydney Laurence, "The Home Guard," 1917. Watercolor, 9' x 12". Private Collection. Photo Anchorage Museum, Chris Arend photographer **134** Frank Schoonover, "Trapper and Dog Team," 1937. Wilmington Trust Company Permanent Collection, Wilmington, Delaware **138** Ellan Young Photography **140–141** William A. Karges Family Trust **148(t)** Dave Cannon/ALLSPORT USA **148(b)** Foto Lobl-Schreyer/FPG International Corp. **149(t)** Simon Bruty 1995/ALLSPORT USA **149(b)** ALLSPORT USA **150(tl)** Mike Powell 1995/ALLSPORT USA **150(tr)** Mike Powell 1995/ALLSPORT USA **150(b)** Vandystadt/ALLSPORT **151(background)** Simon Bruty 1995/ALLSPORT USA **151(inset)** UPI/Corbis-Bettmann **152** UPI/Corbis-Bettman **153** AP/Wide World **158** Hereke Silk Rug. From *All Colour Book of Oriental Carpets and Rugs* by Stanley Reed. Copyright © 1972 by Octopus Books Limitd. Photo: Perez (London) Ltd. **165** Courtesy Bantam Doubleday Dell, Photo: Rob Delroy **167** Stanhope Alexander Forbes, "A Cornish Estuary","Taylor Gallery, London/Bridgeman/Art Resource **171** Barbara Banthien **174** Allen R. Banks, "Sunday Afternoon," 1984. Courtesy of the artist **180–181** Sir John Tenniel drawing of Walrus and Carpenter from "*Alice in Wonderland*" **183** Charles Burchfield, "Childhood's Garden," 1917. Watercolor, 27 x 18¹⁵⁄₁₆ inches. Munson-Williams-Proctor Institute Museum, Utica, N.Y. **186** Courtesy Bantam Doubleday Dell, Photo: Stan Mack **189** Superstock, Inc. **193** Courtesy Farrar, Straus & Giroux **194**, "Pouch," embroidery on cream satin weave silk, late 19th-early 20th century, 25.5 x 9.5 cm. Victoria and Albert Museum, London, T.132.1963/Art Resource **195** Viesti Associates, Inc. **196–197** Paper shadow puppets in a wedding procession, carrying the bride in the traditional sedan marked with the double XI characters meaning "double happiness." Late 19th century, Hebei Province, China, each puppet 4" high. From *Chinese Folk Art: The Small Skills of Carving Insects* by Nancy Zeng Berliner. Copyright © 1986 by Nancy Zeng

Berliner. A New York Graphic Society book published by Little, Brown and Co., Inc. **202** Superstock, Inc. **203(t)** Superstock, Inc. **203(c)** James L. Amos **203(b)** Superstock, Inc. **204(tl)** Superstock, Inc. **204(tr)** Ancient Art & Architecture Collection/Ronald Sheridan Photo-Library **204(b)** Christie's London/ Superstock, Inc. **205(r)** © 1992 Dennis Cox **216–217** Faith Ringgold, *"The Dinner Quilt,"* 1986, dyed, painted, pieced fabric with beads, 48½" x 66". Faith Ringgold Inc. copyright, private collection **217, 272, 292, 322, 328(icon)** Mary Cassatt, "The Boating Party," National Gallery of Art, Washington, D.C./Superstock, Inc. **218** Henry Moore, "Family Group," a bronze sculpture 1948–1949, Museum of Modern Art, A Conger Goodyear Fund. Photo: (c) The Museum of Modern Art, N.Y. **219** Myrleen Ferguson/ PhotoEdit **221** AP/Wide World **223** Maynard Dixon, "Magic Mesa," 1936. Oil on canvas, 30 x 40 inches. Private Collection **227** Eiteljorg Museum of American Indians and Western Art **228** Shelburne Museum, Shelburne, Vermont **231** Edward J. Fraughton **234** National Portrait Gallery, London **236, 241, 250, 253** Scene from Milwaukee Repertory Theater's production of *A Christmas Carol.* Scrooge: James Pickering. Photo: Mark Avery **238, 246** Scene from Milwaukee Repertory Theater's production of *A Christmas Carol.* Scrooge: James Pickering. Crachit: Andrew May. Photo: Jay Westhauser **256** Courtesy Harcourt Brace Jovanovich, Photo: Paul Brewer **257** Illustration from *Lives of the Writers: Comedies, Tragedies (And What the Neighbors Thought)* by Kathleen Krull, illustrated by Kathryn Hewitt. Text copyright © 1994 by Kathleen Krull. Illustrations copyright © 1994 by Kathryn Hewitt. Reproduced by permission of Harcourt Brace & Company. **260** Corbis-Bettmann Archive **261** "Screen Panel depicting Aesop's Fable, "The Fox and The Grapes," Savonnerie Tapestry, mid 18th century. Mobilier National, Paris/Bridgeman Art Library, London/Superstock, Inc. **263** E. J. Detmold, "The Town Mouse and The Country Mouse." Private Collection/ Bridgeman Art Library, London/Superstock, Inc. **266(l)** Joe Viesti/Viesti Associates, Inc. **266(r)** Bob Daemmrich/Stock Boston **266, 267, 268** Superstock, Inc. **267** Joe Viesti/Viesti Associates, Inc. **268(l)** Richard Hutchings/ PhotoEdit **268(r)** Lawrence Migdale **273** Courtesy of Bantam Publishing, Photo by Beth Bergman **275** Superstock, Inc. **279(all)** Culver Pictures Inc. **284** Ben Shahn, "Vacant Lot," 1939. Tempera, 19 x 23 inches. © 1996 Estate of Ben Shahn/Licensed by VAGA, NY **285** Susan Kuklin **286, 289** © 1990 by Maxine B. Rosenberg. Used with permission. **293** Courtesy Harper, Collins Publishers **295** Henry Moore, "Family Group," a bronze sculpture 1948–1949, Museum of Modern Art, A Conger Goodyear Fund. Photo: (c) The Museum of Modern Art, N.Y. **297** Corbis-Bettmann Archive **298** New York Public Library, Astor, Lenox and Tilden Foundations **301** Museo Archeologico Nazionale, NaplesScala/Art Resource **305** Jean-Loup Charmet **306** C.M. Dixon **309** AP/Wide World **311** The Royal Music Barque by James C. Christensen © 1993, The Greenwich Workshop, Inc. Courtesy of the

Greenwich Workshop, Inc., Shelton, CT **316** Museo Archeologico Nazionale, Naples/Scala/Art Resource, New York **322–323** Reproduced from Dorling Kindersley, *The Dorling Kindersley History of the World.*, Published by DK Publishing Inc. **324(b)** Giraudon/Art Resource **324(t)** Civic Museum, Oderzo, Italy/E. T. Archives, London/Superstock, Inc. **326(b)** Illustration by Laurie McGaw from *Secrets of Vesuvius* by Sara C. Bisel with Jane Bisel and Shelley Tanaka, © 1990 A Scholastic/Madison Press Book. **326(t)** O. Louis Mazzatenta/National Geographic Society **327(b)** Borromeo/Art Resource **327(t)** O. Louis Mazzatenta/ National Geographic Society **338–339** Donna Clair, "Wild Asters at Picuris," 1990, oil on canvas **339, 380, 405, 410, 416(icon)** Konstantin Rodko, "Tending the Garden," Superstock, Inc. **340** David Young-Wolff/ PhotoEdit **341(t)** William F. McMahon/Adler Planetarium, Chicago **341(bl)** William F. McMahon/ Adler Planetarium **343** Photo by Wilfredo Q. Castano **344–345** Victor Kerpel, "Winter Surf (Self-Portrait,)" 1993. Courtesy of the artist. **347** David Hockney, "Beach Umbrella," 1971. Acrylic on canvas, 48 x 35¾ inches. © 1971 David Hockney **349** Hess/ Image Bank **351** Jose Carrillo/PhotoEdit **352** Courtesy Harold Orber & Associates, Photo: Catherine Noren **353** Corbis-Bettmann Archive **354** Museum of the City of New York, The J. Clarence Davis Collection **356** National Museum of American Art 1964.1.15/Art Resource **361(b)** Trustees of Amherst College **361(t)** UPI/Corbis-Bettmann **363** Collection of the Museum of Fine Arts, Museum of New Mexico; Gift of the Artist in honor of Teresa Bakos **365** AP/Wide World **371** Christie's, London/Superstock, Inc. **374(t)** Robert Harding Picture Library **374(b)** Library of Congress **375(t)** Mary Evans Picture Library **375(b)** Robert Harding Picture Library **381** Courtesy Little, Brown & Co., Photo: Richard Connelly **382** Faesi/Marine Mammal Images **385** from *It's Our World Too* by Phillip Hoose. © 1993 Phillip Hoose. By permission of Little, Brown & Co. **387** Alan Oddie/PhotoEdit **390, 393** Toledo Museum of Art, Toledo, Ohio; Museum Purchase Fund **397** Michos Tzovaras/Art Resource **400** R.J.Muna/Graphistock **410–411** Jean-Marie Chauvet/Sygma **400(inset)** Altamira Caves, Spain/Bridgeman Art Library London/Superstock, Inc. **411(t-inset)** Erich Lessing/Art Resource **411(b-inset)** Superstock, Inc. **412** Martin Harvey/Wildlife Collection **413(t)** Martin Harvey/Wildlife Collection **413(b)** Bruce Coleman Inc. **414** Bob Daemmrich/Image Works **415(tl)** Michael Francis/ Wildlife Collection **415(tr)** Martin Harvey/Wildlife Collection **415(bl)** Martin Harvey/Wildlife Collection **415(br)** John Giustina/ Wildlife Collection **426–427** Justice: "Liberty in the Form of the Goddess of Youth, giving support to the Bald Eagle in front of the Trenton Arches," c.1800–1815, unknown artist(s) possibly from NY or NJ, silk embroidery, watercolor, sequins and mica on silk. The Daughters of the American Revolution Museum, Washington, D.C., (Gift of New Jersey State Society) **427, 430, 459, 460, 464(icon)** Alexej von Jawlensky, "Head of Young Girl (Madchenkopf)," Christie's, London/Superstock, Inc. **427, 465, 505, 506,**

510(icon) Tsing-Fang Chen, "Bombardment," Lucia Gallery, New York City/Superstock, Inc. **432** © Lena Guyot. In the collection of Cooperstown Bat Co., Cooperstown, N.Y. **439** © 1993 Karen Felicity Berkenfeld **443** Wide World/AP **447** Courtesy Lescher & Lescher, Ltd., Photo: Sigrid Estrada **449** Markisches Museum, Berlin/A.K.G. Berlin/Superstock, Inc. **452** Library of Congress **453, 454, 455** Library of Congress **460** J.Greenberg/Image Works **461(l)** Superstock, Inc. **461(c)** Robert Harding Picture Library **461(r)** Bibliotheque Nationale, Paris/Bridgeman Art Library, London/Superstock, Inc. **462** Corkery/News/Globe Photo, Inc **462(r)** Corbis-Bettmann Archive **462(l)** Corbis-Bettmann Archive **466** Gail Russell **469** Private Collection **472** Thyssen-Boremisza Museum, Madrid/Scala Art Resource **477** Frank Collyer/Stock Illustration Source, Inc. **480** Winslow Williams **483** Ernest Berke **484** James Bama, "Slim Warren, the Old Cowboy," 1994. © 1994 The Greenwich Workshop, Inc., Shelton, CT **486** Fremont Ellis, "The Blue Portal," 1953 (oil on canvas); Stark Museum of Art, Orange, TX **489** Courtesy Scholastic **491** Library of Congress **492** New Haven Colony Historical Society **496** Superstock, Inc. **498** Library of Congress **502** Dan Ostermiller Gallery **506(r)** Bettmann Archive **506(l)** Robert Frerck/Odyssey Productions **507(tl)** Victoria & Albert Museum, London/Art Resource **507(tr)** National Historical Museum, Bucharest/E.T. Archives, London/Superstock, Inc. **507(bl)** Bettmann Archive **507(br)** National Archives, Paris/Giraudon/Art Resource **515** National Portrait Gallery, London **520–521** Henri Rousseau, "Tropical Forest: Battling Tiger and Bull," 1908, oil on canvas, Hermitage State Museum, St. Petersburg/A. Burkatousky/Superstock, Inc. **521, 524, 554, 562, 568(icon)** Paul Klee, "Senecio (Bladgreis)," Offentliche Kunstsammlung, Basle/A.K.G. Berlin/Superstock, Inc. **521, 569, 605, 610, 614 (icon)** Paul Klee, "Wandbild Aus Dem Tempel Der Sehnsucht Dorth," Metropolitan Museum of Art, New York/Christie's London/Superstock, Inc. **523(t)** Superstock, Inc. **523(b)** BIbliotheque National, Paris/A.K.G., Berlin/Superstock, Inc. **525** Courtesy of the author **527** Terry Sirrell/Stock Illustration Source, Inc. **530** Shawn Michienzi/RipSaw **531** Illustration by Harriet Sherman, accompanying the poem "Argument" from *Out Loud* by Eve Merriam. Reprinted by permission of the illustrator. **536** Courtesy of Hadley House, Bloomington, MN **539** Oldham Art Gallery, Lancaster, England/ Bridgeman Art Library, London/Superstock, Inc. **542** Burt Silverman Studios, Inc. **546** Stephen Hamrick, "Getting Warm," Courtesy of Hadley House, Bloomington, MN **547** North Wind Picture Archives **549** Halstead Craig Hannah **555** Courtesy of the author **556** Illustration Courtesy of Chevron Corporation **558** Sheldon Memorial Art Gallery, University of Nebraska, Lincoln, Nebraska Art Association, Collection, Nelle Cochrane Woods Memorial. 1968.N-229. **561** Jeremy Wolff/Grafistock **562(l)** Christie's, London/Superstock, Inc. **562(r)** National Historical Museum, Bucharest/E.T.Archives, London/Superstock, Inc. **563** Biblioteca Estense, Modena, Italy/E. T. Archives, London/Superstock, Inc. **564(b)** Bibliotheque Nationale, Paris/E. T. Archives, London/Superstock, Inc. **564(tl)** Bibliotheque Nationale, Paris/Bridgeman Art Library, London/Superstock, Inc. **564(tr)** Biblioteca Marciana, Venice/E. T. Archives, London/Superstock, Inc. **565** Superstock, Inc. **566** Lee Snider/Image Works **567** Superstock, Inc. **570(l)** Carolyn Soto **570(r)** Everett Collection **573–574** Superstock, Inc. **582** Mary Anne Lloyd/Sharon Kurlansky Associates **590** Superstock, Inc. **591** Collection of the Whitney Museum of American Art, N.Y., Gift of Gertrude Vanderbilt Whitney. **595** Illustration © 1994 by Peter McCarty. From the Book *Frozen Man* by David Getz. Reprinted by permission of Henry Holt and Co., Inc. **597** Paul Hanny/Gamma Liaison **599** Hinterleitner/Gamma Liaison **600(all)** Illustrations © 1994 by Peter McCarty. From the book *Frozen Man* by David Getz. Reprinted by permission of Henry Holt and Co., Inc. **602** Superstock, Inc. **607** Bibliotheque Nationale, Paris/A.K.G., Berlin/Superstock, Inc.